# Evolutionary Economics and Social Complexity Science

## Volume 24

**Editor-in-Chiefs**

Takahiro Fujimoto, Tokyo, Japan
Yuji Aruka, Kyoto, Japan

The Japan Association for Evolutionary Economics (JAFEE) always has adhered to its original aim of taking an explicit "integrated" approach. This path has been followed steadfastly since the Association's establishment in 1997 and, as well, since the inauguration of our international journal in 2004. We have deployed an agenda encompassing a contemporary array of subjects including but not limited to: foundations of institutional and evolutionary economics, criticism of mainstream views in the social sciences, knowledge and learning in socio-economic life, development and innovation of technologies, transformation of industrial organizations and economic systems, experimental studies in economics, agent-based modeling of socio-economic systems, evolution of the governance structure of firms and other organizations, comparison of dynamically changing institutions of the world, and policy proposals in the transformational process of economic life. In short, our starting point is an "integrative science" of evolutionary and institutional views. Furthermore, we always endeavor to stay abreast of newly established methods such as agent-based modeling, socio/econo-physics, and network analysis as part of our integrative links.

More fundamentally, "evolution" in social science is interpreted as an essential key word, i.e., an integrative and /or communicative link to understand and re-domain various preceding dichotomies in the sciences: ontological or epistemological, subjective or objective, homogeneous or heterogeneous, natural or artificial, selfish or altruistic, individualistic or collective, rational or irrational, axiomatic or psychological-based, causal nexus or cyclic networked, optimal or adaptive, micro- or macroscopic, deterministic or stochastic, historical or theoretical, mathematical or computational, experimental or empirical, agent-based or socio/econo-physical, institutional or evolutionary, regional or global, and so on. The conventional meanings adhering to various traditional dichotomies may be more or less obsolete, to be replaced with more current ones vis-à-vis contemporary academic trends. Thus we are strongly encouraged to integrate some of the conventional dichotomies.

These attempts are not limited to the field of economic sciences, including management sciences, but also include social science in general. In that way, understanding the social profiles of complex science may then be within our reach. In the meantime, contemporary society appears to be evolving into a newly emerging phase, chiefly characterized by an information and communication technology (ICT) mode of production and a service network system replacing the earlier established factory system with a new one that is suited to actual observations. In the face of these changes we are urgently compelled to explore a set of new properties for a new socio/economic system by implementing new ideas. We thus are keen to look for "integrated principles" common to the above-mentioned dichotomies throughout our serial compilation of publications. We are also encouraged to create a new, broader spectrum for establishing a specific method positively integrated in our own original way.

*Editors-in-Chief*

Takahiro Fujimoto, Tokyo, Japan
Yuji Aruka, Tokyo, Japan

More information about this series at http://www.springer.com/series/11930

Theodore Mariolis • Nikolaos Rodousakis •
George Soklis

# Spectral Theory of Value and Actual Economies

## Controllability, Effective Demand, and Cycles

 Springer

Theodore Mariolis
Public Administration
Panteion University of Social & Political
Science
Athens, Greece

Nikolaos Rodousakis
Centre of Planning and Economic
Research (KEPE)
Athens, Greece

George Soklis
Centre of Planning and Economic
Research (KEPE)
Athens, Greece

ISSN 2198-4204          ISSN 2198-4212   (electronic)
Evolutionary Economics and Social Complexity Science
ISBN 978-981-33-6259-8        ISBN 978-981-33-6260-4   (eBook)
https://doi.org/10.1007/978-981-33-6260-4

This Springer imprint is published by the registered company Springer Nature Singapore Pte Ltd.
The registered company address is: 152 Beach Road, #21-01/04 Gateway East, Singapore 189721,
Singapore

# Preface and Acknowledgements

If there is no one-way avenue that leads from "factors of production" to "consumption goods", but instead a network of interactions amongst income distribution, value, effective demand, capital accumulation, and technical conditions of production, where effects become causes in their turn, then the Sraffa–Kalecki–Goodwin modelling of endogenous circular causation provides the appropriate context for formulating and dealing with non-self-referential representations of the real-world economies.

This book develops a post-2000 line of research that, on the one hand, couples Piero Sraffa's theory of value with Rudolf Emil Kalman's theory of controllability/observability and, on the other hand, is inspired by the works of Karl Marx, John Maynard Keynes, Michał Kalecki, Nicholas Kaldor, and Richard M. Goodwin. Thus, it first proposes a unified treatment of the income distribution–capital–value problems, then derives meaningful theoretical results consistent with the empirical evidence, and vice versa, and, finally, turns to the issues of distributive–effective demand–technological change dynamics from both political economy and economic policy perspectives.

The arguments in the present book proceed in stages. Chapter 1 maps the structure of the empirical input–output representations of actual economies, i.e. the Supply and Use Tables (the counterpart of pure joint production economies) and the Symmetric Input–Output Tables (the counterpart of single production economies), and critically evaluates the methods that have been proposed to convert the former into the latter. It is thus argued that this conversion rests on the tacit and groundless assumption that there is a single production system hidden in the Supply and Use Tables characterizing the real world, whereas a consistent approach is the straightforward treatment of the Supply and Use Tables on the basis of general joint production models inspired by the John von Neumann and Sraffa contributions.

Chapter 2 shows that Kalman's concepts of controllability and observability articulate a general basis for dealing with central issues of value, capital, and income distribution–growth theory. Thus, it identifies new aspects of the Sraffian theory, emphasizes the generality of this theory, determines the location of the alternative, traditional (i.e. classical, Marxian, Austrian, and neoclassical), and Sraffian theories of national value in the complex plane, and, hence, points out a spectral reduction or post-construction of the value theory. This post-construction forms a typical, mathematical model for the most general value theory to date, i.e. the Sraffian theory, and might provide a representation of the evolution of competing value theories in terms of both the logic and the history of economic thought.

Chapter 3 points out that although the existence of long-period value (i.e. production price)–profit rate curves that are non-monotonic irrespective of the labour vector direction presupposes that the eigenvalue distributions of the system matrix are sharply different from those appearing in actual economies, the Sraffian theory is not only the most general to date but is also empirically relevant. Since actual economies exhibit non-monotonic value–profit rate curves, wage–profit rate curves with alternating curvature, and value–vertically integrated labour reversals, which are analogous to the re-switching phenomenon, they can only be treated through the Sraffian theory. At the same time, however, actual economies are characterized by rather low degrees and relatively low normalized numerical ranks of value controllability: the hitherto available evidence suggests that the degrees of value controllability are no greater than $10^{-18}$ and the normalized numerical ranks of value controllability are no greater than eighteen percent. These findings result from the skew characteristic value distributions of the vertically integrated technical coefficients matrices and indicate that actual economies tend to respond as uncontrollable and unobservable systems, with only a relatively few effectively controllable and observable modes. Finally, this property of almost uncontrollability and unobservability explains, in turn, the specific shape features of the empirical value–wage–profit rate curves that are (re-)positioned, by the traditional value theory, at the heart of the capital theory debate.

Chapter 4 applies the principles of the Sraffian theory to pure joint production or/and open economies, where the "non-substitution theorem" ceases to be of general validity and, therefore, there is an additional source of insurmountable difficulties for the traditional value theory. If, however, we are willing to consider produced means of production, positive profits, non-"golden rule" steady states, heterogeneous labour (primary inputs), and joint-products as "market failures", as well as joint production through the lens of single production, then we are not required to move away from the self-referential world of only one commodity. In the opposite case, the general conclusion is that open, joint-product economies should be treated as the norm, whereas closed, single-product economies and their special properties should be pointed out as limiting paradigms.

Chapter 5 extends the empirical investigation of the shape of wage–profit rate curves and of the relationships amongst "labour values", long-period values, and market values (i.e. market prices) to the case of pure joint production using data from eighty-five Supply and Use Tables for twelve different national economies. The main results are as follows: (i) the systems examined are not "all-productive" and, therefore, do not have the usual properties of single production systems; (ii) about eighty-nine percent of them are not "$r_0$–all-engaging" and, therefore, there is no interval of the profit rate in which they retain the wage (consumption)–profit (growth) rate properties of irreducible single production systems; (iii) the monotonicity of the estimated wage–profit rate curves depends on the choice of the standard of value or *numéraire*, while the downward-sloping wage–profit rate curves appear to be "close" to the linear "trends", and this fact expresses the uncontrollable/unobservable aspects of the real-world economies; (iv) economically irrelevant "additive labour values" (actual long-period values) have been detected in about eight percent (in about twelve percent) of the systems examined, while there are cases where economically irrelevant actual long-period values co-exist with positive "surplus value" (measured in terms of "additive labour values"); and (v) in the economically relevant cases, the estimated actual long-period value (market value)–"additive labour value" deviation, measured by the "normalized $d$–distance", is in the range of eight to sixty-two percent (of sixteen to seventy one percent), while the market value–actual long-period value deviation is in the range of nineteen to seventy-six percent, that is to say, the value deviations are considerably greater than those estimated on the basis of Symmetric Input–Output Tables. Since, in the real world, joint production activities constitute the rule, these empirical findings reinforce the Marx-after-Sraffa theoretical statement that actual economies cannot be coherently analysed in terms of the traditional value theory.

Chapter 6 detects and identifies the conditions under which positive "surplus labour", as defined by Marx, is both necessary and sufficient for positive profits. It is found that these conditions are restrictive and, therefore, the traditional Marxian "exploitation theory of profit" cannot be sustained. Nevertheless, this chapter also argues that a Marx-after-Sraffa re-formulation of the concepts of "time dilation" and "abstract social-international labour", which are involved, explicitly or otherwise, in Marx's analysis, may lead to the proposal that the labour values of commodities are determined by their market prices and are equal to them; therefore, surplus labour is determined by and is equal to actual profits.

Chapter 7 returns to the "outside world" by extending the empirical investigation of the relationships amongst "labour values", as they are *traditionally* defined, long-period values and market values to the framework of "alternative value bases" in both single and pure joint production economies. This extended investigation reveals that there are cases in which "commodity $i$ values" and "additive commodity $i$ values" are better approximations of actual values than "labour values" and "additive labour values", respectively. And taking into account the detection of economically irrelevant long-period values, "additive commodity $i$ values", and/or "additive labour values" in the empirically relevant case of joint production, the findings indicate that the claim that actual economies can be coherently analysed in terms of "labour values" cannot be sustained. In actual fact, the analysis developed so far in this book proves that, in the empirically relevant cases of heterogeneous labour, open economies, and joint production, any attempt to test the classical–Marxian price–"labour value" hypothesis, i.e. the main determinant of commodity prices is the corresponding quantities of labour "embodied", is, at best, circular.

Chapter 8 identifies the specific features of matrix demand multipliers in Sraffian frameworks and their spectral characteristics. The multipliers in Sraffian frameworks include, as special versions or limiting cases, the Kahn–Keynes and Kaldor multipliers, the corresponding multipliers of the traditional input–output analysis and their Marxian versions. This chapter (i) constructs and explores matrix demand multipliers for the case of a closed economy of single production, circulating capital, and homogeneous labour; (ii) shows that there is an autonomous demand–transfer payments curve, which exhibits formal similarities with the consumption (wage)–growth (profit) curve in steady-state capital and growth theory; (iii) extends the analysis to more realistic cases, including those of heterogeneous labour, open economy systems, and pure joint production; and (iv) deals with an open economy model, with heterogeneous capital and linear processes of both single and joint production, from a long-run perspective, and explores the relationships between the exchange rate, the relative commodity prices, and the volume of total employment. Since the multiplier effects of autonomous demand are a central focus of the macroeconomic analysis of actual economies and since in the post-2008 world there are intense, policy-oriented debates on the "size of the fiscal multiplier", this Sraffian analysis is also of interest for both structural and policy studies.

Chapter 9 provides empirical estimations and policy-oriented analysis of (i) the output, import, and employment matrix demand multipliers for two representative "PIIGS economies", i.e. Greece and Spain, and for the Eurozone economy as a whole; and (ii) the medium- and long-run effects of wage and currency devaluations on international price competitiveness and income distribution by focusing exclusively on the input–output configurations of Greece and Italy, i.e. two "PIIGS economies" that are characterized, however, by different levels and structures of production and, at the same time, have experienced significantly different rates of wage devaluation. For this purpose, we use, on the one hand, input–output data from the Supply and Use Tables and the Symmetric Input–Output Tables for the "pre-adjustment" year of 2010 and, on the other hand, input–output models based on the Sraffian framework(s) developed in Chap. 8. The findings seem to be in accordance with the observed deep Southern Eurozone recession, cast doubt on the "horizontal" policy measures implemented in the post-2010 Eurozone economy, and point to the limited effectiveness of both types of devaluation as key levers for the required economic adjustment and recovery. Hence, they rather call for a wider and more flexible strategy framework that includes, on the one hand, per country and sector-specific wage rate changes and demand management policies and, on the other hand, an intra-Eurozone industrial, trade, and currency depreciation policy. In more general terms, since the prevailing debates about capitalist trade liberalization, integration, and holopoiesis ("globalization") are based on the traditional, "main-stream" and "radical", international value theories, the Sraffian theory findings of Chaps. 4, 6, and 9 form the basis for the development of a coherent alternative discourse.

Chapter 10 delves into the analysis of capitalist accumulation cycles and fluctu-ations by investigating Goodwin's distributional conflict or predator–prey model. More specifically, it focuses on (i) the model's stability properties under the assump-tions of a variable elasticity of substitution (VES) production function and endog-enous labour productivity growth; and (ii) the implications of capital heterogeneity under the assumption of a "nominal Phillips curve" or, alternatively, a "real Phillips curve". The inclusion of a VES production function is equivalent to the introduction of a dampening effect, whereas endogenous labour productivity growth produces a destabilizing effect, where neither is, in general, dominant over the other. Contrary to Goodwin's approach, it is also found that both the economic relevance and the dynamic behaviour of the heterogeneous capital model depend on the eigenvalues of the matrix of input–output coefficients: (i) if some eigenvalues are complex, then Goodwin's assumptions about differential (across industries) labour markets and growth rates of the labour force lead to an economically irrelevant system; and (ii) even if we avoid these assumptions, numerical simulations show that the model characterized by a "real Phillips curve" exhibits explosive oscillations, while this is also verified through empirical tests using actual input–output table data. These insights on Goodwin's model in disaggregative forms result from the existence of complicated inter-relationships amongst industries in the empirically relevant case of production of commodities by means of commodities and, hence, underlines the importance of Sraffa's contribution.

Chapter 11 dissects and re-investigates Marx's treatment of capitalist accumulation fluctuations on the basis of post-Keynesian and Sraffian frameworks. It (i) incorporates the Bhaduri–Marglin accumulation function into the Goodwin distributional conflict model and deals with alternative, relevant versions of this extended model; (ii) zeroes in on Marx's so-called "law of the tendency of the profit rate to fall"; (iii) argues that in the twentieth century or, more precisely, since the 1920s, the prevailing "law" was that of non-decreasing capital productivity, which implies that a decrease in the profit rate presupposes a decrease in the share of profits or, in other words, that Marx's "law" fails to hold; and (iv) points out that the profit mass may be strictly increasing even when the normalized profit rate (i.e. "the" profit rate–capacity utilization rate ratio) is strictly decreasing and, therefore, the "long-wave version" of the falling profit rate theory of crisis lacks logical consistency. Hence, it is concluded that Marx's sub-theory of biased technological change (and consequent long-term fall in the profit rate) overdetermines his sub-theories of distributive cycles and of effective demand, while the Sraffa–Kalecki–Goodwin modelling of endogenous circular causation provides the appropriate analytical framework for dealing with the capitalist accumulation process.[1]

In a note dated 15 August 1946, Ludwig Wittgenstein wrote:

> Grasping the difficulty *in its depth* is what is hard. For if you interpret it in a shallow way the difficulty just remains. It has to be pulled out by the root; & that means, you have to start thinking about these things in a new way. [...] The new way of thinking is what is so hard to establish. Once it [i.e. the new way of thinking] is established the old problems disappear; indeed it becomes hard to recapture them. For they are embedded in the way we express ourselves; & if we clothe ourselves in a new form of expression, the old problems are discarded along with the old garment. (*Culture and Value*, 55e)

---

[1]The division of labour amongst the authors was as follows: Nikolaos Rodousakis wrote Chap. 10 and Sect. 11.3; George Soklis wrote Chaps. 1, 5, and 7; and Theodore Mariolis wrote the remaining sections and coordinated the work.

Written on the occasion of the 60th anniversary of the publication of both Sraffa's *Production of Commodities by Means of Commodities* and Kalman's paper "On the General Theory of Control Systems", our book synthesizes those two new ways of *thinking* and further supports the relevance of the resulting synthesis to grasping the difficulties of both the theory and the empirics of value in their depth and implications.

Central topics of this book were presented at workshops of the "Study Group on Sraffian Economics" and at its 1st Conference titled "From the Capital Theory Controversy in the 1960s to Greece's Virtual Bankruptcy in 2010", held at the Panteion University of Athens, 11–12 April 2019. We are grateful to the participants, and in particular to Athanasios Angeloussis, Antonia Chistodoulaki, Charalampos Economidis, Heleni Groza, Fotoula Iliadi, Apostolis Katsinos, Despoina Kesperi, Gregory Kordas, Eirini Leriou, Nikolaos Ntemiroglou, Maria Pantzartzidou, Kostas Papoulis, Eleftheria Rodousaki, Stelios Sfakiotakis, Christos Tsirimokos, Manolis Tzouvelekas, Panagiotis Veltsistas, and Eugenia Zouvela for stimulating questions, very helpful remarks and suggestions.

Furthermore, for criticisms, comments, hints, and insightful discussions on various materials that eventually became this book, we are indebted to Deepankar Basu, Amit Bhaduri, Scott Carter, Paul Cockshott, Gabriel Colletis, Stavros A. Drakopoulos, George Economakis, Peter Flaschel, Takao Fujimoto, Konstantinos N. Konstantakis, Heinz D. Kurz, Costas Lapavitsas, Panayotis G. Michaelides, Murray Milgate, Gary Mongiovi, Thomas Moutos, Sobei H. Oda, Fabio Petri, Dimitri B. Papadimitriou, Bruce Philp, Louis-Philippe Rochon, Neri Salvadori, Bertram Schefold, Susan K. Schroeder, Anwar M. Shaikh, Nicholas Theocarakis, Ioannis Theodossiou, Persefoni Tsaliki, Lefteris Tsoulfidis, Spyros Vassilakis, Roberto Veneziani, Dave Zachariah, and Stefano Zambelli.

Very special thanks are due to Yuji Aruka for his kind interest in our work: he encouraged us to integrate our research by publishing the present book and his help during the project was invaluable. The responsibility for the views expressed herein, errors, and oversights is our own.

Athens, Greece                                                              Theodore Mariolis
September 2020                                                          Nikolaos Rodousakis
                                                                                  George Soklis

# Contents

# About the Authors

**Theodore Mariolis** is Professor of Political Economy in the Department of Public Administration at the Panteion University of Athens, Greece. His main educational and research interests are Political Economy, Input–Output Analysis, International Economics, Theory of Endogenous Economic Fluctuations, and History of Economic Thought. He was Founder & Co-Editor of the journal "Bulletin of Political Economy", and is Director of the "Study Group on Sraffian Economics".

**Nikolaos Rodousakis** is a Research Fellow in the Centre of Planning and Economic Research (KEPE), Athens, Greece. He holds a Degree in 'Public Economics', a M.A. in 'Economics of Production and Intersectoral Relations', and a PhD in 'Economics' from the Department of Public Administration of the Panteion University of Social and Political Sciences, Greece. His main educational and research interests are Political Economy, Input–Output Analysis, and Theory of Endogenous Economic Fluctuations.

**George Soklis** is a Research Fellow in the Centre of Planning and Economic Research (KEPE), Athens, Greece. He holds a Degree in 'Public Economics', a M.A. in 'Economics of Production and Intersectoral Relations', and a PhD in 'Economics' from the Department of Public Administration of the Panteion University of Social and Political Sciences, Greece. His main educational and research interests are Political Economy, Input–Output Analysis, and Tourism Economics.

# Chapter 1
# Empirical Input–Output Representations and Transmutations of Actual Economies

**Abstract** This chapter maps the structure of the empirical input–output representations of actual economies, i.e. the Supply and Use Tables and the Symmetric Input–Output Tables, and critically evaluates the methods that have been proposed to convert the former into the latter. It is argued that (i) all conversion methods rest on the groundless assumption that single production, and not joint production, characterizes the economic structure of the real world; and (ii) a consistent approach is the straightforward treatment of the Supply and Use Tables on the basis of general joint production models inspired by the von Neumann and Sraffa contributions.

**Keywords** Input–output analysis · Joint production · Supply and use tables · Symmetric Input–Output tables · von Neumann–Sraffa-based analysis

## 1.1  Introduction

The representation of actual economies in terms of input–output relationships, where the inter-dependency amongst the different production activities plays a central role, dates back to the *Tableau Économique* of François Quesnay (1972). In this table, Quesnay distinguished two productive sectors (primary production and manufacturing) and three social classes, i.e. the "productive class" (*classe productive*), which is involved in primary production; the "sterile class" (*classe stérile*), involved in manufacturing; and the class of proprietors of land and natural resources (*classe propriétaire*). The modern representation of actual economies and the development of input–output analysis as a distinct area of economics was introduced by Leontief (1936), who constructed the *tableau économique* or, in modern terms, the input–output table for the economy of the United States of America.[1]

---

[1]For a review of the contributions to the foundation of input–output analysis from the Physiocrats to Piero Sraffa, see Kurz et al. (1998). For the *Tableau Économique*, also see Marx (1977).

© Springer Nature Singapore Pte Ltd. 2021
T. Mariolis et al., *Spectral Theory of Value and Actual Economies*, Evolutionary Economics and Social Complexity Science 24,
https://doi.org/10.1007/978-981-33-6260-4_1

1

During the last decades, there has been a significant development, both theoretically and empirically, of input–output analysis, and, today, input–output tables constitute part of the national accounting systems for most countries. The most known form of input–output tables, and the most widely used in empirical studies, are the so-called Symmetric Input–Output Tables (SIOTs). SIOTs represent the inter-sectoral relationships of an economy in which the number of products equals the number of production activities and each product is produced by only one production activity; therefore, SIOTs rule out, by construction, joint production. On the other hand, a less often used form of input–output tables, for empirical applications, is the Supply and Use Tables (SUTs), which constitute a pair of tables: one describes the production of goods and services by the different industries (Supply Table) and the other describes the use of goods and services by the different industries (Use Table). Contrary to the structure of the SIOTs, in the SUTs, there are industries that produce more than one product and products that are produced by more than one industry; therefore, these tables do not rule out joint production. Furthermore, SUTs constitute the core of the modern system of national accounting and also the basis for the derivation of SIOTs under specific assumptions.

This chapter (1) presents the basic characteristics of both the SUTs and SIOTs; (2) critically reviews the methods that have been proposed to convert SUTs into SIOTs; and (3) exposes the essential ideas of the von Neumann–Sraffa-based approach on joint production as a preferable approach to treat SUTs. Section 1.2 presents the basic structure of the SUTs. Section 1.3 presents the basic structure of the SIOTs. Section 1.4 critically reviews and evaluates the methods that have been proposed to convert SUTs into SIOTs. Section 1.5 presents the essential ideas of the von Neumann–Sraffa-based approach on joint production as a way to treat SUTs. Finally, Sect. 1.6 concludes.

## 1.2   The Supply and Use Tables

In 1968 System of National Accounts, United Nations introduced the supply and use framework in the compilation of national accounts (United Nations 1968).[2] This framework forms the basis for the most detailed description of a national economy, providing information about the supply and demand side of the economic system as well as its relations with other national economies. The core of the supply and use framework consists of a pair of tables, known as the Supply and Use Tables (SUTs). The SUTs describe the flows of goods and services produced by the different industries of a national economy, the flows of goods and services with the rest of the world, the structure of the cost of production of each industry, the income generated in the production processes, and the final uses in the economy. The SUTs provide detailed information not only regarding the inter-dependencies

---

[2]What follows draws on Soklis (2005, 2012, Chap. 4).

**Table 1.1** Simplistic supply table

| Industries Products | Industry 1 | Industry 2 | Total | Imports | Total supply |
|---|---|---|---|---|---|
| Product 1 | $M_{11}$ | $M_{12}$ | $\sum_{j=1}^{2} M_{1j}$ | $IM_1$ | $TS_1$ |
| Product 2 | $M_{21}$ | $M_{22}$ | $\sum_{j=1}^{2} M_{2j}$ | $IM_2$ | $TS_2$ |
| Total | $\sum_{i=1}^{2} M_{i1}$ | $\sum_{i=1}^{2} M_{i2}$ | $\sum_{i,j=1}^{2} M_{ij}$ | $\sum_{i=1}^{2} IM_i$ | $TS$ |

amongst the various industries of the national economy but also on basic macroeconomic aggregates, such as gross domestic product, value added, total and intermediate consumption, capital formation, exports, and imports.

The supply table describes the production of goods and services by the different
industries, distinguishing domestic supply from imports per product. The part of the
supply table that describes domestic production of the different industries is called
the "make matrix" of the economy. A simplistic supply table, describing the
production of two commodities by two industries is shown in Table 1.1. Thus, the
make matrix, $\mathbf{M} \equiv [M_{ij}]$ of this particular economy is of dimensions $2 \times 2$.[3]

Each row of the make matrix gives the quantities (in money terms) of each
product produced by the different industries, while each column gives the quantities
of the different products produced by each industry. Thus, $M_{ij}$ denotes the quantity of
product $i$ produced by industry $j$. The on-diagonal elements of the make matrix
describe the so-called primary (or characteristic) product of each industry and the
off-diagonal elements describe the so-called secondary products, where the "primary
product" of an industry is defined as the output of that industry that comprises the
primary source of revenues. The column of imports gives the quantities of total
imports of each commodity, while the last column of the supply table gives the total
supply of the economy (domestic production plus imports) of each commodity. The
last row of the supply table gives the total output of each industry, the total imports,
and the total supply in the economy. Thus, $IM_i$ denotes the imports of product $i$; $TS_i$
the total supply of product $i$ in the economy; and $TS$ the total supply in the economy.

The use table describes the use of goods and services by the different industries,
the income generation per production activity, and the final uses of the production
per category of final demand. The part of the use table that describes intermediate
consumption by product and by industry is called the "use matrix" of the economy.
A simplistic use table, describing the uses of two commodities by two industries is
shown in Table 1.2. Thus, the use matrix, $\mathbf{U} \equiv [U_{ij}]$ of this particular economy is of
dimensions $2 \times 2$.

---

[3]In general, the SUTs need not be "square", i.e. the number of goods and services produced need
not be equal to the producing industries (see, e.g. Eurostat 2008, p. 325; United Nations 1999,
p. 86). Nevertheless, in what follows we assume, for simplicity's sake, that the make and use
matrices are square.

**Table 1.2** Simplistic use table

| Industries / Products | Industry 1 | Industry 2 | Total | Final uses | Total uses |
|---|---|---|---|---|---|
| Product 1 | $U_{11}$ | $U_{12}$ | $\sum_{j=1}^{2} U_{1j}$ | $F_1$ | $TU_1$ |
| Product 2 | $U_{21}$ | $U_{22}$ | $\sum_{j=1}^{2} U_{2j}$ | $F_2$ | $TU_2$ |
| Total intermediate consumption | $\sum_{i=1}^{2} U_{i1}$ | $\sum_{i=1}^{2} U_{i2}$ | $\sum_{i,j=1}^{2} U_{ij}$ | $\sum_{i=1}^{2} F_i$ | $TU$ |
| Value added | $V_1$ | $V_2$ | $\sum_{j=1}^{2} V_j$ | | |
| Total output | $X_1$ | $X_2$ | $\sum_{j=1}^{2} X_j$ | | |

Each row of the use matrix gives the quantities (in money terms) of each product used by the different industries, while each column gives the quantities of the different products used by each industry. Thus, $U_{ij}$ denotes the quantity of product $i$ used by industry $j$. The column of final uses gives the uses of products for final consumption, gross capital formation and exports, while the row of value added gives the components of value added per industry, i.e. compensation of employees, other net taxes on production, consumption of fixed capital, and net operating surplus. The last column of the use table gives the total uses (intermediate consumption plus final uses) by product, while the last row of the table shows the total inputs (intermediate consumption plus value added) by industry and, therefore, is identified with the money value of the total output of each industry. Thus, $F_i$ denotes the quantity of product $i$ used for final demand; $TU_i$ the total use of product $i$ in the economy; $V_j$ the value added in industry $j$; $X_j$ the total output of industry $j$; and $TU$ the total uses in the economy (all data are expressed in monetary units).

By construction of the SUTs, the following identities hold for the supply table:

$$\sum_{j=1}^{2} M_{ij} + IM_i \equiv TS_i \tag{1.1}$$

$$\sum_{i,j=1}^{2} M_{ij} + \sum_{i=1}^{2} IM_i \equiv TS \tag{1.2}$$

From identities (1.1) and (1.2) it follows that it is also holds

$$\sum_{i=1}^{2} TS_i \equiv TS \tag{1.3}$$

By construction of the SUTs, the following identities hold for the use table:

$$\sum_{j=1}^{2} U_{ij} + F_i \equiv TU_i \tag{1.4}$$

$$\sum_{i,j=1}^{2} U_{ij} + \sum_{i=1}^{2} F_i \equiv TU \tag{1.5}$$

$$\sum_{i=1}^{2} U_{ij} + V_j \equiv X_j \tag{1.6}$$

From identities (1.4) and (1.5) it follows that it also holds

$$\sum_{i=1}^{2} TU_i \equiv TU \tag{1.7}$$

The supply and the use tables are connected through the following identity:

$$TS_i \equiv TU_i \tag{1.8}$$

By taking into account identities (1.1) and (1.4), identity (1.8) can be rewritten as

$$\sum_{j=1}^{2} M_{ij} + IM_i \equiv \sum_{j=1}^{2} U_{ij} + F_i \tag{1.9}$$

Thus, taking into account identities (1.3) and (1.7), it also holds

$$TS \equiv TU$$

The supply and the use tables are also connected through the following identity:

$$\sum_{i=1}^{2} M_{ij} \equiv X_j$$

or, by taking into account identity (1.6),

$$\sum_{i=1}^{2} M_{ij} \equiv \sum_{i=1}^{2} U_{ij} + V_j \qquad (1.10)$$

The identities (1.9) and (1.10) can be rewritten in vector–matrix terms as follows:

$$\mathbf{Me} + \mathbf{Im} \equiv \mathbf{Ue} + \mathbf{f} \qquad (1.11)$$

$$\mathbf{e}^{\mathrm{T}}\mathbf{M} \equiv \mathbf{e}^{\mathrm{T}}\mathbf{U} + \mathbf{v}^{\mathrm{T}} \qquad (1.12)$$

where $\mathbf{M} = \begin{bmatrix} M_{11} & M_{12} \\ M_{21} & M_{22} \end{bmatrix}$ is the make matrix; $\mathbf{Im} = \begin{bmatrix} IM_1 \\ IM_2 \end{bmatrix}$ is the vector of imports; $\mathbf{U} = \begin{bmatrix} U_{11} & U_{12} \\ U_{21} & U_{22} \end{bmatrix}$ is the use matrix; $\mathbf{f} = \begin{bmatrix} F_1 \\ F_2 \end{bmatrix}$ is the vector of final demand; $\mathbf{v} = \begin{bmatrix} V_1 \\ V_2 \end{bmatrix}$ is the value added vector; $\mathbf{e} = \begin{bmatrix} 1 \\ 1 \end{bmatrix}$ the column summation vector; and the superscript "T" denotes the transpose.

From the previous, it follows that SUTs constitute a general accounting framework that allows statistical authorities to enter basic economic data in the exact structure in which they are observed. It is interesting to note that despite the fact that SUTs give a very detailed "picture" of the actual economies, they are rarely used in input–output applications in the form presented above.[4] On the other hand, the usual basis for input–output applications are the Symmetric Input–Output Tables (SIOTs ). The main difference between SUTs and SIOTs is that in the SUTs (SIOTs) there are (are no) industries that produce more than one commodity and (nor) commodities that are produced by more than one industry. Thus, the SUTs (SIOTs) allow for (exclude) joint production activities, which constitute a central characteristic of the actual economic world.[5] In the next section we present the main characteristics of the SIOTs.

---

[4]Exceptions can be found in Mariolis and Soklis (2007, 2010, 2018), Mariolis et al. (2018), Soklis (2006, 2011, 2012, 2015). Also see Chaps. 5, 7 and 9 of this book.

[5]It has to be noted that some of the secondary products that appear in the SUTs may result from statistical classification. Therefore, these products do not correspond with the notion of joint production (see, e.g. United Nations 1999, p. 77). However, this fact by no means undermines the empirical importance of joint production (see, e.g. Baumgärtner et al. 2006; Faber et al. 1998; Kurz 2006; Steedman 1984).

**Table 1.3** Simplistic symmetric input–output table

| Products<br>Products | Product 1 | Product 2 | Total | Final uses | Total uses |
|---|---|---|---|---|---|
| Product 1 | $Z_{11}$ | $Z_{12}$ | $\sum_{j=1}^{2} Z_{1j}$ | $F_1$ | $TU_1$ |
| Product 2 | $Z_{21}$ | $Z_{22}$ | $\sum_{j=1}^{2} Z_{2j}$ | $F_2$ | $TU_2$ |
| Total intermediate consumption | $\sum_{i=1}^{2} Z_{i1}$ | $\sum_{i=1}^{2} Z_{i2}$ | $\sum_{i,j=1}^{2} Z_{ij}$ | $\sum_{i=1}^{2} F_i$ | $TU$ |
| Value added | $V_1$ | $V_2$ | $\sum_{j=1}^{2} V_j$ | | |
| Total output | $X_1$ | $X_2$ | $\sum_{j=1}^{2} X_j$ | | |
| Imports | $IM_1$ | $IM_2$ | $\sum_{i=1}^{2} IM_i$ | | |
| Total supply | $TS_1$ | $TS_2$ | $TS$ | | |

## 1.3   The Symmetric Input–Output Tables

The SIOTs are constructed on the basis of assumptions on the relationships between inputs and outputs that have been recorded in the SUTs.[6] The alternative assumptions that have been proposed to convert SUTs into SIOTs will be analytically discussed in Sect. 1.4. Depending on the assumptions used to construct SIOTs, the derived input–output table can either describe the relationships amongst the products of a national economy ("product-by-product" SIOTs) or the relationships amongst the industries of the economy ("industry-by-industry" SIOTs). The choice between the construction of product-by-product tables or industry-by-industry tables depends on the analytical purposes that these tables are intended to be used. Industry-by-industry SIOTs are considered to be closer to statistical sources and actual market transactions, while product-by-product SIOTs are considered as more homogenous in terms of cost structures and production activities (see, e.g. Eurostat 2008, p. 24). The part of the SIOTs table that describes intermediate consumption either by product or by industry is called the "Transactions Matrix" or the "Matrix of Intermediate Inputs" of the economy. A simplistic product-by-product SIOT for an economy producing only two products is shown in Table 1.3.[7] Thus, the transactions matrix, $\mathbf{Z} \equiv [Z_{ij}]$ of this particular economy is of dimensions $2 \times 2$.

Each row of the SIOTs gives the quantities (in money terms) of each product used in the production of the other products of the economy, while each column gives the

---

[6]What follows draws on Soklis (2012, Chap. 3).

[7]What follows can easily be extended in the case of industry-by-industry SIOTs without affecting our main arguments.

quantities of the different products used in the production of each product. Thus, $Z_{ij}$ denotes the quantity of product $i$ used in the production of product $j$. The column of final uses gives the uses of products for final consumption, gross capital formation and exports, while the row of value added gives the components of value added per homogeneous unit of production, i.e. compensation of employees, other net taxes on production, consumption of fixed capital, and net operating surplus. The last column of the SIOTs gives the total uses (intermediate consumption plus final uses) by product, while the last row of the table shows the total supply in the economy, i.e. total output per product plus imports. Thus, $F_i$ denotes the quantity of product $i$ used for final demand; $TU_i$ the total use of product $i$ in the economy; $V_j$ the value added in the production of product $j$; $X_j$ the total output of product $j$; $IM_i$ the imports of product $i$; $TS_i$ the total supply of product $i$; $TU$ the total uses in the economy; and $TS$ the total supply in the economy (all data are expressed in monetary units).

By construction of the SIOTs, the following identities hold:

$$\sum_{j=1}^{2} Z_{ij} + F_i \equiv TU_i \tag{1.13}$$

$$\sum_{i=1}^{2} TU_i \equiv TU \tag{1.14}$$

$$\sum_{i=1}^{2} Z_{ij} + V_j \equiv X_j \tag{1.15}$$

$$TS_i \equiv X_j + IM_i, \quad \forall j = i \tag{1.16}$$

$$\sum_{i=1}^{2} TS_i \equiv TS \tag{1.17}$$

$$TS_i \equiv TU_i \tag{1.18}$$

From identities (1.14), (1.17), and (1.18), it follows that

$$TS \equiv TU$$

From identities (1.13), (1.16), and (1.18), it also follows that

$$X_i + IM_i \equiv \sum_{j=1}^{2} Z_{ij} + F_i \tag{1.19}$$

The identities (1.15) and (1.19) can be rewritten in vector–matrix terms as follows:[8]

$$\mathbf{x}^{\mathrm{T}} \equiv \mathbf{e}^{\mathrm{T}}\mathbf{Z} + \mathbf{v}^{\mathrm{T}}$$

$$\mathbf{x} + \mathbf{Im} \equiv \mathbf{Ze} + \mathbf{f}$$

where $\mathbf{x} = \begin{bmatrix} X_1 \\ X_2 \end{bmatrix}$ is the total output vector; and $\mathbf{Z} = \begin{bmatrix} Z_{11} & Z_{12} \\ Z_{21} & Z_{22} \end{bmatrix}$ is the matrix of intermediate inputs.

From the previous, it follows that the SIOTs describe an economy in which each production process produces only one product and each product is produced by only one production process. Thus, the SIOTs correspond to an economic world of single production. As it has already been mentioned, those tables of single production are derived from the SUTs, which allow for joint production activities, on the basis of specific assumptions on the relationships between inputs and outputs. The alternative assumptions that have been proposed to convert SUTs into SIOTs are discussed in the next section.

## 1.4   Conversion of Supply and Use Tables into Symmetric Input–Output Tables

### 1.4.1   Methods Converting Supply and Use Tables into Product-by-Product Symmetric Input–Output Tables

Since the introduction of SUTs to the System of National Accounts, there has been an ongoing discussion on how these tables can be converted into single production tables (i.e. SIOTs).[9] Most of the discussion has been focused on two alternative assumptions for dealing with the problem at hand: (i) the Product Technology Assumption (PTA); and (ii) the Industry Technology Assumption (ITA).

Leaving aside, for simplicity's sake, the imports of the economy, then the SUTs described by identities (1.11) and (1.12) reduce to the following equations:

$$\mathbf{Me} = \mathbf{Ue} + \mathbf{f} \tag{1.20}$$

$$\mathbf{e}^{\mathrm{T}}\mathbf{M} = \mathbf{e}^{\mathrm{T}}\mathbf{U} + \mathbf{v}^{\mathrm{T}} \tag{1.21}$$

---

[8]The transpose of an $n \times 1$ vector $\boldsymbol{\chi} \equiv [\chi_i]$ is denoted by $\boldsymbol{\chi}^{\mathrm{T}}$, the diagonal matrix formed from the elements of $\boldsymbol{\chi}$ is denoted by $\hat{\boldsymbol{\chi}}$, and $\mathbf{e}$ denotes the summation vector, i.e. $\mathbf{e} \equiv [1, 1, \ldots, 1]^{\mathrm{T}}$.
[9]What follows draws on Mariolis (2008), Soklis (2009, 2012, Chap. 4).

The conversion methods try to transform Eqs. (1.20) and (1.21) into a single production system (SIOTs) described by the following equations:

$$\mathbf{x} = \mathbf{Ze} + \mathbf{f}^* \tag{1.22}$$

$$\mathbf{x}^T = \mathbf{e}^T\mathbf{Z} + \mathbf{v}^{*T} \tag{1.23}$$

where $\mathbf{Z} \equiv [\mathbf{A}(\mathbf{U}, \mathbf{M})\widehat{\mathbf{x}}]$, $\mathbf{A}(\mathbf{U}, \mathbf{M})$ is the technical coefficients matrix that is derived from the conversion of SUTs into SIOTs, and $\mathbf{f}^*$, $\mathbf{v}^{*T}$ are the transformed vectors of final demand and value added, respectively. It should be clear that the conversion of SUTs into SIOTs is meaningful only in the case where the make matrix, $\mathbf{M}$, is non-diagonal, i.e. there are industries with secondary production. In the case where there is no secondary production in the economy, i.e. the matrix $\mathbf{M}$ is diagonal, then the system of Eqs. (1.20) and (1.21) is equivalent to the system of Eqs. (1.22) and (1.23). Hence, the purpose of the conversion methods presented below is, by definition, the elimination of secondary production in the economic system.

### 1.4.1.1   The Product Technology Assumption

The PTA assumes that each industry produces only the total output of the product that is primary to that industry and that each product has its own input structure, irrespective of the industry that produces it. In formal terms, it is assumed that (see, e.g. van Rijckeghem 1967; United Nations 1968, p. 49)[10]

$$\mathbf{A}(\mathbf{U}, \mathbf{M}) = \mathbf{U}\left[\widehat{\mathbf{e}^T\mathbf{M}}\right]^{-1}\left[\widehat{\mathbf{e}^T\mathbf{M}}\right]\mathbf{M}^{-1} = \mathbf{U}\mathbf{M}^{-1} \tag{1.24}$$

and

$$\mathbf{x} = \mathbf{Me} \tag{1.25}$$

Equation (1.24) entails that

$$\mathbf{U} = \mathbf{A}(\mathbf{U}, \mathbf{M})\mathbf{M} \tag{1.26}$$

Post-multiplying Eq. (1.26) by the summation vector gives

$$\mathbf{Ue} = \mathbf{A}(\mathbf{U}, \mathbf{M})\mathbf{Me} \tag{1.27}$$

Substituting Eqs. (1.25) and (1.27) into Eq. (1.20) yields

---

[10]The origins of this method can be found in Edmonston (1952, p. 567).

$$\mathbf{x} = \mathbf{A}(\mathbf{U}, \mathbf{M})\mathbf{x} + \mathbf{f} \tag{1.28}$$

Thus, from Eqs. (1.28) and (1.22) it follows that $\mathbf{f}^* = \mathbf{f}$. From Eqs. (1.26) and (1.21) it follows that

$$\mathbf{e}^{\mathrm{T}}\mathbf{M} = \mathbf{e}^{\mathrm{T}}\mathbf{A}(\mathbf{U}, \mathbf{M})\mathbf{M} + \mathbf{v}^{\mathrm{T}} \tag{1.29}$$

Post-multiplying Eq. (1.29) by $\mathbf{M}^{-1}\left[\widehat{\mathbf{Me}}\right]$ gives

$$\mathbf{e}^{\mathrm{T}}\left[\widehat{\mathbf{Me}}\right] = \mathbf{e}^{\mathrm{T}}\mathbf{A}(\mathbf{U}, \mathbf{M})\left[\widehat{\mathbf{Me}}\right] + \mathbf{v}^{\mathrm{T}}\mathbf{M}^{-1}\left[\widehat{\mathbf{Me}}\right] \tag{1.30}$$

Substituting Eq. (1.25) into Eq. (1.30) we obtain

$$\mathbf{x}^{\mathrm{T}} = \mathbf{e}^{\mathrm{T}}\mathbf{A}(\mathbf{U}, \mathbf{M})\widehat{\mathbf{x}} + \mathbf{v}^{\mathrm{T}}\mathbf{M}^{-1}\widehat{\mathbf{x}} \tag{1.31}$$

From Eqs. (1.31), (1.23), and (1.25) it follows that $\mathbf{v}^{*\mathrm{T}} = \mathbf{v}^{\mathrm{T}}\mathbf{M}^{-1}\left[\widehat{\mathbf{Me}}\right]$. Hence, under the PTA, the joint production system described by Eqs. (1.20) and (1.21) is converted into the single production system described by the following equations:

$$\mathbf{Me} = \mathbf{A}(\mathbf{U}, \mathbf{M})\mathbf{Me} + \mathbf{f} \tag{1.32}$$

and

$$\left[\mathbf{Me}\right]^{\mathrm{T}} = \mathbf{e}^{\mathrm{T}}\mathbf{A}(\mathbf{U}, \mathbf{M})\left[\widehat{\mathbf{Me}}\right] + \mathbf{v}^{\mathrm{T}}\mathbf{M}^{-1}\left[\widehat{\mathbf{Me}}\right] \tag{1.33}$$

### 1.4.1.2   The Industry Technology Assumption

The ITA assumes that each industry produces only the total output of the product that is primary to that industry and that has the same input requirements for any unit of output. In that case, the input structure of each product depends on what industry produces it. In formal terms, it is assumed that (see, e.g. United Nations 1968, pp. 49–50)

$$\mathbf{A}(\mathbf{U}, \mathbf{M}) = \mathbf{U}\left[\widehat{\mathbf{e}^{\mathrm{T}}\mathbf{M}}\right]^{-1}\mathbf{M}^{\mathrm{T}}\left[\widehat{\mathbf{Me}}\right]^{-1} \tag{1.34}$$

and

$$\mathbf{x} = \mathbf{Me} \tag{1.35}$$

Equation (1.34) entails that

$$\mathbf{U} = \mathbf{A(U,M)} \left[ \widehat{\mathbf{Me}} \right] \left[ \mathbf{M^T} \right]^{-1} \left[ \widehat{\mathbf{e^T M}} \right] \tag{1.36}$$

Post-multiplying Eq. (1.36) by the summation vector gives

$$\mathbf{Ue} = \mathbf{A(U,M)Me} \tag{1.37}$$

Substituting Eqs. (1.35) and (1.37) into Eq. (1.20) yields

$$\mathbf{x} = \mathbf{A(U,M)x + f} \tag{1.38}$$

From Eqs. (1.38) and (1.22) it follows that $\mathbf{f^*} = \mathbf{f}$. Substituting Eq. (1.36) into Eq. (1.21) yields

$$\mathbf{e^T M} = \mathbf{e^T A(U,M)} \left[ \widehat{\mathbf{Me}} \right] \left[ \mathbf{M^T} \right]^{-1} \left[ \widehat{\mathbf{e^T M}} \right] + \mathbf{v^T} \tag{1.39}$$

Post-multiplying Eq. (1.39) by $\left[ \widehat{\mathbf{e^T M}} \right]^{-1} \mathbf{M^T}$ gives

$$\mathbf{e^T M} \left[ \widehat{\mathbf{e^T M}} \right]^{-1} \mathbf{M^T} = \mathbf{e^T A(U,M)} \left[ \widehat{\mathbf{Me}} \right] + \mathbf{v^T} \left[ \widehat{\mathbf{e^T M}} \right]^{-1} \mathbf{M^T} \tag{1.40}$$

Substituting Eq. (1.35) into Eq. (1.40) we obtain[11]

$$\mathbf{x^T} = \mathbf{e^T A(U,M)\hat{x}} + \mathbf{v^T} \left[ \widehat{\mathbf{e^T M}} \right]^{-1} \mathbf{M^T} \tag{1.41}$$

From Eqs. (1.41) and (1.23) it follows that $\mathbf{v^{*T}} = \mathbf{v^T} \left[ \widehat{\mathbf{e^T M}} \right]^{-1} \mathbf{M^T}$. Hence, under the ITA, the joint production system described by Eqs. (1.20) and (1.21) is converted into the single production system described by the following equations:

$$\mathbf{Me} = \mathbf{A(U,M)Me + f} \tag{1.42}$$

and

---

[11]Note that $\mathbf{e^T M} \left[ \widehat{\mathbf{e^T M}} \right]^{-1} \mathbf{M^T} = \mathbf{e^T M^T} = [\mathbf{Me}]^T$.

$$[\mathbf{Me}]^{\mathrm{T}} = \mathbf{e}^{\mathrm{T}}\mathbf{A}(\mathbf{U},\mathbf{M})\left[\widehat{\mathbf{Me}}\right] + \mathbf{v}^{\mathrm{T}}\left[\widehat{\mathbf{e}^{\mathrm{T}}\mathbf{M}}\right]^{-1}\mathbf{M}^{\mathrm{T}} \qquad (1.43)$$

### 1.4.1.3  The By-Product Method

The by-product method (Stone 1961, pp. 39–41) assumes that all secondary products are "by-products" and that can be treated as negative inputs of the industries that they are actually produced.[12] The make matrix splits into $\mathbf{M}_1$ and $\mathbf{M}_2$, where $\mathbf{M}_1$ is the diagonal matrix that describes the primary products of each industry and $\mathbf{M}_2$ is the off-diagonal matrix that describes the secondary products of each industry. Thus, it holds

$$\mathbf{M} \equiv \mathbf{M}_1 + \mathbf{M}_2 \qquad (1.44)$$

In mathematical terms, the by-product method assumes that (see, e.g. ten Raa et al. 1984, p. 88)

$$\mathbf{A}(\mathbf{U},\mathbf{M}) = [\mathbf{U} - \mathbf{M}_2]\mathbf{M}_1^{-1} \qquad (1.45)$$

and

$$\mathbf{x} = \mathbf{M}_1\mathbf{e} \qquad (1.46)$$

Equation (1.45) entails that

$$\mathbf{U} - \mathbf{M}_2 = \mathbf{A}(\mathbf{U},\mathbf{M})\mathbf{M}_1 \qquad (1.47)$$

Combining Eqs. (1.44) and (1.20) gives

$$\mathbf{M}_1\mathbf{e} = (\mathbf{U} - \mathbf{M}_2)\mathbf{e} + \mathbf{f} \qquad (1.48)$$

Substituting Eqs. (1.46) and (1.47) into Eq. (1.48) yields

$$\mathbf{x} = \mathbf{A}(\mathbf{U},\mathbf{M})\mathbf{x} + \mathbf{f} \qquad (1.49)$$

From Eqs. (1.22) and (1.49) it follows that $\mathbf{f}^* = \mathbf{f}$. Combining Eqs. (1.44) and (1.21) gives

---

[12]By-products are defined as products that are technologically linked to the production of the primary product of the industry where it is actually produced (Stone 1961, p. 39). The inputs needed for their production are considered to be "low" in relation to the primary product of the industry where they are produced (United Nations 1999, p. 77; Viet 1994).

$$\mathbf{e}^T \mathbf{M}_1 = \mathbf{e}^T \left[ \mathbf{U} - \mathbf{M}_2 \right] + \mathbf{v}^T \tag{1.50}$$

Substituting Eq. (1.45) into Eq. (1.50) yields

$$\mathbf{e}^T \mathbf{M}_1 = \mathbf{e}^T \mathbf{A}(\mathbf{U}, \mathbf{M}) \mathbf{M}_1 + \mathbf{v}^T \tag{1.51}$$

Substituting Eq. (1.46) into Eq. (1.51) yields[13]

$$\mathbf{x}^T = \mathbf{e}^T \mathbf{A}(\mathbf{U}, \mathbf{M}) \widehat{\mathbf{x}} + \mathbf{v}^T \tag{1.52}$$

From Eqs. (1.52) and (1.23) it follows that $\mathbf{v}^{*T} = \mathbf{v}^T$. Thus, it follows that, under the by-product method, the joint production system described by Eqs. (1.20) and (1.21) is converted into the single production system described by the equations

$$\mathbf{M}_1 \mathbf{e} = \mathbf{A}(\mathbf{U}, \mathbf{M}) \mathbf{M}_1 \mathbf{e} + \mathbf{f}$$

and

$$\left[ \mathbf{M}_1 \mathbf{e} \right]^T = \mathbf{e}^T \mathbf{A}(\mathbf{U}, \mathbf{M}) \mathbf{M}_1 + \mathbf{v}^T$$

### 1.4.1.4   Mixed Technology Assumptions

Mixed Technology Assumptions were suggested by Gigantes and Matuszewski (1968) and were incorporated in the 1968 System of National Accounts (United Nations 1968, p. 50). This conversion method assumes that a part of the secondary products should be treated using the PTA and the remaining part should be treated using the ITA. The make matrix splits into the matrices $\mathbf{M}_1$ and $\mathbf{M}_2$ and it is assumed that $\mathbf{M}_1$ includes output that fits the PTA, whereas $\mathbf{M}_2$ includes output that fits the ITA. Thus, it holds

$$\mathbf{M} \equiv \mathbf{M}_1 + \mathbf{M}_2 \tag{1.53}$$

Following Armstrong (1975), we assume that

$$\mathbf{A}_1 = \mathbf{U} \left[ \widehat{\mathbf{M}^T \mathbf{e}} \right]^{-1} \left[ \widehat{\mathbf{M}_1^T \mathbf{e}} \right] \mathbf{M}_1^{-1}$$

and

---

[13]Note that $\mathbf{e}^T \mathbf{M}_1 = [\mathbf{M}_1 \mathbf{e}]^T$ and $\mathbf{M}_1 = \left[ \widehat{\mathbf{M}_1 \mathbf{e}} \right]$.

$$\mathbf{A}_2 = \mathbf{U}\left[\widehat{\mathbf{M}^T\mathbf{e}}\right]^{-1}\mathbf{M}_2^T\left[\widehat{\mathbf{M}_2\mathbf{e}}\right]^{-1}$$

where $\mathbf{A}_1$ is the technical coefficients matrix for outputs included in $\mathbf{M}_1$, while $\mathbf{A}_2$ is the technical coefficients matrix for outputs included in $\mathbf{M}_2$. Then, the technical coefficients matrix of the economy is given by[14]

$$\mathbf{A}(\mathbf{U},\mathbf{M}) = \mathbf{A}_1[\mathbf{I} - \mathbf{D}] + \mathbf{A}_2\mathbf{D}$$

where $\mathbf{D} \equiv \left[\widehat{\mathbf{M}_2\mathbf{e}}\right]\left[\widehat{\mathbf{M}\mathbf{e}}\right]^{-1}$. It can be seen that if $\mathbf{M}_2 = \mathbf{0}$, then $\mathbf{A}(\mathbf{U},\mathbf{M}) = \mathbf{A}_1 = \mathbf{U}\mathbf{M}^{-1}$, which is the PTA. On the other hand, if $\mathbf{M}_1 = \mathbf{0}$, then $\mathbf{A}(\mathbf{U},\mathbf{M}) = \mathbf{A}_2 = \mathbf{U}\left[\widehat{\mathbf{e}^T\mathbf{M}}\right]^{-1}\mathbf{M}^T\left[\widehat{\mathbf{M}\mathbf{e}}\right]^{-1}$, which is the ITA.

On the basis of their critique to the ITA, ten Raa et al. (1984) constructed an alternative mixed technology model, assuming that $\mathbf{M}_2$ includes output that fits the by-product assumption. In mathematical terms, it is assumed that

$$\mathbf{A}(\mathbf{U},\mathbf{M}) = [\mathbf{U} - \mathbf{M}_2]\mathbf{M}_1^{-1} \tag{1.54}$$

and

$$\mathbf{x} = \mathbf{M}_1\mathbf{e} \tag{1.55}$$

Equation (1.54) entails that

$$\mathbf{U} - \mathbf{M}_2 = \mathbf{A}(\mathbf{U},\mathbf{M})\mathbf{M}_1 \tag{1.56}$$

Combining Eqs. (1.53) and (1.20) gives

$$\mathbf{M}_1\mathbf{e} = [\mathbf{U} - \mathbf{M}_2]\mathbf{e} + \mathbf{f} \tag{1.57}$$

Substituting Eqs. (1.55) and (1.56) into Eq. (1.57) yields

$$\mathbf{x} = \mathbf{A}(\mathbf{U},\mathbf{M})\mathbf{x} + \mathbf{f} \tag{1.58}$$

From Eqs. (1.58) and (1.22) it follows that $\mathbf{f}^* = \mathbf{f}$. Combining Eqs. (1.53) and (1.21) gives

$$\mathbf{e}^T\mathbf{M}_1 = \mathbf{e}^T\left[\mathbf{U} - \mathbf{M}_2\right] + \mathbf{v}^T \tag{1.59}$$

Substituting Eq. (1.56) into Eq. (1.59) yields

---

[14]For alternative ways of calculating the technical coefficients matrix, using mixed technology assumptions, see Armstrong (1975, pp. 74–76) and Gigantes (1970, pp. 284–290).

$$\mathbf{e}^T\mathbf{M}_1 = \mathbf{e}^T\mathbf{A}(\mathbf{U},\mathbf{M})\mathbf{M}_1 + \mathbf{v}^T \tag{1.60}$$

Post-multiplying Eq. (1.60) by $\mathbf{M}_1^{-1}\left[\widehat{\mathbf{M}_1\mathbf{e}}\right]$ we obtain

$$\mathbf{e}^T\left[\widehat{\mathbf{M}_1\mathbf{e}}\right] = \mathbf{e}^T\mathbf{A}(\mathbf{U},\mathbf{M})\left[\widehat{\mathbf{M}_1\mathbf{e}}\right] + \mathbf{v}^T\mathbf{M}_1^{-1}\left[\widehat{\mathbf{M}_1\mathbf{e}}\right] \tag{1.61}$$

Substituting Eq. (1.55) into Eq. (1.61) yields

$$\mathbf{x}^T = \mathbf{e}^T\mathbf{A}(\mathbf{U},\mathbf{M})\widehat{\mathbf{x}} + \mathbf{v}^T\mathbf{M}_1^{-1}\widehat{\mathbf{x}} \tag{1.62}$$

From Eqs. (1.62), (1.55), and (1.23) it follows that $\mathbf{v}^{*T} = \mathbf{v}^T\mathbf{M}_1^{-1}\left[\widehat{\mathbf{M}_1\mathbf{e}}\right]$. Thus, it follows that, under the mixed technology model introduced by ten Raa et al. (1984), the joint production system described by Eqs. (1.20) and (1.21) is converted into the single production system described by

$$\mathbf{M}_1\mathbf{e} = \mathbf{A}(\mathbf{U},\mathbf{M})\mathbf{M}_1\mathbf{e} + \mathbf{f}$$

and

$$\left[\mathbf{M}_1\mathbf{e}\right]^T = \mathbf{e}^T\mathbf{A}(\mathbf{U},\mathbf{M})\left[\widehat{\mathbf{M}_1\mathbf{e}}\right] + \mathbf{v}^T\mathbf{M}_1^{-1}\left[\widehat{\mathbf{M}_1\mathbf{e}}\right]$$

### 1.4.1.5  The Transfer Method

The Transfer method was proposed by Stone (1961, pp. 39–41) as an alternative method to treat by-products. This method treats secondary products as if they were bought by the industry where they are "primary" and added to the output of that industry. In formal terms, it is assumed that (see, e.g. Jansen and ten Raa 1990, p. 215)

$$\mathbf{x} = \left[\mathbf{M} + \mathbf{M}_2^T\right]\mathbf{e} \tag{1.63}$$

and

$$\mathbf{A}(\mathbf{U},\mathbf{M}) = \left[\mathbf{U} + \mathbf{M}_2^T\right]\left[\left[\widehat{\mathbf{e}^T\mathbf{M}}\right] + \left[\widehat{\mathbf{M}\mathbf{e}}\right] - \mathbf{M}_1\right]^{-1} \tag{1.64}$$

where $\mathbf{M}_1$ is the diagonal matrix that describes the primary products of each industry and $\mathbf{M}_2$ is the off-diagonal matrix that describes the secondary products of each industry. Equation (1.64) entails that

$$\mathbf{U} + \mathbf{M}_2^T = \mathbf{A}(\mathbf{U}, \mathbf{M}) \left[ \left[ \widehat{\mathbf{e}^T \mathbf{M}} \right] + \left[ \widehat{\mathbf{M} \mathbf{e}} \right] - \mathbf{M}_1 \right] \tag{1.65}$$

Adding $\mathbf{M}_2^T \mathbf{e}$ to both sides of Eq. (1.20) we obtain

$$\left[ \mathbf{M} + \mathbf{M}_2^T \right] \mathbf{e} = \left[ \mathbf{U} + \mathbf{M}_2^T \right] \mathbf{e} + \mathbf{f} \tag{1.66}$$

Substituting Eq. (1.65) into Eq. (1.66) yields

$$\left[ \mathbf{M} + \mathbf{M}_2^T \right] \mathbf{e} = \mathbf{A}(\mathbf{U}, \mathbf{M}) \left[ \left[ \widehat{\mathbf{e}^T \mathbf{M}} \right] + \left[ \widehat{\mathbf{M} \mathbf{e}} \right] - \mathbf{M}_1 \right] \mathbf{e} + \mathbf{f}$$

or[15]

$$\left[ \mathbf{M} + \mathbf{M}_2^T \right] \mathbf{e} = \mathbf{A}(\mathbf{U}, \mathbf{M}) \left[ \mathbf{M} + \mathbf{M}_2^T \right] \mathbf{e} + \mathbf{f} \tag{1.67}$$

Substituting Eq. (1.63) into Eq. (1.67) gives

$$\mathbf{x} = \mathbf{A}(\mathbf{U}, \mathbf{M}) \mathbf{x} + \mathbf{f} \tag{1.68}$$

From Eqs. (1.68) and (1.22) it follows that $\mathbf{f}^* = \mathbf{f}$. Adding $\mathbf{e}^T \mathbf{M}_2^T$ to both sides of Eq. (1.21) we obtain

$$\mathbf{e}^T \left[ \mathbf{M} + \mathbf{M}_2^T \right] = \mathbf{e}^T \left[ \mathbf{U} + \mathbf{M}_2^T \right] + \mathbf{v}^T \tag{1.69}$$

Substituting Eq. (1.65) into Eq. (1.69) yields

$$\mathbf{e}^T \left[ \mathbf{M} + \mathbf{M}_2^T \right] = \mathbf{e}^T \mathbf{A}(\mathbf{U}, \mathbf{M}) \left[ \left[ \widehat{\mathbf{e}^T \mathbf{M}} \right] + \left[ \widehat{\mathbf{M} \mathbf{e}} \right] - \mathbf{M}_1 \right] + \mathbf{v}^T$$

or

$$\mathbf{x}^T = \mathbf{e}^T \mathbf{A}(\mathbf{U}, \mathbf{M}) \widehat{\mathbf{x}} + \mathbf{v}^T \tag{1.70}$$

From Eqs. (1.70) and (1.23) it follows that $\mathbf{v}^{*T} = \mathbf{v}^T$. Hence, it follows that, under the transfer method, the joint production system described by Eqs. (1.20) and (1.21) is converted into the single production system described by

$$\left[ \mathbf{M} + \mathbf{M}_2^T \right] \mathbf{e} = \mathbf{A}(\mathbf{U}, \mathbf{M}) \left[ \mathbf{M} + \mathbf{M}_2^T \right] \mathbf{e} + \mathbf{f}$$

and

---

[15]Note that $\left[ \widehat{\mathbf{e}^T \mathbf{M}} \right] + \left[ \widehat{\mathbf{M} \mathbf{e}} \right] - \mathbf{M}_1 = \left[ \widehat{\mathbf{M} + \mathbf{M}_2^T} \right] \mathbf{e}$.

$$\left[\left[\mathbf{M} + \mathbf{M}_2^T\right]\mathbf{e}\right]^T = \mathbf{e}^T\mathbf{A}(\mathbf{U}, \mathbf{M})\left[\widehat{\mathbf{M} + \mathbf{M}_2^T}\right]\mathbf{e} + \mathbf{v}^T$$

### 1.4.1.6   The ESA Method

The ESA (European System of Integrated Economic Accounts) method (Eurostat 1979, pp. 116–117) recommends that secondary products should be treated as if they were produced by the industries where these products are primary. In formal terms, it is assumed that (see, e.g. Viet 1994, pp. 38–40)

$$\mathbf{x} = \mathbf{Me} \tag{1.71}$$

and

$$\mathbf{A}(\mathbf{U}, \mathbf{M}) = \mathbf{U}\left[\widehat{\mathbf{Me}}\right]^{-1} \tag{1.72}$$

Equation (1.72) entails that

$$\mathbf{U} = \mathbf{A}(\mathbf{U}, \mathbf{M})\left[\widehat{\mathbf{Me}}\right] \tag{1.73}$$

Substituting Eq. (1.73) into Eq. (1.20) yields

$$\mathbf{Me} = \mathbf{A}(\mathbf{U}, \mathbf{M})\mathbf{Me} + \mathbf{f} \tag{1.74}$$

Substituting Eq. (1.71) into Eq. (1.74) gives

$$\mathbf{x} = \mathbf{A}(\mathbf{U}, \mathbf{M})\mathbf{x} + \mathbf{f} \tag{1.75}$$

From Eqs. (1.75) and (1.22) it follows that $\mathbf{f}^* = \mathbf{f}$. Substituting Eq. (1.73) into Eq. (1.21) yields

$$\mathbf{e}^T\mathbf{M} = \mathbf{e}^T\mathbf{A}(\mathbf{U}, \mathbf{M})\left[\widehat{\mathbf{Me}}\right] + \mathbf{v}^T \tag{1.76}$$

Adding $[\mathbf{Me}]^T$ to both sides of Eq. (1.76) and after rearrangement we obtain

$$\left[\mathbf{Me}\right]^T = \mathbf{e}^T\mathbf{A}(\mathbf{U}, \mathbf{M})\left[\widehat{\mathbf{Me}}\right] + \mathbf{v}^T + \left[\mathbf{Me}\right]^T - \mathbf{e}^T\mathbf{M} \tag{1.77}$$

Substituting Eq. (1.71) into Eq. (1.77) yields

$$\mathbf{x}^{\mathrm{T}} = \mathbf{e}^{\mathrm{T}}\mathbf{A}(\mathbf{U},\mathbf{M})\widehat{\mathbf{x}} + \mathbf{v}^{\mathrm{T}} + \left[\mathbf{Me}\right]^{\mathrm{T}} - \mathbf{e}^{\mathrm{T}}\mathbf{M} \tag{1.78}$$

From Eqs. (1.78) and (1.23) it follows that $\mathbf{v}^{*\mathrm{T}} = \mathbf{v}^{\mathrm{T}} + [\mathbf{Me}]^{\mathrm{T}} - \mathbf{e}^{\mathrm{T}}\mathbf{M}$. Consequently, with the use of the ESA method, the joint production system described by Eqs. (1.20) and (1.21) is converted into the single production system described by the equations

$$\mathbf{Me} = \mathbf{A}(\mathbf{U},\mathbf{M})\mathbf{Me} + \mathbf{f}$$

and

$$\left[\mathbf{Me}\right]^{\mathrm{T}} = \mathbf{e}^{\mathrm{T}}\mathbf{A}(\mathbf{U},\mathbf{M})\left[\widehat{\mathbf{Me}}\right] + \mathbf{v}^{\mathrm{T}} + \left[\mathbf{Me}\right]^{\mathrm{T}} - \mathbf{e}^{\mathrm{T}}\mathbf{M}$$

### 1.4.1.7  The Lump-Sum Method

The Lump-Sum (or Aggregation) Method (Office of Statistical Standards 1974, p. 116) treats secondary products as if they were produced as a primary product of the industry that they are actually produced. In formal terms, it is assumed that (see, e.g. Fukui and Seneta 1985, p. 177)

$$\mathbf{x} = \mathbf{M}^{\mathrm{T}}\mathbf{e} \tag{1.79}$$

and

$$\mathbf{A}(\mathbf{U},\mathbf{M}) = \mathbf{U}\left[\widehat{\mathbf{M}^{\mathrm{T}}\mathbf{e}}\right]^{-1} \tag{1.80}$$

Equation (1.80) entails that

$$\mathbf{U} = \mathbf{A}(\mathbf{U},\mathbf{M})\left[\widehat{\mathbf{M}^{\mathrm{T}}\mathbf{e}}\right] \tag{1.81}$$

Substituting Eq. (1.81) into Eq. (1.20) yields

$$\mathbf{Me} = \mathbf{A}(\mathbf{U},\mathbf{M})\mathbf{M}^{\mathrm{T}}\mathbf{e} + \mathbf{f} \tag{1.82}$$

Adding $\mathbf{M}^{\mathrm{T}}\mathbf{e}$ to both sides of Eq. (1.82) and after rearrangement we obtain

$$\mathbf{M}^{\mathrm{T}}\mathbf{e} = \mathbf{A}(\mathbf{U},\mathbf{M})\mathbf{M}^{\mathrm{T}}\mathbf{e} + \mathbf{f} + \left[\mathbf{M}^{\mathrm{T}} - \mathbf{M}\right]\mathbf{e} \tag{1.83}$$

Substituting Eq. (1.79) into Eq. (1.83) yields

$$\mathbf{x} = \mathbf{A}(\mathbf{U}, \mathbf{M})\mathbf{x} + \mathbf{f} + \left[\mathbf{M}^\mathrm{T} - \mathbf{M}\right]\mathbf{e} \tag{1.84}$$

From Eqs. (1.84) and (1.22) it follows that $\mathbf{f}^* = \mathbf{f} + [\mathbf{M}^\mathrm{T} - \mathbf{M}]\mathbf{e}$. Substituting Eq. (1.81) into Eq. (1.21) gives

$$\mathbf{e}^\mathrm{T}\mathbf{M} = \mathbf{e}^\mathrm{T}\mathbf{A}(\mathbf{U}, \mathbf{M})\left[\widehat{\mathbf{M}^\mathrm{T}\mathbf{e}}\right] + \mathbf{v}^\mathrm{T} \tag{1.85}$$

Combining Eqs. (1.79) and (1.85) yields[16]

$$\mathbf{x}^\mathrm{T} = \mathbf{e}^\mathrm{T}\mathbf{A}(\mathbf{U}, \mathbf{M})\widehat{\mathbf{x}} + \mathbf{v}^\mathrm{T} \tag{1.86}$$

From Eqs. (1.86) and (1.23) it follows that $\mathbf{v}^{*\mathrm{T}} = \mathbf{v}^\mathrm{T}$. Hence, under the Lump-Sum Method, the joint production system described by Eqs. (1.20) and (1.21) is converted into the single production system described by the equations

$$\mathbf{M}^\mathrm{T}\mathbf{e} = \mathbf{A}(\mathbf{U}, \mathbf{M})\mathbf{M}^\mathrm{T}\mathbf{e} + \mathbf{f} + \left[\mathbf{M}^\mathrm{T} - \mathbf{M}\right]\mathbf{e}$$

and

$$\left[\mathbf{M}^\mathrm{T}\mathbf{e}\right]^\mathrm{T} = \mathbf{e}^\mathrm{T}\mathbf{A}(\mathbf{U}, \mathbf{M})\left[\widehat{\mathbf{M}^\mathrm{T}\mathbf{e}}\right] + \mathbf{v}^\mathrm{T}$$

### 1.4.1.8    The Redefinition Method

The Redefinition method is used to move outputs and inputs of secondary products, that have distinctive production processes compared to those of the primary products of each industry, to the industries where these products are primary (see, e.g. Viet 1994, p. 40). This method is most suitable to be applied for secondary products that have production processes similar to the respective production processes of the industries where these products are primary. Nevertheless, this method needs additional data on the production of the secondary products that are not always available (see, e.g. United Nations 1999, p. 81).[17]

---

[16]Note that $\mathbf{e}^\mathrm{T}\mathbf{M} = [\mathbf{M}^\mathrm{T}\mathbf{e}]^\mathrm{T}$.

[17]For a presentation of the results that the Redefinition method yielded in the case of the USA input–output tables for the year 1992, see Guo et al. (2002, pp. 11–13).

## 1.4.2    Methods Converting Supply and Use Tables into Industry-by-Industry Symmetric Input–Output Tables

The conversion methods presented so far derive SIOTs where the dimensions of the derived matrix of intermediate inputs and, hence, the technical coefficients matrix, $\mathbf{A}$ $(\mathbf{U}, \mathbf{M})$, is product-by-product, i.e. represents the transactions amongst the different products of the economy. However, following conjugated procedures with those previously presented we may convert SUTs into SIOTs where the dimensions of the derived matrix of intermediate inputs is industry-by-industry, i.e. represents the transactions amongst the different industries of the economy. In what follows we present two such conversion methods, known as the fixed industry sales assumption (FISA) and fixed product sales assumption (FPSA), respectively.

### 1.4.2.1    The Fixed Industry Sales Assumption

The FISA treats secondary products as if they were produced as a primary product of the industry that they are actually produced and assumes that each industry has its own sales structure, irrespective of its product mix. In formal terms, it is assumed that

$$\mathbf{A}(\mathbf{U}, \mathbf{M}) = \left[\widehat{\mathbf{e}^{\mathrm{T}}\mathbf{M}}\right]\mathbf{M}^{-1}\mathbf{U}\left[\widehat{\mathbf{e}^{\mathrm{T}}\mathbf{M}}\right]^{-1} \tag{1.87}$$

and

$$\mathbf{x} = \mathbf{M}^{\mathrm{T}}\mathbf{e} \tag{1.88}$$

Equation (1.87) entails that

$$\mathbf{U} = \mathbf{M}\left[\widehat{\mathbf{e}^{\mathrm{T}}\mathbf{M}}\right]^{-1}\mathbf{A}(\mathbf{U}, \mathbf{M})\left[\widehat{\mathbf{e}^{\mathrm{T}}\mathbf{M}}\right] \tag{1.89}$$

Substituting Eqs. (1.88) and (1.89) into Eq. (1.21) yields

$$\mathbf{x}^{\mathrm{T}} = \mathbf{e}^{\mathrm{T}}\mathbf{M}\left[\widehat{\mathbf{e}^{\mathrm{T}}\mathbf{M}}\right]^{-1}\mathbf{A}(\mathbf{U}, \mathbf{M})\widehat{\mathbf{x}} + \mathbf{v}^{\mathrm{T}}$$

or

$$\mathbf{x}^{\mathrm{T}} = \mathbf{e}^{\mathrm{T}}\mathbf{A}(\mathbf{U}, \mathbf{M})\widehat{\mathbf{x}} + \mathbf{v}^{\mathrm{T}} \tag{1.90}$$

From Eqs. (1.90) and (1.23) it follows that $\mathbf{v}^{*\mathrm{T}} = \mathbf{v}^{\mathrm{T}}$. Substituting Eq. (1.89) into Eq. (1.20) yields

$$\mathbf{Me} = \mathbf{M}\left[\widehat{\mathbf{e}^{\mathrm{T}}\mathbf{M}}\right]^{-1}\mathbf{A}(\mathbf{U},\mathbf{M})\left[\widehat{\mathbf{e}^{\mathrm{T}}\mathbf{M}}\right]\mathbf{e} + \mathbf{f} \tag{1.91}$$

Pre-multiplying Eq. (1.91) by $\left[\widehat{\mathbf{e}^{\mathrm{T}}\mathbf{M}}\right]\mathbf{M}^{-1}$ and taking into account Eq. (1.88), we obtain

$$\mathbf{x} = \mathbf{A}(\mathbf{U},\mathbf{M})\mathbf{x} + \left[\widehat{\mathbf{e}^{\mathrm{T}}\mathbf{M}}\right]\mathbf{M}^{-1}\mathbf{f} \tag{1.92}$$

From Eqs. (1.92) and (1.22) it follows that $\mathbf{f}^* = \left[\widehat{\mathbf{e}^{\mathrm{T}}\mathbf{M}}\right]\mathbf{M}^{-1}\mathbf{f}$. Hence, under the FISA, the joint production system described by Eqs. (1.20) and (1.21) is converted into the single production system described by the following equations:

$$\mathbf{M}^{\mathrm{T}}\mathbf{e} = \mathbf{A}(\mathbf{U},\mathbf{M})\mathbf{M}^{\mathrm{T}}\mathbf{e} + \left[\widehat{\mathbf{e}^{\mathrm{T}}\mathbf{M}}\right]\mathbf{M}^{-1}\mathbf{f} \tag{1.93}$$

and

$$\mathbf{e}^{\mathrm{T}}\mathbf{M} = \mathbf{e}^{\mathrm{T}}\mathbf{A}(\mathbf{U},\mathbf{M})\left[\widehat{\mathbf{e}^{\mathrm{T}}\mathbf{M}}\right] + \mathbf{v}^{\mathrm{T}} \tag{1.94}$$

Comparing Eqs. (1.32) and (1.33) with Eqs. (1.93) and (1.94), i.e. the single production system derived under the PTA with the single production system derived under the FISA, it follows that

$$\mathbf{A}_{\mathrm{I}}(\mathbf{U},\mathbf{M}) = \mathbf{S}\mathbf{A}_{\mathrm{C}}(\mathbf{U},\mathbf{M})\mathbf{S}^{-1}$$
$$\mathbf{f}_{\mathrm{I}}^* = \mathbf{S}\mathbf{f}_{\mathrm{C}}^*$$
$$\boldsymbol{\pi}_{\mathrm{I}}^{*\mathrm{T}} = \boldsymbol{\pi}_{\mathrm{C}}^{*\mathrm{T}}\mathbf{S}^{-1}$$

and

$$\mathbf{x}_{\mathrm{I}} = \mathbf{S}\mathbf{x}_{\mathrm{C}}$$

where $\mathbf{S} \equiv \left[\widehat{\mathbf{e}^{\mathrm{T}}\mathbf{M}}\right]\mathbf{M}^{-1}$, while $\mathbf{A}_{\mathrm{I}}(\mathbf{U},\mathbf{M})$ ($\mathbf{A}_{\mathrm{C}}(\mathbf{U},\mathbf{M})$), $\mathbf{f}_{\mathrm{I}}^*$ ($\mathbf{f}_{\mathrm{C}}^*$), $\boldsymbol{\pi}_{\mathrm{I}}^{*\mathrm{T}} \equiv \left[\mathbf{v}_{\mathrm{I}}^{*\mathrm{T}}\widehat{\mathbf{x}_{\mathrm{I}}}^{-1}\right]$ ($\boldsymbol{\pi}_{\mathrm{C}}^{*\mathrm{T}} \equiv \left[\mathbf{v}_{\mathrm{C}}^{*\mathrm{T}}\widehat{\mathbf{x}_{\mathrm{C}}}^{-1}\right]$), and $\mathbf{x}_{\mathrm{I}}$ ($\mathbf{x}_{\mathrm{C}}$) are the technical coefficients matrix, the transformed vector of final demand, the transformed vector of value added coefficients, and the transformed vector of value added, respectively, derived under the FISA (PTA). These relationships imply that the FISA (PTA) can be derived from PTA (FISA) via a similarity transformation.

### 1.4.2.2 The Fixed Product Sales Assumption

The FPSA treats secondary products as if they were produced as a primary product of the industry that they are actually produced and assumes that each product has its own market shares independent of the industry where it is produced. In formal terms, it is assumed that

$$\mathbf{A}(\mathbf{U}, \mathbf{M}) = \mathbf{M}^{\mathrm{T}} \left[ \widehat{\mathbf{Me}} \right]^{-1} \mathbf{U} \left[ \widehat{\mathbf{e}^{\mathrm{T}}\mathbf{M}} \right]^{-1} \tag{1.95}$$

and

$$\mathbf{x} = \mathbf{M}^{\mathrm{T}} \mathbf{e} \tag{1.96}$$

Equation (1.95) entails that

$$\mathbf{U} = \left[ \widehat{\mathbf{Me}} \right] \left[ \mathbf{M}^{\mathrm{T}} \right]^{-1} \mathbf{A}(\mathbf{U}, \mathbf{M}) \left[ \widehat{\mathbf{e}^{\mathrm{T}}\mathbf{M}} \right] \tag{1.97}$$

Substituting Eqs. (1.96) and (1.97) into Eq. (1.21) yields

$$\mathbf{x}^{\mathrm{T}} = \mathbf{e}^{\mathrm{T}} \left[ \widehat{\mathbf{Me}} \right] \left[ \mathbf{M}^{\mathrm{T}} \right]^{-1} \mathbf{A}(\mathbf{U}, \mathbf{M}) \widehat{\mathbf{x}} + \mathbf{v}^{\mathrm{T}}$$

or

$$\mathbf{x}^{\mathrm{T}} = \mathbf{e}^{\mathrm{T}} \mathbf{M}^{\mathrm{T}} \left[ \mathbf{M}^{\mathrm{T}} \right]^{-1} \mathbf{A}(\mathbf{U}, \mathbf{M}) \widehat{\mathbf{x}} + \mathbf{v}^{\mathrm{T}}$$

or

$$\mathbf{x}^{\mathrm{T}} = \mathbf{e}^{\mathrm{T}} \mathbf{A}(\mathbf{U}, \mathbf{M}) \widehat{\mathbf{x}} + \mathbf{v}^{\mathrm{T}} \tag{1.98}$$

From Eqs. (1.98) and (1.23) it follows that $\mathbf{v}^{*\mathrm{T}} = \mathbf{v}^{\mathrm{T}}$. Substituting Eq. (1.97) into Eq. (1.20) yields

$$\mathbf{Me} = \left[ \widehat{\mathbf{Me}} \right] \left[ \mathbf{M}^{\mathrm{T}} \right]^{-1} \mathbf{A}(\mathbf{U}, \mathbf{M}) \left[ \widehat{\mathbf{e}^{\mathrm{T}}\mathbf{M}} \right] \mathbf{e} + \mathbf{f} \tag{1.99}$$

Pre-multiplying Eq. (1.99) by $\mathbf{M}^{\mathrm{T}} \left[ \widehat{\mathbf{Me}} \right]^{-1}$ and taking into account Eq. (1.96), we obtain

$$\mathbf{x} = \mathbf{A}(\mathbf{U}, \mathbf{M}) \mathbf{x} + \mathbf{M}^{\mathrm{T}} \left[ \widehat{\mathbf{Me}} \right]^{-1} \mathbf{f} \tag{1.100}$$

From Eqs. (1.100) and (1.22) it follows that $\mathbf{f}^* = \mathbf{M}^\mathrm{T}\left[\widehat{\mathbf{Me}}\right]^{-1}\mathbf{f}$. Hence, under the FPSA, the joint production system described by Eqs. (1.20) and (1.21) is converted into the single production system described by the following equations:

$$\mathbf{M}^\mathrm{T}\mathbf{e} = \mathbf{A}(\mathbf{U}, \mathbf{M})\mathbf{M}^\mathrm{T}\mathbf{e} + \mathbf{M}^\mathrm{T}\left[\widehat{\mathbf{Me}}\right]^{-1}\mathbf{f} \tag{1.101}$$

and

$$\mathbf{e}^\mathrm{T}\mathbf{M} = \mathbf{e}^\mathrm{T}\mathbf{A}(\mathbf{U}, \mathbf{M})\left[\widehat{\mathbf{e}^\mathrm{T}\mathbf{M}}\right] + \mathbf{v}^\mathrm{T} \tag{1.102}$$

Comparing Eqs. (1.42) and (1.43) with Eqs. (1.101) and (1.102), i.e. the single production system derived under the ITA with the single production system derived under the FPSA, it follows that

$$\mathbf{A}_\mathrm{I}(\mathbf{U}, \mathbf{M}) = \mathbf{S}\mathbf{A}_\mathrm{C}(\mathbf{U}, \mathbf{M})\mathbf{S}^{-1}$$
$$\mathbf{f}_\mathrm{I}^* = \mathbf{S}\mathbf{f}_\mathrm{C}^*$$
$$\boldsymbol{\pi}_\mathrm{I}^{*\mathrm{T}} = \boldsymbol{\pi}_\mathrm{C}^{*\mathrm{T}}\mathbf{S}^{-1}$$

and

$$\mathbf{x}_\mathrm{I} = \mathbf{S}\mathbf{x}_\mathrm{C}$$

where $\mathbf{S} \equiv \mathbf{M}^\mathrm{T}\left[\widehat{\mathbf{Me}}\right]^{-1}$, while $\mathbf{A}_\mathrm{I}(\mathbf{U}, \mathbf{M})$ $(\mathbf{A}_\mathrm{C}(\mathbf{U}, \mathbf{M}))$, $\mathbf{f}_\mathrm{I}^*$ $(\mathbf{f}_\mathrm{C}^*)$, $\boldsymbol{\pi}_\mathrm{I}^{*\mathrm{T}} \equiv \left[\mathbf{v}_\mathrm{I}^{*\mathrm{T}}\widehat{\mathbf{x}}_\mathrm{I}^{-1}\right]$ $\left(\boldsymbol{\pi}_\mathrm{C}^{*\mathrm{T}} \equiv \left[\mathbf{v}_\mathrm{C}^{*\mathrm{T}}\widehat{\mathbf{x}}_\mathrm{C}^{-1}\right]\right)$, and $\mathbf{x}_\mathrm{I}$ $(\mathbf{x}_\mathrm{C})$ are the technical coefficients matrix, the transformed vector of final demand, the transformed vector of value added coefficients, and the transformed vector of value added, respectively, derived under the FPSA (ITA). These relationships imply that the FPSA (ITA) can be derived from ITA (FISA) via a similarity transformation.

### 1.4.3  Evaluation of the Conversion Methods

The next issue that comes up is which of the conversion methods is the most suitable for the problem at hand. Since there were not any objective criteria to test the consistency of the various methods, Jansen and ten Raa (1990) developed four desirable properties or, alternative, axioms that the various methods converting SUTs into product-by-product SIOTs should fulfil. These properties are:

1. The "material balance property" or, in formal terms,

$$\mathbf{A(U, M)Me = Ue}$$

This property implies that the requirements needed to produce the output should be equal to the actual inputs of the economy.

2. The "financial balance property" or, in formal terms,

$$\mathbf{e^T A(U, M)M = e^T U}$$

This property implies that the input cost of the output should be equal to the cost of the actual inputs.

3. The "price invariance property" or, in formal terms,

$$\mathbf{A(\widehat{p}_b U, \widehat{p}_b M) = \widehat{p}_b A(U, M)\widehat{p}_b^{-1}, \;\; \forall p_b > 0}$$

where $\mathbf{p}_b$ is the price vector relative to the base-year prices. This property implies that whatever the base-year price is, the corresponding technical coefficients matrix should be similar to the matrix $\mathbf{A(U, M)}$.

4. The "scale invariance property" or, in formal terms,

$$\mathbf{A(U\widehat{s}, M\widehat{s}) = A(U, M), \;\; \forall s > 0}$$

This property guarantees that the technical coefficients matrix does not depend on the activity levels of the economy.

Jansen and ten Raa (1990) proved that: (i) the PTA fulfils all the desirable properties; (ii) the ITA fulfils only the material balance property";[18] (iii) the by-product method and the mixed technology model, constructed by ten Raa et al. (1984), fulfil the price and scale invariance properties; (iv) the transfer method does not fulfil any of the properties; (v) the ESA method fulfils the material balance and price invariance properties; and (vi) the lump-sum method fulfils only the scale invariance property.

Following Jansen and ten Raa (1990), Rueda-Cantuche and ten Raa (2009) developed four desirable properties that the conversion methods that derive industry-by-industry SIOTs should fulfil, which are conjugated to those developed by Jansen and ten Raa (1990) for the conversion methods that derive product-by-product SIOTs. These properties are:

---

[18]ten Raa et al. (1984) had shown that the technical coefficients matrix derived under the ITA depends on the base-year prices. In other words, they had proved that the ITA does not fulfil the price invariance property.

1. The material balance property:

$$\mathbf{M}\left[\widehat{\mathbf{e}^{\mathrm{T}}\mathbf{M}}\right]^{-1}\mathbf{A}(\mathbf{U},\mathbf{M})\left[\widehat{\mathbf{e}^{\mathrm{T}}\mathbf{M}}\right]\mathbf{e} = \mathbf{U}\mathbf{e}$$

2. The financial balance property:

$$\mathbf{e}^{\mathrm{T}}\mathbf{M}\left[\widehat{\mathbf{e}^{\mathrm{T}}\mathbf{M}}\right]^{-1}\mathbf{A}(\mathbf{U},\mathbf{M})\left[\widehat{\mathbf{e}^{\mathrm{T}}\mathbf{M}}\right] = \mathbf{e}^{\mathrm{T}}\mathbf{U}$$

3. The price invariance property:

$$\mathbf{A}(\widehat{\mathbf{p}_b}\mathbf{U},\widehat{\mathbf{p}_b}\mathbf{M}) = \widehat{\mathbf{p}_b}\mathbf{M}\left[\widehat{\mathbf{e}^{\mathrm{T}}\mathbf{M}}\right]^{-1}\mathbf{A}(\mathbf{U},\mathbf{M})\left[\widehat{\mathbf{e}^{\mathrm{T}}\mathbf{M}}\right]\left[\widehat{\mathbf{p}_b\mathbf{M}}\right]^{-1}, \quad \forall \mathbf{p}_b > \mathbf{0}$$

4. The scale invariance property:

$$\mathbf{A}(\mathbf{U}\widehat{\mathbf{s}},\mathbf{M}\widehat{\mathbf{s}}) = \mathbf{A}(\mathbf{U},\mathbf{M}), \quad \forall \mathbf{s} > \mathbf{0}$$

Rueda-Cantuche and ten Raa (2009) proved that the FISA fulfils all the desirable properties, while the FPSA fulfils only the financial balance property.

Thus, it is concluded that only the PTA and the FISA fulfil all the desirable properties. However, both the PTA and the FISA can be criticized because (i) they cannot be applied to the case of rectangular SUTs;[19] and (ii) the technical coefficients matrix that is derived from these methods is possible to contain negative elements. In order to overcome the problem of negative coefficients, there have been proposed various procedures for removing the negative coefficients that may appear in the technical coefficients matrix.[20] A well-known method is that proposed by Almon (1970, 2000), which consists of an iterative procedure of changes in the technical coefficients matrix that converges to a (semi-)positive matrix, but convergence is guaranteed only if more than half of the production of each commodity is in its primary industry. However, Almon's method has been criticized for being without economic justification (see ten Raa et al. 1984, p. 93; ten Raa and Rueda-Cantuche 2013). Alternatively, mixed technology models are often used in order to overcome the problem of negative coefficients (see, e.g. Armstrong 1975). Nevertheless, mixed technology models cannot guarantee the derivation of a technical coefficients matrix with non-negative coefficients. Moreover, de Mesnard (2011) has pointed out that even in the case where the technical coefficients matrix derived from PTA or FISA is non-negative, both methods should be rejected as economically irrelevant.

---

[19]That is because those methods require the inversion of the make matrix.

[20]For a detailed review of the available methods to remove negative coefficients, see ten Raa and Rueda-Cantuche (2013, pp. 4–13).

On the basis of the previous analysis it can be concluded that none of the conversion methods can guarantee (i) consistency with the requirements of input–output analysis; and (ii) economically acceptable results. We may find a way out of that problem by accepting that we live in a world where joint production economic activities are common and by making use of general joint production models inspired by von Neumann (1937, 1945) and Sraffa (1960). In the next section we present the essential ideas of the von Neumann–Sraffa-based approach to the case of joint production as a preferable approach to treat SUTs.[21]

## 1.5   The von Neumann–Sraffa-Based Approach

A square linear system of joint production *à la* von Neumann–Sraffa is defined by the pair $\{\mathbf{B}, \mathbf{A}\}$, where $\mathbf{B}$ is the output matrix and $\mathbf{A}$ is the input matrix (both $\mathbf{B}$ and $\mathbf{A}$ are expressed in physical terms). Also, let $\mathbf{d}$ be the vector of final demand (in physical terms), $\boldsymbol{\pi}$ be the vector of value added coefficients, $\mathbf{y}$ be the vector of activity levels, and $\mathbf{p}$ be the vector of market prices. Then we can write

$$\mathbf{By} = \mathbf{Ay} + \mathbf{d} \tag{1.103}$$

and

$$\mathbf{p}^{\mathrm{T}}\mathbf{B} = \mathbf{p}^{\mathrm{T}}\mathbf{A} + \boldsymbol{\pi}^{\mathrm{T}} \tag{1.104}$$

The above system is said to be strictly *viable* if it can produce a physical net surplus of any commodity or, in formal terms,

$$\exists \mathbf{y} \geq \mathbf{0}, \quad \left[\mathbf{B} - \mathbf{A}\right]\mathbf{y} > \mathbf{0}$$

A system $\{\mathbf{B}, \mathbf{A}\}$ is said to be strictly *profitable* if there exists a price vector $\mathbf{p}$ for which all industries are profitable, or, in formal terms,[22]

$$\exists \mathbf{p} \geq \mathbf{0}, \quad \mathbf{p}^{\mathrm{T}}\left[\mathbf{B} - \mathbf{A}\right] > \mathbf{0}^{\mathrm{T}}$$

---

[21]For a detailed exposition of the von Neumann–Sraffa-based analysis and the connection between the works of von Neumann and Sraffa, see Kurz and Salvadori (1995, Chap. 8 and pp. 403–426), Kurz and Salvadori (2001).

[22]In the case of joint production, the conditions of viability and profitability are not equivalent (see Bidard 1986, pp. 55–56). It need hardly be said that, in general, none of the usual laws of single production systems hold true in the case of joint production (see Bidard 1997; Steedman 1982).

A commodity $i$ is said to be *separately producible* if it is possible to produce a net output consisting of a unit of that commodity alone with a non-negative vector of activity levels or, in formal terms,

$$\exists \mathbf{y} \geq \mathbf{0}, \quad \left[\mathbf{B} - \mathbf{A}\right]\mathbf{y} = \mathbf{e}_i$$

where $\mathbf{e}_i$ is a vector whose $i$th element is equal to 1 and all other elements are equal to zero. A system $\{\mathbf{B}, \mathbf{A}\}$ is said to be *all-productive* if all products are separately producible or, in formal terms,

$$\forall \mathbf{d} \geq \mathbf{0}, \quad \exists \mathbf{y} \geq \mathbf{0}, \quad \left[\mathbf{B} - \mathbf{A}\right]\mathbf{y} = \mathbf{d}$$

Thus, if $\{\mathbf{B}, \mathbf{A}\}$ is all-productive, then $[\mathbf{B} - \mathbf{A}]^{-1} \geq \mathbf{0}$ (and *vice versa*). A process, within a system $\{\mathbf{B}, \mathbf{A}\}$, is called *indispensable* if it has to be activated whatever net output is to be produced. An all-productive system whose processes are all indispensable is called *all-engaging*. Formally, the system $\{\mathbf{B}, \mathbf{A}\}$ is all-engaging if the following two properties hold:

$$\exists \mathbf{y} \geq \mathbf{0}, \quad \left[\mathbf{B} - \mathbf{A}\right]\mathbf{y} \geq \mathbf{0}$$

$$\{\exists \mathbf{y} \geq \mathbf{0}, [\mathbf{B} - \mathbf{A}]\mathbf{y} \geq \mathbf{0}\} \Rightarrow \mathbf{y} > \mathbf{0}$$

Thus, if $\{\mathbf{B}, \mathbf{A}\}$ is all-engaging, then $[\mathbf{B} - \mathbf{A}]^{-1} > \mathbf{0}$ (and *vice versa*). As is well known, the concepts of "all-productive" ("all-engaging") systems correspond with systems that retain all the essential properties of reducible (irreducible) single-product systems.[23]

We now return to the actual economic system described by the make and use matrices, i.e. the pair $\{\mathbf{M}, \mathbf{U}\}$. The make and use matrices can be rewritten as

$$\mathbf{M} = \widehat{\mathbf{p}}\mathbf{B}\widehat{\mathbf{y}} \tag{1.105}$$

and

$$\mathbf{U} = \widehat{\mathbf{p}}\mathbf{A}\widehat{\mathbf{y}} \tag{1.106}$$

Analogously, the vectors of final demand and value added can be rewritten as

$$\mathbf{f} = \widehat{\mathbf{p}}\mathbf{d} \tag{1.107}$$

and

---

[23]See Bidard (1996), Kurz and Salvadori (1995, pp. 238–240), Schefold (1978).

$$\mathbf{v}^{\mathrm{T}} = \boldsymbol{\pi}^{\mathrm{T}}\widehat{\mathbf{y}} \tag{1.108}$$

Now, we assume that the physical unit of measurement of each product is that unit which is worth of a monetary unit, i.e. it holds

$$\mathbf{p} = \mathbf{e} \tag{1.109}$$

Substituting Eqs. (1.105), (1.106), (1.107), and (1.109) into Eq. (1.20) we obtain

$$\mathbf{B}\widehat{\mathbf{y}}\mathbf{e} = \mathbf{A}\widehat{\mathbf{y}}\mathbf{e} + \mathbf{d}$$

or

$$\mathbf{B}\mathbf{y} = \mathbf{A}\mathbf{y} + \mathbf{d} \tag{1.110}$$

Finally, substituting Eqs. (1.105), (1.106), (1.108), and (1.109) into Eq. (1.21) we obtain

$$\mathbf{e}^{\mathrm{T}}\mathbf{B}\widehat{\mathbf{y}} = \mathbf{e}^{\mathrm{T}}\mathbf{A}\widehat{\mathbf{y}} + \boldsymbol{\pi}^{\mathrm{T}}\widehat{\mathbf{y}}$$

or

$$\mathbf{e}^{\mathrm{T}}\mathbf{B} = \mathbf{e}^{\mathrm{T}}\mathbf{A} + \boldsymbol{\pi}^{\mathrm{T}} \tag{1.111}$$

Thus, it follows that Eq. (1.110) is equivalent to Eq. (1.103) and, by taking into account Eq. (1.109), it follows that Eq. (1.111) is equivalent to Eq. (1.104). Consequently, the system described by the make and use matrices can be considered as the empirical counterpart of a joint production system *à la* von Neumann–Sraffa. Namely, the make matrix, $\mathbf{M}$, can be considered as the counterpart of the output matrix, $\mathbf{B}$, and the use matrix, $\mathbf{U}$, can be considered as the counterpart of the matrix $\mathbf{A}$ (also see Bidard and Erreygers 1998, pp. 434–436). Therefore, an actual economy will be said to be all-productive (all-engaging) when it holds $[\mathbf{M} - \mathbf{U}]^{-1} \geq \mathbf{0}$ ($[\mathbf{M} - \mathbf{U}]^{-1} > \mathbf{0}$).[24]

The conversion methods try to transform the system described by the pair of matrices $\{\mathbf{M}, \mathbf{U}\}$ into the single production system described by the pair of matrices $\{\mathbf{I}, \mathbf{A}(\mathbf{U}, \mathbf{M})\}$. This means that all conversion methods assume, implicitly or otherwise, that there is a single production system "hidden", i.e. not directly observable, in the SUTs. However, this is a groundless assumption. The awareness of joint

---

[24]The relevant empirical investigation so far has shown that none of the actual systems is all-productive (see Chaps. 5, 7 and 9).

product processes has been already familiar to classical economists, such as Adam Smith (1776, Book 1, Chap. 11).[25] For instance, Jevons (1888, Chap. 5) points out that the cases of joint production form the general rule, to which it is difficult to find important exceptions, while similar points have been stressed more recently (see Baumgärtner et al. 2006; Faber et al. 1998; Kurz 2006; Steedman 1984). Contrary to the approach imposed by the conversion (namely, transmutation) methods, the von Neumann–Sraffa-based analysis of joint production constitutes a straightforward approach, i.e. it does not rule out joint production, which is not based on any of the restrictive (and debatable) assumptions of the conversion methods.

To sum up, given that (1) the pair $\{M, U\}$ can be considered as the empirical counterpart of the pair $\{B, A\}$ and (2) joint production constitutes the empirically relevant case, it would seem reasonable that a straightforward treatment of SUTs, based on the von Neumann–Sraffa-based analysis, to be preferred instead of trying to derive single production tables (i.e. SIOTs).

## 1.6    Concluding Remarks

This chapter mapped the structure of the empirical input–output representations of actual economies, i.e. the Supply and Use Tables (SUTs) and the Symmetric Input–Output Tables (SIOTs). It has been shown that the main difference between these two types of input–output tables is that the SUTs, which constitute the core of the modern systems of national accounting, allow for joint production activities, whereas the SIOTs rule out joint production and are constructed on the basis of specific assumptions on the relationships between inputs and outputs recorded in the SUTs. The review of the alternative methods used to convert SUTs into SIOTs revealed that, despite the differences amongst those methods, they all rest on the tacit assumption that there is a single production system hidden in the SUTs characterizing the real world. It has been argued that this is a groundless assumption, and that a consistent approach is the straightforward treatment of SUTs on the basis of general joint production models inspired by the von Neumann and Sraffa contributions.

## References

Almon, C. (1970). Investment in input–output models and the treatment of secondary products. In A. P. Carter & A. Bródy (Eds.), *Applications of input–output analysis* (pp. 103–116). Amsterdam: North Holland.

---

[25]For a review of the contributions of classical and early neoclassical economists to the analysis of joint production, see Kurz (1986).

Almon, C. (2000). Product-to-product tables via product technology with no negative flows. *Economic Systems Research, 12*(1), 27–43.

Armstrong, A. G. (1975). Technology assumptions in the construction of United Kingdom input–output tables. In R. I. G. Allen & W. F. Gossling (Eds.), *Estimating and projecting input–output coefficients* (pp. 68–93). London: Input–Output Publishing.

Baumgärtner, S., Faber, M., & Schiller, J. (2006). *Joint production and responsibility in ecological economics. On the foundation of environmental policy.* Cheltenham: Edward Elgar.

Bidard, C. (1986). The maximum rate of profits in joint production. *Metroeconomica, 38*(1), 53–66.

Bidard, C. (1996). All-engaging systems. *Economic Systems Research, 8*(4), 323–340.

Bidard, C. (1997). Pure joint production. *Cambridge Journal of Economics, 21*(6), 685–701.

Bidard, C., & Erreygers, G. (1998). Sraffa and Leontief on joint production. *Review of Political Economy, 10*(4), 427–446.

de Mesnard, L. (2011). Negatives in symmetric input–output tables: the impossible quest for the Holy Grail. *The Annals of Regional Science, 46*(2), 427–454.

Edmonston, J. H. (1952). A treatment of multiple-process industries. *The Quarterly Journal of Economics, 66*(4), 557–571.

Eurostat. (1979). *European system of integrated economic accounts (ESA)* (2nd ed.). Luxembourg: Office for the Official Publications of the European Communities.

Eurostat. (2008). *Eurostat manual of supply, use and input–output tables.* Luxembourg: Office for the Official Publications of the European Communities.

Faber, M., Proops, J. L. R., & Baumgärtner, S. (1998). All production is joint production. A thermodynamic analysis. In S. Faucheux, J. Cowdy, & I. Nikolaï (Eds.), *Sustainability and firms: Technological change and the changing regulatory environment* (pp. 131–158). Cheltenham: Edward Elgar.

Fukui, Y., & Seneta, E. (1985). A theoretical approach to the conventional treatment of joint product in input–output tables. *Economics Letters, 18*(2–3), 175–179.

Gigantes, T. (1970). The representation of technology in input–output systems. In A. P. Carter & A. Bródy (Eds.), *Contributions to input–output analysis* (pp. 270–290). Amsterdam: North-Holland.

Gigantes, T., & Matuszewski, T. (1968). *Technology in input–output models.* Paper presented at the Fourth International Conference on Input–Output Techniques, 8–12 January 1968, Geneva.

Guo, J., Lawson, A. M., & Planting, M. A. (2002). *From make–use to symmetric IO tables: An assessment of alternative technology assumptions*, in Paper presented at the 14th International Input–Output Conference, 10–15 October 2002, Montreal Canada. Retrieved 30 Sept, 2019, from http://www.bea.gov/papers/pdf/alttechassump.pdf

Jansen, K. P., & ten Raa, T. (1990). The choice of model in the construction of input–output coefficients matrices. *International Economic Review, 31*(1), 213–227.

Jevons, W. S. (1888). *The theory of political economy* (3rd ed.). London: Macmillan and Co.

Kurz, H. D. (1986). Classical and early neoclassical economists on joint production. *Metroeconomica, 38*(1), 1–37.

Kurz, H. D. (2006). Goods and bads: Sundry observations on joint production waste disposal, and renewable and exhaustible resources. *Progress in Industrial Ecology – An International Journal, 3*(4), 280–301.

Kurz, H. D., Dietzenbacher, E., & Lager, C. (1998). General introduction. In H. D. Kurz, E. Dietzenbacher, & C. Lager (Eds.), *Input–output analysis.* Cheltenham: Edward Elgar.

Kurz, H. D., & Salvadori, N. (1995). *Theory of production. A long-period analysis.* Cambridge: Cambridge University Press.

Kurz, H. D., & Salvadori, N. (2001). Sraffa and von Neumann. *Review of Political Economy, 13*(2), 161–180.

Leontief, W. (1936). Quantitative input and output relations in the economic system of the United States. *The Review of Economics and Statistics, 18*(3), 105–125.

Mariolis, T. (2008). *The conversion of SUTs into SIOTs*. Internal Report of the Study Group on Sraffian Economics, 4 Apr 2008. Athens: Department of Public Administration, Panteion University (in Greek).

Mariolis, T., Ntemiroglou, N., & Soklis, G. (2018). The static demand multipliers in a joint production framework: Comparative findings for the Greek, Spanish and Eurozone economies. *Journal of Economic Structures, 7*, 18.

Mariolis, T., & Soklis, G. (2007). On the empirical validity of the labour theory of value. In T. Mariolis (2010). *Essays on the logical history of political economy* (pp. 231–260). Athens: Matura (in Greek).

Mariolis, T., & Soklis, G. (2010). Additive labour values and prices: Evidence from the supply and use tables of the French, German and Greek Economies. *Economic Issues, 15*(2), 87–107.

Mariolis, T., & Soklis, G. (2018). The static Sraffian multiplier for the Greek economy: Evidence from the supply and use table for the year 2010. *Review of Keynesian Economics, 6*(1), 114–147.

Marx, K. (1977). From the critical history. In F. Engels (Ed.), *Anti-Dühring. Herr Eugen Dühring's revolution in science* (pp. 274–305). Moscow: Progress Publishers.

Office of Statistical Standards. (1974). *Input–output tables for 1970*. Tokyo: Institute for Dissemination of Government Data.

Quesnay, F. (1972). *Quesnay's Tableau economique [1759]*. London: Macmillan.

Rueda-Cantuche, J. M., & ten Raa, T. (2009). The choice of model in the construction of industry coefficients matrices. *Economic Systems Research, 21*(4), 363–376.

Schefold, B. (1978). Multiple product techniques with properties of single product systems. *Journal of Economics, 38*(1–2), 29–53.

Smith, A. (1776). *An inquiry into the nature and causes of the wealth of nations*. London: Strahan and Cadell.

Soklis, G. (2005). *On the make and use matrices in input–output analysis*. Internal Report on Political Economy No. 2, 24 Nov 2005. Athens: Department of Public Administration, Panteion University (in Greek).

Soklis, G. (2006). *Labour values and production prices: Exploration based on the joint production table of the Greek economy for the year 1999*. Master's Thesis, Athens: Department of Public Administration, Panteion University (in Greek).

Soklis, G. (2009). The conversion of the supply and use tables to symmetric input–output tables: A critical review. *Bulletin of Political Economy, 3*(1), 51–70.

Soklis, G. (2011). Shape of wage–profit curves in joint production systems: Evidence from the supply and use tables of the Finnish economy. *Metroeconomica, 62*(4), 548–560.

Soklis, G. (2012). *Labour values, commodity values, prices and income distribution: Exploration based on empirical input–output tables*. Ph.D. Dissertation, Athens: Department of Public Administration, Panteion University (in Greek).

Soklis, G. (2015). Labour versus alternative value bases in actual joint production systems. *Bulletin of Political Economy, 9*(1), 1–31.

Sraffa, P. (1960). *Production of commodities by means of commodities. Prelude to a critique of economic theory*. Cambridge: Cambridge University Press.

Steedman, I. (1982). Joint production and the wage–rent frontier. *The Economic Journal, 92*(2), 377–385.

Steedman, I. (1984). L'importance empirique de la production jointe. In C. Bidard (Ed.), *La production jointe. Nouveaux débats* (pp. 5–20). Paris: Economica.

Stone, R. (1961). *Input–output and national accounts*. Paris: OECD.

ten Raa, T., Chakraborty, D., & Small, J. A. (1984). An alternative treatment of secondary products in input–output analysis. *The Review of Economics and Statistics, 66*(1), 88–97.

ten Raa, T., & Rueda-Cantuche, J. M. (2013). The problem of negatives generated by the commodity technology model in input–output analysis: A review of the solutions. *Journal of Economic Structures, 2*, 5. https://doi.org/10.1186/2193-2409-2-5.

United Nations. (1968). *A system of national accounts*. New York: United Nations.

United Nations. (1999). *Handbook of input–output table. Compilation and analysis. Studies in methods. Handbook of national accounting*. New York: United Nations.

van Rijckeghem, W. (1967). An exact method for determining the technology matrix in a situation with secondary products. *The Review of Economics and Statistics, 49*(4), 607–608.

Viet, V. Q. (1994). Practices in input–output table compilation. *Regional Science and Urban Economics, 24*(1), 27–54.

von Neumann, J. (1937). Über ein ökonomisches Gleichungssystem und eine Verallgemeinerung des Brouwerschen Fixpunktsatzes. In K. Menger (Ed.), *Ergebnisse eines Mathematischen Kolloquiums, 8* (pp. 73–83). Leipzig: Deuticke.

von Neumann, J. (1945). A model of general economic equilibrium. *The Review of Economic Studies, 13*(1), 1–9.

# Chapter 2
# Controllability, Observability and Spectral Post-Construction of the Value Theory

**Abstract** Focusing on Kalman's modern control theory, which is based on the dual concepts of controllability and observability, and on the relationships between the modern and the classical control theories, this chapter restates fundamental structural features of Sraffa's theory of production. Thus, it identifies new aspects of the Sraffian theory, emphasizes the generality of this theory, determines the location of the alternative, traditional and Sraffian value theories in the complex plane and, hence, points out a spectral post-construction of the value theory.

**Keywords** Capital-intensity and value effects · Circulant matrices · Hyper-basic commodities · Modern and classical control theories · Sraffian and traditional value theories

## 2.1 Introduction

In spite of their fundamental conceptual differences, the value theories of the traditional political economy (classical, Marxian, Austrian, and neoclassical) reduce, in essence, to the existence of an unambiguous relationship between, on the one hand, the movement of the long-period relative price of two commodities arising from changes in income distribution and, on the other hand, the difference in the capital intensities of the industries producing these commodities. Since Sraffa's (1960) contribution, it has been gradually recognized, however, that such a relationship does not necessarily exist: Even in a world of fixed technical coefficients and at least three commodities, produced by means of themselves and homogeneous labour, long-period relative prices or "values" (Sraffa 1960, pp. 8–9) can change in a complicated way as income distribution changes. This phenomenon has crucial implications for all the traditional theories of value, capital, income distribution–growth, and international trade, while its investigation led to the formation of a *new* theory of value, which includes the abovementioned relationship between value variation and capital intensity difference as its special or limiting case.

© Springer Nature Singapore Pte Ltd. 2021
T. Mariolis et al., *Spectral Theory of Value and Actual Economies*, Evolutionary
Economics and Social Complexity Science 24,
https://doi.org/10.1007/978-981-33-6260-4_2

Following a line of research that restates fundamental structural features of Piero Sraffa's radical theory of "production of commodities by means of commodities" in terms of Rudolf Emil Kalman's (1960a, b) innovative "general theory of control systems", this chapter identifies new aspects of the Sraffian theory, zeroes in on the spectral characteristics of the relevant Krylov matrices and, finally, reveals that the alternative value theories correspond to specific complex plane locations of the eigenvalues of the technical coefficients matrix. Thus, this chapter also paves the way for a general and unified treatment of the value and capital problems on both theoretical and empirical grounds.[1]

The remainder of the chapter is structured as follows. Section 2.2 outlines Kalman's general or modern control theory and its relationships with the traditional or classical one. Section 2.3 (a) outlines Sraffa's theory and restates its fundamental structural features; (b) models the negative and positive relationships that exist between the Sraffian and the traditional political economy; and (c) points out a spectral reduction or post-construction of the national value theory, i.e. the value theory of closed economies. Finally, Sect. 2.4 concludes.

## 2.2 Two Different System Representations

There are two different languages or methods for representing systems, namely, by means of (1) state variables; and (2) transformed input–output relations. The latter method constitutes the basis for the classical control theory, the keywords of which are Laplace and zed transforms, transfer function, frequency-domain analysis. The former method characterizes the modern control theory, the keywords of which are differential and difference equations with respect to state variables, controllability and observability, state-space analysis.

More specifically, the core, both algebraic and conceptual, of the modern control theory is formed by the dual concepts of controllability and observability that were introduced and developed by Kalman in the late 1950s and early 1960s. In his *Lectures on Controllability and Observability*, given at a Summer School of the "Centro Internazionale Matematico Estivo (C.I.M.E.)", held in Pontecchio (Bologna), 1–9 July 1968, Kalman (1969) depicted the making of the modern control theory as follows:

> The theory of controllability and observability has been developed, one might almost say *reluctantly*, in response to problems generated by technological science, especially in areas related to control, communication, and computers. It seems that the first *conscious* steps to formalize these matters as a separate area of (system-theoretic or mathematical) research

---

[1]The seminal papers in this field are Mariolis (2003), Mariolis and Tsoulfidis (2009). Despite the subsequent unfolding of this line of research and outcomes, there are still misunderstandings about them; for instance, Schefold (2019) states, without evidence or explicit reference, "Anwar Shaikh and his school have undertaken empirical investigations, in particular Theodore Mariolis and Lefteris Tsoulfidis [...]" (p. 32).

were undertaken only as late as 1959, by Kalman (1960a, b). There have been, however, many scattered results before this time [...], and one might confidently assert today that some of the main results have been discovered, more or less independently, in every country which has reached an advanced stage of "development" and it is certain that these same results will be rediscovered again in still more places as other countries progress on the road to development. (p. 5; emphasis added) [...] The writer developed the mathematical definition of controllability with applications to control theory, during the first part of 1959 (Unpublished course notes at Johns Hopkins University, 1958/59.). [...] Formal presentations of the results were made in Mexico City (September, 1959, see Kalman (1960a)) University of California at Berkeley (April, 1969, see Kalman (1960c)), and Moskva (June, 1960, see Kalman (1960b)),[2] and in scientific lectures on many other concurrent occasions in the U.S. As far as the writer is aware, a *conscious* and *explicit* definition of controllability which combines a control-theoretic wording with a precise mathematical criterion was first given in the above references. There are of course many instances of similar ideas arising in related contexts. Perhaps the comments below can be used as the starting point of a more detailed examination of the situation in a seminar in the history of ideas. (p. 134; emphasis added) [...] Let us conclude by stating the writer's own current position as to the significance of controllability as a subject in mathematics: (1) Controllability is basically an algebraic concept. [...] (2) The historical development of controllability was heavily influenced by the interest prevailing in the 1950s in optimal control theory. Ultimately, however, controllability is seen as a relatively minor component of that theory. (3) Controllability as a conceptual tool is indispensable in the discussion of the relationship between transfer functions and differential equations [...] (pp. 140–141)[3]

In the next sections, we deal, in turn, with the two above mentioned methods of system representation.

## 2.2.1 State Variable Representation

### 2.2.1.1 Axiomatization

An important class of linear systems can be represented axiomatically by[4]

$$\psi_{t+1}^{\mathrm{T}} = u_t \beta^{\mathrm{T}} + \psi_t^{\mathrm{T}} \mathbf{A}, \quad t = 0, 1, \ldots \tag{2.1}$$

$$\varepsilon_t = \psi_t^{\mathrm{T}} \delta \tag{2.2}$$

where $\psi_t^{\mathrm{T}}$ denotes the real $1 \times n$ state vector, i.e. the vector that captures the state of the system with $n$ nodes at time $t$, $\mathbf{A}$ the real, time-invariant, $n \times n$ system matrix

---

[2]That is, at the First Congress of the "International Federation of Automatic Control (I.F.A.C.)". For this congress, from the point of view of the history of control theory, see Bissell (2013), Feigenbaum (1961), Friedland (1986, pp. xi and 15–16). However, the observations provided are not always compatible with each other.

[3]Short but extremely informative historical background notes are embedded in the technical, specialized books by Franklin et al. (2015), Friedland (1986).

[4]The transpose of an $n \times 1$ vector $\psi \equiv [\psi_i]$ is denoted by $\psi^{\mathrm{T}}$. The diagonal matrix formed from the elements of $\psi$ will be denoted by $\hat{\psi}$, and $\mathbf{I}$ will denote the $n \times n$ identity matrix.

(also known as the plant coefficient matrix), which describes the inter-action strengths amongst the system components, $u_t$ the input to the system, which constitutes a scalar function of time (also known as the one-dimensional control vector), $\boldsymbol{\beta}^T$ the real, time-invariant, $1 \times n$ input vector (it may identify the nodes controlled by an outside controller who imposes $u_t$), $\boldsymbol{\delta}$ the real, time-invariant, $n \times 1$ output vector, and $\varepsilon_t$ the output of the system (also known as the measurement variable). Equations (2.1) and (2.2) are the dynamical equations of this "single input–single output" system. The continuous-time analogue of these equations is

$$d\boldsymbol{\psi}^T(t)/dt = u(t)\boldsymbol{\beta}^T + \boldsymbol{\psi}^T(t)[\mathbf{A} - \mathbf{I}] \tag{2.3}$$

$$\varepsilon(t) = \boldsymbol{\psi}^T(t)\boldsymbol{\delta} \tag{2.4}$$

where $d\boldsymbol{\psi}^T(t)/dt$ denotes the time derivative of the system's state.

This axiomatic representation is based on Newton's laws of mechanics:

> In dealing with physical phenomena, it is not sufficient to give an empirical description but one must have also some idea of the underlying causes. Without being able to separate in some sense causes and effects, i.e. without the assumption of causality, one can hardly hope for useful results. [...] How is a dynamic system (linear or nonlinear) described? The fundamental concept is the notion of the *state*. By this is meant, intuitively, some quantitative information (a set of numbers, a function, etc.) which is the least amount of data one has to know about the past behavior of the system in order to predict its future behavior. The dynamics is then described in terms of *state transitions*, i.e. one must specify how one state is transformed into another as time passes (Kalman 1960d, pp. 38–39). Macroscopic physical phenomena are commonly described in terms of cause-and-effect relationships. This is the "Principle of Causality". The idea involved here is at least as old as Newtonian mechanics. According to the latter, the motion of a system of particles is fully determined for all future time by the present positions and momenta of the particles and by the present and future forces acting on the system. How the particles actually attained their present positions and momenta is immaterial. Future forces can have no effect on what happens at present. In modern terminology, we say that the numbers which specify the instantaneous position and momentum of each particle represent the *state* of the system. The state is to be regarded always as an abstract quantity (Kalman 1963, p. 154)

Thus, the state of a system is a mathematical structure containing the $n$ variables $\psi_{jt}$, i.e. the so-called state variables. The initial values, $\psi_{j0}$, of these variables and the input, $u_t$, are sufficient for uniquely determining the system behaviour for any $t \geq 0$. The state variables need not be observable and measurable quantities; they may be purely mathematical, abstract, quantities. On the contrary, the input and output of the system are directly observable and measurable quantities, that is, quantities which have a concrete meaning (e.g. physical or economic). It may be said that the input is the force acting on the particles. State space is the $n$-dimensional space, in which the components of the state vector represent its coordinate axes. The choice of state variables, i.e. the choice of the smallest possible set of variables for uniquely determining the future behaviour of the system, is not unique. Nevertheless, a uniquely determined state corresponds to each choice of the said variables.

By definition, this axiomatization is incomplete for systems that include agents' expectations about the future ("acausal systems").[5] In that case, "the future influences the present just as much as the past" (Friedrich Nietzsche) and, therefore, the concept of "*futurität* (futurity)" becomes indispensable (see, e.g. Willke 1993, Chap. 4).

### 2.2.1.2  Strictly Equivalent Representations and Diagonalization

Two representations, $[\mathbf{A}, \boldsymbol{\beta}^{\mathrm{T}}, \boldsymbol{\delta}]$ and $[\mathbf{A}^*, \boldsymbol{\beta}^{*\mathrm{T}}, \boldsymbol{\delta}^*]$, of the same system are said to be "strictly equivalent" when their state vectors, $\boldsymbol{\psi}_t^{\mathrm{T}}$ and $\boldsymbol{\psi}_t^{*\mathrm{T}}$, respectively, are related for all $t$ as

$$\boldsymbol{\psi}_t^{*\mathrm{T}} = \boldsymbol{\psi}_t^{\mathrm{T}} \mathbf{T} \tag{2.5}$$

where $\mathbf{T}$ denotes a time-invariant non-singular matrix. From Eqs. (2.1), (2.2), and (2.5) it follows that strict equivalence implies the following relationships (and vice versa):

$$\mathbf{A}^* = \mathbf{T}^{-1} \mathbf{A} \mathbf{T}$$

$$\boldsymbol{\beta}^{*\mathrm{T}} = \boldsymbol{\beta}^{\mathrm{T}} \mathbf{T}$$

$$\boldsymbol{\delta}^* = \mathbf{T}^{-1} \boldsymbol{\delta}$$

These relationships define a similarity transformation by the matrix $\mathbf{T}$ or, in other words, a change of the coordinate system in the state space.

If $\mathbf{A}$ has a complete set of $n$ linearly independent eigenvectors (diagonalizable matrix), then system (2.1) is strictly equivalent to the system

$$\widetilde{\boldsymbol{\psi}}_{t+1}^{\mathrm{T}} = u_t \widetilde{\boldsymbol{\beta}} + \widetilde{\boldsymbol{\psi}}_t^{\mathrm{T}} \widehat{\boldsymbol{\lambda}}_{\mathrm{A}} \tag{2.6}$$

where

$$\widehat{\boldsymbol{\lambda}}_{\mathrm{A}} = \mathbf{X}_{\mathrm{A}}^{-1} \mathbf{A} \mathbf{X}_{\mathrm{A}} \tag{2.7}$$

denotes the diagonal matrix (spectral matrix) formed from the eigenvalues, $\lambda_{\mathrm{A}j}$, of $\mathbf{A}$, $\mathbf{X}_{\mathrm{A}}$ $\left(\mathbf{X}_{\mathrm{A}}^{-1}\right)$ the matrix formed from the right (the left) eigenvectors of $\mathbf{A}$, known as the modal matrix, $\widetilde{\boldsymbol{\psi}}_t^{\mathrm{T}} \equiv \boldsymbol{\psi}_t^{\mathrm{T}} \mathbf{X}_{\mathrm{A}}$, and $\widetilde{\boldsymbol{\beta}}^{\mathrm{T}} \equiv \boldsymbol{\beta}^{\mathrm{T}} \mathbf{X}_{\mathrm{A}}$. Thus, the modal matrix defines a new coordinate system ("normal coordinates") in which the system matrix is represented by its diagonal eigenvalue matrix and, therefore, the system is

---

[5]For instance, models for exchange rate determination are typical examples of the representation of such systems.

decomposed into a set of *uncoupled* first-order sub-systems, where each of them is associated with a particular system eigenvalue.

If there is not a complete set of eigenvectors, $\mathbf{A}$ cannot be reduced to a diagonal form by a similarity transformation and, therefore, the original system cannot be decomposed into a set of uncoupled first-order sub-systems. It is always possible, however, to find a basis in which $\mathbf{A}$ is almost diagonal (Jordan normal form). In that case, the transformed system (also) contains "chains" of first-order sub-systems (associated with a particular system eigenvalue), where the output of one is the input of another.[6]

Luenberger (1979) emphasizes the importance of the diagonalizing transformation as follows:

> [T]he diagonalization process is invaluable, for it reveals an underlying simplicity of linear systems. Armed with this concept, we know, when faced with what appears to be a *complex interconnected* system, that there is a way to look at it, through a kind of distorted lenses which changes variables, so that it appears simply as a collection of *first-order systems*. Even if we *never find* the diagonalizing transformation, the knowledge that one *exists* profoundly influences our perception of a system and enriches our analysis methodology. (pp. 141–142; emphasis added)

### 2.2.1.3  Equilibrium and Stability

Now assume, for instance, that the system input is time-invariant, i.e. $u_t = u$ and, therefore,

$$\mathbf{\psi}_{t+1}^{\mathrm{T}} = u\mathbf{\beta}^{\mathrm{T}} + \mathbf{\psi}_t^{\mathrm{T}}\mathbf{A} \tag{2.8}$$

An equilibrium point, $\overline{\mathbf{\psi}}^{\mathrm{T}}$, of system (2.8) must satisfy the equation

$$\overline{\mathbf{\psi}}^{\mathrm{T}} = u\mathbf{\beta}^{\mathrm{T}} + \overline{\mathbf{\psi}}^{\mathrm{T}}\mathbf{A} \tag{2.9}$$

Provided that the matrix $[\mathbf{I} - \mathbf{A}]$ is non-singular or, equivalently, that 1 is not an eigenvalue of $\mathbf{A}$, Eq. (2.9) can be uniquely solved for $\overline{\mathbf{\psi}}^{\mathrm{T}}$:

$$\overline{\mathbf{\psi}}^{\mathrm{T}} = u\mathbf{\beta}^{\mathrm{T}}[\mathbf{I} - \mathbf{A}]^{-1}$$

In the opposite case, either there is no equilibrium point (Eq. (2.9) is inconsistent) or there is an infinity of such points.

From Eqs. (2.8) and (2.9) it follows that

---

[6]Non-diagonalizable systems are of measure zero in the set of all systems and, hence, not generic, while given any $\mathbf{A}$ and an arbitrary $e \neq 0$, it is possible to perturb the elements of $\mathbf{A}$ by an amount less than $|e|$ so that the resulting matrix is diagonalizable (see, e.g. Aruka 1990).

$$\boldsymbol{\psi}_{t+1}^{T} - \overline{\boldsymbol{\psi}}^{T} = \left(\boldsymbol{\psi}_{t}^{T} - \overline{\boldsymbol{\psi}}^{T}\right)\mathbf{A}$$

or

$$\boldsymbol{\psi}_{t+1}^{T} - \overline{\boldsymbol{\psi}}^{T} = \left(\boldsymbol{\psi}_{0}^{T} - \overline{\boldsymbol{\psi}}^{T}\right)\mathbf{A}^{t+1}$$

or, since $\mathbf{A}^{t+1} = \mathbf{X_A}\widehat{\boldsymbol{\lambda}}_{\mathbf{A}}^{t+1}\mathbf{X_A^{-1}}$ (see Eq. (2.7)),

$$\left(\boldsymbol{\psi}_{t+1}^{T} - \overline{\boldsymbol{\psi}}^{T}\right)\mathbf{X_A} = \left(\boldsymbol{\psi}_{0}^{T} - \overline{\boldsymbol{\psi}}^{T}\right)\mathbf{X_A}\widehat{\boldsymbol{\lambda}}_{\mathbf{A}}^{t+1}$$

or, setting $\widetilde{\overline{\boldsymbol{\psi}}}^{T} \equiv \overline{\boldsymbol{\psi}}^{T}\mathbf{X_A}$,

$$\widetilde{\boldsymbol{\psi}}_{t+1}^{T} - \widetilde{\overline{\boldsymbol{\psi}}}^{T} = \left(\widetilde{\boldsymbol{\psi}}_{0}^{T} - \widetilde{\overline{\boldsymbol{\psi}}}^{T}\right)\widehat{\boldsymbol{\lambda}}_{\mathbf{A}}^{t+1} \tag{2.10}$$

Equation (2.10) implies, therefore, that the equilibrium point is "asymptotically stable", i.e. for any initial condition, $\boldsymbol{\psi}_{0}^{T}$, the state vector tends to the equilibrium point as time increases, iff the eigenvalues of $\mathbf{A}$ all have moduli less than 1. In that case, the eigenvalues of $[\mathbf{A} - \mathbf{I}]$ all have negative real part (and vice versa); hence, the equilibrium point of the continuous-time system (2.3), with $u(t) = u$, is asymptotically stable.

### 2.2.1.4   Controllability and Observability

The $n$-system (2.1), i.e. the representation $[\mathbf{A}, \boldsymbol{\beta}^{T}]$ of the underlying system, is said to be "completely controllable" if the initial state $\boldsymbol{\psi}_{0}^{T} = \mathbf{0}^{T}$ can be transferred, by application of $u_t$, to any state, in a finite length of time. It is completely controllable iff the Krylov–controllability matrix

$$\mathbf{K} \equiv \left[\boldsymbol{\beta}, \mathbf{A^T}\boldsymbol{\beta}, \ldots, \left(\mathbf{A^T}\right)^{n-1}\boldsymbol{\beta}\right]^{T}$$

has rank equal to $n$ or, equivalently, iff $\boldsymbol{\beta}^{T}$ is not orthogonal to any (real or complex) right eigenvector of $\mathbf{A}$. In that case there is a real vector $\boldsymbol{\eta}$ ("feedback gain") such that the matrix, $\mathbf{A} + \boldsymbol{\eta}\boldsymbol{\beta}^{T}$, of the closed-loop system

$$\boldsymbol{\psi}_{t+1}^{T} = \widetilde{u}_{t}\boldsymbol{\beta}^{T} + \boldsymbol{\psi}_{t}^{T}\mathbf{A}$$

$$\widetilde{u}_{t} \equiv u_{t} + \boldsymbol{\psi}_{t}^{T}\boldsymbol{\eta}$$

has any desired set of eigenvalues (Eigenvalue assignment theorem; Wonhman 1967; Brunovský 1970). It then follows that complete controllability implies stabilizability by closed-loop linear state feedback control (but not vice versa).

By contrast, iff $rank[\mathbf{K}] = m < n$, then the system is said to be "uncontrollable" or, more specifically, "controllable of rank $m$". It can be proved that closed-loop linear state feedback control does not affect the complete controllability, i.e. if the original, open-loop system is completely controllable (is uncontrollable), then the corresponding closed-loop system is also completely controllable (uncontrollable) (Brockett 1965). Iff the dimension of an eigenspace associated with an eigenvalue of $\mathbf{A}$ is larger than 1 or, equivalently, iff $\mathbf{A}$ satisfies a polynomial equation of degree less than $n$, then the system is uncontrollable whatever $\boldsymbol{\beta}^T$ is (Ford and Johnson 1968; Johnson 1966). For instance, consider the following two polar cases:

1. When $\boldsymbol{\beta}^T$ is an eigenvector of $\mathbf{A}$ associated with, say, eigenvalue $\lambda_{\mathbf{A}1}$, i.e. $\boldsymbol{\beta}^T\mathbf{A} = \lambda_{\mathbf{A}1}\boldsymbol{\beta}^T$, it follows that $rank[\mathbf{K}] = 1$ and, when $\boldsymbol{\psi}_0^T = \mathbf{0}^T$,

$$\boldsymbol{\psi}_{t+1}^T = \left(u_0\lambda_{\mathbf{A}1}^t + u_1\lambda_{\mathbf{A}1}^{t-1} + \ldots + u_{t-1}\lambda_{\mathbf{A}1} + u_t\right)\boldsymbol{\beta}^T \tag{2.11}$$

i.e. $\boldsymbol{\psi}_{t+1}^T$ and $\boldsymbol{\beta}^T$ are linearly dependent irrespective of the input sequence, $u_t$. The system is, therefore, controllable of rank 1 irrespective of the rank of $\mathbf{A}$. In that case, or when the feedback gain, $\boldsymbol{\eta}$, is an eigenvector of $\mathbf{A}$ associated with $\lambda_{\mathbf{A}1}$, the eigenvalues of the closed-loop system, $[\mathbf{A} + \boldsymbol{\eta}\boldsymbol{\beta}^T, \boldsymbol{\beta}^T]$, are $\{\lambda_{\mathbf{A}1} + \boldsymbol{\eta}\boldsymbol{\beta}^T, \lambda_{\mathbf{A}2}, \ldots, \lambda_{\mathbf{A}n}\}$.[7]

2. When $rank[\mathbf{A}] = 1$, i.e. $\mathbf{A} = \mathbf{x}\mathbf{y}^T$ and, therefore, the only non-zero eigenvalue of $\mathbf{A}$ equals $\lambda \equiv \mathbf{y}^T\mathbf{x}$, it follows that $rank[\mathbf{K}] = 2$ and, when $\boldsymbol{\psi}_0^T = \mathbf{0}^T$,

$$\boldsymbol{\psi}_{t+1}^T = \left(\boldsymbol{\beta}^T\mathbf{x}\right)\left(u_0\lambda^{t-2} + u_1\lambda^{t-3} + \ldots + u_{t-2}\lambda + u_{t-1}\right)\mathbf{y}^T + u_t\boldsymbol{\beta}^T \tag{2.12}$$

i.e. $\boldsymbol{\psi}_{t+1}^T$ is a linear combination of $\mathbf{y}^T$ and $\boldsymbol{\beta}^T$, irrespective of the input sequence. The system is, therefore, controllable of rank 2, irrespective of the direction of $\boldsymbol{\beta}^T$. These two uncontrollable systems (or, more generally, the low-rank controllable systems) *seem* to have some correspondence with the "autopoietic systems" of living and social systems theory (Mariolis 2010a, pp. 222–223).[8]

---

[7]We apply the following theorem: Let $\mathbf{A}$ be an arbitrary $n \times n$ matrix, with eigenvalues $\{\lambda_{\mathbf{A}1}, \lambda_{\mathbf{A}2}, \ldots, \lambda_{\mathbf{A}n}\}$, counting algebraic multiplicity. Then the eigenvalues of $\mathbf{A} + \boldsymbol{\eta}\boldsymbol{\beta}^T$, where either $\boldsymbol{\beta}^T$ or $\boldsymbol{\eta}$ are eigenvectors of $\mathbf{A}$ associated with $\lambda_{\mathbf{A}1}$, are $\{\lambda_{\mathbf{A}1} + \boldsymbol{\eta}\boldsymbol{\beta}^T, \lambda_{\mathbf{A}2}, \ldots, \lambda_{\mathbf{A}n}\}$, counting algebraic multiplicity (Brauer 1952; also see Soto and Rojo 2006; Ding and Zhou 2007).

[8]As is well known, the term "autpoiesis" has been introduced in 1973 by the biologists Humberto Maturana and Francisco Varela. It comes from the Greek compound word "αὐτό (self)–ποίησις (creation)", and, according to some interpretations, it is inspired by the post-1965 writings of Cornelius Castoriadis. Although this term is extensively used in modern general system theory (for a formal analysis, see, e.g. Dekkers 2015, Chap. 7), there is, to the best of our knowledge, no corresponding general mathematical modelling (nevertheless, see Bourgine and Stewart 2004). In a paper presented at the Third Systems Symposium, "Systems Approach in Biology", Case Institute of Technology, Cleveland, Ohio, 20–21 October 1966, Kalman (1968) argued, "I have an (unproved) theorem which claims that "Systems Technology" = "Artificial Biology"; after all, the aim of the systems theorist is to create systems which approach or perhaps even surpass

The $n$-system (2.1) and (2.2), i.e. the representation $[\mathbf{A}, \boldsymbol{\delta}]$, is said to be "completely observable" if the knowledge of $\varepsilon_t$, over a finite interval of time, is sufficient to determine the initial state, $\boldsymbol{\psi}_0^\mathrm{T}$. It is completely observable iff the Krylov–observability matrix

$$\mathbf{K}^\mathrm{O} \equiv \left[\boldsymbol{\delta}, \mathbf{A}\boldsymbol{\delta}, \dots, \mathbf{A}^{n-1}\boldsymbol{\delta}\right]$$

has rank $n$ or, equivalently, iff $\boldsymbol{\delta}$ is not orthogonal to any (real or complex) left eigenvector of $\mathbf{A}$.[9] By contrast, iff $rank[\mathbf{K}^\mathrm{O}] = m^\mathrm{O} < n$, then the system is said to be "unobservable" or, more specifically, "observable of rank $m^\mathrm{O}$". Closed-loop linear state feedback control can affect complete observability.

Similarity transformations do not affect either controllability or observability, since

$$\mathbf{K}^* \equiv \left[\boldsymbol{\beta}^*, \mathbf{A}^{*\mathrm{T}}\boldsymbol{\beta}^*, \dots, \left(\mathbf{A}^{*\mathrm{T}}\right)^{n-1}\boldsymbol{\beta}^*\right]^\mathrm{T} = \mathbf{K}\mathbf{T}$$

$$\mathbf{K}^{\mathrm{O}*} \equiv \left[\boldsymbol{\delta}^*, \mathbf{A}^*\boldsymbol{\delta}^*, \dots, \mathbf{A}^{*n-1}\boldsymbol{\delta}^*\right] = \mathbf{T}^{-1}\mathbf{K}^\mathrm{O}$$

Hence, using the Sylvester rank inequality, i.e., for instance,

$$rank[\mathbf{K}] + rank[\mathbf{T}] - n \leq rank[\mathbf{K}\mathbf{T}] \leq \min\left\{rank[\mathbf{K}], rank[\mathbf{T}]\right\}$$

we get

$$rank[\mathbf{K}^*] = rank[\mathbf{K}] \text{ and } rank\left[\mathbf{K}^{\mathrm{O}*}\right] = rank\left[\mathbf{K}^\mathrm{O}\right]$$

Thus, it also follows that system (2.1) and (2.2) is both completely controllable and completely observable iff the Hankel matrix

---

capabilities normally observed only in the living world. The aims of the systems theorists are not unlike those of the biologists, though we must remember that the two groups work under very different kinds of constraints. The systems theorist does not claim that computers will provide ready-made models for explaining the brain, but he is optimistic that the methods devised to gain a deep understanding of inanimate computers will have some relevance to the understanding of living computers. (p. 222) [...] The ideas of realizability theory [i.e. Kalman's general control theory] have already become an essential part of systems technology, that is, of artificial biology; it seems unthinkable (to me) that a real understanding of real biology can be had without systematic, computer-aided model building. And that task will surely require a mathematical apparatus [...] (p. 231)".

[9]The rank-eigenvector conditions for controllability/observability are known as "Popov–Belevitch–Hautus tests or criteria" (Popov 1966; Belevitch 1968; Hautus 1969).

$$\mathbf{KK}^O = \mathbf{K}^*\mathbf{K}^{O*}$$

has full rank.

Iff system (2.1) is completely controllable, then it is not strictly equivalent to a system of the type

$$\left[\boldsymbol{\psi}_{1t+1}^{*T}, \boldsymbol{\psi}_{2t+1}^{*T}\right] = u_t\left[\boldsymbol{\beta}_1^{*T}, \mathbf{0}_2^T\right] + \left[\boldsymbol{\psi}_{1t}^{*T}, \boldsymbol{\psi}_{2t}^{*T}\right]\begin{bmatrix} \mathbf{A}_{11}^* & \mathbf{0}_{12} \\ \mathbf{A}_{21}^* & \mathbf{A}_{22}^* \end{bmatrix}$$

where $\boldsymbol{\psi}_{1t}^{*T}$, $\boldsymbol{\psi}_{2t}^{*T}$ are $1 \times n_1$ and $1 \times n_2$ vectors, respectively, and $n_1 + n_2 = n$ (Kalman controllability decomposition). That is, it is not possible to find a coordinate system in which the state variables are separated into two groups, $\boldsymbol{\psi}_{1t}^{*T}$, and $\boldsymbol{\psi}_{2t}^{*T}$, such that group 2 is not affected either by group 1 or by the input to the system.

On the other hand, iff system (2.1) and (2.2) is completely observable, then it is not strictly equivalent to a system of the type

$$\left[\boldsymbol{\psi}_{1t+1}^{*T}, \boldsymbol{\psi}_{2t+1}^{*T}\right] = u_t\left[\boldsymbol{\beta}_1^{*T}, \boldsymbol{\beta}_2^{*T}\right] + \left[\boldsymbol{\psi}_{1t}^{*T}, \boldsymbol{\psi}_{2t}^{*T}\right]\begin{bmatrix} \mathbf{A}_{11}^* & \mathbf{A}_{12}^* \\ \mathbf{0}_{21} & \mathbf{A}_{22}^* \end{bmatrix}$$

$$\varepsilon_t = \left[\boldsymbol{\psi}_{1t}^{*T}, \boldsymbol{\psi}_{2t}^{*T}\right]\begin{bmatrix} \boldsymbol{\delta}_1^* \\ \mathbf{0}_2 \end{bmatrix}$$

where $\boldsymbol{\psi}_{1t}^{*T}$, $\boldsymbol{\psi}_{2t}^{*T}$ are $1 \times n_1$ and $1 \times n_2$ vectors, respectively, and $n_1 + n_2 = n$ (Kalman observability decomposition). That is, it is not possible to find a coordinate system in which the state variables are separated into two groups, such that group 2 does not affect either group 1 or the output of the system.

It then follows that, iff system (2.1) and (2.2) is both uncontrollable and unobservable, then it is strictly equivalent to a system of the type

$$\boldsymbol{\psi}_{t+1}^{*T} = u_t\left[\boldsymbol{\beta}_1^{*T}, \boldsymbol{\beta}_2^{*T}, \mathbf{0}_3^T, \mathbf{0}_4^T\right] + \boldsymbol{\psi}_t^{*T}\begin{bmatrix} \mathbf{A}_{11}^* & \mathbf{0}_{12} & \mathbf{0}_{13} & \mathbf{0}_{14} \\ \mathbf{A}_{21}^* & \mathbf{A}_{22}^* & \mathbf{0}_{23} & \mathbf{0}_{24} \\ \mathbf{A}_{31}^* & \mathbf{0}_{32} & \mathbf{A}_{33}^* & \mathbf{0}_{34} \\ \mathbf{A}_{41}^* & \mathbf{A}_{42}^* & \mathbf{A}_{43}^* & \mathbf{A}_{44}^* \end{bmatrix} \quad (2.13)$$

$$\varepsilon_t = \boldsymbol{\psi}_t^{*T}\begin{bmatrix} \mathbf{0}_1 \\ \boldsymbol{\delta}_2^* \\ \mathbf{0}_3 \\ \boldsymbol{\delta}_4^* \end{bmatrix} \quad (2.14)$$

where the $n_1$-sub-system 1 is completely controllable but unobservable, the $n_2$-sub-system 2 is both completely controllable and completely observable, the $n_3$-sub-system 3 is both uncontrollable and unobservable, the $n_4$-sub-system 4 is uncontrollable but completely observable, and $n_1 + n_2 + n_3 + n_4 = n$. The actual values of the possible non-zero vectors and matrices depend on the choice of the similarity matrix, $\mathbf{T}$, whereas the dimensions of the corresponding, four mutually exclusive, sub-systems are uniquely determined (Kalman general decomposition theorem; Gilbert 1963; Kalman 1962, 1963, 1982).

Finally, it is noted that:

1. Many authors define a system as "completely controllable or controllable to the origin" (as "completely reachable or controllable from the origin") if any initial state (if $\boldsymbol{\psi}_0^{\mathrm{T}} = \mathbf{0}^{\mathrm{T}}$) can be transferred to zero (to any state) in a finite length of time by an appropriate input sequence. The choice $\boldsymbol{\psi}_0^{\mathrm{T}} = \mathbf{0}^{\mathrm{T}}$ is for convenience only; when $rank[\mathbf{K}] = n$, it is possible to drive the system from any initial sate to any specified state within a finite number of "steps". Respectively, two concepts of observability can be found in the literature, that is, observability using future outputs, which is usually called "observability", and observability using past outputs, which is usually called "constructibility". When $\mathbf{A}$ is non-singular, controllability coincides with reachability, and constructibility coincides with observability (Kalman et al. 1969, pp. 40–41; Kailath 1980, pp. 95–99).

2. Similar definitions and treatments apply both for the continuous-time system (where, amongst other features, controllability and observability are always equivalent to reachability and constructibility, respectively), and the "multi-input–multi-output" systems. Furthermore, they form the basis for dealing with (a) linear time-varying systems; and (b) non-linear systems.[10]

### 2.2.1.5   Almost Uncontrollability and Unobservability

The previous approach provides only a *yes/no* criterion for complete controllability and observability, while uncontrollable and/or unobservable systems are of measure zero in the set of all systems and, thus, not generic[11] or, in other words, systems are *almost always* controllable and observable (Kalman et al. 1963; for a more recent discussion, see Cowan et al. 2012). However,

> [i]n the *real* world [. . .] it may not be possible to make such sharp distinctions. An electrical bridge network, for example, is uncontrollable (or unobservable) for one discrete combination of its parameters. [. . .] The problem with the standard definition of controllability and observability is that it can lead to discontinuous functions of the system parameters: an arbitrarily small change in a system parameter can cause an abrupt change in the rank of the matrix by which controllability or observability is determined. It would be desirable to have definitions which can vary continuously with the parameters of the system and thus can reflect the *degree of controllability* of the system. Kalman et al. (1963) recognized the need

---

[10]See Antsaklis and Michel (2006), Kailath (1980), Lohmiller and Slotine (1998), Slotine and Li (1991), Van Willigenburg and De Koning (2008). For various versions of the concepts of controllability and observability, and their relevance to economic analysis and policy, see Aoki (1976, 1989), Hansen and Sargent (2008), Holly and Hallet (1989), Martos (1990), McFadden (1969), Wohltmann (1981, 1985).

[11]Compare with the class of non-diagonalizable systems (footnote 6 of this chapter).

and suggested using the determinant of the corresponding test matrix [...] as a measure of the degree of controllability or observability. Friedland (1975), noting that basing the degree of controllability or observability on the determinant of the test matrix suffers from sensitivity to the scaling of the state variables, suggested using the ratio of the smallest of the singular values to the largest as a preferable measure. Moore (1981) subsequently elaborated upon this suggestion. (Friedland 1986, p. 220; emphasis added)

In this connection, therefore, a diagonalizable matrix $\mathbf{A}\left(= \mathbf{X_A}\widehat{\boldsymbol{\lambda}_A}\mathbf{X_A^{-1}}\right)$ can be decomposed as (spectral decomposition)

$$\mathbf{A} = \sum_{j=1}^{n} \lambda_{Aj}\left(\mathbf{y}_{Aj}^T\mathbf{x}_{Aj}\right)^{-1}\mathbf{x}_{Aj}\mathbf{y}_{Aj}^T \qquad (2.15)$$

where $\mathbf{x}_{Aj}$ $\left(\mathbf{y}_{Aj}^T\right)$ denotes the right (the left) eigenvector of $\mathbf{A}$ associated with $\lambda_{Aj}$. Equation (2.15) implies, in turn, that the controllability matrix can be expressed as a product of three matrices:

$$\mathbf{K} = \mathbf{V}\widehat{\widehat{\boldsymbol{\beta}}}\mathbf{X_A^{-1}}$$

where $\mathbf{V} \equiv (\lambda_{Aj})^{i-1}$ denotes the Vandermonde matrix of the eigenvalues of $\mathbf{A}$, and $\widehat{\widehat{\boldsymbol{\beta}}}$ the diagonal matrix formed from the elements of $\widetilde{\boldsymbol{\beta}}^T (\equiv \boldsymbol{\beta}^T\mathbf{X_A})$. Consequently, the determinant of $\mathbf{K}$ is given by

$$\det[\mathbf{K}] = \det[\mathbf{V}]\det\left[\widehat{\widehat{\boldsymbol{\beta}}}\right]\det\left[\mathbf{X_A^{-1}}\right] \qquad (2.16)$$

where

$$\det[\mathbf{V}] = \prod_{1 \leq i < j \leq n} \left(\lambda_{Aj} - \lambda_{Ai}\right) \qquad (2.17)$$

Finally, the "degree of controllability" is defined as

$$DC \equiv \sigma_{Kn}\sigma_{K1}^{-1} \qquad (2.18)$$

where $0 \leq DC < 1$, and $\sigma_{K1}$, $\sigma_{Kn}$ denote the largest and the smallest singular values of $\mathbf{K}$, respectively, while $DC^{-1}$ equals the "condition number" of $\mathbf{K}$ (the degree of observability is defined analogously). When $DC = 0$, the system is uncontrollable; otherwise, it is completely controllable. Nevertheless, when the value of $DC$ is "very small", the controllability is "weak" or "poor"; in other words, the system is said to be "almost uncontrollable".

Finally, the distance between a completely controllable system $[\mathbf{A}, \boldsymbol{\beta}^{\mathrm{T}}]$ and the nearest uncontrollable system $[\mathbf{A} + \Delta\mathbf{A}, \boldsymbol{\beta}^{\mathrm{T}} + \Delta\boldsymbol{\beta}^{\mathrm{T}}]$, where $\Delta\mathbf{A}, \Delta\boldsymbol{\beta}^{\mathrm{T}}$ denote allowed perturbations, is defined as

$$d\left(\mathbf{A}, \boldsymbol{\beta}^{\mathrm{T}}\right) \equiv \min \left\| \Delta\mathbf{A}, \Delta\boldsymbol{\beta}^{\mathrm{T}} \right\|_2$$

where $\|\bullet\|_2$ denotes the Euclidean norm of $\bullet$ (spectral norm for matrices). An upper bound for this distance is given by

$$d(\mathbf{A}, \boldsymbol{\beta}^{\mathrm{T}}) \leq \min \left\{ (1 + \|\mathbf{C_A}\|_2 \sigma_{\mathrm{K}h}^{-1}) \sigma_{\mathrm{K}h+1} \right\}, \quad h = 1, 2, \ldots, n-1 \qquad (2.19)$$

where $\mathbf{C_A}$ denotes a companion matrix of $\mathbf{A}$, while $\|\mathbf{C_A}\|_2 = \sigma_{\mathrm{C_A}1}$.[12] An upper bound for the distance, $d(\mathbf{A}, \boldsymbol{\beta}^{\mathrm{T}}, \boldsymbol{\delta})$, between a completely controllable and, at the same time, observable system and the nearest both uncontrollable and unobservable system is given by

$$d\left(\mathbf{A}, \boldsymbol{\beta}^{\mathrm{T}}, \boldsymbol{\delta}\right) \leq \min \left\{ d_{\mathrm{I}}, d_{\mathrm{II}} \right\}$$

where

$$d_{\mathrm{I}} \leq \min \left\{ \left( \|\mathbf{C_A}\|_2 \sigma_{\mathrm{K}h+1} + \min \left\{ \sigma_{\mathrm{N}1}, \sigma_{\mathrm{K}^{\mathrm{O}}1} \sigma_{\mathrm{K}h} \right\} \right) \sigma_{\mathrm{K}1h}^{-1} + \sigma_{\mathrm{K}h+1} \right\}$$

$$d_{\mathrm{II}} \leq \min \left\{ \left( \|\mathbf{C_A}\|_2 \sigma_{\mathrm{K}^{\mathrm{O}}h+1} + \min \left\{ \sigma_{\mathrm{N}1}, \sigma_{\mathrm{K}1} \sigma_{\mathrm{K}^{\mathrm{O}}h} \right\} \right) \sigma_{\mathrm{K}^{\mathrm{O}}h}^{-1} + \sigma_{\mathrm{K}^{\mathrm{O}}h+1} \right\}$$

and $\mathbf{N} \equiv \mathbf{K}\mathbf{K}^{\mathrm{O}}$ (Boley and Lu 1984, p. 774; Boley and Lu 1986, pp. 250–251; Clotet et al. 2001, pp. 556–563).[13]


## 2.2.2  Transfer Function Representation

Let $\zeta$ be a complex variable and let

$$y \equiv \sum_{t=0}^{+\infty} y_t \zeta^{-t} \qquad (2.20)$$

be the unilateral $\zeta$-transform of a given sequence of numbers $y_t$ (Ragazzini and Zadeh 1952). Provided that series (2.20) converges, the $\zeta$-transform converts a sequence of numbers defined in the time domain to an expression defined in the

---

[12]It goes without saying that the corresponding upper bound for the distance between a completely observable system and the nearest unobservable system is determined analogously.

[13]For a comprehensive review of alternative approaches, see Datta (2004, pp. 183–191).

complex $\zeta$-domain, and $\zeta$ is usually called "complex frequency". From this definition it follows that, if the sequences $y_{I_t}$ and $y_{II_t}$ have the $\zeta$-transforms $y_I$ and $y_{II}$,
respectively, then the $\zeta$-transform (a) of $y_{I_t} + y_{II_t}$ is $y_I + y_{II}$; (b) of $\alpha y_{I_t}$ is $\alpha y_I$; and (c) of
$y_{I_{t+1}}$ is $\zeta y_I - \zeta y_{I0}$.

Application of the $\zeta$-transform to Eqs. (2.1) and (2.2), with $\boldsymbol{\psi}_0^T = \mathbf{0}^T$ and for det
$[\zeta\mathbf{I} - \mathbf{A}] \neq 0$, finally yields

$$\boldsymbol{\psi}^T = u\boldsymbol{\beta}^T[\zeta\mathbf{I} - \mathbf{A}]^{-1} \tag{2.21}$$

and

$$\varepsilon u^{-1} = \boldsymbol{\beta}^T[\zeta\mathbf{I} - \mathbf{A}]^{-1}\boldsymbol{\delta}$$

or

$$\varepsilon u^{-1} = (\boldsymbol{\beta}^T\mathrm{adj}[\zeta\mathbf{I} - \mathbf{A}]\boldsymbol{\delta})(\det[\zeta\mathbf{I} - \mathbf{A}])^{-1} \tag{2.22}$$

where the right-hand side of Eq. (2.22) gives the transfer function of the system. This
function seems, therefore, to be a proper rational function of degree $n$, which relates
the $\zeta$-transform, $\varepsilon$, of the output to the $\zeta$-transform, $u$, of the input. The roots of the
denominator, i.e. the eigenvalues of $\mathbf{A}$, are called the "poles" of the system, while the
roots of the numerator are the "zeros". The location of the poles and zeros in the $\zeta$-
complex plane determines the transient response of the system, which can be derived
by applying the inverse $\zeta$-transform to the transfer function.

The Laplace transform is the continuous-time counterpart of the $\zeta$-transform. The
Laplace transform of a function $y(t)$ is defined by

$$y \equiv \int_0^{+\infty} y(t)e^{-st}dt \tag{2.23}$$

where $s$ denotes a complex variable. From this definition it follows that, if the
functions $y_I(t)$ and $y_{II}(t)$ have the Laplace transforms $y_I$ and $y_{II}$, respectively, then
the Laplace transform (a) of $y_I(t) + y_{II}(t)$ is $y_I + y_{II}$; (b) of $\alpha y_I(t)$ is $\alpha y_I$; and (c) of $dy_I(t)/dt$ is $sy_I - y_I(0)$.

Application of the Laplace transform to the continuous-time system (2.3) and
(2.4), with $\boldsymbol{\psi}^T(t) = \mathbf{0}^T$ and for $\det[(1 + s)\mathbf{I} - \mathbf{A}] \neq 0$, finally yields

$$\boldsymbol{\psi}^T = u\boldsymbol{\beta}^T[(1 + s)\mathbf{I} - \mathbf{A}]^{-1} \tag{2.24}$$

and

$$\varepsilon u^{-1} = \boldsymbol{\beta}^{\mathrm{T}}[(1+s)\mathbf{I} - \mathbf{A}]^{-1}\boldsymbol{\delta}$$

or

$$\varepsilon u^{-1} = \left(\boldsymbol{\beta}^{\mathrm{T}}\mathrm{adj}[(1+s)\mathbf{I} - \mathbf{A}]\boldsymbol{\delta}\right)\left(\det[(1+s)\mathbf{I} - \mathbf{A}]\right)^{-1} \qquad (2.25)$$

where the right-hand side of Eq. (2.25) gives the transfer function of the system. As in the discrete-time case, this function seems, therefore, to be a proper rational function of degree $n$, which relates the Laplace transform of the output to the Laplace transform of the input. The roots of the denominator, i.e. the eigenvalues of $[\mathbf{A} - \mathbf{I}]$, are called the poles of the system, while the roots of the numerator are the zeros. The location of the poles and zeros in the $s$-complex plane determines the transient response of the system, which can be derived by applying the inverse Laplace transform to the transfer function.[14]

In his *Lectures*, Kalman (1969) stressed that

[t]here has been a vigorous tradition in engineering (especially in electrical engineering in the United States during 1950–1960) that seeks to phrase all results of the theory of linear constant dynamical systems in the language of the Laplace transform. Textbooks in this area often try to motivate their biased point of view by claiming that "the Laplace transform reduces the analytical problem of solving a differential equation to an algebraic problem". When directed to a mathematician, such claims are highly misleading because the mathematical *ideas* of the Laplace transform are never in fact used. The ideas which *are* actually used belong to classical complex function theory: properties of rational functions, the partial-fraction expansion, residue calculus, etc. More importantly, the word "algebraic" is used in engineering in an archaic sense and the actual (modern) algebraic content of engineering education and practice as related to linear systems is very meager. For example, the crucial concept of the *transfer function* is usually introduced via heuristic arguments based on linearity or "defined" purely formally as "the ratio of Laplace transforms of the output over the input". To do the job *right*, and to recognize the transfer function as a natural and purely algebraic gadget, requires a drastically new point of view [. . .]. (p. 78)

### 2.2.3 State Variable Versus Transfer Function Representation

Iff the system $[\mathbf{A}, \boldsymbol{\beta}^{\mathrm{T}}, \boldsymbol{\delta}]$ (the system $[\mathbf{A} - \mathbf{I}, \boldsymbol{\beta}^{\mathrm{T}}, \boldsymbol{\delta}]$) is both completely controllable and completely observable, then the transfer function contains all the information which characterises its dynamic behaviour or, equivalently, the knowledge of the transfer function is sufficient for the unique determination of the dynamic Eqs. (2.1) and (2.2) (Eqs. (2.3) and (2.4)). In the opposite case, Kalman general decomposition

---

[14]For the early applications of the transfer function modelling to economic analysis and policy, see Allen (1956, Chap. 9), Lange (1970), Leeson (2000), and the review papers by Chatelain and Ralf (2020), Turnovsky (2011).

theorem and Eq. (2.22) or, respectively, Eq. (2.25) imply that (setting $s' = \zeta$ or, respectively, $1 + s$)

$$\varepsilon u^{-1} = \left(\boldsymbol{\beta}^{*T}\mathbf{T}^{-1}\right)\left[s'\mathbf{I} - \left[\mathbf{TA}^*\mathbf{T}^{-1}\right]\right]^{-1}(\mathbf{T\delta})$$

or, since $[s'\mathbf{I} - [\mathbf{TA}^*\mathbf{T}^{-1}]]^{-1} = \mathbf{T}[s'\mathbf{I} - \mathbf{A}^*]^{-1}\mathbf{T}^{-1}$,

$$\varepsilon u^{-1} = \boldsymbol{\beta}^{*T}[s'\mathbf{I} - \mathbf{A}^*]^{-1}\boldsymbol{\delta}^*$$

or, finally,

$$\varepsilon u^{-1} = \boldsymbol{\beta}_2^{*T}\left[s'\mathbf{I}_2 - \mathbf{A}_{22}^*\right]^{-1}\boldsymbol{\delta}_2^* \tag{2.26}$$

where the $1 \times n$ vector $\boldsymbol{\beta}^{*T}[s'\mathbf{I} - \mathbf{A}^*]^{-1}$ represents only the completely controllable sub-systems 1 and 2, while the $n \times 1$ vector $[s'\mathbf{I} - \mathbf{A}^*]^{-1}\boldsymbol{\delta}^*$ represents only the completely observable sub-systems 2 and 4. Hence, as Eq. (2.26) implies, the transfer function represents only the completely controllable and completely observable sub-system, i.e. sub-system 2 (Gilbert 1963; Kalman 1963; Popov 1963, 1970).

Thus, it can be concluded that the state variable representation and the transfer function representation are not necessarily equivalent, while Friedland (1986) notes that

> [t]he classical period of control theory, characterized by frequency-domain analysis, is still going strong, and is now in a "neoclassical" phase – with the development of various sophisticated techniques for multivariable systems. But concurrent with it is the *modern* period, which began in the late 1950s and early 1960s. (p. 9) [...] Starting in the mid 1970s, new impetus was imparted to frequency-domain methods for multivariable systems through the efforts of a number of investigators centered in Great Britain around [Howard H.] Rosenbrock and [Alistair G. J.] MacFarlane. Among the fruits of this effort was a growing recognition that frequency-domain methods and state-space methods enhance and complement each other. The burgeoning theory of robust control systems, which was started only in the past few years, is further evidence of the symbiosis of frequency-domain and state-space methods. (p. 113)

### 2.2.4 Numerical Examples

The following three numerical examples illustrate the points made above:[15]

---

[15]Example 2.1 is provided by Paige (1981, p. 132). Examples 2.2 and 2.3 are based on examples provided by Friedland (1986, pp. 190–193 and 213) and Kalman (1963, pp. 166–168), respectively.

***Example 2.1***
Consider the system:

$$\mathbf{A} = \begin{bmatrix} 1 & 0 & \cdots & 0 \\ 0 & 2^{-1} & \cdots & 0 \\ \vdots & \vdots & \ddots & \vdots \\ 0 & 0 & \cdots & 2^{1-n} \end{bmatrix}, \quad \boldsymbol{\beta}^{\mathrm{T}} \equiv [1, 1, \ldots, 1]$$

It follows that $\mathbf{X_A} = \mathbf{I}$, the $(i, j)$th element of the controllability matrix, $\mathbf{K}$, is $2^{(i-1)(1-j)}$, $rank[\mathbf{K}] = n$, i.e. the system is completely controllable, and $\mathbf{K} = \mathbf{V}$ (see Eqs. (2.16) and (2.17)). For $n = 10$, we get

$$\det[\mathbf{K}] = \det[\mathbf{V}] \cong -3.039 \times 10^{-41}$$

The largest and the three smallest singular values of $\mathbf{K}$ are

$$\sigma_{K1} \cong 3.630, \sigma_{K8} \cong 0.712 \times 10^{-7}, \sigma_{K9} \cong 0.364 \times 10^{-9}, \sigma_{K10} \cong 0.613 \times 10^{-12}$$

Finally, the degree of controllability (see Eq. (2.18)) is

$$DC = \sigma_{K10}\sigma_{K1}^{-1} \cong 1.688 \times 10^{-13}$$

On a computer with machine precision no smaller than $10^{-12}$, we will conclude that the system is uncontrollable. In actual fact, however, a perturbation of $10^{-3}$ must be made to $\mathbf{A}$ to obtain an uncontrollable system (which is very large compared with $10^{-12}$).

***Example 2.2***
Consider the continuous-time system:

$$\mathbf{A} - \mathbf{I} = \begin{bmatrix} 2 & -2 & -2 & -2 \\ 3 & -3 & -2 & -2 \\ 2 & 0 & -4 & -2 \\ 1 & 0 & 0 & -5 \end{bmatrix}, \quad \boldsymbol{\beta}^{\mathrm{T}} = [1, -2, 2, -1], \quad \boldsymbol{\delta} = \begin{bmatrix} 7 \\ 6 \\ 4 \\ 2 \end{bmatrix}$$

It follows that

$$\boldsymbol{\beta}^{\mathrm{T}} adj[(1 + s)\mathbf{I} - \mathbf{A}]\boldsymbol{\delta} = 24 + 26s + 9s^2 + s^3$$

$$\det[(1 + s)\mathbf{I} - \mathbf{A}] = 24 + 50s + 35s^2 + 10s^3 + s^4$$

and, therefore, the transfer function is given by

$$\varepsilon u^{-1} = \left(24 + 26s + 9s^2 + s^3\right)\left(24 + 50s + 35s^2 + 10s^3 + s^4\right)^{-1}$$

Hence, it appears that the transfer function is a proper rational function of degree 4. However, factoring both the denominator and the numerator yields

$$\varepsilon u^{-1} = (4+s)(3+s)(2+s)[(4+s)(3+s)(2+s)(1+s)]^{-1}$$

or

$$\varepsilon u^{-1} = (1+s)^{-1}$$

that is, due to three pole–zero *cancellations*, the transfer function is, in fact, a rational function of degree 1.

This "peculiar" phenomenon is explained as follows. The system is both uncontrollable and unobservable, since $\boldsymbol{\beta}^T$ (since $\boldsymbol{\delta}$) is orthogonal to two right (to two left) eigenvectors of $\mathbf{A} - \mathbf{I}$, i.e.

$$\boldsymbol{\beta}^T \mathbf{X_A} = [0, 1, 0, 1], \quad \mathbf{X_A^{-1}} \boldsymbol{\delta} = [0, 0, 1, 1]^T$$

where

$$\mathbf{X_A} = \begin{bmatrix} 1 & 2 & 3 & 4 \\ 1 & 2 & 3 & 3 \\ 1 & 2 & 2 & 2 \\ 1 & 1 & 1 & 1 \end{bmatrix}, \quad \mathbf{X_A^{-1}} = \begin{bmatrix} 0 & 0 & -1 & 2 \\ 0 & -1 & 2 & -1 \\ -1 & 2 & -1 & 0 \\ 1 & -1 & 0 & 0 \end{bmatrix}$$

Therefore,

$$rank[\mathbf{K}] = rank \begin{bmatrix} 1 & -2 & 2 & -1 \\ -1 & 4 & -6 & 3 \\ 1 & -10 & 18 & -9 \\ -1 & 28 & -54 & 27 \end{bmatrix} = 2$$

$$rank\left[\mathbf{K^O}\right] = rank \begin{bmatrix} 7 & -10 & 16 & -28 \\ 6 & -9 & 15 & -27 \\ 4 & -6 & 10 & -18 \\ 2 & -3 & 5 & -9 \end{bmatrix} = 2$$

$$rank\left[\mathbf{KK^O}\right] = rank \begin{bmatrix} 1 & -1 & 1 & -1 \\ -1 & 1 & -1 & 1 \\ 1 & -1 & 1 & -1 \\ -1 & 1 & -1 & 1 \end{bmatrix} = 1$$

$$\boldsymbol{\beta}^T[(1+s)\mathbf{I} - \mathbf{A}]^{-1}\mathbf{x_{A1}} = \boldsymbol{\beta}^T[(1+s)\mathbf{I} - \mathbf{A}]^{-1}\mathbf{x_{A3}} = 0 \qquad (2.27)$$

$$\mathbf{y}_{A1}^{T}[(1+s)\mathbf{I} - \mathbf{A}]^{-1}\boldsymbol{\delta} = \mathbf{y}_{A2}^{T}[(1+s)\mathbf{I} - \mathbf{A}]^{-1}\boldsymbol{\delta} = 0 \qquad (2.28)$$

Hence, the system is strictly equivalent to the diagonal system

$$\mathbf{X}_{A}^{-1}\mathbf{A}\mathbf{X}_{A} - \mathbf{I} = \hat{\boldsymbol{\lambda}}_{A} - \mathbf{I} = \begin{bmatrix} -4 & 0 & 0 & 0 \\ 0 & -3 & 0 & 0 \\ 0 & 0 & -2 & 0 \\ 0 & 0 & 0 & -1 \end{bmatrix}, \boldsymbol{\beta}^{T}\mathbf{X}_{A}, \mathbf{X}_{A}^{-1}\boldsymbol{\delta}$$

where eigen-system 1 is unaffected by the input and invisible in the output, eigen-system 2 is affected by the input but invisible in the output, eigen-system 3 is unaffected by the input but visible in the output, and eigen-system 4 is affected by the input and visible in the output. This diagonal system has the Kalman general decomposition form (Eqs. (2.13) and (2.14)), and the transfer function represents eigen-system 4, which is the only controllable and observable mode of the underlying system. Friedland (1986) makes the following apt remark:

> The system in the foregoing example is asymptotically stable: all its poles are in the left half-plane, so the consequences of the system being unobservable and uncontrollable are innocuous. Any initial conditions on the uncontrollable and unobservable states decay harmlessly to zero. But suppose that one of the uncontrollable or unobservable subsystems were *unstable*. The resulting behavior could well be disastrous: a random disturbance, no matter how small, which establishes a nonzero initial state will send the subsystem off to infinity. Murphy's law par excellence! (pp. 193–194)

Now consider the system $[\mathbf{A} - \mathbf{I}, \boldsymbol{\beta}'^{T}, \boldsymbol{\delta}]$, where

$$\Delta\boldsymbol{\beta}^{T} \equiv \boldsymbol{\beta}'^{T} - \boldsymbol{\beta}^{T} = [0.001, 0, 0, 0]$$

This system is completely controllable. The transfer function is given by

$$\varepsilon u^{-1} = (1+s)^{-1}\left[1 + \Delta\beta_{1}(11 + 7s)(2 + s)^{-1}\right]$$

or

$$\varepsilon u^{-1} = (2.011 + 1.007s)[(1 + s)(2 + s)]^{-1}$$

and represents eigen-systems 3 and 4. The determinant of the ("new") controllability matrix, $\mathbf{K}'$, and its components are

$$\det[\mathbf{K}'] \cong 3.621 \times 10^{-5},\ \det\left[\hat{\boldsymbol{\beta}}'\right] \cong 3.018 \times 10^{-6},\ \det[\mathbf{X}_{A}^{-1}] = 1$$

while

$$rank\left[\mathbf{K}'\mathbf{K}^O\right] = rank\begin{bmatrix} 1.007 & -1.010 & 1.016 & -1.028 \\ -1.010 & 1.016 & -1.028 & 1.052 \\ 1.016 & -1.028 & 1.052 & -1.100 \\ -1.028 & 1.052 & -1.100 & 1.196 \end{bmatrix} = 2$$

The singular values of $\mathbf{K}'$ are

$$\sigma_{\mathbf{K}'1} \cong 70.732, \sigma_{\mathbf{K}'2} \cong 1.919, \sigma_{\mathbf{K}'3} \cong 6.246 \times 10^{-3}, \sigma_{\mathbf{K}'4} \cong 4.272 \times 10^{-5}$$

and the degree of controllability is

$$DC \cong 6.041 \times 10^{-7}$$

Finally, the Frobenius companion matrix of $[\mathbf{A} - \mathbf{I}]$ is

$$\begin{bmatrix} 0 & 0 & 0 & -24 \\ 1 & 0 & 0 & -50 \\ 0 & 1 & 0 & -35 \\ 0 & 0 & 1 & -10 \end{bmatrix}$$

and its largest singular value is approximately equal to 66.347. Hence, according to relation (2.19), the distance to the nearest uncontrollable pair is no greater than

$$\min\{3.718, 0.222, 0.454\} = 0.222$$

As Boley and Lu (1986) stress:

> For most systems [...] the entries of the companion [matrix] are larger than 1, so [relation (2.19)] would be dominated by the second term $\|\mathbf{C_A}\|_2\sigma_{\mathbf{K}h}^{-1}\sigma_{\mathbf{K}h+1}$. This formula shows that the size of the perturbation $d(\mathbf{A}, \boldsymbol{\beta}^T)$ is not bounded by the smallest singular value of $\mathbf{K}$; rather it is bounded by the ratio between two consecutive singular values. To find a small real perturbation to obtain an uncontrollable system, one must find a gap among the singular values. (pp. 250–251; using our symbols)

### Example 2.3

Consider the discrete-time system:

$$\mathbf{A} = \begin{bmatrix} -3 & 26 & 30 & 30 \\ -3 & 36 & 39 & 43 \\ 1 & -3 & -2 & -3 \\ 0 & -25 & -27 & -32 \end{bmatrix}, \boldsymbol{\beta}^T = [3, -2, 0, 0], \boldsymbol{\delta} = \begin{bmatrix} -5 \\ -8 \\ 1 \\ 5 \end{bmatrix}$$

The system is both uncontrollable and unobservable, since $\boldsymbol{\beta}^T$ ($\boldsymbol{\delta}$) is orthogonal to two right (left) eigenvectors of $\mathbf{A}$, i.e.

$$\boldsymbol{\beta}^{\mathrm{T}}\mathbf{X_A} = [0, -2, 0, -20], \quad \mathbf{X_A^{-1}\delta} = [0, -1/2, 3/2, 0]^{\mathrm{T}}$$

where

$$\mathbf{X_A} = \begin{bmatrix} -10 & -8 & -6 & -50 \\ -15 & -11 & -9 & -65 \\ 1 & 1 & 1 & 1 \\ 12 & 8 & 6 & 47 \end{bmatrix}, \mathbf{X_A^{-1}} = \begin{bmatrix} 1/2 & -1/10 & -3/10 & 2/5 \\ -3/2 & 5/3 & 2 & 2/3 \\ 1 & -3/2 & -1/2 & -1 \\ 0 & -1/15 & -1/5 & -1/15 \end{bmatrix}$$

Therefore,

$$\mathrm{rank}[\mathbf{K}] = \mathrm{rank}[\mathbf{K^O}] = 2, \ \mathrm{rank}[\mathbf{KK^O}] = 1$$

and the system is strictly equivalent to the diagonal system

$$\mathbf{X_A^{-1}AX_A} = \widehat{\boldsymbol{\lambda}}_\mathbf{A} = \begin{bmatrix} -3 & 0 & 0 & 0 \\ 0 & -1 & 0 & 0 \\ 0 & 0 & 1 & 0 \\ 0 & 0 & 0 & 2 \end{bmatrix}, \boldsymbol{\beta}^{\mathrm{T}}\mathbf{X_A}, \mathbf{X_A^{-1}\delta} \qquad (2.29)$$

where eigen-system 1 is both uncontrollable and unobservable, eigen-system 2 is both controllable and observable, eigen-system 3 is uncontrollable but observable, and sub-system 4 is controllable but unobservable.

Changing coordinates by $\mathbf{T_I}$ or, alternatively, $\mathbf{T_{II}}$, where

$$\mathbf{T_I} \equiv \begin{bmatrix} 2 & 1 & -2 & -6 \\ 3 & 1 & -3 & -9 \\ 0 & 0 & 0 & 1 \\ -2 & -1 & 3 & 6 \end{bmatrix}, \mathbf{T_{II}} \equiv \begin{bmatrix} 3 & 1 & -5 & -6 \\ 4 & 1 & -15/2 & -9 \\ 0 & 0 & 1/2 & 1 \\ -3 & -1 & 6 & 6 \end{bmatrix}$$

we get

$$\mathbf{T_I^{-1}AT_I} = \begin{bmatrix} 2 & 0 & 0 & 0 \\ 4 & -1 & 0 & 0 \\ 1 & 0 & -3 & 0 \\ -1 & 1 & -2 & 1 \end{bmatrix}, \boldsymbol{\beta}^{\mathrm{T}}\mathbf{T_I} = [0, 1, 0, 0], \ \mathbf{T_I^{-1}\delta}$$
$$= [0, 1, 0, 1]^{\mathrm{T}} \qquad (2.30)$$

or, respectively,

$$\mathbf{T}_{II}^{-1}\mathbf{A}\mathbf{T}_{II} = \begin{bmatrix} 2 & 0 & 0 & 0 \\ 1 & -1 & 0 & 0 \\ 1 & 0 & -3 & 0 \\ -1/2 & 1 & 0 & 1 \end{bmatrix}, \ \boldsymbol{\beta}^{\mathrm{T}}\mathbf{T}_{II} = [1,1,0,0], \ \mathbf{T}_{II}^{-1}\boldsymbol{\delta}$$

$$= [0,1,0,1]^{\mathrm{T}} \tag{2.31}$$

Systems (2.29), (2.30) and (2.31) have the Kalman general decomposition form, where sub-system 2 (corresponding to eigenvalue $-1$) is the only controllable and observable sub-system. Hence, the transfer function provides no information about two asymptotically stable modes and one unstable mode of the system:

$$\boldsymbol{\beta}^{\mathrm{T}}[\zeta\mathbf{I} - \mathbf{A}]^{-1} = (1+\zeta)^{-1}\left[3, -2(-4+\zeta)(-2+\zeta)^{-1}, 12(-2+\zeta)^{-1}, 4(-2+\zeta)^{-1}\right]$$

$$[\zeta\mathbf{I} - \mathbf{A}]^{-1}\boldsymbol{\delta} = [(-1+\zeta)(1+\zeta)]^{-1}[-(13+5\zeta), -(19+8\zeta), 2+\zeta, (13+5\zeta)]^{\mathrm{T}}$$

and

$$\varepsilon u^{-1} = (1+\zeta)^{-1}$$

## 2.3   The Sraffian Representation of Linear Economies

### 2.3.1   The Stationary Value and Quantity Systems

Consider a closed, linear economy involving only single products and circulating capital (Sraffa 1960, Part I). We assume that (unless otherwise stated):

1. The labour and technical coefficients of production are fixed.
2. The economy is strictly profitable or, equivalently, viable, and diagonalizable.
3. Each commodity enters directly and/or indirectly into the production of all commodities. That is, all commodities are "basics", and the matrix of direct technical coefficients is irreducible.
4. The value of a commodity obtained as an output at the end of the production period is the same as the value of that commodity used as an input at the beginning of that period (stationary values).
5. The net product is distributed to profits and wages that are paid at the end of the common production period, and there are no savings out of this income.
6. Labour may be treated as homogeneous because relative wage rates are invariant.
7. Both the profit (or interest) rate and the capital accumulation (or growth) rate are

uniform.

On the basis of these assumptions, the value side of the economy can be described by[16]

$$\mathbf{p}^T = w\mathbf{l}^T + (1 + r)\mathbf{p}^T\mathbf{A} \tag{2.32}$$

where $\mathbf{A}$ $(\geq \mathbf{0})$ now denotes the $n \times n$ matrix of direct technical coefficients, with $\lambda_{A1} < 1$, $\mathbf{p}^T$ a $1 \times n$ vector of long-period values, $w$ the money wage rate, $\mathbf{l}^T$ $(> \mathbf{0}^T)$ the $1 \times n$ vector of direct labour coefficients, and $r$ the uniform profit rate.

At $r = -1$ we obtain

$$\mathbf{p}^T = w\mathbf{l}^T$$

i.e. the value vector is proportional to the vector of direct labour coefficients. At $r = 0$ we obtain

$$\mathbf{p}^T = w\mathbf{l}^T + \mathbf{p}\mathbf{A}^T$$

or, solving for $\mathbf{p}^T$,

$$\mathbf{p}^T = w\mathbf{v}^T$$

where

$$\mathbf{v}^T \equiv \mathbf{l}^T[\mathbf{I} - \mathbf{A}]^{-1}$$

denotes the vector of "vertically integrated" labour coefficients (Pasinetti 1973; Sraffa 1960, Appendix A) or of the so-called "labour values", i.e. the vector of direct and indirect labour requirements per unit of net output for each commodity, and $[\mathbf{I} - \mathbf{A}]^{-1} > \mathbf{0}$. That is, values are proportional to vertically integrated labour coefficients, which represent "employment multipliers" (in the sense of Kahn 1931).

At $w = 0$ we obtain

$$\mathbf{p}^T = (1 + r)\mathbf{p}\mathbf{A}^T$$

---

[16]The symbol $\lambda_{A1}$ will denote the Perron–Frobenius (P–F) eigenvalue of a semi-positive $n \times n$ matrix $\mathbf{A} \equiv [a_{ij}]$, and $(\mathbf{x}_{A1}^T, \mathbf{y}_{A1})$ the corresponding eigenvectors, while $\lambda_{Ak}$, $k = 2, \ldots, n$ and $|\lambda_{A2}| \geq |\lambda_{A3}| \geq \ldots \geq |\lambda_{An}|$, will denote the non-dominant eigenvalues, and $(\mathbf{x}_{Ak}^T, \mathbf{y}_{Ak})$ the corresponding eigenvectors. Finally, $\mathbf{e}$ will denote the summation vector, i.e. $\mathbf{e} \equiv [1, 1, \ldots, 1]^T$, and $\mathbf{e}_i$ the $i$th unit vector.

i.e. values are proportional to the cost of means of production. Since a non-positive value vector is economically irrelevant, it follows that $(1 + r)^{-1}$ is the P–F eigenvalue of $\mathbf{A}$, or

$$r = R \equiv \lambda_{A1}^{-1} - 1$$

and $\mathbf{p}^T$ is the corresponding left eigenvector. Iff $-1 \le r < R$, then

$$\mathbf{p}^T = w\mathbf{l}^T[\mathbf{I} - (1 + r)\mathbf{A}]^{-1}$$

or

$$\mathbf{p}^T = w\left[\mathbf{l}^T + (1 + r)\mathbf{l}^T\mathbf{A} + (1 + r)^2\mathbf{l}^T\mathbf{A}^2 + \ldots\right] \qquad (2.33)$$

This formula is the reduction of values to physical quantities of labour, weighted with the compounded profit rate appropriate to their conceptual dates of application, or to "dated quantities of direct labour" (Sraffa 1960, pp. 34–35). The series is finite iff no commodity enters, directly or indirectly, into its own production (Austrian-type models). In that case, $\mathbf{A}$ is strictly triangular and, therefore, nilpotent, i.e. there exists a positive integer number $\nu < n$, such that $\mathbf{A}^\nu = \mathbf{0}$, and the system of production can be represented by a single flow input–point output process of finite duration (Burmeister 1974; Hagemann and Kurz 1976; Sraffa 1960, pp. 93–94).[17]

If $\mathbf{l}^T$ is the P–F eigenvector of $\mathbf{A}$, i.e. $\mathbf{l}^T\mathbf{A} = \lambda_{A1}\mathbf{l}^T$, then Eq. (2.33) reduces to

$$\mathbf{p}^T = w\mathbf{l}^T(1 + R)(R - r)^{-1}$$

or,

$$\mathbf{p}^T = w\mathbf{v}^T R(R - r)^{-1}$$

i.e. the value vector is proportional to the vector of direct labour coefficients and, at the same time, to the vector of vertically integrated labour coefficients. This corresponds to the "equal value compositions of capital" case.[18] In any other case, the entire value vector cannot be proportional to that of vertically integrated labour coefficients at a positive level of the profit rate (Mainwaring 1974, pp. 93–101;

---

[17]This assumed structure of production is present even in a popular, "Austrian" essay by Read (1958).

[18]Or Ricardo (1817)–Marx (1894)–Dmitriev (1898)–Samuelson (1962) special case. When the real wage rate is considered as exogenously given (as in classical and Marxian frameworks), it is possible to determine the direct and indirect requirements of commodity $i$ necessary to produce one unit of each commodity as gross output or, in other words, the "commodity $i$ values" (see Chap. 7 of this book). In that case, therefore, there are $n$ "commodity $i$ value theories", which are formally similar to the labour value theory.

Sraffa 1960, Chap. 3). Thus, it can be stated that $r = 0$ or $\mathbf{l}^T\mathbf{A} = \lambda_{\mathbf{A}1}\mathbf{l}^T$ implies that the so-called labour value theory holds true, and $w = 0$ implies that the so-called capital value theory holds true, while the "capital–labour value theory" (Gilibert 1998) applies to all other cases. Commodity values are proportional to "labour values" also when the vector of profits per unit activity level is proportional to the vector of direct labour coefficients; in that case, however, the profit rates differ across industries (also see, e.g. Okishio 1963, pp. 289–291).

After rearrangement, Eq. (2.32) becomes[19]

$$\mathbf{p}^T = w\mathbf{v}^T + r\mathbf{p}^T\mathbf{H}$$

or

$$\mathbf{p}^T = w\mathbf{v}^T + \rho\mathbf{p}^T\mathbf{J} \tag{2.34}$$

or, iff $0 \leq \rho < 1$,

$$\mathbf{p}^T = w\mathbf{v}^T[\mathbf{I} - \rho\mathbf{J}]^{-1} = w[\mathbf{v}^T + \rho\mathbf{v}^T\mathbf{J} + \rho^2\mathbf{v}^T\mathbf{J}^2 + \ldots] \tag{2.35}$$

where $\mathbf{H} \equiv \mathbf{A}[\mathbf{I} - \mathbf{A}]^{-1}$ $(> \mathbf{0})$ denotes the vertically integrated technical coefficients matrix, $\rho \equiv rR^{-1}$ the relative profit rate, and $\mathbf{J} \equiv R\mathbf{H}$ the normalized vertically integrated technical coefficients matrix, with $\lambda_{\mathbf{J}1} = R\lambda_{\mathbf{H}1} = 1$ (since $R = \lambda_{\mathbf{H}1}^{-1}$). Finally, the moduli of the normalized non-dominant eigenvalues of system (2.34) are less than those of system (2.32): If $\lambda_{\mathbf{A}k}$ is positive, then $\lambda_{\mathbf{A}k} < \lambda_{\mathbf{A}1}$. If $\lambda_{\mathbf{A}k}$ is negative or complex, then $|\lambda_{\mathbf{A}k}| \leq \lambda_{\mathbf{A}1}$ (the equality holds iff $\mathbf{A}$ is imprimitive, i.e. has more than one eigenvalue on its spectral circle)[20] and $|1 - \lambda_{\mathbf{A}k}| > 1 - |\lambda_{\mathbf{A}k}|$. Hence,

$$|\lambda_{\mathbf{J}k}| = R|\lambda_{\mathbf{A}k}||1 - \lambda_{\mathbf{A}k}|^{-1} < \left(|\lambda_{\mathbf{A}k}|\lambda_{\mathbf{A}1}^{-1}\right)(1 - \lambda_{\mathbf{A}1})(1 - |\lambda_{\mathbf{A}k}|)^{-1} \leq |\lambda_{\mathbf{A}k}|\lambda_{\mathbf{A}1}^{-1}$$

or

$$|\lambda_{\mathbf{J}k}| < |\lambda_{\mathbf{A}k}|\lambda_{\mathbf{A}1}^{-1}$$

holds for all $k$.

---

[19]The following formulations draw on Mariolis (1993, Chap. 5), Mariolis and Tsoulfidis (2016, Chap. 2), Steedman (1999).

[20]Matrix $\mathbf{A}$ is primitive iff

$$\mathbf{A}^{n^2-2n+2} > \mathbf{0}$$

or, equivalently, iff it is acyclic (see, e.g. Meyer 2001, pp. 674–680).

Equation (2.35) represents the reduction of values to dated quantities of normalized vertically integrated labour, and implies that each element in the vector of "labour-commanded" values (Smith 1776),

$$\mathbf{p}_w^T \equiv w^{-1}\mathbf{p}^T = \mathbf{v}^T[\mathbf{I} - \rho\mathbf{J}]^{-1} \tag{2.36}$$

is a strictly increasing and convex function of $\rho$, tending to plus (to minus) infinity as $\rho$ approaches 1 from below (from above):

$$\dot{\mathbf{p}}_w^T \equiv d\mathbf{p}_w^T/d\rho = \mathbf{p}_w^T\mathbf{J}[\mathbf{I} - \rho\mathbf{J}]^{-1}$$

(also see Sraffa 1960, pp. 38–39).

If commodity $\mathbf{z}$, with $\mathbf{v}^T\mathbf{z} = 1$, is chosen as the standard of value or *numéraire*, i.e. $\mathbf{p}^T\mathbf{z} = 1$, then Eqs. (2.34) and (2.35) imply

$$w = W - \rho k_{\mathbf{z}} = 1 - \rho k_{\mathbf{z}} \tag{2.37}$$

$$w(\rho) = \left(\mathbf{v}^T[\mathbf{I} - \rho\mathbf{J}]^{-1}\mathbf{z}\right)^{-1} = \det[\mathbf{I} - \rho\mathbf{J}]\left(\mathbf{v}^T\mathrm{adj}[\mathbf{I} - \rho\mathbf{J}]\mathbf{z}\right)^{-1} \tag{2.38}$$

and

$$\mathbf{p}^T(\rho) = \left(\mathbf{v}^T[\mathbf{I} - \rho\mathbf{J}]^{-1}\mathbf{z}\right)^{-1}\mathbf{v}^T[\mathbf{I} - \rho\mathbf{J}]^{-1} \tag{2.39}$$

where

$$W \equiv \mathbf{p}^T\mathbf{z}(\mathbf{v}^T\mathbf{z})^{-1} = 1$$

and

$$k_{\mathbf{z}} \equiv \mathbf{p}^T\mathbf{J}\mathbf{z}(\mathbf{v}^T\mathbf{z})^{-1} = \mathbf{p}^T\mathbf{J}\mathbf{z} \tag{2.40}$$

Post-multiplying Eq. (2.34) by Sraffa's (1960, Chaps. 4 and 5) Standard commodity (SSC), i.e. $\mathbf{s} \equiv [\mathbf{I} - \mathbf{A}]\mathbf{x}_{\mathbf{A1}}\ (> \mathbf{0})$, with $\mathbf{l}^T\mathbf{x}_{\mathbf{A1}} = 1$, gives

$$\mathbf{p}^T\mathbf{s} = w\mathbf{v}^T\mathbf{s} + \rho\mathbf{p}^T\mathbf{J}\mathbf{s}$$

or, since $\mathbf{v}^T\mathbf{s} = 1$ and $\mathbf{J}\mathbf{s} = \mathbf{s}$,

$$w = (1 - \rho)\mathbf{p}^T\mathbf{s} \tag{2.41}$$

where $\mathbf{p}^T\mathbf{s}$ equals the value of net output (measured in terms of $\mathbf{z}$) of the Sraffian Standard system (SSS). It then follows that

$$\rho = 1 - w\left(\mathbf{p}^T\mathbf{s}\right)^{-1}$$

equals the share of profits in the SSS, and $R$ equals the net output–capital ratio in the SSS. Hence, $k_{\mathbf{z}}$ (see Eq. (2.40)) equals the ratio of the capital–net output ratio in the vertically integrated industry producing the *numéraire* commodity to the capital–net output ratio in the SSS.

Equation (2.38) gives a trade-off between $w$ and $\rho$, $0 \leq \rho < 1$, known as the "wage–relative profit rate curve". More specifically:

1. Equations (2.36), (2.37), (2.38) and (2.41) imply that

$$\dot{w} = -k_{\mathbf{z}} - \rho \dot{k}_{\mathbf{z}} \tag{2.42}$$

$$\dot{w} = -w\mathbf{p}^T\mathbf{J}[\mathbf{I} - \rho\mathbf{J}]^{-1}\mathbf{z}$$

and

$$\dot{w} = -\mathbf{p}^T\mathbf{s} + (1 - \rho)\dot{\mathbf{p}}^T\mathbf{s}$$

2. At $\rho = 0$ we obtain $w(0) = 1$, $\mathbf{p}^T(0) = \mathbf{v}^T$, $k_{\mathbf{z}}(0) = \mathbf{p}^T(0)\mathbf{J}\mathbf{z}$, and

$$\dot{w}(0) = -k_{\mathbf{z}}(0) = -1 + \dot{\mathbf{p}}^T(0)\mathbf{s} < 0 \tag{2.43}$$

In the other extreme case, i.e. at $\rho = 1$, we obtain $w(1) = 0$

$$\mathbf{p}^T(1) = \left(\mathbf{y}_{\mathbf{J}1}^T\mathbf{z}\right)^{-1}\mathbf{y}_{\mathbf{J}1}^T \tag{2.44}$$

$k_{\mathbf{z}}(1) = 1$, and

$$\dot{w}(1) = -\mathbf{p}^T(1)\mathbf{s} = -\left(\mathbf{y}_{\mathbf{J}1}^T\mathbf{z}\right)^{-1}\mathbf{y}_{\mathbf{J}1}^T\mathbf{s} = -\left(1 + \dot{k}_{\mathbf{z}}(1)\right) < 0 \tag{2.45}$$

That is, the slope, $-\dot{w}R^{-1}$, of the wage–profit rate curve: (a) at $\rho = 0$ represents the capital–labour ratio in the vertically integrated industry producing the *numéraire* commodity; and (b) at $\rho = 1$ represents the capital–labour ratio in the SSS. At any other value of the profit rate this slope no longer represents a capital–labour ratio (except by a fluke). Finally, for $w \geq 0$ and $\rho > 1$, it follows that $\mathbf{p}^T\mathbf{s} \leq 0$ (see Eq. (2.41)) and, therefore, at least one long-period value is negative.

3. If $\mathbf{v}^T$ ($\mathbf{l}^T$) is the P–F eigenvector of $\mathbf{J}$ (of $\mathbf{A}$) or, alternatively, if SSC is chosen as

the *numéraire*, i.e. $\mathbf{z} = \mathbf{s}$, then $k_\mathbf{z} = \mathbf{p}^T\mathbf{s} = 1$ and

$$w = w^S \equiv 1 - \rho \tag{2.46}$$

i.e. the wage–relative profit rate curve is linear, as in a one-commodity world. When $\mathbf{z} = \mathbf{s}$ , Eqs. (2.34), (2.35) and (2.44) imply

$$\mathbf{p}^T = (1 - \rho)\mathbf{v}^T + \rho\mathbf{p}^T\mathbf{J} \tag{2.47}$$

$$\mathbf{p}^T = (1 - \rho)\left[\mathbf{v}^T + \rho\mathbf{v}^T\mathbf{J} + \rho^2\mathbf{v}^T\mathbf{J}^2 + \ldots\right] \tag{2.48}$$

and

$$\mathbf{p}^T(1) = \left(\mathbf{y}_{\mathbf{J}1}^T[\mathbf{I} - \mathbf{A}]\mathbf{x}_{\mathbf{A}1}\right)^{-1}\mathbf{y}_{\mathbf{J}1}^T$$

or, since

$$[\mathbf{I} - \mathbf{A}]\mathbf{x}_{\mathbf{A}1} = (1 - \lambda_{\mathbf{A}1})\mathbf{x}_{\mathbf{A}1}$$

and matrices $\mathbf{A}$ and $\mathbf{J}$ have the same set of eigenvectors,

$$\mathbf{p}^T(1) = \left[(1 - \lambda_{\mathbf{A}1})\mathbf{y}_{\mathbf{J}1}^T\mathbf{x}_{\mathbf{J}1}\right]^{-1}\mathbf{y}_{\mathbf{J}1}^T \tag{2.49}$$

Equation (2.47) indicates that $p_j$ is a convex combination of $v_j$ and $\mathbf{p}^T\mathbf{J}\mathbf{e}_j$, where the latter equals the ratio of means of production in the vertically integrated industry producing commodity $j$ to means of production in the SSS. Equation (2.48) gives the long-period values, expressed in terms of SSC, as polynomial functions of $\rho$.[21] Sraffa (1960) remarks

> it is curious that we should thus be enabled to use a standard [of value, i.e. $\mathbf{s}$,] without knowing what it consists of. (p. 32)[22]

4. Equation (2.42) implies that

---

[21]If wages are paid *ex ante*, then the wage–relative profit rate curve is non-linear, i.e.

$$w = (1 + R\rho)^{-1}(1 - \rho)$$

and $\rho$ is no greater than the share of profits in the SSS. Nevertheless, Eq. (2.47) holds true. For the issue of the timing of wage payments, see Harris (1981), Steedman (1977, pp. 103–105).

[22]Compare with the remark by David G. Luenberger on the importance of the diagonalizing transformation (Sect. 2.2.1.2).

$$-(\dot{w} + k_{\mathbf{z}}) = \rho \dot{k}_{\mathbf{z}}$$

On the other hand, when the wage–relative profit rate curve is concave (convex) to the origin, it necessarily holds that

$$-\dot{w} \geq (\leq) k_{\mathbf{z}}$$

or

$$-(\dot{w} + k_{\mathbf{z}}) \geq (\leq) 0$$

It then follows that

$$\ddot{w} \leq (\geq) 0 \Leftrightarrow \dot{k}_{\mathbf{z}} \geq (\leq) 0$$

i.e. a strictly concave (strictly convex) wage–relative profit rate curve involves a—so-called—"negative (positive) price Wicksell effect" (Robinson 1953, p. 95), which appears as incompatible (as compatible) with the neoclassical one-commodity "parable" relations. In the *general* case, however, the wage–relative profit rate curve is a ratio between a polynomial of the $n$th degree and one of the $(n - 1)$th degree in $\rho$ (see Eq. (2.38)) and, therefore, may admit up to $3n - 6$ inflection points; and the long-period values are ratios of polynomials of degree $(n - 1)$ in $\rho$ (see Eq. (2.39)) and, therefore, may admit up to $2n - 4$ extreme points (though it is not certain that the inflection and extreme points will all occur in the interval $0 \leq \rho \leq 1$; Garegnani 1970, p. 419). It then follows that, for $n \geq 3$, both $k_{\mathbf{z}}$ and $\mathbf{p}^{\mathrm{T}}\mathbf{s}$ can change in a complicated way as $\rho$ changes.

These fundamental value relationships remain valid for the cases of (a) fixed capital *à la* Leontief (1953)–Bródy (1970); and (b) differential profit rates (provided that the sectoral profit rates exhibit a stable structure in relative terms). For instance, in the former case, $\mathbf{v}^{\mathrm{T}}$ and $\mathbf{H}$ should be replaced by $\mathbf{l}^{\mathrm{T}}[\mathbf{I} - (\mathbf{A} + \mathbf{A}^D)]^{-1}$ and $\mathbf{A}^C[\mathbf{I} - (\mathbf{A} + \mathbf{A}^D)]^{-1}$, respectively, where $\mathbf{A}^D$ denotes the matrix of depreciation coefficients, and $\mathbf{A}^C$ the matrix of capital stock coefficients. Nevertheless, the said value relationships do not necessarily remain valid for pure joint production and/or open economies (see Chap. 4 of the present book).

Finally, the stationary quantity side of the economy can be described by

$$\mathbf{I}\mathbf{x} = c\mathbf{f} + (1 + g)\mathbf{A}\mathbf{x}, \mathbf{l}^{\mathrm{T}}(\mathbf{I}\mathbf{x}) = 1 \tag{2.50}$$

where $\mathbf{x}$ denotes the $n \times 1$ vector of activity levels, $\mathbf{I}\mathbf{x} (= \mathbf{x})$ the $n \times 1$ vector of gross outputs per unit of labour employed, $c$ the level of consumption per unit of labour employed, $\mathbf{f}$ an exogenously given $n \times 1$ commodity vector representing the uniform, across income types, consumption pattern, and $g$ the uniform growth rate. Equations (2.50) imply

$$[\mathbf{I} - \mathbf{A}]\mathbf{x} = c\mathbf{f} + g\mathbf{A}\mathbf{x}$$

or, setting $\mathbf{y} \equiv [\mathbf{I} - \mathbf{A}]\mathbf{x}$,

$$\mathbf{y} = c\mathbf{f} + g\mathbf{H}\mathbf{y}$$

or, finally,

$$\mathbf{y} = c\mathbf{f} + \phi\mathbf{J}\mathbf{y}, \, \mathbf{v}^{\mathsf{T}}\mathbf{y} = 1 \tag{2.51}$$

where $\mathbf{y}$ denotes the vector of net outputs per unit of labour employed, $\phi \equiv gG^{-1}$ the relative growth rate, and $G (= R)$ the maximum uniform growth rate, i.e. the growth rate corresponding to $[c = 0, \mathbf{x} > \mathbf{0}]$. Equations (2.51) imply that there is a trade-off between $c$ and $\phi$, i.e. the "consumption–relative growth rate curve". More specifically, this curve is given by

$$c(\phi) = \left(\mathbf{v}^{\mathsf{T}}[\mathbf{I} - \phi\mathbf{J}]^{-1}\mathbf{f}\right)^{-1} \tag{2.52}$$

while

$$\mathbf{y}(\phi) = c[\mathbf{I} - \phi\mathbf{J}]^{-1}\mathbf{f} = \left(\mathbf{v}^{\mathsf{T}}[\mathbf{I} - \phi\mathbf{J}]^{-1}\mathbf{f}\right)^{-1}[\mathbf{I} - \phi\mathbf{J}]^{-1}\mathbf{f} \tag{2.53}$$

Since the consumption–relative growth rate curve is formally equivalent to the wage–relative profit rate curve (see Eqs. (2.38) and (2.52)), and Eq. (2.53) is formally equivalent to Eq. (2.39), it follows that the previous analysis also applies to the quantity side of the economy.

In steady, equilibrium growth, investment adjusts to savings (classical viewpoint) or savings adjust to investment (post-Keynesian viewpoint). Hence,

$$\phi = s_p\rho \tag{2.54}$$

or, respectively,

$$\rho = s_p^{-1}\phi \tag{2.55}$$

where $s_p$, $0 < s_p \leq 1$, denotes the savings ratio out of profits. That is, Eq. (2.54) or, respectively, Eq. (2.55) reflects the saving–investment mechanism and, hence, provides the link between the two sides of the economy.[23]

---

[23]It is noted that, when there is not a uniform, across income types, consumption pattern or when the uniform consumption pattern depends on relative commodity values, the quantity and value sides cannot, in general, be separated; see, e.g. Kurz and Salvadori (1995, pp. 102–104 and Chap. 15).

## 2.3.2 Controllability and Observability of Sraffian Economies

Consider the following dynamic versions of the Sraffian value system:

$$\mathbf{p}_{t+1}^{\mathrm{T}} = w_{t+1}\mathbf{v}^{\mathrm{T}} + \rho^{\mathrm{n}}\mathbf{p}_t^{\mathrm{T}}\mathbf{J}, t = 0, 1, \ldots \tag{2.56}$$

$$\varepsilon_t = \mathbf{p}_t^{\mathrm{T}}\mathbf{z} \tag{2.57}$$

or, alternatively,

$$d\mathbf{p}^{\mathrm{T}}(t)/dt = (w(t) + dw(t)/dt)\mathbf{v}^{\mathrm{T}} + \mathbf{p}^{\mathrm{T}}(t)[\rho^{\mathrm{n}}\mathbf{J} - \mathbf{I}] \tag{2.58}$$

$$\varepsilon(t) = \mathbf{p}^{\mathrm{T}}(t)\mathbf{z} \tag{2.59}$$

where $\rho^{\mathrm{n}}$ denotes the exogenously given nominal relative profit rate, the output of the system, $\varepsilon$, is the value of the *numéraire* commodity, $\mathbf{z}$, and $\left[w_0 = 0, \mathbf{p}_0^{\mathrm{T}} = \mathbf{0}^{\mathrm{T}}\right]$ or $[w(0) = 0, \mathbf{p}^{\mathrm{T}}(0) = \mathbf{0}^{\mathrm{T}}]$, respectively.[24]

Application of the $\zeta$-transform (see Eq. (2.20)), with $\zeta = \rho^{\mathrm{n}}\rho^{-1}$, to Eqs. (2.56) and (2.57) or, alternatively, application of the Laplace transform (see Eq. (2.23)), with $s = \rho^{\mathrm{n}}\rho^{-1} - 1$, to Eqs. (2.58) and (2.59) finally yields

$$\mathbf{p}^{\mathrm{T}} = w\mathbf{v}^{\mathrm{T}}[\mathbf{I} - \rho\mathbf{J}]^{-1}$$

$$\varepsilon w^{-1} = \mathbf{v}^{\mathrm{T}}[\mathbf{I} - \rho\mathbf{J}]^{-1}\mathbf{z}$$

From these equations it follows that the stationary value system constitutes the $s'-$ transformed dynamic value system, where $s' = \rho^{\mathrm{n}}\rho^{-1}$ or $s' = \rho^{\mathrm{n}}\rho^{-1} - 1$, respectively. More specifically, given the analysis in Sect. 2.2, it can be stated that:

1. The labour-commanded price vector (see Eq. (2.36)) is the ratio of the $s'-$ transform of the state vector to the $s'-$ transform of the input (see Eqs. (2.21) and (2.24)).
2. The reciprocal of the wage–relative profit rate curve (Eq. (2.38)) is the transfer function of the dynamic value system (see Eqs. (2.22) and (2.25)).

---

Steedman (1979) remarks, "Consumer "preferences" are intangible and may be employed as a *deus ex machina* to explain anything—and thus nothing. Again, little can be said concerning the effects of differences in relative prices on aggregate consumption patterns, since relative price differences are inextricably related to differences in income distribution. It is thus reasonable to treat the proportions in which consumption commodities are consumed as exogenously determined, admitting that one cannot explain them." (p. 16).

[24]For the analytic treatment of the value model(s), as well as of the corresponding quantity model (s), see Solow (1952, 1959), Takayama (1985, Chaps. 4 and 6). Since the state variables are assumed to be non-negative, these systems belong to the class of "positive dynamic systems", which exhibits specific properties; see Farina and Rinaldi (2011), Krause (2015). Heterogeneous labour can be modelled by means of multi-input systems.

3. The economic meaning of this transformation is that $[w, \mathbf{p}^T]$ is the present value of the sequence $[w_t, \mathbf{p}_t^T]$ or of $[w(t), \mathbf{p}^T(t)]$, and $\rho^n \rho^{-1} - 1$ is the discount rate (Mariolis 2003).
4. Due to the duality between the value system and the quantity system, it follows that the reciprocal of the consumption–relative growth rate curve (see Eq. (2.52)) is the transfer function of the dynamic quantity system.
5. The wage–relative profit rate curve represents only the completely controllable and completely observable sub-system of the value side, while the consumption–relative growth rate curve represents only the completely controllable and completely observable sub-system of the quantity side. The value system is completely controllable iff the $n \times n$ matrix of the first $n$ dated quantities of normalized vertically integrated labour, i.e.

$$\mathbf{K} \equiv \left[ \mathbf{v}, \mathbf{J}^T \mathbf{v}, \ldots, \left( \mathbf{J}^T \right)^{n-1} \mathbf{v} \right]^T$$

has rank equal to $n$ or, equivalently, iff $\mathbf{v}^T$ is not orthogonal to any right eigenvector of $\mathbf{J}$. And it is completely observable iff the $n \times n$ matrix of the first $n$ dated quantities of means of production in the normalized vertically integrated industry producing the the *numéraire* commodity, i.e.

$$\mathbf{K}^O \equiv \left[ \mathbf{z}, \mathbf{Jz}, \ldots, \mathbf{J}^{n-1} \mathbf{z} \right]$$

has rank equal to $n$ or, equivalently, iff $\mathbf{z}$ is not orthogonal to any left eigenvector of $\mathbf{J}$. On the other hand, the quantity system is completely controllable iff the $n \times n$ matrix of the first $n$ dated quantities of means of production in the normalized vertically integrated industry producing the unit of consumption, i.e.

$$\mathbf{K}_q \equiv \left[ \mathbf{f}, \mathbf{Jf}, \ldots, \mathbf{J}^{n-1} \mathbf{f} \right]$$

has rank equal to $n$ or, equivalently, iff $\mathbf{f}$ is not orthogonal to any left eigenvector of $\mathbf{J}$. And it is completely observable iff the $n \times n$ matrix

$$\mathbf{K}_q^O \equiv \left[ \mathbf{v}, \mathbf{J}^T \mathbf{v}, \ldots, \left( \mathbf{J}^T \right)^{n-1} \mathbf{v} \right]^T = \mathbf{K}$$

has rank equal to $n$ or, equivalently, iff $\mathbf{v}^T$ is not orthogonal to any right eigenvector of $\mathbf{J}$. It then follows that (a) the value system is completely controllable iff the quantity system is completely observable; and (b) when the unit of consumption is used as the *numéraire*, it holds $\mathbf{K}^O = \mathbf{K}_q$ and, therefore, the value system is completely observable iff the quantity system is completely controllable.[25]

6. From the transformation of the value system (2.32), with $\mathbf{p}^T\mathbf{z} = 1$, into the Kalman general decomposition form (see Eqs. (2.13), (2.14) and (2.26)), it follows that (a) the value sub-vectors corresponding to the uncontrollable and unobservable sub-system and to the uncontrollable and completely observable sub-system are both equal to zero; and (b) the P–F eigenvalue of the matrix of direct technical coefficients is an eigenvalue of the completely controllable and completely observable sub-system.

Furthermore, it can be proved that, when the value system is completely controllable, the stationary value vectors (given by Eq. (2.39)) relative to any $n$ distinct values of the profit rate ($0 \leq \rho < 1$) are linearly independent (analogously, the same holds true for the quantity side). Therefore, the curve $\mathbf{p}^T(\rho)$ is entirely contained in a space of dimension $n$, and cuts any space of dimension $n'(< n)$ in no more than $n'$ points. Hence, the value movement arising from changes in income distribution can be characterized as—somewhat—"erratic". By contrast, when the value system is controllable of rank $m$ ($< n$), the stationary value vectors relative to any $m + 1$ distinct values of the profit rate are linearly dependent and, therefore, the curve $\mathbf{p}^T(\rho)$ is entirely contained in a space of dimension $m$. In that case, there are $n - m$ vectors $\mathbf{z}'$ such that $\mathbf{K}\mathbf{z}' = \mathbf{0}$ and, therefore, $\mathbf{p}^T(\rho)\mathbf{z}' = 0$ (see Eq. (2.35)). Hence, a change of *numéraire*, from $\mathbf{z}$ to $\mathbf{z} + \alpha\mathbf{z}'$, where $\alpha$ is a given scalar, has no effect on the wage–relative profit rate curve (and on the stationary values).[26] In a word, then, we have the following pairs of "opposites": controllability (uncontrollability) implies unpredictable (predictable) stationary value and wage movements arising from changes in the profit rate. And predictability decreases with increasing rank of controllability.

Finally, when some non-basic commodities exist, $\mathbf{A}$ is reducible and, therefore, can be transformed by the same permutation of rows and columns into the form

---

[25]In the 1970s, Bertram Schefold introduced the following concept of "regularity" of a production technique: A production technique $[\mathbf{A}, \mathbf{l}^T]$ is said to be "regular" iff (a) $\mathbf{l}^T$ is not orthogonal to any right eigenvector of $\mathbf{A}$; and (b) there exists exactly one right eigenvector (up to a factor) associated with each eigenvalue of $\mathbf{A}$. Equivalently, iff the matrix

$$\left[\mathbf{l}, \mathbf{A}^T\mathbf{l}, \ldots, \left(\mathbf{A}^T\right)^{n-1}\mathbf{l}\right]^T$$

has rank equal to $n$ (Schefold 1971, 1976). Condition (b) is superfluous (see Sect. 2.2.1.4, and especially the papers by David A. Ford and Carroll D. Johnson).

[26]For the proofs and further properties, see Bidard and Ehrbar (2007), Kurz and Salvadori (1995, Chap. 6), Miyao (1977), Schefold (1976).

$$\begin{bmatrix} \mathbf{A}_{11} & \mathbf{A}_{12} \\ \mathbf{0}_{21} & \mathbf{A}_{22} \end{bmatrix}$$

where the square and irreducible matrix $\mathbf{A}_{11}$ refers to basics, and $\mathbf{A}_{12}$ denotes the matrix of direct technical coefficients of basics entering into the production of non-basics; the square non-negative matrix $\mathbf{A}_{22}$ refers to non-basics, and is either irreducible ("self-reproducing non-basics") or reducible (Sraffa 1960, Appendix B; Sraffa and Newman 1962; Kurz and Salvadori 1995, pp. 82–84). In that case, the stationary value system takes the form

$$\left[ \mathbf{p}_1^T, \mathbf{p}_2^T \right] = w \left[ \mathbf{l}_1^T, \mathbf{l}_2^T \right] + (1 + r) \left[ \mathbf{p}_1^T, \mathbf{p}_2^T \right] \begin{bmatrix} \mathbf{A}_{11} & \mathbf{A}_{12} \\ \mathbf{0}_{21} & \mathbf{A}_{22} \end{bmatrix}$$

$$\left[ \mathbf{p}_1^T, \mathbf{p}_2^T \right] \begin{bmatrix} \mathbf{z}_1 \\ \mathbf{z}_2 \end{bmatrix} = 1$$

Hence, when the *numéraire* consists of basic commodities only (i.e. $\mathbf{z}_2 = \mathbf{0}_2$), the value system is unobservable.

The following two numerical examples illustrate some of the points made above:[27]

### Example 2.4
Consider the economy:

$$\mathbf{J} = 11^{-1} \begin{bmatrix} 3 & 4 & 4 \\ 4 & 3 & 4 \\ 4 & 4 & 3 \end{bmatrix}, \mathbf{v}^T = 11^{-1}[34, 44, 54], \mathbf{z} = 12^{-1}[1, 1, 1]$$

There is a repeated eigenvalue, $\lambda_{J2} = \lambda_{J3} = -11^{-1}$, and this eigenvalue has two linearly independent eigenvectors, i.e. $\mathbf{x}_{J2} = \chi_2[-1, 0, 1]^T$ and $\mathbf{x}_{J3} = \chi_3[-1, 1, 0]^T$, where $\chi_2, \chi_3$ denote arbitrary non-zero scalars. Hence, there exists an eigenvector of $\mathbf{J}$ that is orthogonal to $\mathbf{v}^T$: For $\chi_3 = -2\chi_2$, it holds

$$\mathbf{v}^T(\mathbf{x}_{J2} + \mathbf{x}_{J3}) = \chi_2 \mathbf{v}^T[1, -2, 1]^T = 0$$

and, therefore,

$$\mathbf{v}^T[\mathbf{I} - \rho\mathbf{J}]^{-1}(\mathbf{x}_{J2} + \mathbf{x}_{J3}) = 0$$

or

----

[27]Example 2.4 is based on numerical examples provided by Schefold (1976, p. 30, footnote 8), Miyao (1977, p. 159). Example 2.5 is based on Mariolis (1993, pp. 85–94).

$$\mathbf{p}_w^{\mathrm{T}}(\mathbf{x}_{J2} + \mathbf{x}_{J3}) = 0$$

(compare with Eq. (2.27)). It then follows that the value system is controllable of rank 2, both $w^{-1}p_1$ and $w^{-1}p_3$ are not rational functions of degree $n - 1 (= 2)$ but of degree $n - 2 (= 1)$, $w^{-1}p_2 = v_2$, and $w^{-1}(p_1 + p_3) = 2v_2$.

On the other hand, $\mathbf{z}$ is SSC and, therefore,

$$\mathbf{y}_{J1}^{\mathrm{T}}[\mathbf{I} - \rho\mathbf{J}]^{-1}\mathbf{z} = \mathbf{y}_{J2}^{\mathrm{T}}[\mathbf{I} - \rho\mathbf{J}]^{-1}\mathbf{z} = 0$$

(compare with Eq. (2.28)). It then follows that the value system is observable of rank 1, and, for $\rho \neq -11$ (i.e. $r \neq (\lambda_{A2,3}^{-1} - 1)R$), the wage–relative profit rate curve is

$$w = (1 - \rho)(11 + \rho)^2(11 + \rho)^{-2}$$

or

$$w = w^{\mathrm{S}} \equiv 1 - \rho$$

(see Eq. (2.46)). A change of *numéraire*, from $\mathbf{z}$ to

$$\mathbf{z} + \alpha\left[\chi_2^{-1}\mathbf{x}_{J2} - 2\chi_3^{-1}\mathbf{x}_{J3}\right] = 12^{-1}[1 + 12\alpha, 1 - 24\alpha, 1 + 12\alpha]^{\mathrm{T}}$$

has no effect on the wage–relative profit rate curve, while, for $-12^{-1} \leq \alpha \leq 24^{-1}$, the new *numéraire* does not include negative quantities. [28] If $\mathbf{f} = \mathbf{z}$, then the quantity system is controllable of rank 1, and observable of rank 2.

Finally, changing coordinates by

$$\mathbf{T} = \begin{bmatrix} 12^{-1} & \tau_{12} & 1 \\ 12^{-1} & \tau_{22} & -2 \\ 12^{-1} & \tau_{32} & 1 \end{bmatrix}, \ \tau_{12} \neq \tau_{32}$$

the value system is reduced to the following Kalman general decomposition form:

---

[28]Regarding the Standard commodity in pure joint production economies, Sraffa (1960) remarks that negative quantities "can be interpreted, by analogy with the accounting concept, as liabilities or debts, while the positive components will be regarded as assets. Thus a Standard commodity which includes both positive and negative quantities can be adopted as money of account without too great a stretch of the imagination provided that the unit is conceived as representing, like a share in a company, a fraction of each asset and of each liability, the latter in the shape of an obligation to deliver without payment certain quantities of particular commodities." (p. 48).

$$\mathbf{J}^* \equiv \mathbf{T}^{-1}\mathbf{J}\mathbf{T} = \begin{bmatrix} 1 & (48/11)(\tau_{12} + \tau_{22} + \tau_{32}) & 0 \\ 0 & -11^{-1} & 0 \\ 0 & 0 & -11^{-1} \end{bmatrix}$$

$$\mathbf{v}^{*\mathrm{T}} \equiv \mathbf{v}^{\mathrm{T}}\mathbf{T} = [1, v_1\tau_{12} + v_2\tau_{22} + v_3\tau_{32}, 0]$$

$$\mathbf{z}^* \equiv \mathbf{T}^{-1}\mathbf{z} = [1, 0, 0]^{\mathrm{T}}$$

where sub-system 1 is both controllable and observable, sub-system 2 is controllable but unobservable, and sub-system 3 is uncontrollable and unobservable (there is no sub-system that is uncontrollable and observable).

The transformed system $[\mathbf{J}^*, \mathbf{v}^{*\mathrm{T}}, \mathbf{z}^*]$ involves only one basic commodity, i.e. a "hyper-basic commodity" (Mariolis and Tsoulfidis 2014, p. 221), which is no more than SSC, and two *economically* irrelevant non-basic commodities ("hyper-non-basics"). For $\rho \neq -11$, the value solution, $\mathbf{p}^{*\mathrm{T}}(\rho) \equiv \mathbf{p}^{\mathrm{T}}(\rho)\mathbf{T}$, to this system is

$$p_1^*(\rho) = 1$$

$$p_2^*(\rho) = 4\tau_{22} + 2(11 + \rho)^{-1}[\tau_{12}(17 + 7\rho) + 3\tau_{32}(9 - \rho)]$$

and

$$p_3^*(\rho) = 0$$

### Example 2.5

Consider the reducible economy:

$$\mathbf{A} = \begin{bmatrix} 0.5 + e & 1 & 1 \\ 0 & 0.4 & 0.1 \\ 0 & 0.1 & 0.4 \end{bmatrix}, \quad -0.5 < e < 0.5, \quad \mathbf{l}^{\mathrm{T}} = [1, l_2, l_3]$$

The eigenvalues of $\mathbf{A}$ are $\{0.5 + e, 0.5, 0.3\}$. We distinguish between the following three cases:

1. When

$$0 < e < 0.5, l_2 = 2e^{-1} - l_3, l_3 \neq e^{-1}$$

the value system is controllable of rank 2 (when $l_2 = l_3 = e^{-1}$, $\mathbf{l}^{\mathrm{T}}$ equals the left P–F eigenvector of $\mathbf{A}$ and, therefore, the value system is controllable of rank 1). Hence, when

$$\mathbf{z} = [0.5 - e, 0, 0]^{\mathrm{T}}$$

the wage–profit rate curve is

$$w = 1 - (1 + 2e)(1 - 2e)^{-1}r$$

while a change of *numéraire*, from $\mathbf{z}$ to

$$\mathbf{z} + \alpha\left[-2e^{-1}, 1, 1\right]^{\mathrm{T}} = \left[0.5 - \alpha 2e^{-1} - e, \alpha, \alpha\right]^{\mathrm{T}}$$

where $\alpha[-2e^{-1}, 1, 1]^{\mathrm{T}}$ is the right eigenvector corresponding to $\lambda_{\mathbf{A}2} = 0.5$, has no effect on this curve. Finally, for

$$0 < \alpha < 0.25e(1 - 2e)$$

the new *numéraire* vector is positive.

2. When

$$-0.5 < e < 0, l_2 = l_3$$

the value system is controllable of rank 2 (since the left P–F eigenvector of $\mathbf{A}$ is $[0, 1, 1]$, the rank of the controllability matrix *cannot* be less than 2). Hence, when

$$\mathbf{z} = -0.25(1 - l_3 e)^{-1}e\left[-2e^{-1}, 1, 1\right]^{\mathrm{T}}$$

where $[-2e^{-1}, 1, 1]^{\mathrm{T}}$ is, now, the P–F eigenvector, the wage–profit rate curve is

$$w = 1 - r$$

while a change of *numéraire*, from $\mathbf{z}$ to

$$\mathbf{z} + \alpha[0, -1, 1]^{\mathrm{T}}$$

where $\alpha[0, -1, 1]^{\mathrm{T}}$ is the right eigenvector corresponding to the eigenvalue 0.3 (for $e < -0.2, \lambda_{\mathbf{A}2} = 0.3$), has no effect on this curve. Finally, for

$$0.25(1 - l_3 e)^{-1}e < \alpha < -0.25(1 - l_3 e)^{-1}e$$

the new *numéraire* vector is positive.

3. When $e = 0$, the economy is non-diagonalizable, and its Jordan normal form is

$$\mathbf{A}^* \equiv \mathbf{T}^{-1}\mathbf{A}\mathbf{T} = \begin{bmatrix} 0.5 & 1 & 0 \\ 0 & 0.5 & 0 \\ 0 & 0 & 0.3 \end{bmatrix}, \mathbf{l}^{*T} \equiv \mathbf{l}^T\mathbf{T} = [1, 0.5(l_2 + l_3), l_3 - l_2]$$

where

$$\mathbf{T} \equiv \begin{bmatrix} 1 & 0 & 0 \\ 0 & 0.5 & -1 \\ 0 & 0.5 & 1 \end{bmatrix}$$

This form implies that, when $l_2 = l_3$, the value system is controllable of rank 2 (since the left P–F eigenvector of $\mathbf{A}$ is [0, 1, 1], the rank of the controllability matrix cannot be less than 2). Hence, when $l_2 = l_3$ and

$$\mathbf{z} = [0.5, 0, 0]^T$$

the wage–profit rate curve is

$$w = 1 - r$$

while a change of *numéraire*, from $\mathbf{z}$ to

$$\mathbf{z} + \alpha[0, -1, 1]^T = [0.5, -\alpha, \alpha]^T$$

has no effect on this curve. In this case, therefore, the new *numéraire* is necessarily no semi-positive.

Finally, it is noted that when (a) $e = 0$; and (b) the *numéraire* is (semi-)positive and includes non-basics, it follows that $\mathbf{p}^T(1)\mathbf{s} = 0$ and, therefore, $\dot{w}(1) = 0$ and $\dot{k}_z(1) = -1$ (see Eq. (2.45)). This "peculiar" situation results from the assumption

of a uniform price for all the units of a commodity and a uniform rate of profits on all the means of production. (Sraffa 1960, p. 91)

See, for instance, Fig. 2.1, where $\mathbf{l}^T = [1, 2, 10]$ and $\mathbf{z} = [1, 1, 0]^T$:

$$\mathbf{p}^T(1) = [0, 86/7, 86/7], \quad \dot{\mathbf{p}}^T(1) = 14^{-1}[-43, 43, 43]$$

and, due to the numerical values chosen, the value of commodity 3 has a minimum in the economically relevant interval of the profit rate, i.e. at

$$r = \left(439 - 8\sqrt{415}\right)/291 \cong 0.949$$

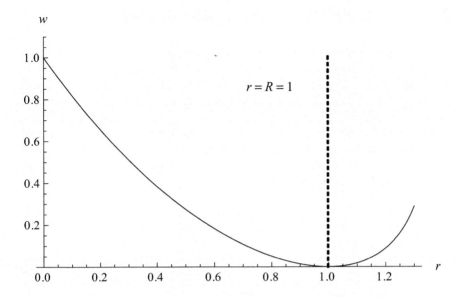

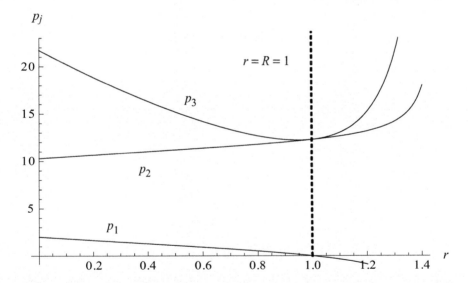

**Fig. 2.1**  The wage–value–profit rate curves in a reducible three-industry economy, where the P–F eigenvalue of the non-basic part equals the P–F eigenvalue of the basic system

### 2.3.3   *Traditional Versus Sraffian Value Theories*

As we have seen above, in the Ricardo–Marx–Dmitriev–Samuelson "equal value compositions of capital case", $\mathbf{l}^T$ ($\mathbf{v}^T$) is the left P–F eigenvector of $\mathbf{A}$ (of $\mathbf{J}$). Therefore, the value vector, measured in terms of a *numéraire* commodity $\mathbf{z}$, $\mathbf{p}^T\mathbf{z} = \mathbf{v}^T\mathbf{z}$, is equal to the vector of vertically integrated labour coefficients, i.e. $\mathbf{p}^T(\rho) = \mathbf{p}^T(0) = \mathbf{p}^T(1)$ or, in other words, the so-called labour value theory (LVT) appears to hold true. In that case, the value system is controllable of rank 1 irrespective of the rank of $\mathbf{J}$ (compare with Eq. (2.11)).[29]

In the simplest two-industry economy, i.e. reducible and without self-reproducing non-basics, $\mathbf{A}$ takes the form

$$\mathbf{A} = \begin{bmatrix} a_{11} & a_{12} \\ 0 & 0 \end{bmatrix}, \ a_{11} < 1$$

This system corresponds to the Marx (1885)–Fel'dman (1928)–Mahalanobis (1953) model(s) or, in more traditional terms, to the Samuelson (1962)–Hicks (1965)–Spaventa (1970) "corn–tractor" model. When values are normalized by setting $p_2 = v_2$, where

$$v_2 = l_1 a_{12}(1 - a_{11})^{-1} + l_2$$

we get

$$p_1 = v_2 a_{11} l_1 [a_{11}(l_2 - \Delta_I) - \rho(1 - a_{11})\Delta_I]^{-1} \tag{2.60}$$

$$k_z = [\Delta_{II} - \rho(\Delta_{II} - 1)]^{-1} \tag{2.61}$$

$$w = w^S [1 + \rho(\Delta_{II}^{-1} - 1)]^{-1} \tag{2.62}$$

where

$$\Delta_I \equiv a_{11} l_2 - a_{12} l_1$$

$$\Delta_{II} \equiv a_{11}(l_2 - \Delta_I)(a_{12} l_1)^{-1}, \ l_2 > \Delta_I$$

and $\Delta_{II} > 1$ iff $\Delta_I > 0$, i.e. iff the capital-commodity industry is more capital-intensive than the consumption-commodity (*numéraire*) industry. Differentiation of Eqs. (2.60), (2.61) and (2.62), with respect to $\rho$, gives

---

[29]Analogously, the same applies to the validity of the "commodity $i$ value theories".

$$\{\dot{p}_1 > (<)\, 0, \dot{k}_z > (<)\, 0, \ddot{w} < (>)\, 0\} \Leftrightarrow \Delta_I > (<)\, 0$$

When both commodities are basic, and $p_2 = v_2$, we finally get

$$\{\dot{p}_1 > (<)\, 0, \dot{k}_z > (<)\, 0, \ddot{w} < (>)\, 0\} \Leftrightarrow \Delta_{III} > (<)\, 0 \Leftrightarrow \Delta_{IV} > (<)\, 0$$

where

$$\Delta_{III} \equiv (l_1 a_{11} + l_2 a_{21}) l_1^{-1} - (l_1 a_{12} + l_2 a_{22}) l_2^{-1}$$
$$\Delta_{IV} \equiv (p_1 a_{11} + v_2 a_{21}) l_1^{-1} - (p_1 a_{12} + v_2 a_{22}) l_2^{-1}$$

Hence, it can be stated that, in the two-industry case, the functions $p_j(\rho)$ are necessarily monotonic and, therefore, the direction of relative value movement is governed only by the differences in the relevant capital intensities ("capital-intensity effect"), as in the various versions of the traditional value theory (TVT), i.e. classical (Ricardo 1817, Chap. 1), Marxian (Marx 1894, Chaps. 11 and 12), Austrian (Böhm-Bawerk 1959, vol. 2, pp. 86 and 356–358; Weizsäcker 1977), and neoclassical (see, e.g. Kemp 1973; Stolper and Samuelson 1941).

Finally, when $rank[\mathbf{J}] = 1$, i.e.

$$\mathbf{J} = \left(\mathbf{y}_{J1}^T \mathbf{x}_{J1}\right)^{-1} \mathbf{x}_{J1} \mathbf{y}_{J1}^T$$

and, therefore, $\lambda_{Jk} = 0$, the Woodbury matrix identity[30] implies that

---

[30]Let $\mathbf{A}$ be an arbitrary non-singular $n \times n$ matrix and let $\boldsymbol{\chi}$, $\boldsymbol{\psi}$ be arbitrary $n$-vectors. Then

$$\det[\mathbf{A} - \boldsymbol{\chi}\boldsymbol{\psi}^T] = \left(1 - \boldsymbol{\psi}^T \mathbf{A}^{-1} \boldsymbol{\chi}\right)\det[\mathbf{A}]$$

and, iff $\boldsymbol{\psi}^T \mathbf{A}^{-1} \boldsymbol{\chi} \neq 1$,

$$[\mathbf{A} - \boldsymbol{\chi}\boldsymbol{\psi}^T]^{-1} = \mathbf{A}^{-1} + \left(1 - \boldsymbol{\psi}^T \mathbf{A}^{-1} \boldsymbol{\chi}\right) \mathbf{A}^{-1} \boldsymbol{\chi}\boldsymbol{\psi}^T \mathbf{A}^{-1}$$

When $\mathbf{A} = \mathbf{I}$, it follows that

$$\det[\mathbf{I} - \boldsymbol{\chi}\boldsymbol{\psi}^T] = \left(1 - \boldsymbol{\psi}^T \boldsymbol{\chi}\right)^{-1}$$

and, iff $\boldsymbol{\psi}^T \boldsymbol{\chi} \neq 1$,

$$[\mathbf{I} - \boldsymbol{\chi}\boldsymbol{\psi}^T]^{-1} = \mathbf{I} + \left(1 - \boldsymbol{\psi}^T \boldsymbol{\chi}\right)^{-1} \boldsymbol{\chi}\boldsymbol{\psi}^T$$

(see, e.g. Meyer 2001, p. 124).

$$[\mathbf{I} - \rho\mathbf{J}]^{-1} = \mathbf{I} + (1 - \rho)^{-1}\rho(\mathbf{y}_{\mathbf{J}1}^{\mathrm{T}}\mathbf{x}_{\mathbf{J}1})^{-1}\mathbf{x}_{\mathbf{J}1}\mathbf{y}_{\mathbf{J}1}^{\mathrm{T}}$$

Hence, from Eqs. (2.38) and (2.39) it follows that both the wage–relative profit rate curve and the long-period values are either rational functions of degree 1 (homographic functions) or linear. More specifically, when $\mathbf{y}_{\mathbf{J}1}^{\mathrm{T}}$ and $\mathbf{x}_{\mathbf{J}1}$ are normalized by setting

$$\mathbf{y}_{\mathbf{J}1}^{\mathrm{T}}[\mathbf{I} - \mathbf{A}]\mathbf{x}_{\mathbf{J}1} = \mathbf{v}^{\mathrm{T}}[\mathbf{I} - \mathbf{A}]\mathbf{x}_{\mathbf{J}1} = 1$$

we get

$$w = w^{\mathrm{S}}\left[1 + \rho(\mathbf{y}_{\mathbf{J}1}^{\mathrm{T}}\mathbf{z} - 1)\right]^{-1}$$

and

$$\mathbf{p}^{\mathrm{T}} = \left[1 + \rho(\mathbf{y}_{\mathbf{J}1}^{\mathrm{T}}\mathbf{z} - 1)\right]^{-1}\left[(1 - \rho)\mathbf{p}^{\mathrm{T}}(0) + \rho(\mathbf{y}_{\mathbf{J}1}^{\mathrm{T}}\mathbf{z})\mathbf{p}^{\mathrm{T}}(1)\right]$$

when $\mathbf{z} = \mathbf{s}$, it holds that $\mathbf{y}_{\mathbf{J}1}^{\mathrm{T}}\mathbf{z} = 1$ (see Eq. (2.44)) and, therefore, $w = w^{\mathrm{S}}$ and

$$\mathbf{p}^{\mathrm{T}} = (1 - \rho)\mathbf{p}^{\mathrm{T}}(0) + \rho\mathbf{p}^{\mathrm{T}}(1) \tag{2.63}$$

namely, $\mathbf{p}^{\mathrm{T}}$ is a convex combination of the extreme, economically relevant, values of the value vector (compare with Eq. (2.12)). The essential characteristics of a rank-one economy, i.e. $rank[\mathbf{J}] = 1$, are as follows:

1. Its value system is controllable of rank 2, irrespective of the direction of $\mathbf{p}^{\mathrm{T}}(0)$.
2. The Schur triangularization theorem (see, e.g. Meyer 2001, pp. 508–509) implies that it can be transformed, via a semi-positive similarity matrix $\mathbf{T}$, into

$$\mathbf{J}^* \equiv \mathbf{T}^{-1}\mathbf{J}\mathbf{T} = \begin{bmatrix} 1 & \left[\mathbf{J}_{12}^*\right]_{1\times(n-1)} \\ \mathbf{0}_{(n-1)\times 1} & \mathbf{0}_{(n-1)\times(n-1)} \end{bmatrix} \tag{2.64}$$

where the first column of $\mathbf{T}$ is $\mathbf{x}_{\mathbf{J}1}$, while the remaining columns are arbitrary, and the vector $\mathbf{J}_{12}^*$ is necessarily positive. If, for instance,

$$\mathbf{T} \equiv [\mathbf{x}_{\mathbf{J}1}, \mathbf{e}_2, \ldots, \mathbf{e}_n]$$

then

$$\mathbf{J}_{12}^* = \left(\mathbf{y}_{\mathbf{J}1}^{\mathrm{T}}\mathbf{x}_{\mathbf{J}1}\right)^{-1}\left[y_{2\mathbf{J}1}, y_{3\mathbf{J}1}, \ldots, y_{n\mathbf{J}1}\right]$$

Namely, a rank-one economy is strictly equivalent to an economically *relevant* and generalized $(1 \times n - 1)$ Marx–Fel'dman–Mahalanobis economy (compare with Example 2.4) and, therefore, behaves as a reducible two-industry economy without self-reproducing non-basics (Mariolis 2013, pp. 5195–5196; Mariolis 2015, p. 270). Consequently, on the one hand, the value side is "a little" more complex than that of a LVT economy and, at the same time, much simpler than that of a completely controllable economy. In fact, its value side corresponds to that of the TVT. On the other hand, a rank-one economy can be fully described by a triangular matrix with only $n$ positive technical coefficients and, therefore, its production structure is "a little" more complex than that of Austrian-type economies, where the technical coefficients matrix is, by assumption, strictly triangular.

However, leaving aside the abovementioned unrealistic or restrictive cases, changes in income distribution can activate complex capital re-valuation effects, which imply that the direction of relative value movement is governed not only by the differences in the relevant capital intensities but also by the movement of the relevant capital intensities ("value effect") arising from changes in relative long-period values. As Sraffa (1960) pointed out,

> the means of production of an industry are themselves the product of one or more industries which may in their turn employ a still lower proportion of labour to means of production (and the same may be the case with these latter means of production; and so on) (pp. 14–15). [...] [A]s the wages fall the price of the product of a low-proportion [...] industry may rise or it may fall, or it may even alternate in rising and falling, relative to its means of production (p. 15). [...] The reduction to dated labour terms [see Eq. (2.33) or Eq. (2.35)] has some bearing on the attempts that have been made to find in the "period of production" an independent measure of the quantity of capital which can be used, without arguing in a circle, for the determination of prices and of the shares in distribution. But the case just considered seems conclusive in showing the impossibility of aggregating the "periods" belonging to the several quantities of labour into a single magnitude which could be regarded as representing the quantity of capital. The reversals in the direction of the movement of relative prices, in the face of unchanged methods of production, cannot be reconciled with *any* notion of capital as measurable quantity independent of distribution and prices. (p. 38)

Indeed, differentiating Eq. (2.34) with respect to $\rho$, and invoking Eq. (2.42), finally gives

$$\dot{p}_j = v_j R(\text{CIE} + \text{VE}) \qquad (2.65)$$

where

$$\text{CIE} \equiv \kappa_j - \kappa_\mathbf{z}$$

denotes the capital-intensity effect, $\kappa_j \equiv v_j^{-1} \mathbf{p}^{\mathrm{T}} \mathbf{H} \mathbf{e}_j$ the capital intensity of the vertically integrated industry producing commodity $j$, $\kappa_\mathbf{z} \equiv R^{-1} k_\mathbf{z} \ (= \mathbf{p}^{\mathrm{T}} \mathbf{H} \mathbf{z})$ equals the capital intensity of the vertically integrated industry producing the *numéraire* commodity, and

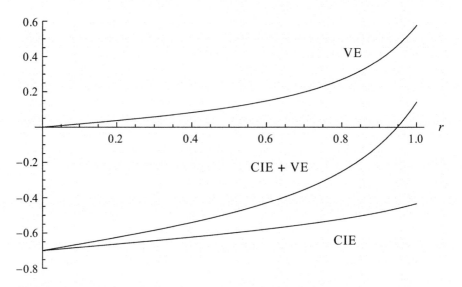

**Fig. 2.2** Example of exact compensation between the capital-intensity and the value effects

$$\text{VE} \equiv \rho\big(\dot{\kappa}_j - \dot{\kappa}_{\mathbf{z}}\big) = \rho\Big(v_j^{-1}\dot{\mathbf{p}}^{\mathsf{T}}\mathbf{He}_j - \dot{\mathbf{p}}^{\mathsf{T}}\mathbf{Hz}\Big)$$

denotes the Sraffian or value effect, which depends on the *entire* economic system and, therefore, is not predictable at the level of any single industry. When SSC is chosen as the *numéraire*, the value movement can be "observed as in a vacuum" (Sraffa 1960, p. 18), in the sense that the capital-intensity effect reduces to

$$\text{CIE} \equiv \kappa_j - R^{-1}$$

where $R^{-1}$ is now equal to the capital intensity of the SSS, while $\dot{\kappa}_{\mathbf{z}} = 0$ and, therefore, the value effect reduces to

$$\text{VE} \equiv \rho\dot{\kappa}_j$$

Hence, it must be concluded that, when these two effects have opposite signs, i.e. CIE > (<) 0 and VE < (>) 0, the traditional statement about the direction of relative value movements does not necessarily hold true, while the underlying phenomena call for a new approach to value theory and, therefore, form the basis of the "Sraffian value theory" (SVT). See, for instance, Fig. 2.2, which is associated with the numerical example depicted in Fig. 2.1 and the value of commodity 3: the capital-intensity effect is negative, the value effect is positive, while the two effects exactly compensate each other at $r \cong 0.949$.[31]

Both in reducible and irreducible economies, non-monotonic value movements need not imply capital intensity reversals for the relevant industries. On the other hand, from Eqs. (2.34) and (2.37) or, when SSC is chosen as the *numéraire*, from Eq. (2.47), we get

$$p_j v_j^{-1} - 1 = \rho R \left( \kappa_j - \kappa_{\mathbf{z}} \right)$$

or, respectively,

$$p_j v_j^{-1} - 1 = \rho R \left( \kappa_j - R^{-1} \right)$$

that is, in any case,

$$p_j v_j^{-1} - 1 = \rho R \text{CIE}$$

It then follows that a value–vertically integrated labour reversal, i.e. a reversal in the sign of the difference: $p_j - v_j$, necessarily implies:

1. The "transmutation" of the vertically integrated industry $j$ from a labour (capital)-intensive industry, relative to the vertically integrated industry producing the *numéraire* commodity, into a capital (labour)-intensive one. Therefore, in contrast to the TVT, the identification of an industry as "labour (or capital)-intensive" makes sense only with respect to a given profit rate.[32]
2. A non-monotonic value movement. Let $\rho_j^*$, $0 < \rho_j^* < 1$, be a value of the relative profit rate at which CIE $= 0$ and, therefore $p_j = v_j$. Since at $\rho = 0$, $p_j$ equals $v_j$, Rolle's theorem implies that, in the interval $\left( 0, \rho_j^* \right)$, there is at least one change in the direction of the movement of $p_j$. For instance, consider the Sraffa–Pasinetti

---

[31]This formulation is based on Parys (1982), Mariolis (1993, Chap. 6), Mariolis (1997, 2010a, pp. 150–159). For further theoretical and empirical analyses, see Mariolis and Tsoulfidis (2009, 2011), Mariolis et al. (2013).

[32]In a recent paper, Eatwell (2019) emphasizes that although "[t]here have been numerous attempts since 1870s to develop a neoclassical theory of the rate of profit [...] there is no neoclassical theory of the rate of profit.". It may be noted in this context that, regarding the dynamic value system (see Eq. (2.56)), Solow (1959) remarks: "Counting the wage rate and the interest rate there are $n + 2$ time-profiles and only $n$ equations. As usual, we could divide each equation through by the wage rate and solve only for relative prices. That still leaves the interest rate undetermined, which is only right and proper since nothing has been said about the supply of saving or the disposition of income or the banking system or the desire for liquidity, or any of the other forces we normally incorporate in a theory of interest. I propose to let the interest rate hang, and to treat it as an arbitrary function of time. We can solve for relative prices in terms of the interest rate and the parameters of the system." (p. 36).

numerical example of the "old wine" (commodity "a") and the "oak chest" (commodity "b"),[33] where

$$p_a = w100(1 + 0.25\rho)^8(1 - \rho)^{-1}, \quad v_a = 100$$

$$p_b = w[120 + 5(1 + 0.25\rho)^{25}](1 - \rho)^{-1}, \quad v_b = 125$$

It follows that $p_a = p_b$ at $\rho = \rho_1 \cong 0.141$ and at $\rho = \rho_2 \cong 0.646$; and when commodity b is chosen as the *numéraire*, i.e. $p_b v_b^{-1} = 1$, it follows that $p_a v_a^{-1} = 1$ at $\rho_a^* \cong 0.756$ (see Fig. 2.3). Hence, as Sraffa (1962) stresses, the "old wine–oak chest" example

> is a crucial test for the [traditional] ideas of a quantity of capital and of [an average] period of production. [. . .] One can only wonder what is the good of a quantity of capital or a period of production which, since it depends on the rate of interest [the rate of profits], cannot be used for its traditional purpose, which is to determine the rate of interest [the rate of profits]. (pp. 478–479)

Finally, when alternative production methods exist (and $n \geq 2$), the value effect implies that (a) a higher profit rate can be associated with higher capital intensity; and/or (b) a production technique can be cost-minimizing over more than one interval of the profit rate. These two phenomena, widely known as "reverse capital deepening" and "re-switching of techniques", respectively, further demonstrate that the neoclassical or Austrian school attempts to start from a given "quantity of capital" or an "average period of production", in order to determine the profit or interest rate, are ill-founded. For instance, consider the above Sraffa–Pasinetti numerical example, but now assume that the value equations refer to the *same* commodity, which can be produced by two alternative systems-technologies ("a" and "b") as their net final product. Thus, adapting Sraffa's (1960) relevant remark, we can then write

> [a]t any given level of the general rate of profits, the [technology] that produces at a lower [value] is of course the most profitable of the two for a producer who builds a new plant. The two curves [in the first graph of Fig. 2.3] show how the [value] of the commodity as produced by the two alternative [technologies] varies with rate of profits (the [value], or cost of production, being expressed in terms of an arbitrarily chosen standard [of value]). The points of intersections were the [values] are equal correspond to the switching from one to the other [technology] as rate of profits changes. There may be one or more such intersections within the range of possible rates of profit, *by analogy* with what we have seen in the case of two *distinct* commodities (§48); if on the other hand there is no intersection, one of the [technologies] is unprofitable in all circumstances and may be disregarded. (pp. 81–82; emphasis added)

Indeed, setting $p_a = p_b = 1$ (*numéraire* equation), we get the "mirror image", which is displayed in the first graph of Fig. 2.4: the two wage–relative profit rate curves

---

[33]In fact, we "merge" the two numerical examples provided by Pasinetti (1966, pp. 504–508) and Sraffa (1960, pp. 37–38).

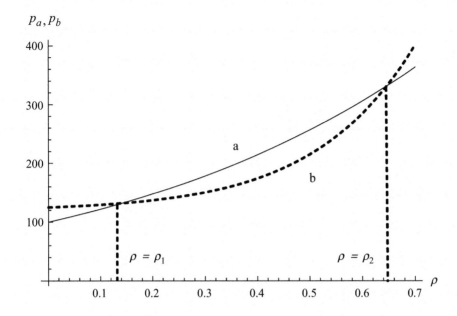

*Numéraire*: Sraffa's Standard commodity

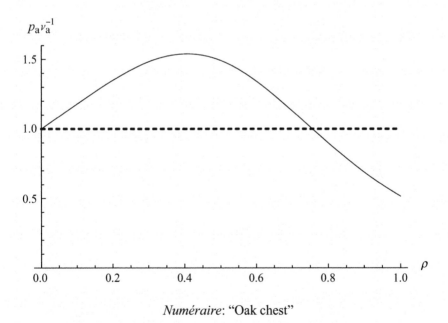

*Numéraire*: "Oak chest"

**Fig. 2.3** The Sraffa–Pasinetti "old wine–oak chest" numerical example: commodity values, in terms of Sraffa's Standard commodity, as functions of the relative profit rate; and value–vertically integrated labour reversal

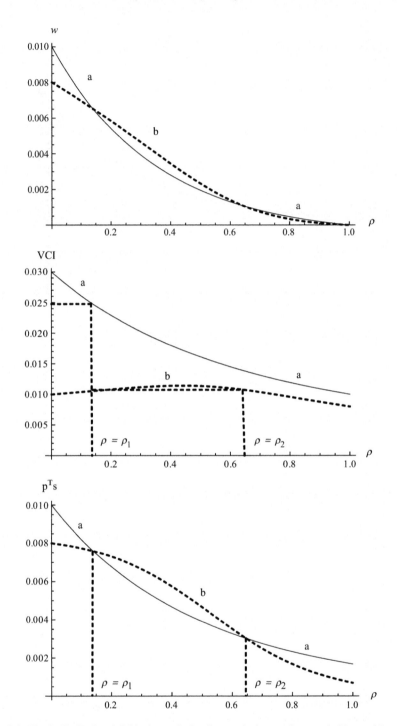

**Fig. 2.4** The Sraffa–Pasinetti "old wine–oak chest" numerical example: re-switching and "reverse capital deepening" phenomena

intersect each other three times, i.e. at $\rho = \rho_1, \rho_2, 1$. And the other two graphs in Fig. 2.4, which display the vertically integrated capital intensities, $VCI \equiv \mathbf{p}^T\mathbf{J}\mathbf{z}$ $(\mathbf{v}^T\mathbf{z})^{-1}$, of the two systems, and the corresponding values of net output of the SSS, $\mathbf{p}^T\mathbf{s} = w(1 - \rho)^{-1}$ (see Eq. (2.41)), as functions of $\rho$, indicate that the second switch-point, $\rho = \rho_2$, is associated with "reverse capital deepening". Furthermore, when there are more than two technologies, a monotonic relationship between the profit rate and capital intensity may not exist even when there is no re-switching, while it is possible for two different profit rates to give the same capital intensity, even when there is no re-switching on or below the outer envelope of the wage–profit rate curves, i.e. re-switching is a sufficient, but not necessary, condition for "reverse capital deepening".[34]

At the same time, these two phenomena fatally undermine the neoclassical analysis of demand and supply for "capital and labour" and, thus, the explanation of the distributive variables as the service prices of the "production factors" that reflect their "scarcities". In effect, all statements and relationships derived from an aggregate production function or average production period framework cannot, in general, be extended beyond a world where: (a) there are no produced means of production; or (b) there are produced means of production, while the profit rate on the value of those means of production is zero; or, finally, (c) that profit rate is positive, while the economy produces one and only one, single or composite, commodity. In that no-value-effect world, there would also be classical and Marxian value statements that would be necessarily valid.[35]

It can be concluded, therefore, that the failures of the TVT result from the existence of complex inter-industry linkages in the realistic case of production of commodities *and* positive profits by means of commodities. In a note written on January 16, 1946, Piero Sraffa remarked that

> if the "*Labour Theory of Value*" applied exactly throughout, *then, and only then*, would the "*marginal product of capital*" theory work! (Sraffa Papers D3/12/16: 34; cited in Kurz 1998, p. 447. Also see Kurz 2009, pp. 274–275)

Many people like to comment that Sraffa's one or the other partial finding is not so novel. As with Kalman's work, what sets Sraffa's work apart is the consciousness of the meaning, significance and implications of both previous and own findings or, in other words, the overall supervision of their scientific fields. And both works were confronted with reluctance, while Sraffa's is still confronted with it.

---

[34]See the illustration provided by Pasinetti (1966, pp. 515–516) under Sraffa's suggestion, and Garegnani (1970). For systematic investigations of the possibility and probability of re-switching and "reverse capital deepening", see Aruka (2000) and Mainwaring and Steedman (2000), respectively. Yuji Aruka's approach rather follows or, alternatively, is in accordance with Sraffa's (1960, pp. 80–81) abovementioned remark. Lynn Mainwaring and Ian Steedman focus on two-industry models, and conclude that the highest probability of re-switching is observed in the case of wage–profit rate curves of relatively *low* concavity.

[35]For comprehensive analytical treatments, see various entries in Eatwell et al. (1990), Garegnani (1984), Harcourt (1972), Salvadori and Stedman (1985), Steedman (1977, 1994).

## 2.3.4   The Spectral Post-Construction of the National Value Theory

Leaving aside the abovementioned three unrealistic or restrictive cases, i.e. (a) $\mathbf{p}^T(0)$ $\mathbf{J} = \mathbf{p}^T(0)$; (b) $n = 2$; and (c) *rank*[$\mathbf{J}$] $= 1$, and using, for instance, SSC as the *numéraire*, Eqs. (2.46)–(2.49) and the spectral decomposition of $\mathbf{J}$, i.e.

$$\mathbf{J} = \left(\mathbf{y}_{\mathbf{J}1}^T \mathbf{x}_{\mathbf{J}1}\right)^{-1} \mathbf{x}_{\mathbf{J}1} \mathbf{y}_{\mathbf{J}1}^T + \sum_{k=2}^{n} \lambda_{\mathbf{J}k} \left(\mathbf{y}_{\mathbf{J}k}^T \mathbf{x}_{\mathbf{J}k}\right)^{-1} \mathbf{x}_{\mathbf{J}k} \mathbf{y}_{\mathbf{J}k}^T \qquad (2.66)$$

imply that, from a value theory viewpoint, it suffices to focus on the following seven ideal-type (in the Weberian sense) cases:[36]

**Case 1:** The economy *tends* to be decomposed into $n$ quasi-similar self-reproducing vertically integrated industries, i.e. $\mathbf{J} \approx \mathbf{I}$ (consider Hartfiel and Meyer 1998). It follows that $\lambda_{\mathbf{J}k} \approx 1$ (see Eq. (2.66)) and $\mathbf{p}^T \approx \mathbf{p}^T(0)$. Hence, irrespective of the direction of $\mathbf{p}^T(0)$, the economy tends to be controllable of rank 1 and to behave as a one-industry economy, while the LVT tends to hold true.

**Case 2:** There are strong quasi-linear dependencies amongst the non-labour conditions of production in all the vertically integrated industries, i.e. $\mathbf{J} \approx \left(\mathbf{y}_{\mathbf{J}1}^T \mathbf{x}_{\mathbf{J}1}\right)^{-1} \mathbf{x}_{\mathbf{J}1} \mathbf{y}_{\mathbf{J}1}^T, |\lambda_{\mathbf{J}k}| \approx 0$ (see Eq. (2.66)). Hence, irrespective of the direction of $\mathbf{p}^T(0)$, the economy tends to be controllable of rank 2 and to behave as a reducible two-industry economy without self-reproducing non-basics, while the value vector tends to be a linear function of the profit rate (see Eq. (2.63)).

A different way to approach this case is: If the elements of $\mathbf{J}$ are identically and independently distributed, then Bródy's (1997) conjecture implies that $|\lambda_{\mathbf{J}2}|$ tends to zero, with speed $n^{-0.5}$, when $n$ tends to *infinity*. This conjecture indicates that, in the case of—endogenous or exogenous—disturbances, the speed of (decentralized) convergence to the equilibrium value and quantity vectors increases statistically with the number of produced commodities. Hence, a market economy of a large size converges to equilibrium more quickly than one of a smaller size, and this issue is not unrelated to the so-called "socialist calculation debate".[37] In his last response to this debate, Lange (1967) supported:

> [T]he market may be considered as one of the oldest historical devices for solving simultaneous equations. [...] It may be interesting to compare the relative merits of the market and of the computer in a socialist economy. The computer has the undoubted advantage of much

---

[36]What follows draws on Mariolis (2019a, b, c, 2021). The first five cases have been extensively analyzed in the literature: Mariolis (2015), Mariolis and Tsoulfidis (2009, 2011, 2014, 2016, Chap. 5). Thus, here we report, without detailed proofs, the main findings that are directly relevant for our present purposes. To the best of our knowledge, the other two cases have not been addressed in the literature. Examples illustrating these two cases are given in the Appendix at the end of this chapter.

[37]As Sun (2008) shows, Bródy's conjecture can be proved using theorems provided by Goldberg et al. (2000) (also see Mariolis and Tsoulfidis 2016, Chap. 6). We will return to Bródy's conjecture in Chap. 3.

greater speed. The market is a cumbersome and slow-working servo-mechanism. Its iteration process operates with considerable time-lags and oscillations and may not be convergent at all. This is shown by cobweb cycles, inventory and other reinvestment cycles as well as by the general business cycle. Thus the Walrasian *tâtonnements* are full of unpleasant fluctuations and may also prove to be divergent. In this respect the electronic computer shows an unchallenged superiority. [. . .] All this, however, does not mean that the market has not its relative merits. First of all, even the most powerful electronic computers have a limited capacity. There may be (and there are) economic processes so complex in terms of the number of commodities and the type of equations involved that no computer can tackle them. Or it may be too costly to construct computers of such large capacity. In such cases nothing remains but to use the old-fashioned market servo-mechanism which has a much broader working capacity. (pp. 159–160)

**Case 3:** Consider the following rank-one perturbation of the LVT economy, $\mathbf{J} = \mathbf{I}$ (see Case 1):

$$\mathbf{J} \approx \left(1 + \boldsymbol{\psi}^{\mathrm{T}}\boldsymbol{\chi}\right)^{-1}\left[\mathbf{I} + \boldsymbol{\chi}\boldsymbol{\psi}^{\mathrm{T}}\right] (\geq \mathbf{0})$$

It follows that[38]

$$\lambda_{\mathbf{J}k} \approx \left(1 + \boldsymbol{\psi}^{\mathrm{T}}\boldsymbol{\chi}\right)^{-1}$$

and

$$\mathbf{p}^{\mathrm{T}} \approx \left(1 - \rho\lambda_{\mathbf{J}k}\right)^{-1}\left[(1 - \rho)\mathbf{p}^{\mathrm{T}}(0) + \rho(1 - \lambda_{\mathbf{J}k})\mathbf{p}^{\mathrm{T}}(1)\right]$$

namely, $p_j$ tend to be homographic functions and, therefore, monotonic. Hence, for

$$-\infty << \boldsymbol{\psi}^{\mathrm{T}}\boldsymbol{\chi} << 0 \text{ or } 0 << \boldsymbol{\psi}^{\mathrm{T}}\boldsymbol{\chi} << +\infty$$

the economy tends to behave as a two-industry economy with only basic commodities, and the TVT tends to hold true. As $\boldsymbol{\psi}^{\mathrm{T}}\boldsymbol{\chi} \to 0 \; (\boldsymbol{\psi}^{\mathrm{T}}\boldsymbol{\chi} \to \pm\infty)$, we obtain Case 1 (Case 2).

**Case 4:** Consider the following rank-two perturbation of the LVT economy:

$$\mathbf{J} \approx (1 + \lambda_{\boldsymbol{\psi}1})^{-1}\left[\mathbf{I} + \sum_{\kappa=1}^{2}\boldsymbol{\chi}_{\kappa}\boldsymbol{\psi}_{\kappa}^{\mathrm{T}}\right]$$

where $\boldsymbol{\chi}_{\kappa}$, $\boldsymbol{\psi}_{\kappa}^{\mathrm{T}}$, are semi-positive vectors (or two pairs of complex conjugate vectors), and

---

[38]Consider the theorem mentioned in footnote 7.

$$\boldsymbol{\Psi} \equiv [\boldsymbol{\psi}_1, \boldsymbol{\psi}_2]^T [\boldsymbol{\chi}_1, \boldsymbol{\chi}_2]$$

(in either case, $\boldsymbol{\Psi}$ is a $2 \times 2$ matrix with only real eigenvalues). It follows that $n - 2$ non-dominant eigenvalues of $\mathbf{J}$ tend to equal

$$(1 + \lambda_{\boldsymbol{\psi}1})^{-1}$$

and the remaining tends to equal

$$(1 + \lambda_{\boldsymbol{\psi}2})(1 + \lambda_{\boldsymbol{\psi}1})^{-1}$$

(consider Ding and Zhou 2008, p. 635). Hence, the economy tends to behave as a three-industry economy; and the same holds true when $\lambda_{\mathbf{J}k} \approx \alpha_k \pm i\beta_k$, where $i \equiv \sqrt{-1}$ and $0 << |\beta_k|$, for all $k$.[39]

**Case 5**: The sub-dominant eigenvalues are complex:

$$\lambda_{\mathbf{J}2,3} = \alpha_{2,3} \pm i\beta_{2,3}, \ \ 0 << |\beta_{2,3}|$$

and

$$\lambda_{\mathbf{J}4} \approx \ldots \approx \lambda_{\mathbf{J}n} \approx 0$$

Hence, the economy tends to behave as a reducible four-industry economy without self-reproducing non-basics. Both in Cases 4 and 5, the value functions *may* be non-monotonic.

**Case 6**: Matrix $\mathbf{J}$ is *doubly* stochastic, i.e. $\mathbf{e}^T \mathbf{J} = \mathbf{e}^T$ and $\mathbf{J}\mathbf{e} = \mathbf{e}$. From Eq. (2.49) it follows that

$$\mathbf{p}^T(1) = [(1 - \lambda_{\mathbf{A}1})n]^{-1} (\mathbf{l}^T\mathbf{e})\mathbf{e}^T$$

or, since $\mathbf{v}^T\mathbf{e} = (1 - \lambda_{\mathbf{A}1})^{-1}(\mathbf{l}^T\mathbf{e})$ and $\mathbf{p}^T(0) = \mathbf{v}^T$,

$$\mathbf{p}^T(1) = \bar{p}(0)\mathbf{e}^T \qquad\qquad (2.67)$$

where $\bar{p}(0) \equiv n^{-1}(\mathbf{p}^T(0)\mathbf{e})$ equals the arithmetic mean of the vertically integrated labour coefficients. Hence, if there is a commodity whose vertically integrated labour coefficient equals the arithmetic mean of the vertically integrated labour

---

[39] Any complex number is an eigenvalue of a positive $3 \times 3$ circulant matrix (Minc 1988, p. 167). For the properties of the circulant matrices, see Davis (1979).

coefficients, then, by Rolle's theorem, its value curve will necessarily have at least one stationary point in the economically relevant interval of the profit rate.[40]

**Case 7**: Since $\mathbf{A} = [\mathbf{I} + \mathbf{H}]^{-1}\mathbf{H}$, there is no good economic reason for supposing that $\mathbf{J}$ is doubly stochastic. It should be noted, however, that:

1. Any doubly stochastic matrix can be expressed as a convex combination of at most $(n - 1)^2 + 1$ permutation matrices (see, e.g. Minc 1988, pp. 117–122).
2. Matrix $\mathbf{J}$ is similar to the *column* stochastic matrix $\mathbf{M} \equiv \widehat{\mathbf{y}}_{\mathbf{J1}}\mathbf{J}\widehat{\mathbf{y}}_{\mathbf{J1}}^{-1}$:

$$\mathbf{e}^{\mathrm{T}}\mathbf{M} = \mathbf{y}_{\mathbf{J1}}^{\mathrm{T}}\mathbf{J}\widehat{\mathbf{y}}_{\mathbf{J1}}^{-1} = \mathbf{y}_{\mathbf{J1}}^{\mathrm{T}}\widehat{\mathbf{y}}_{\mathbf{J1}}^{-1} = \mathbf{e}^{\mathrm{T}}$$

The elements of $\mathbf{M}$ are independent of both the choice of physical measurement units and the normalization of $\mathbf{y}_{\mathbf{J1}}^{\mathrm{T}}$. Matrix $\mathbf{M}$ can be conceived of as a matrix of the relative shares of the capital goods in the cost of outputs, evaluated at $\rho = 1$, or, alternatively, as derived from $\mathbf{J}$ by changing the units in which the various commodity quantities are measured (Ara 1963; Mariolis 2010b).[41] Moreover, the Dmitriev and Dynkin (1946) and Karpelevich (1951) inequalities for stochastic matrices imply that

$$\alpha_k + |\beta_k| \tan\left(\pi n^{-1}\right) \leq 1 \tag{2.68}$$

for each eigenvalue $\lambda_{\mathbf{M}k} (= \lambda_{\mathbf{J}k}) = \alpha_k \pm i\beta_k$.

3. Finally, when there is only one commodity input in each industry (i.e. industry $\kappa$, $\kappa = 1, 2, \ldots, n - 1$, produces the input for industry $\kappa + 1$, and industry $n$ produces the input for industry 1), $\mathbf{A}$ is imprimitive or "cyclic". Therefore, $\mathbf{M}$ is circulant and doubly stochastic (see Mariolis and Tsoulfidis 2016, pp. 165–167).

Thus, hereafter, we consider a "*basic* circulant" perturbation of the LVT economy, i.e.

---

[40]See Example 2.6 (which is a generalization of Example 2.4) in the Appendix at the end of this chapter.

[41]When $rank[\mathbf{J}] = 1$, all the columns of $\mathbf{M}$ are equal to each other (Mariolis and Tsoulfidis 2009, p. 10; Iliadi et al. 2014, p. 40). It may also be noted that, when

$$\mathbf{M} \approx \mathbf{G} \equiv \alpha\mathbf{S} + (1 - \alpha)\boldsymbol{\omega}\mathbf{e}^{\mathrm{T}}$$

where $\mathbf{G}$ is a column stochastic matrix, known as a "Google matrix", $\mathbf{S}$ denotes a column stochastic matrix, $\alpha$ a real number such that $0 < \alpha < 1$, known as a "damping factor", and $\boldsymbol{\omega}$ a semi-positive vector normalized by setting $\mathbf{e}^{\mathrm{T}}\boldsymbol{\omega} = 1$, it follows that $|\lambda_{\mathbf{M}2}| \approx |\lambda_{\mathbf{G}2}| \leq \alpha$ (Haveliwala and Kamvar 2003). Setting

$$\alpha = (1 + \boldsymbol{\psi}^{\mathrm{T}}\boldsymbol{\chi})^{-1}, \ \mathbf{S} = \mathbf{I}, \ \boldsymbol{\omega} = (\boldsymbol{\psi}^{\mathrm{T}}\boldsymbol{\chi})^{-1}\boldsymbol{\chi}$$

and replacing $\mathbf{e}^{\mathrm{T}}$ by $\boldsymbol{\psi}^{\mathrm{T}}$, we obtain Case 3.

$$\mathbf{J} \approx \mathbf{C} \equiv c\mathbf{I} + (1 - c)\mathbf{\Pi}$$

where $0 \leq c < 1$, $\mathbf{\Pi} \equiv$ circ$[0, 1, 0, \ldots, 0]$ is the basic circulant permutation (or shift) matrix (post-multiplying any matrix by $\mathbf{\Pi}$ shifts its columns one place to the right), and $\mathbf{\Pi}^n = \mathbf{I}$.

The eigenvalues of the circulant doubly stochastic matrix $\mathbf{C}$ are $c + (1 - c)\theta^\kappa$, where $\kappa = 0, 1, \ldots, n - 1$, $\theta \equiv \exp(2\pi i n^{-1})$, and

$$\theta^\kappa = \cos\left(2\pi\kappa n^{-1}\right) + i\sin\left(2\pi\kappa n^{-1}\right)$$

are the $n$ distinct roots of unity. It then follows that:

1. The eigenvalues of $\mathbf{C}$ are the vertices of a regular $n$–gon, and $\mathbf{C}$ is that stochastic matrix that has an "extremal eigenvalue" on the segment joining the points 1 and $\theta$ (Dmitriev and Dynkin 1946; Karpelevich 1951).[42] This eigenvalue is a sub-dominant eigenvalue, which satisfies relation (2.68) as an *equality*.

2. For $0 < c < 1$, the moduli of the eigenvalues of $\mathbf{C}$ are given by

$$\sqrt{c^2 + 2c(1 - c)\cos\left(2\pi\kappa n^{-1}\right) + (1 - c)^2}$$

or, equivalently,

$$\sqrt{1 + 2c(1 - c)\left[\cos\left(2\pi\kappa n^{-1}\right) - 1\right]}$$

which is a symmetric function with respect to $c = 0.5$ and $\kappa'$, $\kappa''$, where $\kappa' + \kappa'' = n$ (Davis 1979, pp. 119–120). The modulus of the sub-dominant eigenvalues occurs for $\kappa = 1, n - 1$. When $n$ is even, i.e. $n = 2\mu$, the smallest modulus occurs for $\kappa = \mu$, and equals $|1 - 2c|$, while when $n$ is odd, $n = 2\mu + 1$, the smallest modulus occurs for $\kappa = \mu, \mu + 1$. Finally, $\mathbf{C}$ has rank $n - 1$ iff $n$ is even and $c = 0.5$ (Davis 1979, p. 147). For instance, Fig. 2.5 displays the location of the eigenvalues of $\mathbf{C}$ in the complex plane, for $n = 3, 6, 7$ and $c = 0, 0.25, 0.75$.[43]

Now we turn to the value side of the economies $[\mathbf{C}, \mathbf{p}^\mathbf{T}(0)]$, $0 \leq c < 1$. Ignoring the approximation error, Eq. (2.47) reduces to

$$\mathbf{p}^\mathbf{T} = (1 - \gamma)\mathbf{p}^\mathbf{T}(0) + \gamma\mathbf{p}^\mathbf{T}\mathbf{\Pi} \tag{2.69}$$

where $\gamma \equiv (1 - c)\rho(1 - \rho c)^{-1}$, $0 \leq \gamma \leq 1$. Hence, since $\mathbf{\Pi}^n = \mathbf{I}$, Eq. (2.48) reduces to

---

[42] A number $\lambda$ is called extremal eigenvalue if (a) it belongs to the set of eigenvalues of a stochastic matrix; and (b) $\alpha\lambda$ does not belong to this set, whenever $\alpha > 1$.

[43] Furthermore, see Example 2.7 in the Appendix at the end of this chapter.

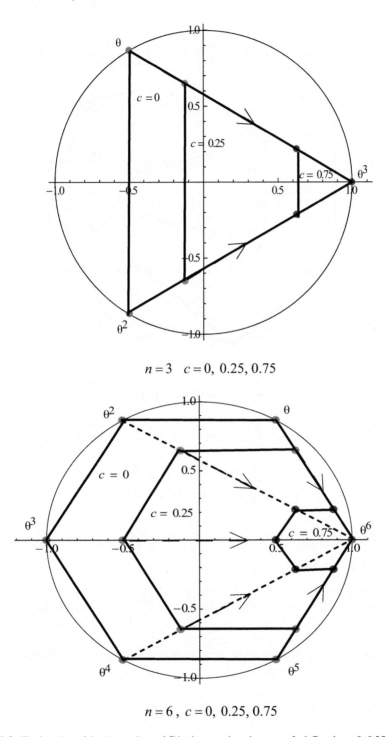

$n = 3$   $c = 0,\ 0.25,\ 0.75$

$n = 6$, $c = 0,\ 0.25,\ 0.75$

**Fig. 2.5** The location of the eigenvalues of **C** in the complex plane: $n = 3, 6, 7$ and $c = 0, 0.25, 0.75$

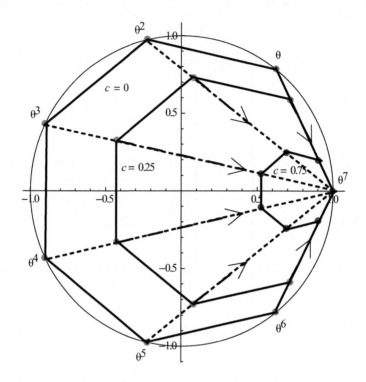

$$n = 7, \ c = 0, \ 0.25, \ 0.75$$

**Fig. 2.5** (continued)

$$\mathbf{p}^{\mathrm{T}} = (1 - \gamma)(1 - \gamma^n)^{-1}\mathbf{p}^{\mathrm{T}}(0)[\mathbf{I} + \gamma\mathbf{\Pi} + \gamma^2\mathbf{\Pi}^2 + \cdots + \gamma^{n-1}\mathbf{\Pi}^{n-1}]$$

or, since $(1 - \gamma)(1 - \gamma^n)^{-1} = (1 + \gamma + \gamma^2 + \ldots + \gamma^{n-1})^{-1}$,

$$\mathbf{p}^{\mathrm{T}} = (1 + \gamma + \gamma^2 + \cdots + \gamma^{n-1})^{-1}\mathbf{p}^{\mathrm{T}}(0)[\mathbf{I} + \gamma\mathbf{\Pi} + \gamma^2\mathbf{\Pi}^2 + \cdots + \gamma^{n-1}\mathbf{\Pi}^{n-1}] \quad (2.70)$$

From Eqs. (2.69) and (2.70) it follows that:

1. Although matrix $\mathbf{C}$ is irreducible, long-period values reduce to a *finite* series of dated quantities of normalized vertically integrated labour. Hence, it can be stated that these "basic circulant economies" bear some characteristic similarities with Sraffa's "old wine–oak chest" example.
2. In fact, because of the structure of the economies' matrices, long-period values are governed by the terms

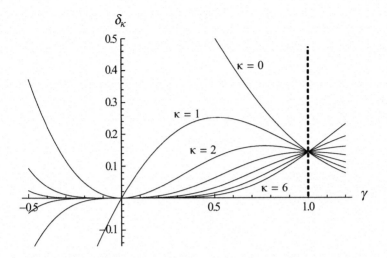

**Fig. 2.6** The rational function terms that govern the long-period values in basic circulant economies: $n = 7$, $-0.5 \leq \gamma \leq 1.2$

$$\delta_\kappa \equiv (1 + \gamma + \gamma^2 + \cdots + \gamma^{n-1})^{-1} \gamma^\kappa, \quad \kappa = 0, 1, \ldots, n-1$$

where the denominator has either no real roots (when $n$ is odd) or one real root (i.e. $-1$, when $n$ is even). The first derivative of $\delta_\kappa$ with respect to $\gamma$ is

$$\dot{\delta}_\kappa = (1 - \gamma^n)^{-2} \gamma^{\kappa-1} (\varepsilon_\kappa + \zeta_\kappa)$$

where

$$\varepsilon_\kappa \equiv \kappa - (1 + \kappa)\gamma$$

defines a linear function, and

$$\zeta_\kappa \equiv [(n - \kappa) - (n - \kappa - 1)\gamma]\gamma^n$$

defines a polynomial function. Hence, we get $\dot{\delta}_0(0) = -1$, $\dot{\delta}_1(0) = 1$ and $\dot{\delta}_\kappa(0) = 0$, for $\kappa \geq 2$, while

$$\dot{\delta}_\kappa(1) = (2n)^{-1}(1 + 2\kappa - n)$$

Moreover, when $\kappa \geq 2$ is even (is odd), $\delta_\kappa$ has a minimum (an inflection point) at $\gamma = 0$. Finally, iff $1 \leq \kappa < 2^{-1}(n - 1)$ and $n \geq 4$, then the equation $\varepsilon_\kappa + \zeta_\kappa = 0$ has two roots in the interval $[0, 1]$, i.e. $\gamma = \gamma_\kappa^*$ (unique), where $0 < \gamma_\kappa^* < 1$, at which $\delta_\kappa$ is maximized, and $\gamma = 1$ (repeated), where $\dot{\varepsilon}_\kappa(1) + \dot{\zeta}_\kappa(1) = 0$ (in all other cases, it has, in the said interval, the roots 0 and/or 1). For instance, Fig. 2.6 displays the terms $\delta_\kappa$

as functions of $\gamma$, for $n = 7$: $\gamma_1^* \cong 0.517$, $\gamma_2^* \cong 0.768$, and $\delta_3$ has a maximum at $\gamma = 1$. The values $\gamma_\kappa^*$ tend to the values of the sequence $(1 + \kappa)^{-1}\kappa$ as $n$ tends to infinity and, therefore, the maximum values of $\delta_\kappa$ tend to the values of the sequence $(1 + \kappa)^{-(1 + \kappa)}\kappa^\kappa$.

3. Long-period values tend to $\mathbf{p}^T(0)\mathbf{\Pi}^{n-1}$ as $\gamma$ tends to plus or minus infinity. Iff there exists a non-zero value of $\gamma$, say $\gamma^{**}$, such that $p_j(\gamma^{**}) = p_j(0)$, then

$$p_j(\gamma^{**}) = \mathbf{p}^T(\gamma^{**})\mathbf{\Pi e}_j = p_{j-1}(\gamma^{**})$$

where $j = 1, 2, \ldots, n$ and $p_0(\gamma^{**}) \equiv p_n(\gamma^{**})$.

4. Finally, differentiation of Eq. (2.69) with respect to $\rho$ gives

$$\dot{\mathbf{p}}^T = -\dot{\gamma}(\mathbf{p}^T(0) - \mathbf{p}^T\mathbf{\Pi}) + \gamma\dot{\mathbf{p}}^T\mathbf{\Pi} \tag{2.71}$$

$$\dot{\mathbf{p}}^T\mathbf{e} = 0 \tag{2.72}$$

where $\dot{\gamma} \equiv (1 - c)(1 - \rho c)^{-2} > 0$, the difference $\mathbf{p}^T\mathbf{\Pi} - \mathbf{p}^T(0)$ represents the capital-intensity effect, while the term $\gamma\dot{\mathbf{p}}^T\mathbf{\Pi}$ represents the value effect (see Eq. (2.65)). Now, it suffices to focus on the extreme, economically relevant, values of $\rho$:

a. At $\rho = 0$ Eq. (2.71) reduces to

$$\dot{\mathbf{p}}^T(0) = -(1 - c)^{-1}\mathbf{p}^T(0)\mathbf{D} \tag{2.73}$$

where $\mathbf{D} \equiv \mathbf{I} - \mathbf{\Pi}$ is a circulant double-centered matrix, since all its columns and rows sum to zero, i.e. $\mathbf{e}^T\mathbf{D} = \mathbf{0}^T$, $\mathbf{De} = \mathbf{0}$, and $rank[\mathbf{D}] = n - 1$.

b. At $\rho = 1$ Eq. (2.71) reduces to

$$\dot{\mathbf{p}}^T(1) = -(1 - c)^{-1}(\mathbf{p}^T(0) - \mathbf{p}^T(1)\mathbf{\Pi}) + \dot{\mathbf{p}}^T(1)\mathbf{\Pi}$$

or, rearranging terms and invoking Eq. (2.67) and $\mathbf{e}^T\mathbf{\Pi} = \mathbf{e}^T$,

$$\dot{\mathbf{p}}^T(1)\mathbf{D} = -(1 - c)^{-1}\mathbf{p}^T(0)\mathbf{F} \tag{2.74}$$

where

$$\mathbf{F} \equiv \mathbf{I} - n^{-1}(\mathbf{ee}^T)$$

is the centering matrix, which is symmetric and idempotent (multiplication of any vector by the centering matrix has the effect of subtracting its arithmetic mean from every element). The solution to Eqs. (2.72) and (2.74) is given by

$$\dot{\mathbf{p}}^{\mathrm{T}}(1) = -(1-c)^{-1}\mathbf{p}^{\mathrm{T}}(0)\mathbf{F}\mathbf{D}^{+}$$

or

$$\dot{\mathbf{p}}^{\mathrm{T}}(1) = -(1-c)^{-1}\mathbf{p}^{\mathrm{T}}(0)\mathbf{D}^{+} \tag{2.75}$$

where $\mathbf{D}^{+}$ denotes the Moore–Penrose inverse of $\mathbf{D}$, which is, in our case, a circulant double-centered matrix satisfying $\mathbf{D}\mathbf{D}^{+} = \mathbf{D}^{+}\mathbf{D} = \mathbf{F}$.[44] Moreover, when $n$ is even, $n = 2\mu$, the explicit expression for matrix $\mathbf{D}^{+}$ can be written as

$$\mathbf{D}^{+} = (4\mu)^{-1}\mathrm{circ}[2\mu - 1, 2\mu - 3, 2\mu - 5, \ldots, -(2\mu - 3), -(2\mu - 1)] \tag{2.76}$$

while when $n$ is odd, $n = 2\mu + 1$, it can be written as

$$\mathbf{D}^{+} = (2\mu + 1)^{-1}\mathrm{circ}[\mu, \mu - 1, \mu - 2, \ldots, -(\mu - 1), -\mu] \tag{2.77}$$

(consider Davis 1979, pp. 148–149). The elements of the first row of $-\mathbf{D}^{+}$ are equal to

$$\dot{\delta}_{\kappa}(1) = (2n)^{-1}(1 + 2\kappa - n), \quad \kappa = 0, 1, \ldots, n - 1$$

Hence, it is easy to check that Eqs. (2.73)–(2.77) imply that, when $n \geq 3$ and $p_j(0) < p_{j+1}(0), j = 1, 2, \ldots, n - 1$, there is at least one element of $\dot{\mathbf{p}}^{\mathrm{T}}$, say $\dot{p}_h$, such that $\dot{p}_h(0)\dot{p}_h(1) < 0$, *irrespective* of the direction of $\mathbf{p}^{\mathrm{T}}(0)$. Then, by Bolzano's theorem, it follows that $p_h$ necessarily has at least one extreme point in the interval $(0, 1)$.[45]

These seven ideal-type cases (and their possible combinations) indicate that the location of the non-dominant eigenvalues in the complex plane could be considered as an index for the underlying inter-industry linkages. More specifically, the analysis showed that, ignoring the approximation error, the alternative value theories can be represented *algebraically* as "perturbations" of the so-called LVT, i.e. of Case 1. Cases 2 and 3 correspond to the TVT, while Cases 4, 5 and 6 fall into the SVT.

---

[44]There is an algebraic analogue of Eqs. (2.72) and (2.74) in electrical network theory: $\dot{\mathbf{p}}^{\mathrm{T}}(1)$ and $-(1-c)^{-1}\mathbf{p}^{\mathrm{T}}(0)\mathbf{F}$ correspond to the vectors of voltages and currents, respectively; Eqs. (2.72) and (2.74) correspond to Kirchhoff's voltage law and Ohm's law, respectively; $\mathbf{D}$ and $\mathbf{D}^{+}$ correspond to the matrices of admittance and impedance, respectively (see Sharpe and Styan 1965). It may also be noted that the basic circulant permutaion matrix and circulant doubly stochastic matrices can be detected in Lévi-Strauss's (1967, Chaps. 11 and 15) analysis of kinship and marriage.

[45]See Examples 2.8, 2.9 and 2.10 in the Appendix at the end of this chapter.

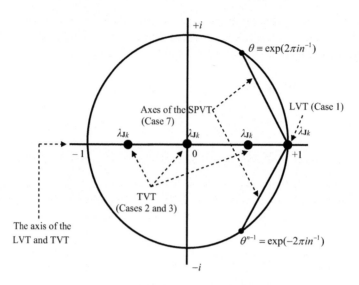

**Fig. 2.7** The complex plane location of the polar value theories

Finally, it could be said that Case 7, i.e. the basic circulant perturbation of the LVT economy, corresponds to the "Sraffian polar value theory" (SPVT), since in that case the value–profit rate relationship is non-monotonic whatever the vector of vertically integrated labour coefficients is. Hence, Fig. 2.7 displays the location of the polar value theories, i.e. LVT, TVT, and SPVT, in the complex plane.

## 2.4  Synopsis and Final Remarks

Developing the restatement of fundamental structural features of Piero Sraffa's theory of production of commodities and positive profits by means of commodities in terms of Rudolf Emil Kalman's general theory of control systems, this chapter:

1. Showed that Kalman's concepts of controllability and observability articulate a general basis for dealing with central issues of value, capital and income distribution–growth theory.
2. Further operationalized Sraffa's critical transcendence of the traditional political economy, by shedding new light on the value–income–technology relationships.
3. Identified new aspects of the Sraffian theory, by generalizing both the concept of basic commodities and the (in)famous "old wine–oak chest" example, and proved that this theory is the most general to date.
4. Pointed out a spectral reduction or post-construction of the alternative national value theories that forms a typical, mathematical model for the Sraffian theory. Hence, this post-construction might provide a representation of the evolution of competing value theories in terms of both the logic and the history of economic thought.

5. More specifically, it revealed that the alternative national value theories correspond to specific production structures and, therefore, to specific spectral characteristics of the value controllability matrix and complex plane locations of the
eigenvalues of the technical coefficients matrix. Thus, it showed that these value
theories can be represented algebraically and, furthermore, understood concep-
tually as "perturbations" of the so-called labour value theory (or, equivalently, of
the "commodity $i$ value theories"), which is a polar theory that holds true when,
and only when, the rank of the value controllability matrix equals one.

Since only little can be said a priori about the dominating spectral characteristics
of real-world value controllability matrices, and almost nothing was said in this
chapter about the joint production of commodities by means of domestically produced and imported commodities, which is the rule in economic reality (see
Chap. 1), it is absolutely necessary to (re)turn to the "outside world" and also to
examine actual input–output data. We will follow these paths in the next chapters of
this book.

## Appendix: Additional Examples

### Example 2.6

Consider the following $3 \times 3$ doubly stochastic and irreducible economies:

$$\mathbf{J} = \begin{bmatrix} \alpha & \beta & 1 - \alpha - \beta \\ \delta & \varepsilon & 1 - \delta - \varepsilon \\ 1 - \alpha - \delta & 1 - \beta - \varepsilon & \alpha + \beta + \delta + \varepsilon - 1 \end{bmatrix}$$

where $\mathbf{p}^{\mathrm{T}}(0) \neq \mathbf{p}^{\mathrm{T}}(1)$.

Iff $\alpha = \varepsilon$ and $\beta = \delta = 2^{-1}(1 - \alpha)$, then $\mathbf{J}$ is circulant with a repeated eigenvalue,
$\lambda_{\mathrm{J2}} = \lambda_{\mathrm{J3}} = (3\alpha - 1)/2$, and this eigenvalue has two linearly independent eigenvec-
tors, i.e. $\mathbf{x}_{\mathrm{J2}} = \chi_2[-1, 0, 1]^{\mathrm{T}}$ and $\mathbf{x}_{\mathrm{J3}} = \chi_3[-1, 1, 0]^{\mathrm{T}}$. Since $\mathbf{x}_{\mathrm{J2}} + \mathbf{x}_{\mathrm{J3}}$ is also an
eigenvector, there exists an eigenvector of $\mathbf{J}$ that is orthogonal to any given $\mathbf{p}^{\mathrm{T}}(0)$.
Therefore, $rank[\mathbf{K}] = 2$, the economies are uncontrollable whatever $\mathbf{p}^{\mathrm{T}}(0)$ is, and $p_j$
are not rational functions of degree $n - 1 \, (= 2)$ but of degree $n - 2 \, (= 1)$. More
specifically, when $\mathbf{p}^{\mathrm{T}}(0)\mathbf{x}_{\mathrm{J2}} = 0$ or $\mathbf{p}^{\mathrm{T}}(0)\mathbf{x}_{\mathrm{J3}} = 0$, Eq. (2.47) implies that $p_1 = p_3$ or
$p_1 = p_2$, respectively. When $\mathbf{p}^{\mathrm{T}}(0)\mathbf{x}_{\mathrm{J}k} \neq 0$, it follows that

$$\mathbf{p}^{\mathrm{T}}\mathbf{x}_{\mathrm{J2}}\left(\mathbf{p}^{\mathrm{T}}\mathbf{x}_{\mathrm{J3}}\right)^{-1} = \mathbf{p}^{\mathrm{T}}(0)\mathbf{x}_{\mathrm{J2}}\left(\mathbf{p}^{\mathrm{T}}(0)\mathbf{x}_{\mathrm{J3}}\right)^{-1}$$

or

$$p_2 = \eta p_1 + (1 - \eta)p_3$$

where

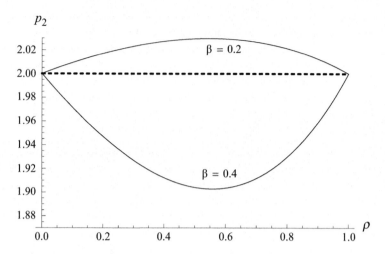

**Fig. 2.8** Non-monotonic value–relative profit rate curves in $3 \times 3$ doubly stochastic economies, where $p_2(0) = (p_1(0) + p_3(0))/2$

$$\eta \equiv (p_3(0) - p_2(0))(p_3(0) - p_1(0))^{-1} \qquad (2.78)$$

Iff $p_2(0) = \bar{p}(0)$, then $\eta = 1/2$ and, therefore, $p_2 = (p_1 + p_3)/2 = p_2(0)$.

It should be added that, when $\lambda_{J2} = \lambda_{J3}$, the Schur triangularization theorem implies that $\mathbf{J}$ can be transformed, via the semi-positive similarity matrix $\mathbf{T} \equiv [\mathbf{x}_{J1}, \mathbf{e}_2, \mathbf{e}_3]$, into

$$\mathbf{J}^* \equiv \mathbf{T}^{-1}\mathbf{J}\mathbf{T} = \begin{bmatrix} 1 & (1-\alpha)/2 & (1-\alpha)/2 \\ 0 & (3\alpha-1)/2 & 0 \\ 0 & 0 & (3\alpha-1)/2 \end{bmatrix}$$

Hence, when $\alpha > 1/3$, the original economies are strictly equivalent to triangular economies involving only one hyper-basic commodity, i.e. SSC, and an economically relevant diagonal hyper-non-basic part. When $\alpha = 1/3$, $\mathbf{J}^*$ turns to a triangular matrix (see Eqs. (2.63) and (2.64)).

By contrast, when $\lambda_{J2} \neq \lambda_{J3}$ and $p_2(0) = \bar{p}(0)$, $p_2$ has an extreme point in the economically relevant interval of the profit rate, i.e. at

$$\rho^* \equiv \left[ 1 + \sqrt{3}\sqrt{(1-\alpha)(1-\varepsilon)} - \beta\delta \right]^{-1}$$

See, for instance, Fig. 2.8, where $\alpha = \varepsilon = 0.5$, $\beta = 0.2$ or $0.4$, $\delta = 0.1$, and $\mathbf{p}^{\mathrm{T}}(0) = [1, 2, 3]$. When $\beta = 0.2$, $\det[\mathbf{K}] = -0.414$ and the degree of controllability, $DC$, is approximately equal to $0.010$ (see Eqs. (2.16) and (2.18)), while when

$\beta = 0.4$, $\det[\mathbf{K}] = 1.134$ and $DC \cong 0.029$. Also note that, when $p_2(0) \neq \bar{p}(0)$, all six value curves may be monotonic.

### Example 2.7
Figure 2.9 displays the moduli of the eigenvalues of $\mathbf{C}$, for $n = 7$, $500$ and $c = 0.1$, $0.3$, $0.5$. Figure 2.10 displays the modulus of the sub-dominant eigenvalues of $\mathbf{C}$ as a function of $c$, $0 < c \leq 0.5$, and $n$, $3 \leq n \leq 50$.

### Example 2.8
Consider the following economies: $\mathbf{J} = \mathbf{C}$, where $p_j(0) < p_{j+1}(0)$. When $n = 6$, i.e. $\mu = 3$, it necessarily follows that $\dot{p}_\mu(0)\dot{p}_\mu(1) < 0$, since

$$\dot{p}_3(0) = (1 - c)(p_2(0) - p_3(0)) < 0$$

and

$$\dot{p}_3(1) = [12(1 - c)]^{-1}[5(p_4(0) - p_3(0)) + 3(p_5(0) - p_2(0)) + p_6(0) - p_1(0)] > 0$$

When $n = 7$, i.e. $\mu = 3$, it necessarily follows that $\dot{p}_\mu(0)\dot{p}_\mu(1) < 0$ and $\dot{p}_{\mu+1}(0)\dot{p}_{\mu+1}(1) < 0$, since

$$\dot{p}_3(0) = (1 - c)(p_2(0) - p_3(0)) < 0$$
$$\dot{p}_4(0) = (1 - c)(p_3(0) - p_4(0)) < 0$$

and

$$\dot{p}_3(1) = [7(1 - c)]^{-1}[3(p_4(0) - p_3(0)) + 2(p_5(0) - p_2(0)) + p_6(0) - p_1(0)] > 0$$
$$\dot{p}_4(1) = [7(1 - c)]^{-1}[3(p_5(0) - p_4(0)) + 2(p_6(0) - p_3(0)) + p_7(0) - p_2(0)] > 0$$

### Example 2.9
Consider the following economies: $\mathbf{J} = \mathbf{C}$, $n = 3$, where $p_j(0) < p_{j+1}(0)$. It follows that, in the economically relevant interval of $\gamma$, $p_1(\gamma)$ and $p_3(\gamma)$ are monotonic, while $p_2(\gamma)$ is minimized at

$$\gamma^* \equiv -\eta + \sqrt{1 - \eta + \eta^2}$$

where $\eta < 1$ (see Eq. (2.78)) and $d\gamma^*/d\eta < 0$. Since $\gamma$ increases (decreases) with $\rho$ (with $c$), the relevant value of the profit rate, i.e.

$$\rho^* = \gamma^*[1 - c(1 - \gamma^*)]^{-1}$$

increases with $c$. Finally, $p_2(\gamma) = p_2(0)$ at $\gamma = 0$ and at

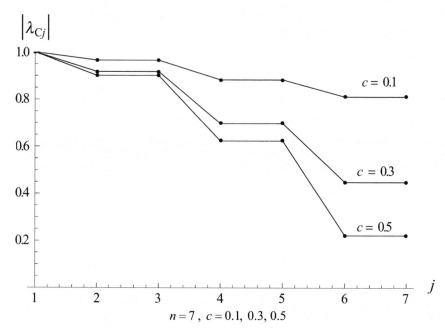

$n = 7$ , $c = 0.1, 0.3, 0.5$

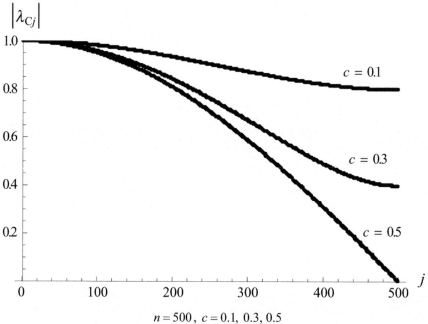

$n = 500$ , $c = 0.1, 0.3, 0.5$

**Fig. 2.9** The moduli of the eigenvalues of **C**: $n = 7, 500$ and $c = 0.1, 0.3, 0.5$

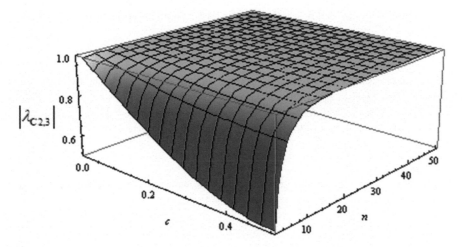

**Fig. 2.10** The modulus of the sub-dominant eigenvalues of $\mathbf{C}$ as a function of $c$ and $n$: $0 < c \leq 0.5$ and $3 \leq n \leq 50$

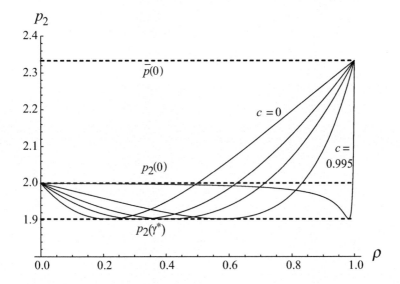

**Fig. 2.11** Non-monotonic value–relative profit rate curves in $3 \times 3$ basic circulant economies

$$\gamma^{**} \equiv \eta^{-1} - 1$$

where $\gamma^{**} > \gamma^*$, while $\gamma^{**} \leq 1$ iff $\eta \geq 1/2$ or, equivalently, $p_2(0) \leq \bar{p}(0)$. See, for instance, Fig. 2.11, where $\mathbf{p}^T(0) = [1, 2, 4]$ and $c$ is in the range of 0 to 0.995; $\eta = 2/3$, $\gamma^* = \left(\sqrt{7} - 2\right)/3 \cong 0.215$, $p_2(\gamma^*) = \left(11 - 2\sqrt{7}\right)/3 \cong 1.903$ and $\gamma^{**} = 0.5$.

It should be noted that $n \times n$ doubly stochastic circulant economies of the form

$$c_1 \mathbf{I} + c_2 \mathbf{\Pi} + c_3 \mathbf{\Pi}^2 + \cdots + c_n \mathbf{\Pi}^{n-1}, \quad (c_2, c_3, \ldots, c_{n-1}) > 0$$

do not necessarily generate non-monotonic value curves. For instance, consider Example 2.6 ($\lambda_{J2} = \lambda_{J3}$) or the following $3 \times 3$ cases: (a) $c_1 = 0$, $c_2 = 0.6$, $c_3 = 0.4$; and (b) $c_1 = 0.6$, $c_2 = 0.25$, $c_3 = 0.15$, with $\mathbf{p}^{\mathrm{T}}(0) = [1, 2, 4]$, and take into account the structure of the relevant matrices $\mathbf{D}^+$ (compare with Eqs. (2.76) and (2.77)).

### Example 2.10
Consider the following economies: $\mathbf{J} = \mathbf{C}$, $n = 4$, where $\mathbf{p}^{\mathrm{T}}(0) = [1, 5, 4, p_4(0)]$ and $p_4(0) > 5$. It follows that $p_3(\gamma) = p_3(0)$ at $\gamma = 0$ and at

$$\gamma_{1,2}^{**} \equiv \left[ (\eta_1^{-1} - 1)/2 \right] \mp \sqrt{\left[ (\eta_1^{-1} - 1)^2/4 \right] + (\eta_2^{-1} - 1)} \qquad (2.79)$$

where

$$\eta_1 \equiv (p_4(0) - p_3(0))(p_4(0) - p_1(0))^{-1}, \quad 0 < \eta_1 < 1$$

$$\eta_2 \equiv (p_4(0) - p_3(0))(p_4(0) - p_2(0))^{-1}, \quad \eta_2 > 1$$

and, therefore, that $0 < \gamma_{1,2}^{**} \leq 1$ for $6 \leq p_4(0) \leq 6.25$. More specifically, for $p_4(0) = 6$ we get $\gamma_1^{**} = 1/2$ and $\gamma_2^{**} = 1$, while for $p_4(0) = 6.25$ we get $\gamma_1^{**} = \gamma_2^{**} = 2/3$.

Hence, when, for instance, $p_4(0) = 6.1$, we get $\gamma_{1,2}^{**} = (15 \mp \sqrt{15})/21$, i.e. $\gamma_1^{**} \cong 0.530$, $\gamma_2^{**} \cong 0.899$; $p_3(\gamma)$ has two extreme points, i.e. at $\gamma_1^* \cong 0.183$ and at $\gamma_2^* \cong 0.712$, while $p_2(\gamma)$ is minimized at $\gamma^* \cong 0.689$. The graphs in Fig. 2.12 display $p_3(\rho)$ for values of $c$ in the range of 0 to 0.90 (note that $\dot{p}_3(0)\dot{p}_3(1) > 0$), and the value difference $p_3(\gamma) - p_2(\gamma)$, which equals zero at $\gamma = \gamma_{1,2}^{**}$ and at $\gamma = 1$ (compare with Fig. 3 in Sraffa 1960, p. 38).

Now, assume that $\mathbf{p}^{\mathrm{T}}(0)$ is arbitrary but $\mathbf{p}^{\mathrm{T}}(0) \neq \mathbf{p}^{\mathrm{T}}(1)$. The determinant of the controllability matrix is given by

$$\det[\mathbf{K}] = -(1 - c)^6 P_0 P_1 P_2$$

where $-(1 - c)^6 = \det[\mathbf{V}]\det\left[\mathbf{X}_{\mathbf{J}}^1\right]$ (see Eq. (2.16)),

$$P_0 \equiv -\sum_{j=1}^{4} p_j(0)$$

and

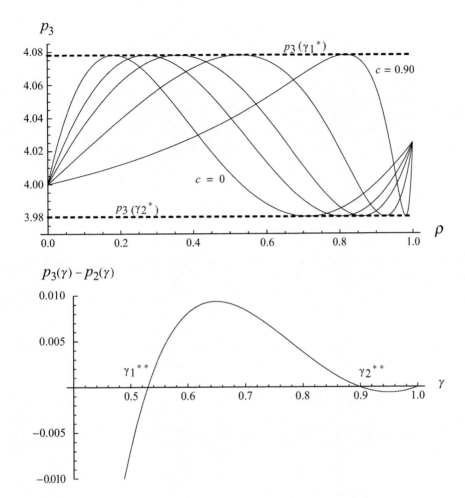

**Fig. 2.12** Possible non-monotonic value–relative profit rate curves; and value difference in $4 \times 4$ basic circulant economies

$$P_1 \equiv p_1(0) - p_2(0) + p_3(0) - p_4(0)$$

$$P_2 \equiv (p_1(0) - p_3(0))^2 + (p_2(0) - p_4(0))^2$$

Hence, these economies are uncontrollable iff either $P_1(0)$ ($rank[\mathbf{K}] = 3$) or $P_2 = 0$ ($rank[\mathbf{K}] = 2$):

1. When $P_1 = 0$:

   a. $p_j(\gamma)$ are rational functions of degree $n - 2 \, (= 2)$, and

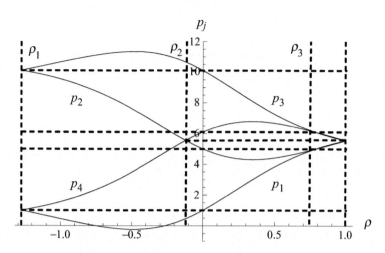

**Fig. 2.13** The value–relative profit rate curves in a controllable of rank 3 basic circulant economy: $n = 4$, $c = 0$, $\eta_1^{-1} (= -51/40) \leq \rho \leq 1$, $\rho_1 \equiv \eta_1^{-1}$, $\rho_2 \equiv -(1 + \eta_1)(1 - \eta_1)^{-1}$ and $\rho_3 \equiv -\eta_1$

$$p_1(\gamma) + p_3(\gamma) = p_2(\gamma) + p_4(\gamma) = p_1(0) + p_3(0)$$

b. $p_1(\gamma) = p_1(0)$, $p_3(\gamma) = p_3(0)$ at $\gamma = 0$ or at $\gamma = 0$ and at $\gamma = \eta_1^{-1}$ (consider Eq. (2.79), with $\eta_1^{-1} = \eta_2^{-1} - 1$; this latter equation implies $P_1 = 0$, but not vice versa).

c. $p_1(\gamma) = p_3(\gamma)$ at $\gamma = 1$ or at $\gamma = 1$ and at

$$\gamma = (1 - \eta_1)(1 + \eta_1)^{-1}$$

d. $p_2(\gamma) = p_2(0)$, $p_4(\gamma) = p_4(0)$ at $\gamma = 0$ or at $\gamma = 0$ and at $\gamma = -\eta_1$.

e. $p_2(\gamma) = p_4(\gamma)$ at $\gamma = 1$ or at $\gamma = 1$ and at

$$\gamma = -(1 + \eta_1)(1 - \eta_1)^{-1}$$

f. $\dot{p}_1(\gamma) = 0$, $\dot{p}_3(\gamma) = 0$ at $\gamma = 0$ or at

$$\gamma = -\eta_1 \mp \sqrt{1 + \eta_1^2}$$

g. $\dot{p}_2(\gamma) = 0$, $\dot{p}_4(\gamma) = 0$ at $\gamma = 0$ or at $\gamma = \mp 1$ or, finally, at

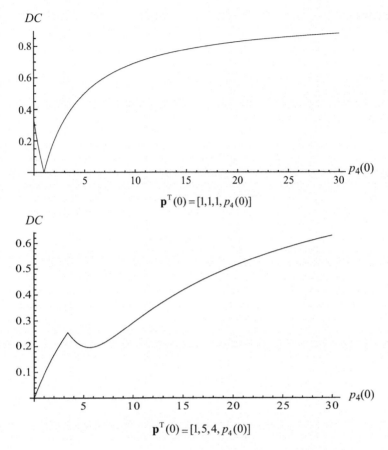

**Fig. 2.14** The degree of controllability of a $4 \times 4$ basic circulant economy ($c = 0$) as a function of $p_4(0)$

$$\gamma = \eta_1^{-1} \left( 1 \mp \sqrt{1 + \eta_1^2} \right)$$

See, for instance, Fig. 2.13, where $c = 0$, $\mathbf{p}^T(0) = [1, 5, 10.1, 6.1]$ and, therefore, $\eta_1 = -40/51$.

2. When $P_2 = 0$, $p_j(\gamma)$ are rational functions of degree $n - 3 \, (= 1)$, $p_1(\gamma) = p_3(\gamma)$ and $p_2(\gamma) = p_4(\gamma)$.

Finally, the graphs in Fig. 2.14 display the degree of controllability, $DC$, as a function of $p_4(0)$, for $c = 0$ and $\mathbf{p}^T(0) = [1, 1, 1, p_4(0)]$ or, alternatively, $\mathbf{p}^T(0) = [1, 5, 4, p_4(0)]$: $DC = 0$ at $p_4(0) = 1$ or $DC = 0$ at $p_4(0) = 0$, respectively, while $DC$ tends to 1 as $p_4(0)$ tends to plus infinity.

# References

Allen, R. G. D. (1956). *Mathematical economics*. New York: St. Martin's Press.

Antsaklis, P. J., & Michel, A. N. (2006). *Linear systems*. Boston: Birkhäuser.

Aoki, M. (1976). *Optimal control and system theory in dynamic economic analysis*. Amsterdam: North Holland.

Aoki, M. (1989). *Optimization of stochastic systems. Topics in discrete-time systems* (2nd ed.). New York: Academic Press.

Ara, K. (1963). A note on input–output matrices. *Hitotsubashi Journal of Economics, 3*(2), 68–70.

Aruka, Y. (1990). *Perturbation theorems on the linear production model and some properties of eigenprices*. The Australian National University, Faculty of Economics, Working Papers in Economics and Econometrics, Working Paper No. 203.

Aruka, Y. (2000). Possibility theorems on reswitching of techniques and the related issues of price variations. *Bulletin of Economic Research. Chuo University, 30*, 79–119. Reprinted in Y. Aruka (Ed.). (2011). *Complexities of production and interacting human behaviour* (pp. 67–111). Heidelberg: Physica–Verlag.

Belevitch, V. (1968). *Classical network theory*. San Francisco: Holden-Day.

Bidard, C., & Ehrbar, H. G. (2007). Relative prices in the classical theory: Facts and figures. *Bulletin Political Economy, 1*(2), 161–211.

Bissell, C. (2013). *Control in the Cold War: The genesis and early years of the International Federation of Automatic Control*. Paper presented at the 24th International Congress of the History of Science, Technology and Medicine, 21–28 July 2013, Manchester, UK. Retrieved Nov 17, 2017, from http://oro.open.ac.uk/39906/.

Böhm-Bawerk, E. V. (1959). *Capital and interest*. South Holland: Libertarian Press.

Boley, D., & Lu, W.-S. (1984). Quasi-Kalman decomposition and its relation to state feedback. In *1984 American control conference* (pp. 772–775). San Diego: Institute of Electrical and Electronics Engineers.

Boley, D., & Lu, W.-S. (1986). Measuring how far a controllable system is from an uncontrollable one. *Institute of Electrical and Electronics Engineers Transactions on Automatic Control, 31* (3), 249–251.

Bourgine, P., & Stewart, J. (2004). Autopoiesis and cognition. *Artificial Life, 10*(3), 327–345.

Brauer, A. (1952). Limits for the characteristic roots of a matrix. IV: Applications to stochastic matrices. *Duke Mathematical Journal, 19*(1), 75–91.

Brockett, R. W. (1965). Poles, zeros, and feedback: State space interpretation. *Institute of Electrical and Electronics Engineers Transactions on Automatic Control, 10*(2), 129–135.

Bródy, A. (1970). *Proportions, prices and planning. A mathematical restatement of the labor theory of value*. Budapest: Akadémiai Kiadó, and Amsterdam: North-Holland.

Bródy, A. (1997). The second eigenvalue of the Leontief matrix. *Economic Systems Research, 9*(3), 253–258.

Brunovský, P. (1970). A classification of linear controllable systems. *Kybernetika, 6*(3), 173–188.

Burmeister, E. (1974). Synthesizing the Neo-Austrian and alternative approaches to capital theory: A survey. *Journal of Economic Literature, 12*(2), 413–456.

Chatelain, J.-B., & Ralf, K. (2020). *How macroeconomists lost control of stabilization policy: Towards dark ages*. Mimeo. Retrieved Mar 30, 2020, from https://www.researchgate.net/publication/336103794.

Clotet, J., Garcia-Planas, M. I., & Magret, M. D. (2001). Estimating distances from quadruples satisfying stability properties to quadruples not satisfying them. *Linear Algebra and its Applications, 332–334*, 541–567.

Cowan, N. J., Chastain, E. J., Vilhena, D. A., Freudenberg, J. S., & Bergstrom, C. T. (2012). Nodal dynamics, not degree distributions, determine the structural controllability of complex networks. *PLoS One, 7*(6), e38398. https://doi.org/10.1371/journal.pone.0038398.

Datta, B. N. (2004). *Numerical methods for linear control systems. Design and analysis*. Amsterdam: Elsevier Academic Press.

Davis, P. J. (1979). *Circulant matrices*. New York: John Wiley & Sons.

Dekkers, R. (2015). *Applied systems theory*. Heidelberg: Springer.

Ding, J., & Zhou, A. (2007). Eigenvalues of rank-one updated matrices with some applications. *Applied Mathematics Letters, 20*(12), 1223–1226.

Ding, J., & Zhou, A. (2008). Characteristic polynomials of some perturbed matrices. *Applied Mathematics and Computation, 199*(2), 631–636.

Dmitriev, V. K. (1898). The theory of value of David Ricardo: An attempt at a rigorous analysis. In V. K. Dmitriev (1974). *Economic essays on value, competition and utility* (pp. 37–95). Edited with an introduction by D. M. Nuti, London: Cambridge University Press.

Dmitriev, N. A., & Dynkin, E. (1946). On characteristic roots of stochastic matrices. *Izvestiya Rossiiskoi Akademii Nauk SSSR Seriya Matematicheskaya, 10*(2), 167–184 (in Russian; English translation in Swift, J. (1972). *The location of characteristic roots of stochastic matrices*. M.Sc. Thesis, Montreal: McGill University).

Eatwell, J. (2019). "Cost of production" and the theory of the rate of profit. *Contributions to Political Economy, 38*(1), 1–11.

Eatwell, J., Milgate, M., & Newman, P. (Eds.). (1990). *The new Palgrave: Capital theory*. London: Macmillan.

Farina, L., & Rinaldi, S. (2011). *Positive linear systems. Theory and applications*. New York: John Wiley & Sons.

Feigenbaum, E. A. (1961). Soviet cybernetics and computer sciences, 1960. *Communications of the Association for Computing Machinery, 4*(12), 566–579.

Fel'dman, G. A. (1928). On the theory of growth rates of national income. In N. Spulber (Ed.), *Foundations of soviet strategy for economic growth: Selected soviet essays, 1924–1930* (pp. 174–199). Bloomington: Indiana University Press.

Ford, D. A., & Johnson, C. D. (1968). Invariant subspaces and the controllability and observability of linear dynamical systems. *Society for Industrial and Applied Mathematics Journal on Control, 6*(4), 553–558.

Franklin, G. F., Powell, J. D., Emami-Naeini, A., & Sanjay, H. S. (2015). *Feedback control of dynamic systems* (7th ed.). London: Pearson.

Friedland, B. (1975). Controllability index based on conditioning number. *Journal of Dynamic Systems, Measurement, and Control, 97*(4), 444–445.

Friedland, B. (1986). *Control system design. An introduction to state-space methods*. New York: McGraw-Hill.

Garegnani, P. (1970). Heterogeneous capital, the production function and the theory of distribution. *The Review of Economic Studies, 37*(3), 407–436.

Garegnani, P. (1984). On some illusory instances of "marginal products". *Metroeconomica, 36* (2–3), 143–160.

Gilbert, E. G. (1963). Controllability and observability in multivariable control systems. *Society for Industrial and Applied Mathematics Journal on Control, 1*(2), 128–151.

Gilibert, G. (1998). Necessary price. In H. D. Kurz & N. Salvadori (Eds.), *The Elgar companion to classical economics L–Z* (pp. 166–176). Cheltenham: Edward Elgar.

Goldberg, G., Okunev, P., Neumann, M., & Schneider, H. (2000). Distribution of subdominant eigenvalues of random matrices. *Methodology and Computing in Applied Probability, 2*(2), 137–151.

Hagemann, H., & Kurz, H. D. (1976). The return of the same truncation period and reswitching of techniques in neo-Austrian and more general models. *Kyklos, 29*(4), 678–708.

Hansen, L. P., & Sargent, T. J. (2008). *Robustness*. Princeton: Princeton University Press.

Harcourt, G. C. (1972). *Some Cambridge controversies in the theory of capital*. Cambridge: Cambridge University Press.

Harris, D. J. (1981). On the timing of wage payments. *Cambridge Journal of Economics, 5*(4), 369–381.

Hartfiel, D. J., & Meyer, C. D. (1998). On the structure of stochastic matrices with a subdominant eigenvalue near 1. Linear Algebra and its Applications, 272(1–3), 193–203.

Hautus, M. L. (1969). Controllability and observability conditions of linear autonomous systems. *Indagationes Mathematicae, 72*(5), 443–448.

Haveliwala, T. H., & Kamvar, S. D. (2003). *The second eigenvalue of the Google matrix (technical report 2003-20).* Stanford: Computer Science Department, Stanford University.

Hicks, J. R. (1965). *Capital and growth.* Oxford: Oxford University Press.

Holly, S., & Hallet, A. H. (1989). *Optimal control, expectations and uncertainty.* Cambridge: Cambridge University Press.

Iliadi, F., Mariolis, T., Soklis, G., & Tsoulfidis, L. (2014). Bienenfeld's approximation of production prices and eigenvalue distribution: Further evidence from five European economies. *Contributions to Political Economy, 33*(1), 35–54.

Johnson, C. D. (1966). Invariant hyperplanes for linear dynamical systems. *Institute of Electrical and Electronics Engineers Transactions on Automatic Control, 11*(1), 113–116.

Kahn, R. F. (1931). The relation of home investment to unemployment. *The Economic Journal, 41* (162), 173–198.

Kailath, T. (1980). *Linear systems.* Englewood Cliffs, NJ: Prentice-Hall.

Kalman, R. E. (1960a). Contributions to the theory of optimal control. *Boletín de la Sociedad Matémática Mexicana, 5*(2), 102–119.

Kalman, R. E. (1960b). On the general theory of control systems. *International Federation of Automatic Control Proceedings Volumes, 1*(1), 491–502.

Kalman, R. E. (1960c). Lecture notes on control system theory (by M. Athans and G. Lendaris). University of California, at Berkeley.

Kalman, R. E. (1960d). A new approach to linear filtering and prediction problems. *Transactions of the American Society of Mechanical Engineers. Journal of Basic Engineering, 82D*(1), 35–45.

Kalman, R. E. (1962). Canonical structure of linear dynamical systems. *Proceedings of the National Academy of Sciences of the United States of America, 48*(4), 596–600.

Kalman, R. E. (1963). Mathematical description of linear dynamical systems. *Society for Industrial and Applied Mathematics Journal on Control, 1*(2), 152–192.

Kalman, R. E. (1968). New developments in system theory relevant to biology. In M. D. Mesarović (Ed.), *Systems theory and biology* (pp. 222–232). Berlin: Springer.

Kalman, R. E. (1969). *Lectures on controllability and observability, CIME Summer Course, Bologna, 1968.* Cremonese, Rome. Reprinted in E. Evangelisti (Ed.). (2011). *Controllability and observability* (pp. 1–149). Springer: Heidelberg.

Kalman, R. E. (1982). On the computation of the reachable/observable canonical form. *Society for Industrial and Applied Mathematics Journal on Control and Optimization, 20*(2), 258–260.

Kalman, R. E., Ho, Y. C., & Narendra, K. S. (1963). Controllability of linear dynamic systems. *Contributions to Differential Equations, 1*(2), 189–213.

Kalman, R. E., Falb, P. L., & Arbib, M. A. (1969). *Topics in mathematical system theory* (Vol. 1). New York: McGraw-Hill.

Karpelevich, F. I. (1951). On the characteristic roots of matrices with non-negative elements. *Izvestiya Rossiiskoi Akademii Nauk SSSR Seriya Matematicheskaya, 15*(4), 361–383 (in Russian; English translation in Swift, J. (1972). *The location of characteristic roots of stochastic matrices.* M.Sc. Thesis, Montreal: McGill University).

Kemp, M. C. (1973). Heterogeneous capital goods and long-run Stolper–Samuels on theorems. *Australian Economic Papers, 12*(21), 253–260.

Krause, U. (2015). *Positive dynamical systems in discrete time. Theory, models, and applications.* Berlin: Walter de Gruyter GmbH.

Kurz, H. D. (1998). Against the current: Sraffa's unpublished manuscripts and the history of economic thought. *Journal of the History of Economic Thought, 5*(3), 437–451.

Kurz, H. D. (2009). Preparing the edition of Piero Sraffa's *Unpublished Papers and Correspondence. Cahiers d'économie politique/Papers in Political Economy, 57*(2), 261–278.

Kurz, H. D., & Salvadori, N. (1995). *Theory of production. A long-period analysis.* Cambridge: Cambridge University Press.

Lange, O. (1967). The computer and the market. In C. H. Feinstein (Ed.), *Socialism, capitalism and economic growth: Essays presented to Maurice Dobb* (pp. 158–161). Cambridge: Cambridge University Press.

Lange, O. (1970). *Introduction to economic cybernetics*. Oxford: Pergamon Press.

Leeson, R. (Ed.). (2000). *A.W.H Phillips: Collected works in contemporary perspective*. Cambridge: Cambridge University Press.

Leontief, W. (1953). *Studies in the structure of the American economy*. New York: Oxford University Press.

Lévi-Strauss, C. (1967). *Les structures élémentaires de la parenté*. Berlin: Mouton de Gruyter.

Lohmiller, W., & Slotine, J.-J. E. (1998). On contraction analysis for non-linear systems. *Automatica, 34*(6), 683–696.

Luenberger, D. G. (1979). *Introduction to dynamic systems. Theory, models, and applications*. New York: Wiley.

Mahalanobis, P. C. (1953). Some observations on the process of growth of national income. *Sankhyā, 12*(4), 307–312.

Mainwaring, L. (1974). *A neo-Ricardian analysis of trade*. Ph.D. Thesis, Manchester: University of Manchester.

Mainwaring, L., & Steedman, I. (2000). On the probability of re-switching and capital reversing in a two-sector Sraffian model. In H. D. Kurz (Ed.), *Critical essays on Piero Sraffa's legacy in economics* (pp. 323–354). Cambridge: Cambridge University Press.

Mariolis, T. (1993). *The neo-Ricardian theory of foreign trade. Critical approach*. Ph.D. Dissertation, Athens: Department of Public Administration, Panteion University (in Greek).

Mariolis, T. (1997). On the Stolper–Samuelson theorem in heterogeneous capital models: Addendum. Πολιτική Οικονομία/*Political Economy. Review of Political Economy and Social Sciences, 1*, 113–120 (in Greek).

Mariolis, T. (2003). Controllability, observability, regularity, and the so-called problem of transforming values into prices of production. *Asian–African Journal of Economics and Econometrics, 3*(2), 113–127.

Mariolis, T. (2010a). *Essays on the logical history of political economy*. Athens: Matura (in Greek).

Mariolis, T. (2010b). Norm bounds for a transformed price vector in Sraffian systems. *Applied Mathematical Sciences, 4*(9–12), 551–574.

Mariolis, T. (2013). Applying the mean absolute eigen-deviation of labour commanded prices from labour values to actual economies. *Applied Mathematical Sciences, 7*(104), 5193–5204.

Mariolis, T. (2015). Norm bounds and a homographic approximation for the wage–profit curve. *Metroeconomica, 66*(2), 263–283.

Mariolis, T. (2019a). *Piero Sraffa's fundamental theorems and the traditional political economy*. Paper written for the preparation of the 1st Conference of the Study Group on Sraffian Economics: "From the Capital Theory Controversy in the 1960s to Greece's Virtual Bankruptcy in 2010", 11–12 April 2019, Panteion University, Athens, Greece (in Greek). Retrieved Mar 30, 2020, from https://www.researchgate.net/publication/330397024.

Mariolis, T. (2019b). *The "second wave" of the Sraffian critical transcendence of the traditional political economy*. Paper presented at the 1st Conference of the Study Group on Sraffian Economics: "From the Capital Theory Controversy in the 1960s to Greece's Virtual Bankruptcy in 2010", 11–12 April 2019, Panteion University, Athens, Greece (in Greek).

Mariolis, T. (2019c). *The location of the value theories in the complex plane and the degree of regularity-controllability of actual economies*. MPRA Paper No 96972. Retrieved Mar 30, 2020, from https://mpra.ub.uni-muenchen.de/96972/.

Mariolis, T. (2021). Competing theories of value: A spectral analysis. *Contributions to Political Economy, 40*(1) (forthcoming).

Mariolis, T., & Tsoulfidis, L. (2009). Decomposing the changes in production prices into "capital-intensity" and "price" effects: Theory and evidence from the Chinese economy. *Contributions to Political Economy, 28*(1), 1–22.

Mariolis, T., & Tsoulfidis, L. (2011). Eigenvalue distribution and the production price–profit rate relationship: Theory and empirical evidence. *Evolutionary and Institutional Economics Review, 8*(1), 87–122.

Mariolis, T., & Tsoulfidis, L. (2014). On Bródy's conjecture: Theory, facts and figures about instability of the US economy. *Economic Systems Research, 26*(2), 209–223.

Mariolis, T., & Tsoulfidis, L. (2016). *Modern classical economics and reality. A spectral analysis of the theory of value and distribution*. Tokyo: Springer.

Mariolis, T., Soklis, G., & Zouvela, E. (2013). Testing Böhm-Bawerk's theory of capital: Some evidence from the Finnish economy. *The Review of Austrian Economics, 26*(2), 207–220.

Martos, B. (1990). *Economic control structures. A non-Walrasian approach*. Amsterdam: North Holland.

Marx, K. (1885). *Das Kapital. Kritik der politischen Oekonomie. Zweiter Band. Buch II: Der Cirkulationsprocess des Kapital. Herausgegeben von F. Engels*. Hamburg: Verlag von Otto Meissner.

Marx, K. (1894). *Das Kapital. Kritik der politischen Oekonomie. Dritter Band, erster Theil. Buch III: Der Gesammtprocess der kapitalistischen Produktion Kapitel I bis XXVIII (Bd. 3 von 4). Herausgegeben von F. Engels*. Hamburg: Verlag von Otto Meissner.

McFadden, D. (1969). On the controllability of decentralized macroeconomic systems. The assignment problem. In H. W. Kuhn & G. P. Szegö (Eds.), *Mathematical systems theory and economics* (pp. 221–239). Berlin: Springer–Verlag.

Meyer, C. D. (2001). *Matrix analysis and applied linear algebra*. New York: Society for Industrial and Applied Mathematics.

Minc, H. (1988). *Nonnegative matrices*. New York: John Wiley & Sons.

Miyao, T. (1977). A generalization of Sraffa's standard commodity and its complete characterization. *International Economic Review, 18*(1), 151–162.

Moore, B. (1981). Principal component analysis in linear systems: Controllability, observability, and model reduction. *Institute of Electrical and Electronics Engineers Transactions on Automatic Control, 26*(1), 17–32.

Okishio, N. (1963). A mathematical note on Marxian theorems. *Weltwirtschaftliches Archiv, 91*, 287–299. Reprinted in N. Okishio (1993). *Essays on political economy* (pp. 27–39). Edited by M. Krüger & P. Flaschel. Frankfurt am Main: Peter Lang.

Paige, C. C. (1981). Properties of numerical algorithms related to computing controllability. *Institute of Electrical and Electronics Engineers Transactions on Automatic Control, 26*(1), 130–138.

Parys, W. (1982). The deviation of prices from labor values. *The American Economic Review, 72* (5), 1208–1212.

Pasinetti, L. L. (1966). Changes in the rate of profit and switches of techniques. *Quarterly Journal of Economics, 80*(4), 503–517.

Pasinetti, L. L. (1973). The notion of vertical integration in economic analysis. *Metroeconomica, 25* (1), 1–29.

Popov, V. M. (1963). Solution of a new stability problem for controlled systems. *Automation and Remote Control, 24*(1), 1–23.

Popov, V. M. (1966). *Hiperstabilitatea sistemelor automate*. Bucharest: Editura Academiei Republicii Socialiste România. Revised and augmented editions in: Russian (Moscow: Nauka, 1970), French (Paris: Dunod, 1973), English (Berlin: Springer–Verlag, 1973).

Popov, V. M. (1970). Some properties of the control systems with irreducible matrix-transfer functions. In J. A. Yorke (Ed.), *Seminar on differential equations and dynamical systems, II. Seminar lectures at the University of Maryland 1969* (pp. 169–180). Berlin: Springer–Verlag.

Ragazzini, J. R., & Zadeh, L. A. (1952). The analysis of sampled-data systems. *Transactions of the American Institute of Electrical Engineers, Part II: Applications and Industry, 71*(5), 225–234.

Read, L. E. (1958). I, pencil: My family tree as told to Leonard E. Read. *The Freeman: Ideas on Liberty, 8*(12), 32–37.

Ricardo, D. (1817). *On the principles of political economy and taxation.* In D. Ricardo (1951–1973). *The works and correspondence of David Ricardo* (Vol. 1). Edited by P. Sraffa with the collaboration of M. H. Dobb, Cambridge: Cambridge University Press.

Robinson, J. V. (1953). The production function and the theory of capital. *The Review of Economic Studies, 21*(2), 81–106.

Salvadori, N., & Stedman, I. (1985). Cost functions and produced means of production: Duality and capital theory. *Contributions to Political Economy, 4*(1), 79–90.

Samuelson, P. A. (1962). Parable and realism in capital theory: The surrogate production function. *The Review of Economic Studies, 29*(3), 193–206.

Schefold, B. (1971). *Mr. Sraffa on joint production.* Ph.D. Thesis, Basle: University of Basle.

Schefold, B. (1976). Relative prices as a function of the profit rate: A mathematical note. *Zeitschrift für Nationalökonomie/Journal of Economics, 36*(1–2), 21–48. Reprinted in B. Schefold (1997). *Normal prices, technical change and accumulation* (pp. 46–75). London: Macmillan.

Schefold, B. (2019). The transformation of values into prices on the basis of random systems revisited. *Evolutionary and Institutional Economics Review, 16*(2), 261–302.

Sharpe, G., & Styan, G. (1965). Circuit duality and the general network inverse. *Institute of Electrical and Electronics Engineers Transactions on Circuit Theory, 12*(1), 22–27.

Slotine, J.-J. E., & Li, W. (1991). *Applied nonlinear control.* Englewood Cliffs: Prentice-Hall.

Smith, A. (1776). *An inquiry into the nature and causes of the wealth of nations.* London: Strahan and Cadell.

Solow, R. (1952). On the structure of linear models. *Econometrica, 20*(1), 29–46.

Solow, R. M. (1959). Competitive valuation in a dynamic input–output system. *Econometrica, 27* (1), 30–53.

Soto, R. L., & Rojo, O. (2006). Applications of a Brauer theorem in the nonnegative inverse eigenvalue problem. *Linear Algebra and its Applications, 416*(2–3), 844–856.

Spaventa, L. (1970). Rate of profit, rate of growth, and capital intensity in a simple production model. *Oxford Economic Papers, 22*(2), 129–147.

Sraffa, P. (1960). *Production of commodities by means of commodities. Prelude to a critique of economic theory.* Cambridge: Cambridge University Press.

Sraffa, P. (1962). Production of commodities: A comment. *The Economic Journal, 72*(286), 477–479.

Sraffa, P., & Newman, P. (1962). Exchange of letters, published as an Appendix to K. Bharadwaj (1970). On the maximum number of switches between two production systems. *Schweizerische Zeitschrift für Volkswirtschaft und Statistik/Revue suisse d'Economie politique et de Statistique, 106*(4), 409–429.

Steedman, I. (1977). *Marx after Sraffa.* London: New Left Books.

Steedman, I. (1979). *Trade amongst growing economics.* Cambridge: Cambridge University Press.

Steedman, I. (1994). "Perverse" behaviour in a "one commodity" model. *Cambridge Journal of Economics, 18*(3), 299–311.

Steedman, I. (1999). Vertical integration and "reduction to dated quantities of labour". In G. Mongiovi & F. Petri (Eds.), *Value distribution and capital. Essays in honour of Pierangelo Garegnani* (pp. 314–318). London: Routledge.

Stolper, W. F., & Samuelson, P. A. (1941). Protection and real wages. *The Review of Economic Studies, 9*(1), 58–73.

Sun, G.-Z. (2008). The first two eigenvalues of large random matrices and Brody's hypothesis on the stability of large input–output systems. *Economic Systems Research, 20*(4), 429–432.

Takayama, A. (1985). *Mathematical economics* (2nd ed.). Cambridge: Cambridge University Press.

Turnovsky, S. J. (2011). Stabilization theory and policy: 50 years after the Phillips curve. *Economica, 78*(309), 67–88.

Van Willigenburg, L. G., & De Koning, W. L. (2008). Linear systems theory revisited. *Automatica, 44*(7), 1686–1696.

Weizsäcker, C. C. V. (1977). Organic composition of capital and average period of production. *Revue d'Economie Politique, 87*(2), 198–231.

Willke, H. (1993). *Systemtheorie. Eine Einführung in die Grundprobleme der Theorie sozialer Systeme*. Stuttgart: Gustav Fischer Verlag.

Wohltmann, H. W. (1981). Complete, perfect, and maximal controllability of discrete economic systems. *Zeitschrift für Nationalökonomie/Journal of Economics, 41*(1–2), 39–58.

Wohltmann, H. W. (1985). On the controllability of continuous-time macroeconomic models. *Zeitschrift für Nationalökonomie/Journal of Economics, 45*(1), 47–66.

Wonhman, W. M. (1967). On pole assignment in multi-input controllable linear systems. *Institute of Electrical and Electronics Engineers Transactions on Automatic Control, 12*(6), 660–665.

# Chapter 3
# The Capital Theory Debate and the Almost Uncontrollability and Unobservability of Actual Economies

**Abstract** Despite the fact that the actual economies are characterized by rather low degrees and numerical ranks of value controllability, the key stylized findings on empirical value–wage–profit rate curves point out that these economies cannot be coherently analysed in terms of the traditional value theory. Hence, on the one hand, the Sraffian theory is not only the most general to date, but is also empirically relevant. On the other hand, the actual economies constitute almost uncontrollable and unobservable systems, and this explains, in turn, the specific shape features of the empirical value–wage–profit rate curves that are at the heart of the capital theory debate.

**Keywords** Almost uncontrollability and unobservability · Capital theory debate · Empirical relevance of the Sraffian theory · Skew characteristic value distributions · Spectral decompositions of the value system

> [W]hat is it that always is, but never comes to be, and what is it that comes to be but never is? The former, since it is always consistent, can be grasped by the intellect with the support of a reasoned account, while the latter is the object of belief, supported by unreasoning sensation, since it is generated and passes away, but never really is. Now, anything created is necessarily created by some cause, because nothing can possibly come to be without there being something that is responsible for its coming to be. —Plato, *Timaeus* (Plato (2008). *Timaeus and Critias*. Oxford: Oxford University Press.)

## 3.1 Introduction

The value–wage–profit rate system of quite diverse actual economies (but, *ex hypothesis*, linear and single-product), or, to be more precise, of their Symmetric Input–Output Tables (SIOTs) simulacra, has been examined in a relatively large

© Springer Nature Singapore Pte Ltd. 2021
T. Mariolis et al., *Spectral Theory of Value and Actual Economies*, Evolutionary Economics and Social Complexity Science 24,
https://doi.org/10.1007/978-981-33-6260-4_3

number of studies. The key stylized findings were that, in the economically relevant interval of the profit rate:[1]

i. Non-monotonic value–profit rate curves *do* occur. Nevertheless, they are not significantly more than 20% of the tested cases, while, expressed in terms of Sraffa's Standard commodity (SSC), they have no more than one extreme point. Cases of reversal in the direction of deviation between long-period values and vertically integrated labour coefficients (V–VLR) also occur, but are rarer.

ii. Wage–profit rate curves with alternating curvature *do* occur. Nevertheless, despite the presence of considerable deviations from the equal value compositions of capital case (see Sect. 2.3.1), these curves are near-linear, in the sense that the correlation coefficients between the distributive variables tend to be above 99%, and their second derivatives change sign no more than once or, very rarely, twice, irrespective of the *numéraire* chosen.

iii. Therefore, the approximation of the empirical value–wage–profit rate curves through low-order formulae (ranging from linear to quadratic) works well. Moreover, the "*actual* relative profit rate" is usually no greater than 0.5 and, most of the time, it is in the range of 0.3 to 0.4, implying that polynomial approximations of the "actual long-period values", through dated quantities of vertically integrated labour (see Eq. (2.35)), require the inclusion of just a few terms.[2]

iv. Since actual economies are characterized by complex inter-industry linkages, alternative production methods, and the production of many commodities and positive profits by means of many commodities, the aforementioned shapes of the value–wage–profit rate curves seem to be *paradoxical*. However, they can be explained by the fact that, across countries and over time, both the moduli of the first non-dominant eigenvalues and the first non-dominant singular values of the vertically integrated technical coefficients matrices, $\mathbf{J}$, fall quite rapidly, whereas the rest constellate in much lower values, forming "long tails". More specifically:

   a. The majority of the non-dominant eigenvalues are crowded at very low values and bounded in a relatively small region of the unit circle. In point of fact, both the eigenvalue moduli and the singular values follow exponentially decaying trends, in the case of circulating capital, or a nearly "L-shaped form", in the case of the presence of fixed capital stocks (treated, however,

---

[1] Mariolis and Tsoulfidis (2016a, Chaps. 3 and 5) and the references therein. Also see Li (2017, Chaps. 7 and 8).

[2] The terms "actual relative profit rate" and "actual long-period values" are used to signify the relative profit rate and long-period commodity values that correspond to the "actual" real wage rate vector, where the latter is estimated, under the usual convenient assumptions, on the basis of the available input–output data. It is also noted that, taking into account that the relative profit rate is no greater than the share of profits in the Sraffian Standard system (see Sect. 2.3.1), the abovementioned figures for the actual relative profit rate seem to be in accordance with many well-known estimations of the share of profits (approximated by the net operating surplus) in actual economies.

in terms of the Leontief–Bródy approach). Hence, although *rank*[**J**] $= n$ holds true, the numerical rank, or "effective dimensions", of matrices **J** are much lower than $n$.

b. The complex (as well as the negative) eigenvalues *tend* to appear in the lower ranks, i.e. their modulus is relatively small. However, even in the cases where they appear in the higher ranks, i.e. second or third rank, the real part is much larger than the imaginary part. In the rarer cases where the imaginary part of an eigenvalue exceeds the real one, not only is their ratio relatively small, but also the modulus of the eigenvalue can be considered as a negligible quantity. In general, the imaginary part gets progressively smaller. Consequently, the distribution of the moduli is a fair representation of the eigenvalue distribution.

c. Although the aggregation level of the SIOTs affects both the central tendency and skewness of the eigenvalue distributions, the moduli of the higher non-dominant eigenvalues exhibit small relative changes that go to either direction. Hence, the aggregation level does not affect the specific shape features of the empirical value–wage–profit rate curves.

d. These findings suggest that the elements of actual technical coefficients matrices cannot be considered as identically and independently distributed and, therefore, do not provide empirical support for Bródy's conjecture.[3] At the same time, however, they reveal that, regardless of the aggregation level of the SIOTs, actual economies can be represented in terms of a "core" of only a few "hyper-basic industries" (see Sect. 2.3.2) that conditions the motion of the entire economic system in the case of—endogenous or exogenous—disturbances.[4]

Applying the analysis developed in Chap. 2 of this book, this chapter provides a unified treatment of the value–capital problem on both theoretical and empirical grounds. In particular, it looks deeper into the key stylized findings of the empirical studies, and zeroes in on the spectral "imprint" of actual value–wage–profit rate systems by detecting the singular value configuration of the relevant controllability matrices. Hence, it further supports the recently proposed link between the tendency of actual economies to respond as uncontrollable systems and the specific shape features of the empirical value–wage–profit rate curves (Mariolis and Tsoulfidis 2018).

The remainder of the chapter is structured as follows. Section 3.2 constructs spectral decompositions and alternative approximations of the value–wage–profit rate system. Section 3.3 presents and evaluates newer evidence that suggests the empirical relevance of the Sraffian value theory and, at the same time, the almost uncontrollability and unobservability of actual economies. Finally, Sect. 3.4 concludes.

---

[3]See Sect. 2.3.4 (Case 2).

[4]The logic of this finding has been used or applied in a number of quite diverse empirical studies; see, e.g. Konstantakis et al. (2017), Lin III (2016), Michaelides et al. (2018).

## 3.2   Spectral Decompositions of the Value–Wage–Profit Rate System

### 3.2.1   Fundamental Forms

Consider the Sraffian economy presented in Sect. 2.3.1. When (i) the value side is completely controllable, i.e. $\mathbf{1}^T\mathbf{x}_{\mathbf{J}k} \neq 0$ for all $k$ (which is the empirically relevant case); (ii) the eigenvectors, $\mathbf{y}_{\mathbf{J}i}^T$ and $\mathbf{x}_{\mathbf{J}i}$, are normalized by setting

$$\mathbf{y}_{\mathbf{J}i}^T[\mathbf{I} - \mathbf{A}]\mathbf{x}_{\mathbf{J}i} = \mathbf{v}^T[\mathbf{I} - \mathbf{A}]\mathbf{x}_{\mathbf{J}i} = 1$$

and (iii) long-period values are normalized by setting

$$\mathbf{p}^T\mathbf{z} = \mathbf{v}^T\mathbf{z} = 1$$

it follows that the wage–relative profit rate curve (WPC) and the value–relative profit rate curves (VPCs) can be expressed in the following spectral forms (Mariolis and Tsoulfidis 2011, pp. 91–92):

$$w = \left[(1-\rho)^{-1}d_1 + \Lambda_k^w\right]^{-1}, \Lambda_k^w \equiv \sum_{k=2}^{n}(1-\rho\lambda_{\mathbf{J}k})^{-1}d_k, \sum_{i=1}^{n}d_i = 1, d_1$$

$$= \mathbf{y}_{\mathbf{J}1}^T\mathbf{z} \tag{3.1}$$

$$\mathbf{p}^T = w[(1-\rho)^{-1}\mathbf{y}_{\mathbf{J}1}^T + \Lambda_k^p], \Lambda_k^p \equiv \sum_{k=2}^{n}(1-\rho\lambda_{\mathbf{J}k})^{-1}\mathbf{y}_{\mathbf{J}k}^T, \sum_{i=1}^{n}\mathbf{y}_{\mathbf{J}i}^T = \mathbf{v}^T \tag{3.2}$$

where $\Lambda_k^w, \Lambda_k^p$ represent the effects of non-dominant eigenvalues on WPC and VPCs, respectively, the $d_i$ denote the coordinates of $\mathbf{z}$ in terms of the right eigen-basis $[\mathbf{I} - \mathbf{A}]\mathbf{x}_{\mathbf{J}i}, \mathbf{p}^T(0) = \mathbf{v}^T$, and $\mathbf{p}^T(1) = d_1^{-1}\mathbf{y}_{\mathbf{J}1}^T$ (also see Eq. (2.44)).

If there are strong quasi-linear dependencies amongst the non-labour conditions of production in all the vertically integrated industries, then

$$\mathbf{J} \approx (\mathbf{y}_{\mathbf{J}1}^T\mathbf{x}_{\mathbf{J}1})^{-1}\mathbf{x}_{\mathbf{J}1}\mathbf{y}_{\mathbf{J}1}^T, \ |\lambda_{\mathbf{J}k}| \approx 0$$

Hence, from Eqs. (3.1) and (3.2) it follows that

$$\Lambda_k^w \approx 1 - d_1$$

$$\Lambda_k^p \approx \mathbf{v}^T - \mathbf{y}_{\mathbf{J}1}^T = \mathbf{p}^T(0) - d_1\mathbf{p}^T(1)$$

and, therefore, both the WPC and the VPCs tend to be homographic functions:

$$w \approx \left[(1-\rho)^{-1}d_1 + (1-d_1)\right]^{-1}$$

or

$$w \approx w^S[1 + \rho(d_1 - 1)]^{-1} \tag{3.3}$$

where $w^S \equiv 1 - \rho$ is the Sraffian linear WPC, while the right-hand side of approximation (3.3) is strictly concave (strictly convex) to the origin iff $d_1 < (>) 1$; and

$$\mathbf{p}^T \approx w^S[1 + \rho(d_1 - 1)]^{-1}\left[(1-\rho)^{-1}d_1\mathbf{p}^T(1) + \mathbf{p}^T(0) - d_1\mathbf{p}^T(1)\right]$$

or

$$\mathbf{p}^T \approx [1 + \rho(d_1 - 1)]^{-1}\left[(1-\rho)\mathbf{p}^T(0) + \rho d_1\mathbf{p}^T(1)\right] \tag{3.4}$$

Relations 3.3 and 3.4 imply that the economy tends to be controllable of rank 2 and strictly equivalent to an economically relevant and generalized $(1 \times n - 1)$ Marx–Fel'dman–Mahalanobis economy and, therefore, to behave as a reducible two-industry economy without self-reproducing non-basics (see Sects. 2.3.3 and 2. 3.4). These rank-one approximations have the following properties:

i. Their accuracy is directly related to the magnitudes of $|\lambda_{\mathbf{J}k}|^{-1}$
ii. They are exact at the extreme, economically relevant, values of $\rho$.
iii. When $rank[\mathbf{J}] = 1$ they become exact for all $\rho$.

Then the absolute deviation, $|w - w^S|$, of the WPC from $w^S$, is maximized at

$$\rho = \left(-1 + \sqrt{d_1}\right)\left(-1 + d_1\right)^{-1}$$

where

$$\max\left|w - w^S\right| = \left|1 - \sqrt{d_1}\right|\left(1 + \sqrt{d_1}\right)^{-1} \tag{3.5}$$

while the mean value of this deviation is

$$MAD \equiv \int_0^1 \left|(w - w^S)\right|d\rho = \left|-(1 - d_1^2 + 2d_1 \ln d_1)\right|\left[2(-1 + d_1)^2\right]^{-1} \tag{3.6}$$

As $d_1$ tends either to zero or to plus infinity, the right-hand side of Eq. (3.5) tends to 1, while the right-hand side of Eq. (3.6) tends to $2^{-1}$ (Mariolis 2015a, pp. 280–282; Mariolis and Tsoulfidis 2016b, pp. 302–303).

When, for instance, SSC is chosen as the *numéraire*, it follows that $d_1 = 1, d_k = 0$, Eq. (3.1) reduces to $w = w^S$, and Eq. (3.2) reduces to

$$\mathbf{p}^{ST} = \mathbf{p}^{ST}(1) + (1 - \rho)\mathbf{\Lambda}_k^{\mathbf{p}} \tag{3.7}$$

where $\mathbf{p}^{ST}$ denotes the value vector in terms of SSC, and $\mathbf{p}^{ST}(1) = \mathbf{y}_{\mathbf{J}1}^T$. Substituting $(1 - \rho\lambda_{\mathbf{J}k})^{-1} = 1 + \rho\lambda_{\mathbf{J}k}(1 - \rho\lambda_{\mathbf{J}k})^{-1}$ into Eq. (3.7) yields

$$\mathbf{p}^{ST} = LP + NLP \tag{3.8}$$

where

$$LP \equiv (1 - \rho)\mathbf{p}^T(0) + \rho\mathbf{p}^{ST}(1)$$

and

$$NLP \equiv (1 - \rho)\rho \sum_{k=2}^{n} \lambda_{\mathbf{J}k}(1 - \rho\lambda_{\mathbf{J}k})^{-1}\mathbf{y}_{\mathbf{J}k}^T$$

Equation (3.8) defines an additive decomposition of the value vector, $\mathbf{p}^{ST}$, into linear and non-linear parts. The linear part (i) tends to be insensitive to the profit rate when the economy tends to the equal value compositions of capital case; (ii) gives the correct values for $\mathbf{p}^{ST}$ at the extreme values of $\rho$; and (iii) corresponds to the Sraffian Standard system. On the other hand, the non-linear part (i) does not exist in the equal value compositions of capital case; (ii) tends to zero when the economy tends to be controllable of rank 2; (iii) equals zero at the extreme values of $\rho$; (iv) may contain elements with more than one extreme point; and (v) corresponds to the non-Sraffian Standard systems, the normalized maximum uniform profit (and growth) rates of which equals $\lambda_{\mathbf{J}k}^{-1}$.[5] More specifically, post-multiplying Eq. (3.8) by the diagonal matrix $\left[\widehat{\mathbf{p}}^T(0)\right]^{-1}$ gives

$$\boldsymbol{\pi}^{ST} = (1 - \rho)\mathbf{e}^T(0) + \rho\boldsymbol{\pi}^{ST}(1) + NLP\left[\widehat{\mathbf{p}}^T(0)\right]^{-1}$$

where

---

[5]For the non-Sraffian Standard systems-commodities, see Sraffa (1960, pp. 30–31, 48 and 53–54), Goodwin (1976), Aruka (1991), and Sect. 10.4 of the present book.

$$\boldsymbol{\pi}^{\mathrm{ST}} \equiv \mathbf{p}^{\mathrm{ST}} \left[ \hat{\mathbf{p}}^{\mathrm{T}}(0) \right]^{-1}$$

and

$$\boldsymbol{\pi}^{\mathrm{ST}}(1) \equiv \mathbf{p}^{\mathrm{ST}}(1) \left[ \hat{\mathbf{p}}^{\mathrm{T}}(0) \right]^{-1}$$

Let $\theta_{\mathrm{L}}$ and $d_{\mathrm{L}}$ be the angle and the Euclidean distance, respectively, between the unit-length vectors $\boldsymbol{\pi}^{\mathrm{ST}}(1) \left\| \boldsymbol{\pi}^{\mathrm{ST}}(1) \right\|_2^{-1}$ and $\mathbf{e}^{\mathrm{T}} \| \mathbf{e}^{\mathrm{T}} \|_2^{-1}$. Then

$$d_{\mathrm{L}} \equiv \sqrt{2(1 - \cos \theta_{\mathrm{L}})}$$

is a measure of the deviation from the equal value compositions of capital case, which is independent of any choice of *numéraire* and physical measurement units.[6] Analogously, for $0 < \rho < 1$, the Euclidean distance between $\boldsymbol{\pi}^{\mathrm{ST}} \| \boldsymbol{\pi}^{\mathrm{ST}} \|_2^{-1}$ and the unit-length vector formed from

$$(1 - \rho)\mathbf{e}^{\mathrm{T}}(0) + \rho \boldsymbol{\pi}^{\mathrm{ST}}(1)$$

is a measure of the deviation from the corresponding controllable of rank 2 economy.

### 3.2.2 Alternative Approximations

Based on Eq. (3.8), we can now construct the following three, different approximations for the value vector $\mathbf{p}^{\mathrm{ST}}$:

i. *Eigenvalue decomposition approximation*: When the moduli of the last $n - \nu$ eigenvalues, $2 \leq \nu \leq n - 1$, are sufficiently small that can be considered as negligible, Eq. (3.8) reduces to

$$\mathbf{p}^{\mathrm{ST}} \approx \mathrm{LP} + \sum_{k=2}^{\nu} f_k(\rho) \mathbf{y}_{\mathbf{j}k}^{\mathrm{T}} \tag{3.9}$$

where

---

[6]This class of measures is known as " $d$ – distances" (see Mariolis and Soklis 2010, p. 94; 2011; Steedman and Tomkins 1998).

$$f_k(\rho) \equiv \sum_{k=2}^{\nu} (1-\rho)\rho\lambda_{\mathbf{J}k}(1-\rho\lambda_{\mathbf{J}k})^{-1}$$

When $\lambda_{\mathbf{J}k}$ is positive (negative), the non-linear term $f_k(\rho)$ is a semi-positive (semi-negative) and strictly concave (strictly convex) function of $\rho$, which is maximized (minimized) at

$$\rho^* \equiv \left(1 - \sqrt{1-\lambda_{\mathbf{J}k}}\right)\lambda_{\mathbf{J}k}^{-1}$$

where

$$-1 + \sqrt{2} < \rho^* < 1$$

and

$$-3 + 2\sqrt{2} < f_k(\rho^*) < 1$$

since $|\lambda_{\mathbf{J}k}| < 1$. Relation (3.9) defines a " $\nu$-th order eigenvalue decomposition approximation", which is exact at the extreme values of $\rho$. In fact, the right-hand side of relation (3.9) is the value vector associated with the rank–$\nu$, truncated system $[\mathbf{J}^A, \mathbf{p}^T(0)]$, where

$$\mathbf{J}^A \equiv \mathbf{X_J}\widehat{\lambda}_{\mathbf{J}}^{[\nu]}\mathbf{X_J}^{-1}$$

$\mathbf{X_J}$ denotes the modal matrix for $\mathbf{J}$, and $\widehat{\lambda}_{\mathbf{J}}^{[\nu]}$ is derived from $\widehat{\lambda}_{\mathbf{J}}$ (the diagonal matrix formed from the eigenvalues of $\mathbf{J}$) by replacing the last $n - \nu$ eigenvalues by zeroes (Mariolis and Tsoulfidis 2011, pp. 99–100; 2016a, pp. 161–162).

ii. *Singular value decomposition approximation*: An alternative rank–$\nu$ approximation can be deduced from the singular value decomposition of $\mathbf{J}$, i.e.

$$\mathbf{J} = \mathbf{U}\widehat{\mathbf{\sigma}}_{\mathbf{J}}\mathbf{W}^T$$

where $\mathbf{U}$ and $\mathbf{W}^T$ are real and orthogonal $n \times n$ matrices (i.e. $\mathbf{U}^T = \mathbf{U}^{-1}$ and $\mathbf{W}^T = \mathbf{W}^{-1}$), and $\widehat{\mathbf{\sigma}}_{\mathbf{J}} \equiv [\sigma_{\mathbf{J}j}]$ is the diagonal matrix formed from the singular values of $\mathbf{J}$. The columns of $\mathbf{U}$ (of $\mathbf{W}$) are particular choices of the right eigenvectors of $\mathbf{JJ}^T$ (of $\mathbf{J}^T\mathbf{J}$), which is a positive symmetric matrix. The non-zero singular values of $\mathbf{J}$ are the square roots of the non-zero eigenvalues of either $\mathbf{JJ}^T$ or $\mathbf{J}^T\mathbf{J}$, and, therefore,[7]

---

[7]See, e.g. Horn and Johnson (1991, Chap. 3), and take into account that $\mathbf{J}$ is similar to the column stochastic matrix $\widehat{\mathbf{y}}_{\mathbf{J}1}\mathbf{J}\widehat{\mathbf{y}}_{\mathbf{J}1}^{-1}$ (see Sect. 2.3.4, Case 7).

$$\sqrt{n} \geq \sigma_{\mathbf{J}1} \geq \lambda_{\mathbf{J}1} = 1 > |\lambda_{\mathbf{J}k}| \geq \sigma_{\mathbf{J}n}$$

$$|\det\mathbf{J}| = \prod_{i=1}^{n} \sigma_{\mathbf{J}i} = \left|\prod_{i=1}^{n} \lambda_{\mathbf{J}i}\right|$$

$$rank[\mathbf{J}] = rank[\widehat{\boldsymbol{\sigma}}_{\mathbf{J}}] \geq rank\left[\widehat{\boldsymbol{\lambda}}_{\mathbf{J}}\right]$$

Now let $\widehat{\boldsymbol{\sigma}}_{\mathbf{J}}^{[\nu]}$ be the matrix derived from $\widehat{\boldsymbol{\sigma}}_{\mathbf{J}}$ by replacing the last $n - \nu$ singular values by zeroes. Then the matrix

$$\overline{\mathbf{J}}^{A} \equiv \mathbf{U}\widehat{\boldsymbol{\sigma}}_{\mathbf{J}}^{[\nu]}\mathbf{W}^{\mathrm{T}} \tag{3.10}$$

is the closest rank–$\nu$ matrix to $\mathbf{J}$ in both the spectral and the Frobenius (F) norms (Schmidt–Eckart–Young Theorem):

$$\left\|\mathbf{J} - \overline{\mathbf{J}}^{A}\right\|_{2} = \sigma_{\mathbf{J}\nu+1}$$

$$\left\|\mathbf{J} - \overline{\mathbf{J}}^{A}\right\|_{F} = \sqrt{\sigma_{\mathbf{J}\nu+1}^{2} + \ldots + \sigma_{\mathbf{J}n}^{2}}$$

Thus, a "$\nu$-th order singular value decomposition approximation" is given by the value vector associated with the truncated system $\left[\overline{\mathbf{J}}^{A}, \mathbf{p}^{\mathrm{T}}(0)\right]$, while this approximation is not necessarily exact at $\rho = 1$ (Mariolis and Tsoulfidis 2016a, pp. 162–167). Finally, the index of "inseparability",

$$\varepsilon_{\mathbf{J}\nu}(\sigma) \equiv 1 - \sum_{i=1}^{\nu} \sigma_{\mathbf{J}i}^{2}\left(\sum_{i=1}^{n} \sigma_{\mathbf{J}i}^{2}\right)^{-1}, \quad 0 \leq \varepsilon_{\mathbf{J}\nu}(\sigma) < 1 \tag{3.11}$$

is a convenient scalar-valued measure of the truncation error. Low values of $\varepsilon_{\mathbf{J}\nu}(\sigma)$, say less than 0.010, indicate that $\overline{\mathbf{J}}^{A}$ represents $\mathbf{J}$ adequately (see Treitel and Shanks 1971, pp. 12–15).[8]

iii. *Polynomial approximation*: Equation (3.8) can be written as

$$\mathbf{p}^{\mathrm{ST}} = \mathbf{LP} + (1 - \rho)\sum_{k=2}^{n}\left(\rho\lambda_{\mathbf{J}k} + \rho^{2}\lambda_{\mathbf{J}k}^{2} + \rho^{3}\lambda_{\mathbf{J}k}^{3} + \ldots\right)\mathbf{y}_{\mathbf{J}k}^{\mathrm{T}} \tag{3.12}$$

Post-multiplying

---

[8]Both $\mathbf{J}^{A}$ and $\overline{\mathbf{J}}^{A}$ may contain negative elements (unless $\nu = 1$).

$$\sum_{k=2}^{n} \mathbf{y}_{\mathbf{J}k}^{\mathrm{T}} = \mathbf{p}^{\mathrm{T}}(0) - \mathbf{p}^{\mathrm{ST}}(1)$$

by $\mathbf{J}^h$, $h = 0, 1, \ldots$, gives

$$\sum_{k=2}^{n} \lambda_{\mathbf{J}k}^{h} \mathbf{y}_{\mathbf{J}k}^{\mathrm{T}} = \mathbf{p}^{\mathrm{T}}(0)\mathbf{J}^h - \mathbf{p}^{\mathrm{ST}}(1) \tag{3.13}$$

Moreover, for any semi-positive $n$−vector $\boldsymbol{\psi}^{\mathrm{T}}$, $\boldsymbol{\psi}^{\mathrm{T}}\mathbf{J}^h$ tends to the left Perron–Frobenius (P–F) eigenvector of $\mathbf{J}$ as $h$ tends to infinity, i.e.

$$\lim_{h \to +\infty} \boldsymbol{\psi}^{\mathrm{T}}\mathbf{J}^h = \left[ \left( \boldsymbol{\psi}^{\mathrm{T}}\mathbf{x}_{\mathbf{J}1} \right) \left( \mathbf{y}_{\mathbf{J}1}^{\mathrm{T}}\mathbf{x}_{\mathbf{J}1} \right)^{-1} \right] \mathbf{y}_{\mathbf{J}1}^{\mathrm{T}} \tag{3.14}$$

while an upper bound on the rate of convergence is given by $\|\boldsymbol{\Gamma}\|_{\infty} < bc^h$, where

$$\boldsymbol{\Gamma} \equiv \mathbf{J}^h - \left( \mathbf{y}_{\mathbf{J}1}^{\mathrm{T}}\mathbf{x}_{\mathbf{J}1} \right)^{-1} \mathbf{x}_{\mathbf{J}1}\mathbf{y}_{\mathbf{J}1}^{\mathrm{T}}$$

the norm $\|\boldsymbol{\Gamma}\|_{\infty}$ denotes the maximum of the absolute values of the elements of $\boldsymbol{\Gamma}$, and $b$ represents a positive constant, which depends on $\mathbf{J}$ and $c$, for any $c$ such that $|\lambda_{\mathbf{J}2}| < c < 1$ (see, e.g. Horn and Johnson, 1990, p. 501).[9] Therefore, for a sufficiently large value of $m$ such that

$$\mathbf{p}^{\mathrm{T}}(0)\mathbf{J}^m \approx \mathbf{p}^{\mathrm{T}}(0)\mathbf{J}^{m+1} \approx \ldots \approx \mathbf{p}^{\mathrm{ST}}(1)$$

it follows from Eqs. (3.12) and (3.13) that

$$\mathbf{p}^{\mathrm{ST}} \approx \left[ (1 - \rho)\mathbf{p}^{\mathrm{T}}(0) \sum_{h=0}^{m-1} \rho^h \mathbf{J}^h \right] + \rho \left[ 1 - (1 - \rho)\left( 1 + \rho + \ldots + \rho^{m-2} \right) \right] \mathbf{p}^{\mathrm{ST}}(1)$$

or

$$\mathbf{p}^{\mathrm{ST}} \approx \left[ (1 - \rho)\mathbf{p}^{\mathrm{T}}(0) \sum_{h=0}^{m-1} \rho^h \mathbf{J}^h \right] + \rho^m \mathbf{p}^{\mathrm{ST}}(1)$$

or, rearranging terms,

---

[9] The closer to zero $|\lambda_{\mathbf{J}2}||\lambda_{\mathbf{J}1}|^{-1} (= |\lambda_{\mathbf{J}2}|)$ is, the faster is the convergence to the P–F eigenvector, i.e. the convergence is asymptotically exponential, at a rate at *least* as fast as $\log|\lambda_{\mathbf{J}2}|^{-1}$. The number $|\lambda_{\mathbf{J}2}|^{-1}\lambda_{\mathbf{J}1}$ is known as the the "smallest damping ratio", in population dynamics theory, and can be considered as a lower measure of the intrinsic resilience of the state vector to disturbance (for critical remarks on this and alternative measures, see Keyfitz and Caswell 2005, pp. 165–175; Stott et al. 2011, pp. 960–961).

$$\mathbf{p}^{\text{ST}} \approx \mathbf{p}^{\text{T}}(0) + \sum_{h=1}^{m-1} \rho^h \left(\mathbf{p}^{\text{T}}(0)\mathbf{J}^h - \mathbf{p}^{\text{T}}(0)\mathbf{J}^{h-1}\right) + \rho^m \left(\mathbf{p}^{\text{ST}}(1) - \mathbf{p}^{\text{T}}(0)\mathbf{J}^{m-1}\right) \quad (3.15)$$

Relation (3.15) coincides with Bienenfeld's (1988) polynomial approximation for $\mathbf{p}^{\text{ST}}$:

(a) It is exact at the extreme values of $\rho$.
(b) For $m \geq 2$, it gives the correct slope of the VPCs at $\rho = 0$. This correct slope is (see Eq. (3.7))

$$\dot{\mathbf{p}}^{\text{ST}}(0) = -\mathbf{\Lambda}_k^{\text{P}}(0) + \dot{\mathbf{\Lambda}}_k^{\text{P}}(0) = -\left(\mathbf{p}^{\text{T}}(0) - \mathbf{p}^{\text{ST}}(1)\right) + \left(\mathbf{p}^{\text{T}}(0)\mathbf{J} - \mathbf{p}^{\text{ST}}(1)\right)$$

or

$$\dot{\mathbf{p}}^{\text{ST}}(0) = -\mathbf{p}^{\text{T}}(0) + \mathbf{p}^{\text{T}}(0)\mathbf{J}$$

(c) Its accuracy is directly related to the rate of convergence in Eq. (3.14), which is, in turn, directly related to the magnitudes of $|\lambda_{\mathbf{J}k}|^{-1}$.

Finally, since

$$w^{-1}\left(\mathbf{p}^{\text{T}}\mathbf{z}\right) = \left(w^{\text{S}}\right)^{-1}\left(\mathbf{p}^{\text{ST}}\mathbf{z}\right)$$

the WPC in terms of commodity $\mathbf{z}$ can be expressed as

$$w = w^{\text{S}}\left(\mathbf{p}^{\text{ST}}\mathbf{z}\right)^{-1}$$

Hence, approximation (3.15), $d_1 = \mathbf{y}_{\mathbf{J}_1}^{\text{T}}\mathbf{z}$ and $\mathbf{p}^{\text{ST}}(1) = \mathbf{y}_{\mathbf{J}_1}^{\text{T}}$ imply that

$$w \approx w^{\text{S}}\left[1 + \sum_{h=1}^{m-1} \rho^h\left(\mathbf{p}^{\text{T}}(0)\mathbf{J}^h - \mathbf{p}^{\text{T}}(0)\mathbf{J}^{h-1}\right)\mathbf{z} + \rho^m\left(d_1 - \mathbf{p}^{\text{T}}(0)\mathbf{J}^{m-1}\mathbf{z}\right)\right]^{-1}$$

The essential characteristics of this approximate WPC are as follows:

i. It is a *proper* rational function of degree $m$, and exact at the extreme values of $\rho$, while its accuracy is directly related to the magnitudes of $|\lambda_{\mathbf{J}k}|^{-1}$.
ii. It gives the correct slope of the WPC at $\rho = 1$ (see Eq. (2.45)). For $m \geq 2$, it gives the correct slope at $\rho = 0$ (see Eq. (2.43)).
iii. For $m \geq 2$, it may admit up to $2m - 1$ inflection points. Setting $m = 1$, it reduces to approximation (3.3). And setting $m = 2$, it reduces to

$$w \approx w^{A} \equiv w^{S}\left[1 + \rho(\mathbf{p}^{T}(0)\mathbf{Jz} - 1) + \rho^{2}(d_{1} - \mathbf{p}^{T}(0)\mathbf{Jz})\right]^{-1} \qquad (3.16)$$

Let $\rho_{\kappa}$, $\kappa = 1, 2, 3$, be the roots of equation $\ddot{w}^{A} = 0$, let $\Delta$ be the discriminant of the numerator of $\ddot{w}^{A}$, and set $\alpha \equiv \mathbf{p}^{T}(0)\mathbf{Jz}$, $\alpha \neq d_{1}$. It is easily checked that

$$\rho_{1}\rho_{2}\rho_{3} = (\alpha^{2} - d_{1})(\alpha - d_{1})^{-2}$$

$$\rho_{1}\rho_{2} + \rho_{1}\rho_{3} + \rho_{2}\rho_{3} = 3\alpha(\alpha - d_{1})^{-1}$$

$$\rho_{1} + \rho_{2} + \rho_{3} = 3$$

$$\Delta = -432d_{1}^{2}\left[(1 + \alpha)^{2} - 4d_{1}\right](\alpha - d_{1})^{4} \qquad (3.17)$$

It then follows that:

(a) All the roots are real and distinct iff $d_{1} > 4^{-1}(1 + \alpha)^{2}$, where $\alpha^{2} < \alpha < 4^{-1}(1 + \alpha)^{2}$ for $0 < \alpha < 1$, while $\alpha < 4^{-1}(1 + \alpha)^{2} < \alpha^{2}$ for $\alpha > 1$.

(b) The second-order approximate curve (3.16) has at most one inflection point in the interval $0 \leq \rho \leq 1$. More specifically, that inflection point occurs when $\alpha < (>)\ 1$ and $d_{1} \geq (\leq)\ 2^{-1}(1 + \alpha)$ or $d_{1} \leq (\geq)\ \alpha^{2}$.

## 3.3  Empirical Evidence

### 3.3.1  Linear Approximations

The application of our analysis to the SIOT of the United Kingdom economy for the year 1990 ($n = 33$), by distinguishing between the cases of circulating and fixed capital (*à la* Leontief–Bródy), gave the following results:[10]

i. In the circulating capital case (CC case hereafter), the normalized $d$–distance between $\mathbf{p}^{ST}(1)$ and $\mathbf{1}^{T}$, and between $\mathbf{p}^{ST}(1)$ and $\mathbf{p}^{T}(0)$ is 0.446 and 0.240, respectively.[11] In the fixed capital case (FC case hereafter), the figures are 0.557 and 0.435, respectively. It then follows that these systems deviate considerably from the equal value compositions of capital case. Moreover, in the CC case the "actual" relative profit rate is 0.310, while in the FC case, it is 0.281.

---

[10]This section is based on Mariolis and Tsoulfidis (2016b). For the available input–output data as well as the construction of the relevant variables, see the Appendix in that paper (pp. 319–320).

[11]In our case, the theoretically maximum value of the $d$– distance is

$$\sqrt{2\left[1 - (\sqrt{n})^{-1}\right]}$$

Thus, the normalized $d$– distance is defined in terms of this maximum value.

ii. The VPCs, expressed in terms of SSC, are in most cases monotonic: there are seven cases (or $7/66 \cong 11\%$ of the cases tested) of non-monotonic value movement (with no more than one extreme point), and three cases (or 5%) of V–VLRs (see Sect. 2.3.3). Both phenomena occur at values of $\rho$ that are greater than the actual one. The graphs in Fig. 3.1 display the $p_j^S (p_j(0))^{-1}$ curves that are non-monotonic. It is thus observed that, in the CC case, industries 5 and 20 (industry 31) are "transmuted" (is "transmuted") into capital (labour)-intensive, relative to the Sraffian Standard system, whereas industry 8 (industry 28) remains capital (labour)-intensive. In the FC case, industries 15 and 30 remain capital-intensive.

iii. Figure 3.2 displays the normalized errors in the linear approximation, i.e.

$$(LP_j - p_j^S)(p_j(0))^{-1} = -NLP_j(p_j(0))^{-1}, \quad j = 1, 2, \ldots, 33$$

as functions of the relative profit rate (see Eq. (3.8)). A visual inspection of Fig. 3.2 reveals that, in both cases, the majority of the errors is concentrated in narrow bands and, therefore, this "crude" approximation is not without some validity (especially in the FC case, where the errors are less than $\pm 0.043$).

It was also found that: (a) Only a single curve, corresponding to industry 2 ("Mining and quarrying") in the CC case, crosses the horizontal axis (at $\rho \cong 0.639$; see the second graph in Fig. 3.2); (b) in the CC case, the means of the absolute normalized errors in this approximation, i.e.

$$MAE_j \equiv \int_0^1 \left| \left( LP_j - p_j^S \right) (p_j(0))^{-1} \right| d\rho$$

are in the range of 0.0003 to 0.089 (the arithmetic mean value is 0.019, and the standard deviation is 0.019); and (c) in the FC case, the $MAE_j$ are in the range of 0.0002 to 0.028 (the arithmetic mean value is 0.008, and the standard deviation is 0.007).

iv. Figure 3.3 displays the WPCs (see Eq. (3.1)) measured in terms of three alternative *numéraires* that are of particular significance, i.e. the actual gross output, net output, and real wage rate vectors, and the $w^S$ curve, which is depicted by a dashed line. This figure also reports the sign of the second derivative, $\ddot{w}$, the maximum absolute deviation from the straight line, max| $w - w^S$|, and the mean value of this deviation,

$$MAD \equiv \int_0^1 \left| (w - w^S) \right| d\rho$$

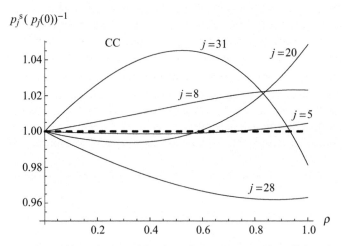

$j = 5$ ("Wood products and furniture"), 8 ("Drugs and medicines"),
20 ("Other transport"), 28 ("Restaurants and hotels") and 31 ("Finance and insurance")

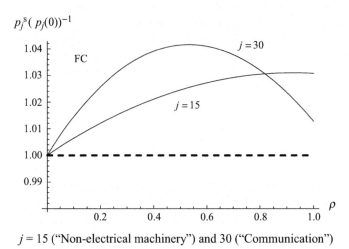

$j = 15$ ("Non-electrical machinery") and 30 ("Communication")

**Fig. 3.1** The non-monotonic normalized value–relative profit rate curves: UK economy, year 1990

It is thus observed that there is only one inflection point, which occurs at a "low" value of $\rho$ and, in fact, less than the actual one, while, as experiments showed, the relevant value effects, in the six cases already examined, are relatively weak and, therefore, for "*low*" values of $\rho$, we can safely write

$$w = 1 - \mathbf{p}^{\mathrm{T}}\mathbf{J}\mathbf{z} \approx 1 - \mathbf{p}^{\mathrm{T}}(0)\mathbf{J}\mathbf{z}$$

(see Eqs. (2.37) and (2.40)).

$(\mathrm{LP}_j - p_j^S)(p_j(0))^{-1}$

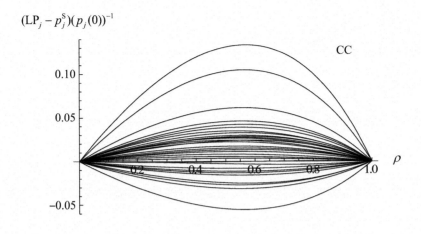

$(\mathrm{LP}_2 - p_2^S)(p_2(0))^{-1}$

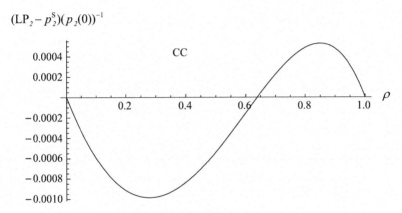

$(\mathrm{LP}_j - p_j^S)(p_j(0))^{-1}$

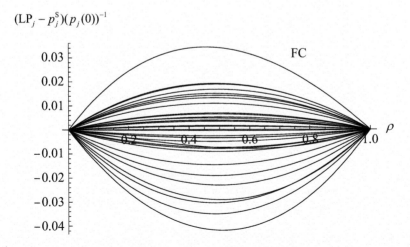

**Fig. 3.2** The normalized errors in the linear approximation of values as functions of the relative profit rate: UK economy, year 1990

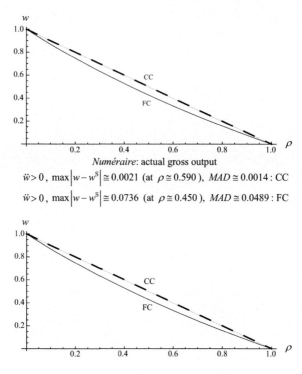

*Numéraire*: actual gross output

$\ddot{w} > 0$, $\max\left|w - w^S\right| \cong 0.0021$ (at $\rho \cong 0.590$), $MAD \cong 0.0014$ : CC

$\ddot{w} > 0$, $\max\left|w - w^S\right| \cong 0.0736$ (at $\rho \cong 0.450$), $MAD \cong 0.0489$ : FC

*Numéraire*: actual net output

$\ddot{w} < (>) \ 0$ for $\rho < (>) \rho^* \cong 0.164$, $\max\left|w - w^S\right| \cong 0.0022$ (at $\rho \cong 0.630$), $MAD \cong 0.0014$ : CC

$\ddot{w} > 0$, $\max\left|w - w^S\right| \cong 0.0443$ (at $\rho \cong 0.460$), $MAD \cong 0.0294$ : FC

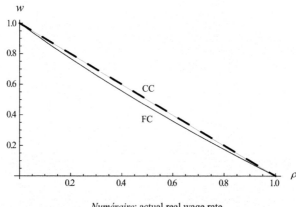

*Numéraire*: actual real wage rate

$\ddot{w} > 0$, $\max\left|w - w^S\right| \cong 0.0020$ (at $\rho \cong 0.380$), $MAD \cong 0.0012$ : CC

$\ddot{w} > 0$, $\max\left|w - w^S\right| \cong 0.0312$ (at $\rho \cong 0.450$), $MAD \cong 0.0207$ : FC

**Fig. 3.3** The wage–relative profit rate curves in terms of composite commodities: UK economy, year 1990

Further experiments, with all the individual commodities as *numéraires*, gave somewhat similar results. For instance, consider Figure 3.4, which displays the deviations of the WPCs, measured in terms of individual commodity $j$, from the $w^S$ curve as functions of $\rho$. It is added that, in the CC case, (a) the WPCs in terms of commodities $j = 5, 20$, and 31 cross (as expected) the $w^S$ curve at the points where occur V–VLRs (see the relevant graphs in Figs. 3.1 and 3.4), while an inflection point appears on each WPC for $0.57 < \rho < 0.70$, i.e. at values of $\rho$ which are greater than the actual one; (b) an inflection point also appears on the WPCs in terms of commodities $j = 6$ ("Paper, paper products and printing"), 11 ("Non-metallic mineral products"), and 22 ("Aircraft"), for $0.10 < \rho < 0.30$, i.e. at values of $\rho$ which are less than the actual one; (c) the maximum value of $\max|w^j - w^S|$ is 0.140 (for $j = 13$ ("Non-ferrous metals") and 23 ("Professional goods"); the relevant *MADs* are 0.092); and (d) the areas under the WPCs are in the range of 0.408 to 0.593 (the arithmetic mean value is 0.490, and the standard deviation is 0.049). In the FC case, (a) an inflection point appears on the WPCs in terms of commodities $j = 19$ ("Shipbuilding and repairing"), 21 ("Motor vehicles"), 28 and 29 ("Transport and storage"); for $j = 19$, 21, and 28 it occurs at $\rho \cong 0.25, 0.25$, and 0.22, respectively, i.e. at values of $\rho$ which are less than the actual one, while for $j = 29$, it occurs at $\rho \cong 0.32$, i.e. at a value of $\rho$ which is greater than the actual one; (b) the maximum value of $\max|w^j - w^S|$ is 0.310 (for $j = 2$ ; the relevant *MAD* is 0.201); and (c) the areas under the WPCs are in the range of 0.299 to 0.643 (the arithmetic mean value is 0.487, and the standard deviation is 0.083).

Summing up, the WPCs alternate in curvature in eleven cases (or $11/72 \cong 15\%$ of the cases tested), in 7 cases (or 10 %) the inflection point occurs at values of $\rho$ which are less than the actual one, while it has not been found any case where the curvature switches more than once.

v. All the above findings clearly suggest that the actual economy under consideration behaves as a low-dimensional economy, that is, with no more than three industries. This statement *per se* refers to the economically relevant interval of $\rho$, and relies on the detected monotonicity of the VPCs and inflection points of the WPCs, not on the near-linearity of the latter curves (even in controllable of rank 2 economies, the WPC may deviate considerably from the straight line; see Eqs. (3.5) and (3.6)).

As the spectral Eqs. (3.1) and (3.2) indicate, this experimental finding, which is in line with the overall available empirical evidence on the topic, can be connected to the characteristic value distributions of matrices **J**. Thus, Figs. 3.5 and 3.6 (the horizontal axes are plotted in logarithmic scale) display the moduli of the eigenvalues and the normalized singular values, $\sigma_{Ji}\sigma_{J1}^{-1}$, respectively, as well as the relevant arithmetic (*AM*) and geometric (*GM*) means of the non-zero non-dominant values, and the indexes of inseparability (see Eq. (3.11)). It is noted that:

(a) As is well known, the geometric mean is more appropriate for detecting the central tendency of an exponential set of numbers. In our case, it can be written as

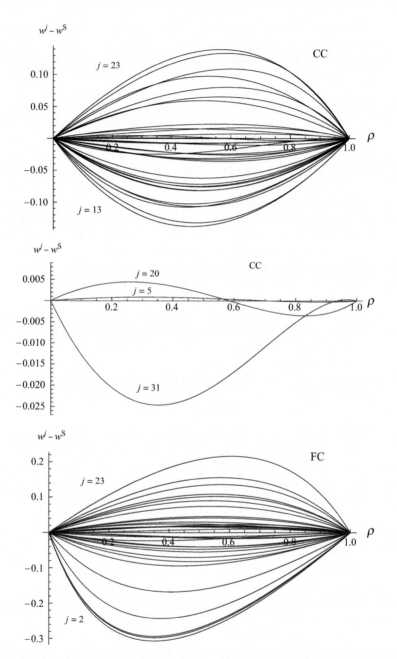

**Fig. 3.4** The deviations of the wage–relative profit rate curves, in terms of individual commodities, from the straight line as functions of the relative profit rate: UK economy, year 1990

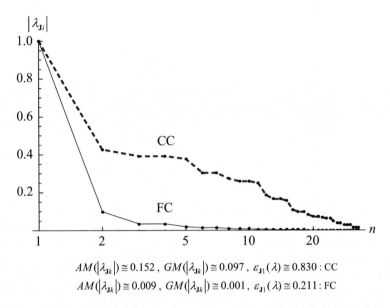

$$AM(|\lambda_{Jk}|) \cong 0.152, \ GM(|\lambda_{Jk}|) \cong 0.097, \ \varepsilon_{J1}(\lambda) \cong 0.830 : CC$$
$$AM(|\lambda_{Jk}|) \cong 0.009, \ GM(|\lambda_{Jk}|) \cong 0.001, \ \varepsilon_{J1}(\lambda) \cong 0.211 : FC$$

**Fig. 3.5** The moduli of the eigenvalues of the normalized vertically integrated technical coefficients matrices: UK economy, year 1990

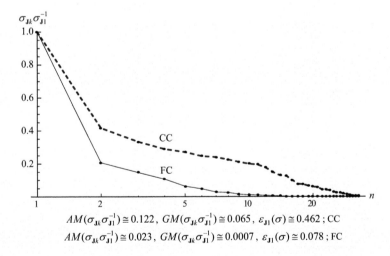

$$AM(\sigma_{Jk}\sigma_{J1}^{-1}) \cong 0.122, \ GM(\sigma_{Jk}\sigma_{J1}^{-1}) \cong 0.065, \ \varepsilon_{J1}(\sigma) \cong 0.462 ; CC$$
$$AM(\sigma_{Jk}\sigma_{J1}^{-1}) \cong 0.023, \ GM(\sigma_{Jk}\sigma_{J1}^{-1}) \cong 0.0007, \ \varepsilon_{J1}(\sigma) \cong 0.078 ; FC$$

**Fig. 3.6** The normalized singular values of the normalized vertically integrated technical coefficients matrices: UK economy, year 1990

$$GM = |\det[\mathbf{J}]|^{(n-1)^{-1}} = \left(\prod_{i=1}^{n} \sigma_{\mathbf{J}i}\right)^{(n-1)^{-1}}$$

(b) We define the index of inseparability associated with the P–F eigenvalue or, in other words, with the linear approximation for the value vector as

$$\varepsilon_{\mathbf{J}1}(\lambda) \equiv 1 - \lambda_{\mathbf{J}1}\left(\sum_{i=1}^{n} |\lambda_{\mathbf{J}i}|\right)^{-1} = 1 - \left(1 + \sum_{k=2}^{n} |\lambda_{\mathbf{J}k}|\right)^{-1}$$

Moreover, it is interesting to remark that the modulus of the second eigenvalue (that the second normalized singular value) of the FC model is much lower than that of the CC model, i.e. 0.099 (0.207) versus 0.427 (0.417). This finding is closely related to the fact that the matrix of capital stock coefficients, $\mathbf{A}^C$, which contains many zero and near-zero elements, imposes its reducibility form *and* spectral attributes onto the matrix $\mathbf{H}^C \equiv \mathbf{A}^C[\mathbf{I} - \mathbf{A}]^{-1}$. This claim may be ascertained by merely comparing the graphs and the levels of the indexes in Figs. 3.5 and 3.6 with those in Fig. 3.7, which displays the moduli of the normalized eigenvalues and the normalized singular values of $\mathbf{A}^C$ (the horizontal axis is plotted in logarithmic scale). The Sylvester rank inequality implies that

$$rank\left[\mathbf{A}^C\right] + rank[\mathbf{I} - \mathbf{A}] - n \leq rank\left[\mathbf{H}^C\right] \leq \min\left\{rank\left[\mathbf{A}^C\right], rank[\mathbf{I} - \mathbf{A}]\right\}$$

and, in our case,

$$rank[\mathbf{A}^C] = 30, \quad |\lambda_{\mathbf{A}^C 2}||\lambda_{\mathbf{A}^C 1}^{-1}| \cong 0.285, \quad |\lambda_{\mathbf{A}^C 3,4}||\lambda_{\mathbf{A}^C 1}^{-1}| \cong 0.055,$$

$$\sigma_{\mathbf{A}^C 2}\sigma_{\mathbf{A}^C 1}^{-1} \cong 0.302, \quad \sigma_{\mathbf{A}^C 3}\sigma_{\mathbf{A}^C 1}^{-1} \cong 0.236,$$

$rank[\mathbf{H}^C] = 30$, $rank[\mathbf{I} - \mathbf{A}] = 33$. Thus, matrix $\mathbf{H}^C$ is reducible without self-reproducing non-basics, and the decay of its trailing characteristic values is remarkably faster than that of the characteristic values of $\mathbf{H} \equiv \mathbf{A}[\mathbf{I} - \mathbf{A}]^{-1}$. These characteristic value configurations indicate that the *effective* dimensions of the system matrices are relatively low and, therefore, our statements about the shapes of the value–wage–profit rate curves of the UK economy would not be so sensitive to the *numéraire* choice.

vi. Having established that

$$\mathbf{J}^A \equiv \left(\mathbf{y}_{\mathbf{J}1}^T\mathbf{x}_{\mathbf{J}1}\right)^{-1}\mathbf{x}_{\mathbf{J}1}\mathbf{y}_{\mathbf{J}1}^T$$

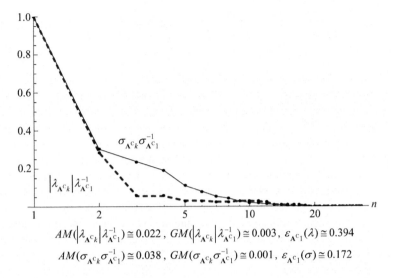

$$AM(\left|\lambda_{A^{c_k}}\right|\lambda_{A^{c_1}}^{-1}) \cong 0.022, \ GM(\left|\lambda_{A^{c_k}}\right|\lambda_{A^{c_1}}^{-1}) \cong 0.003, \ \varepsilon_{A^{c_1}}(\lambda) \cong 0.394$$

$$AM(\sigma_{A^{c_k}}\sigma_{A^{c_1}}^{-1}) \cong 0.038, \ GM(\sigma_{A^{c_k}}\sigma_{A^{c_1}}^{-1}) \cong 0.001, \ \varepsilon_{A^{c_1}}(\sigma) \cong 0.172$$

**Fig. 3.7** The moduli of the normalized eigenvalues, and the normalized singular values of the capital stock coefficients matrix: UK economy, year 1990

is a good *first* approximation of $\mathbf{J}$, in the sense that both matrices give rise to VPCs close to each other, we shall focus on the FC case and apply the Schur decomposition (see Eq. (2.64)) to these matrices. It then follows that:

(a). Consider the triangular, semi-positive, and rank-1 matrix

$$\mathbf{J}^{A*} \equiv \mathbf{T}^{-1}\mathbf{J}^A\mathbf{T} = \mathbf{T}^{-1}[\mathbf{J} - \mathbf{E}]\mathbf{T}$$

where

$$\mathbf{E} \equiv \sum_{k=2}^{n} \lambda_{Jk} \left(\mathbf{y}_{Jk}^{T}\mathbf{x}_{Jk}\right)^{-1} \mathbf{x}_{Jk}\mathbf{y}_{Jk}^{T}$$

is the error matrix (see Eq. (2.66)), and

$$\mathbf{T} \equiv [\mathbf{x}_{J1}, \mathbf{e}_2, \dots, \mathbf{e}_n]$$

is the similarity matrix. The first row of $\mathbf{J}^{A*}$ is

| 1.000 | 0.792 | 0.355 | 0.302 | 0.297 | 0.362 | 0.463 | 0.384 | 0.654 | 0.370 | 0.356 |
|-------|-------|-------|-------|-------|-------|-------|-------|-------|-------|-------|
| 0.350 | 0.321 | 0.345 | 0.305 | 0.463 | 0.346 | 0.348 | 0.535 | 0.331 | 0.432 | 0.227 |
| 0.292 | 0.284 | 0.673 | 0.279 | 0.345 | 0.283 | 0.374 | 0.346 | 0.455 | 1.234 | 0.420 |

(b). The first row of the non-triangular, non-semi-positive and rank-30 matrix $\mathbf{J}^* \equiv \mathbf{T}^{-1}\mathbf{J}\mathbf{T}$ is

| 1.000 | 0.791 | 0.336 | 0.276 | 0.299 | 0.375 | 0.366 | 0.302 | 0.555 | 0.309 | 0.286 |
| 0.302 | 0.283 | 0.296 | 0.295 | 0.358 | 0.293 | 0.318 | 0.346 | 0.280 | 0.337 | 0.208 |
| 0.281 | 0.265 | 0.715 | 0.290 | 0.382 | 0.391 | 0.425 | 0.205 | 0.550 | 1.575 | 0.694 |

(c). The Euclidean norm of the difference between these rows is 0.585. The spectral norm of matrix $\mathbf{J}^* - \mathbf{J}^{A*}$ is 0.760, while that of matrix $\mathbf{J} - \mathbf{J}^A$ is 0.631.

Since, on the one hand, $\mathbf{J}^A$ is a good approximation of $\mathbf{J}$ , and on the other hand, the first row of $\mathbf{J}^{A*}$ is a good approximation of the first row of $\mathbf{J}^*$, it follows that the essential value–profit rate-information embedded in the original-actual economy is captured by the first row of $\mathbf{J}^*$ and extracted in the first row of $\mathbf{J}^{A*}$. Hence, the controllable of rank 2 economy, defined by the rank-1 matrix $\mathbf{J}^{A*}$, and producing a pure capital good (which is no more than SSC) and $n - 1$ pure consumption goods, tends to be a fairly representative simulacrum of the actual economy.

Finally, the same holds true for the singular value decomposition rank-one approximation matrix of $\mathbf{J}$ (Eq. (3.10)), with $\nu = 1$): consider the triangular, semi-positive, normalized, and rank-1 matrix

$$\overline{\mathbf{J}}^{A*} \equiv \overline{\mathbf{T}}^{-1}\left(\lambda_{\overline{\mathbf{J}}^A_1}^{-1}\overline{\mathbf{J}}^A\right)\overline{\mathbf{T}}$$

where

$$\overline{\mathbf{T}} = [\mathbf{x}_{\overline{\mathbf{J}}^A_1}, \mathbf{e}_2, \ldots, \mathbf{e}_n], \quad \lambda_{\overline{\mathbf{J}}^A_1} \cong 0.973$$

The first row of $\overline{\mathbf{J}}^{A*}$ is

| 1.000 | 0.799 | 0.371 | 0.313 | 0.320 | 0.402 | 0.405 | 0.360 | 0.605 | 0.356 | 0.321 |
| 0.329 | 0.304 | 0.324 | 0.314 | 0.414 | 0.322 | 0.340 | 0.488 | 0.302 | 0.378 | 0.214 |
| 0.295 | 0.293 | 0.720 | 0.295 | 0.376 | 0.360 | 0.423 | 0.248 | 0.532 | 1.414 | 0.602 |

The Euclidean norm of the difference between this row and the first row of $\mathbf{J}^*$ is 0.286. The spectral norm of matrix $\mathbf{J}^* - \overline{\mathbf{J}}^{A*}$ is 0.627, while that of matrix $\mathbf{J} - \lambda_{\overline{\mathbf{J}}^A_1}^{-1}\overline{\mathbf{J}}^A$ is 0.548.

### 3.3.2  Higher-Order Approximations

The test of the second-order approximate WPC (Eq. (3.16)), measured in terms of the actual real wage rate vector, with data from ten flow SIOTs of the Greek economy ($n = 19$), spanning the period 1988–1997, gave the results summarized in Table 3.1.[12] This table reports:

i. The actual relative profit rates, $\rho^a$.
ii. The actual, $\rho^*$, and the estimated, $\rho^{*e}$, values of $\rho$, $0 \le \rho \le 1$, at which the inflection points occur.
iii. The signs of the discriminant, $\Delta$, and of $1 - \alpha$ (see Eq. (3.17)).
iv. The mean of the absolute error in this approximation, i.e.

$$MAE \equiv \int\limits_0^1 \left|w - w^A\right| d\rho$$

v. The Euclidean angles (measured in degrees) between $\mathbf{p}^{ST}(1)$ and $\mathbf{p}^T(0)\mathbf{J}^m$, $m = 0$, 1, 2, which are denoted by $\theta_m$.
vi. The modulus of the first two non-dominant eigenvalues, $|\lambda_{J2}|$, $|\lambda_{J3}|$, and the arithmetic ($AM$) and geometric ($GM$) means of the moduli of the non-dominant eigenvalues.

**Table 3.1** Indicators and determinants of the accuracy of the second-order approximate wage–relative profit rate curve: Greek economy, 1988–1997

| | 1988 | 1989 | 1990 | 1991 | 1992 | 1993 | 1994 | 1995 | 1996 | 1997 |
|---|---|---|---|---|---|---|---|---|---|---|
| $\rho^a$ | 0.411 | 0.414 | 0.399 | 0.409 | 0.420 | 0.388 | 0.421 | 0.419 | 0.423 | 0.438 |
| $\rho^*$ | 0.269 | 0.300 | 0.360 | 0.302 | 0.534 | 0.385 | 0.336 | 0.110 | 0.200 | – ($\ddot{w} < 0$) |
| $\rho^{*e}$ | 0.275 | 0.298 | 0.311 | 0.299 | 0.410 | 0.325 | 0.302 | 0.216 | 0.247 | 0.136 |
| $\Delta$ | <0 | <0 | <0 | <0 | <0 | <0 | <0 | <0 | <0 | <0 |
| $1 - \alpha$ | >0 | >0 | >0 | >0 | <0 | >0 | >0 | >0 | >0 | >0 |
| $MAE$ | 0.007 | 0.009 | 0.008 | 0.007 | 0.004 | 0.007 | 0.008 | 0.006 | 0.006 | 0.005 |
| $\theta_0$ | 29.3 ° | 31.1 ° | 30.4 ° | 30.0 ° | 25.3 ° | 26.5 ° | 27.8 ° | 28.1 ° | 27.3 ° | 26.4 ° |
| $\theta_1$ | 15.0° | 16.6 ° | 15.7 ° | 14.8 ° | 10.3 ° | 13.3 ° | 13.7 ° | 13.1 ° | 12.5 ° | 10.8 ° |
| $\theta_2$ | 6.4 ° | 8.3 ° | 7.7 ° | 7.2 ° | 4.3 ° | 6.7 ° | 6.9 ° | 5.9 ° | 5.7 ° | 4.7 ° |
| $|\lambda_{J2}|$ | 0.643 | 0.683 | 0.675 | 0.657 | 0.624 | 0.667 | 0.678 | 0.655 | 0.664 | 0.641 |
| $|\lambda_{J3}|$ | 0.416 | 0.436 | 0.418 | 0.397 | 0.443 | 0.433 | 0.420 | 0.390 | 0.390 | 0.350 |
| $AM$ | 0.168 | 0.175 | 0.176 | 0.176 | 0.185 | 0.174 | 0.171 | 0.161 | 0.167 | 0.157 |
| $GM$ | 0.086 | 0.086 | 0.088 | 0.087 | 0.089 | 0.081 | 0.088 | 0.074 | 0.074 | 0.073 |

---

[12]This section is based on Mariolis (2015b), Mariolis and Tsoulfidis (2011, pp. 113–115). For the available input–output data as well as the construction of the relevant variables, see Tsoulfidis and Mariolis (2007, pp. 435–437), Mariolis (2013, p. 5199).

From these findings, the associated numerical results and the hitherto analysis, we conclude that:

i. Although the systems deviate considerably from the equal value compositions of capital case (consider the values of $\theta_0$), the approximation works pretty well. With the exception of the year 1997, both curves switch from convex to concave at "adjacent" values of the relative profit rate (the errors $|\rho^{*e} - \rho^*|$ are in the range of 0.002 to 0.124), and the *MAEs* are no greater than 0.010. The graphs in Fig. 3.8 are sufficiently representative and display the actual (depicted by a solid line) and the approximate (depicted by a dotted line) WPCs for the years 1989 (where *MAE*, $\theta_m$ and $|\lambda_{J2}|$ exhibit their highest values) and 1997 (where $\ddot{w} < 0$).

ii. In all systems, $\mathbf{p}^T(0)\mathbf{J}^m$ tend quickly to $\mathbf{p}^{ST}(1)$, and the moduli of the first non-dominant eigenvalues fall quite rapidly, whereas the rest constellate in much lower values, forming a "long tail". In fact, as it has already been pointed out (Mariolis and Tsoulfidis 2011, pp. 104–105), the moduli of the eigenvalues follow an exponential pattern of the form

$$y = \gamma_0 + \gamma_1 \exp(x^{-0.2}), \quad \gamma_0 < 0, \quad \gamma_1 > 0$$

where $y$ stands for the moduli of the eigenvalues, whereas $x$ stands for the respective ranking of the moduli, and $\gamma_0, \gamma_1$ are parameters to be estimated; in the present case, $-1.738 \leq \gamma_0 \leq -1.827$, $0.986 \leq \gamma_1 \leq 1.040$ and the R-squared are in the range of 0.975 to 0.991. These findings indicate that the accuracy of this second-order approximation would *not* be so sensitive to the *numéraire* choice.

Finally, in terms of SSC, there are thirty-six (or 36/190 $\cong$ 19%) VPCs that are non-monotonic (with one extreme point), and twenty-nine cases (or 15 %) of V–VLRs, while both phenomena do not always occur at values of $\rho$ that are greater than the actual one (Tsoulfidis and Mariolis 2007, p. 432). For instance, the graphs in Fig. 3.9 correspond to the year 1994, and display the actual normalized non-monotonic VPCs (depicted by solid lines), their third-order eigenvalue decomposition approximation (depicted by dotted lines; see Eq. (3.9), with $\nu = 3$),[13] and, finally, their Bienenfeld's quadratic approximation (depicted by dashed lines; see Eq. (3.15), with $m = 2$). Moreover, in Table 3.2 we report (i) the actual and approximate values of $\rho$ at which occur extreme points and V–VLRs and (ii) the mean of the relative error (*MRE*) between approximate and actual curves. It is thus observed that both approximations work well.

It should, however, be added that, in terms of the corresponding actual net output vectors, there are in total three VPCs that display *two* extreme points (and the total number of non-monotonic VPCs is forty-four or 23%; Mariolis 2015a, pp. 271–274).

---

[13]The non-linear terms have no more than one extreme point.

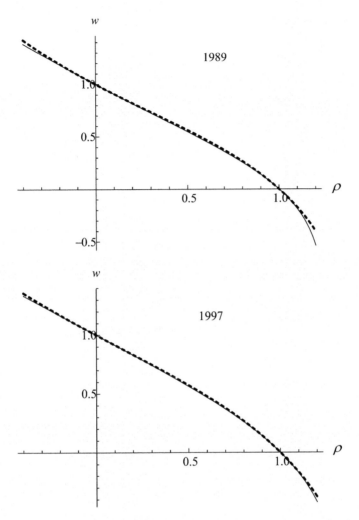

**Fig. 3.8** Actual and second-order approximate wage–relative profit rate curves, measured in terms of the actual real wage rate vector: Greek economy, years 1989 and 1997

### 3.3.3 Controllability Characteristics

To look deeper into the key stylized findings of the empirical studies, we will deal with data from ten flow SIOTs of five European economies, i.e. Denmark (for the years 2000 and 2004; $n = 56$), Finland (for the years 1995 and 2004; $n = 57$), France (for the years 1995, $n = 58$, and 2005, $n = 57$), Germany (for the years 2000 and 2002; $n = 57$), and Sweden (for the years 1995, $n = 53$, and 2005, $n = 51$).[14] These

---

[14]This section is based on Mariolis (2019, pp. 19–22; 2021).

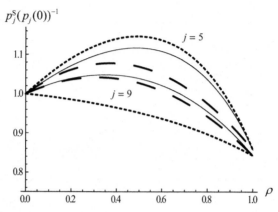

$j = 5$ ("Food products and beverage and tobacco products") and 9 ("Manufacture of coke")

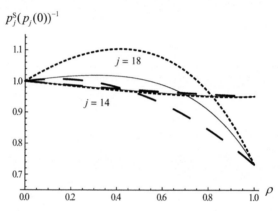

$j = 14$ ("Machinery and equipment") and 18 ("Hotel and restaurant services")

**Fig. 3.9** Actual normalized non-monotonic value–profit rate curves, third-order eigenvalue decomposition approximation, and Bienenfeld's quadratic approximation: Greek economy, year 1994

**Table 3.2** Accuracy indicators of the third-order eigenvalue decomposition and Bienenfeld's quadratic approximations for the non-monotonic value curves: Greek economy, 1994

|  | $j = 5$ | $j = 9$ | $j = 14$ | $j = 18$ |
|---|---|---|---|---|
| Actual |  |  |  |  |
| Extreme point | 0.488 | 0.352 | 0.938 | 0.313 |
| V–VLR | 0.856 | 0.680 | > 1 | 0.546 |
| $\nu = 3$ |  |  |  |  |
| Extreme point | 0.491 | > 1 | 0.902 | 0.415 |
| V–VLR | 0.874 | > 1 | > 1 | 0.754 |
| MRE | 1.8% | 5.7% | 0.2% | 6.2% |
| $m = 2$ |  |  |  |  |
| Extreme point | 0.373 | 0.315 | > 1 | 0.137 |
| V–VLR | 0.746 | 0.629 | > 1 | 0.274 |
| MRE | 3.3% | 0.8% | 0.3% | 3.8% |

SIOTs have been firstly used by Iliadi et al. (2014), and their basic findings are as follows:

i. Non-monotonic VPCs, expressed in terms of SSC, are observed in about 105/559 or 19% of the tested cases. There is no VPC with more than one extreme point.
ii. Bienenfeld's quadratic approximation for $\mathbf{p}^{ST}$ works extremely well. More specifically, (a) the arithmetic means of the means of the relative errors between the actual and the approximate VPCs are in the range of 0.30% to 7.10%; and (b) there are statistically significant relationships between the distribution of $|\lambda_{\mathbf{J}k}|$ and indicators of the accuracy of Bienenfeld's approximation.
iii. The effective dimensions of the actual economies under consideration are between 2 and 3.

Since the findings are in absolute accordance with those detected in other studies of quite diverse actual single-product economies, this data sample could be considered as sufficiently representative. Hence, in Table 3.3 we report:

i. The normalized $d$–distances between $\mathbf{p}^{ST}(1)$ and $\mathbf{l}^T$, and between $\mathbf{p}^{ST}(1)$ and $\mathbf{p}^T(0)$, which are denoted by $ND_{\mathrm{I}}$ and $ND_{\mathrm{II}}$, respectively.
ii. $|\lambda_{\mathbf{J}2}|$, $|\lambda_{\mathbf{J}3}|$, $|\lambda_{\mathbf{J}n}|$, the arithmetic ($AM$) and the geometric ($GM$) means of the moduli of the non-dominant eigenvalues of $\mathbf{J}$ (reproduced from Iliadi et al. 2014, pp. 42 and 43, respectively).
iii. The ratio between the smallest and the largest singular values, $\sigma_{\mathbf{J}n}\sigma_{\mathbf{J}1}^{-1}$, of $\mathbf{J}$.
iv. The numbers of non-monotonic VPCs and of V–VLRs, denoted by "N-M" and "Rev.", respectively. It then follows that, in total, there are 63/559 or 11% cases of V–VLRs.
v. The absolute values of the determinant of the value controllability matrices, $\mathbf{K}$, (see Sect. 2.3.2) and of the determinant of the Vandermonde matrices, $\mathbf{V}$, of the eigenvalues of $\mathbf{J}$ (see Eqs. (2.16) and (2.17)).
vi. The degree of controllability, $DC \equiv \sigma_{\mathbf{K}n}\sigma_{\mathbf{K}1}^{-1}$ (Eq. (2.18)).
vii. The relative or normalized numerical rank of controllability, $NNRC$, defined as

$$NNRC(\bar{\tau}) \equiv 100n^{-1}NR(\mathbf{K}, \bar{\tau})$$

where $NR(\mathbf{K}, \bar{\tau})$ denotes the numerical rank of $\mathbf{K}$, i.e. the number of singular values of $\mathbf{K}$ that are larger than $\bar{\tau}\sigma_{\mathbf{K}1}$, and $\bar{\tau}$ denotes the chosen level of tolerance.
viii. The largest "spread", $\min\{\sigma_{\mathbf{K}h}^{-1}\sigma_{\mathbf{K}h+1}\}$, $h = 1, 2, \ldots, n - 1$, between two consecutive singular values of $\mathbf{K}$, the spectral norm, $\|\mathbf{C}_{\mathbf{J}}\|_2$, of the Frobenius companion matrix of $\mathbf{J}$, and the relevant upper bound for the distance, $d(\mathbf{J}, \mathbf{p}^T(0))$, to the nearest uncontrollable value system (see relation (2.19) and Example 2.2).

Finally, Fig. 3.10 (reproduced from Iliadi et al. 2014, p. 45) displays the location of the eigenvalues of all matrices $\mathbf{J}$ in the complex plane; Fig. 3.11 (the horizontal

**Table 3.3** Spectral and controllability characteristics of actual economies: five European economies, ten Symmetric Input–Output Tables

| | Denmark | | Finland | | France | | Germany | | Sweden | |
|---|---|---|---|---|---|---|---|---|---|---|
| | 2000 $n=56$ | 2004 $n=56$ | 1995 $n=57$ | 2004 $n=57$ | 1995 $n=58$ | 2005 $n=57$ | 2000 $n=57$ | 2002 $n=57$ | 1995 $n=53$ | 2005 $n=51$ |
| $ND_{\mathrm{I}}$ | 0.686 | 0.792 | 0.838 | 0.915 | 0.782 | 0.801 | 0.731 | 0.729 | 0.765 | 0.923 |
| $ND_{\mathrm{II}}$ | 0.419 | 0.502 | 0.557 | 0.729 | 0.478 | 0.483 | 0.472 | 0.485 | 0.408 | 0.404 |
| $|\lambda_{J2}|$ | 0.522 | 0.638 | 0.597 | 0.850 | 0.611 | 0.588 | 0.570 | 0.610 | 0.532 | 0.422 |
| $|\lambda_{J3}|$ | 0.486 | 0.502 | 0.433 | 0.503 | 0.529 | 0.453 | 0.497 | 0.516 | 0.434 | 0.390 |
| $|\lambda_{Jn}|$ | $6 \times 10^{-4}$ | $1 \times 10^{-3}$ | $1 \times 10^{-3}$ | $3 \times 10^{-4}$ | $3 \times 10^{-5}$ | $1 \times 10^{-3}$ | $1 \times 10^{-3}$ | $6 \times 10^{-3}$ | $3 \times 10^{-3}$ | $9 \times 10^{-4}$ |
| $AM$ | 0.118 | 0.108 | 0.100 | 0.103 | 0.131 | 0.128 | 0.178 | 0.178 | 0.098 | 0.099 |
| $GM$ | 0.069 | 0.065 | 0.047 | 0.047 | 0.059 | 0.076 | 0.106 | 0.111 | 0.050 | 0.052 |
| $\sigma_{Jn}\sigma_{J1}^{-1}$ | $9 \times 10^{-5}$ | $1 \times 10^{-3}$ | $1 \times 10^{-3}$ | $5 \times 10^{-5}$ | $10^{-5}$ | $2 \times 10^{-4}$ | $9 \times 10^{-5}$ | $4 \times 10^{-4}$ | $5 \times 10^{-4}$ | $10^{-4}$ |
| N-M | 13 (23%) | 18 (32%) | 9 (16%) | 13 (23%) | 11 (19%) | 8 (14%) | 9 (16%) | 7 (12%) | 11 (21%) | 6 (12%) |
| Rev. | 5 (9%) | 13 (23%) | 6 (11%) | 13 (23%) | 6 (10%) | 2 (4%) | 7 (12%) | 3 (5%) | 5 (9%) | 3 (6%) |
| $|\det[\mathbf{K}]|$ | $10^{-782}$ | $10^{-793}$ | $10^{-727}$ | $10^{-740}$ | $10^{-741}$ | $4 \times 10^{-744}$ | $10^{-728}$ | $10^{-722}$ | $2 \times 10^{-727}$ | $6 \times 10^{-721}$ |
| $|\det[\mathbf{V}]|$ | $2 \times 10^{-647}$ | $3 \times 10^{-657}$ | $3 \times 10^{-674}$ | $2 \times 10^{-674}$ | $3 \times 10^{-681}$ | $2 \times 10^{-672}$ | $1 \times 10^{-659}$ | $4 \times 10^{-646}$ | $3 \times 10^{-610}$ | $3 \times 10^{-591}$ |
| $DC$ | $6 \times 10^{-19}$ | $6 \times 10^{-19}$ | $8 \times 10^{-19}$ | $1 \times 10^{-19}$ | $5 \times 10^{-19}$ | $8 \times 10^{-19}$ | $9 \times 10^{-20}$ | $6 \times 10^{-19}$ | $5 \times 10^{-19}$ | $3 \times 10^{-20}$ |
| $NNRC(10^{-4})$ | 9% | 11% | 11% | 11% | 10% | 11% | 11% | 11% | 9% | 10% |
| $NNRC(10^{-2})$ | 5% | 5% | 5% | 7% | 5% | 5% | 5% | 5% | 6% | 6% |
| $\min\{\sigma_{Kih}\sigma_{Kih+1}\}$ | 0.062 | 0.076 | 0.088 | 0.065 | 0.061 | 0.061 | 0.046 | 0.059 | 0.058 | 0.025 |
| $\|\mathbf{C}_J\|_2$ | 98.772 | 65.568 | 61.543 | 74.761 | 401.115 | 326.957 | 2235.710 | 2048.705 | 37.710 | 36.686 |
| $d(\mathbf{J},\mathbf{p}^{\mathrm{T}}(0))$ | 6.178 | 5.027 | 5.431 | 4.867 | 25.085 | 20.211 | 103.437 | 120.886 | 2.194 | 0.910 |

**Fig. 3.10** The complex plane location of the eigenvalues of all normalized vertically integrated technical coefficients matrices: five European economies, ten Symmetric Input–Output Tables

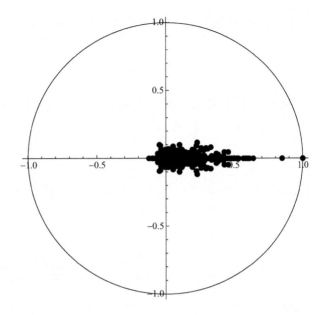

axis is plotted in logarithmic scale) displays the normalized singular values, $\sigma_{Kj}\sigma_{K1}^{-1}$, of all matrices $\mathbf{K}$; and, as an illustration, Fig. 3.12 displays the singular value spreads, $\sigma_{Kh}^{-1}\sigma_{Kh+1}$, for the German (for the year 2002) and Swedish (for the year 2005) economies.

### 3.3.4 Evaluation

From all these results, it is deduced that:

i. Non-monotonic VPCs appear when the value and the capital-intensity effects work in opposite directions, and the former dominate the latter. Moreover, the WPCs curves can alternate in curvature, even when the value effect along these curves is weak. Finally, the V–VLRs (a) imply that the identification of a vertically integrated industry as "labour (or capital)-intensive" makes no a priori sense; and (b) are analogous to the re-switching of techniques phenomenon and, therefore, indicate that there is no reason to consider that the empirical probability of this phenomenon is negligible. Since actual economies exhibit non-monotonic VPCs, WPCs with alternating curvature and V–VLRs, they cannot be coherently analysed in terms of the traditional value theory.

ii. There is a not insignificant number of studies that cast doubt on the empirical importance of re-switching in terms of either WPCs constructed from SIOTs for different years and/or the outer envelope of the WPCs corresponding to different countries and years (as if the available SIOTs belong to a uniform, across space

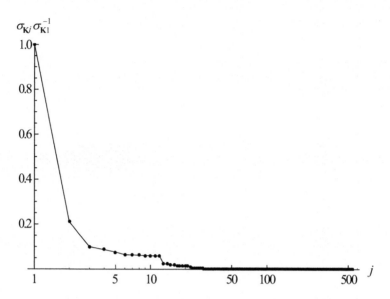

**Fig. 3.11** The normalized singular values of all value controllability matrices: five European economies, ten Symmetric Input–Output Tables

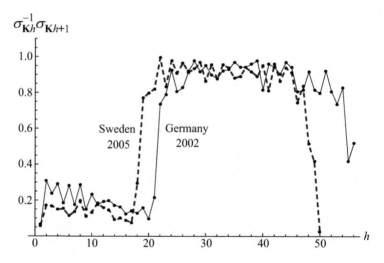

**Fig. 3.12** The singular value spreads of the value controllability matrices: German (year 2002) and Swedish (year 2005) economies

and time, technology). It should be remembered, however, that, as Kurz and Salvadori (1995, p. 450) stress, "[l]eaving aside data problems and the conceptual difficulties concerning the required "translation" of empirical "facts" into the categories of the analytical framework", Sraffa's re-switching argument "refers to the technical knowledge *at a given moment of time*". Hence, given that the hitherto available input–output data refer to different times and economic spaces, the empirical importance of Sraffa's argument cannot be either disconfirmed or confirmed on the basis of the aforesaid approach. By contrast, *if* the key issue is "to decide whether the real world is nearer to the idealized polar cases represented by (a) the neoclassical parable or (b) the simple re-switching paradigm" (Samuelson 1980, p. 576),[15] then our findings suggest that the real world is far from the former case and, therefore, close to the latter case.

iii. The existence of fairly good, low-order approximations to the V–WPCs is not, it need hardly be said, sufficient to restore the traditional value theory. Therefore, only the Sraffian value theory offers a sound empirical basis, although the eigenvalue distributions of the actual matrices $\mathbf{J}$ sharply differ from those of the basic circulant economies, which correspond to the Sraffian *polar* value theory.[16] In fact, the actual eigenvalue distributions can be viewed as mixed combinations of the ideal-type Cases 4 and 5 presented in Sect. 2.3.4.

iv. The actual single-product economies are characterized by rather low degrees and normalized numerical ranks of value controllability (and, therefore, of quantity observability). This primarily results from the skew characteristic value distributions of the actual matrices $\mathbf{J}$ and implies that these economies constitute almost uncontrollable and unobservable systems both in value and quantity terms (see Table 3.3 and Fig. 3.11; compare with Fig. 2.14).[17] It is added that Mariolis and Veltsistas (2020) and Veltsistas (2020) used input–output data from the "World Input–Output Database" (one hundred and seventy-two SIOTs from forty-three countries, spanning the period 2000–2014), and found that: (a) the ratios $\sigma_{\mathbf{J}n}\sigma_{\mathbf{J}1}^{-1}$ are in the range of $10^{-14}$ to $10^{-4}$; (b) the degrees of value controllability are in the range of $10^{-21}$ to $10^{-18}$; and (c) for a tolerance of $10^{-4}$ (of $10^{-2}$), the normalized numerical ranks of value controllability are in the range of 7% to 18% (of 4% to 9%). Finally, we also experimented with the input–output data used by Soklis (2011), i.e. ten Supply and Use Tables (SUTs) of the Finnish economy (for the years 1995 through 2004; $n = 57$),[18] and the results were also similar. For instance, when the value controllability matrix is formed from the matrices $\mathbf{A}[\mathbf{B} - \mathbf{A}]^{-1}$ and the vectors $\mathbf{l}^T[\mathbf{B} - \mathbf{A}]^{-1}$, where $\mathbf{B}$ denotes the output coefficients matrix, the degrees of controllability are in the range of $10^{-93}$ to $10^{-27}$, while, when the value controllability matrix is formed from $\mathbf{A}\mathbf{B}^{-1}$ and $\mathbf{l}^T\mathbf{B}^{-1}$, the degrees of controllability are in the range of $10^{-28}$ to

---

[15]Cited by Cohen (1993, p. 155). Zambelli (2004, p. 107, footnote 2) aptly observes that re-switching is a sub-case of the—much more general—*non*-neoclassical case.

[16]Compare Fig. 2.5 with Fig. 3.10, and Figs. 2.9 and 2.10 with Fig. 3.5 and the eigenvalue distribution characteristics reported in Tables 3.1 and 3.3.

[17]Experiments with controllability matrices formed from pseudo-random vectors $\mathbf{p}^T(0)$ and the abovementioned actual matrices $\mathbf{J}$ lead to degrees of controllability of the order of $10^{-19}$. These pseudo-random vectors were generated by *Mathematica*; see
  https://reference.wolfram.com/language/tutorial/PseudorandomNumbers.html.

[18]See Sect. 5.3.1 of this book.

$10^{-20}$. Thus, the finding that actual economies constitute almost uncontrollable and unobservable systems is further supported.


## 3.4  Concluding Remarks

It has been shown that, although the existence of value–profit rate curves that are non-monotonic irrespective of the labour vector direction presupposes eigenvalue distributions sharply different from those appearing in actual economies, the Sraffian theory is not only the most general to date, but is also empirically relevant. Since actual economies exhibit non-monotonic value–profit rate curves, wage–profit rate curves with alternating curvature, and value–vertically integrated labour reversals, which are analogous to the re-switching phenomenon, they can only be treated through the Sraffian theory.

At the same time, actual economies are characterized by rather low degrees and relatively low normalized numerical ranks of value controllability. More specifically, the hitherto available evidence suggests that the degrees of value controllability are no greater than $10^{-18}$ and, for a tolerance of $10^{-4}$ (of $10^{-2}$), the normalized numerical ranks of value controllability are no greater than 9% (than 18%). These findings result from the skew characteristic value distributions of the vertically integrated technical coefficients matrices, and indicate that actual economies constitute almost uncontrollable and unobservable systems. And the almost uncontrollability and unobservability of actual economies explain, in turn, the specific shape features of the empirical value–wage–profit rate curves that are (re-)positioned, by the traditional value theory, at the heart of the capital theory debate. It then follows that a lot is lost by one-commodity world postulations, embedded, explicitly or otherwise, in all the traditional value theories, whereas there is room for using low-dimensional models, with three basic commodities and many non-self-reproducing non-basics, as surrogates for actual economic systems.

It is not unexpected that, despite their different theoretical backgrounds, many scholars rather view the economy as

> a complex web of contractual relations that reflect the anticipations and plans of the various participants. Metaphorically, it is far more like a gigantic erector set running throughout a 200-room mansion, with each piece connected to pieces in many different rooms. Changes made at one point will exert effects throughout the system, and will do so with varying time delays. *And no one person will be able to apprehend the entire apparatus* [. . .]. Moreover, shifts taking place at one point can be the consequence of earlier shifts elsewhere, and there is no assurance about the consequences of additional changes made at that point. (Buchanan et al. 1978, p. 25)

It seems that the finding that the actual economies tend to respond as uncontrollable and unobservable systems, with only a relatively few effectively controllable and observable modes, is not irrelevant for a critical systematization and factualization of this view(s).

Future research work should (i) expand the empirical analysis of the joint production economies using data from the Supply and Use Tables; (ii) delve into the proximate determinants of the uncontrollable/unobservable aspects of real-world economies, and draw their broader implications for both political economy and economic policy issues; and (iii) heuristically look for eigenvalue locations in the complex plane that could lead to new versions of the value theory.

# References

Aruka, Y. (1991). Generalized Goodwin's theorems on general coordinates. *Structural Change and Economic Dynamics, 2*(1), 69–91. Reprinted in Y. Aruka (Ed.). (2011). *Complexities of production and interacting human behaviour* (pp. 39–66). Heidelberg: Physica–Verlag.

Bienenfeld, M. (1988). Regularity in price changes as an effect of changes in distribution. *Cambridge Journal of Economics, 12*(2), 247–255.

Buchanan, J. M., Burton, J., & Wagner, R. E. (1978). *The consequences of Mr Keynes.* London: Institute of Economic Affairs.

Cohen, A. J. (1993). Samuelson and the 93% scarcity theory of value. In M. Baranzini & G. C. Harcourt (Eds.), *The Dynamics of the Wealth of Nations. Growth, Distribution and Structural Change. Essays in Honour of Luigi Pasinetti* (pp. 149–172). London: Palgrave Macmillan.

Goodwin, R. M. (1976). Use of normalized general co-ordinates in linear value and distribution theory. In K. R. Polenske & J. V. Skolka (Eds.), *Advances in input–output analysis* (pp. 581–602). Cambridge, MA: Ballinger.

Horn, R. A., & Johnson, C. R. (1990). *Matrix analysis.* Cambridge: Cambridge University Press.

Horn, R. A., & Johnson, C. R. (1991). *Topics in matrix analysis.* Cambridge: Cambridge University Press.

Iliadi, F., Mariolis, T., Soklis, G., & Tsoulfidis, L. (2014). Bienenfeld's approximation of production prices and eigenvalue distribution: Further evidence from five European economies. *Contributions to Political Economy, 33*(1), 35–54.

Keyfitz, N., & Caswell, H. (2005). *Applied mathematical demography.* New York: Springer.

Konstantakis, K. N., Soklis, G., & Michaelides, P. G. (2017). Tourism expenditures and crisis transmission: A general equilibrium GVAR analysis with network theory. *Annals of Tourism Research, 66,* 74–94.

Kurz, H. D., & Salvadori, N. (1995). *Theory of production. A long-period analysis.* Cambridge: Cambridge University Press.

Li, B. (2017). *Linear theory of fixed capital and China's economy. Marx, Sraffa and Okishio.* Singapore: Springer.

Linn, J. B., III. (2016). Reverse-engineering the business cycle with Petri nets. *OECD Journal: Journal of Business Cycle Measurement and Analysis, 2015*(2), 1–28.

Mariolis, T. (2013). Applying the mean absolute eigen-deviation of labour commanded prices from labour values to actual economies. *Applied Mathematical Sciences, 7*(104), 5193–5204.

Mariolis, T. (2015a). Norm bounds and a homographic approximation for the wage–profit curve. *Metroeconomica, 66*(2), 263–283.

Mariolis, T. (2015b). Testing Bienenfeld's second-order approximation for the wage–profit curve. *Bulletin of Political Economy, 9*(2), 161–170.

Mariolis, T. (2019). *The location of the value theories in the complex plane and the degree of regularity-controllability of actual economies.* MPRA Paper No 96972. Retrieved Mar 30, 2020, from https://mpra.ub.uni-muenchen.de/96972/.

Mariolis, T. (2021). Competing theories of value: A spectral analysis. *Contributions to Political Economy, 40*(1) (forthcoming).

Mariolis, T., & Soklis, G. (2010). Additive labour values and prices of production: Evidence from the supply and use tables of the French, German and Greek economies. *Economic Issues, 15*(2), 87–107.

Mariolis, T., & Soklis, G. (2011). On constructing numeraire-free measures of price–value deviation: A note on the Steedman–Tomkins distance. *Cambridge Journal of Economics, 35*(3), 613–618.

Mariolis, T., & Tsoulfidis, L. (2011). Eigenvalue distribution and the production price–profit rate relationship: Theory and empirical evidence. *Evolutionary and Institutional Economics Review, 8*(1), 87–122.

Mariolis, T., & Tsoulfidis, L. (2016a). *Modern classical economics and reality. A spectral analysis of the theory of value and distribution.* Tokyo: Springer.

Mariolis, T., & Tsoulfidis, L. (2016b). Capital theory "paradoxes" and paradoxical results: Resolved or continued? *Evolutionary and Institutional Economics Review, 13*(2), 297–322.

Mariolis, T., & Tsoulfidis, L. (2018). Less is more: Capital theory and almost irregular-uncontrollable actual economies. *Contributions to Political Economy, 37*(1), 65–88.

Mariolis, T., & Veltsistas, P. (2020). *Celebrating 60 years of Rudolf E. Kálmán's and Piero Sraffa's theories: Real-world price systems are almost uncontrollable.* MPRA Paper No 99648 (in Greek). Retrieved May 12, 2020, from https://mpra.ub.uni-muenchen.de/96972/.

Michaelides, P. G., Tsionas, E. G., & Konstantakis, K. N. (2018). Debt dynamics in Europe: A network general equilibrium GVAR approach. *Journal of Economic Dynamics and Control, 93*, 175–202.

Samuelson, P. A. (1980). *Economics* (11th ed.). New York: McGrawHill.

Soklis, G. (2011). Shape of wage–profit curves in joint production systems: Evidence from the supply and use tables of the Finnish economy. *Metroeconomica, 62*(4), 548–560.

Sraffa, P. (1960). *Production of Commodities by Means of Commodities. Prelude to a Critique of Economic Theory.* Cambridge: Cambridge University Press.

Steedman, I., & Tomkins, J. (1998). On measuring the deviation of prices from values. *Cambridge Journal of Economics, 22*(3), 379–385.

Stott, I., Townley, S., & Hodgson, D. J. (2011). A framework for studying transient dynamics of population projection matrix models. *Ecology Letters, 14*(9), 959–970.

Treitel, S., & Shanks, J. L. (1971). The design of multistage separable planar filters. *Institute of Electrical and Electronics Engineers Transactions on Geoscience Electronics, 9*(1), 10–27.

Tsoulfidis, L., & Mariolis, T. (2007). Labour values, prices of production and the effects of income distribution: Evidence from the Greek economy. *Economic Systems Research, 19*(4), 425–437.

Veltsistas, P. (2020). *Eigenvalue distribution and the degree of regularity-controllability of actual economies: Evidence from the WIOD 2000–2014.* Master's Thesis, Athens: Department of Public Administration, Panteion University (in Greek). Retrieved May 12, 2020, from https://www.researchgate.net/publication/341043862.

Zambelli, S. (2004). The 40% neoclassical aggregate theory of production. *Cambridge Journal of Economics, 28*(1), 99–120.

# Chapter 4
# Value Theory, Joint Production, and International Trade Issues

**Abstract** The application of the principles of the Sraffian theory to joint production or/and open economies further reveals the inner limits of the traditional value theory: it is found that many statements make no sense or are not verified. If, however, we are willing to consider produced means of production, positive profits, non-"golden rule" steady states, heterogeneous labour (primary inputs), and joint-products as "market failures", as well as joint production through the lens of single production, then we are not required to move away from the classical–Marxian–neoclassical one-commodity world. In the opposite case, a specific analysis of each particular issue must be made, and the general conclusion is that open, joint-product economies should be treated as the norm, whereas closed, single-product economies and their special properties should be pointed out as limiting paradigms.

**Keywords** Downward output supply curve · Harrod–Balassa–Samuelson effect · Law of comparative advantage · No wage–profit rate trade-off · Non-substitution theorem

## 4.1 Introduction

Pure joint production of commodities by means of domestically produced and imported commodities is the rule in economic reality. Both aspects of this rule, i.e. joint production and foreign trade, imply that, in general, relative commodity prices depend on the pattern of final demand or, formally speaking, the "non-substitution theorem" (which was first studied by Dmitriev 1974) is not of general validity. Therefore, there is an additional source of conceptual and analytical difficulties for the traditional value theory.

This chapter applies the Sraffian analysis of (i) joint production and (ii) the price effects of sectoral productivity changes to open economies, and, thus, deals with some of these difficulties. More specifically, Sect. 4.2 focuses on the possibilities of a positive correlation between the distributive variables and of a downward output supply curve in joint production economies and pinpoints the consequences for the

© Springer Nature Singapore Pte Ltd. 2021
T. Mariolis et al., *Spectral Theory of Value and Actual Economies*, Evolutionary Economics and Social Complexity Science 24,
https://doi.org/10.1007/978-981-33-6260-4_4

international value theory. Section 4.3 examines the validity of the "Harrod–Balassa–Samuelson effect or productivity bias hypothesis" in a world with heterogeneous capital commodities. Finally, Sect. 4.4 concludes.

## 4.2  Aspects and Implications of Pure Joint Production

### 4.2.1  Closed Economy

Consider the closed, $n-$ commodity economy described in Sect. 2.3.1, but assume now that the economy has $n$ linear processes of pure joint production. Hence, the following von Neumann (1937, 1945)–Sraffa (1960) equations and inequalities need to be satisfied:

$$\mathbf{p}^T\mathbf{B} \leqq w\mathbf{l}^T(1+r)\mathbf{p}^T\mathbf{A} \tag{4.1}$$

$$\mathbf{p}^T\mathbf{B}\mathbf{x} = w\mathbf{l}^T\mathbf{x} + (1+r)\mathbf{p}^T\mathbf{A}\mathbf{x} \tag{4.2}$$

$$\mathbf{p}^T\mathbf{f} = 1 \tag{4.3}$$

$$\mathbf{B}\mathbf{x} \geq c(\mathbf{l}^T\mathbf{x})\mathbf{f} + (1+g)\mathbf{A}\mathbf{x} \tag{4.4}$$

$$\mathbf{p}^T\mathbf{B}\mathbf{x} = c(\mathbf{l}^T\mathbf{x})\mathbf{p}^T\mathbf{f} + (1+g)\mathbf{p}^T\mathbf{A}\mathbf{x} \tag{4.5}$$

$$\mathbf{p}^T \geq \mathbf{0}^T, \ \ \mathbf{x} \geq \mathbf{0}, \ \ [w,c] \geq \mathbf{0}^T \tag{4.6}$$

where $\mathbf{p}^T$ denotes the price vector, $\mathbf{B}$ the output coefficient matrix, $w$ the uniform money wage rate, $r\,(\geq 0)$ the exogenously given uniform profit rate, $\mathbf{l}^T$, $\mathbf{A}$ the direct labour coefficients vector and input coefficients matrix, respectively, $\mathbf{x}$ the vector of activity levels, $\mathbf{f}$ an exogenously given $n \times 1$ commodity vector representing the uniform, across income types, consumption pattern,[1] $g$ ($\geq 0$) the exogenously given uniform growth rate, and $c$ the level of consumption per unit of labour employed. Relation (4.1) implies that no process is able to pay extra profits. Equation (4.2) implies, also because of relations (4.6), that when a process is not able to pay the ruling profit rate, it is not operated. Relation (4.4) implies that the "requirements for use" (Sraffa 1960, p. 43, footnote 2), i.e. the demand for capital accumulation and consumption, are satisfied.[2] Equation (4.5), also because of relations (4.6), is the

---

[1] The relaxation of these two assumptions regarding consumption demand is not absolutely necessary for our present purposes (thus, it is left to the reader; also see Chap. 2, footnote 23).

[2] As Salvadori and Steedman (1988a) remark, "Sraffa's phrase "requirements for use" is not a standard term in economic analysis and Sraffa provides no explication of this phrase. Thus one is obliged to be cautious in offering an interpretation. Nevertheless it might seem that Sraffa was seeking to de-emphasize the subjective elements in the determination of the pattern of output, without denying them" (p. 168, footnote 2).

"rule of free goods", i.e. overproduced commodities fetch a zero price. Finally, Eq. (4.3) fixes the *numéraire*; hence, $w$ also symbolizes the level of the real wage rate. Close inspection of this system can reveal that, primarily when $g < r$ (non-"golden rule" steady state), there are fundamental and significant structural differences between the cases of single and joint production, implying that the laws governing the behaviour of single production economies do not apply to all joint production economies.[3]

To begin with, consider a viable and profitable (see Sect. 1.5) $n \times n$ joint production economy in which *all* processes operate and, therefore, we can safely write:

$$\mathbf{p}^T\mathbf{B} = w\mathbf{l}^T + (1 + r)\mathbf{p}^T\mathbf{A} \tag{4.7}$$

(i) According to Marx, "labour values" satisfy: (a) actuality, i.e. they are defined by reference to the processes actually used in the economy considered; (b) additivity, i.e. the "labour value" of the gross output, whether from a single process, an industry, or a whole sector of the economy, is equal to the sum of the "labour values" of the various means of production used up plus the "live labour" performed; (c) uniqueness, i.e. they are uniquely determined; and (d) positivity. However, as Sraffa (1960) stressed,

> in the case of joint-products there is no obvious criterion for apportioning the labour among individual products, and indeed it seems doubtful whether it makes any sense to speak of a *separate* quantity of labour as having gone to produce one of a number of *jointly* produced commodities. (p. 56)

Hence, one possible way forward would be to define "labour values", $\mathbf{v}^T$, as the labour-commanded prices corresponding to zero profits (see Eq. (4.7)), i.e.

$$w^{-1}\mathbf{p}^T\mathbf{B} = \mathbf{l}^T + w^{-1}\mathbf{p}^T\mathbf{A}$$

or, setting $\mathbf{v}^T \equiv w^{-1}\mathbf{p}^T$,

$$\mathbf{v}^T\mathbf{B} = \mathbf{l}^T + \mathbf{v}^T\mathbf{A}$$

or, provided that $[\mathbf{B} - \mathbf{A}]$ is non-singular,

---

[3]It is often overlooked that Sraffa's (1960) three chapters on "Joint Production" do *not* provide a general treatment of this issue but "are in the main a preliminary to the discussion of Fixed Capital and Land in Chaps. X and XI" (p. 43, footnote 1). For general treatments, see Bidard (1991, Part 2; 1997), Kurz and Salvadori (1995, Chaps. 7, 8, and 9) and the references (and historical notes) therein. Finally, for critical remarks and broader discussions on the "golden rule hypothesis", see Latham (1975), Goodwin (1972), Nuti (1970).

$$\mathbf{v}^{T} = \mathbf{l}^{T}[\mathbf{B} - \mathbf{A}]^{-1} \tag{4.8}$$

The values thus defined are called "additive labour values": they satisfy actuality, additivity, and represent "employment multipliers" (in the sense of Kahn 1931; also see Sraffa 1960, p. 60), i.e. $v_{j}$ equals the labour required to produce a net output consisting of commodity $j$ alone. However, they can be non-uniquely determined (when $[\mathbf{B} - \mathbf{A}]$ is singular) or negative; more specifically, some $v_{j}$ are negative iff a non-negative linear combination of some processes yields a greater net output per unit of labour employed than a non-negative linear combination of the remaining ones (Filippini and Filippini 1982, pp. 387–388). And the possible negativity of $v_{j}$ and/or of the corresponding matrix of vertically integrated technical coefficients, $\mathbf{H} \equiv \mathbf{A}[\mathbf{B} - \mathbf{A}]^{-1}$, does not imply that the labour requirement, or the requirement for some capital stocks, is negative for a commodity but that the net output of the economy cannot contain only that commodity. Hence, it is concluded that, when joint production is allowed for, the aforesaid set of Marxian properties (a) to (d) is not necessarily self-consistent (Steedman 1975, 1976a, 1976b).

(ii) Equation (4.7) can be written as

$$\mathbf{p}^{T}[\mathbf{B} - \mathbf{A}] = w\mathbf{l}^{T} + r\mathbf{p}^{T}\mathbf{A} \tag{4.9}$$

When the system $\{(1 + r_{0})\mathbf{B}, \mathbf{A}\}$, where $r_{0} > -1$, is "all-engaging" (see Sect. 1.5), i.e. when

$$\mathbf{E}(r_{0}) \equiv [\mathbf{B} - (1 + r_{0})\mathbf{A}]^{-1} = [\mathbf{B} - \mathbf{A}]^{-1}[\mathbf{I} - r_{0}\mathbf{H}]^{-1} > \mathbf{0}$$

the system $\{\mathbf{B}, \mathbf{A}\}$ is called "$r_{0}-$ all-engaging" (Schefold 1978; Bidard 1996). In that case, subtracting $r_{0}\mathbf{p}^{T}\mathbf{A}$ from both sides of Eq. (4.9), then post-multiplying by $\mathbf{E}(r_{0})$, and setting $\boldsymbol{\Phi}(r_{0}) \equiv \mathbf{A}\mathbf{E}(r_{0})$ gives

$$\mathbf{p}^{T} = w\mathbf{l}^{T}\mathbf{E}(r_{0}) + (r - r_{0})\mathbf{p}^{T}\boldsymbol{\Phi}(r_{0})$$

from which it follows that: When the system $\{\mathbf{B}, \mathbf{A}\}$ is $r_{0}-$ all-engaging, there is a closed interval of the profit rate in which the economy retains all the wage (consumption)–profit (growth) rate properties of irreducible single production economies, and this interval is: $[r_{0}, R_{0}]$, where $R_{0} \equiv r_{0} + \lambda_{\boldsymbol{\Phi}(r_{0})1}^{-1}$, and $\lambda_{\boldsymbol{\Phi}(r_{0})1}^{-1}$ denotes the Perron–Frobenius eigenvalue of $\boldsymbol{\Phi}(r_{0})$. Finally, the system is $r_{0}-$ all-engaging iff there exist $[\lambda, \boldsymbol{\chi}, \boldsymbol{\psi}] > \mathbf{0}$, where $\boldsymbol{\chi}$ is determined up to a factor, such that

$$\lambda\mathbf{B}\boldsymbol{\chi} = \mathbf{A}\boldsymbol{\chi}$$

and

$$\lambda \psi^T B = \psi^T A$$

(Bidard 1996, p. 328).[4] In that case, $\lambda^{-1} - 1 \, (= R_0)$ represents the maximum feasible growth (and profit) rate, as defined by von Neumann (1937, 1945), $\psi^T$ the associated long-period price vector, and $\chi$ the associated vector of activity levels or, alternatively, the vector of activity levels of Sraffa's (1960, Chap. 8) Standard system.

The following two numerical examples further highlight some of the specific features of joint production economies.[5]

***Example 4.1: No w–r trade-off***
Consider the following economy:

$$\mathbf{B} = \begin{bmatrix} 13.05 & 12.95 \\ 2.95 & 4.05 \end{bmatrix}, \quad \mathbf{A} = \begin{bmatrix} 12 & 12 \\ 2 & 3 \end{bmatrix}, \quad \mathbf{l}^T = [1, 1],$$

$$\mathbf{f} = [1, 1]^T, \quad g = 0$$

It is obtained that

$$[\mathbf{B} - \mathbf{A}] > \mathbf{0}, \quad [\mathbf{B} - \mathbf{A}]^{-1} = \begin{bmatrix} 5.25 & -4.75 \\ -4.75 & 5.25 \end{bmatrix}, \quad v_1 = v_2 = 1/2$$

$$\mathbf{H} = \mathbf{A}\mathbf{B}^{-1}[\mathbf{I} - \mathbf{A}\mathbf{B}^{-1}]^{-1} = \begin{bmatrix} 6 & 6 \\ -3.75 & 6.25 \end{bmatrix}$$

the matrix $[\mathbf{B} - (1 + r)\mathbf{A}]^{-1}$ contains negative elements, and the eigenvalues of $\mathbf{A}\mathbf{B}^{-1}$ (and of $\mathbf{H}$) are complex. Therefore, the system is not $r_0-$ all-engaging, while the "additive labour values" are all positive.

For $0 \leq r \leq 0.1$, both processes operate and, therefore, commodity prices are determined by Eqs. (4.3) and (4.7), which imply that

$$p_1 = (1 - 10r)(2 - 10r)^{-1} \geq 0, \quad p_2 = (2 - 10r)^{-1} > 0 \qquad (4.10)$$

and

$$w = (2 - 24.5r + 120r^2)(2 - 10r)^{-1} \qquad (4.11)$$

i.e. commodity prices are all positive for $0 \leq r < 0.1$, and the $w - r$ curve is strictly decreasing (increasing) for $0 \leq r < r'$ (for $r' < r \leq 0.1$), where

---

[4]For an analytical investigation of the $2 \times 2$ case, see Abraham-Frois and Berrebi (1984).

[5]These examples have been built by correcting and modifying, respectively, two numerical examples provided by Bidard (1997, pp. 689–690) and further examined by Mariolis (2004a, 2010, Essay 2; 2019) and Mariolis and Soklis (2018). For other specific features of the joint production economies, see Chaps. 5, 6, 7, 8, and 9 of this book.

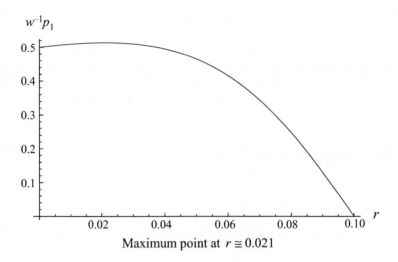

Maximum point at $r \cong 0.021$

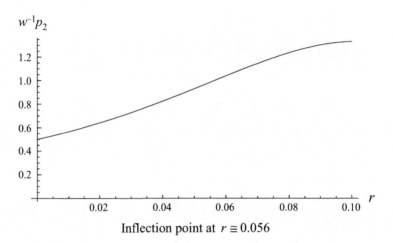

Inflection point at $r \cong 0.056$

**Fig. 4.1** The labour-commanded prices as functions of the profit rate: $0 \leq r < 0.1$

$$r' \equiv 0.2 - \left( \sqrt{57}/60 \right) \cong 0.074$$

For $r > 0.1$, only process 1 operates, $p_1 = 0$ (overproduced commodity), and the $w - r$ curve is linear and strictly decreasing, i.e.

$$w = 0.95 - 2r, \quad \dot{w} \equiv dw/dr = -2 \qquad (4.12)$$

The graphs in Figs. 4.1 and 4.2 display the labour-commanded prices

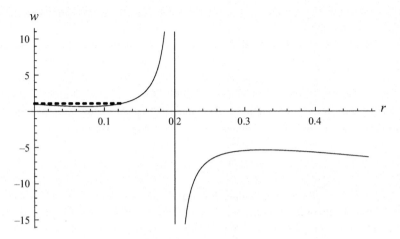

The algebraic wage–profit rate curve

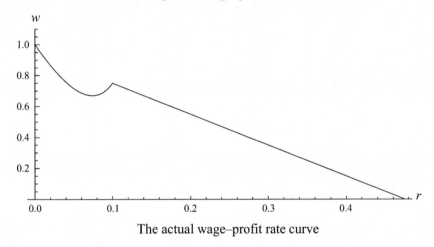

The actual wage–profit rate curve

**Fig. 4.2** The algebraic and the actual wage–profit rate curves: $0 \leq r \leq 0.475$

$$w^{-1}\mathbf{p}^{\mathrm{T}} = \mathbf{l}^{\mathrm{T}}[\mathbf{B} - (1+r)\mathbf{A}]^{-1}$$

as functions of the profit rate (for $0 \leq r < 0.1$) and the algebraic and the actual $w - r$ curves (for $0 \leq r \leq 0.475$; see Eqs. (4.11) and (4.12)), respectively (compare with Fig. 2.1).[6]

---

[6]The non-monotonic $w - r$ curves analysed by, for instance, Filippini and Filippini (1984, pp. 57–62) have no specific economic content and are, therefore, unreal: the authors, on the one hand, do not take into account the requirements for use, and, on the other hand, assume that all the available processes operate. That is to say, those curves are algebraic $w - r$ curves.

The monotonicity of the $w - r$ curve is not without consequences for the traditional value theory:

(i) If the real wage rate is treated as a datum, then to any $w$ in the open interval

$$(w(r') = -2.35 + 0.4\sqrt{57} \cong 0.670, \quad w(0.1) = 0.75)$$

there corresponds a unique value for the Marxian "rate of exploitation of workers", measured in terms of "additive labour values" (see Eq. (4.8)), i.e.

$$\left(w\mathbf{v}^{\mathrm{T}}\mathbf{f}\right)^{-1} - 1 = w^{-1} - 1$$

and two economically relevant values for $[r, \mathbf{p}^{\mathrm{T}}]$.[7] Hence, the logic of Marx's (1991, Part 2) "transformation problem", i.e. "transformation of the rate of exploitation into the profit rate" and, therefore, "transformation of labour values into production prices", breaks down. Nevertheless, a non-monotonic $w - r$ curve is only sufficient, but not necessary, for this type of breakdown (consider the $2 \times 2$ joint production numerical example and analysis provided by Steedman 1992). It is rather surprising that modern Marxist economists do not systematically focus on joint production, whereas a century ago, Hilferding (1981, Chap. 11) and Lenin (1917, pp. 198–200) insisted on its importance.

(ii) From Eqs. (4.3), (4.8), and (4.9) it follows that

$$w = \left(\mathbf{v}^{\mathrm{T}}\mathbf{f}\right)^{-1} - r\kappa_{\mathbf{f}} \tag{4.13}$$

where $\kappa_{\mathbf{f}} \equiv (\mathbf{p}^{\mathrm{T}}\mathbf{Hf})(\mathbf{v}^{\mathrm{T}}\mathbf{f})^{-1}$ ($> 0$) denotes the capital intensity of the vertically integrated consumption goods—*numéraire* industry. Hence, for $r > 0$, it necessarily holds that

$$w(0) = \left(\mathbf{v}^{\mathrm{T}}\mathbf{f}\right)^{-1} > w(r) \tag{4.14}$$

Differentiation of Eq. (4.13) with respect to the profit rate gives

$$\dot{w} = -\kappa_{\mathbf{f}} - r\dot{\kappa}_{\mathbf{f}}$$

or

---

[7]For $r > 0.1$, we obtain

$$v_1 1.05 + v_2 0.95 = 1$$

and, therefore, "labour values" are not uniquely determined.

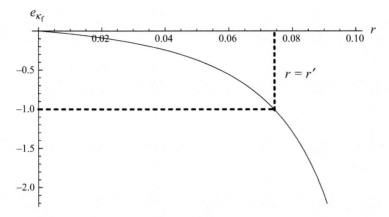

**Fig. 4.3** The elasticity of capital intensity as a function of the profit rate: at $r = r'$, $e_{\kappa_f} = -1$ and, therefore, $\dot{w} = 0$

$$\dot{w} = -\kappa_f(1 + e_{\kappa_f})$$

where $e_{\kappa_f} \equiv \dot{\kappa}_f(r/\kappa_f)$ denotes the elasticity of $\kappa_f$ with respect to the profit rate. Hence, a "*positive* price Wicksell effect" (see Sect. 2.3.1), i.e. $\dot{\kappa}_f < 0$ or, equivalently,

$$\ddot{w} > 0 \tag{4.15}$$

is a necessary condition for a non-monotonic $w - r$ curve, while a necessary and sufficient condition is $e_{\kappa_f} < -1$ (for our numerical example, see Fig. 4.3). Finally, at $r = 0$, the slope of such a curve is necessarily negative, since[8]

$$\dot{w}(0) = -\kappa_f(0) < 0 \tag{4.16}$$

According now to the neoclassical theory, the "factor price frontier" can be derived from the "total cost function" (Samuelson 1962; Burmeister and Kuga 1970; Diewert 1971). Conversely, "total cost functions" are—supposed to be—homogeneous of degree one, non-decreasing, and concave in "factor prices", while, using Shephard's (1953) lemma, the underlying "production function" can be derived from the "total cost function". Although the phenomenon of non-monotonic wage–profit rate curves involves a "positive price Wicksell effect", it seriously undermines the basis of the

---

[8]In 2 × 2 economies, $\ddot{w} \neq 0$; hence, Eqs. (4.14) and (4.15) imply that a necessary condition for a non-monotonic $w - r$ curve is that the eigenvalues of **H** are complex. Thus, it is not unexpected that the 2 × 2, no $w - r$ trade-off, numerical example analysed by d'Autume (1988, pp. 343–344) has the same production structure as the present example. According to d'Autume (1986, 1988), when we adopt the viewpoint of the "general equilibrium theory", the only real paradox, specific to the joint production case, is the possibility that, outside the "golden rule" path, the $w - r$ curve is non-monotonic.

aforesaid neoclassical double inferences (or "dualities") and, therefore, the construction of approximate "surrogate production functions" from "near-linear"[9] wage–profit rate curves.[10]

***Example 4.2: Downward output supply curves and $r_0$ – all-engaging system***
Consider the following economy:

$$\mathbf{B} = \begin{bmatrix} 5 & 8 \\ 8 & 3 \end{bmatrix}, \quad \mathbf{A} = \begin{bmatrix} 1 & 3 \\ 3 & 0 \end{bmatrix}, \quad \mathbf{l}^T = [1, 1], \quad \mathbf{f} = [1, 1]^T, \quad g = 0$$

It is obtained that

$$[\mathbf{B} - \mathbf{A}] > 0, \quad [\mathbf{B} - \mathbf{A}]^{-1} = 13^{-1} \begin{bmatrix} -3 & 5 \\ 5 & -4 \end{bmatrix}, \quad v_1 = 2/13, \quad v_2 = 1/13$$

$$\mathbf{H} = 13^{-1} \begin{bmatrix} 12 & -7 \\ -9 & 15 \end{bmatrix}$$

The eigenvalues of $\mathbf{AB}^{-1}$ (and of $\mathbf{H}$) are all positive, and the determinant of $[\mathbf{B} - (1 + r)\mathbf{A}]$ equals zero at

$$r = \left(9 \mp \sqrt{29}\right)/6 \cong 0.602, 2.398$$

Moreover, $[\mathbf{B} - (1 + r)\mathbf{A}]^{-1} > \mathbf{0}$ for

$$5/3 \cong 1.667 < r < R_0 \equiv \left(9 + \sqrt{29}\right)/6$$

i.e. the system is $r_0$– all-engaging, $(1 + R_0)^{-1}$ equals the sub-dominant eigenvalue of $\mathbf{AB}^{-1}$, while $[\mathbf{I} - r\mathbf{H}]^{-1} > 0$ for

$$13/12 \cong 1.083 < r < R_0$$

and the "additive labour values" are all positive.

For $0 \le r < 1/2$, the relative output supply curve is upward (see Fig. 4.4, where "S", "D" indicate the relative supply and demand curves, respectively, "[1], [2]" the corresponding processes, and $q_1/q_2$ denotes the relative quantity of commodities). It then follows that both processes operate, and

---

[9]See Chaps. 3 and 5 of the present book.
[10]It may be noted that, in our numerical example, $p_1/p_2$ is a linear function of the profit rate (defined by Eq. (4.10)), and the mean of the relative error between the actual $w - r$ curve (defined by Eq. (4.11)) and its Taylor linear approximation about $r = 0$, i.e. $w \approx 1 - 7.25r$, is almost 1.85%.

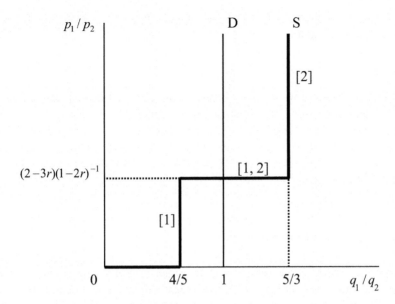

**Fig. 4.4** The output supply–demand equilibrium: $0 \leq r < 1/2$, upward output supply curves

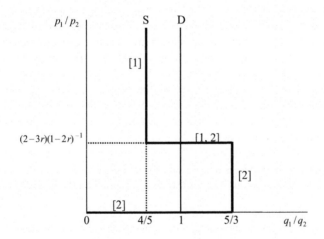

**Fig. 4.5** The output supply–demand equilibria: $2/3 < r \leq R_0$, downward output supply curves

$$p_1 = (2 - 3r)(3 - 5r)^{-1}, \quad p_2 = (1 - 2r)(3 - 5r)^{-1}, \quad \dot{p}_1 > 0 \qquad (4.17)$$

$$w = (13 - 27r + 9r^2)(3 - 5r)^{-1}, \quad w > 0, \quad \dot{w} < 0, \ddot{w} > 0 \qquad (4.18)$$

At $r = 1/2$, both processes operate, $p_1 = 1, p_2 = 0$, and $w = 3.5$. For $1/2 < r < 2/3$, only process 1 operates, $p_1 = 1, p_2 = 0$, and $w = 4 - r$. At $r = 2/3$, both processes operate, $p_1 = 0, p_2 = 1$, and $w = 3$. For $2/3 < r \leq R_0$, the relative output supply curve is downward (see Fig. 4.5) and, therefore, there are two solutions: (i) both processes operate, and Eqs. (4.17) and (4.18) hold (with $w \geq 0$ and $\ddot{w} < 0$);[11] or (ii) only process 2 operates, and

$$p_1 = 0, \quad p_2 = 1, \quad w = 3 \tag{4.19}$$

Finally, for $r > R_0$, only process 2 operates, and Eqs. (4.19) hold. The graphs in Fig. 4.6 display, therefore, the algebraic and the actual $w - r$ curves.

It has been shown, therefore, that the co-existence of positive "additive labour values" with an interval of $r$ ($> 0$) in which the system is $r_0$– all-engaging, $[\mathbf{I} - r\mathbf{H}]^{-1} > 0$, and the output supply curve is downward cannot be ruled out (also see Salvadori and Steedman 1988b).[12]

### 4.2.2 Open Economies

Consider two closed economies, A and B, which have the same production processes, but different profit rates. We assume that both labour and money (financial) capital are perfectly immobile internationally, and that, for each economy, the profit rate is the same in no- and with-free trade equilibria. The profit rate in economy K ($= A, B$) will be denoted by $r^K$, and the corresponding autarky price ratio will be denoted by $p^K \equiv p_1^K/p_2^K$. Thus, we focus on the issues of (i) international "specialization", as a particular issue of the cost-minimization choice of technique; and (ii) the validity of the "law of comparative advantage". The term "specialization" pertains to processes, not to commodities, while "comparative advantage" is determined by the relative no-trade price ratios (therefore, it depends on income distribution) and not (like Ricardo) by the relative "labour value" ratios. Thus, by "law of comparative advantage" we mean that each economy exports the commodity which is relatively cheapest to produce.[13]

In fact, the present von Neumann–Sraffa modelling is general enough to incorporate alternative assumptions about trade impediments and mobility, and ways of closing the system. For instance, the study of Emmanuel's (1969, 1975) model case,

---

[11]Such a sign change of $\ddot{w}$ is impossible in the corresponding single production case (i.e. two commodities and one production technique).

[12]Compare with Debreu (1984, p. 50). According to Kehoe (1985), the only economically interpretable restrictions that imply uniqueness of equilibrium in models of economic competition are either that the demand side behaves like a single consumer or that the supply side satisfies the "nonsubstitution theorem"; also see Mas-Colell (1985, Chap. 6).

[13]For the bases of the Ricardian, neoclassical, and Sraffian theories of open economies, as well as for their negative and positive relationships, see Baldone (2000), Giammanco (1998), Mainwaring (1974a), Parrinello (1970), Ravix (1979, 1990), Sraffa (1930), Steedman (1979a, Chaps. 1 and 2; 1979b, Essay 1; 1999), Steedman and Metcalfe (1973a, 1973b, 1981). For a comprehensive von Neumann analysis of the "small", growing open economy case (i.e. a growing economy facing given world prices and a world economy growing at least as fast as the economy under consideration), see Steedman (1979c).

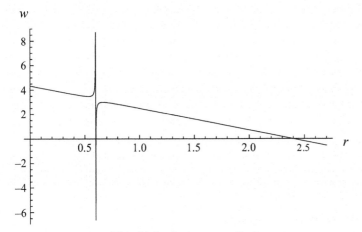

The algebraic wage–profit rate curve

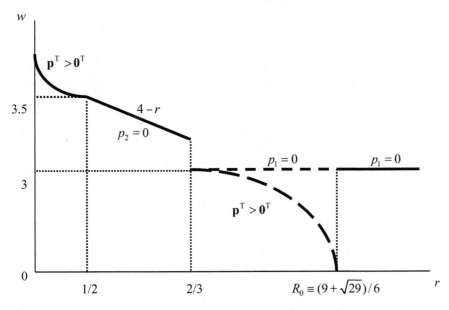

The actual wage–profit rate curve

**Fig. 4.6** The algebraic and the actual wage–profit rate curves: $r \geq 0$

where the national wage rates are determined from outside the system, by domestic factors (historical, socio-political, and institutional), and, at the same time, the perfect international mobility of money capital leads to the equalization of the national profit rates, can be based on Brewer's (1985) enlightening analysis, i.e. the corresponding re-formulation of our system of relations (4.1) to (4.6). Conversely, given what has been said about "labour values" and the monotonicity of the wage–profit rate curves (Sect. 4.2.1; also see Chaps. 5 and 6), it is not necessary to consider the relevant theories of "unequal exchange (or of transfer) of labour quantities (or of surplus value)" (either Marxist or non-Marxist). Nevertheless, some of them (e.g. Manoilescu 1929; Stefanidis 1930) are both original and interesting as theories of "domestic distortions", "infant-economy protection", and "circular and cumulative causation of the development process".[14]

It should also be clarified from the outset that the key for interpreting various traditional neoclassical statements about open, joint-product economies is:

> [V]alid joint-products theorems may often be obtained from valid single-products theorems by deleting "commodity prices" and "net outputs" from these latter and replacing those terms by "process revenues" and "process activity levels" respectively: the difficulties arise in framing joint-products theorems which *do* refer to "commodity prices" and "net outputs". (Steedman 1982, p. 383, footnote 1)[15]

### *Example 4.3: No higher w–r combination*

Consider Example 4.1, and assume that $r^A = 0.05\,(< r')$, $r^B = 0.095\,(> r')$. From Eqs. (4.10) and (4.11) it follows that

$$p^A = 0.5, \quad w^A = 43/60, \quad p^B = 0.05, \quad w^B = 1511/2100 > w^A$$

Let $p^* \equiv \left(p_1^*/p_2^*\right)$ be the international price ratio, and let $w_j^K$ be the real wage in economy K, when it specializes in process $j = 1, 2$. From our numerical data, it is obtained that

$$\left\{w_j^A > w^A \Leftrightarrow p^* < p^A\right\} \text{ and } \left\{w_1^A > (<)\, w_2^A \Leftrightarrow p^* > (<)\, p^A\right\} \qquad (4.20)$$

$$\left\{w_j^B > w^B \Leftrightarrow p^* < p^B\right\} \text{ and } \left\{w_1^B > (<)\, w_2^B \Leftrightarrow p^* > (<)\, p^B\right\} \qquad (4.21)$$

Therefore, there are only two possible specialization patterns:

$P_I$: $p^* < p^B$, process 1 does not operate, i.e. both economies specialize in process 2, and $w_2^K > w^{K}$.[16]

---

[14]On Mihail Manoilescu's and Dimosthenis Stefanidis's contributions, see Hagen (1958) and Mariolis (2018), respectively. For the neoclassical theory of "domestic distortions" and "infant-economy protection", see, e.g. Chacholiades (1978, Chaps. 20 and 21).

[15]For a more recent, non-Sraffian exchange on the topic, see Jones (1992) and Samuelson (1992), while Jones (2012) notes: "In early discussions of activity analysis [...] activities allowed *joint production* (i.e., production processes involving not only multiple inputs, but also multiple outputs). [...] In trade theory the lack of joint production insures an asymmetry between inputs (many) and outputs (one) that is the basis for the Stolper–Samuelson theorem (1941). As to its effect on the factor-price equalization theorem, opinions differ. For example, see Samuelson (1992) and Jones (1992)" (p. 151, footnote 2).

[16]In single production economies also, it is entirely possible for international equilibrium price ratios to exist, which do not lie between the corresponding autarky price ratios (Steedman 1979a, pp. 115–116). However, this presupposes that more than two commodities are produced.

$P_{II}$: $p^* = p^B$, economy A specializes in process 2 $\left(w_2^A > w^A\right)$, while economy B uses any linear combination of processes 1, 2, and, thus, the real wage rate does not increase.

However, pattern $P_I$ does not satisfy consumption demand (1/1) and, consequently, only pattern $P_{II}$ corresponds to the situation of international equilibrium. Moreover, in the case of $P_{II}$ satisfaction of demand proportions is possible only when economy B specializes in process 1, and because (easily proven) economy A exports commodity 2, while economy B exports commodity 1, it follows that the law of comparative advantage still holds.

It may be added that there are also the following three specialization patterns that satisfy consumption demand:

$P_{III}$: $p^* < p^B$, economy A (economy B) specializes in process 1 (process 2), $w_j^K > w^K$, and the law of comparative advantage fails to hold.

$P_{IV}$: $p^* < p^B$, economy A (economy B) specializes in process 2 (process 1), $w_j^K > w^K$, and the said law holds.

$P_V$: $p^* = p^B$, economy A (economy B) specializes in process 1 (process 2), $w_1^A > w^A$, $w_2^B = w^B$, and the said law fails to hold.

Nevertheless, these three patterns are not actual, precisely because they rule out the operation of some process, which pays extra profits at the associated price vector. The existence of such patterns, i.e. non-dominant patterns, is also possible in the single production case (Steedman 1979a, pp. 47 and 110–118). However, more than two commodities must be produced.

Finally, the reduction in total consumption per unit of labour employed in economy B, i.e. the appearance of negative "specialization gain", which can be easily ascertained, does not reflect a feature of joint production economies, but rather a specific feature of *all*, both closed and open, production of commodities and positive profits by means of commodities economies. Namely, outside the "golden rule" path, the cost-minimization choice of technique is not necessarily optimal with respect to consumption per unit of labour employed. According to Rodrik (2011),

> [i]n the economist's jargon, the resources used in international exchanges must be valued at their true social opportunity costs rather than at prevailing market prices. These two accounting schemes coincide only when markets internalize all social costs, distributional considerations can be shunted aside, and other social and political objectives are not at stake; they don't otherwise (pp. 53–54). [...] Recall one of the points I made when we discussed the gains from trade. A profitable exchange between a buyer and a seller is only desirable for society as a whole when prices reflect the full social (opportunity) costs involved in the exchange. (p. 112)

A few decades ago, however, Metcalfe and Steedman (1974) proved that a positive interest (profit) rate is equivalent in its effects to a "factor market distortion" (i.e. divergence between relative commodity prices and "opportunity costs") and, therefore, the "specialization gain" can be negative (even for all free-trading economies).[17]

It has been shown, therefore, that the existence of joint production may have the following implications:

(i)  An economy is in a position to attain the highest possible $w - r$ combination iff it chooses one, and only one, specialization.
(ii) The "simultaneous" attainment of the highest possible $w - r$ combination from both economies requires that they choose the same specialization.
(iii) It is possible that the aforesaid specialization pattern does not satisfy consumption demand. In that case, the international price ratio coincides with either economy's pre-trade price ratio and, therefore, one of the two economies takes the place of the so-called "large country". As is well known, the "large–small country" equilibrium can occur not only in the textbook "Ricardian" theory (see, e.g. Jones and Weder 2017, Chaps. 4 and 5), or in more complicated versions of it (consider, e.g. Scarf and Wilson 2005), but also in the Sraffian modelling of single production economies (Steedman 1979b, pp. 107–108). In our case, however, the equilibrium $p^* = p^B$ is the "rule", because the only possible patterns are $P_I$ and $P_{II}$; at the same time, "country B" is completely specialized and "loses from specialization".

We could assume that if "we choose": $(r^A, r^B) < r' \cong 0.074$, and consequently our investigation will be restricted to those intervals of $r$, in which the $w - r$ curve is strictly decreasing, the properties of the single production economies will re-appear. However, this is not correct: consider Fig. 4.7, in which the straight line marked 1 (marked 2) depicts the $w - r$ combinations which correspond to process 1 (to process 2), for given commodity prices, i.e.

$$w_j \equiv \left\{ p_1 \left[ b_{1j} - (1+r)a_{1j} \right] + p_2 \left[ b_{2j} - (1+r)a_{2j} \right] \right\} l_j^{-1}$$

or, since $p_1 f_1 + p_2 f_2 = 1$,

$$w_j = \left\{ p \left[ b_{1j} - (1+r)a_{1j} \right] + \left[ b_{2j} - (1+r)a_{2j} \right] \right\} \left[ (p f_1 + f_2) l_j \right]^{-1} \qquad (4.22)$$

where $p \equiv p_1/p_2$. The intersection points of these straight lines necessarily lie in the actual $w - r$ curve. At $r = 0.01$ (at $r = -1/90$), the straight line 1 (line 2) is tangent to the actual $w - r$ curve. Finally, the straight line 1 (the straight line 2) always passes through the point $\Delta$ (the notional point $\Gamma$).[18] Thus, it is verified that

[17]For further on the "gains from free trade", i.e. "specialization gain" and "transition (from autarky to free trade) gain", the possibility of negative "overall gain from free trade" and the consequent implications for the theories of "economic integration" and economic policy, see Mainwaring (1976a, 1979, 1991, Chap. 2), Mariolis (2000, 2005a, 2005b), Montani (2010, 2012), Steedman (1979a, 1979b, 2018).

[18]Compare with Fig. 2 in Mainwaring (1974b, p. 541).

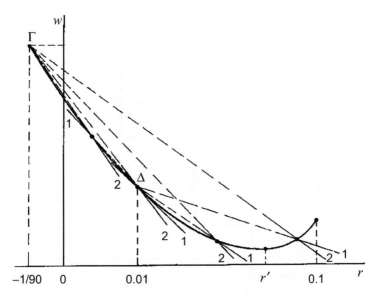

**Fig. 4.7** The actual $w - r$ curve and the linear $w - r$ curves for each process: a $2 \times 2$, closed and joint production economy

$$w_1 > (<) \, w \Leftrightarrow p^* > (<) \, p, \quad \text{for } r < 0.01$$

$$w_1 > (<) \, w \Leftrightarrow p^* < (>) \, p, \quad \text{for } r > 0.01$$

$$r = 0.01 \Leftrightarrow w_1 = w = 0.93$$

and

$$w_2 > (<) \, w \Leftrightarrow p^* < (>) \, p$$

It follows, therefore, that, with respect to the issue of international specialization, the system behaves as a single production system when, and only when, $r < 0.01$, and when, for instance, $0 < r^A < r^B < 0.01$, the international price ratio is not uniquely determined (see Fig. 4.8, where "S" indicates now the international relative supply curve), positive (negative) "specialization gain" appears in economy A (in economy B), and the law of comparative advantage holds (however, not all the properties of single production economies appear, for the matrix $[\mathbf{B} - (1 + r)\mathbf{A}]^{-1}$ contains negative elements). This kind of non-unique determination of the price ratio is due to the consumption demand features and can occur, for instance, in the so-called "classical system with choice of technology" (Simpson 1975, Chap. 14), which is the closed economy–*heterogeneous* labour counterpart of the textbook "Ricardian" model (also see Ricardo 1817, p. 136, footnote), and in closed, joint-product economies (see Kurz and Salvadori 1995, p. 224).

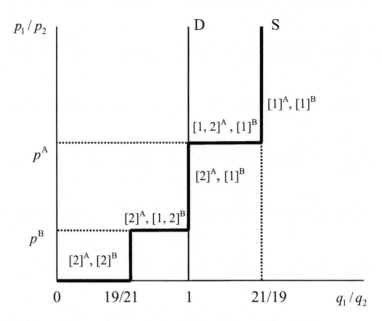

**Fig. 4.8** The international output supply–demand equilibria: $0 < r^A < r^B < 0.01$

As shown by Mainwaring (1974b, 1976b), within the context of single production economies the following holds:

> To each point on any real [actual] wage–rate of profit frontier there corresponds a particular set of relative prices of the commodities. Taking those relative prices as fixed, we may draw a hypothetical, linear wage–profit frontier for each process separately. It is clear that these hypothetical frontiers must intersect at the corresponding point on the actual wage–profit frontier. In addition [...] the absolute slope of the actual frontier, at the point in question, must lie between the maximum and minimum absolute slopes of the hypothetical frontiers [...]. In the special "labour theory of value" case, of course, the relative prices are independent of distribution and hence each hypothetical frontier is the same whichever point on the actual frontier one starts from. And so each hypothetical frontier coincides with all the others and with the actual frontier—hence this last is linear also. (Salvadori and Steedman 1988c, p. 482)

This fundamental property of $2 \times 2$ single production economies is expressed algebraically as follows (we disregard the "labour theory of value" case): Since

$$\dot{w} = s_1 + C = s_2 + D, \quad \dot{w} < 0, \quad s_1 < 0, \quad s_2 < 0$$

and

$$CD < 0 \tag{4.23}$$

it follows that

$$|s_2| < |\dot{w}| < |s_1| \text{ or } |s_1| < |\dot{w}| < |s_2|$$

where $\dot{w}$ denotes the slope of the actual "frontier", $s_1$, $s_2$ the slopes of the aforesaid "hypothetical frontiers", and $C$, $D$ magnitudes which depend on technical conditions of production, the profit rate, and the composition of workers' consumption.

In the irreducible single production case, where the validity of $\dot{w} < 0$ is always given, the "crucial condition" is condition (4.23). By contrast, in the joint production case, none of the said conditions is given *a priori*. For instance, in our numerical example it holds that

(i)   $0 \leq r < 0.01$: $\dot{w} < 0$, $C < 0$, and $D > 0$;
(ii)  $r = 0.01$: $\dot{w} < 0$, $C = 0$, and $D > 0$;[19]
(iii) $0.01 < r < r'$: $\dot{w} < 0$, $C > 0$, and $D > 0$;
(iv)  $r = r'$: $\dot{w} = 0$, $C > 0$, and $D > 0$; and
(v)   $r' < r < 0.1$: $\dot{w} > 0$, $C > 0$, and $D > 0$

where

$$\dot{w} = -\left(\mathbf{p}^T \mathbf{A}[\mathbf{B} - (1+r)\mathbf{A}]^{-1}\mathbf{f}\right)\left(\mathbf{1}^T[\mathbf{B} - (1+r)\mathbf{A}]^{-1}\mathbf{f}\right)^{-1}$$

$$s_j \equiv -(p_1 a_{1j} + p_2 a_{2j})l_j^{-1} < 0$$

$$C \equiv \{\dot{p}_1[b_{11} - (1+r)a_{11}] + \dot{p}_2[b_{21} - (1+r)a_{21}]\}l_1^{-1}$$

$$D \equiv \{\dot{p}_1[b_{12} - (1+r)a_{12}] + \dot{p}_2[b_{22} - (1+r)a_{22}]\}l_2^{-1}$$

and

$$\dot{p}_1 f_1 + \dot{p}_2 f_2 = 0$$

Moreover, given that, when both processes operate, the relations

$$\dot{w} = s_1 + C = s_2 + D, \quad s_1 < 0, \quad s_2 < 0$$

always hold, we conclude that, in the joint production case, the following conditions generally hold:

$$\dot{w} \geq 0 \Rightarrow \{C > 0, D > 0\}$$

$$CD < 0 \Rightarrow \dot{w} < 0$$

$$\{C < 0 \text{ or (and) } D < 0\} \Rightarrow \dot{w} < 0$$

---

[19] See point $\Delta$ in Fig. 4.7. At point $\Gamma$ it holds that $D = 0$.

$$[\mathbf{B} - (1 + r)\mathbf{A}]^{-1} \geq \mathbf{0} \Rightarrow \{\dot{w} < 0, CD < 0\}$$

It has been shown, therefore, that, with respect to the issue of international specialization, the "peculiar" behaviour of joint production economies is due to the fact that it is possible for

$$\dot{w} \geq 0 \Rightarrow \{C > 0, D > 0\} \ \text{ or } \ CD > 0 \nRightarrow \dot{w} \geq 0$$

to hold.[20] Joint production economies can behave like single production economies, in the sense that $\dot{w} < 0$, $CD < 0$, even when the matrix $[\mathbf{B} - (1 + r)\mathbf{A}]^{-1}$ contains negative elements. Conversely, when this matrix is (semi-)positive, joint production economies retain all the wage (consumption)–profit (growth) rate properties of single production economies.

Finally, it should not be forgotten that, when joint production is allowed for, non-negative correlations amongst the distributive variables are possible even when there are no produced means of production and interest charges, while this phenomenon has various implications for the non-Sraffian theories, e.g.

> an import tariff can "harm" both factors (contrary to the Stolper–Samuelson theorem) and [...] a factor supply increase can, at constant commodity prices, provoke an increase in the output of both commodities (contrary to the Rybczynski theorem) [...]. Hence a number of familiar results from "marginalist" theory are not readily generalizable to the joint production case—i.e., to the empirically relevant case. The same is true of familiar ideas relating to neutral Hicksian technical progress. Such progress can, in the presence of joint production, shift an upward sloping wage–rent frontier inwards towards the origin and can, at both constant relative factor prices and constant relative commodity prices, lead to results quite different from those predicted (correctly) in the single-products case [...]. (Salvadori and Steedman 1988a, pp. 188–189)

### Example 4.4: Non-validity of the law of comparative advantage
Consider Example 4.2, and assume that

$$2/3 < r^A < r^B < R_0 \equiv \left(9 + \sqrt{29}\right)/6$$

and that the closed economies use both processes. These imply that $\dot{w}^K < 0$ (see Eq. (4.18)),

$$\{C > 0, D < 0\} \Rightarrow |s_2| < |\dot{w}| < |s_1| \tag{4.24}$$

---

[20]We recall, therefore, Ricardo's (1817) view, "[T]he rate of profits can never be increased but by a fall in wages, and that there can be no permanent fall of wages but in consequence of a fall of the necessaries on which wages are expended. If, therefore, by the extension of foreign trade, or by improvements in machinery, the food and necessaries of the labourer can be brought to market at a reduced price, profits will rise." (p. 132).

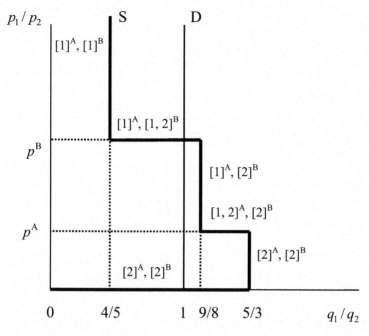

**Fig. 4.9** The international output supply–demand equilibria: $2/3 < r^A < r^B < R_0$, downward supply curve

(see relation (4.23)), and the specialization patterns are determined by the relations $\dot{p}_1 > 0$ and (4.24). It emerges from the demand composition, however, either that both economies specialize in process 2 (in which case Eq. (4.19) hold) or that economy A specializes in process 1, while economy B uses both processes (see Fig. 4.9). In the latter case, the international price ratio equals $p^B$, and economy A exports commodity 2, while economy B exports commodity 1. Consequently, the law of comparative advantage fails to hold; and for $5/3 < r^A$, the non-validity of this law and the positivity of matrix $[\mathbf{B} - (1 + r)\mathbf{A}]^{-1}$ co-exist.

By contrast, for $0 < r^A < r^B < 1/2$, the possible specialization patterns are determined by the relations $\dot{p}_1 > 0$ and

$$\{C < 0, D > 0\} \Rightarrow |s_1| < |\dot{w}| < |s_2|$$

(compare with relation (4.24)).[21] The international price ratio equals $p^A$, economy A uses both processes and exports commodity 1, while economy B specializes in process 1 and exports commodity 2 (see Fig. 4.10). That is, the international relative supply curve is upward, and the law of comparative advantage holds.

---

[21]Such a sign change of $\{C, D\}$ is impossible in the corresponding single production case.

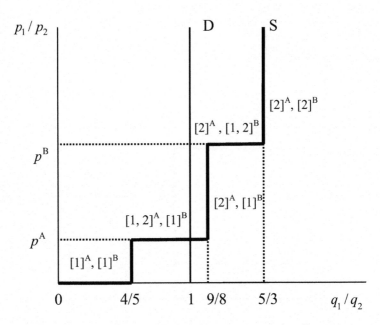

**Fig. 4.10** The international output supply–demand equilibrium: $0 < r^A < r^B < 1/2$, upward supply curve

If we consider all those models in the context of which this law holds, we may conclude that its non-validity is due to the existence of a downward output supply curve. More specifically, the said existence is a necessary but not a sufficient condition for the non-validity of this law, while a necessary and sufficient condition is that the international equilibrium is "unstable" (in the traditional, Walrasian sense).[22]

To deal with the case of downward output supply curves, we assume that, for given $r$ and $g$, with $r > g$, the following holds:

(i) $[B - (1 + g)A] > 0$, which implies that

$$[b_{11} - (1 + g)a_{11}][b_{21} - (1 + g)a_{21}]^{-1}$$
$$< (>) [b_{12} - (1 + g)a_{12}][b_{22} - (1 + g)a_{22}]^{-1} \qquad (4.25)$$

(ii) $p_1/p_2 > 0$, which implies that

$$l_2[b_{11} - (1 + r)a_{11}] < (>) l_1[b_{12} - (1 + r)a_{12}] \qquad (4.26)$$

and

---

[22]There are also cases of non-validity of this law, which are attributed to features of consumption demand only (see, e.g. Chacholiades 1978, pp. 149–151).

$$l_1[b_{22} - (1 + r)a_{22}] < (>) \, l_2[b_{21} - (1 + r)a_{21}] \qquad (4.27)$$

For there to be a downward output supply curve, it must also hold that (see Eq. (4.22))

$$dw_1/dp > (<) \, dw_2/dp$$

which implies that

$$
\begin{aligned}
\{l_2[b_{11} - (1 + r)a_{11}] - l_1[b_{12} - (1 + r)a_{12}]\}f_2 > (<) \\
\{l_2[b_{21} - (1 + r)a_{21}] - l_1[b_{22} - (1 + r)a_{22}]\}f_1
\end{aligned}
\qquad (4.28)
$$

It is thus concluded that nothing prevents the existence of downward output supply curves. Conversely, when there are no produced means of production, i.e. $\mathbf{A} = \mathbf{0}$, or, alternatively, when $r = g$, relations (4.25) to (4.28) cannot hold simultaneously.

As pointed out by John Stanley Metcalfe and Ian Steedman, these two conditions (i.e. $\mathbf{A} = \mathbf{0}$ or $r = g$) are "crucial" also with respect to the possibility of downward-sloping supply curves appearing in the context of a Heckscher–Ohlin–Samuelson (H–O–S) type model of *single* production, i.e. with two commodities, which are used both as means of production and as means of consumption, consumers having identical, homothetic preferences, infinitely many production techniques, zero net accumulation, fixed supplies of two homogeneous primary inputs, and a positive profit (or interest) rate. Thus, they finally concluded that, when the profit rate is the same in both economies, nothing can be said *a priori* about (i) the relationship between "factor prices" and the "factor-intensity" of production methods; and (ii) the shape of the relative supply curve. This makes the H–O–S theorem invalid in its "price" form and means that uniqueness of international equilibrium is to be regarded as a special case. And with different profit rates in the two economies, free trade in commodities would not, in general, equalize real wages and rents as between the economies or, in other words, the "factor price" equalization theorem (Samuelson 1948) is not of general validity (see Steedman 1979b, pp. 15–46).[23]

## 4.3   Sectoral Productivity Changes and the Harrod–Balassa–Samuelson Effect

The real world seems to be characterized by systematic changes in real exchange rates, that is, permanent deviations from "purchasing power parity theory" (or doctrine). Harrod (1933, Chap. 4), Balassa (1964), and Samuelson (1964) have

---

[23] Also see Metcalfe and Steedman (1981) and Montet (1979). Nevertheless, there are H–O–S type theorems which fail to hold even when $r = g = 0$ and there are at least two primary inputs and only one produced input (Steedman 2005; Opocher and Steedman 2015, Chap. 2).

proposed an explanation of the said deviations, which is based on international productivity differences. More specifically, the so-called "Harrod–Balassa–Samuelson effect or productivity bias hypothesis"[24] (H–B–S effect hereafter) is a tendency for countries with higher "total factor productivity" in tradable commodities compared with non-tradables to have higher long-period price levels. Thus, deviations from "purchasing power parity theory" reflect international differences in the long-period relative price of non-tradables.

Following the exposition of the H–B–S effect proposed by Obstfeld and Rogoff (1998, pp. 199–216), which is more general than the original treatment by Balassa (1964) and Samuelson (1964), we will first investigate the relationship between long-period relative prices and sectoral "total factor productivities", within a closed economy framework and then deal with the H–B–S effect.[25]

### 4.3.1  Relative Prices and Productivity Changes

Consider the closed, $n-$ commodity economy described in Sect. 2.3.1, but assume now the existence of neoclassical, constant returns to scale production functions (see, e.g. Burmeister and Dobell 1970, Chaps. 1 and 3):

$$x_j = \tau_j F_j(K_{1j}, K_{2j}, \ldots, K_{nj}, L_j), \quad j = 1, 2, \ldots, n$$

where $x_j$ denotes the gross output of the $j$ th industry, $L_j$, $K_{ij}$ the inputs of labour and the $i$ th capital commodity, respectively, used to produce the $j$ th commodity, and $\tau_j$ a positive parameter, which measures "total factor productivity" in the $j$ th industry. Since the functions $F_j$ are homogeneous of degree one, unit outputs are given by

$$1 = \tau_j F_j(a_{1j}, a_{2j}, \ldots, l_j) \tag{4.29}$$

where $a_{ij} \equiv K_{ij} X_j^{-1}$ and $l_j \equiv L_j X_j^{-1}$. Finally, assume that the economy is in a competitive and steady-state equilibrium.

The first-order conditions for cost-minimization imply that

$$\tau_j p_j(\partial F_j/\partial a_{ij}) = (1 + r)p_i, \quad \tau_j p_j(\partial F_j/\partial l_j) = w \tag{4.30}$$

where $p_j$ denotes the output price of commodity $j$, and $(1 + r)p_i$ the gross "rental rate" for the $i$ th capital commodity. Given the interest (profit) rate from outside the system, the coefficients $a_{ij}$, $l_j$ and the equilibrium commodity prices (in terms of the money wage rate) are uniquely determined by Eqs. (4.29) and (4.30) ("non-

---

[24]Or, according to Samuelson (1994), "Ricardo–Viner–Harrod–Balassa–Samuelson–Penn–Bhagwati effect".

[25]What follows draws on Mariolis (2008), Mariolis et al. (2015).

substitution theorem"; see, e.g. Burmeister and Dobell 1970, Chap. 9). Obviously, in equilibrium it holds that

$$\mathbf{p}^T = w\mathbf{l}^T + (1 + \bar{r})\mathbf{p}^T\mathbf{A} \tag{4.31}$$

where $\mathbf{p}^T$ ($> \mathbf{0}^T$) denotes the equilibrium commodity price vector, $\mathbf{l}^T$, $\mathbf{A}$ the equilibrium values of the direct labour and technical coefficients, respectively, and $\bar{r}$ the exogenously given value of the interest rate ($0 < \bar{r} < R \equiv \lambda_{A1}^{-1} - 1$).

Let $\widehat{\psi}$ denote the logarithmic derivative for any positive variable $\psi$, and consider a rise in the sectoral productivity shifters ("Hicks-neutral technical change"). Differentiation of Eq. (4.29) gives

$$\sum_{i=1}^{n} \tau_j \left[ (\partial F_j / \partial a_{ij}) da_{ij} + (\partial F_j / \partial l_j) dl_j \right] = -\widehat{\tau}_j$$

and substituting conditions (4.30) yields

$$\sum_{i=1}^{n} (1 + \bar{r}) p_i da_{ij} + w dl_j = -p_j \widehat{\tau}_j \tag{4.32}$$

Let $\mathbf{\Theta}_K$ denote the $n \times n$ matrix of the relative shares of the capital commodities in the price of outputs, i.e.

$$\mathbf{\Theta}_K \equiv [\theta_{ij}], \quad \theta_{ij} \equiv (1 + \bar{r}) p_i a_{ij} p_j^{-1}$$

and let $\mathbf{\theta}_L^T$ denote the $1 \times n$ vector of the relative shares of labour in the price of outputs, i.e.

$$\mathbf{\theta}_L^T \equiv [\theta_{Lj}], \quad \theta_{Lj} \equiv w l_j p_j^{-1}$$

It then follows that

$$\mathbf{e}^T = \mathbf{\theta}_L^T + \mathbf{e}^T \mathbf{\Theta}_K$$

or

$$\mathbf{e}^T = \mathbf{\theta}_L^T [\mathbf{I} - \mathbf{\Theta}_K]^{-1} \tag{4.33}$$

where $\mathbf{e}^T$ denotes the summation vector, $[\mathbf{I} - \mathbf{\Theta}_K]^{-1}$ is positive, since $(1 + \bar{r})\mathbf{A}$ and $\mathbf{\Theta}_K$ are similar matrices ($\mathbf{\Theta}_K = \widehat{\mathbf{p}}[(1 + \bar{r})\mathbf{A}]\widehat{\mathbf{p}}^{-1}$), while $\bar{r} < \lambda_{A1}^{-1} - 1$, and $0 < Z \equiv \det [\mathbf{I} - \mathbf{\Theta}_K] < 1$ (Holley 1951).[26]

---

[26]$Z = 1$ iff $\mathbf{A}$ is strictly triangular and, therefore, nilpotent (as in the Austrian-type models).

From Eqs. (4.31) and (4.32), and the definitions of the relative shares of the capital commodities and labour, we obtain

$$\hat{\mathbf{p}}^{\mathrm{T}} = \hat{w}\boldsymbol{\theta}_L^{\mathrm{T}} + \hat{\mathbf{p}}^{\mathrm{T}}\boldsymbol{\Theta}_{\mathrm{K}} - \hat{\boldsymbol{\tau}}^{\mathrm{T}}, \quad \hat{\boldsymbol{\tau}}^{\mathrm{T}} \equiv [\hat{\tau}_1, \hat{\tau}_2, \ldots, \hat{\tau}_n]$$

or, solving for $\hat{\mathbf{p}}^{\mathrm{T}}$ and invoking Eq. (4.33),

$$\hat{\mathbf{p}}^{\mathrm{T}} = \hat{w}\mathbf{e}^{\mathrm{T}} - \hat{\boldsymbol{\tau}}^{\mathrm{T}}[\mathbf{I} - \boldsymbol{\Theta}_{\mathrm{K}}]^{-1}$$

or, finally,

$$\hat{\mathbf{p}}^{\mathrm{T}} - \hat{w}\mathbf{e}^{\mathrm{T}} = -\hat{\boldsymbol{\tau}}^{\mathrm{T}}[\mathbf{I} - \boldsymbol{\Theta}_{\mathrm{K}}]^{-1} \tag{4.34}$$

where the right-hand side of this equation equals the logarithmic derivative of the sum of the series of Sraffa's (1960) "dated quantities of direct labour".

Now it suffices to consider the following two cases:
(i) When $n = 2$, Eq. (4.34) implies that

$$[\hat{w} - \hat{p}_1, \hat{w} - \hat{p}_2] = [\hat{\tau}_1(1 - \theta_{22}) + \hat{\tau}_2\theta_{21}, \hat{\tau}_1\theta_{12} + \hat{\tau}_2(1 - \theta_{11})]Z^{-1} \tag{4.35}$$

and

$$\hat{p}_1 - \hat{p}_2 = (\hat{\tau}_2\theta_{L1} - \hat{\tau}_1\theta_{L2})Z^{-1} \tag{4.36}$$

Hence, when commodity 1 is at least as "labour-intensive" as commodity 2 (i.-e. $\theta_{L1} \geq \theta_{L2}$), faster productivity growth in industry 2 than in industry 1 (i.e. $\hat{\tau}_2 > \hat{\tau}_1$) will push the relative price of commodity 1 upward over time (and *vice versa*). In other words, increased productivities will increase real wage (see Eq. (4.35)), and as a result lead to an increase in the relative price of commodity 1 (unambiguously, when $\theta_{L1} \geq \theta_{L2}$ and $\hat{\tau}_2 > \hat{\tau}_1$ hold). However, in general, the labour intensity difference depends on the ratio of sectoral productivities.[27] Therefore, when, for instance, $\theta_{L1} > \theta_{L2}$ holds initially, and $\hat{\tau}_2 > \hat{\tau}_1$, a reversal of the range of the sectoral labour intensities may take place, which will bring a change in the sign of $\hat{p}_1 - \hat{p}_2$. In the case where $K_{11} = K_{12} = 0$ ("corn–tractor" model or, in the words of Obstfeld and Rogoff 1998, pp. 204–205, commodity 1 "cannot be transformed into capital"), and commodity 2 is the *numéraire*, it follows that

$$\hat{w} = \hat{\tau}_2\theta_{L2}^{-1}$$

and

---

[27]For simplicity, the reader may consider the fixed input coefficients case.

$$\hat{p}_1 = \hat{w}\theta_{L1} - \hat{\tau}_1 = \hat{\tau}_2\theta_{L1}\theta_{L2}^{-1} - \hat{\tau}_1$$

Finally, when commodities are produced by unassisted labour alone (as in the textbook "Ricardian" theory and in Balassa 1964),

$$\hat{p}_1 = \hat{\tau}_2 - \hat{\tau}_1$$

The definite prediction of the movement of relative prices presupposes (a) the existence of a one-to-one relation between the signs of $\hat{p}_1 - \hat{p}_2$ and of $\hat{\tau}_2\theta_{L1} - \hat{\tau}_1\theta_{L2}$; and (b) the independence of the sign of $\theta_{L1} - \theta_{L2}$ from the value of $\tau_2\tau_1^{-1}$. We have seen that in a world with two capital commodities, only the first of these presuppositions is always given. Now we shall see that with more capital commodities the first presupposition is not always given.[28]

(ii) When $n = 3$ and, for instance, $\hat{\tau}_1 \neq \hat{\tau}_2 = \hat{\tau}_3$, Eq. (4.34) implies that

$$\hat{p}_1 - \hat{p}_2 = [(1 - \theta_{33})(\hat{\tau}_2\theta_{L1} - \hat{\tau}_1\theta_{L2}) + \theta_{32}(\hat{\tau}_2\theta_{L1} - \hat{\tau}_1\theta_{L3}) + \hat{\tau}_2\theta_{31}(\theta_{L3} - \theta_{L2})]Z^{-1}$$
(4.37)

$$\hat{p}_1 - \hat{p}_3 = [(1 - \theta_{22})(\hat{\tau}_2\theta_{L1} - \hat{\tau}_1\theta_{L3}) + \theta_{23}(\hat{\tau}_2\theta_{L1} - \hat{\tau}_1\theta_{L2}) + \hat{\tau}_2\theta_{21}(\theta_{L2} - \theta_{L3})]Z^{-1}$$
(4.38)

$$\hat{p}_2 - \hat{p}_3 = [\theta_{12}(\hat{\tau}_2\theta_{L1} - \hat{\tau}_1\theta_{L3}) + \theta_{13}(\hat{\tau}_1\theta_{L2} - \hat{\tau}_2\theta_{L1}) + \hat{\tau}_2(1 - \theta_{11})(\theta_{L2} - \theta_{L3})]Z^{-1}$$
(4.39)

Assume that $\theta_{L1} \geq (\theta_{L2}, \theta_{L3})$ and $\hat{\tau}_2 > \hat{\tau}_1$. In the extreme case where $\theta_{L1} = \theta_{L2} = \theta_{L3}$, it follows that $\hat{p}_1 > \hat{p}_2$ and $\hat{p}_1 > \hat{p}_3$, while the sign of $\hat{p}_2 - \hat{p}_3$ is the same as that of $\theta_{12} - \theta_{13}$. When $\theta_{L2} > (<)\,\theta_{L3}$, it follows that $\hat{p}_1 > \hat{p}_3$ (that $\hat{p}_1 > \hat{p}_2$), while the signs of $\hat{p}_1 - \hat{p}_2$ (of $\hat{p}_1 - \hat{p}_3$) and $\hat{p}_2 - \hat{p}_3$ are not known a priori. Finally, in the other extreme case of a uniform rate of "total factor productivity" change, i.e. $\hat{\tau}^T = \hat{\tau}e^T$, and when, for instance, $\theta_{L1} = \theta_{L2}$, it follows that

$$\hat{p}_1 - \hat{p}_2 = \hat{\tau}(\theta_{L1} - \theta_{L3})(\theta_{32} - \theta_{31})Z^{-1}$$
$$\hat{p}_2 - \hat{p}_3 = \hat{\tau}(\theta_{L2} - \theta_{L3})(1 - \theta_{11} + \theta_{12})Z^{-1}$$

Consequently, in the case in which there are at least three commodities (and even when all industries share a common rate of "total factor productivity" change) it is not possible to formulate a definite prediction.

It is thus concluded that the movement of the relative price of two commodities is determined by the range of relative shares of labour in the industries producing these commodities, in the industries producing the means of production of these

---

[28]The two-sector case is often used for the analysis of real phenomena (such as inflation differentials across Eurozone economies).

commodities, in the industries producing the means of production of the aforesaid means of production, and so on, ad infinitum. Or, in other words, it is determined by the relative movement of the sums of the series of "dated quantities of direct labour", which are needed to produce these commodities. However, because in general it is not possible to say anything more about the relation between the movement of relative commodity prices and the range of relative shares of labour in all the aforementioned industries, and also because this range depends (in an ambiguous way) on the growth rates of productivity *and* on the value of the interest rate, it follows that the attempt to formulate a definite prediction is not only doomed to failure but is also devoid of economic sense.

The issue at hand is formally equivalent to that of price movements arising from non-uniform changes in the sectoral profit rates or from changes in the uniform profit rate (see Chaps. 2 and 3 of the present book). The former case corresponds to $\hat{\boldsymbol{\tau}}^T \neq \hat{\tau} \mathbf{e}^T$, while the latter to $\hat{\boldsymbol{\tau}}^T = \hat{\tau} \mathbf{e}^T$, and our present analysis also implies that, in a world with heterogeneous capital commodities, the Stolper–Samuelson theorem and, therefore, the "factor price" equalization theorem are not of general validity.[29] It should finally be noted that, in the joint production case, $\hat{\boldsymbol{\tau}}^T \geq \mathbf{0}^T$ does not necessarily imply that $\hat{w} \mathbf{e}^T > \hat{\mathbf{p}}^T$, i.e. productivity growth does not necessarily lead to an increase in the real wage rate (Steedman 1985).

### 4.3.2   The Harrod–Balassa–Samuelson Effect

We assume that there are two "small" economies, "Home" and "Foreign", and only three commodities: commodity 1 is non-tradable, while commodities 2 and 3 are tradable. Thus, the international price of commodity 3 in terms of commodity 2, $\pi_3/\pi_2$, is given by world markets.[30] Furthermore, in accordance with Obstfeld and Rogoff (1998, pp. 202–216),[31] we introduce the following assumptions:

*Assumption 1*: There are no impediments to trade.

*Assumption 2*: Labour is perfectly immobile internationally, whereas money capital is perfectly mobile internationally. Thus, the interest rate is given by world markets.

---

[29] On the invalidity of these two theorems, also see Mainwaring (1976b, 1978), Steedman (1979b, Essays 5), Steedman and Metcalfe (1973b). Nevertheless, the prices of the non-Sraffian Standard commodities (see Sects. 3.2.1 and 10.4 of the present book), in terms of the Sraffian Standard commodity, are strictly decreasing functions of the profit rate and, therefore, in accordance with these two theorems (Mariolis 2004b; Mariolis and Tsoulfidis 2011, pp. 93–96).

[30] The relaxation of the assumption regarding "small" economies complicates the analysis (without substantially changing its basic conclusion), because it implies that $\pi_3/\pi_2$ is determined in terms of international relative supply and demand.

[31] Their model is a two-sector model. The existence of a second tradable commodity necessitates the introduction of additional assumptions.

*Assumption 3*: The technologies are identical across economies in the sense that the production function of a sector is the same in both economies. Hence, given Assumption 2, the without-trade relative prices are the same in both economies ($\mathbf{p}^T = \mathbf{p}^{*T}$; an asterisk denotes a foreign variable).

*Assumption 4*: The Home, I, and Foreign, I*, price levels, or cost-of-living indexes, are

$$I = p_1^\beta p_2^\gamma p_3^\delta, \quad I^* = (p_1^*)^\beta (p_2^*)^\gamma (p_3^*)^\delta \qquad (4.40)$$

where $\beta, \gamma$ are positive constants, $\delta \equiv 1 - \beta - \gamma \, (> 0)$, and

$$p_2 = p_2^* = \pi_2 = 1$$

i.e. commodity 2 is the *numéraire*.

*Assumption 5*: It holds that (for instance)

$$p_2/p_3 \leq \pi_2/\pi_3$$

Since each economy exports the commodity which is relatively cheapest to produce, in the with-trade equilibria the economies produce either commodities 1 and 2 or all the commodities.

*Assumption 6*: In the with-trade equilibria it holds that

$$\widehat{\tau}_1 > \widehat{\tau}_1^*, \quad \widehat{\tau}_2 = \widehat{\tau}_3 > \widehat{\tau}_2^* = \widehat{\tau}_3^*, \quad \widehat{\tau}_2 - \widehat{\tau}_2^* > \widehat{\tau}_1 - \widehat{\tau}_1^* \qquad (4.41)$$

i.e. Home's productivity-growth advantage in tradable sectors exceeds its productivity-growth advantage in the non-tradable sector.

*Assumption 7*: The non-tradable commodity is at least as "labour-intensive" as the tradable commodities.[32]

On the basis of these assumptions, the following holds: When the economies produce commodities 1 and 2, Eqs. (4.36), (4.40), and (4.41) imply that

---

[32]Traditionally, it is argued that, *"Empirically*, nontraded goods tend to be at least as labour-intensive as traded goods, so the condition $\theta_{L1} \geq (\theta_{L2}, \theta_{L3})$ [using our symbols] holds *in practice.* Furthermore, productivity growth in nontradables *historically* has been lower than in tradables. One reason for relatively low productivity growth in the nontradables sector is its substantial overlap with *services*, which are inherently less susceptible to standardization and mechanization than are manufactures or agriculture" (Obstfeld and Rogoff 1998, p. 209; emphasis added. Also see the relevant Special Issue of the *Review of International Economics* 1994). However, these observations are highly disputable: consider what was said on the basis of Eq. (4.34), as well as the fact that the empirically relevant case of joint production creates a new kind of insurmountable problems for the traditional approaches. For instance, in that case, (i) the definition of a commodity as "relatively labour-intensive" makes no sense; (ii) relative prices depend on the demand conditions; and (iii) productivity growth does not necessarily lead to an increase in the real wage rate.

$$\hat{I} - \hat{I}^* = \beta\big[(\hat{\tau}_2 - \hat{\tau}_2^*)\theta_{L1} - (\hat{\tau}_1 - \hat{\tau}_1^*)\theta_{L2}\big]Z^{-1} > 0$$

and, therefore, the H–B–S effect is verified. However, when both economies produce all the commodities, Eqs. (4.37) and (4.39), with $\hat{p}_2 = \hat{p}_3 = 0$, and (4.40) imply that

$$\hat{I} - \hat{I}^* = \beta\big(\hat{\tau}_2 - \hat{\tau}_2^*\big)(\theta_{L3} - \theta_{L2})(\theta_{12}\theta_{L3} - \theta_{13}\theta_{L2})^{-1}$$

and, therefore, the H–B–S effect is not necessarily verified.[33]

Now, *ceteris paribus*, let us assume that instead of Assumption 3 the following holds: Both economies' sectoral gross outputs are proportional to the same functions $F_j$, but with different "total factor productivities". More specifically, let us assume that

$$\tau_1 > \tau_1^*, \quad \tau_2 = \tau_3 > \tau_2^* = \tau_3^*, \quad \tau_2/\tau_2^* > \tau_1/\tau_1^*$$

i.e. Home's productivity advantage in tradable sectors exceeds its productivity advantage in the non-tradable sector. In this case the range of the without-trade relative prices is not known *a priori* (consider Eq. (4.39)). Thus, for instance, we assume that

$$p_3^* < \pi_3 < p_3$$

i.e. in the with-trade equilibria Home (Foreign) exports commodity 2 (commodity 3). Equations (4.37)–(4.40) imply that

$$\hat{I} - \hat{I}^* = \beta\big[\hat{\tau}_2\theta_{L1}Z^{-1} - \hat{\tau}_2^*\theta_{L1}^*Z^{*-1} - \big(\hat{\tau}_1\theta_{L2}Z^{-1} - \hat{\tau}_1^*\theta_{L3}^*Z^{*-1}\big)\big]$$

where

$$Z^* \equiv \big(1 - \theta_{11}^*\big)\theta_{L3}^* + \theta_{13}^*\theta_{L1}^*$$

and

$$K_{1j} = 0 \Rightarrow \theta_{L2}Z^{-1} = \theta_{L3}^*Z^{*-1} = 1 \qquad (4.42)$$

---

[33]It should be noted that $\theta_{L2} = \theta_{L3}$ implies that

$$\hat{w} = \hat{\tau}_1\theta_{L1}^{-1} = \hat{\tau}_2\theta_{L2}^{-1} = \hat{w}^*, \quad \hat{I} = \hat{I}^* = 0$$

while $\theta_{12} = \theta_{13}$ implies that $\theta_{L2} = \theta_{L3}$.

Consequently, the H–B–S effect is not necessarily verified, even when Eqs. (4.42) hold.[34] Assuming additionally that $\hat{\tau}_2 > \hat{\tau}_1$ and $\hat{\tau}_2^* > \hat{\tau}_1^*$, the only thing we know is that both I and I* rise.[35]

## 4.4 Synopsis and Final Remarks

The application of the principles of the Sraffian theory of international value to joint production economies, with only one primary input (homogeneous labour) and constant returns to scale, showed that these economies, in contrast with the corresponding single production economies, display two specific features, which are independent of each other:

(i) There is not always a pattern of international specialization, which would entail the increase of the real wage rate in all free-trading economies, while the existence of such a pattern depends on the values of the distributive variables. Conversely, joint production economies can behave like single production economies (with respect to the issue of international specialization) even when they are not $r_0$– all-engaging systems. These are attributed to the properties that the wage–profit rate curve of a joint production economy may have and that are completely different to those that correspond to single production economies.

(ii) The law of comparative advantage does not always hold, while its validity depends on the values of the distributive variables. This is attributed to the fact that the existence of a downward output supply curve is entirely possible in joint production economies. In particular, the co-existence of positive "additive labour values" with an interval of the profit rate in which the system is $r_0$– all-engaging and the output supply curve is downward cannot be ruled out.

In combination with other general features of all production of commodities and positive profits by means of commodities economies (such as the possibility of "negative gains from free trade"), these two specific features of joint production economies further reveal the inner limits of the traditional value theory.

---

[34]Both Balassa (1964, pp. 585–586) and Samuelson (1964, pp. 147–148) refer to the non-tradable commodities as services. Thus, in the relevant literature it is considered that Eq. (4.42) are in accordance with this reference. Of course, all these are simplifications (also see Steedman 1979a, pp. 99–105).

[35]The hitherto available empirical evidence on the relative price effects of total productivity shift (see Eq. (4.34)), with $\hat{\tau}^T = \hat{\tau} e^T$) suggests that the direction of the price movements is, more often than not, governed by the labour cost condition, while this is reduced to the "skew distribution" (see Chap. 3 of this book) of the eigenvalues of the matrices, $\Theta_K$, of the relative shares of the capital commodities (Mariolis et al. 2015). The empirical evidence on the H–B–S effect provides rather mixed findings, while, for instance, according to Tica and Družić (2006), "[t]he growing body of evidence makes it difficult to ignore the HBS theory and definitely points towards professional rethinking about the contemporary significance of the Harrod–Balassa–Samuelson theory." (p. 15).

It has also been shown that the Harrod–Balassa–Samuelson effect cannot, in general, be extended beyond the self-referential world of only one commodity. It is thus not expected that the inclusion in the model of the process of economic growth, the conditions of demand (removing the assumption about "small" economies), additional primary "factors" (such as labour of different kinds and land of different qualities), fixed capital, and pure joint-products would lead to a different conclusion. The so-called alternative approach, proposed by Kravis and Lipsey (1983, 1988) and Bhagwati (1984), while reaching the same conclusion as Balassa (1964) and Samuelson (1964), is based on the concept of "capital" as a primary input and, consequently, on the existence of a strictly increasing function between the "capital"–labour ratio and the real wage rate. That is, it is explicitly based on the traditional theory(-ies) and, therefore, the examination of this "alternative approach" is not necessary. Finally, given the direct analytical relationships amongst the H–B–S effect, the Stolper–Samuelson theorem, and the "factor price" equalization theorem, it also follows that these theorems are not of general validity, and the reason for this triple breakdown is that there is not necessarily an unambiguous relationship between the movement of the long-period relative price of two commodities, on the one hand, and the ratios of relative labour shares to growth rates of total productivity in the industries producing these commodities, on the other hand. This is, it could now be stated, the *full* message of Piero Sraffa's analysis of the relative price movements.

Since the prevailing debates about capitalist trade liberalization, integration, and holopoiesis ("globalization") are based, explicitly or otherwise, on the traditional, "mainstream" and "radical", international value theories, the Sraffian theory findings of this chapter (as well as those of Chaps. 6 and 9) form the basis for the development of a coherent alternative discourse.

# References

Abraham-Frois, G., & Berrebi, E. (1984). Taux de profit minimum dans les modèles de production. In C. Bidard (Ed.), *La production jointe. Nouveaux débats* (pp. 211–229). Paris: Economica.

Balassa, B. (1964). The purchasing-power parity doctrine: A reappraisal. *Journal of Political Economy, 72*(6), 584–596.

Baldone, S. (2000). A comment on Steedman. In T. Cozzi & R. Marchionatti (Eds.), *Piero Sraffa's political economy: A centenary estimate* (pp. 359–361). London: Routledge.

Bhagwati, J. N. (1984). Why are services cheaper in the poor countries? *The Economic Journal, 94*(374), 279–286.

Bidard, C. (1991). *Prix, reproduction, rareté*. Paris: Dunod.

Bidard, C. (1996). All-engaging systems. *Economic Systems Research, 8*(4), 323–340.

Bidard, C. (1997). Pure joint production. *Cambridge Journal of Economics, 21*(6), 685–701.

Brewer, A. (1985). Trade with fixed real wages and mobile capital. *Journal of International Economics, 18*(1–2), 177–186.

Burmeister, E., & Dobell, R. A. (1970). *Mathematical theories of economic growth.* New York: Macmillan.

Burmeister, E., & Kuga, K. (1970). The factor-price frontier, duality and joint production. *The Review of Economic Studies, 37*(1), 11–19.

Chacholiades, M. (1978). *International trade theory and policy.* Singapore: McGraw-Hill.

d'Autume, A. (1986). Le rôle intime de la demande dans la production jointe. In R. Arena & J.-L. Ravix (Eds.). (1990). *Sraffa, trente ans après* (pp. 245–256). Paris: Presses Universitaires de France.

d'Autume, A. (1988). La production jointe: Le point de vue de la théorie de l'équilibre général. *Revue Économique, 39*(2), 325–347.

Debreu, G. (1984). *Théorie de la valeur. Analyse axiomatique de l'équilibre économique. Suivi d'un inédit en français: Existence d'un équilibre concurrentiel* (2ᵉ éd.). Paris: Dunod.

Diewert, W. E. (1971). An application of the Shephard duality theorem: A generalized Leontief production function. *Journal of Political Economy, 79*(3), 481–507.

Dmitriev, V. K. (1974). *Economic essays on value, competition and utility.* Edited with an introduction by D. M. Nuti. London: Cambridge University Press.

Emmanuel, A. (1969). *L'échange inégal: essai sur les antagonismes dans les rapports économiques internationaux.* Paris: François Maspero.

Emmanuel, A. (1975). *Unequal exchange revisited.* Discussion Paper No. 77, Institute of Development Studies, University of Sussex.

Filippini, C., & Filippini, L. (1982). Two theorems on joint production. *The Economic Journal, 92* (366), 386–390.

Filippini, C., & Filippini, L. (1984). La frontière de prix des facteurs dans les modèles de production jointe. In C. Bidard (Ed.), *La production jointe. Nouveaux débats* (pp. 52–64). Paris: Economica.

Giammanco, M. D. (1998). Scarcity of resources in a Sraffian framework of international trade. *Metroeconomica, 49*(3), 300–318.

Goodwin, R. M. (1972). Capitalism's golden rule. *Bulletin of the Conference of Socialist Economist, 2*(2), 56. Reprinted in R. M. Goodwin (1982). *Essays in Economic Dynamics* (pp. 171–172). London: Palgrave Macmillan.

Hagen, E. E. (1958). An economic justification of protectionism. *The Quarterly Journal of Economics, 72*(4), 496–514.

Harrod, R. F. (1933). *International economics.* London: James Nisbet and Cambridge University Press.

Hilferding, R. (1981). *Finance capital. A study of the latest phase of capitalist development.* Edited with an introduction by T. Bottomore from translations by M. Watnick and S. Gordon. London: Routledge & Kegan Paul.

Holley, J. L. (1951). Note on the inversion of the Leontief Matrix. *Econometrica, 19*(3), 317–320.

Jones, R. W. (1992). Jointness in production and factor-price equalization. *Review of International Economics, 1*(1), 10–18.

Jones, R. W. (2012). General equilibrium theory and competitive trade models. *International Journal of Economic Theory, 8*(2), 149–164.

Jones, R. W., & Weder, R. (Eds.). (2017). *200 Years of Ricardian trade theory. Challenges of globalization.* Cham: Springer.

Kahn, R. F. (1931). The relation of home investment to unemployment. *The Economic Journal, 41* (162), 173–198.

Kehoe, T. J. (1985). Multiplicity of equilibria and comparative statics. *The Quarterly Journal of Economics, 100*(1), 119–147.

Kravis I. B., & Lipsey R. E. (1983). *Towards an explanation of national price levels.* Princeton Studies in International Financial, no. 52. Princeton: Princeton University Press.

Kravis, I. B., & Lipsey, R. E. (1988). National price levels and the prices of tradables and nontradables. *The American Economic Review. Papers and Proceedings of the One-Hundredth Annual Meeting of the American Economic Association, 78*(2), 474–478.

Kurz, H. D., & Salvadori, N. (1995). *Theory of production. A long-period analysis.* Cambridge: Cambridge University Press.

Latham, R. W. (1975). The golden rule of accumulation under alternative savings assumptions. *Oxford Economic Papers, 27*(3), 462–469.

Lenin, V. I. (1917). Imperialism, the highest stage of capitalism. A popular outline. In V. I. Lenin (Ed.), *Collected works* (Vol. 22, pp. 185–304). Moscow: Progress Publishers.

Mainwaring, L. (1974a). *A neo-Ricardian analysis of trade.* Ph.D. Thesis, Manchester: University of Manchester.

Mainwaring, L. (1974b). A neo-Ricardian analysis of international trade. *Kyklos, 27*(3), 537–553. Reprinted in I. Steedman (Ed.). (1979). *Fundamental issues in trade theory* (pp. 110–122). London: Macmillan.

Mainwaring, L. (1976a). The correction of neo-Ricardian trade losses. *Economia Internazionale/ International Economics, 29*(1), 92–99.

Mainwaring, L. (1976b). Relative prices and "factor price" equalisation in a heterogeneous capital goods model. *Australian Economic Papers, 15*(26), 109–118. Reprinted in I. Steedman (Ed.). (1979). *Fundamental issues in trade theory* (pp. 77–89). London: Macmillan.

Mainwaring, L. (1978). The interest rate equalisation theorem with non-traded goods. *Journal of International Economics, 8*(1), 11–19. Reprinted in I. Steedman (Ed.), (1979). *Fundamental issues in trade theory* (pp. 90–98). London: Macmillan.

Mainwaring, L. (1979). On the transition from autarky to trade. In I. Steedman (Ed.). (1979). *Fundamental issues in trade theory* (pp. 131–141). London: Macmillan.

Mainwaring, L. (1991). *Dynamics of uneven development.* Aldershot: Edward Elgar.

Manoilescu, M. (1929). *Théorie du protectionism et de l'échange international.* Paris: M. Giard.

Mariolis, T. (2000). The division of labour in European Monetary Union: Absolute versus comparative advantage. *European Research Studies, 3*(1–2), 79–90.

Mariolis, T. (2004a). Pure joint production and international trade: A note. *Cambridge Journal of Economics, 28*(3), 449–456.

Mariolis, T. (2004b). A Sraffian approach to the Stolper–Samuelson theorem. *Asian African Journal of Economics and Econometrics, 4*(1), 1–11.

Mariolis, T. (2005a). *A neo-Ricardian critique of the traditional static theory of trade, customs unions and common markets.* MPRA Paper No. 23088. Retrieved May 12, 2020, from https://mpra.ub.uni-muenchen.de/23088/.

Mariolis, T. (2005b). Endogenous growth and ambiguous steady-state gains from free trade. *Indian Development Review. An International Journal of Development Economics, 3*(1), 15–27.

Mariolis, T. (2008). Heterogeneous capital goods and the Harrod–Balassa–Samuelson effect. *Metroeconomica, 59*(2), 238–248.

Mariolis, T. (2010). *Essays on the logical history of political economy.* Athens: Matura (in Greek).

Mariolis, T. (2018). Dimosthenis S. Stefanidis: The Greek pioneer of the theory of "unequal exchange" and cumulative causation in international economics. In T. Mariolis (Ed.), *Essays on the work of Dimitris Batsis: "The heavy industry in Greece"* (pp. 157–168). Athens: Tziola Publications (in Greek).

Mariolis, T. (2019). *The "second wave" of the Sraffian critical transcendence of the traditional political economy.* Paper presented at the 1st Conference of the Study Group on Sraffian Economics: "From the Capital Theory Controversy in the 1960s to Greece's Virtual Bankruptcy in 2010", 11–12 April 2019, Panteion University, Athens, Greece (in Greek).

Mariolis, T., & Soklis, G. (2018). *The non-monotonic wage–profit curve and its implications for the traditional political economy.* Paper presented at the 20th Conference of the Greek Historians of Economic Thought, 1–2 June 2018, University of Thessalia, Volos, Greece (in Greek).

Mariolis, T., & Tsoulfidis, L. (2011). Eigenvalue distribution and the production price–profit rate relationship: Theory and empirical evidence. *Evolutionary and Institutional Economics Review, 8*(1), 87–122.

Mariolis, T., Rodousakis, N., & Christodoulaki, A. (2015). Input–output evidence on the relative price effects of total productivity shift. *International Review of Applied Economics, 29*(2), 150–163.

Marx, K. (1991). *Capital. A critique of political economy. Volume Three.* Harmondsworth: Penguin Books.

Mas-Colell, A. (1985). *The theory of general economic equilibrium. A differentiable approach.* Cambridge: Cambridge University Press.

Metcalfe, J. S., & Steedman, I. (1974). A note on the gain from trade. *Economic Record, 50*(4), 581–595. Reprinted in I. Steedman (Ed.). (1979). *Fundamental issues in trade theory* (pp. 47–63). London: Macmillan.

Metcalfe, J. S., & Steedman, I. (1981). On two production possibility frontiers. *Metroeconomica, 33* (1-2-3), 1–19.

Montani, G. (2010). The Neoricardian theory of economic integration. *Bulletin of Political Economy, 4*(1), 31–43.

Montani, G. (2012). World trade and world money: A Neoricardian outlook on global economy. *Bulletin of Political Economy, 6*(1), 1–17.

Montet, C. (1979). Reswitching and primary input use: A comment. *The Economic Journal, 89* (355), 642–647.

Nuti, D. M. (1970). Capitalism, socialism and steady growth. *The Economic Journal, 80*(317), 32–57.

Obstfeld, M., & Rogoff, K. (1998). *Foundations of international macroeconomics.* Cambridge, MA: MIT Press.

Opocher, A., & Steedman, I. (2015). *Full industry equilibrium. A theory of the industrial long run.* Cambridge: Cambridge University Press.

Parrinello, S. (1970). Introduzione ad una teoria neoricardiana del commercio internazionale. *Studi Economici, 25*(3–4), 267–321.

Ravix, J. T. (1979). Note sur la théorie ricardienne du commerce international. *Cahiers d'économie politique/Papers in Political Economy, 5,* 101–117.

Ravix, J. T. (1990). Prix internationaux et spécialisation dans les analyses post-sraffaiennes du commerce international. In R. Arena & J.-L. Ravix (Eds.), *Sraffa, trente ans après* (pp. 413–425). Paris: Presses Universitaires de France.

Review of International Economics. (1994). Special issue: Thirty years of the Balassa–Samuelson model. *Review of International Economics, 2*(3).

Ricardo, D. (1817). *On the principles of political economy and taxation.* In D. Ricardo (1951–1973). *The works and correspondence of David Ricardo* (Vol. 1). Edited by P. Sraffa with the collaboration of M. H. Dobb. Cambridge: Cambridge University Press.

Rodrik, D. (2011). *The globalization paradox. Why global markets, states, and democracy can't coexist.* Oxford: Oxford University Press.

Salvadori, N., & Steedman, I. (1988a). Joint production analysis in a Sraffian framework. *Bulletin of Economic Research, 40*(3), 165–195.

Salvadori, N., & Steedman, I. (1988b). A note about the interest rate and the revenue function. *Eastern Economic Journal, 14*(2), 153–156.

Salvadori, N., & Steedman, I. (1988c). No reswitching? No switching! *Cambridge Journal of Economics, 12*(4), 481–486.

Samuelson, P. A. (1948). International trade and the equalisation of factor prices. *The Economic Journal, 58*(230), 163–184.

Samuelson, P. A. (1962). Parable and realism in capital theory: The surrogate production function. *The Review of Economic Studies, 29*(3), 193–206.

Samuelson, P. A. (1964). Theoretical notes on trade problems. *The Review of Economics and Statistics, 46*(2), 145–154.

Samuelson, P. A. (1992). Factor-price equalization by trade in joint and non-joint production. *Review of International Economics, 1*(1), 1–9.

Samuelson, P. A. (1994). Facets of Balassa-Samuelson thirty years later. *Review of International Economics, 2*(3), Special issue: Thirty years of the Balassa–Samuelson model, 201–226.

Scarf, H. E., & Wilson, C. A. (2005). Uniqueness of equilibrium in the multicountry Ricardo model. In T. J. Kehoe, T. N. Srinivasan, & J. Whalley (Eds.), *Frontiers in applied general equilibrium modeling. In honor of Herbert Scarf* (pp. 24–44). Cambridge: Cambridge University Press.

Schefold, B. (1978). Multiple product techniques with properties of single product systems. *Journal of Economics, 38*(1–2), 29–53.

Shephard, R. W. (1953). *Cost and production functions*. Princeton, NJ: Princeton University Press.

Simpson, D. (1975). *General equilibrium analysis*. Oxford: Basil Blackwell.

Sraffa, P. (1930). An alleged correction of Ricardo. *The Quarterly Journal of Economics, 44*(3), 539–544.

Sraffa, P. (1960). *Production of commodities by means of commodities. Prelude to a critique of economic theory*. Cambridge: Cambridge University Press.

Steedman, I. (1975). Positive profits with negative surplus value. *The Economic Journal, 85*(337), 114–123.

Steedman, I. (1976a). Positive profits with negative surplus value: A reply. *The Economic Journal, 86*(343), 604–607.

Steedman, I. (1976b). Positive profits with negative surplus value: A reply to Wolfstetter. *The Economic Journal, 86*(344), 873–876.

Steedman, I. (1979a). *Trade amongst growing economies*. Cambridge: Cambridge University Press.

Steedman, I. (Ed.). (1979b). *Fundamental issues in trade theory*. London: Macmillan.

Steedman, I. (1979c). The von Neumann analysis and the small open economy. In I. Steedman (Ed.), *Fundamental issues in trade theory* (pp. 142–158). London: Macmillan.

Steedman, I. (1982). Joint production and the wage–rent frontier. *The Economic Journal, 92*(366), 377–385.

Steedman, I. (1985). Joint production and technical progress. *Political Economy. Studies in the Surplus Approach, 1*(1), 127–138.

Steedman, I. (1992). Joint production and the "New Solution" to the transformation problem. *Indian Economic Review, 27*, Special number in memory of Sukhamoy Chakravarty, 123–127.

Steedman, I. (1999). Production of commodities by means of commodities and the open economy. *Metroeconomica, 50*(3), 260–276. Reprinted in T. Cozzi & R. Marchionatti (Eds.). (2000). *Piero Sraffa's political economy: A centenary estimate* (pp. 239–253). London: Routledge.

Steedman, I. (2005). The comparative statics of industry-level produced-input-use in HOS trade theory. *Review of Political Economy, 17*(3), 465–470.

Steedman, I. (2018). Foreign trade. In *The new Palgrave. A dictionary of economics* (3rd ed., pp. 4878–4887). London: Palgrave Macmillan.

Steedman, I., & Metcalfe, J. S. (1973a). On foreign trade. *Economia Internazionale/International Economics, 26*(3–4), 516–528. Reprinted in I. Steedman (Ed.). (1979). *Fundamental issues in trade theory* (pp. 99–119). London: Macmillan.

Steedman, I., & Metcalfe, J. S. (1973b). The non-substitution theorem and international trade theory. *Australian Economic Papers, 12*(21), 267–269. Reprinted in I. Steedman (Ed.). (1979). *Fundamental issues in trade theory* (pp. 123–126). London: Macmillan.

Steedman, I., & Metcalfe, J. S. (1981). On duality and basic commodities in an open economy. *Australian Economic Papers, 20*(36), 133–141.

Stefanidis, D. (1930). *The inflow of foreign capital and its economic and political consequences*. Thessaloniki (in Greek).

Stolper, W. F., & Samuelson, P. A. (1941). Protection and real wages. *The Review of Economic Studies, 9*(1), 58–73.

Tica, J., & Družić, I. (2006). *The Harrod–Balassa–Samuelson effect: A survey of empirical evidence*. EFZG Working Paper Series, No. 06–7/686, 1–38.

von Neumann, J. (1937). Über ein ökonomisches Gleichungssystem und eine Verallgemeinerung des Brouwerschen Fixpunktsatzes. In K. Menger (Ed.), *Ergebnisse eines Mathematischen Kolloquiums, 8* (pp. 73–83). Leipzig: Deuticke.

von Neumann, J. (1945). A model of general economic equilibrium. *The Review of Economic Studies, 13*(1), 1–9.

# Chapter 5
# Empirical Pitfalls of the Traditional Value Theory: Joint Production and Actual Economies

**Abstract** This chapter extends the empirical investigation of the shape of wage–profit rate curves and of the relationships amongst "labour values", long-period values, i.e. production prices, and market values to the case of joint production using data from eighty-five Supply and Use Tables for twelve different national economies. It is found that (i) the considered systems do not have the usual properties of single production systems; (ii) the monotonicity of the estimated wage–profit rate curves depends on the choice of the *numéraire*; and (iii) there are cases in which the vectors of "additive labour values" and/or actual long-period values are economically irrelevant. The evaluation of the results reveals the inner limits of the traditional value theory and, therefore, that actual economies cannot be coherently analysed in terms of that theory.

**Keywords** Actual economies · Joint production · Traditional value theory · Value deviations · Wage–profit rate curves

## 5.1 Introduction

Classical and Marxian value theories support the view that "labour values" are the main determinants of long-period values and market values. Since Sraffa's (1960) contribution, it has been gradually recognized that, in the linear single production–homogeneous labour case, the conditions of production and the real wage rate suffice to determine long-period values without any reference to "labour values".[1] Moreover, the exploration of the problem of choice of techniques by Sraffa (1960, Chap. 12) demonstrated the possibility that a higher profit rate can be associated with higher capital intensity and/or that a production technique can be cost-minimizing over more than one interval of the profit rate (see Sect. 2.3.3 of the

---

[1]For an exhaustive Sraffa-based critique of the Marxian labour value theory, see Steedman (1977, 1985, 2008).

© Springer Nature Singapore Pte Ltd. 2021
T. Mariolis et al., *Spectral Theory of Value and Actual Economies*, Evolutionary
Economics and Social Complexity Science 24,
https://doi.org/10.1007/978-981-33-6260-4_5

present book). As is well known, these two phenomena, widely known as "reverse capital deepening" and "re-switching of techniques", respectively, have crucial implications for the traditional value theory (classical, Marxian, Austrian, and neoclassical); for instance, they indicate that, on the one hand, the attempts of the neoclassical or Austrian school to start from a given "quantity of capital" or an "average period of production", in order to determine the profit or interest rate, are ill-founded, and, on the other hand, that an analysis of the cost-minimization problem in terms of "labour values" can be incompatible with that in terms of long-period values.

During the last decades, a significant number of empirical studies have explored, using input–output table data, (a) the shape of wage–profit rate ($w - r$) curves constructed for different years and/or the outer envelope of the $w - r$ curves corresponding to different national economies and years (as if the available input–output data belong to a uniform, across space and time, technology); and (b) the relationships amongst "labour values", actual long-period values (ALPVs), i.e. production prices that correspond to the "actual" real wage rate (estimated on the basis of the available input–output data), and market values (MVs).[2] The central conclusions of these studies are the following:

(i). The $w - r$ curves are near-linear, in the sense that the correlation coefficients between the distributive variables tend to be above 99%, and do not display many curvatures, i.e. their second derivatives change sign no more than once or, very rarely, twice, irrespective of the *numéraire* chosen.

(ii). The vectors of "labour values" are quite close to ALPVs and MVs, as this can be judged by alternative measures of value deviation.

On the basis of these findings, it is *usually* argued that phenomena such as reverse capital deepening and re-switching of techniques, highlighted by the Sraffian theory, constitute mathematical curiosities rather than real possibilities of actual economic systems. The same line of argument suggests that although the basic propositions of the traditional value theory are not true in general, they appear to be a good approximation to reality.

To the best of our knowledge, all the empirical studies that explore the shape of $w - r$ curves and/or value deviations are based on data from Symmetric Input–Output Tables and, therefore, on models of single production (see Chap. 1). However, in the real world, joint production constitutes the rule, whereas single production activities are the exception. Hence, the extension of the empirical investigation to the joint production case is necessary.

This chapter extends the empirical investigation of the shape of $w - r$ curves and of the relationships amongst "labour values" and actual values, i.e. ALPVs and MVs, to the case of joint production. Section 5.2 presents the analytic framework. Section 5.3 explores (i) the shape of $w - r$ curves using data from the Supply and

---

[2]For a critical presentation and interpretation, see Mariolis and Tsoulfidis (2016, Chaps. 3 and 5) and Chaps. 2 and 3 of the present book. Also see Li (2017), who focuses on fixed capital modelling.

Use Tables (SUTs) of the Finnish economy (for the years 1995 through 2004) and (ii) the relationships amongst "labour values", ALPVs, and MVs using data from eighty-five SUTs for twelve different national economies, i.e. Denmark, Finland, France, FYROM (former), Germany, Greece, Hungary, Japan, Portugal, Slovenia, Sweden, and the USA.[3] Finally, Sect. 5.4 concludes.

## 5.2   The Analytic Framework

### 5.2.1   Wage–Profit Rate Curves in Joint Production Economies

We assume a closed, square, and linear system of joint production with circulating capital and homogeneous labour, which is not an input to the household sector. The net product is distributed to profits and wages that are paid at the beginning of the production period and there are no savings out of this income. The givens in our analysis are (i) the vector of MVs and (ii) the technical conditions of production, i.e. the triplet $\{\mathbf{B}, \mathbf{A}, \mathbf{l}^T\}$, where $\mathbf{B}$ represents the $n \times n$ make matrix, $\mathbf{A}$ the $n \times n$ use matrix, and $\mathbf{l}^T$ the $1 \times n$ vector of employment levels process by process.[4] On the basis of these assumptions, the long-period values, $\mathbf{p}$, are given by

$$\mathbf{p}^T\mathbf{B} = (1 + r)(w\mathbf{l}^T + \mathbf{p}^T\mathbf{A}) \tag{5.1}$$

$$\mathbf{p}^T\mathbf{z} = 1 \tag{5.2}$$

where $r$ is the uniform profit rate, $w$ the money wage rate, and $\mathbf{z}$ the standard of value or *numéraire*. Provided that $[\mathbf{B} - (1 + r)\mathbf{A}]$ is non-singular, Eqs. (5.1) and (5.2) imply that

$$w = [(1 + r)\mathbf{l}^T\mathbf{E}(r)\mathbf{z}]^{-1} \tag{5.3}$$

where $\mathbf{E}(r) \equiv [\mathbf{B} - (1 + r)\mathbf{A}]^{-1}$. Equation (5.3) gives a $w - r$ curve for this economy. By contrast with single production systems, when joint production is allowed for, $\mathbf{E}(r)$ may contain negative elements. However, in the case where $[\mathbf{B}-\mathbf{A}]^{-1} > \mathbf{0}$ ($[\mathbf{B}-\mathbf{A}]^{-1} \geq \mathbf{0}$), the system $\{\mathbf{B}, \mathbf{A}\}$ is called "all-engaging" ("all-productive") and is characterized by $\mathbf{E}(r) > \mathbf{0}$ ($\mathbf{E}(r) \geq \mathbf{0}$) for $0 \leq r \leq R$, where $R$ is the only positive root of $\det[\mathbf{B} - (1 + r)\mathbf{A}]$ associated with a positive eigenvector.[5] Therefore, when

---

[3]For the available SUTs as well as the construction of the relevant variables, see the Appendix at the end of this chapter.

[4]The transpose of an $n \times 1$ vector $\boldsymbol{\chi} \equiv [\chi_i]$ is denoted by $\boldsymbol{\chi}^T$, the diagonal matrix formed from the elements of $\boldsymbol{\chi}$ is denoted by $\hat{\boldsymbol{\chi}}$, and $\mathbf{e}$ denotes the summation vector, i.e. $\mathbf{e} \equiv [1, 1, \ldots, 1]^T$.

[5]See Sects. 1.5 and 4.2.1 of this book.

the system $\{\mathbf{B}, \mathbf{A}\}$ is all-engaging (all-productive), it holds $\mathbf{p}^T > \mathbf{0}^T$ ($\mathbf{p}^T \geq \mathbf{0}^T$) for $0 \leq r \leq R$ and the $w - r$ curve is downward-sloping. Conversely, when $[\mathbf{B} - \mathbf{A}]^{-1}$ contains negative elements, nothing guarantees the existence of an interval of $r$ in which long-period values are (semi-)positive.[6] Moreover, even if such an interval exists, the monotonicity of the $w - r$ curve is *a priori* unknown and may depend on the adopted normalization condition.[7] In that case it is important to study whether the "labour-commanded" values, $\mathbf{p}_w^T \equiv w^{-1}\mathbf{p}^T$, are directly related to the profit rate, because if each element of the vector of labour-commanded values is a strictly increasing function of the profit rate, then the $w - r$ curve is strictly decreasing irrespective of the *numéraire* chosen. As is well known, some labour-commanded values are inversely related to the profit rate iff there exists a non-negative linear combination of processes that yields a greater $r$ – net output than a non-negative linear combination of the remaining ones, while the input values of the former combination are lower (see Filippini and Filippini 1982, pp. 389–390; Salvadori and Steedman 1988, p. 181).

### 5.2.2 Values in Joint Production Economies

Now, we further assume that the real wage rate, which is represented by the $n \times 1$ vector $\mathbf{b}$, is exogenously given.[8] Then, Eq. (5.1) can be rewritten as

$$\mathbf{p}^T\mathbf{B} = (1+r)\left(w\mathbf{l}^T + \mathbf{p}^T\mathbf{A}\right) \tag{5.4}$$

$$w = \mathbf{p}^T\mathbf{b} \tag{5.5}$$

From Eqs. (5.4) and (5.5) it follows that

$$\mathbf{p}^T\mathbf{B} = (1+r)\mathbf{p}^T\mathbf{C} \tag{5.6}$$

where $\mathbf{C} \equiv [\mathbf{b}\mathbf{l}^T + \mathbf{A}]$ represents the "augmented" use matrix. Provided that $\mathbf{B}$ is non-singular, Eq. (5.6) implies that

$$(1+r)^{-1}\mathbf{p}^T = \mathbf{p}^T\mathbf{C}\mathbf{B}^{-1} \tag{5.7}$$

---

[6]Some long-period values are negative at a given profit rate iff there exists a non-negative linear combination of processes that yields a greater $r$ – net output (i.e. gross output minus $(1 + r)$ times the production inputs) than a non-negative linear combination of the remaining ones (see Filippini and Filippini 1982, pp. 387–388; Salvadori and Steedman 1988, p. 179).

[7]For the implications of upward-sloping $w - r$ curves, see Sects. 4.2 and 8.5.2 of this book.

[8]What follows draws on Mariolis (2006), Mariolis and Soklis (2007, 2010).

where $(1 + r)^{-1}$ is an eigenvalue of the matrix $\mathbf{CB}^{-1}$, and $\mathbf{p}^T$ is the corresponding left eigenvector.

The vector of "additive labour values" (ALVs), $\mathbf{v}^T \equiv [v_j]$ (see Sect. 4.2.1) and the corresponding total "surplus value", $S$, are given by the following equations:

$$\mathbf{v}^T \mathbf{B} = \mathbf{l}^T + \mathbf{v}^T \mathbf{A} \tag{5.8}$$

$$S = \mathbf{v}^T \mathbf{u} \tag{5.9}$$

where $\mathbf{u} \equiv [\mathbf{B} - \mathbf{C}]\mathbf{e}$ represents the surplus product. Provided that $[\mathbf{B} - \mathbf{A}]$ is non-singular, Eqs. (5.8) and (5.9) imply that

$$\mathbf{v}^T = \mathbf{l}^T [\mathbf{B} - \mathbf{A}]^{-1} \tag{5.10}$$

$$S = \left(1 - \mathbf{v}^T \mathbf{b}\right) \mathbf{l}^T \mathbf{e} \tag{5.11}$$

From Eq. (5.10) it follows that $\mathbf{v}^T$ is uniquely determined, while from Eq. (5.11) it follows that $S$ is positive iff the unit "labour value of labour power", $\mathbf{v}^T \mathbf{b}$, is less than 1.

Nevertheless, nothing guarantees the derivation of a (semi-)positive solution for $[r, \mathbf{p}^T, \mathbf{v}^T]$ from Eqs. (5.7) and (5.10).[9] Thus, in the case of joint production, is *a priori* unknown if the empirical investigation of the relationships amongst ALVs, ALPVs, and MVs is economically relevant. However, in the case of all-engaging (all-productive) systems (see Sect. 5.2.1), the ALVs and the ALPVs are uniquely determined and positive (semi-positive). Finally, it should be stressed that any "complication" related to joint production, i.e. non-squareness, inconsistency, or non-unique economically relevant solution for $[r, \mathbf{p}^T]$ and/or $\mathbf{v}^T$ (see Bidard 1986a; Steedman 1977, Chaps. 12 and 13), can be adequately handled on the basis of general joint production models inspired by von Neumann (1937, 1945) and Sraffa (1960).

## 5.3 Empirical Investigation

### 5.3.1 Wage–Profit Rate Curves in Actual Joint Production Economies

The application of the analysis exposed in Sect. 5.2.1 to the SUTs of the Finnish economy (for the years 1995 through 2004) gives the following results:[10]

(i). The matrices $[\mathbf{B} - \mathbf{A}]$ are non-singular and, therefore, invertible.

---

[9]See Fujimoto and Krause (1988), Hosoda (1993).

[10]What follows draws on Soklis (2011, 2012, pp. 159–176; 2019).

(ii). The matrices $[\mathbf{B} - \mathbf{A}]^{-1}$ contain negative elements. Consequently, the systems under consideration are not all-productive and, therefore, they do not have the usual properties of single production systems.

The next issue that comes up is whether the systems under consideration are "$r_0-$ all-engaging", i.e. characterized by $\mathbf{E}(r_0) > \mathbf{0}$ for some $r_0 > -1$ (see Sect. 4.2.1). As is well known, $\mathbf{E}(r) > \mathbf{0}$ is a sufficient condition for the existence of an interval of $r$ in which a joint production system retains all the wage (consumption)–profit (growth) rate properties of irreducible single production systems.[11] The investigation can be based on the following theorem (Bidard 1996, p. 328): Consider the eigen-systems associated with the pair $\{\mathbf{B}, \mathbf{A}\}$, namely

$$\lambda \mathbf{B}\chi = \mathbf{A}\chi$$

$$\lambda \boldsymbol{\psi}^{\mathrm{T}}\mathbf{B} = \boldsymbol{\psi}^{\mathrm{T}}\mathbf{A}$$

The system $\{\mathbf{B}, \mathbf{A}\}$ is $r_0-$ all-engaging iff there exist $[\lambda, \chi, \boldsymbol{\psi}] > \mathbf{0}$, where $\chi$ is determined up to a factor. In that case, $\lambda^{-1} - 1$ represents the maximum feasible growth (and profit) rate, as defined by von Neumann (1937, 1945), $\boldsymbol{\psi}^{\mathrm{T}}$ the associated long-period value vector, and $\chi$ the associated vector of activity levels or, alternatively, the vector of activity levels of Sraffa's (1960, Chap. 8) standard system.

The estimation of the characteristic values and vectors associated with the pairs $\{\mathbf{B}, \mathbf{A}\}$ of the Finnish economy gives the following results: The eigen-systems for the years 1995 through 2004 have 16 (1995), 14 (1996), 24 (1997), 15 (1998), 16 (1999), 18 (2000), 22 (2001), 15 (2002), 28 (2003), and 20 (2004) positive and simple eigenvalues, respectively. However, there are no positive left and right eigenvectors and, therefore, the considered systems are *not* $r_0-$ all-engaging. Nevertheless, it is worth noting that the sub-dominant (dominant) eigenvalue of the pair $\{\mathbf{B}, \mathbf{A}\}$ for the year 2001 (2002) is positive ($\lambda_2 \cong 0.77$ (2001), $\lambda_1 \cong 0.79$ (2002)) and associated with a positive left eigenvector. Since the eigenequation $\lambda \boldsymbol{\psi}^{\mathrm{T}}\mathbf{B} = \boldsymbol{\psi}^{\mathrm{T}}\mathbf{A}$ corresponds to the system of long-period values for a zero wage, one may, speaking somewhat loosely, conceive of $R_2 = \lambda_2^{-1} - 1 \cong 0.30$ ($R_1 = \lambda_1^{-1} - 1 \cong 0.27$) as a *meaningful* theoretical maximum profit rate for the year 2001 (year 2002).[12]

As mentioned above, $\mathbf{E}(r) > \mathbf{0}$ is a sufficient condition for the existence of an interval of $r$ in which the $w - r$ curves are downward-sloping. However, even if $\mathbf{E}(r)$ contains negative elements, it is entirely possible for $\mathbf{1}^{\mathrm{T}}\mathbf{E}(r) \geq \mathbf{0}^{\mathrm{T}}$ (or, equivalently,

---

[11]It is important to note that this attribute of the considered systems is independent of the composition and the level of the real wage rate and, therefore, does not rely on our hypothesis that there are no savings out of wages. Furthermore, since the matrices $[\mathbf{B} - \mathbf{A}]^{-1}$ contain negative elements, it follows that the systems under consideration can be $r_0-$ all-engaging only for some $r_0 > 0$.

[12]It may also be added that the dominant eigenvalue of the pair $\{\mathbf{B}, \mathbf{A}\}$ for the year 2001 is positive ($\lambda_1 \cong 0.924$) and is associated with non-positive right and left eigenvectors. Thus, it follows that the long-period values would be infinite at $R_1 = \lambda_1^{-1} - 1 \cong 0.082$ (Sraffa 1960, pp. 53–54; Bidard 1986b).

**Table 5.1** Economically relevant profit rate intervals: Finnish economy, period 1995–2004

| Year | $\mathbf{l}^T\mathbf{E}(r) > \mathbf{0}^T$ |
|------|-----------------------|
| 1995 | $0 \leq r \leq 0.14$ |
| 1996 | $0 \leq r < 0.01$ |
| 1997 | $0 \leq r \leq 0.11$ |
| 1998 | $0 \leq r \leq 0.05$ |
| 1999 | – |
| 2000 | $0.03 \leq r \leq 0.23$ |
| 2001 | $0.09 \leq r \leq 0.29$ |
| 2002 | $0.25 \leq r \leq 0.26$ |
| 2003 | – |
| 2004 | – |

$\mathbf{P}^T \geq \mathbf{0}^T$) to hold for some $r$. In what follows, we investigate whether such intervals of the profit rate exist in the Finnish economy. Calculations are performed by varying profit rate from zero to one ($0 \leq r \leq 1$) with step equal to $0.01$.[13] The results of the investigation are reported in Table 5.1. It is found that there exists an interval of $r$, such that $\mathbf{l}^T\mathbf{E}(r) \geq \mathbf{0}^T$, for the years 1995 through 1998 and 2000 through 2002. The larger interval is found for the years 2000 and 2001 ($0.03 \leq r \leq 0.23$ and $0.09 \leq r \leq 0.29$, respectively), while the smallest interval is found for the year 1996 ($0 \leq r \leq 0.01$).

In what follows, we estimate the $w - r$ curves for the years 1995, 1997, 2000, and 2001 of the Finnish economy associated with the intervals of the profit rate reported in Table 5.1.[14] The $w - r$ curves are obtained on the basis of Eq. (5.3), while each of the commodities described in the SUTs of the Finish economy is used as *numéraire*. Thus, we obtain 57 $w - r$ curves for each year plus the curves obtained using the vectors of gross output, net ouptut, and real wage rate as *numéraires*. Firstly, we examine the monotonicity of the curves. Secondly, we examine the curvature of the downward-sloping $w - r$ curves, i.e. whether these curves are convex or concave to the origin, and we detect the points where the curvature switches from convex to concave or *vice versa*. Lastly, we examine the linearity of the downward-sloping $w - r$ curves by using Pearson's correlation coefficient. Calculations are performed by varying profit rate from its "minimum" to its "maximum" with step equal to $0.001$. The numerical results of the analysis are reported in Tables 5.2 and 5.3. Table 5.2 reports the results for the years 1995 and 1997, while Table 5.3 reports the results for the years 2000 and 2001. The first column of these tables indicates the CPA code of the commodity that is used as *numéraire*, while the second column

---

[13]Since we have found a meaningful maximum profit rate, we restrict our investigation to the interval $0 \leq r \leq 0.30$ ($0 \leq r \leq 0.27$) for the year 2001 (2002). Nevertheless, the choice of the interval of $r$ in which we apply our investigation for the remaining years, is, necessarily, conventional.

[14]We exclude from our investigation the years 1996, 1998, and 2002 because the intervals of the profit rate, in which the systems give economically relevant results, can be considered as quite "small".

**Table 5.2** Wage–profit rate curves: Finnish economy, years 1995 and 1997

| Numéraire-commodity (CPA) | Monotonicity, year 1995 | Curvature, year 1995 | \|ρl, year 1995 | Monotonicity, year 1997 | Curvature, year 1997 | \|ρl, year 1997 |
|---|---|---|---|---|---|---|
| 01 | ↗ | CX | 99.91% | ↗ | CX | 99.94% |
| 02 | ↗ | CX | 99.96% | ↗ | CX | 99.98% |
| 05 | ↗ | CX | 99.93% | ↗ | CX | 99.96% |
| 10 | ↗ | CX | 99.93% | ↗ | CX | 99.95% |
| 13 | ↗ | CX | 99.94% | ↗ | CX | 99.95% |
| 14 | ↗ | CX | 99.94% | ↗ | CX | 99.97% |
| 15 | ↗ | CX | 99.91% | ↗ | CX | 99.94% |
| 16 | ↗ | CX | 99.93% | ↗ | CX | 99.97% |
| 17 | ↗ | CX | 99.95% | ↗ | CX | 99.98% |
| 18 | ↗ | CX | 99.95% | ↗ | CX | 99.97% |
| 19 | ↗ | CX | 99.94% | ↗ | CX | 99.97% |
| 20 | ↗ | CX | 99.95% | ↗ | CX | 99.97% |
| 21 | ↗ | CX | 99.92% | ↗ | CX | 99.96% |
| 22 | ↗ | CX | 99.95% | ↗ | CX | 99.97% |
| 23 ⊕ 11 | ↗ | CX | 99.81% | ↗ | CX | 99.89% |
| 24 | ↗ | CX | 99.93% | ↗ | CX | 99.96% |
| 25 | ↗ | CX | 99.95% | ↗ | CX | 99.98% |
| 26 | ↗ | CX | 99.96% | ↗ | CX | 99.97% |
| 27 | ↗ | CX | 99.87% | ↗ | CX | 99.90% |
| 28 | ↗ | CX | 99.96% | ↗ | CX | 99.98% |
| 29 | ↗ | CX | 99.95% | ↗ | CX | 99.96% |
| 30 | ↗ | CX | 99.86% | ↗ | CX | 99.90% |
| 31 | ↗ | CX | 99.94% | ↗ | CX | 99.97% |
| 32 | ↗ | CX | 99.91% | ↗ | CX | 99.94% |
| 33 | ↗ | CX | 99.95% | ↗ | CX | 99.97% |

| | | | | | | |
|---|---|---|---|---|---|---|
| 34 | ↗ | CX | 99.94% | ↗ | CX | 99.97% |
| 35 | ↗ | CX | 99.95% | ↗ | CX | 99.97% |
| 36 | ↗ | CX | 99.96% | ↗ | CX | 99.98% |
| 37 | ↗ | – | – | ↗ | – | – |
| 40 | ↗ | CX | 99.95% | ↗ | CX | 99.98% |
| 41 | ↗ | CX | 99.97% | ↗ | CX | 99.98% |
| 45 | ↗ | CX | 99.96% | ↗ | CX | 99.98% |
| 50 | ↗ | CX | 99.97% | ↗ | CX | 99.98% |
| 51 | ↗ | CX | 99.97% | ↗ | CX | 99.98% |
| 52 | ↗ | CX | 99.97% | ↗ | CX | 99.98% |
| 55 | ↗ | CX | 99.96% | ↗ | CX | 99.97% |
| 60 | ↗ | CX | 99.98% | ↗ | CX/CV (7.5%) | 100.00% |
| 61 | ↗ | CX | 99.95% | ↗ | CX | 99.98% |
| 62 | ↗ | CX | 99.96% | ↗ | CX | 99.98% |
| 63 | ↗ | CX | 99.95% | ↗ | CX | 99.97% |
| 64 | ↗ | CX | 99.97% | ↗ | CX | 99.98% |
| 65 | ↗ | CX | 99.97% | ↗ | CX | 99.98% |
| 66 | ↗ | CX | 99.95% | ↗ | CX | 99.97% |
| 67 | ↗ | CX | 99.96% | ↗ | CX | 99.98% |
| 70 | ↗ | CX | 99.92% | ↗ | CX | 99.95% |
| 71 | ↗ | CX | 99.96% | ↗ | CX | 99.98% |
| 72 | ↗ | CX | 99.97% | ↗ | CX | 99.98% |
| 73 | ↗ | CX | 99.97% | ↗ | CX | 99.98% |
| 74 | ↗ | CX | 99.97% | ↗ | CX | 99.98% |
| 75 | ↗ | CX | 99.97% | ↗ | CX | 99.98% |
| 80 | ↗ | CX | 99.97% | ↗ | CX | 99.98% |
| 85 | ↗ | CX | 99.97% | ↗ | CX | 99.98% |

(continued)

**Table 5.2** (continued)

| Numéraire-commodity (CPA) | Monotonicity, year 1995 | Curvature, year 1995 | \|ρ\|, year 1995 | Monotonicity, year 1997 | Curvature, year 1997 | \|ρ\|, year 1997 |
|---|---|---|---|---|---|---|
| 90 | ↗ | CX | 99.96% | ↗ | CX | 99.98% |
| 91 | ↗ | CX | 99.97% | ↗ | CX | 99.98% |
| 92 | ↗ | CX | 99.97% | ↗ | CX | 99.98% |
| 93 | ↗ | CX | 99.98% | ↗ | CX | 99.99% |
| 95 | ↗ | CX | 99.94% | ↗ | CX | 99.96% |
| Real Wage Rate | ↗ | CX | 99.96% | ↗ | CX | 99.98% |
| Gross Output | ↗ | CX | 99.93% | ↗ | CX | 99.97% |
| Net Output | ↗ | CX | 99.94% | ↗ | CX | 99.97% |

**Table 5.3** Wage–profit rate curves: Finnish economy, years 2000 and 2001

| Numéraire-commodity (CPA) | Monotonicity, year 2000 | Curvature, year 2000 | $\|\rho\|$, year 2000 | Monotonicity, year 2001 | Curvature, year 2001 | $\|\rho\|$, year 2001 |
|---|---|---|---|---|---|---|
| 01 | ↘ | CX/CV (12.1%) | 99.67% | ↘ | CV/CX (10.3%)/CV (15.5%) | 98.46% |
| 02 | ↘ | CX/CV (6.7%) | 98.15% | ↘ | CV/CX (9.8%)/CV (12%) | 94.52% |
| 05 | ↘ | CX/CV (10.6%) | 99.45% | ↘ | CV/CX (9.9%)/CV (16.2%) | 97.67% |
| 10 | ↘ | CX/CV (9.4%) | 99.28% | ↘ | CV/CX (10.2%)/CV (15.1%) | 97.40% |
| 13 | ↘ | CV/CX (3.2%)/CV (5.9%) | 98.78% | ↘ | CV/CX (11.3%)/CV (12.9%) | 96.20% |
| 14 | ↘ | CX/CV (9.2%) | 99.43% | ↘ | CX/CV (14.4%) | 98.02% |
| 15 | ↘ | CX/CV (12.2%) | 99.67% | ↘ | CV/CX (10.3%)/CV (16.3%) | 98.18% |
| 16 | ↘ | CX/CV (9.7%) | 99.28% | ↘ | CV/CX (9.9%)/CV (16.2%) | 98.01% |
| 17 | ↘ | CX/CV (7.4%) | 98.90% | ↘ | CV/CX (10.6%)/CV (12.2%) | 96.70% |
| 18 | ↘ | CX/CV (8.6%) | 98.93% | ↘ | CV/CX (10%)/CV (14.6%) | 96.63% |
| 19 | ↘ | CX/CV (9.1%) | 99.12% | ↘ | CV/CX (10.2%)/CV (14.7%) | 96.78% |
| 20 | ↘ | CX/CV (8.8%) | 99.04% | ↘ | CV/CX (12.2%)/CV (13.2%) | 96.49% |
| 21 | ↘ | CV/CX (3.6%)/CV (10.0%) | 99.44% | ↘ | CV/CX (10.4%)/CV (13.4%) | 97.80% |

(continued)

**Table 5.3** (continued)

| Numéraire-commodity (CPA) | Monotonicity, year 2000 | Curvature, year 2000 | $\|\rho\|$, year 2000 | Monotonicity, year 2001 | Curvature, year 2001 | $\|\rho\|$, year 2001 |
|---|---|---|---|---|---|---|
| 22 | ↘ | CV/CX (3.2%)/CV (12.7%) | 99.77% | ↘ | CV/CX (9.8%)/CV (15.2%) | 96.64% |
| 23 ⊕ 11 | ↘ | CX/CV (21.2%) | 99.51% | ↘ | CV/CX (9.3%) | 99.33% |
| 24 | ↘ | CX/CV (9.1%) | 99.44% | ↘ | CV/CX (11.2%)/ CV (13.3%) | 97.98% |
| 25 | ↘ | CX/CV (8.1%) | 99.07% | ↗ ↘ (9.2%) | – | – |
| 26 | ↘ | CV/CX (4.9%)/CV (8.0%) | 99.10% | ↗ ↘ (10.6%) | – | – |
| 27 | ↘ | CX/CV (12.0%) | 99.71% | ↘ | CV/CX (10.4%)/ CV (16.9%) | 98.58% |
| 28 | ↘ | CX/CV (9.1%) | 99.30% | ↘ | CV/CX (11.2%)/ CV (15.1%) | 97.58% |
| 29 | ↘ | CX/CV (10.4%) | 99.39% | ↘ | CV/CX (10.2%)/ CV (17.3%) | 97.84% |
| 30 | ↘ | CX | 99.40% | ↘ | CV/CX (9.4%)/CV (19.5%) | 99.41% |
| 31 | ↘ | CX/CV (11.3%) | 99.53% | ↘ | CV/CX (10.8%)/ CV (17.4%) | 98.30% |
| 32 | ↘ | CX/CV (14.3%) | 99.84% | ↘ | CV/CX (10%)/CV (20.5%) | 99.20% |
| 33 | ↘ | CX/CV (6.0%) | 98.92% | ↘ | CV/CX (10.3%)/ CV (17.2%) | 97.95% |
| 34 | ↘ | CX/CV (9.7%) | 99.26% | ↘ | CV/CX (11.3%)/ CV (15.6%) | 97.20% |
| 35 | ↘ | CX/CV (10.4%) | 99.38% | ↘ | CV/CX (10.8%)/ | 97.98% |

(continued)

**Table 5.3**  (continued)

| Numéraire-commodity (CPA) | Monotonicity, year 2000 | Curvature, year 2000 | \|ρ\|, year 2000 | Monotonicity, year 2001 | Curvature, year 2001 | \|ρ\|, year 2001 |
|---|---|---|---|---|---|---|
| | | | | | CV (17.1%) | |
| 36 | ↘ | CX/CV (8.7%) | 99.04% | ↘ | CV/CX (11.5%)/ CV (14.0%) | 96.73% |
| 37 | ↗ | – | – | ↗ ↘ (24.9%) | – | – |
| 40 | ↘ | CX/CV (6.3%) | 99.50% | ↘ | CV | 99.03% |
| 41 | ↘ | CX/CV (4.8%) | 98.42% | ↘ | CV | 95.36% |
| 45 | ↘ | CV/CX (3.4%)/CV (8.5%) | 98.97% | ↘ | CV | 96.74% |
| 50 | ↘ | CV | 98.30% | ↘ | CV | 95.41% |
| 51 | ↘ | CV | 98.44% | ↘ | CV | 95.94% |
| 52 | ↘ | CV | 97.57% | ↘ | CV | 94.32% |
| 55 | ↘ | CX/CV (8.0%) | 98.92% | ↘ | CV/CX (10.4%)/ CV (14.4%) | 96.55% |
| 60 | ↘ | CV | 98.19% | ↘ | CV | 95.34% |
| 61 | ↘ | CX/CV (6.9%) | 99.16% | ↘ | CV | 97.87% |
| 62 | ↘ | CV/CX (3.2%)/CV (4.5%) | 99.33% | ↘ | CV | 98.56% |
| 63 | ↘ | CX/CV (6.6%) | 98.67% | ↘ | CV/CX (10.7%)/ CV (12.7%) | 96.15% |
| 64 | ↘ | CX/CV (7.3%) | 98.54% | ↘ | CV/CX (11.2%)/ CV (13.7%) | 95.74% |
| 65 | ↘ | CV | 97.51% | ↘ | CV | 94.57% |
| 66 | ↘ | CX/CV (4.9%) | 97.10% | ↘ | CV/CX (9.4%)/CV (15.4%) | 95.94% |
| 67 | ↘ | CX/CV (4.9%) | 97.85% | ↘ | CV/CX (10.0%)/ CV (15.1%) | 95.77% |
| 70 | ↘ | CX/CV (9.1%) | 99.25% | ↘ | CV/CX (11.2%)/ | 97.51% |

(continued)

**Table 5.3** (continued)

| Numéraire-commodity (CPA) | Monotonicity, year 2000 | Curvature, year 2000 | $\|\rho\|$, year 2000 | Monotonicity, year 2001 | Curvature, year 2001 | $\|\rho\|$, year 2001 |
|---|---|---|---|---|---|---|
| | | | | | CV (15.4%) | |
| 71 | ↘ | CV | 99.03% | ↘ | CV/CX (11.4%)/ CV (13.2%) | 96.43% |
| 72 | ↘ | CV/CX (3.2%)/CV (3.6%) | 97.34% | ↘ | CV/CX (10.0%)/ CV (14.3%) | 95.22% |
| 73 | ↘ | CX/CV (5.2%) | 97.32% | ↘ | CV/CX (10.1%)/ CV (14.3%) | 94.99% |
| 74 | ↘ | CV | 98.18% | ↘ | CV/CX (10.3%)/ CV (13.5%) | 95.63% |
| 75 | ↘ | CX/CV (7.2%) | 98.21% | ↘ | CV/CX (10.2%)/ CV (13.9%) | 94.74% |
| 80 | ↘ | CX/CV (7.8%) | 98.15% | ↘ | CV/CX (9.8%)/CV (14.6%) | 94.28% |
| 85 | ↘ | CX/CV (7.4%) | 97.99% | ↘ | CV/CX (10.4%)/ CV (14.0%) | 93.96% |
| 90 | ↘ | CV | 98.92% | ↘ | CV/CX (10.9%)/ CV (12.1%) | 96.24% |
| 91 | ↘ | CX/CV (6.6%) | 97.97% | ↘ | CV/CX (9.9%)/CV (12.9%) | 93.88% |
| 92 | ↘ | CX/CV (7.0%) | 98.40% | ↘ | CV/CX (10.3%)/ CV (13.4%) | 95.05% |
| 93 | ↘ | CV | 99.16% | ↘ | CV | 96.27% |
| 95 | ↘ | CX | 99.89% | ↘ | CX | 99.90% |
| Real Wage Rate | ↘ | CV/CX (3.2%)/CV (5.5%) | 98.72% | ↘ | CV | 96.33% |

(continued)

**Table 5.3** (continued)

| Numéraire-commodity (CPA) | Monotonicity, year 2000 | Curvature, year 2000 | $\lvert\rho\rvert$, year 2000 | Monotonicity, year 2001 | Curvature, year 2001 | $\lvert\rho\rvert$, year 2001 |
|---|---|---|---|---|---|---|
| Gross Output | ↗↘ (3.4%) | – | – | ↗↘ (12.2%) | – | – |
| Net Output | ↘ | CV | 97.11% | ↗↘ (10.1%) | – | – |

reports the monotonicity of the $w - r$ curves. The symbol ↘ (↗) indicates that a curve is strictly decreasing (increasing) for the whole interval of $r$, while ↗↘ (•) indicates that a curve is alternately increasing and decreasing, and • indicates the value of $r$ where the monotonicity is reversed.[15] The third column reports the curvature of the $w - r$ curves. The abbreviation CX (CV) denotes that a curve is convex (concave) for the whole interval of $r$, while CX/CV (•) (CV/CX (•)) indicates that a curve switches from convex (concave) to concave (convex) at $r = •$. Furthermore, CV/CX (•) /CV (○) indicates that a curve switches from concave to convex at $r = •$ and re-switches to concave at $r = ○$.[16] Finally, the fourth column reports the absolute values of Pearson's correlation coefficient, $\lvert\rho\rvert$, between $w$ and $r$.

### 5.3.1.1 Monotonicity

(i). The $w - r$ curves for the years 1995 and 1997 are strictly decreasing, except for the case where product 37 ("secondary raw materials") is used as numéraire. In the latter case, the corresponding curves are strictly increasing.

(ii). The curves for the year 2000 are strictly decreasing, except for the case where product 37 or the gross output is used as numéraire. When product 37 (gross output) is used as numéraire, the corresponding curve is strictly increasing (alternately increasing and decreasing).

(iii). The curves for the year 2001 are strictly decreasing, except for the cases where product 25 ("rubber and plastic products") or 26 ("other non-metallic mineral products") or 37 or gross output or net output is used as numéraire. In the latter cases, the corresponding curves are alternately increasing and decreasing.

Thus, we obtain strictly decreasing curves in about 96.25% of the tested cases. Additionally, we observe that when product 37, which is the "primary" product of the "recycling" industry, is used as numéraire, we derive non-strictly decreasing curves for all the tested cases.[17]

---

[15]It is interesting to note that it has not been found any case where the monotonicity of a $w - r$ curve is alternately decreasing and increasing.

[16]It is worth noting that it has not been found any case where a $w - r$ curve switches from convex to concave and then re-switches to convex.

[17]As it has been argued, Recycling is an activity that would not exist if there were no joint products (Steedman 1984). In this regard, it is worth mentioning that the "secondary" production of the

## 5.3.1.2    Curvature

(i). The curves for the year 1995 are convex for the whole interval of $r$.

(ii). The curves for the year 1997 are convex for the whole interval of $r$, except for the case where product 60 ("land transport; transport via pipeline services") is used as *numéraire*. In the latter case, the curve switches from convex to concave at $r = 0.075$.

(iii). The investigation of the curves for the year 2000 gives (a) 38 curves that switch from convex to concave; (b) 10 curves that are concave for the whole interval of ; (c) 8 curves that switch from concave to convex and re-switch to concave; and (d) 2 curves that are convex for the whole interval of $r$.

(iv). The investigation of the curves for the year 2001 gives (a) 40 curves that switch from concave to convex and re-switch to concave; (b) 12 curves that are concave for the whole interval of $r$; (c) 1 curve that switches from convex to concave; (d) 1 curve that switches from concave to convex; and (e) 1 curve that is convex for the whole interval of $r$.

Thus, we observe that the curves for the years 1995 and 1997 are in about 99.14% of the tested cases convex for the whole interval of $r$, whereas the curves for the years 2000 and 2001 alternate in curvature in about 77.88% of the tested cases. However, it has not been found any case where the curvature switches more than two times.

## 5.3.1.3    Linearity

The absolute value of the correlation coefficient between $w$ and $r$ for the years 1995, 1997, 2000, and 2001 is in the range of 99.81% to 99.98%, 99.89% to 100.00%, 97.10% to 99.89%, and 93.88% to 99.90%, respectively. Thus, it can be said that the $w - r$ curves for the years 1995 and 1997 are near-linear, whereas we obtain curves with lesser correlation coefficients for the years 2000 and 2001. Leaving aside the detection of upward-sloping curves, these results are in accordance with those obtained by Petrović (1991) on the basis of the Symmetric Input–Output Tables of the Yugoslavian economy for the years 1976 and 1978. More specifically, Petrović found that (a) in *most* cases the curvature of the curves switches no more than two times; and (b) the correlation coefficient between $w$ and $r$ for the year 1976 (1978) is in the range of 97.51% to 99.98% (96.61% to 99.99%).

---

Recycling industry of the Finnish economy is more than 96% of the total production of that industry, while the total secondary production of all industries is less than 7% of the total production of the economy, for each year of our analysis.

#### 5.3.1.4    Visual Representation of Wage–Profit Rate Curves

In order to get a picture of the $w - r$ curves of the Finnish economy, in Figs. 5.1, 5.2, 5.3, and 5.4 we display some of these curves.[18] In Fig. 5.1 (Fig. 5.2) we display the $w - r$ curves for the year 1995 (1997) associated with the *numéraire* (a) 23 $\oplus$ 11 (i.e. the product that results from the aggregation of the product "coke, refined petroleum products, and nuclear fuels" with the product "crude petroleum and natural gas; services incidental to oil and gas extraction excluding surveying"); (b) 37 ("secondary raw materials"); (c) 60 ("land transport; transport via pipeline services"); and (d) real wage rate, respectively.[19] In Fig. 5.3 we display the $w - r$ curves for the year 2000 associated with the *numéraire* (a) 37; (b) 45 ("construction work"); (c) 50 ("trade, maintenance, and repair services of motor vehicles and motorcycles; retail sale of automotive fuel"); and (d) real wage rate, respectively. Finally, in Fig. 5.4 we display the $w - r$ curves for the year 2001 associated with the *numéraire* (a) 02 ("products of forestry, logging, and related services"); (b) 26

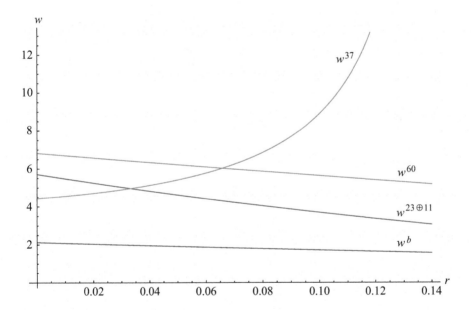

**Fig. 5.1** Wage–profit rate curves: Finnish economy, year 1995

---

[18]For the construction of each figure, 10,000 sample points are used.

[19]The symbol $w^i$ denotes the wage rate expressed in terms of commodity $i$, where $i$ is the CPA code of the respective commodity. Furthermore, the symbol $w^b$ ($w^x$) denotes the wage rate expressed in terms of the consumption basket (the gross output). It should be noted that, in fact, there is no contradiction between the shapes of the detected non-decreasing $w - r$ curves and relations (4.14), (4.15), and (4.16).

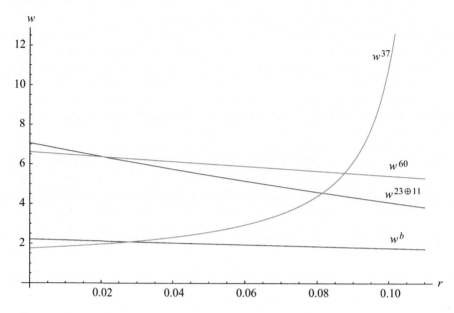

**Fig. 5.2** Wage–profit rate curves: Finnish economy, year 1997

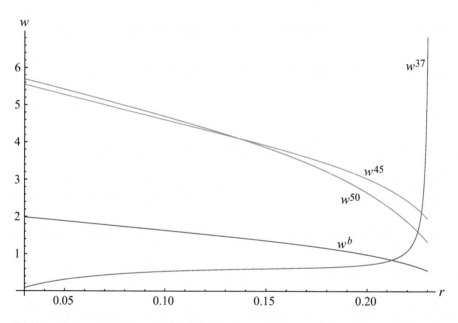

**Fig. 5.3** Wage–profit rate curves: Finnish economy, year 2000

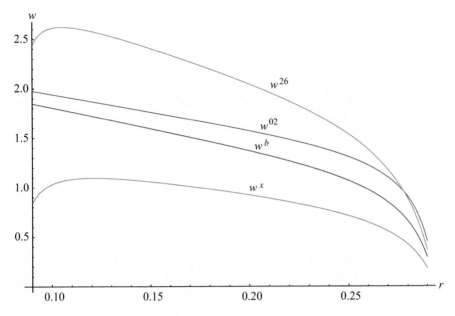

**Fig. 5.4** Wage–profit rate curves: Finnish economy, year 2001

("other non-metallic mineral products"); (c) gross output; and (d) real wage rate, respectively.

### 5.3.1.5   Sensitivity Analysis

In the following we investigate whether the above results are robust to the choice of precision in the numerical calculations. Thus, we examine whether there exists an interval of $r > 0$ such that $\mathbf{p}_w^T > \mathbf{0}^T$ with step equal to 0.0001 (instead of 0.01) and we find that the labour-commanded values for the years 2000 and 2001 are *also* positive for $0.0247 \leq r \leq 0.0300$ and $0.0825 \leq r \leq 0.0900$, respectively (compare with the results reported in Table 5.1). The investigation of the monotonicity of the $w - r$ curves, within the above intervals of $r$, reveals that in *most* cases there exists an interval of $r$ in which the $w - r$ curves are increasing. More specifically, it is found that, with the exception of the case where commodity 14 ("other mining and quarrying products") or 66 ("insurance and pension funding services, except compulsory social security services") or 95 ("private households with employed persons") is used as *numéraire*, the $w - r$ curves for the year 2000 are alternately increasing and decreasing. Furthermore, with the exception of the case where commodity 14 or 95 is used as *numéraire*, the $w - r$ curves for the year 2001 are alternately increasing and decreasing. In other words, it is found that there exists an interval of $r$ in which 54/57 (55/57) of the labour-commanded values for the year 2000 (2001) are inversely related to $r$. In Fig. 5.5 we display the $w - r$ curves for the year 2000 (for $0.0247 \leq r \leq 0.0250$) associated with the *numéraire* (a) 13 ("metal

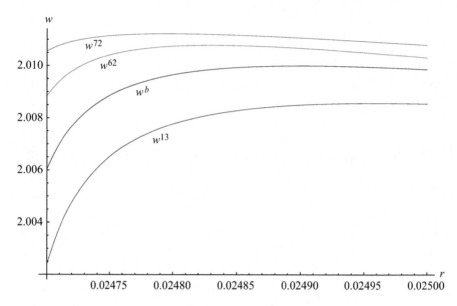

**Fig. 5.5**  Wage–profit rate curves: Finnish economy, year 2000

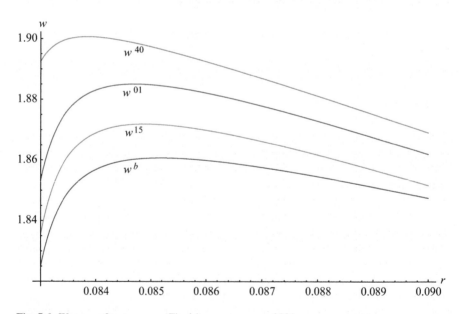

**Fig. 5.6**  Wage–profit rate curves: Finnish economy, year 2001

ores"); (b) 62 ("air transport services"); (c) 72 ("computer and related services"); and
(d) real wage rate, respectively, while in Fig. 5.6 we display the $w - r$ curves for the
year 2001 (for $0.0825 \leq r \leq 0.0900$) associated with the *numéraire* (a) 01 ("products
of agriculture, hunting, and related services"); (b) 15 ("food products and

beverages"); (c) 40 ("electrical energy, gas, steam, and hot water"); and (d) real wage rate, respectively.

Thus, it follows that the empirical results can be extremely sensitive to the choice of precision in calculations.

### 5.3.2 Values in Actual Joint Production Economies

The results from the application of the analysis exposed in Sect. 5.2.2 to the SUTs of the Danish (for the years 2000 and 2004), Finnish (for the years 1995 through 2004), French (for the years 1995 and 2005), FYROM (for the year 2005), German (for the years 1997 through 2005), Greek (for the years 1995 through 1999), Hungarian (for the years 2001 through 2004), Japanese (for the years 1970, 1975, 1980, 1985, 1990, 1995, and 2000), Portuguese (for the years 1995 through 2004), Slovenian (for the years 2002 through 2005), Swedish (for the years 1995 through 2005), and the USA (for the years 1998 through 2007) economies are summarized in Table 5.4.[20] The first column of the table indicates the country and the reference year of the analysis.[21] The second column reports whether the systems under consideration are all-productive, i.e. whether it holds $[\mathbf{B} - \mathbf{A}]^{-1} > \mathbf{0}$. The third column reports whether the ALVs of the economies under consideration are economically relevant, i.e. whether it holds $\mathbf{v}^{\mathrm{T}} \geq \mathbf{0}^{\mathrm{T}}$. The fourth column reports whether the "surplus values" are positive, i.e. whether it holds $\mathbf{v}^{\mathrm{T}}\mathbf{b} < 1$, as well as the level of the "labour value of labour power". The fifth column reports whether the ALPVs of the economies are economically relevant as well as the level of the actual profit rate for the cases where it holds $\mathbf{p}^{\mathrm{T}} \geq \mathbf{0}^{\mathrm{T}}$. The sixth column reports whether the considered systems are $r_0-$ all-engaging, i.e. whether there exists $r > 0$ such that $\mathbf{E}(r) > \mathbf{0}$, as well as the interval of profit rate in which it holds $\mathbf{E}(r) > \mathbf{0}$. Finally, the symbol $*$ indicates affirmation, whereas the symbol $\times$ indicates negation. For example, the second row of the table indicates that the economy of Denmark for the year 2000 is not all-productive nor $r_0-$ all-engaging, while it holds $\mathbf{v}^{\mathrm{T}} \geq \mathbf{0}^{\mathrm{T}}$, $\mathbf{v}^{\mathrm{T}}\mathbf{b} \cong 0.48 < 1$, and $\mathbf{p}^{\mathrm{T}} \geq \mathbf{0}^{\mathrm{T}}$ at $r \cong 35\%$.

From the evaluation of the results of the previous analysis we arrive at the following conclusions:

(i). The matrices $[\mathbf{B} - \mathbf{A}]$ and $\mathbf{B}$ are non-singular in all the economies under consideration. Consequently, the vectors of ALVs can be uniquely estimated from Eq. (5.10) and the vectors of ALPVs can be estimated from Eq. (5.7).

---

[20]What follows draws on Mariolis and Soklis (2007, 2010), Soklis (2006, 2012, pp. 140–158; 2019).

[21]In the case of the US economy, there are available two sets of SUTs for each year. The symbol R indicates SUTs of the US economy that have been constructed using the redefinition method (see the Appendix at the end of this chapter).

**Table 5.4** Summary Table

| Country (Year) | $[\mathbf{B} - \mathbf{A}]^{-1} > 0$ | $\mathbf{v} \geq 0$ | $\mathbf{v}^{\mathrm{T}}\mathbf{b} < 1$ | $\mathbf{p} \geq 0$ | $E(r) > 0$ |
|---|---|---|---|---|---|
| Denmark (2000) | × | * | * ($\mathbf{v}^{\mathrm{T}}\mathbf{b} \cong 0.48$) | * ($r \cong 35\%$) | × |
| (2004) | × | * | * ($\mathbf{v}^{\mathrm{T}}\mathbf{b} \cong 0.49$) | * ($r \cong 34\%$) | * ($98.1\% \leq r \leq 99.0\%$) |
| Finland (1995) | × | * | * ($\mathbf{v}^{\mathrm{T}}\mathbf{b} \cong 0.47$) | × | × |
| (1996) | × | * | * ($\mathbf{v}^{\mathrm{T}}\mathbf{b} \cong 0.46$) | × | × |
| (1997) | × | * | * ($\mathbf{v}^{\mathrm{T}}\mathbf{b} \cong 0.45$) | × | × |
| (1998) | × | * | * ($\mathbf{v}^{\mathrm{T}}\mathbf{b} \cong 0.45$) | × | × |
| (1999) | × | × | * ($\mathbf{v}^{\mathrm{T}}\mathbf{b} \cong 0.45$) | × | × |
| (2000) | × | × | * ($\mathbf{v}^{\mathrm{T}}\mathbf{b} \cong 0.47$) | * ($r \cong 20\%$) | × |
| (2001) | × | × | * ($\mathbf{v}^{\mathrm{T}}\mathbf{b} \cong 0.44$) | * ($r \cong 26\%$) | × |
| (2002) | × | × | * ($\mathbf{v}^{\mathrm{T}}\mathbf{b} \cong 0.44$) | * ($r \cong 24\%$) | × |
| (2003) | × | × | * ($\mathbf{v}^{\mathrm{T}}\mathbf{b} \cong 0.45$) | × | × |
| (2004) | × | × | * ($\mathbf{v}^{\mathrm{T}}\mathbf{b} \cong 0.44$) | × | × |
| France (1995) | × | * | * ($\mathbf{v}^{\mathrm{T}}\mathbf{b} \cong 0.48$) | * ($r \cong 33\%$) | * ($87\% \leq r \leq 96\%$) |
| (2005) | × | * | * ($\mathbf{v}^{\mathrm{T}}\mathbf{b} \cong 0.48$) | * ($r \cong 32\%$) | * ($78\% \leq r \leq 90\%$) |
| FYROM (2005) | × | * | * ($\mathbf{v}^{\mathrm{T}}\mathbf{b} \cong 0.38$) | * ($r \cong 37\%$) | × |
| Germany (1997) | × | * | * ($\mathbf{v}^{\mathrm{T}}\mathbf{b} \cong 0.50$) | * ($r \cong 28\%$) | × |
| (1998) | × | * | * ($\mathbf{v}^{\mathrm{T}}\mathbf{b} \cong 0.49$) | * ($r \cong 28\%$) | × |
| (1999) | × | * | * ($\mathbf{v}^{\mathrm{T}}\mathbf{b} \cong 0.49$) | * ($r \cong 29\%$) | × |
| (2000) | × | * | * ($\mathbf{v}^{\mathrm{T}}\mathbf{b} \cong 0.48$) | * ($r \cong 35\%$) | × |
| (2001) | × | * | * ($\mathbf{v}^{\mathrm{T}}\mathbf{b} \cong 0.48$) | * ($r \cong 37\%$) | × |
| (2002) | × | * | * ($\mathbf{v}^{\mathrm{T}}\mathbf{b} \cong 0.48$) | * ($r \cong 37\%$) | × |
| (2003) | × | * | * ($\mathbf{v}^{\mathrm{T}}\mathbf{b} \cong 0.47$) | * ($r \cong 37\%$) | × |
| (2004) | × | * | * ($\mathbf{v}^{\mathrm{T}}\mathbf{b} \cong 0.46$) | * ($r \cong 38\%$) | × |

(continued)

**Table 5.4**  (continued)

| Country (Year) | $[\mathbf{B} - \mathbf{A}]^{-1} > \mathbf{0}$ | $\mathbf{v} \geq \mathbf{0}$ | $\mathbf{v}^\mathrm{T}\mathbf{b} < 1$ | $\mathbf{p} \geq \mathbf{0}$ | $E(r) > 0$ |
|---|---|---|---|---|---|
| (2005) | × | * | * ($\mathbf{v}^\mathrm{T}\mathbf{b} \cong 0.45$) | * ($r \cong 38\%$) | × |
| Greece (1995) | × | * | * ($\mathbf{v}^\mathrm{T}\mathbf{b} \cong 0.28$) | × | × |
| (1996) | × | * | * ($\mathbf{v}^\mathrm{T}\mathbf{b} \cong 0.28$) | * ($r \cong 45\%$) | × |
| (1997) | × | * | * ($\mathbf{v}^\mathrm{T}\mathbf{b} \cong 0.29$) | * ($r \cong 46\%$) | × |
| (1998) | × | * | * ($\mathbf{v}^\mathrm{T}\mathbf{b} \cong 0.30$) | × | × |
| (1999) | × | × | * ($\mathbf{v}^\mathrm{T}\mathbf{b} \cong 0.16$) | × | × |
| Hungary (2001) | × | * | * ($\mathbf{v}^\mathrm{T}\mathbf{b} \cong 0.47$) | * ($r \cong 22\%$) | × |
| (2002) | × | * | * ($\mathbf{v}^\mathrm{T}\mathbf{b} \cong 0.45$) | * ($r \cong 25\%$) | × |
| (2003) | × | * | * ($\mathbf{v}^\mathrm{T}\mathbf{b} \cong 0.46$) | * ($r \cong 27\%$) | × |
| (2004) | × | * | * ($\mathbf{v}^\mathrm{T}\mathbf{b} \cong 0.46$) | * ($r \cong 29\%$) | × |
| Japan (1970) | × | * | * ($\mathbf{v}^\mathrm{T}\mathbf{b} \cong 0.31$) | * ($r \cong 42\%$) | × |
| (1975) | × | * | * ($\mathbf{v}^\mathrm{T}\mathbf{b} \cong 0.42$) | * ($r \cong 32\%$) | × |
| (1980) | × | * | * ($\mathbf{v}^\mathrm{T}\mathbf{b} \cong 0.41$) | * ($r \cong 31\%$) | × |
| (1985) | × | * | * ($\mathbf{v}^\mathrm{T}\mathbf{b} \cong 0.34$) | * ($r \cong 34\%$) | × |
| (1990) | × | * | * ($\mathbf{v}^\mathrm{T}\mathbf{b} \cong 0.41$) | * ($r \cong 38\%$) | × |
| (1995) | × | * | * ($\mathbf{v}^\mathrm{T}\mathbf{b} \cong 0.39$) | * ($r \cong 39\%$) | × |
| (2000) | × | * | * ($\mathbf{v}^\mathrm{T}\mathbf{b} \cong 0.42$) | * ($r \cong 39\%$) | × |
| Portugal (1995) | × | * | * ($\mathbf{v}^\mathrm{T}\mathbf{b} \cong 0.45$) | * ($r \cong 20\%$) | × |
| (1996) | × | * | * ($\mathbf{v}^\mathrm{T}\mathbf{b} \cong 0.45$) | * ($r \cong 21\%$) | × |
| (1997) | × | * | * ($\mathbf{v}^\mathrm{T}\mathbf{b} \cong 0.42$) | * ($r \cong 27\%$) | * ($32\% \leq r \leq 33\%$) |
| (1998) | × | * | * ($\mathbf{v}^\mathrm{T}\mathbf{b} \cong 0.41$) | * ($r \cong 27\%$) | × |
| (1999) | × | * | * ($\mathbf{v}^\mathrm{T}\mathbf{b} \cong 0.42$) | * ($r \cong 29\%$) | × |

(continued)

**Table 5.4** (continued)

| Country (Year) | $[\mathbf{B} - \mathbf{A}]^{-1} > 0$ | $\mathbf{v} \geq 0$ | $\mathbf{v}^{\mathrm{T}}\mathbf{b} < 1$ | $\mathbf{p} \geq 0$ | $E(r) > 0$ |
|---|---|---|---|---|---|
| (2000) | × | * | * ($\mathbf{v}^{\mathrm{T}}\mathbf{b} \cong 0.44$) | * ($r \cong 35\%$) | × |
| (2001) | × | * | * ($\mathbf{v}^{\mathrm{T}}\mathbf{b} \cong 0.44$) | * ($r \cong 34\%$) | × |
| (2002) | × | * | * ($\mathbf{v}^{\mathrm{T}}\mathbf{b} \cong 0.44$) | * ($r \cong 34\%$) | × |
| (2003) | × | * | * ($\mathbf{v}^{\mathrm{T}}\mathbf{b} \cong 0.44$) | * ($r \cong 35\%$) | × |
| (2004) | × | * | * ($\mathbf{v}^{\mathrm{T}}\mathbf{b} \cong 0.43$) | * ($r \cong 35\%$) | × |
| Slovenia (2002) | × | * | * ($\mathbf{v}^{\mathrm{T}}\mathbf{b} \cong 0.60$) | * ($r \cong 18\%$) | × |
| (2003) | × | * | * ($\mathbf{v}^{\mathrm{T}}\mathbf{b} \cong 0.58$) | * ($r \cong 21\%$) | × |
| (2004) | × | * | * ($\mathbf{v}^{\mathrm{T}}\mathbf{b} \cong 0.58$) | * ($r \cong 22\%$) | × |
| (2005) | × | * | * ($\mathbf{v}^{\mathrm{T}}\mathbf{b} \cong 0.56$) | * ($r \cong 24\%$) | × |
| Sweden (1995) | × | * | * ($\mathbf{v}^{\mathrm{T}}\mathbf{b} \cong 0.44$) | * ($r \cong 37\%$) | * ($85\% \leq r \leq 89\%$) |
| (1996) | × | * | * ($\mathbf{v}^{\mathrm{T}}\mathbf{b} \cong 0.46$) | * ($r \cong 35\%$) | * ($87\% \leq r \leq 91\%$) |
| (1997) | × | * | * ($\mathbf{v}^{\mathrm{T}}\mathbf{b} \cong 0.45$) | * ($r \cong 36\%$) | * ($86\% \leq r \leq 89\%$) |
| (1998) | × | * | * ($\mathbf{v}^{\mathrm{T}}\mathbf{b} \cong 0.45$) | * ($r \cong 35\%$) | * ($86\% \leq r \leq 90\%$) |
| (1999) | × | * | * ($\mathbf{v}^{\mathrm{T}}\mathbf{b} \cong 0.45$) | * ($r \cong 35\%$) | * ($87\% \leq r \leq 91\%$) |
| (2000) | × | * | * ($\mathbf{v}^{\mathrm{T}}\mathbf{b} \cong 0.47$) | * ($r \cong 20\%$) | × |
| (2001) | × | * | * ($\mathbf{v}^{\mathrm{T}}\mathbf{b} \cong 0.49$) | * ($r \cong 21\%$) | × |
| (2002) | × | * | * ($\mathbf{v}^{\mathrm{T}}\mathbf{b} \cong 0.49$) | * ($r \cong 19\%$) | × |
| (2003) | × | * | * ($\mathbf{v}^{\mathrm{T}}\mathbf{b} \cong 0.48$) | * ($r \cong 17\%$) | × |
| (2004) | × | * | * ($\mathbf{v}^{\mathrm{T}}\mathbf{b} \cong 0.48$) | * ($r \cong 15\%$) | × |
| (2005) | × | * | * ($\mathbf{v}^{\mathrm{T}}\mathbf{b} \cong 0.48$) | * ($r \cong 12\%$) | × |
| USA (1998) | × | * | * ($\mathbf{v}^{\mathrm{T}}\mathbf{b} \cong 0.52$) | * ($r \cong 35\%$) | × |
| (1999) | × | * | * ($\mathbf{v}^{\mathrm{T}}\mathbf{b} \cong 0.52$) | * ($r \cong 35\%$) | × |

(continued)

**Table 5.4**  (continued)

| Country (Year) | $[\mathbf{B} - \mathbf{A}]^{-1} > 0$ | $\mathbf{v} \geq 0$ | $\mathbf{v}^{\mathrm{T}}\mathbf{b} < 1$ | $\mathbf{p} \geq 0$ | $E(r) > 0$ |
|---|---|---|---|---|---|
| (2000) | × | * | * ($\mathbf{v}^{\mathrm{T}}\mathbf{b} \cong 0.53$) | * ($r \cong 34\%$) | × |
| (2001) | × | * | * ($\mathbf{v}^{\mathrm{T}}\mathbf{b} \cong 0.53$) | * ($r \cong 34\%$) | × |
| (2002) | × | * | * ($\mathbf{v}^{\mathrm{T}}\mathbf{b} \cong 0.52$) | * ($r \cong 35\%$) | × |
| (2003) | × | * | * ($\mathbf{v}^{\mathrm{T}}\mathbf{b} \cong 0.52$) | * ($r \cong 36\%$) | × |
| (2004) | × | * | * ($\mathbf{v}^{\mathrm{T}}\mathbf{b} \cong 0.51$) | * ($r \cong 37\%$) | × |
| (2005) | × | * | * ($\mathbf{v}^{\mathrm{T}}\mathbf{b} \cong 0.52$) | * ($r \cong 35\%$) | × |
| (2006) | × | * | * ($\mathbf{v}^{\mathrm{T}}\mathbf{b} \cong 0.50$) | * ($r \cong 37\%$) | × |
| (2007) | × | * | * ($\mathbf{v}^{\mathrm{T}}\mathbf{b} \cong 0.50$) | * ($r \cong 37\%$) | × |
| (1998R) | × | * | * ($\mathbf{v}^{\mathrm{T}}\mathbf{b} \cong 0.52$) | * ($r \cong 35\%$) | × |
| (1999R) | × | * | * ($\mathbf{v}^{\mathrm{T}}\mathbf{b} \cong 0.52$) | * ($r \cong 35\%$) | × |
| (2000R) | × | * | * ($\mathbf{v}^{\mathrm{T}}\mathbf{b} \cong 0.53$) | * ($r \cong 34\%$) | × |
| (2001R) | × | * | * ($\mathbf{v}^{\mathrm{T}}\mathbf{b} \cong 0.53$) | * ($r \cong 34\%$) | × |
| (2002R) | × | * | * ($\mathbf{v}^{\mathrm{T}}\mathbf{b} \cong 0.52$) | * ($r \cong 35\%$) | × |
| (2003R) | × | * | * ($\mathbf{v}^{\mathrm{T}}\mathbf{b} \cong 0.52$) | * ($r \cong 36\%$) | × |
| (2004R) | × | * | * ($\mathbf{v}^{\mathrm{T}}\mathbf{b} \cong 0.51$) | * ($r \cong 38\%$) | × |
| (2005R) | × | * | * ($\mathbf{v}^{\mathrm{T}}\mathbf{b} \cong 0.50$) | * ($r \cong 38\%$) | × |
| (2006R) | × | * | * ($\mathbf{v}^{\mathrm{T}}\mathbf{b} \cong 0.50$) | * ($r \cong 37\%$) | × |
| (2007R) | × | * | * ($\mathbf{v}^{\mathrm{T}}\mathbf{b} \cong 0.50$) | * ($r \cong 37\%$) | × |

(ii). The matrices $[\mathbf{B} - \mathbf{A}]^{-1}$ contain negative elements. Consequently, the systems under consideration are not all-productive and, therefore, they do not have the usual properties of single production systems.

(iii). There have been detected economically irrelevant vectors of ALVs in 7/85 of the considered systems, i.e. in about 8.2% of the tested cases, and in 2/12 of the countries involved in our analysis, i.e. in about 16.7% of the tested cases.

More specifically, the vectors of ALVs of the Finnish economy for the years 1999 through 2004 contain a negative element, which corresponds to the primary product of industry 37 ("recycling"), while the vector of ALVs of the Greek economy for the year 1999 contains five negative elements, which correspond to the primary products of the following industries: 01 ("agriculture, hunting, and related service activities"); 11 ("extraction of crude petroleum and natural gas; service activities incidental to oil and gas extraction excluding surveying"); 23 ("manufacture of coke, refined petroleum products, and nuclear fuels"); 61 ("water transport"); and 67 ("activities auxiliary to financial intermediation").

(iv). The "surplus values" are positive for all the systems under consideration. In most cases, the "labour value of labour power" is in the range of 0.4 to 0.5 and, therefore, the Marxian "rate of surplus value", $(\mathbf{v}^T\mathbf{b})^{-1} - 1$, is in the range of 100% to 150%. The largest "labour value of labour power" is about 0.60 (and, therefore, the smallest "rate of surplus value" is about 66.7%) and corresponds to the Slovenian economy for the year 2002, while the smallest "labour value of labour power" is about 0.16 (and, therefore, the largest "rate of surplus value" is about 525.0%) and corresponds to the Greek economy for the year 1999. Leaving aside the Greek economy, the smallest "labour value of labour power" is about 0.31 (and, therefore, the "rate of surplus value" is about 222.6%) and corresponds to the Japanese economy for the year 1970. However, given that the largest "labour value of labour power" detected in the Greek economy is about 0.30 (which corresponds to the year 1998 and to a "rate of surplus value" of about 233.3%), it follows that the Greek economy is characterized by the largest "rates of surplus value".

(v). Except for the cases of the Finnish (for the years 1995 through 1999 and 2003 through 2004) and Greek (for the years 1995 and 1998 through 1999) economies, the systems of long-period values have unique and positive solutions for $[r, \mathbf{p}^T]$. Thus, we detect that positive "surplus value" co-exists with economically irrelevant $[r, \mathbf{p}^T]$ in 10/85 of the considered systems, i.e. in about 11.8% of the tested cases, and in 2/12 of the countries involved in our analysis, i.e. in about 16.7% of the tested cases.

(vi). In the case of the Finnish economy (for the years 2000 and 2001), $(1 + r)^{-1}$ constitute the sub-dominant eigenvalues of the matrices $\mathbf{CB}^{-1}$, while in all the remaining cases $(1 + r)^{-1}$ constitute the dominant eigenvalues of $\mathbf{CB}^{-1}$. More specifically, it is found that in most cases the actual uniform profit rate is in the range of 30% to 40%. The largest profit rates detected are 45% and 46% and correspond to the SUTs of the Greek economy for the years 1996 and 1997, respectively. The smallest profit rate detected is 12% and corresponds to the SUTs of the Swedish economy for the year 2005. Leaving aside the Greek economy, the largest profit rate is equal to 42% and corresponds to the SUTs of the Japanese economy for the year 1970, while the second largest profit rate is equal to 39% and corresponds to the SUTs if the Japanese economy for the years 1995 and 2000.

(vii). In the case of the Danish (for the year 2004), French (for the years 1995 and 2005), Portuguese (for the year 1997), and Swedish (for the years 1995 through 1999) economies, there exists $r > 0$ such that $\mathbf{E}(r) > \mathbf{0}$ and, therefore, these systems are $r_0-$ all-engaging. Thus, it is found that 76/85 of the considered systems, i.e. about 89.4% of the systems under consideration, and 8/12 of the countries involved, i.e. about 66.7% of the economies, are *not* $r_0-$ all-engaging. Moreover, although the detected $r_0-$ all-engaging systems are characterized by economically relevant solutions for $[r, \mathbf{p}^{\mathrm{T}}]$, the estimated actual uniform profit rates do not belong to the interval of $r$ in which it holds $\mathbf{E}(r) > \mathbf{0}$. Finally, it is noted that, with the exception of the Portuguese economy, the aforementioned systems are $r_0-$ all-engaging for $r > 78\%$.

(viii). The actual relative profit rate, $\rho \equiv rR^{-1}$, of the Danish economy for the year 2004 is equal to 34%; that of the French economy is equal to 34% (for the year 1995) and 36% (for the year 2005); that of the Portuguese economy for the year 1997 is equal to 82%; and that of the Swedish economy is equal to 42% (for the year 1995), 38% (for the year 1996), 40% (for the year 1997), 39% (for the year 1998), and 38% (for the year 1999). Thus, leaving aside the Portuguese economy, the actual relative profit rates are in the range of 34% to 42%.

Next, we estimate the value deviations for the cases where the estimated vector of ALVs and/or ALPVs is economically relevant. A crucial issue concerning the estimation of value deviations is the choice of a theoretical appropriate measure of deviation. As is well known, the results obtained on the basis of the traditional measures of deviation (such as "correlation coefficient", "mean absolute deviation", "mean absolute weighted deviation", "root-mean-square-percent-error"), which have been widely used in the relevant literature, depend on the arbitrary choice of either the *numéraire* or the physical measurement units.[22] Conversely, the so-called $d-$ distance, introduced by Steedman and Tomkins (1998, pp. 381–382), constitutes a measure of value deviation that is free from *numéraire* and measurement-unit dependence. The $d-$distance between ALPVs and ALVs is defined as

$$d \equiv \sqrt{2(1 - \cos\theta)}$$

where $\theta$ is the Euclidean angle between the vectors $\mathbf{p}^{\mathrm{T}}\widehat{\mathbf{v}}^{-1}$ and $\mathbf{e}$, $\widehat{\mathbf{v}}$ a diagonal matrix formed from the elements of $\mathbf{v}$, and $\mathbf{p}^{\mathrm{T}}\widehat{\mathbf{v}}^{-1}$ the ratio of ALPVs to ALVs.[23] Since the

---

[22]For a detailed discussion of the problem of measuring the value deviations, see Mariolis (2011, 2013), Mariolis and Soklis (2011), Mariolis and Tsoulfidis (2016, Chap. 4), Steedman and Tomkins (1998).

[23]Analogously, the $d-$distance between MVs and ALVs (ALPVs) is estimated on the basis of the Euclidean angle between the vectors $[\mathbf{p}^{\mathrm{M}}]^{\mathrm{T}}\widehat{\mathbf{v}}^{-1}$ ($[\mathbf{p}^{\mathrm{M}}]^{\mathrm{T}}\widehat{\mathbf{p}}^{-1}$) and $\mathbf{e}$, where $\mathbf{p}^{\mathrm{M}}$ denores the vector of MVs.

theoretical maximum value of $\cos\theta$ equals $(\sqrt{n})^{-1}$, the theoretical maximum value of the $d-$ distance, $D$, equals

$$\sqrt{2\left[1 - (\sqrt{n})^{-1}\right]}$$

and, therefore, we may define the "normalized $d-$distance" as $dD^{-1}$ (Mariolis and Soklis 2010, p. 94).[24] Thus, in what follows we use $dD^{-1}$ as a measure of value deviation. The estimated value deviations are reported in Table 5.5. The first column of the table indicates the country and the reference year of the analysis. The second column reports the normalized $d-$distance (as a percentage) between ALPVs and ALVs. The third column reports the deviations between MVs and ALVs. The fourth column reports the deviations between MVs and ALPVs. Finally, the blank cells in the table correspond to cases where the ALVs and/or the ALPVs are economically irrelevant.

From the results reported in Table 5.5, we arrive at the following conclusions:

(i). The ALPV–ALV deviation is in the range of 8.3% to 61.6%. The smallest deviation corresponds to the Slovenian economy for the year 2002, while the largest deviation corresponds to the Swedish economy for the year 2005. Moreover, the average ALPV–ALV deviation, i.e. the sum of the deviations divided by the number of the estimations, is about 19.0%.

(ii). The MV–ALV deviation is in the range of 16.4% to 71.3%. The smallest deviation corresponds to the Slovenian economy for the year 2005, while the largest deviation corresponds to the Finnish economy for the year 1996. Moreover, the average MV–ALV deviation is about 36.7%.

(iii). The MV–ALPV deviation is in the range of 19.0% to 75.9%. The smallest deviation corresponds to the Slovenian economy for the year 2005, while the largest deviation corresponds to the Finnish economy for the year 2002. Moreover, the average MV–ALPV deviation is about 34.8%.

## 5.4  Concluding Remarks

The extension of the empirical investigation of the shape of wage–profit rate curves and of the relationships amongst "labour values" and actual values to the joint production case gave the following results:

---

[24]Mariolis and Soklis (2011) have shown that there exist an infinite number of *numéraire*-free measures of value deviation (in the sense of Steedman and Tomkins 1998) and the choice amongst them depends either on the theoretical viewpoint or the aim of the observer.

**Table 5.5** Value Deviations (%)

| Country (Year) | ALPVs–ALVs | MVs–ALVs | MVs–ALPVs |
|---|---|---|---|
| Denmark (2000) | 11.4 | 66.4 | 64.5 |
| (2004) | 10.7 | 52.4 | 46.7 |
| Finland (1995) | – | 27.5 | – |
| (1996) | – | 71.3 | – |
| (1997) | – | 30.8 | – |
| (1998) | – | 30.0 | – |
| (1999) | – | – | – |
| (2000) | – | – | 37.7 |
| (2001) | – | – | 34.2 |
| (2002) | – | – | 75.9 |
| (2003) | – | – | – |
| (2004) | – | – | – |
| France (1995) | 11.0 | 66.5 | 68.0 |
| (2005) | 11.4 | 33.6 | 33.9 |
| FYROM (2005) | 18.2 | 34.5 | 24.2 |
| Germany (1997) | 19.8 | 43.5 | 38.4 |
| (1998) | 21.4 | 43.1 | 38.0 |
| (1999) | 19.2 | 42.0 | 37.7 |
| (2000) | 10.7 | 43.0 | 43.7 |
| (2001) | 11.7 | 43.9 | 45.3 |
| (2002) | 11.5 | 43.9 | 45.9 |
| (2003) | 11.7 | 44.8 | 46.7 |
| (2004) | 12.0 | 43.2 | 44.2 |
| (2005) | 12.2 | 42.3 | 43.6 |
| Greece (1995) | – | 65.9 | – |
| (1996) | 35.3 | 66.6 | 57.3 |
| (1997) | 32.1 | 67.1 | 66.6 |
| (1998) | – | 65.7 | – |
| (1999) | – | – | – |
| Hungary (2001) | 23.0 | 24.8 | 27.0 |
| (2002) | 31.7 | 19.7 | 22.5 |
| (2003) | 18.9 | 22.5 | 23.4 |
| (2004) | 19.8 | 23.0 | 24.4 |
| Japan (1970) | 25.6 | 48.5 | 43.4 |
| (1975) | 18.4 | 44.9 | 44.1 |

(continued)

**Table 5.5** (continued)

| Country (Year) | ALPVs–ALVs | MVs–ALVs | MVs–ALPVs |
|---|---|---|---|
| (1980) | 19.1 | 47.9 | 49.0 |
| (1985) | 17.9 | 49.7 | 50.9 |
| (1990) | 18.2 | 46.2 | 52.2 |
| (1995) | 16.2 | 48.9 | 52.5 |
| (2000) | 16.3 | 44.2 | 47.8 |
| Portugal (1995) | 35.7 | 47.9 | 46.1 |
| (1996) | 33.0 | 44.2 | 42.7 |
| (1997) | 31.3 | 42.1 | 41.1 |
| (1998) | 30.2 | 42.0 | 42.3 |
| (1999) | 22.9 | 42.4 | 43.0 |
| (2000) | 13.7 | 38.1 | 40.4 |
| (2001) | 13.8 | 34.8 | 36.9 |
| (2002) | 15.1 | 34.8 | 37.3 |
| (2003) | 15.5 | 34.6 | 37.0 |
| (2004) | 16.3 | 33.3 | 36.1 |
| Slovenia (2002) | 8.3 | 33.4 | 29.7 |
| (2003) | 9.2 | 31.7 | 28.4 |
| (2004) | 13.5 | 18.0 | 19.4 |
| (2005) | 18.5 | 16.4 | 19.0 |
| Sweden (1995) | 11.8 | 27.9 | 29.6 |
| (1996) | 11.1 | 27.3 | 29.1 |
| (1997) | 11.9 | 27.0 | 29.4 |
| (1998) | 11.5 | 25.6 | 28.2 |
| (1999) | 11.8 | 25.3 | 28.4 |
| (2000) | 56.9 | 24.2 | 22.7 |
| (2001) | 52.4 | 25.6 | 23.7 |
| (2002) | 51.8 | 25.5 | 22.4 |
| (2003) | 61.1 | 24.7 | 23.1 |
| (2004) | 59.5 | 23.7 | 23.0 |
| (2005) | 61.6 | 20.5 | 23.3 |
| USA (1998) | 10.3 | 27.7 | 22.8 |
| (1999) | 10.1 | 29.2 | 24.6 |
| (2000) | 9.7 | 29.7 | 24.5 |
| (2001) | 9.9 | 30.1 | 24.8 |
| (2002) | 10.0 | 29.2 | 24.2 |
| (2003) | 10.3 | 30.8 | 25.1 |
| (2004) | 10.8 | 31.6 | 25.2 |
| (2005) | 10.4 | 33.5 | 27.8 |

(continued)

**Table 5.5** (continued)

| Country (Year) | ALPVs–ALVs | MVs–ALVs | MVs–ALPVs |
|---|---|---|---|
| (2006) | 11.1 | 29.8 | 24.5 |
| (2007) | 11.1 | 29.7 | 24.0 |
| (1998R) | 10.2 | 27.5 | 23.6 |
| (1999R) | 9.9 | 29.2 | 25.3 |
| (2000R) | 9.7 | 29.5 | 24.9 |
| (2001R) | 9.8 | 29.9 | 25.5 |
| (2002R) | 9.8 | 29.1 | 24.8 |
| (2003R) | 10.2 | 30.8 | 25.7 |
| (2004R) | 10.5 | 31.6 | 25.8 |
| (2005R) | 10.7 | 32.9 | 27.1 |
| (2006R) | 10.9 | 29.8 | 24.8 |
| (2007R) | 11.0 | 29.6 | 24.2 |

(i). The systems examined are not all-productive and, therefore, the actual economies under consideration do not have the usual properties of single production systems.

(ii). About 89.4% (or 76/85) of the systems examined are not $r_0-$ all-engaging. Moreover, in the detected $r_0-$ all-engaging systems, the estimated actual uniform profit rates do not belong to the interval of the profit rate in which the systems are $r_0-$all-engaging.

(iii). The monotonicity of the estimated wage–profit rate curves depends on the choice of the *numéraire*, while upward-sloping relationships exist even for "low" values of the profit rate.

(iv). The downward-sloping wage–profit rate curves appear to be "close" to the linear "trends", and this fact expresses the uncontrollable/unobservable aspects of the real-world economies (see Chaps. 2 and 3 of the present book).

(v). All the estimated "surplus values" are positive. However, economically irrelevant "additive labour values" (actual long-period values) have been detected in about 8.2% (11.8%) of the systems examined. Thus, cases exist where economically irrelevant actual long-period values co-exist with positive "surplus value".

(vi). In the economically relevant cases, the estimated actual long-period value (market value)–"additive labour value" deviation is in the range of 8.3% to 61.6% (16.4% to 71.3%), while the market value–actual long-period value deviation is in the range of 19.0% to 75.9%.

Since, in the real world, joint production activities constitute the rule, these empirical findings reinforce the Marx-after-Sraffa theoretical statement that actual economies cannot be coherently analysed in terms of the traditional value theory.

## Appendix: A Note on the Data

### *Data Sources*

With the exception of the SUTs of the Japanese, Slovenian (for the years 2004 and 2005), and US economies, the SUTs used in the analysis were retrieved through Eurostat's website, http://ec.europa.eu/eurostat. The SUTs of the Japanese economy were obtained through the website of the Cabinet Office of Japan, http://www.cao.go.jp; the SUTs of the Slovenian economy for the years 2004 through 2005 were obtained through the website of the national statistical service of Slovenia, http://www.stat.si; and the SUTs of the US economy were available through the Bureau of Economic Analysis website, http://www.bea.gov. The levels of sectoral employment of the Danish, Finnish, French, FYROM (former), and German economies were included in the SUTs, while those of the rest of the economies were obtained through the national statistical agencies' websites. With the exception of the Japanese and US economies, the SUTs describe 59 products, which are classified according to CPA (Classification of Products by Activity) and 59 industries, which are classified according to NACE (General Industrial Classification of Economic Activities within the European Communities). The described products and their correspondence to CPA are the following:

1. (CPA: 01). Products of agriculture, hunting, and related services
2. (02). Products of forestry, logging, and related services
3. (05). Fish and other fishing products; services incidental of fishing
4. (10). Coal and lignite; peat
5. (11). Crude petroleum and natural gas; services incidental to oil and gas extraction excluding surveying
6. (12). Uranium and thorium ores
7. (13). Metal ores
8. (14). Other mining and quarrying products
9. (15). Food products and beverages
10. (16). Tobacco products
11. (17). Textiles
12. (18). Wearing apparel; furs
13. (19). Leather and leather products
14. (20). Wood and products of wood and cork (except furniture); articles of straw and plaiting materials
15. (21). Pulp, paper, and paper products
16. (22). Printed matter and recorded media
17. (23). Coke, refined petroleum products, and nuclear fuels
18. (24). Chemicals, chemical products, and man-made fibres
19. (25). Rubber and plastic products
20. (26). Other non-metallic mineral products
21. (27). Basic metals
22. (28). Fabricated metal products, except machinery and equipment

23. (29). Machinery and equipment n.e.c.
24. (30). Office machinery and computers
25. (31). Electrical machinery and apparatus n.e.c.
26. (32). Radio, television, and communication equipment and apparatus
27. (33). Medical, precision and optical instruments, watches and clocks
28. (34). Motor vehicles, trailers, and semi-trailers
29. (35). Other transport equipment
30. (36). Furniture; other manufactured goods n.e.c.
31. (37). Secondary raw materials
32. (40). Electrical energy, gas, steam, and hot water
33. (41). Collected and purified water, distribution services of water
34. (45). Construction work
35. (50). Trade, maintenance, and repair services of motor vehicles and motorcycles; retail sale of automotive fuel
36. (51). Wholesale trade and commission trade services, except motor vehicles and motorcycles
37. (52). Retail trade services, except motor vehicles and motorcycles; repair services of personal and household goods
38. (55). Hotel and restaurant services
39. (60). Land transport; transport via pipeline services
40. (61). Water transport services
41. (62). Air transport services
42. (63). Supporting and auxiliary transport services; travel agency services
43. (64). Post and telecommunication services
44. (65). Financial intermediation services, except insurance and pension funding services
45. (66). Insurance and pension funding services, except compulsory social security services
46. (67). Services auxiliary to financial intermediation
47. (70). Real estate services
48. (71). Renting services of machinery and equipment without operator and of personal and household goods
49. (72). Computer and related services
50. (73). Research and development services
51. (74). Other business services
52. (75). Public administration and defence services; compulsory social security services
53. (80). Education services
54. (85). Health and social work services
55. (90). Sewage and refuse disposal services, sanitation and similar services
56. (91). Membership organization services n.e.c.
57. (92). Recreational, cultural, and sporting services
58. (93). Other services
59. (95). Private households with employed persons

The SUTs of the Japanese economy describe 24 products and industries. The described products are the following:

1. Agriculture, forestry, and fishing
2. Mining
3. Food products and beverages
4. Textiles
5. Pulp, paper, and paper products
6. Chemicals
7. Petroleum and coal products
8. Non-metallic mineral products
9. Basic metals
10. Fabricated metal products
11. Machinery
12. Electrical machinery, equipment, and supplies
13. Transport equipment
14. Precision instruments
15. Other manufacturing products
16. Construction
17. Electricity, gas, and water supply
18. Wholesale and retail trade
19. Finance and insurance
20. Real estate
21. Transport and communications
22. Service activities
23. Government services
24. Private non-profit services to households

Finally, the SUTs of the US economy describe 65 products and industries. The described products are the following:

1. Farms
2. Forestry, fishing, and related activities
3. Oil and gas extraction
4. Mining, except oil and gas
5. Support activities for mining
6. Utilities
7. Construction
8. Wood products
9. Non-metallic mineral products
10. Primary metals
11. Fabricated metal products
12. Machinery
13. Computer and electronic products
14. Electrical equipment, appliances, and components
15. Motor vehicles, bodies and trailers, and parts

16. Other transportation equipment
17. Furniture and related products
18. Miscellaneous manufacturing
19. Food and beverage and tobacco products
20. Textile mills and textile product mills
21. Apparel and leather and allied products
22. Paper products
23. Printing and related support activities
24. Petroleum and coal products
25. Chemical products
26. Plastics and rubber products
27. Wholesale trade
28. Retail trade
29. Air transportation
30. Rail transportation
31. Water transportation
32. Truck transportation
33. Transit and ground passenger transportation
34. Pipeline transportation
35. Other transportation and support activities
36. Warehousing and storage
37. Publishing industries, except internet (includes software)
38. Motion picture and sound recording industries
39. Broadcasting and telecommunications
40. Data processing, internet publishing, and other information services
41. Federal Reserve banks, credit intermediation, and related activities
42. Securities, commodity contracts, and investments
43. Insurance carriers and related activities
44. Funds, trusts, and other financial vehicles
45. Real estate
46. Rental and leasing services and lessors of intangible assets
47. Legal services
48. Computer systems design and related services
49. Miscellaneous professional, scientific, and technical services
50. Management of companies and enterprises
51. Administrative and support services
52. Waste management and remediation services
53. Educational services
54. Ambulatory health care services
55. Hospitals and nursing and residential care facilities
56. Social assistance
57. Performing arts, spectator sports, museums, and related activities
58. Amusements, gambling, and recreation industries
59. Accommodation
60. Food services and drinking places

61. Other services, except government
62. Federal general government
63. Federal government enterprises
64. State and local general government
65. State and local government enterprises

## *Construction of Variables*

### Denmark

All the elements associated with product/industry 12 ("mining of uranium and thorium ores") in the SUTs of the Danish economy equal zero and, therefore, we remove them from our analysis. Furthermore, all the elements associated with products 10 ("coal and lignite; peat") and 13 ("metal ores") equal zero and, therefore, we remove them from our analysis, while there are elements associated with industries 10 and 13 that are positive. In order to derive "square" make and use matrices, we aggregate industries 10 and 13 with industry 11 ("extraction of crude petroleum and natural gas").[25] Thus, we derive make and use matrices of dimensions $56 \times 56$.

### Finland

All the elements associated with product/industry 12 in the SUTs of the Finnish economy equal zero and, therefore, we remove them from our analysis. Furthermore, all the elements associated with product/industry 11 in the make matrix equal zero, and, therefore, we remove them from our analysis, while there are elements associated with product 11 in the use matrix that are positive. In order to derive square make and use matrices, we aggregate product 11 with the "primary product" ("coke, refined petroleum products, and nuclear fuels") of industry 23 ("manufacture of coke, refined petroleum products, and nuclear fuels"). This choice is based on the fact that product 11 is mainly used by industry 23. Thus, we derive make and use matrices of dimensions $57 \times 57$.

### France

All the elements associated with product 37 ("secondary raw materials") in the SUTs of the French economy equal zero and, therefore, we remove them from our analysis, while there are elements associated with industry 37 that are positive. In order to derive square make and use matrices, we aggregate industry 37 with industry

---

[25] It need hardly be said that the SUTs are not necessarily square (also see Chap. 1).

27 ("basic metals"). This choice is based on the fact that the largest part of the production of industry 37 consists of the primary product of industry 27. Moreover, in the SUTs for the year 2005 the elements associated with product/industry 12 equal zero, and, therefore, we remove them from our analysis. Thus, we derive make and use matrices of dimensions 58 × 58 and 57 × 57 for the years 1995 and 2005, respectively.

## FYROM

All the elements associated with products/industries 12 and 95 ("private households with employed persons") of the FYROM economy equal zero and, therefore, we remove them from our analysis. Thus, we derive make and use matrices of dimensions 57 × 57.

## Germany

All the elements associated with product/industry 12 in the SUTs of the German economy equal zero and, therefore, we remove them from our analysis. Furthermore, all the elements associated with product/industry 13 in the make matrix equal zero, and, therefore, we remove them from our analysis, while there are elements associated with product 13 in the use matrix that are positive. In order to derive square make and use matrices, we aggregate product 13 with product 27. This choice is based on the fact that product 13 is mainly used by industry 27. Thus, we derive make and use matrices of dimensions 57 × 57.

## Greece

All the elements associated with product/industry 12 in the SUTs of the Greek economy equal zero and, therefore, we remove them from our analysis. Thus, we derive make and use matrices of dimensions 58 × 58.

## Hungary

All the elements associated with products/industries 12 and 95 of the Hungarian economy equal zero and, therefore, we remove them from our analysis. Furthermore, the data for the levels of sectoral employment for the year 2001 correspond to 48 industries. In order to derive make and use matrices compatible with the dimensions of the employment data, we aggregate (a) product/industry 10 with products/industries 11, 13, and 14 ("other mining and quarrying products"); (b) product/industry 15 ("food products and beverages") with product/industry 16 ("tobacco products"); (c) product/industry 36 ("furniture; other manufactured goods n.e.c.")

with product/industry 37; (d) product/industry 40 ("electrical energy, gas, steam, and hot water") with product/industry 41 ("collected and purified water, distribution services of water"); and (e) product/industry 90 ("sewage and refuse disposal services, sanitation, and similar services") with products/industries 91 ("membership organization services n.e.c."), 92 ("recreational, cultural, and sporting services"), and 93 ("other services"). Thus, we derive make and use matrices of dimensions 48 × 48 for the year 2001 and of dimensions 57 × 57 for the years 2002 through 2004.

## Japan

In the case of the SUTs of the Japanese economy, no aggregations are needed. Thus, the make and use matrices are of dimensions 24 × 24.

## Portugal

The data for the levels of sectoral employment of the Portuguese economy for the years 1995 through 2001 correspond to 48 industries. In order to derive make and use matrices compatible with the dimensions of the employment data, we aggregate (a) product/industry 10 with products/industries 11, 12, 13, and 14; (b) product/ industry 15 with product/industry 16; (c) product/industry 36 with product/industry 37; (d) product/industry 40 with product/industry 41; and (e) product/industry 90 with products/industries 91, 92, 93, and 95. Moreover, all the elements associated with product/industry 12 in the SUTs for the years 2002 through 2004 equal zero and, therefore, we remove them from our analysis. Furthermore, all the elements associated with industries 10 and 11 equal zero, while there are elements associated with products 10 and 11 that are positive. In order to derive square make and use matrices, we aggregate products 10 and 11 with product 13. Thus, we derive make and use matrices of dimensions 48 × 48 for the years 1995 through 2001 and of dimensions 56 × 56 for the years 2002 through 2004.

## Slovenia

The SUTs of the Slovenian economy for the years 2002 through 2003 describe 59 products/industries, while those for the years 2004 through 2005 are aggregated to 30 products/industries. However, the data for the levels of sectoral employment for the years 2002 through 2003 correspond to 55 industries. In order to derive make and use matrices compatible with the dimensions of the employment data, we aggregate (a) product/industry 10 with products/industries 11 and 12; (b) product/ industry 13 with product/industry 14; and (c) product/industry 15 with product/ industry 16. Thus, we derive make and use matrices of dimensions 55 × 55 for the years 2002 through 2003 and of dimensions 30 × 30 for the years 2004 through 2005.

## Sweden

Due to confidentiality issues, the SUTs of the Swedish economy for the years 1995 through 1999 are available with the following aggregations: (a) product/industry 13 with product/industry 14; (b) product/industry 15 with product/industry 16; and (c) product/industry 50 ("trade, maintenance, and repair services of motor vehicles and motorcycles; retail sale of automotive fuel") with products/industries 51 ("wholesale trade and commission trade services, except motor vehicles and motorcycles") and 52 ("retail trade services, except motor vehicles and motorcycles; repair services of personal and household goods"). Moreover, the available data for the levels of sectoral employment correspond to 50 industries. In order to derive make and use matrices compatible with the dimensions of the employment data, we aggregate (a) product/industry 10 with products/industries 11, 12, 13, and 14; (b) product/industry 31 ("electrical machinery and apparatus n.e.c.") with product/industry 32 ("radio, television, and communication equipment and apparatus"); and (c) product/industry 73 ("research and development services") with product/industry 74 ("other business services"). Furthermore, due to confidentiality issues, the SUTs for the years 2000 through 2005 are available with the following aggregations (a) product/industry 13 with product/industry 14; (b) product/industry 15 with product/industry 16; (c) product/industry 50 with products/industries 51 and 52; and (d) product/industry 73 with product/industry 74. Also, all the elements associated with industry 11 equal zero, while there are elements associated with product 11 that are positive. In order to derive square make and use matrices, we aggregate product 11 with product 23. This choice is based on the fact that product 11 is mainly used by industry 23. Thus, we derive make and use matrices of dimensions 50 × 50 for the years 1995 through 1999 and of dimensions 51 × 51 for the years 2000 through 2005.

## USA

In the case of the US economy, there are available two "sets" of SUTs: (a) the SUTs before the application of the "redefinition method"; and (b) the SUTs after the application of the redefinition method. The redefinition method constitutes a procedure that moves outputs and inputs of secondary products that have distinctive production processes compared to those of the primary products of each industry to the industries where these products are primary (also see Chap. 1). Since this procedure reduces the secondary production that is reported in the SUTs, we apply our analysis in both sets of SUTs in order to explore the sensitivity of our results to the application of the redefinition method. Thus, we derive two sets of make and use matrices of dimensions 65 × 65.

With the exception of the cases of the Danish (for the year 2000), US, Japanese, and Finnish economies, the goods and services in the supply tables are measured at current "basic prices", while the intermediate costs in the use tables are measured in current "purchasers' prices". The derivation of SUTs at basic prices in the latter cases is based on the method proposed by United Nations (1999, Chap. 3 and pp. 228–229). The MVs of all products are taken to be equal to 1; that is to say, the physical unit of measurement of each product is that unit which is worth of a monetary unit. Thus, the make matrix can be considered as the empirical counterpart of the output matrix, $\mathbf{B}$, and the use matrix can be considered as the empirical counterpart of the input matrix, $\mathbf{A}$ (also see Chap. 1).

It need hardly be said that, in the real world, labour is not homogeneous and, therefore, the available levels of sectoral employment correspond to heterogeneous labour. However, in the case of economic systems with heterogeneous labour, any attempt to explore the actual value–"labour value" deviation(s) is devoid of economic sense (see Steedman 1977, Chap. 7 and pp. 178–179; 1985). Thus, in accordance with most of the relevant empirical studies, we use wage differentials to homogenize the sectoral employment (see, e.g. Kurz and Salvadori 1995, pp. 322–325; Sraffa 1960, pp. 10–11), i.e. the $j$-th element of the vector of employment levels process by process, $\mathbf{l}$, is determined by $l_j = L_j(w_j^M/w_{\min}^M)$. Alternatively, the homogenization of employment could be achieved, *for instance*, through the economy's average wage; in fact, the empirical results are robust to alternative normalizations with respect to homogenization of labour inputs. The described reductions of course are only meaningful when the relative wages express with precision the differences in skills and intensity of labour that is employed by each sector of the economy. In any other case the choice of homogenization procedure is, of necessity, arbitrary. Furthermore, by assuming that workers do not save and that their consumption has the same composition as the vector of the final consumption expenditures of the household sector, $\mathbf{h}$, directly obtained from the SUTs, the vector of the real wage rate, $\mathbf{b} \equiv [b_i]$, is determined as follows: $\mathbf{b} = (w_{\min}^M/\mathbf{e}^T\mathbf{h})\mathbf{h}$, where $\mathbf{e}^T \equiv [1, 1, \ldots, 1]$ denotes the row summation vector identified with the vector of MVs. Finally, it is noted that the available SUTs do not include inter-industry data on fixed capital stocks and on non-competitive imports. As a result, our investigation is restricted to a closed economy with circulating capital.

# References

Bidard, C. (1986a). Is von Neumann square? *Zeitschrift für Nationalökonomie, 46*(4), 407–419.
Bidard, C. (1986b). The maximum rate of profits in joint production. *Metroeconomica, 38*(1), 53–66.
Bidard, C. (1996). All-engaging systems. *Economic Systems Research, 8*(4), 323–340.
Filippini, C., & Filippini, L. (1982). Two theorems on joint production. *The Economic Journal, 92* (366), 386–390.
Fujimoto, T., & Krause, U. (1988). More theorems on joint production. *Journal of Economics, 48* (2), 189–196.

Hosoda, E. (1993). Negative surplus value and inferior processes. *Metroeconomica, 44*(1), 29–42.

Kurz, H. D., & Salvadori, N. (1995). *Theory of production. A long-period analysis*. Cambridge: Cambridge University Press.

Li, B. (2017). *Linear theory of fixed capital and China's economy. Marx, Sraffa and Okishio.* Singapore: Springer.

Mariolis, T. (2006). *Prices and labour values in the SUT. Internal Report of the Study Group on Sraffian Economics.* Athens: Department of Public Administration, Panteion University. (in Greek).

Mariolis, T. (2011). A simple measure of price–labour value deviation. *Metroeconomica, 62*(4), 605–611.

Mariolis, T. (2013). Applying the mean absolute eigen-deviation of labour commanded prices from labour values to actual economies. *Applied Mathematical Sciences, 7*(104), 5193–5204.

Mariolis, T., & Soklis, G. (2007). On the empirical validity of the labour theory of value. In T. Mariolis (Ed.), (2010). *Essays on the logical history of political economy* (pp. 231–260). Athens: Matura,. (in Greek).

Mariolis, T., & Soklis, G. (2010). Additive labour values and prices: Evidence from the supply and use tables of the French, German and Greek Economies. *Economic Issues, 15*(2), 87–107.

Mariolis, T., & Soklis, G. (2011). On constructing numéraire-free measures of price–value deviation: a note on the Steedman–Tomkins distance. *Cambridge Journal of Economics, 35*(3), 613–618.

Mariolis, T., & Tsoulfidis, L. (2016). *Modern classical economics and reality. A spectral analysis of the theory of value and distribution.* Tokyo: Springer.

Petrović, P. (1991). Shape of a wage profit curve, some methodology and empirical evidence. *Metroeconomica, 42*(2), 413–429.

Salvadori, N., & Steedman, I. (1988). Joint production analysis in a Sraffian framework. *Bulletin of Economic Research, 40*(3), 165–195.

Soklis, G. (2006). *Labour values and production prices: Exploration based on the joint production table of the Greek economy for the year 1999.* Master's Thesis, Athens: Department of Public Administration, Panteion University (in Greek)

Soklis, G. (2011). Shape of wage–profit curves in joint production systems: Evidence from the supply and use tables of the Finnish economy. *Metroeconomica, 62*(4), 548–560.

Soklis, G. (2012). *Labour values, commodity values, prices and income distribution: Exploration based on empirical input–output tables.* Ph.D. Dissertation. Department of Public Administration, Pantheon University, Athens. (in Greek).

Soklis, G. (2019). *The empirical weakness of the traditional political economy.* Paper presented at the 1st Conference of the Study Group on Sraffian Economics: "From the Capital Theory Controversy in the 1960s to Greece's Virtual Bankruptcy in 2010", 11–12 April 2019, Panteion University, Athens, Greece (in Greek).

Sraffa, P. (1960). *Production of commodities by means of commodities. Prelude to a critique of economic theory.* Cambridge: Cambridge University Press.

Steedman, I. (1977). *Marx after Sraffa.* London: New Left Books.

Steedman, I. (1984). L'importance empirique de la production jointe. In C. Bidard (Ed.), *La production jointe. Nouveaux débats* (pp. 5–20). Paris: Economica.

Steedman, I. (1985). Heterogeneous labour, money wages and Marx's theory. *History of Political Economy, 17*(4), 551–574.

Steedman, I. (2008). Marx after Sraffa and the open economy. *Bulletin of Political Economy, 2*(2), 165–174.

Steedman, I., & Tomkins, J. (1998). On measuring the deviation of prices from values. *Cambridge Journal of Economics, 22*(3), 379–385.

United Nations. (1999). *Handbook of input–output table. Compilation and analysis. Studies in methods. Handbook of national accounting.* United Nations, New York: Department for Economic and Social Affairs, Statistics Division, Series F, No. 74.

von Neumann, J. (1937). Über ein ökonomisches Gleichungssystem und eine Verallgemeinerung des Brouwerschen Fixpunktsatzes. In K. Menger (Ed.), *Ergebnisse eines Mathematischen Kolloquiums* (Vol. 8, pp. 73–83). Leipzig: Deuticke.

von Neumann, J. (1945). A model of general economic equilibrium. *The Review of Economic Studies, 13*(1), 1–9.

# Chapter 6
# Time Dilation, Abstract Social-International Labour, and Profit

**Abstract** The conditions under which positive "surplus labour", as defined by Marx, is both necessary and sufficient for positive profits are found to be restrictive and, therefore, the traditional Marxian "exploitation theory of profit" cannot be sustained. Nevertheless, a Marx-after-Sraffa re-formulation of the concepts of "exploitation", as a "time dilation", and "abstract social-international labour", as the "substance of value", may lead to the proposal that the labour values of commodities are determined by their market prices and are equal to them; therefore, surplus labour, measured in terms of "abstract social-international labour", is determined by and is equal to actual profits.

**Keywords** Abstract social-international labour · Exploitation theory of profit · Fixed point · Integrated wage-goods sector · Time dilation

> Hence when all such inventions were already established, the sciences which do not aim at giving pleasure or at the necessities of life were discovered, and first in the places where men first began to have leisure.—Aristotle, *Metaphysics* (Ross, W. D. (1928). Aristotle, *Metaphysica*. In W. D. Ross (Ed.), *Aristotle, Works* (Vol. VIII, 2d ed.). Oxford: The Clarendon Press)

## 6.1 Introduction

Marx tried to show that the "exploitation of workers", as measured by "surplus value" ("surplus labour, unpaid labour"), is the "exclusive source of profit" or, in other words, that the existence of positive profits is explained by the existence of positive "surplus value". Within this "exploitation theory of profit", "surplus value" is measured in terms of the so-called "labour values", while the "labour value" of a commodity is defined as the quantity of labour "crystalized (or embodied)" in one unit of that commodity, and "surplus value" is defined as the "labour value" of the "surplus product". However, in his analysis of the "forms of value", Marx (1991, Chap. 1)

© Springer Nature Singapore Pte Ltd. 2021
T. Mariolis et al., *Spectral Theory of Value and Actual Economies*, Evolutionary Economics and Social Complexity Science 24,
https://doi.org/10.1007/978-981-33-6260-4_6

also introduces the concept of "abstract social labour" (also see Goldmann 1958; Krause 1982; Rubin 1972), which involves (or tends to involve) a rather different definition of "labour value" than that of "embodied labour". Inevitably, therefore, this ambiguity about the meaning of the term "labour value" (for a critical analysis, see Steedman 1985) has been reflected in the relevant literature. For instance, in the first Soviet official textbook of political economy, by the Academy of Sciences of the USSR (1957), we read

> Commodities of different kinds have only one characteristic in common which makes it possible to compare them for purposes of exchange, and it is that they are all *products of labour.* Underlying the equivalence of two commodities which are exchanged against each other is the social labour expended in producing them. [...] *Value* is the social labour of commodity producers embodied in a commodity. That the value of commodities embodies the social labour expended in producing them is borne out by some generally known facts. [...] A commodity has a *two-fold character:* in one aspect it is a use-value and in another it is a value. The two-fold character of the commodity is caused by the *two-fold nature of the labour* embodied in the commodity. [...] Labour expended in a definite form is *concrete labour.* Concrete labour creates the use-value of a commodity. [...] The labour of commodity producers, considered as expenditure of human labour-power generally, without regard to its concrete form, is *abstract labour.* Abstract labour forms the value of a commodity. Abstract and concrete labour are two aspects of the labour embodied in a commodity (pp. 65–66).

We also read:

> In commodity production, products are produced not for personal consumption but for sale. The social character of labour is here expressed by means of the comparison of one commodity with another, and this comparison takes place through the reducing of concrete forms of labour to the abstract labour which forms the value of a commodity. This process takes place spontaneously, without any sort of common plan, behind the backs of the commodity producers. [...] The magnitude of the value of a commodity is determined not by the individual labour-time expended by a particular commodity producer in producing a commodity, but by the socially-necessary labour-time. *Socially-necessary labour-time* is the time needed for the making of any commodity under average social conditions of production, i.e., with the average level of technique and average skill and intensity of labour. It corresponds to the conditions of production under which the greatest bulk of goods of a particular kind are produced. Socially-necessary labour-time changes as a result of the growth of the productivity of labour (pp. 67–68).

On the other hand, Sraffa (1960) clarifies that, within his analysis,

> the ratios which satisfy the conditions of production have been called "values" or "prices" rather than, as might be thought more appropriate, "costs of production". [...] Such classical terms as "necessary price", "natural price" or "price of production" would meet the case, but value and price have been preferred as being shorter and in the present context (which contains no reference to market prices) no more ambiguous. [...] [*I*]*n general* the use of the term "cost of production" has been avoided in this work, as well as the term "capital" in its quantitative connotation, at the cost of some tiresome circumlocution. This is because these terms have come to be inseparably linked with the supposition that they stand for quantities that can be measured independently of, and prior to, the determination of the prices of the products. (Witness the "real costs" of Marshall and the "quantity of capital" which is implied in the marginal productivity theory.) Since to achieve freedom from such presuppositions

has been one of the aims of this work, avoidance of the terms seemed the only way of not prejudicing the issue (pp. 8–9).[1]

And Steedman (1991), in his dense essay "The Irrelevance of Marxian Values", concludes that

Sraffa's work [...] shows with great clarity that real wages and the conditions of production suffice to determine the rate of profit, *no quantity evaluated in terms of labour values being of the slightest relevance to that determination* (p. 205). [...] [A]ll labour-value magnitudes are purely derivative of other quantities—physical inputs, outputs, real wages, employment levels, etc.—and can thus never tell us anything not already told by these anterior quantities. It may well be crucial to move on to explain why they, in turn, are what they are but the merely derivative value magnitudes cannot possibly assist us in that task. Contemporary economists can learn much from the classical economists—both questions and answers—but they should consign Marx's labour-value magnitudes to the past (p. 221).

The present chapter (i) detects and identifies those restrictive conditions under which positive "surplus labour" is both necessary and sufficient for positive profits; (ii) argues, thus, that Marx's theory of profit cannot be sustained; and (iii) shows an alternative approach, based on a re-formulation of the concepts of "exploitation" and "abstract social labour", which concludes that surplus labour is determined by and is equal to actual profits. Section 6.2 examines Marx's theory of profit. Section 6.3 develops the alternative approach. Finally, Sect. 6.4 concludes.

## 6.2  On Marx's Theory of Profit

Consider a closed, linear economy involving only single products, circulating capital, "basic" commodities, and homogeneous labour (see Chap. 2). We assume that:

(i). The technical coefficients of production are fixed.
(ii). The economy is viable, i.e. the Perron–Frobenius (P–F) eigenvalue, $\lambda_{A1}$, of the irreducible $n \times n$ matrix of direct technical coefficients, $\mathbf{A}$ ( $\geq \mathbf{0}$), is less than 1.
(iii). The price of a commodity obtained as an output at the end of the production period is the same as the price of that commodity used as an input at the beginning of that period (stationary prices).

---

[1]In *Tractatus Logico-Philosophicus* (1922), Ludwig Wittgenstein states: "The simple signs employed in propositions are called names. [(3.202)]. A name means an object. The object is its meaning [...]. [(3.203)]. [...]. In a proposition a name is the representative of an object. [(3.22)]". In *Philosophical Investigations*, he states: "For a *large* class of cases—though not for all—in which we employ the word "meaning" it can be defined thus: the meaning of a word is its use in the language. And the *meaning* of a name is sometimes explained by pointing to its *bearer*." (§43), while in the *Preface* (1945) of that book, we read: "I am indebted to that which a teacher of this university, Mr. P. Sraffa, for many years unceasingly practised on my thoughts. I am indebted to *this* stimulus for the most consequential ideas of this book."

(iv). The net product is distributed to profits and wages that are paid at the beginning of the common production period, and there are no savings out of this income.

(v). Labour is not an input to the household sector.[2]

On the basis of these assumptions, the price side of the economy can be described by

$$\mathbf{p}^T = w\mathbf{l}^T + \mathbf{p}^T\mathbf{A} + \boldsymbol{\pi}^T$$

or

$$\mathbf{p}^T = \mathbf{p}^T\left[\mathbf{d}\mathbf{l}^T + \mathbf{A}\right] + \boldsymbol{\pi}^T = \mathbf{p}^T\mathbf{C}[\mathbf{I} + \widehat{\mathbf{r}}] \tag{6.1}$$

where $\mathbf{p}^T (> \mathbf{0}^T)$ denotes a $1 \times n$ vector of market prices, $w = \mathbf{p}^T\mathbf{d}$ the money wage rate, $\mathbf{d} (\geq \mathbf{0})$ the $n \times 1$ commodity vector representing the real wage rate, $\mathbf{l}^T (> \mathbf{0}^T)$ the $1 \times n$ vector of direct labour coefficients, $\boldsymbol{\pi}^T \equiv [\pi_j]$ the vector of profits per unit activity level, $\mathbf{C} \equiv [c_{ij}] \equiv \mathbf{d}\mathbf{l}^T + \mathbf{A}$ the "augmented" matrix of direct socio-technical coefficients, $\mathbf{I}$ the $n \times n$ identity matrix, and $\widehat{\mathbf{r}}$ the $n \times n$ diagonal matrix of the sectoral profit rates.

The quantity side of the economy can be described by

$$\mathbf{u} \equiv \mathbf{y} - \mathbf{d}L = [\mathbf{I} - \mathbf{C}]\mathbf{x} = \mathbf{C}\widehat{\mathbf{g}}\mathbf{x} + \mathbf{c}_p \tag{6.2}$$

where $\mathbf{u}$ denotes the surplus product, $\mathbf{y} \equiv [\mathbf{I} - \mathbf{A}]\mathbf{x}$ the net output vector, $\mathbf{x} (> \mathbf{0})$ the vector of activity levels (or intensity vector), $L \equiv \mathbf{l}^T\mathbf{x}$ the volume of total employment, $\widehat{\mathbf{g}}$ the diagonal matrix of the sectoral growth rates, $\mathbf{C}\widehat{\mathbf{g}}\mathbf{x}$ the net investment vector, and $\mathbf{c}_p$ the vector of consumption out of profits.

Equations (6.1) and (6.2) imply that

$$[\mathbf{I} - \mathbf{C}]\mathbf{x}^j = \mathbf{C}\widehat{\mathbf{g}}\mathbf{x}^j + \mathbf{c}_p^j + \mathbf{E}^j \tag{6.3}$$

and

$$\pi_j\mathbf{x}^j = \mathbf{p}^T\mathbf{C}\widehat{\mathbf{g}}\mathbf{x}^j + \mathbf{p}^T\mathbf{c}_p^j + \mathbf{p}^T\mathbf{E}^j \tag{6.4}$$

where $\mathbf{I}\mathbf{x}^j (= \mathbf{x}^j)$, $\mathbf{c}_p^j$, $\mathbf{E}^j$ denote the gross output vector, vector of consumption out of profits and net "export" vector, respectively, of the $j$ th process. When $\mathbf{p}^T\mathbf{E}^j > (<) 0$, the $j$ th process lends (borrows).

If $\mathbf{v}^T \equiv \mathbf{l}^T[\mathbf{I} - \mathbf{A}]^{-1} (> \mathbf{0})$ denotes the so-called vector of "labour values", $\widetilde{\mathbf{x}}$ denotes the so-called "necessary intensity vector", i.e. the vector satisfying the equation

---

[2]What follows draws on Mariolis (1999, 2006, 2016, 2018).

$$\widetilde{\mathbf{x}} = \mathbf{A}\widetilde{\mathbf{x}} + L\mathbf{d}$$

or

$$\widetilde{\mathbf{x}} = L[\mathbf{I} - \mathbf{A}]^{-1}\mathbf{d}$$

for a given vector of activity levels, $\mathbf{x}$, and

$$\mathbf{l}^T\widetilde{\mathbf{x}} = L\mathbf{v}^T\mathbf{d}$$

denotes the corresponding "necessary labour", then

$$S \equiv L - \mathbf{l}^T\widetilde{\mathbf{x}} = L(1 - \mathbf{v}^T\mathbf{d}) \tag{6.5}$$

$$S_u \equiv L - L\mathbf{v}^T\mathbf{d} = L(1 - \mathbf{v}^T\mathbf{d})$$

$$S_v \equiv \mathbf{v}^T\mathbf{u} = L(1 - \mathbf{v}^T\mathbf{d})$$

$$e_S \equiv S(\mathbf{l}^T\widetilde{\mathbf{x}})^{-1} = (\mathbf{v}^T\mathbf{d})^{-1} - 1 \tag{6.6}$$

denote Marx's total "surplus labour", "unpaid labour", "surplus value", and "rate of surplus labour (or rate of exploitation)", respectively (see Marx 1982, Chaps. 9 and 18; Fujimori 1982, pp. 4–13). Consequently, $S_v = S_u = S$.

Finally, from Eq. (6.1) we obtain

$$\mathbf{p}^T = \mathbf{p}^T\mathbf{d}\mathbf{v}^T + \boldsymbol{\pi}^T[\mathbf{I} - \mathbf{A}]^{-1}$$

or, post-multiplying by $\mathbf{d}L$, and rearranging terms,

$$L(1 - \mathbf{v}^T\mathbf{d})\mathbf{p}^T\mathbf{d} = \boldsymbol{\pi}^T[\mathbf{I} - \mathbf{A}]^{-1}\mathbf{d}L$$

or, recalling Eq. (6.5),

$$(SL^{-1})\mathbf{p}^T\mathbf{d} = \boldsymbol{\pi}^T[\mathbf{I} - \mathbf{A}]^{-1}\mathbf{d} \tag{6.7}$$

which provides an explicit relationship between $\boldsymbol{\pi}^T$ and $S$.

### 6.2.1 The Basic Counter-Argument

From Eqs. (6.1), (6.3), (6.4), and (6.7), and the P–F theorems for semi-positive matrices, it follows that:

(i). Positive "surplus labour" is a necessary, but not a sufficient, condition for the existence of positive profits in every process, i.e.

$$S > (\leq)0 \Leftrightarrow \left\{ \exists(\not\exists)\, \mathbf{p}^T : \boldsymbol{\pi}^T > (\geq)\, \mathbf{0}^T \right\} \tag{6.8}$$

This is the so-called "fundamental Marxian theorem" (Dmitriev 1898, p. 62; Okishio 1955, pp. 75–78; Morishima and Seton 1961, pp. 207–209).

(ii). $S = 0$ does not necessarily imply that $\boldsymbol{\pi}^T = \mathbf{0}^T$ (that $\mathbf{u} = \mathbf{0}$) unless $\mathbf{p}^T$ (unless $\mathbf{x}$) is the P–F eigenvector of $\mathbf{C}$. Moreover, the co-existence of positive (non-positive) "surplus labour" and non-positive (positive) total profits, $\boldsymbol{\pi}^T\mathbf{x} = \mathbf{p}^T\mathbf{u}$, cannot be ruled out. In this case, however, $\mathbf{u}$, $\boldsymbol{\pi}^T$, and $\widehat{\mathbf{g}}$ contain negative elements, while a non-profitable process does not necessarily reproduce on a diminishing scale:

$$\left\{ \pi_j \leq 0,\, \mathbf{C}\widehat{\mathbf{g}}\mathbf{x}^j \geq \mathbf{0} \right\} \Rightarrow \mathbf{p}^T\mathbf{E}^j < 0$$

(iii). If $\boldsymbol{\pi}^T$ is proportional to $\mathbf{l}^T$, i.e. $\boldsymbol{\pi}^T = \alpha\mathbf{l}^T$, then $\mathbf{p}^T$ is proportional to $\mathbf{v}^T$, i.e.

$$\mathbf{p}^T = (w + \alpha)\mathbf{v}^T$$

or, in words, commodities are exchanged "as products of labour" (Marx); therefore,

$$(w + \alpha)\left(1 - \mathbf{v}^T\mathbf{d}\right)\mathbf{l}^T = \boldsymbol{\pi}^T$$

or

$$(w + \alpha)\left(SL^{-1}\right)\mathbf{l}^T = \boldsymbol{\pi}^T$$

Hence, in this—non-capitalist—case, $S > 0$ is both necessary and sufficient for $\boldsymbol{\pi}^T > \mathbf{0}^T$ (Marx 1982, Chap. 7).

Now consider the vertically integrated industry producing the total real wages (WI) or "integrated wage-goods sector" (Garegnani 1984, p. 313; also see Sect. 2.3.1 of the present book), and let $\mathbf{x}_W$, $\mathbf{y}_W$, $\mathbf{u}_W$ be the intensity vector, net output vector, and surplus product, respectively, of the WI. It then follows that:

(i). $\mathbf{y}_W = L\mathbf{d}$ and, therefore, $\mathbf{x}_W$ equals the "necessary intensity vector", $\widetilde{\mathbf{x}}$ ($=L[\mathbf{I} - \mathbf{A}]^{-1}\mathbf{d}$), and

$$\mathbf{u}_W = L\left(1 - \mathbf{v}^T\mathbf{d}\right)\mathbf{d} = S\mathbf{d}$$

Hence, the WI is a quasi-one-commodity economy, in the sense that $\mathbf{u}_W$ is proportional to $\mathbf{y}_W$, i.e.

$$\mathbf{u}_W = \left(SL^{-1}\right)\mathbf{y}_W \tag{6.9}$$

Equation (6.9) implies, in turn, that

$$\mathbf{v}^T\mathbf{u}_W = \left[\left(\mathbf{l}^T\mathbf{x}_W\right)\left(\mathbf{p}^T\mathbf{y}_W\right)^{-1}\right]\mathbf{p}^T\mathbf{u}_W$$

which corresponds to Marx's (1991, Chap. 9) "double equality" (i.e. "total price equals total labour value" and "total profits equal total surplus value").

(ii). The average profit rate, $r_W$, in the WI is given by

$$r_W \equiv \left(\mathbf{p}^T\mathbf{u}_W\right)\left(\mathbf{p}^T\mathbf{C}\mathbf{x}_W\right)^{-1}$$

or, invoking Eq. (6.6),

$$r_W = e_S(c_W + 1)^{-1} \tag{6.10}$$

where

$$c_W \equiv \left(\mathbf{p}^T\mathbf{H}\mathbf{y}_W\right)\left(w\mathbf{v}^T\mathbf{y}_W\right)^{-1}, \quad \mathbf{H} \equiv \mathbf{A}[\mathbf{I} - \mathbf{A}]^{-1}$$

denote the "price composition of capital" in the WI and the vertically integrated technical coefficients matrix, respectively. Hence, from Eqs. (6.9) and (6.10) we obtain that

$$S > 0 \iff \{\mathbf{u}_W \geq \mathbf{0}, \; 0 < r_W < e_S\}$$

If a uniform profit rate, $r$, is assumed, then Eq. (6.1) becomes

$$\mathbf{p}^T = (1 + r)\mathbf{p}^T\mathbf{C} \tag{6.11}$$

where $\mathbf{p}^T$ now denotes a vector of production prices. Basically, there are two mathematically equivalent, but economically different, fixed-point determinations of $[r, \mathbf{p}^T]$:

(i). Since a non-positive price vector is economically irrelevant, it follows that

$$(1+r)^{-1} = \lambda_{C1} \tag{6.12}$$

and $\mathbf{p}^T$ is the P–F eigenvector of $\mathbf{C}$, i.e. the unique positive fixed point of the linear transformation defined by Eq. (6.11). Therefore, Eqs. (6.11) and (6.12) determine a unique, positive solution for $[r, \mathbf{p}^T]$, provided only that $\lambda_{C1} < 1$, and, hence, the sign of profits is independent of the economy's gross output composition. This is a fixed-point determination, on the basis of the "augmented" matrix of direct socio-technical coefficients and the relevant P–F theorems, which makes no reference to any "labour values".

(ii). Equation (6.11) can be rewritten as

$$\mathbf{p}^T = (1+r)w\mathbf{v}^T + r\mathbf{p}^T\mathbf{H}$$

or, iff $r < R \equiv \lambda_{H1}^{-1} = \lambda_{A1}^{-1} - 1$,

$$\mathbf{p}^T = (1+r)w\mathbf{v}^T[\mathbf{I} - r\mathbf{H}]^{-1} \tag{6.13}$$

where

$$[\mathbf{I} - r\mathbf{H}]^{-1} = \mathbf{I} + r\mathbf{H} + r^2\mathbf{H}^2 + \ldots > \mathbf{0}$$

From Eq. (6.10) we obtain that

$$r_W = \left(1 - \mathbf{v}^T\mathbf{d}\right)\left(\mathbf{p}^T\mathbf{d}\right)\left(\mathbf{p}^T\mathbf{H}\mathbf{d} + w\mathbf{v}^T\mathbf{d}\right)^{-1}$$

or, recalling $w = \mathbf{p}^T\mathbf{d}$,

$$r_W = \left(1 - \mathbf{v}^T\mathbf{d}\right)\left(w^{-1}\mathbf{p}^T\mathbf{H}\mathbf{d} + \mathbf{v}^T\mathbf{d}\right)^{-1} \tag{6.14}$$

Substituting Eq. (6.13) into the right-hand side of Eq. (6.14), setting $r = r_W$ and rearranging terms, yields

$$1 - (1+r)\mathbf{v}^T\mathbf{d} = r(1+r)\mathbf{v}^T[\mathbf{I} - r\mathbf{H}]^{-1}\mathbf{H}\mathbf{d}$$

or

$$1 - \mathbf{v}^T\mathbf{d} = r\left[(1+r)\mathbf{v}^T[\mathbf{I} - r\mathbf{H}]^{-1}\mathbf{H}\mathbf{d} + \mathbf{v}^T\mathbf{d}\right] \tag{6.15}$$

where the right-hand side of Eq. (6.15) is a strictly increasing and convex function of $r$, which tends to plus infinity as $r$ approaches $\lambda_{H1}^{-1}$ from below. Hence, Eq. (6.15)

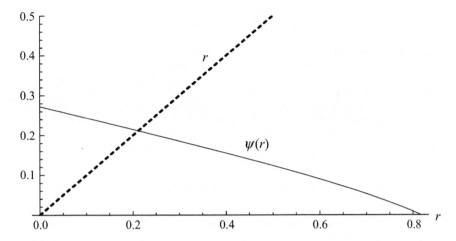

**Fig. 6.1** The fixed-point determination of the uniform profit rate on the basis of the vertically integrated industry producing the total real wages: Greek economy, year 1988; $r \cong 0.212 < e_S \cong 0.573$, $\lambda_{\mathbf{H}1}^{-1} \cong 0.818$

determines a unique, positive, finite value for the profit rate, provided only that $\mathbf{v}^{\mathrm{T}}\mathbf{d} < 1$ or, equivalently, $S > 0$, and this value is the fixed point of the function

$$\psi(r) \equiv (1 - \mathbf{v}^{\mathrm{T}}\mathbf{d})\left[(1 + r)\mathbf{v}^{\mathrm{T}}[\mathbf{I} - r\mathbf{H}]^{-1}\mathbf{H}\mathbf{d} + \mathbf{v}^{\mathrm{T}}\mathbf{d}\right]^{-1}, \quad r < \lambda_{\mathbf{H}1}^{-1}$$

i.e. $r = \psi(r)$ (for instance, see Fig. 6.1, which is based on data from the Greek economy and for the year 1988; see Sect. 3.3.2). Thus, it can be stated that[3]

$$\left[r, \mathbf{p}^{\mathrm{T}}\right] > \mathbf{0}^{\mathrm{T}} \Leftrightarrow S > 0$$

It has been shown, therefore, that, if prices are not proportional to the production prices, then positive "surplus labour" is neither necessary nor sufficient for positive total profits; positive "surplus labour" is necessary and sufficient for positive profits in the WI. Nevertheless, if prices are proportional to the production prices, then the sectoral profit rates equal the profit rate in the WI; hence, positive "surplus labour" appears as a necessary and sufficient condition for the existence of positive prices yielding a positive profit rate.

Finally, it could be added that, according to Marx,

[c]apital itself is the moving contradiction, [in] that it presses to reduce labour time to a minimum, while it posits labour time, on the other side, as sole measure and source of

---

[3]Dmitriev (1898) remarks, "Hardly anyone will dispute (although discussion of this question is not within the competence of political economy [footnote 1 of the original text]) that the *only* process determining the level of profit at the *present time* is the process of production of the means of subsistence of the workers (*capitale alimento*)." (p. 73).

wealth. Hence it diminishes labour time in the necessary form so as to increase it in the superfluous form; hence posits the superfluous in growing measure as a condition—question of life or death—for the necessary (Marx 1993, p. 706). Nevertheless there are limits, which cannot be overcome, to the compensation for a decrease in the number of workers employed, i.e. a decrease in the amount of variable capital advanced, provided by a rise in the rate of surplus-value, i.e. the lengthening of the working day. [...] This self-evident [...] law is of importance for the explanation of many phenomena, arising from the tendency of capital to reduce as much as possible the number of workers employed, i.e. the amount of its variable component, the part which is changed into labour-power (we shall develop this tendency later on [Chap. 25, Sects. 1 and 3]), which stands in contradiction with its other tendency to produce the greatest possible mass of surplus-value (Marx 1982, pp. 419–420). [...] [T]here is an immanent contradiction in the application of machinery to the production of surplus-value, since, of the two factors of the surplus-value created by a given amount of capital, one, the rate of surplus-value, cannot be increased except by diminishing the other, the number of workers (Marx 1982, p. 531).

In the one-commodity case, total "surplus labour" per unit of gross output is given by (see Eq. (6.5))

$$Sx^{-1} = l(1 - vd)$$

or, since $v = l(1 - A)^{-1}$,

$$Sx^{-1} = l - l^2(1 - A)^{-1}d$$

If $A$ and $d$ are considered as exogenously given, then Cournot's (1838, pp. 52–62) "law of maximization" implies that $Sx^{-1}$ is maximized at

$$\bar{l} \equiv (2d)^{-1}(1 - A)$$

or, equivalently,

$$\bar{v} \equiv (2d)^{-1}$$

which implies, in turn, that

$$e_S = 1, \quad Sx^{-1} = (1 - A)(4d)^{-1}$$

(for instance, see Fig. 6.2). Nevertheless, if $l$ decreases continuously (which would be compatible with the criterion of cost-minimization) and tends to zero, then both $e_S$ and the "composition of capital" increase without limit, and $r$ increases continuously.[4] And in a viable, fully automated economy, $\{A < 1, l = 0\}$, the profit rate is positive and equal to its maximum feasible value, i.e. $r = R \equiv A^{-1} - 1$ or, in the

---

[4]As is well known, changes in the technical production conditions are directly related to "Marx's law of the tendency of the profit rate to fall". We will return to this issue in Chap. 11.

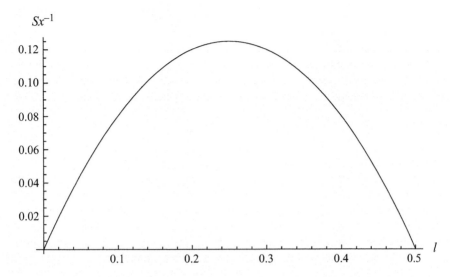

**Fig. 6.2** The total "surplus labour" per unit of gross output as a function of the direct labour coefficient: $A = 0.5$, $d = 1$ and, therefore, $\bar{l} = 0.25$

multi-commodity case, $r = R \equiv \lambda_{A1}^{-1} - 1$, although there is no "surplus labour" (Dmitriev 1898, pp. 62–64). All these suggest that there are additional problems of internal inconsistency in Marx's overall argument about the technical production conditions—"surplus labour"—profit relationships.

### 6.2.2 Some Extensions

Now we extend the analysis to the cases of (i) reducibility; (ii) heterogeneous labour; and (iii) pure joint production. It is thus shown that the conversion of $S > 0$ into a necessary and sufficient condition for $[r, \mathbf{p}^T] > \mathbf{0}^T$ is not always possible.

#### 6.2.2.1 Reducibility

Assume that (i) there are $n + 1$ commodities; (ii) Eq. (6.11) is associated with the first $n$ commodities; (iii) the $n + 1$st commodity is a "self-reproducing non-basic" (in the sense of Sraffa 1960, Appendix B); and (iv) "surplus labour" is positive or, equivalently, $\lambda_{C1} < 1$. Then the $n + 1$st price is determined by

$$p_{n+1} = (1 + r)(\mathbf{p}^T \boldsymbol{\varphi} + p_{n+1}\phi) \qquad (6.16)$$

where $\boldsymbol{\varphi}$ denotes a column vector, and $\phi < 1$.

Now the two fixed-point determinations of $[r, \mathbf{p}^T]$ are not always equivalent to each other, while the latter (i.e. on the basis of the WI) is economically irrelevant: from Eqs. (6.11) and (6.16) it follows that the profit rate is determined by

$$(1 + r)^{-1} = \max\{\lambda_{C1}, \phi\}$$

and, therefore, there is a unique, positive solution for $[r, \mathbf{p}^T]$ iff $\phi < \lambda_{C1}$.[5]

It then follows that $S > 0$ is necessary, but not sufficient, for $r > 0$. With differential profit rates, $S = 0$ is compatible with a semi-positive vector of profits (compare with relations (6.8)), i.e. with zero (with positive) profit in every process of the WI (in the non-basic process). This results from the fact that there is no connection between "surplus labour" and the profits in those processes which play no role (direct or indirect) in the production of the wage bundle.

### 6.2.2.2  Heterogeneous Labour

Assume that there are $m$ types of labour. Let $\mathbf{D}$ be the $n \times m$ matrix of the real wage rates, and let $\mathbf{L}$ be the $m \times 1$ vector of the volume of employments. If the augmented matrix of direct socio-technical coefficients is irreducible, then we can safely write

$$r = r_W = (\mathbf{p}^T\mathbf{DS})(\mathbf{p}^T[\mathbf{H} + \mathbf{DV}]\mathbf{DL})^{-1}, \quad \mathbf{p}^T > \mathbf{0}^T$$

where $\mathbf{V}$ denotes the $m \times n$ matrix of "labour values", and $\mathbf{S}$ the $m \times 1$ vector of "surplus labours", while $\mathbf{DS}$ equals the surplus product of the WI.

In this case the WI ceases to be a quasi-one-commodity economy. Hence, $\mathbf{S} \geq \mathbf{0}$ is sufficient, but not necessary, for $\mathbf{DS} \geq \mathbf{0}$ and, therefore, $\mathbf{S} \geq \mathbf{0}$ does not become a necessary condition for $r > 0$.[6]

---

[5]If $\phi \geq \lambda_{C1}$, then $\mathbf{p}^T = \mathbf{0}^T$ and $p_{n+1} > 0$ (also see Sect. 2.3.2). Okishio (1961) handles the issue as follows: "it is wrong to say that production techniques in non-basic industries have no relation to the general [uniform] rate of profit at all. [...] [W]hile production techniques in non-basic industries have no influence upon the general level of profit, they are concerned whether the general level of profit itself exists or not" (pp. 93–94).

[6]Also consider the $2 \times 2$ numerical examples provided by Morishima (1978, pp. 306–307), where $\mathbf{u}$ and $\mathbf{S}$ contain a negative element, while $\mathbf{DS}$ equals zero or is positive, and by Krause (1981, p. 65), where $\mathbf{u}$, $\mathbf{S}$, and $\mathbf{DS}$ contain a negative element, while $r > 0$.

### 6.2.2.3  Pure Joint Production

Consider an economy producing $n$ commodities by $n$ linear processes of joint production, i.e. a "square", profitable and productive system of joint production defined by the triplet $\{\mathbf{B}, \mathbf{A}, \mathbf{l}^T\}$, where $\mathbf{B}$ denotes the $n \times n$ output matrix (see Chaps. 4 and 5). Moreover, in order to be in a position to compare this system directly with irreducible single-product systems, assume that we can safely write

$$r = r_W = S\left(\mathbf{p}^T\mathbf{d}\right)\left(\mathbf{p}^T\left[\mathbf{H} + \mathbf{d}\mathbf{v}^T\right]L\mathbf{d}\right)^{-1}, \quad \mathbf{p}^T > \mathbf{0}^T \tag{6.17}$$

where $\mathbf{H}$ now equals $\mathbf{A}[\mathbf{B} - \mathbf{A}]^{-1}$, $\mathbf{v}^T$ now equals $\mathbf{l}^T[\mathbf{B} - \mathbf{A}]^{-1}$ and denotes the vector of "additive labour values" (see Sect. 4.2.1), and $S$ now denotes the total "surplus labour" ("unpaid labour, surplus value") in terms of the "additive labour values", while $S\mathbf{d}$ equals the surplus product of the WI.

It goes without saying that $S > 0$ is necessary and sufficient for the (semi-) positivity of $S\mathbf{d}$. However, it is neither necessary nor sufficient for the positivity of the denominator in Eq. (6.17) and, thus, $S > (<) 0$ is compatible with negative (with positive) profits. By contrast, if the WI can produce the exact amount of commodities received as wages, i.e. if $\mathbf{x}_W \geq \mathbf{0}$, then positive "surplus labour" appears as a necessary and sufficient condition for $r > 0$ (regardless of whether or not $\mathbf{v}^T$ contains non-positive elements).[7]

Now we turn to a "rectangular" economy in which $m$ processes operate (Fujimori 1982, Chap. 3). The intensity vector of the WI can be defined by

$$[\mathbf{B} - \mathbf{A}]\mathbf{x}_W = L\mathbf{d} \tag{6.18}$$

where $\mathbf{x}_W$ is now an $m \times 1$ vector. If Eq. (6.18) is consistent, then the general solution is

$$\mathbf{x}_W = L\mathbf{K}^-\mathbf{d} + [\mathbf{I}_m - \mathbf{K}^-\mathbf{K}]\boldsymbol{\chi}$$

where $\mathbf{K} \equiv \mathbf{B} - \mathbf{A}$, $\mathbf{K}^-$ is a (1)-inverse of $\mathbf{K}$, i.e. $\mathbf{K}\mathbf{K}^-\mathbf{K} = \mathbf{K}$, $\mathbf{I}_m$ is the $m \times m$ identity matrix, and $\boldsymbol{\chi}$ is an arbitrary $m$−vector (see, e.g. Barnett 1990, pp. 260–273). In that case, the WI is a quasi-one-commodity economy, i.e.

---

[7]The (in)famous $2 \times 2$ numerical examples provided by Steedman (1975, pp. 115–117) imply that the denominator in Eq. (6.17) is negative and $\{S < 0, r > 0\}$ or $\{S > 0, r < 0\}$. The former case also occurs in the attractive $3 \times 3$ numerical example provided by Hosoda (1993, pp. 37–39). Finally, in Steedman's (1975, pp. 117–118) examples there is a case in which the said denominator equals zero and $\{S = 0, \mathbf{p}^T > \mathbf{0}^T, r > 0\}$; consequently, $r_W$ is an indeterminate (in terms of production prices) and, therefore, Eq. (6.17) do not hold.

$$\mathbf{u}_W = \left(L - \mathbf{l}^T\mathbf{x}_W\right)\mathbf{d} = S\mathbf{d}$$

Consequently, if there is a semi-positive solution for $\mathbf{x}_W$, then positive "surplus *labour*" is a necessary and sufficient condition for $\mathbf{u}_W \geq \mathbf{0}$ and, therefore, for $r\,(=r_W) > 0$. However, if there is a non-positive solution for $\mathbf{x}_W$, profit and "surplus labour" can be of opposite sign. If Eq. (6.18) is inconsistent, then we can write

$$L\mathbf{h} = \mathbf{K}\mathbf{x}_W - L\mathbf{d} \qquad\qquad (6.19)$$

where $\mathbf{h}$ denotes the "residual". In that case, the WI is not a quasi-one-commodity economy, i.e.

$$\mathbf{u}_W = S\mathbf{d} + L\mathbf{h}$$

and therefore $r$ and $S$ can be of opposite sign.[8] Finally, suppose that "labour values" are given by (Fujimori 1982, p. 48)

$$\mathbf{v}^T\mathbf{K} = \mathbf{l}^T \qquad\qquad (6.20)$$

which is dual to Eq. (6.18). If Eq. (6.20) is consistent, then $\mathbf{v}^T$ is a vector of "additive labour values". In that case, "surplus value", $S_v$, equals "unpaid labour", $S_u$, while Eq. (6.19) implies that "surplus value" is given by

$$S_v\,(= S_u) = L - L\mathbf{l}^T\mathbf{K}^-\mathbf{d} = S + L\mathbf{v}^T\mathbf{h}$$

from which it follows that, if Eq. (6.18) is consistent (i.e. $\mathbf{h} = \mathbf{0}$), then $S_u$ necessarily equals $S$. Hence, it can be stated that the traditional relationship between profits and "exploitation" cannot be established unless: (i) the net output of the WI contains only the total real wages; and (ii) the "labour value" system is consistent. The fact that the former condition is necessary and sufficient (is necessary) for the validity of the said relationship in terms of "surplus labour" (in terms of "unpaid labour, surplus value") indicates that Marx's theory of profit is implicitly based on the concept of the WI.[9]

---

[8]There is a difference between the case where Eq. (6.18) has a non-positive solution and the case where Eq. (6.18) is inconsistent. In the latter case, $S = 0$ can be compatible with $r\,(= r_W) \neq 0$.

[9]It could be shown (Mariolis 2006, pp. 7–8) that our (counter-)arguments also apply to an alternative approach to Marx's theory of profit proposed by Morishima (1974), and Morishima and Catephores (1978, Chap. 2). It is also noted that, within that alternative approach, "labour values" are (i) non-additive; (ii) not necessarily related to the processes actually used in the economy considered; and (iii) axiomatically defined as non-negative (see Steedman 1976, 1977, Chap. 13).

## 6.3 Time Dilations and Abstract Social-International Labour

Consider, for instance, the following single-product, viable and "cyclic", two-commodity economy:[10]

$$\mathbf{A} = \begin{bmatrix} 0 & a_{12} \\ a_{21} & 0 \end{bmatrix}, \quad a_{12}a_{21} < 1, \quad \mathbf{l}^{\mathrm{T}} = [l_1, l_2], \quad \mathbf{d} = [d_1, d_2]^{\mathrm{T}}$$

Let $\omega_i^i$, $\omega_j^i$ be the quantities of labour actually expended (directly and indirectly) in industry $i$ to produce one unit of commodity $i$ and to obtain, through market exchange, one unit of commodity $j$ $(i \neq j)$, respectively. Then we can write

$$\omega_i^i = \omega_j^i a_{ji} + l_i$$

and

$$\omega_j^i = p_j p_i^{-1} \omega_i^i$$

which imply that

$$\omega_i^i = l_i \left(1 - p_j p_i^{-1} a_{ji}\right)^{-1}$$

that is,

$$\omega_1^1 = p l_1 (p - a_{21})^{-1}, \quad \omega_2^1 = l_1 (p - a_{21})^{-1} \tag{6.21}$$

$$\omega_2^2 = l_2 (1 - p a_{12})^{-1}, \quad \omega_1^2 = p l_2 (1 - p a_{12})^{-1} \tag{6.22}$$

where $p \equiv p_1 p_2^{-1}$, $a_{21} < p < a_{12}^{-1}$, denotes the relative market price of the two commodities. For instance, assume that

$$a_{12} = 0.5, \quad a_{21} = 1, \quad l_1 = l_2 = 1, \quad d_1 = d_2 = 0.1$$

$$g_1 = s_{p1} r_1, \quad g_2 = s_{p2} r_2, \quad g_1 = g_2$$

where $s_{pj}$ denotes the savings ratio out of profits in industry $j$. It is obtained that

---

[10]What follows also applies to open economies (consider Steedman 2008; compare with Okishio and Nakatani 1985).

$$v_1 = 4, \quad v_2 = 3, \quad v \equiv v_1 v_2^{-1} \cong 1.333, \quad r = r_1 = r_2 \cong 0.096 \Leftrightarrow p \cong 1.354$$

$$[r_1, r_2] > \mathbf{0}^{\mathrm{T}} \Leftrightarrow c_{21}(1 - c_{11})^{-1} \cong 1.222 < p < (1 - c_{22})c_{12}^{-1} = 1.5$$

$$p = c_{21}(1 - c_{11})^{-1} \Leftrightarrow \left\{ r_1 = 0, r_2 = \left[ c_{22} + c_{21}c_{12}(1 - c_{11})^{-1} \right]^{-1} - 1 = 0.2 \right\}$$

$$p = (1 - c_{22})c_{12}^{-1} \Leftrightarrow \left\{ r_1 = \left[ c_{11} + c_{12}c_{21}(1 - c_{22})^{-1} \right]^{-1} - 1 = 0.2, r_2 = 0 \right\}$$

and[11]

$$p = \left[ 57(1 - s) + 5\sqrt{3}f(s) \right] \left[ 12(9 + s) \right]^{-1} \tag{6.23}$$

where

$$f(s) \equiv \sqrt{75 + 202s + 75s^2}, \quad s \equiv s_{p2}s_{p1}^{-1} = r_1 r_2^{-1}$$

Figures 6.3 and 6.4 display $\omega_i^i$, $\omega_j^i$ (see Eqs. (6.21) and (6.22)) and the profit rates (consider Eq. (6.1)), respectively, as functions of $p$, while Fig. 6.5 displays $p$ as a function of $s$ $(= r_1 r_2^{-1}$; see Eq. (6.23)).

From this analysis, we deduce that:

(i). Since $\mathbf{v}^{\mathrm{T}}\mathbf{y} = \mathbf{l}^{\mathrm{T}}\mathbf{x}$ and

$$\boldsymbol{\omega}^{1\mathrm{T}}\mathbf{y}^1 = \mathbf{l}^{\mathrm{T}}\mathbf{x}^1 = \mathbf{v}^{\mathrm{T}}\mathbf{y}^1, \quad \boldsymbol{\omega}^{1\mathrm{T}} \equiv [\omega_1^1, \omega_2^1], \quad \mathbf{y}^1 \equiv [\mathbf{I} - \mathbf{A}]\mathbf{x}^1$$

$$\boldsymbol{\omega}^{2\mathrm{T}}\mathbf{y}^2 = \mathbf{l}^{\mathrm{T}}\mathbf{x}^2 = \mathbf{v}^{\mathrm{T}}\mathbf{y}^2, \quad \boldsymbol{\omega}^{2\mathrm{T}} \equiv [\omega_1^2, \omega_2^2], \quad \mathbf{y}^2 \equiv [\mathbf{I} - \mathbf{A}]\mathbf{x}^2$$

it follows that

---

[11]Iff

$$c_{21}(1 - c_{11})^{-1} = (1 - c_{22})c_{12}^{-1},$$

then $r = 0$ (also see Sect. 7.2.1).

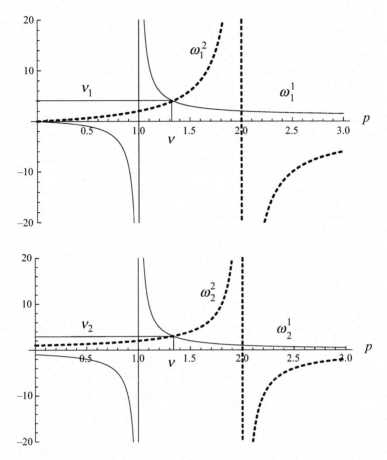

**Fig. 6.3** The quantities of labour actually expended in the two industries as functions of the relative commodity price, $p \equiv p_1 p_2^{-1}$

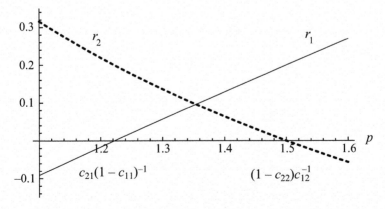

**Fig. 6.4** The profit rates as functions of the relative commodity price, $p \equiv p_1 p_2^{-1}$

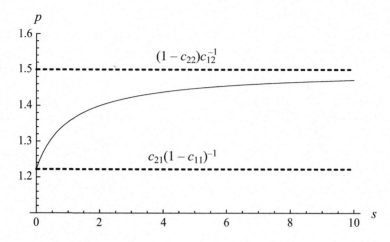

**Fig. 6.5** The relative commodity price, $p \equiv p_1 p_2^{-1}$, as a function of the relative savings ratio, $s \equiv s_{p2} s_{p1}^{-1}$

$$\boldsymbol{\omega}^{1T}\mathbf{y}^1 + \boldsymbol{\omega}^{2T}\mathbf{y}^2 = \mathbf{l}^T\mathbf{x}$$

and

$$\left[\boldsymbol{\omega}^{1T} - \mathbf{v}^T\right]\mathbf{y}^1 = 0$$
$$\left[\boldsymbol{\omega}^{2T} - \mathbf{v}^T\right]\mathbf{y}^2 = 0$$

Moreover, $\omega_i^i = \omega_i^j = v_i$ iff $p = v$. Hence, when $p \neq v$, the traditional definition of $\mathbf{v}^T$, as the vector of the quantities of labour "embodied" or "crystalized" in the different commodities, is vague.

(ii). Profits in industry 1 are positive iff

$$w l_1 < p_1 - p_2 a_{21} \tag{6.24}$$

or

$$w < (p_1 - p_2 a_{21}) l_1^{-1} = \mathbf{p}^T\mathbf{y}^1 \left(\mathbf{l}^T\mathbf{x}^1\right)^{-1} \tag{6.25}$$

or, equivalently,

$$\mathbf{l}^T\mathbf{x}^1 < w^{-1}\mathbf{p}^T\mathbf{y}^1 \tag{6.26}$$

The right-hand side of condition (6.25) equals the net labour productivity in this industry; the right-hand side of condition (6.26) can be conceived of as the working time necessary to buy the net output of this industry, while the left-hand side can be conceived of as the total working time. Hence, the difference

$$w^{-1}\mathbf{p}^T\mathbf{y}^j - \mathbf{1}^T\mathbf{x}^j$$

could be conceived of as a "time dilation" and, therefore, the "rate of exploitation" of workers in industry $j$ could be defined as

$$e^j \equiv \left(w^{-1}\mathbf{p}^T\mathbf{y}^j - \mathbf{1}^T\mathbf{x}^j\right)\left(\mathbf{1}^T\mathbf{x}^j\right)^{-1} \tag{6.27}$$

namely, as a percentage time dilation. Thus, the "rate of exploitation" of workers in the economy could be defined as

$$e \equiv \left(w^{-1}\mathbf{p}^T\mathbf{y} - \mathbf{1}^T\mathbf{x}\right)\left(\mathbf{1}^T\mathbf{x}\right)^{-1} \tag{6.28}$$

or

$$e = e^1\left(\mathbf{1}^T\mathbf{x}^1\right)\left(\mathbf{1}^T\mathbf{x}\right)^{-1} + e^2\left(\mathbf{1}^T\mathbf{x}^2\right)\left(\mathbf{1}^T\mathbf{x}\right)^{-1}$$

It then follows that total profits are positive iff

$$w < \mathbf{p}^T\mathbf{y}\left(\mathbf{1}^T\mathbf{x}\right)^{-1}$$

or, equivalently, iff $e > 0$, while $e^1 = e^2$ iff $p = v$ (in that case, $e = e_S$). Marx's "rate of exploitation" can be rewritten as

$$e_S = \left[(w^{-1}p_1 - v_1)v_1^{-1}\right](v_1 d_1)\left(\mathbf{v}^T\mathbf{d}\right)^{-1} + \left[(w^{-1}p_2 - v_2)v_2^{-1}\right](v_2 d_2)\left(\mathbf{v}^T\mathbf{d}\right)^{-1}$$

that is, as a convex combination of the percentage time dilations

$$\left(w^{-1}p_j - v_j\right)v_j^{-1}$$

However, these percentage time dilations involve $v_j$ and are, therefore, notional-hypothetical.

We borrow the term "time dilation" from Einstein's "special principle of relativity". In that context, "time dilation" is defined as "the "slowing down" of a clock as determined by an observer who is in relative motion with respect to that clock" (*Encyclopaedia Britannica*), while the percentage time dilation is given by

$$\left[1 - (v/c)^2\right]^{-1/2} - 1 = (1/2)(v/c)^2 + (3/8)(v/c)^4 + (5/16)(v/c)^6 + \dots$$

where $v$ denotes the relative velocity of the observers, $c$ the speed of light in a vacuum, which, according to "special relativity", "serves as the single limiting velocity in the universe, being an upper bound to the propagation speed of signals and to the speeds of all material particles" (*Encyclopaedia Britannica*), and, therefore, $v/c \leq 1$. For $v/c > 1$, this percentage time dilation becomes a complex number, i.e.

$$-i\left[(v/c)^2 - 1\right]^{-1/2} - 1, \quad i \equiv \sqrt{-1}$$

and this fact rather suggest the internal consistency of the "special principle of relativity". There is, therefore, an *analogical* correspondence between the "normalized relative velocity", $v/c$, and the "relative profit rate" (Sect. 2.3.1 and Chap. 3 of this book), $r/R$: for instance, when $v << c$, the solution of the classical physics equations tends to be quantitatively valid, and when $r << R$, the solution of the traditional "labour value theory" equations tends to be quantitatively valid. It need hardly be stressed, however, that

> one cannot exorcise internal inconsistency in an argument merely by asserting that certain magnitudes may be approximately equal! (Steedman 1991, p. 206)

And in the empirically relevant case of joint production, the elements of $w^{-1}\mathbf{p}^T$ (and, therefore, both $e$ and $e_S$) are not necessarily strictly increasing functions of the profit rate (see Sect. 4.2.1 and Chap. 5 of the present book).

(iii). Since $w = \mathbf{p}^T\mathbf{d}$, condition (6.24) can be rewritten as

$$(p_1 d_1 + p_2 d_2)l_1(p_1 - p_2 a_{21})^{-1} < 1$$

or, invoking Eq. (6.21),

$$\boldsymbol{\omega}^{1T}\mathbf{d} < 1 \qquad (6.29)$$

or, invoking Eq. (6.27),

$$(1 + e^1)\boldsymbol{\omega}^{1T}\mathbf{d} = 1, \quad e^1 > 0$$

The corresponding profitability condition for industry 2 is

$$\boldsymbol{\omega}^{2T}\mathbf{d} < 1 \qquad (6.30)$$

or

$$(1 + e^2)\boldsymbol{\omega}^{2T}\mathbf{d} = 1, \quad e^2 > 0$$

Conditions (6.29) and (6.30) looks like the Marx–Dmitriev profitability condition, according to which the unit "labour value of labour power" is less than the "new value" produced by one unit of "labour power" or, equivalently, it takes less than one unit of "labour power" to produce one unit of "labour power". However, conditions (6.29) and (6.30) involve a relative market price, $p$. Finally, the corresponding profitability condition for the economy is

$$\left(\boldsymbol{\omega}^{1\mathrm{T}}\mathbf{d}\right)\left(\mathbf{p}^{\mathrm{T}}\mathbf{y}^{1}\right)\left(\mathbf{p}^{\mathrm{T}}\mathbf{y}\right)^{-1} + \left(\boldsymbol{\omega}^{2\mathrm{T}}\mathbf{d}\right)\left(\mathbf{p}^{\mathrm{T}}\mathbf{y}^{2}\right)\left(\mathbf{p}^{\mathrm{T}}\mathbf{y}\right)^{-1} < 1$$

or

$$(1+e)\left[(\boldsymbol{\omega}^{1\mathrm{T}}\mathbf{d})(\mathbf{p}^{\mathrm{T}}\mathbf{y}^{1})(\mathbf{p}^{\mathrm{T}}\mathbf{y})^{-1} + (\boldsymbol{\omega}^{2\mathrm{T}}\mathbf{d})(\mathbf{p}^{\mathrm{T}}\mathbf{y}^{2})(\mathbf{p}^{\mathrm{T}}\mathbf{y})^{-1}\right] = 1, \quad e > 0$$

Thus, it can be concluded that it is $\boldsymbol{\omega}^{1\mathrm{T}}$ and $\boldsymbol{\omega}^{2\mathrm{T}}$ (and not $\mathbf{v}^{\mathrm{T}}$) that are relevant to the issue of profit.

Nevertheless, an alternative approach could take into consideration Marx's concept of "abstract social labour". Marx (1982) remarked that

[m]en do not [...] bring the products of their labour into relation with each other as values because they see these objects merely as the material integuments of homogeneous human labour. The reverse is true: by equating their different products to each other in exchange as values, they equate their different kinds of labour as human labour. They do this without being aware of it. Value, therefore, does not have its description branded on its forehead; it rather transforms every product of labour into a social hieroglyphic. Later on, men try to decipher the hieroglyphic, to get behind the secret of their own social product: for the characteristic which objects of utility have of being values is as much men's social product as is their language (pp. 166–167).

And some years later, in a book written in close contact with Marx, Engels (1977) concluded:

Therefore when I say that a commodity has a particular value, I say (1) that it is a socially useful product; (2) that it has been produced by a private individual for private account; (3) that, although a product of individual labour, it is nevertheless at the same time and as it were unconsciously and involuntarily, also a product of social labour and, be it noted, of a definite quantity of this labour, ascertained in a social way, through exchange; (4) I express this quantity not in labour itself, in so and so many labour-hours, but *in another commodity*. If therefore I say that this clock is worth as much as that piece of cloth and each of them is worth fifty shillings, I say that an equal quantity of social labour is contained in the clock, the cloth and the money. I therefore assert that the social labour-time represented in them has been socially measured and found to be equal. But not directly, absolutely, as labour-time is usually measured, in labour-hours or days, etc., but in a roundabout way, through the medium of exchange, relatively. That is why I cannot express this definite quantity of labour-time in labour-hours—how many of them remains unknown to me—but also only in a roundabout way, relatively, in another commodity, which represents an equal quantity of social labour-time. The clock is worth as much as the piece of cloth (pp. 372–373).

Hence, it could be stated that, through market exchange, the heterogeneous quantities of "concrete private labours" actually expended in the production of one unit of commodity $i$ are equated with the quantities of concrete private labours actually expended in the production of $p_i p_j^{-1}$ units of commodity $i$.[12] Thus, they are transmuted into equal quantities of a—logically—*new* kind of homogeneous labour, namely, of "abstract social labour" and, therefore, constitute, say, $\beta$ units of abstract social labour, where $\beta$ denotes an arbitrary positive number. If, therefore, abstract social labour is the "substance of value" (Marx) and, consequently, value is measured in units of abstract social labour, then the unit labour value of commodity $i$ is $\beta$, and the unit labour value of commodity $j$ is $(p_j p_i^{-1})\beta$, which imply, in turn, that labour values are proportional to actual prices. Nevertheless, the aforementioned arbitrary measurement of abstract social labour is useless and meaningless, since, in actual fact, exchange is mediated by money and, consequently, money constitutes the measure of labour value, while the unit of money constitutes the unit of measurement of abstract social labour.[13]

According to this re-formulation, therefore, (i) money is the necessary form of existence of concrete private-national labours, which have been transmuted into abstract social-international labour; (ii) the labour values of commodities (including "labour powers") are determined by their market prices and are equal to them; (iii) market prices reflect *all* the features of the established—national and international—society, and constitute, therefore, its one-dimensional (monetary) simulacrum (consider Chap. 4 of this book; for a nice, although verbal, formulation, see Bukharin 1921, Chap. 4, Sect. 4); and (iv) surplus labour (unpaid labour, surplus value) is determined by and is equal to profits. For instance, in the case of homogeneous labour, total surplus labour is positive iff the "new value" produced by one unit of "labour power", $\mathbf{p}^T \mathbf{y}(\mathbf{l}^T \mathbf{x})^{-1}$, is greater than the unit labour value of "labour power", $w$. And in the case of heterogeneous labour, the "rate of exploitation" of workers in the economy is given by (see Eq. (6.28))

$$e = \widetilde{w}^{-1}\mathbf{p}^T\mathbf{y}\left(\widetilde{w}^{-1}\mathbf{w}^T\mathbf{L}\right)^{-1} - 1$$

where $\mathbf{w}^T$ denotes the $1 \times m$ vector of money wage rates, $\widetilde{w} \equiv \mathbf{w}^T\boldsymbol{\gamma}$, $\boldsymbol{\gamma}$ an arbitrary (semi-)positive $m \times 1$ vector or "bundle" of labours, and $\widetilde{w}^{-1}\mathbf{w}^T\mathbf{L}$ the homogenized (by means of wages differentials) total employment. The value of $e$ is independent of the arbitrary choice of $\boldsymbol{\gamma}$, and total profits are positive iff $e > 0$.

---

[12]In the general case, these quantities cannot be uniquely determined.

[13]Consider, for instance, the "large–small country" equilibrium of the textbook "Ricardian" theory of foreign trade (see Sect. 4.2.2, Example 4.3, of the present book): the heterogeneous quantities of "concrete national labours" actually expended in the production of individual units of one and the same commodity are transmuted into "abstract international labour". Hence, in the general case, it is not only the various commodities that become commensurate, but also the individual units of any commodity.

## 6.4 Concluding Remarks

It has been shown that positive "surplus labour", as defined by Marx, is both necessary and sufficient for the existence of positive profits iff (i) the economy is irreducible; (ii) there is a vertically integrated industry that (a) can produce the exact amount of commodities received as wages; and (b) constitutes a quasi-one-commodity system; and (iii) prices equal the production prices. In that case, it could be said, using Marx's (1983) metaphorical observation on the "mystical differential calculus of Newton and Leibnitz", that positive profits appear

> like a fruit beside the mother who had previously borne her (*als Frucht neben ihrer Mutter, bevor diese geschwängert war*) (p. 87).

Given that these conditions are restrictive, it follows that either the "exploitation of workers" is not the "exclusive source of profit" or that "surplus labour" provides no adequate measure of the "exploitation of workers" in capitalist economies, where "labour takes the form of [money] capital" and, therefore, the products of concrete private-national labours "are exchanged as products of capitals" (Marx).

On the other hand, a Marx-after-Sraffa re-formulation of the concepts of "time dilation" and "abstract social-international labour", which are involved, explicitly or otherwise, in Marx's analysis, may lead to the proposal that the labour values of commodities are determined by their market prices and are equal to them; therefore, surplus labour is determined by and is equal to actual profits.

## References

Academy of Sciences of the USSR. (1957). *Political economy. Textbook issued by the Institute of Economics of the Academy of Sciences of the USSR.* London: Lawrence & Wishart. Retrieved November 30, 2019, from https://www.marxists.org/subject/economy/authors/pe/index.htm

Barnett, S. (1990). *Matrices. Methods and applications.* Oxford: Clarendon Press.

Bukharin, N. I. (1921). *Historical materialism. A system of sociology.* Retrieved November 30, 2019, from https://www.marxists.org/archive/bukharin/works/1921/histmat/index.htm

Cournot, A. (1838). *Recherches sur les principes mathématiques de la théorie des richesses.* Paris: L. Hachette.

Dmitriev, V. K. (1898). The theory of value of David Ricardo: an attempt at a rigorous analysis. In V. K. Dmitriev ([1904] 1974) (Ed.), *Economic essays on value, competition and utility.* Edited with an introduction by D. M. Nuti (pp. 37–95). London: Cambridge University Press.

Engels, F. (1977). Anti-Dühring. Herr Eugen Dühring's revolution in science. Progress Publishers, Moscow

Fujimori, Y. (1982). *Modern analysis of value theory.* Berlin: Springer.

Garegnani, P. (1984). Value and distribution in the classical economists and Marx. *Oxford Economic Papers, 36*(2), 291–325.

Goldmann, L. (1958). La réification. In L. Goldmann (1959) (Ed.), *Recherches dialectiques* (pp. 64–106). Paris: Éditions Gallimard

Hosoda, E. (1993). Negative surplus value and inferior processes. *Metroeconomica, 44*(1), 29–42.

Krause, U. (1981). Marxian inequalities in a von Neumann setting. *Journal of Economics, 41*(1–2), 59–67.

Krause, U. (1982). *Money and abstract labour. On the analytical foundations of political economy*. London: New Left Books and Verso Editions.

Mariolis, T. (1999). The so-called problem of transforming values into prices. *Political Economy. Review of Political Economy and Social Sciences, 5*, 45–58.

Mariolis, T. (2006). A critical note on Marx's theory of profits. *Asian–African Journal of Economics and Econometrics, 6*(1), 1–11.

Mariolis, T. (2016). The time dilation: Einstein, Marx and Sraffa. *Xenophon, 1*, 48–56. (in Greek).

Mariolis, T. (2018). Mean and "third man argument" in the Aristotelian theory of exchange values. *Statistical Review, Journal of the Greek Statistical Association*, 11–12, Special issue in honor of Professor Ioannis Vavouras, 142–160 (in Greek)

Marx, K. (1993). *Grundrisse. Foundations of the critique of political economy (rough draft)*. Harmondsworth: Penguin Books.

Marx, K. (1982). Capital. A critique of political economy (Vol. 1). Harmondsworth: Penguin Books.

Marx, K. (1991). *Capital. A critique of political economy* (Vol. 3). Harmondsworth: Penguin Books.

Marx, K. (1983). In S. Yanovskaya (Ed.), *Mathematical manuscripts of Karl Marx*. London: New Park Publications Ltd.

Morishima, M. (1974). Marx in the light of modern economic theory. *Econometrica, 42*(4), 611–632.

Morishima, M. (1978). S. Bowles and H. Gintis on the Marxian theory of value and heterogeneous labour. *Cambridge Journal of Economic, 2*(3), 305–309.

Morishima, M., & Catephores, G. (1978). *Value, exploitation and growth*. London: McGraw-Hill.

Morishima, M., & Seton, F. (1961). Aggregation in Leontief matrices and the labour theory of value. *Econometrica, 29*(2), 203–220.

Okishio, N. (1955). Monopoly and the rates of profit. *Kobe University Economic Review, 1*, 71–88. Reprinted in N. Okishio (1993) *Essays on political economy*. Edited by M. Krüger & P. Flaschel. Peter Lang, Frankfurt am Main, pp 381–398

Okishio, N. (1961). Technical change and the rate of profit. *Kobe University Economic Review, 7*, 85–99. Reprinted in N. Okishio (1993). *Essays on political economy*. Edited by M. Krüger & P. Flaschel. Peter Lang, Frankfurt am Main, pp 359–373

Okishio, N., & Nakatani, T. (1985). A measurement of the rate of surplus value in Japan: the 1980 case. *Kobe University Economic Review, 31*, 1–13. Reprinted in Okishio N (1993) *Essays on political economy*. Edited by M. Krüger & P. Flaschel. Peter Lang, Frankfurt am Main, pp 61–73

Rubin, I. I. (1972). *Essays on Marx's theory of value*. Detroit: Black and Red Books.

Sraffa, P. (1960). *Production of commodities by means of commodities. Prelude to a critique of economic theory*. Cambridge: Cambridge University Press.

Steedman, I. (1975). Positive profits with negative surplus value. *The Economic Journal, 85*(337), 114–123.

Steedman, I. (1976). Positive profits with negative surplus value: A reply. *The Economic Journal, 86*(343), 604–608.

Steedman, I. (1977). *Marx after Sraffa*. London: New Left Books.

Steedman, I. (1985). Heterogeneous labour, money wages, and Marx's theory. *History of Political Economy, 17*(4), 551–574.

Steedman, I. (1991). The irrelevance of Marxian values. In G. A. Caravale (Ed.), *Marx and modern economic analysis* (Vol. 1, pp. 205–221). Aldershot: Edward Elgar.

Steedman, I. (2008). Marx after Sraffa and the open economy. *Bulletin of Political Economy, 2*(2), 165–174.

# Chapter 7
# Arguing in Circles: Alternative Value Bases and Actual Economies

**Abstract** This chapter extends the empirical investigation of the relationships amongst "labour values", as they are traditionally defined, long-period values, i.e. production prices, and market values to the framework of "alternative value bases" in both single and joint production systems. It is found that there exist vectors of "commodity values" and "additive commodity values" that are better approximations of actual values than "labour values" and "additive labour values", respectively. Moreover, in the empirically relevant case of joint production, cases were found where the exploration of the relationships amongst long-period values, "commodity values", and/or "labour values" is without economic meaning. Hence, the empirical claim that actual economies can be coherently analysed in terms of "labour values" cannot be sustained.

**Keywords** Actual economies · Alternative value bases · Joint production · Single production · Value deviations

## 7.1 Introduction

During the last decades, a significant number of studies have explored, using input–output table data, the empirical relationships amongst "labour values" (LVs), as they are traditionally defined in the classical–Marxian literature, actual long-period values (ALPVs), i.e. production prices that correspond to the "actual" real wage rate (estimated on the basis of the available input–output data), and market values (MVs).[1] The central conclusion of these studies is that LVs are quite close to ALPVs and MVs, while these results are *usually* interpreted as giving empirical support to the "labour theory of value" as an analytical tool for understanding the

---

[1] For a critical presentation and interpretation, see Mariolis and Tsoulfidis (2016, Chaps. 3 and 5); also see Chap. 5 of the present book.

© Springer Nature Singapore Pte Ltd. 2021
T. Mariolis et al., *Spectral Theory of Value and Actual Economies*, Evolutionary Economics and Social Complexity Science 24,
https://doi.org/10.1007/978-981-33-6260-4_7

laws of motion of modern economies. However, leaving aside the issue of how the latest argument could actually be supported, there are *at least* two objections:

(i).  It is well known that any "basic commodity" (in the sense of Sraffa 1960, pp. 7–8) can be considered as a "value base" and, therefore, it is possible to define the so-called "commodity *i* values" (see, e.g. Gintis and Bowles 1981, pp. 18–21; Roemer 1986, pp. 24–26), i.e. the direct and indirect requirements of commodity *i* necessary to produce one unit of each commodity as gross output. Therefore, the issue that arises is that, strictly speaking, there is no empirical reason to prefer *a priori* the labour theory of value as the most relevant amongst the "alternative value theories".

(ii). The aforementioned studies are based on data from Symmetric Input–Output Tables (SIOTs) and, therefore, on models of single production (see Chap. 1). Thus, the extension of the analysis to the joint production case is necessary.[2]

This chapter extends the empirical investigation of the relationships amongst LVs and actual values (AVs), i.e. ALPVs and MVs, to the framework of "alternative value bases" both in single and joint production systems. Section 7.2 explores the relationships amongst AVs, LVs, and "commodity values" (CVs) in single production and provides empirical evidence using data from the SIOTs of the French and Swedish economies for the years 1995 and 2005. Section 7.3 extends the analysis to the case of joint production and provides empirical evidence using data from the Supply and Use Tables (SUTs) of the Finnish (for the year 2004) and Japanese (for the year 2000) economies. Finally, Sect. 7.4 concludes.


## 7.2   Single Production

### 7.2.1   The Analytic Framework

We assume a closed, linear system with only single production activities, circulating capital, and homogeneous labour, which is not an input to the household sector.[3] The net product is distributed to profits and wages that are paid at the beginning of the common production period and there are no savings out of this income.[4] All commodities are basic and there are no alternative production techniques. The system is viable, i.e. the Perron–Frobenius eigenvalue, $\lambda_{A1}$, of the $n \times n$ matrix of

---

[2]As far as we know, the only studies that have explored value deviations in actual joint production economies are those of Mariolis and Soklis (2007, 2010), Soklis (2006, 2012). Their findings are not in line with those of the relevant studies on the issue, i.e. they detect value deviations that are considerably greater than those estimated on the basis of SIOTs, while cases were found where the exploration of value deviations is without economic meaning (also see Chap. 5 of the present book).

[3]What follows draws on Mariolis (2001), Soklis (2009, 2014).

[4]We hypothesize that wages are paid *ante factum* and that there are no savings out of this income in order to follow most of the empirical studies on this topic.

direct technical coefficients, **A**, is less than 1. Finally, the givens in our analysis are (i) the technical conditions of production, i.e. the pair $\{\mathbf{A}, \mathbf{l}\}$, where $\mathbf{l}^{\mathrm{T}}$ is the $1 \times n$ vector of direct labour coefficients; and (ii) the real wage rate, which is represented by the $n \times 1$ vector **b**. On the basis of these assumptions, we can write

$$\mathbf{v}^{\mathrm{T}} = \mathbf{l}^{\mathrm{T}} + \mathbf{v}^{\mathrm{T}}\mathbf{A} \tag{7.1}$$

$$\mathbf{p}^{\mathrm{T}} = (1 + r)\left(w\mathbf{l}^{\mathrm{T}} + \mathbf{p}^{\mathrm{T}}\mathbf{A}\right) \tag{7.2}$$

$$w = \mathbf{p}^{\mathrm{T}}\mathbf{b} \tag{7.3}$$

where $\mathbf{v}^{\mathrm{T}}$, $\mathbf{p}^{\mathrm{T}}$ are the vectors of LVs and ALPVs, respectively, $w$ the money wage rate, and $r$ the uniform profit rate. Moreover, the LV of the real wage bundle, i.e. the direct and indirect input requirements of labour necessary to produce one unit of labour, is given by

$$\omega \equiv \mathbf{v}^{\mathrm{T}}\mathbf{b}$$

Equations (7.1)–(7.3) imply that

$$\mathbf{v}^{\mathrm{T}} = \mathbf{l}^{\mathrm{T}}[\mathbf{I} - \mathbf{A}]^{-1} \tag{7.4}$$

$$(1 + r)^{-1}\mathbf{p}^{\mathrm{T}} = \mathbf{p}^{\mathrm{T}}\mathbf{C} \tag{7.5}$$

where $\mathbf{C} \equiv [\mathbf{b}\mathbf{l}^{\mathrm{T}} + \mathbf{A}]$ represents the "augmented" matrix of direct socio-technical coefficients. Thus, LVs can be estimated from Eq. (7.4). Each element, $v_j$, of the vector of LVs expresses the "vertically integrated labour coefficient" (Pasinetti 1973) for commodity $j$, i.e. the direct and indirect labour requirements per unit of net output for commodity $j$. Finally, since a non-positive vector of ALPVs is economically irrelevant, Eq. (7.5) implies that $(1 + r)^{-1}$ is the Perron–Frobenius eigenvalue of **C**, and $\mathbf{p}^{\mathrm{T}}$ is the corresponding left eigenvector.

Now, we define the "extended" $m \times m$ $(m = n + 1)$ matrix $\mathbf{D} \equiv [d_{ij}]$ as

$$\mathbf{D} \equiv \begin{bmatrix} \mathbf{A} & \mathbf{b} \\ \mathbf{l}^{\mathrm{T}} & 0 \end{bmatrix}$$

which is also known as the "complete" or "full" matrix (Bródy 1970).[5] Thus, we can re-write the vector of LVs as follows:

---

[5]Due to our assumption that labour is not an input to the household sector, the $(m, m)$th element of matrix **D** equals zero.

$$\mathbf{v}^\mathrm{T} = \mathbf{v}^\mathrm{T}\mathbf{D}_{(m)} + \mathbf{d}_m^\mathrm{T}$$

where $\mathbf{D}_{(m)}$ denotes the matrix derived from $\mathbf{D}$ by extracting its $m$ th row and column and $\mathbf{d}_m^\mathrm{T}$ denotes the $m$ th row of $\mathbf{D}$ if we extract its $m$ th element. Therefore, it can be easily seen that $\mathbf{D}_{(m)} = \mathbf{A}$ and $\mathbf{d}_m^\mathrm{T} = \mathbf{l}^\mathrm{T}$. Furthermore, the LV of the real wage bundle is given by

$$\omega \equiv \mathbf{d}_m^\mathrm{T}\left[\mathbf{I} - \mathbf{D}_{(m)}\right]^{-1}\mathbf{d}^m$$

where $\mathbf{d}^m$ denotes the $m$ th column of $\mathbf{D}$ if we extract its $m$ th element, i.e. $\mathbf{d}^m = \mathbf{b}$. However, labour is just one of the $m$ production inputs that can be considered as a value base. In general, the vector of "commodity $i$ values" is given by

$$\mathbf{v}_i^\mathrm{T} = \mathbf{v}_i^\mathrm{T}\mathbf{D}_{(i)} + \mathbf{d}_i^\mathrm{T} \tag{7.6}$$

where $\mathbf{v}_i^\mathrm{T} \equiv \left[v_1^i, v_2^i, \ldots, v_{i-1}^i, v_{i+1}^i, \ldots, v_m^i\right]$, $v_j^i$ denotes the "commodity $i$ value" of commodity $j$, i.e. the total (direct and indirect) requirements of commodity $i$ necessary to produce one unit of gross output of commodity $j$, $\mathbf{D}_{(i)}$ denotes the matrix derived from $\mathbf{D}$ by extracting its $i$ th row and column, and $\mathbf{d}_i^\mathrm{T}$ denotes the $i$ th row of $\mathbf{D}$ if we extract its $i$ th element (and, therefore, represents the vector of direct input requirements of commodity $i$). For example, assume that $n = 2$ and, therefore, $\mathbf{D}$ is a $3 \times 3$ matrix, i.e.

$$\mathbf{D} = \begin{bmatrix} a_{11} & a_{12} & b_1 \\ a_{21} & a_{22} & b_2 \\ l_1 & l_2 & 0 \end{bmatrix}$$

Then, the vector of "commodity 1 values" is given by

$$\mathbf{v}_1^\mathrm{T} = \mathbf{v}_1^\mathrm{T}\mathbf{D}_{(1)} + \mathbf{d}_1^\mathrm{T} \tag{7.7}$$

where $\mathbf{v}_1^\mathrm{T} = \left[v_2^1, v_3^1\right]$, $\mathbf{D}_{(1)} = \begin{bmatrix} a_{22} & b_2 \\ l_2 & 0 \end{bmatrix}$ and $\mathbf{d}_1^\mathrm{T} = [a_{12}, b_1]$. From Eq 7.7 we obtain

$$v_2^1 = v_2^1 a_{22} + v_3^1 l_2 + a_{12} \tag{7.8}$$

and

$$v_3^1 = v_2^1 b_2 + b_1 \tag{7.9}$$

Equation (7.8) gives the direct and indirect requirements of commodity 1 necessary to produce one unit of commodity 2 as gross output, while Eq. (7.9) gives the direct and indirect requirements of commodity 1 necessary to produce one unit of labour. Analogously, we may obtain the vector of "commodity 2 values" by extracting the second row and column of matrix $\mathbf{D}$. Finally, by extracting the third row and column of $\mathbf{D}$ we may obtain the vector of LVs. Thus, in general, the vector of "commodity $i$ values" is obtained from Eq. (7.6) as follows:

$$\mathbf{v}_i^T = \mathbf{d}_i^T \left[ \mathbf{I} - \mathbf{D}_{(i)} \right]^{-1} \tag{7.10}$$

while the total input requirements of commodity $i$ necessary to produce one unit of itself is given by

$$\omega_i \equiv \mathbf{v}_i^T \mathbf{d}^i + c_{ii}$$

where $\mathbf{d}^i$ denotes the $i$ th column of $\mathbf{D}$ if we extract its $i$ th element, and $\varepsilon_i \equiv (1 - \omega_i)/\omega_i$ may be defined as the "rate of exploitation" of commodity $i$ (also see Gintis and Bowles 1981, p. 18). Moreover, it can be shown that the conditions

$$r > 0, \omega_i < 1, \ \lambda_{\mathbf{D}1} < 1$$

where $\lambda_{\mathbf{D}1}$ denotes the Perron–Frobenius eigenvalue of $\mathbf{D}$, are all equivalent (see Bródy 1970, Part 1).[6] Finally, it is worth mentioning that, over the last decades, it has been recognized that the concept of total requirements for gross output is important in analysing the inter-dependence amongst the industries of an economy (see Milana 1985; Szyrmer 1986, 1992; Szyrmer and Walker 1983), while Mariolis and Rodousaki (2011) have argued that this concept was introduced by Vladimir K. Dmitriev (1898) in his essay on the theory of value in Ricardo.

Following Mariolis (2000, 2001), we may now explore the theoretical relationships between AVs and "commodity $i$ values". We begin with the system of AVs (see Eqs. (7.2) and (7.3)), which we can re-write, on the basis of the complete matrix, $\mathbf{D}$, as follows:

$$\pi^T = \pi^T \mathbf{D} + \mathbf{k}^T \tag{7.11}$$

where $\pi^T \equiv [\mathbf{p}^T, w]$ is the "complete" (in the sense of Bródy 1970) AVs vector, $\mathbf{k}^T \equiv \pi^T \mathbf{D} \mathbf{R}$ is the vector of sectoral profit coefficients,

---

[6]Note that the aforesaid condition constitutes a general profitability condition ("generalized commodity exploitation theorem"), which includes the well-known "fundamental Marxian theorem" (Sect. 6.2.1 of the present book).

$$\mathbf{R} \equiv \begin{bmatrix} \hat{\mathbf{r}} & 0 \\ 0 & 0 \end{bmatrix}$$

and $\hat{\mathbf{r}}$ is an $n \times n$ diagonal matrix formed by the sectoral profit rates. Equation (7.11) may be written as

$$\pi_i^T = \pi_i^T \mathbf{D}_{(i)} + p_i \mathbf{d}_i^T + \mathbf{k}_i^T \tag{7.12}$$

$$p_i = \pi_i^T \mathbf{d}^i + p_i d_{ii} + k_i \tag{7.13}$$

where $\pi_i^T \equiv [p_1, p_2, \ldots, p_{i-1}, p_{i+1}, \ldots, p_m]$ $(\mathbf{k}_i^T \equiv [\pi_i^T \mathbf{D}_{(i)} + p_i \mathbf{d}_i^T] \mathbf{R}_{(i)})$ is the vector derived from $\pi^T$ $(\mathbf{k}^T)$ if we extract its $i$ th element, $\mathbf{R}_{(i)}$ is the $n \times n$ diagonal matrix derived from $\mathbf{R}$ by extracting its $i$ th row and column, and $p_i$ $(k_i)$ is the $i$ th element of $\pi^T$ $(\mathbf{k}^T)$. Equations (7.12) and (7.13) may be interpreted as the reduction of the "production costs" (or, more precisely, the values; see Sraffa 1960, pp. 8–9) to the "production cost" (the value) of commodity $i$ (see Dmitriev 1898, pp. 61–64). From Eq. (7.12) we obtain

$$\pi_i^T = p_i \mathbf{d}_i^T [\mathbf{I} - \mathbf{D}_{(i)}]^{-1} + \mathbf{k}_i^T [\mathbf{I} - \mathbf{D}_{(i)}]^{-1}$$

or, recalling Eq. (7.10),

$$\pi_i^T = p_i \mathbf{v}_i^T + \mathbf{k}_i^T [\mathbf{I} - \mathbf{D}_{(i)}]^{-1} \tag{7.14}$$

Substituting $\mathbf{k}_i^T \equiv [\pi_i^T \mathbf{D}_{(i)} + p_i \mathbf{d}_i^T] \mathbf{R}_{(i)}$ into Eq. (7.14) and after rearrangement we obtain

$$\pi_i^T = \mathbf{v}_i^T \mathbf{T}_{(i)}$$

where

$$\mathbf{T}_{(i)} \equiv p_i [\mathbf{I} - \mathbf{D}_{(i)}] [\mathbf{I} + \mathbf{R}_{(i)}] [\mathbf{I} - \mathbf{D}_{(i)} [\mathbf{I} + \mathbf{R}_{(i)}]]^{-1}$$

is a linear operator "transforming commodity $i$ values" into AVs. If

$$\pi_i^T = \pi_m^T = \mathbf{p}^T$$

i.e. AVs are reduced to the AV of labour, then we obtain $\mathbf{p}^T = \mathbf{v}^T \mathbf{T}_{(m)}$, where $\mathbf{T}_{(m)} \equiv w[\mathbf{I} - \mathbf{A}][\mathbf{I} + \hat{\mathbf{r}}][\mathbf{I} - \mathbf{A}[\mathbf{I} + \hat{\mathbf{r}}]]^{-1}$ is the so-called linear operator transforming LVs into AVs (Pasinetti 1977, Chap. 5, Appendix; Reati 1986).[7]

When $\hat{\mathbf{r}} = \mathbf{0}$ and, therefore, $\mathbf{k}^T = \mathbf{0}^T$, Eq. (7.14) implies that

$$\pi_i^T = p_i \mathbf{v}_i^T$$

Thus, in this case, "commodity $i$ values" are proportional to AVs. Finally, in the *special* case where the vectors of sectoral profit coefficients, $\mathbf{k}_i^T$, and direct input requirements of commodity $i$, $\mathbf{d}_i^T$, are linearly dependent, i.e. $\mathbf{k}_i^T = z\mathbf{d}_i^T$, where $z$ is a positive real number, then from Eq. (7.14) we obtain

$$\pi_i^T = (p_i + z)\mathbf{v}_i^T$$

Therefore, in this special case, "commodity $i$ values" are proportional to AVs.

### 7.2.2 Empirical Investigation

Although alternative value bases are usually neglected in the empirical investigation of the relationships between AVs and LVs, the few studies that have attempted to incorporate "alternative values" in their analysis conclude that LVs are by far better approximations of AVs than alternative values and, therefore, there is an empirical basis for preferring labour as a value base. Nevertheless, the estimated alternative values in those studies do not correspond to the notion of CVs as defined by Eq. (7.6), the main difference being that they do not take into account the quantity of labour that enters into the production of the commodities. That is because the procedure that has been followed to calculate alternative values is to delete the $i$ th row and column of matrix $\mathbf{A}$ and to substitute the direct labour inputs in Eq. (7.1) with alternative direct inputs, i.e. the $i$ th row of matrix $\mathbf{A}$. However, this calculation does not take into account the quantity of labour, measured in terms of commodity $i$, that enters into the production of the commodities. For instance, in the $2 \times 2$ example of Sect. 7.2.1, the term $v_3^1 l_2$ in Eq. (7.8) would not exist, and Eq. (7.9) could not be defined. Since in the actual economic systems labour enters directly and indirectly into the production of all the commodities, it follows that the aforesaid estimation does not measure the "commodity $i$ values". On the other hand, Manresa et al. (1998) have estimated the total (direct and indirect) requirements of energy

---

[7] In fact, however, these operators are not (and could not be) price/money-free and, therefore, "transform" a price, i.e. $w$ or, respectively, $p_i$, into other prices, i.e. $\mathbf{p}^T$ or, respectively, $\pi_i^T$ (Mariolis 2003a). For the theoretical investigation of the relationships between AVs and LVs, also see Bidard and Ehrbar (2007), Parys (1982). For a norm bound approach, see Mariolis (2010), while Sect. 6.3 of the present book proposes an "abstract social labour" approach.

necessary to produce one unit of gross output of each commodity, i.e. "energy values", in the economy of Catalonia for the year 1987 on the basis of Eq. (7.6). Although the purpose of that study was not the empirical investigation of the relationships between AVs and LVs, it demonstrated that commodities' commodity content, or CVs, can be estimated by the same system of equations as LVs and showed the practical feasibility and usefulness of the estimation. Therefore, as far as we know, the empirical relationships between AVs and CVs have not been investigated.

In what follows, we estimate the value deviations in single production economies using data from the SIOTs of the French and Swedish economies for the years 1995 and 2005.[8] The vectors of "commodity $i$ values" of the economies are estimated from Eq. (7.10), while the vectors of ALPVs are estimated from eigen-system (7.5). A crucial issue concerning the empirical investigation of the relationships between AVs and "commodity $i$ values" is the choice of a theoretical appropriate measure of value deviations. As is well known, the results obtained on the basis of the traditional measures of value deviation (such as "correlation coefficient", "mean absolute deviation", "mean absolute weighted deviation", "root-mean-square-percent-error"), which have been widely used in the relevant literature, depend on the arbitrary choice of either the *numéraire* or the physical measurement units.[9] On the other hand, the so-called $d-$distance constitutes a measure of value deviation that is free from *numéraire* and measurement-unit dependence: it is defined as

$$d \equiv \sqrt{2(1 - \cos\theta)}$$

where $\theta$ is, in our case, the Euclidean angle between the vectors $\boldsymbol{\pi}_i^T \widehat{\mathbf{v}}_i^{-1}$ and $\mathbf{e}$, $\widehat{\mathbf{v}}_i$ a diagonal matrix formed from the elements of $\mathbf{v}_i$ and $\boldsymbol{\pi}_i^T \widehat{\mathbf{v}}_i^{-1}$ the ratio of ALPVs to "commodity $i$ values".[10] Thus, in what follows, we use the "normalized $d-$distance", $dD^{-1}$, as a measure of value deviation, where

$$D \equiv \sqrt{2\left[1 - \left(\sqrt{n}\right)^{-1}\right]}$$

is the theoretically maximum value of the $d-$distance.

---

[8]For the available input–output data as well as the construction of relevant variables, see the Appendix at the end of this chapter.

[9]See Sect. 5.3.2 of this book.

[10]The $d-$ distance between MVs and "commodity $i$ values" is estimated on the basis of the Euclidean angle between the vectors $[\boldsymbol{\pi}_i^M]^T \widehat{\mathbf{v}}_i^{-1}$ and $\mathbf{e}$, where $[\boldsymbol{\pi}_i^M]^T \equiv [p_1^M, p_2^M, \ldots, p_{i-1}^M, p_{i+1}^M, \ldots, p_m^M]$ denotes the vector of MVs. Since MVs are taken to be equal to 1 (see the Appendix at the end of this chapter), it follows that for $i \neq m$ we get $[\boldsymbol{\pi}_i^M]^T = [1, 1, 1, 1, \ldots, w_{\min}^M]$, while for $i = m$ we get $[\boldsymbol{\pi}_m^M]^T = \mathbf{e}^T$.

### 7.2.2.1 France

The main results from the application of the previous analysis to the input–output tables of the French economy for the years 1995 and 2005 are reported in Tables 7.1 and 7.2, and Figs. 7.1 and 7.2. Tables 7.1 and 7.2 report the largest and smallest value deviations for the year 1995 and 2005, respectively. The first row of each table refers to the deviations of AVs from LVs, while the remaining rows report the deviations of AVs from CVs.[11] The last row refers to the average deviations of AVs from CVs, i.e. the sum of the deviations divided by the total number of commodities that are used as value bases.

In order to get a complete picture of the value deviations, in Fig. 7.1 (in Fig. 7.2) we display the deviations of the vector of ALPVs (MVs) from each vector of CVs for both years of our analysis. The deviations for the year 1995 (year 2005) are measured in the vertical (horizontal) axis, while the AV–LV deviations are taken as the origin of the axes. The points below (above) the horizontal axes indicate AV–CV deviations less (greater) than the AV–LV deviations for the year 1995, while the points on the left (right) side of the vertical axes indicate AV–CV deviations less (greater) than the AV–LV deviations for the year 2005. Thus, it follows that the points on the lower-left (upper-right) quadrants of the figures indicate vectors of CVs that are better (worse) approximations of AVs than LVs for both years of our analysis.

From Tables 7.1 and 7.2, Figs. 7.1 and 7.2, and the associated numerical results, we arrive at the following conclusions:

(i). The ALPV (MV)–LV deviation for the year 1995 is almost 11.3% (65.6%), while that for the year 2005 is almost 11.5% (31.7%). Also, the actual "relative profit rate", $\rho \equiv (rR^{-1})$, where $R \equiv \lambda_{A1}^{-1} - 1$ denotes the maximum profit rate, is almost 35.8% ($r \cong 32.2\%$, $R \cong 89.9\%$) for the year 1995 and almost 36.0% for the year 2005 ($r \cong 30.8\%$, $R \cong 85.5\%$).[12]

(ii). The average deviation of ALPVs (MVs) from CVs is almost 15.6% (66.2%) for the year 1995 and almost 15.6% (34.1%) for the year 2005.

(iii). The deviations of ALPVs from the vectors of CVs associated with commodities 50 ("Trade, maintenance and repair services of motor vehicles and motorcycles; retail sale of automotive fuel"), 51 ("Wholesale trade and commission trade services, except of motor vehicles and motorcycles"), 52 ("Retail trade services, except of motor vehicles and motorcycles; repair services of personal and household goods"), 60 ("Land transport; transport via pipeline services"), and 74 ("Other business services") are less than the corresponding

---

[11]The value deviations that are found to be less than the corresponding AV–LV deviations are indicated by bold characters.

[12]It should be noted that all the relevant empirical studies have found a relative profit rate that is in the range of 17% to 40%, an ALPV–LV deviation that is in the range of 6% to 20%, and a MV–LV deviation that is in the range of 7% to 37%. Consequently, our results regarding the MV–LV deviations for the year 1995 show a significant divergence from those reported in similar studies.

**Table 7.1** Value deviations: French economy, year 1995

| Value bases | $dD^{-1}$ (%) | | Value bases | $dD^{-1}$ (%) | |
|---|---|---|---|---|---|
| | ALPVs vs. "commodity $i$ values" | MVs vs. "commodity $i$ values" | | ALPVs vs. "commodity $i$ values" | MVs vs. "commodity $i$ values" |
| Labour | 11.3 | 65.6 | "Post and telecommunication services" CPA: 64 | 15.6 | 70.4 |
| "Coal and lignite; peat" CPA:10 | 17.4 | **58.4** | "Financial intermediation services" CPA: 65 | 14.6 | 70.1 |
| "Crude petroleum and natural gas" CPA: 11 | 18.9 | **57.4** | "Insurance and pension funding services" CPA: 66 | 11.6 | 68.1 |
| "Metal ores" CPA: 13 | 24.3 | **48.4** | "Services auxiliary to financial intermediation" CPA: 67 | 15.6 | 70.7 |
| "Other mining and quarrying products" CPA: 14 | 21.5 | **61.0** | "Real estate services" CPA: 70 | 12.4 | 67.7 |
| "Printed matter and recorded media" CPA: 22 | 16.8 | 70.1 | "Computer and related services" CPA: 72 | 15.3 | 71.5 |
| "Coke, refined petroleum products, and nuclear fuels" CPA: 23 | 16.8 | **57.5** | "Research and development services" CPA: 73 | 24.1 | 69.2 |

| Product | | |
|---|---|---|
| "Other non-metallic mineral products" CPA: 26 | 16.2 | **57.5** |
| "Electrical energy, gas, steam, and hot water" CPA: 40 | 13.1 | **51.3** |
| "Construction work" CPA: 45 | 21.8 | **30.1** |
| "Trade, maintenance and repair services of motor vehicles and motorcycles" CPA: 50 | **8.8** | 67.4 |
| "Wholesale trade and commission trade services" CPA: 51 | **6.2** | 67.9 |
| "Retail trade services" CPA: 52 | **7.3** | 67.4 |
| "Hotel and restaurant services" CPA: 55 | 12.0 | 67.5 |
| "Land transport; transport via pipeline services" CPA: 60 | **9.4** | 68.0 |
| "Other business services" CPA: 74 | **10.8** | **62.0** |
| "Sewage and refuse disposal services" CPA: 90 | 14.7 | 70.2 |
| "Membership organization services n.e.c." CPA: 91 | 14.4 | 72.2 |
| "Recreational, cultural and sporting services" CPA: 92 | 13.3 | 67.1 |
| "Other services" CPA: 93 | 14.3 | 67.4 |
| "Private households with employed persons" CPA: 95 | 13.2 | 66.1 |
| Average value deviations | 15.6 | 66.2 |

**Table 7.2** Value deviations: French economy, year 2005

| Value bases | $dD^{-1}$ (%) | | Value bases | $dD^{-1}$ (%) | |
|---|---|---|---|---|---|
| | ALPVs vs. "commodity $i$ values" | MVs vs. "commodity $i$ values" | | ALPVs vs. "commodity $i$ values" | MVs vs. "commodity $i$ values" |
| Labour | 11.5 | 31.7 | "Post and telecommunication services" CPA: 64 | 14.5 | **27.6** |
| "Coal and lignite; peat" CPA:10 | 19.4 | 40.9 | "Financial intermediation services" CPA: 65 | 14.8 | **17.7** |
| "Crude petroleum and natural gas" CPA: 11 | 20.1 | 39.2 | "Insurance and pension funding services" CPA: 66 | **11.5** | **29.4** |
| "Metal ores" CPA: 13 | 24.8 | 44.8 | "Services auxiliary to financial intermediation" CPA: 67 | 15.4 | **31.1** |
| "Other mining and quarrying products" CPA: 14 | 22.4 | 39.1 | "Real estate services" CPA: 70 | 12.4 | **19.7** |
| "Printed matter and recorded media" CPA: 22 | 16.9 | **30.9** | "Computer and related services" CPA: 72 | 15.1 | **26.0** |
| "Coke, refined petroleum products and nuclear fuels" CPA: 23 | 17.6 | 38.0 | "Research and development services" CPA: 73 | 24.6 | 46.0 |
| "Other non-metallic mineral products" CPA: 26 | 16.3 | 35.0 | "Other business services" CPA: 74 | **9.6** | **26.7** |

| Category | | | Category | | |
|---|---|---|---|---|---|
| "Electrical energy, gas, steam and hot water" CPA: 40 | 13.6 | 34.2 | "Sewage and refuse disposal services" CPA: 90 | 14.4 | **23.5** |
| "Construction work" CPA: 45 | 18.1 | **20.6** | "Membership organization services n.e.c." CPA: 91 | 22.6 | 32.8 |
| "Trade, maintenance and repair services of motor vehicles and motorcycles" CPA: 50 | **9.7** | 34.6 | "Recreational, cultural, and sporting services" CPA: 92 | 13.0 | **25.9** |
| "Wholesale trade and commission trade services" CPA: 51 | **7.8** | 33.3 | "Other services" CPA: 93 | 14.2 | **29.5** |
| "Retail trade services" CPA: 52 | **9.1** | 36.4 | "Private households with employed persons" CPA: 95 | 13.3 | **20.3** |
| "Hotel and restaurant services" CPA: 55 | 11.8 | **30.1** | Average value deviations | 15.6 | 34.1 |
| "Land transport; transport via pipeline services" CPA: 60 | **10.4** | 36.8 | | | |

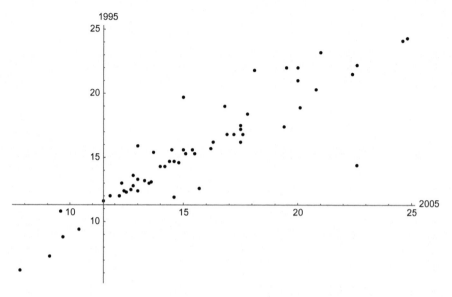

**Fig. 7.1** ALPV–CV deviations (%): French economy, years 1995 and 2005

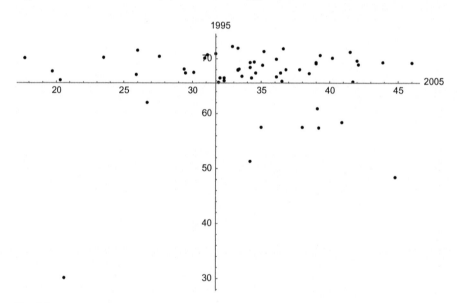

**Fig. 7.2** MV–CV deviations (%): French economy, years 1995 and 2005

ALPV–LV deviation for both years of our analysis. Furthermore, the deviation of ALPVs from the vector of CVs associated with commodity 66 ("Insurance and pension funding services") is less than the corresponding production ALPV–LV deviation for the year 2005.

(iv). The deviations of MVs from the vectors of CVs associated with commodities 45 ("Construction work") and 74 ("Other business services") are less than the corresponding MV–LV deviation for both years of our analysis. Furthermore, the deviations of MVs from the vectors of CVs associated with commodities (a) 10 ("Coal and lignite; peat"), 11 ("Crude petroleum and natural gas"), 13 ("Metal ores"), 14 ("Other mining and quarrying products"), 23 ("Coke, refined petroleum products and nuclear fuels"), 26 ("Other non-metallic mineral products"), and 40 ("Electrical energy, gas, steam and hot water") for the year 1995; and (b) 22 ("Printed matter and recorded media"), 55 ("Hotel and restaurant services"), 64 ("Post and telecommunication services"), 65 ("Financial intermediation services"), 66 ("Insurance and pension funding services"), 67 ("Services auxiliary to financial intermediation"), 70 ("Real estate services"), 72 ("Computer and related services"), 90 ("Sewage and refuse disposal services"), 92 ("Recreational, cultural and sporting services"), 93 ("Other services"), and 95 ("Private households with employed persons") for the year 2005 are less than the corresponding MV–LV deviations.

(v). The smallest ALPV–"commodity $i$ value" deviation for the year 1995 (2005) is 6.2% (7.8%) and corresponds to the vector of "commodity $i$ values" associated with commodity "Wholesale trade and commission trade services, except of motor vehicles and motorcycles", while the smallest MV–"commodity $i$ value" deviation for the year 1995 (2005) is almost 30.1% (17.7%) and corresponds to the vector of "commodity $i$ values" associated with the commodity "Construction work" ("Financial intermediation services").

(vi). The largest ALPV–"commodity $i$ value" deviation for the year 1995 (2005) is 24.3% (24.8%) and corresponds to the vector of "commodity $i$ values" associated with the commodity "Metal ores", while the largest MV–"commodity $i$ value" deviation for the year 1995 (2005) is 72.2% (46.0%) and corresponds to the vector of "commodity $i$ values" associated with the commodity "Membership organization services n.e.c." ("Research and development services").

### 7.2.2.2 Sweden

The main results obtained for the case of the Swedish economy are reported in Tables 7.3 and 7.4, and Figs. 7.3 and 7.4, which are constructed with the same logic as Tables 7.1 and 7.2, and Figs. 7.1 and 7.2, respectively, in Sect. 7.2.2.1.

From Tables 7.3 and 7.4, Figs. 7.3 and 7.4, and the associated numerical results, we arrive at the following conclusions:

(i). The deviation of the vector of ALPVs (MVs) from the vector of LVs for the year 1995 is almost 10.7% (24.4%), while that for the year 2005 is almost 10.4% (16.6%). Furthermore, the actual relative profit rate, $\rho$, is almost 39.1%

**Table 7.3** Value deviations: Swedish economy, year 1995

| | $dD^{-1}$ (%) | |
| Value bases | ALPVs vs. "commodity $i$ values" | MVs vs. "commodity $i$ values" |
| --- | --- | --- |
| Labour | 10.7 | 24.4 |
| "Products of forestry" CPA:02 | 22.1 | **24.0** |
| "Wearing apparels; Furs" CPA: 18 | 13.1 | **22.7** |
| "Basic metals" CPA: 27 | 25.4 | 35.9 |
| "Secondary raw Materials" CPA: 37 | 23.6 | 35.7 |
| "Energy products" CPA: 40 | 11.3 | **24.2** |
| "Services of water" CPA: 41 | 15.3 | 27.3 |
| "Construction work" CPA: 45 | 16.8 | **17.6** |
| "Wholesale and retail trade services" CPA: 50 $\oplus$ 51 $\oplus$ 52 | **8.3** | 26.4 |
| "Financial intermediation services" CPA: 65 | 11.4 | **20.3** |
| "Insurance services" CPA: 66 | 13.2 | **22.0** |
| "Real estate services" CPA: 70 | 14.3 | 25.8 |
| Average value deviations | 16.4 | 28.7 |

($r \cong 33.6\%$, $R \cong 85.9\%$) for the year 1995 and almost 36.8% for the year 2005 ($r \cong 29.7\%$, $R \cong 80.7\%$).[13]

(ii). The average deviation of ALPVs (MVs) from CVs is in the area of 16.4% (28.7%) for the year 1995 and in the area of 15.6% (20.8%) for the year 2005.

(iii). The deviation of ALPVs from the vector of CVs associated with the aggregate commodity of industries[14] 50 ("Trade, maintenance and repair services of motor vehicles and motorcycles; retail sale of automotive fuel"), 51 ("Wholesale trade and commission trade services, except of motor vehicles and motorcycles"), and 52 ("Retail trade services, except of motor vehicles and motorcycles; repair services of personal and household goods") is less than the corresponding ALPV–LV deviation for both years of our analysis.

---

[13]Note that these results are in accordance with the findings of the relevant empirical studies.

[14]For the degree of sectoral disaggregation of Sweden's input–output tables, see the Appendix at the end of this chapter.

**Table 7.4**  Value deviations: Swedish economy, year 2005

| Value bases | $dD^{-1}$ (%) | |
| --- | --- | --- |
| | ALPVs vs. "commodity $i$ values" | MVs vs. "commodity $i$ values" |
| Labour | 10.4 | 16.6 |
| "Products of forestry" CPA:02 | 22.9 | 24.6 |
| "Wearing apparels; furs" CPA: 18 | 12.2 | 17.5 |
| "Basic metals" CPA: 27 | 23.5 | 29.1 |
| "Secondary raw materials" CPA: 37 | 23.3 | 30.3 |
| "Energy products" CPA: 40 | 10.8 | **14.6** |
| "Services of water" CPA: 41 | 15.1 | **15.1** |
| "Construction work" CPA: 45 | 16.0 | **12.7** |
| "Wholesale and retail trade services" CPA: 50 $\oplus$ 51 $\oplus$ 52 | **7.9** | 17.5 |
| "Financial intermediation services" CPA: 65 | 11.7 | **12.0** |
| "Insurance services" CPA: 66 | 12.7 | **13.6** |
| "Real estate services" CPA: 70 | 13.1 | **15.9** |
| Average value deviations | 15.6 | 20.8 |

(iv). The deviations of MVs from the vectors of CVs associated with commodities 40 ("Energy products"), 45 ("Construction work"), 65 ("Financial intermediation services"), and 66 ("Insurance services") are less than the corresponding MV–LV deviation for both years of our analysis. Furthermore, the deviations of MVs from the vectors of CVs associated with commodities (a) 02 ("Products of forestry") and 18 ("Wearing apparels") for the year 1995; and (b) 41 ("Services of water") and 70 ("Real estate services") for the year 2005 are less than the corresponding MV–LV deviations.

(v). The smallest ALPV–"commodity $i$ value" deviation for the year 1995 (2005) is 8.3% (7.9%) and corresponds to the vector of CVs associated with the aggregate commodity of the sectors 50, 51, and 52, while the smallest MV– "commodity $i$ value" deviation for the year 1995 (2005) is almost 17.6% (12.0%) and corresponds to the vector of CVs associated with the commodity "Construction work" ("Financial intermediation services").

(vi). The largest ALPV–"commodity $i$ value" deviation for the year 1995 (2005) is 25.4% (23.5%) and corresponds to the vector of CVs associated with the

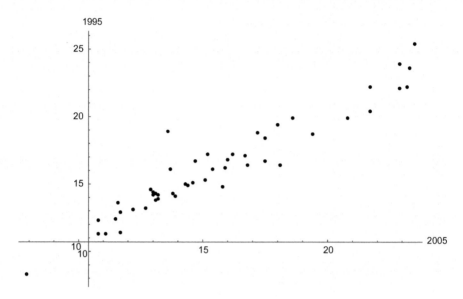

**Fig. 7.3**  ALPV–CV deviations (%): Swedish economy, years 1995 and 2005

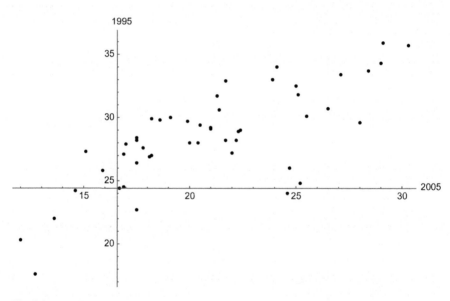

**Fig. 7.4**  MV–CV deviations (%): Swedish economy, years 1995 and 2005

commodity "Basic metals", while the largest MV–"commodity *i* value" deviation for the year 1995 (2005) is 35.9% (30.3%) and corresponds to the vector of CVs associated with the commodity "Basic metals" ("Secondary raw materials").

## 7.3  Joint Production

### 7.3.1  The Analytic Framework

Consider the joint production economy described in Sect. 5.2.[15] The givens in our analysis are (i) the vector of MVs; (ii) the technical conditions of production, i.e. the triplet $\{\mathbf{B}, \mathbf{A}, \mathbf{l}\}$, where $\mathbf{B}$ represents the $n \times n$ make matrix, $\mathbf{A}$ the $n \times n$ use matrix, and $\mathbf{l}^T$ the $1 \times n$ vector of employment levels process by process; and (iii) the real wage rate, which is represented by the $n \times 1$ vector $\mathbf{b}$. On the basis of these assumptions, the ALPVs, $\mathbf{p}$, are given by

$$\mathbf{p}^T \mathbf{B} = (1+r)(w\mathbf{l}^T + \mathbf{p}^T \mathbf{A}) \tag{7.15}$$

$$w = \mathbf{p}^T \mathbf{b} \tag{7.16}$$

From Eqs. (7.15) and (7.16) it follows that

$$\mathbf{p}^T \mathbf{B} = (1+r)\mathbf{p}^T \mathbf{C} \tag{7.17}$$

where $\mathbf{C} \equiv [\mathbf{b}\mathbf{l}^T + \mathbf{A}]$ now represents the "augmented" use matrix. Provided that $\mathbf{B}$ is non-singular, Eq. (7.17) implies that

$$(1+r)^{-1}\mathbf{p}^T = \mathbf{p}^T \mathbf{C}\mathbf{B}^{-1} \tag{7.18}$$

where $(1+r)^{-1}$ is now an eigenvalue of the matrix $\mathbf{C}\mathbf{B}^{-1}$, and $\mathbf{p}^T$ is the corresponding left eigenvector.

The vector of "additive labour values" (ALVs), $\mathbf{v}^T \equiv [v_j]$ (see Sect. 4.2.1), is given by the following equation:

$$\mathbf{v}^T \mathbf{B} = \mathbf{l}^T + \mathbf{v}^T \mathbf{A} \tag{7.19}$$

Now, we define the extended $m \times m$ ($m = n + 1$) input and output matrices as $\mathbf{D}$ and $\mathbf{V}$, respectively, where

$$\mathbf{D} \equiv \begin{bmatrix} \mathbf{A} & \mathbf{b} \\ \mathbf{l}^T & 0 \end{bmatrix}$$

and

---

[15]What follows draws on Mariolis (2003b), Soklis (2012, Chaps. 2 and 6; 2015).

$$V \equiv \begin{bmatrix} \mathbf{B} & 0 \\ 0 & 1 \end{bmatrix}$$

On the basis of these matrices, we may write

$$\boldsymbol{\omega}_i^T \mathbf{V} = \boldsymbol{\omega}_i^T \mathbf{D}_{(i)} + \mathbf{d}_i^T \qquad (7.20)$$

where $\boldsymbol{\omega}_i^T \equiv [\omega_1^i, \omega_2^i, \dots, \omega_m^i]$, $\omega_j^i$ denotes the "additive commodity $i$ value of commodity $j$" (Mariolis 2003b), i.e. the total (direct and indirect) requirements of commodity $i$ necessary to produce one unit of commodity $j$ as net product, $\mathbf{D}_{(i)}$ denotes the matrix derived from $\mathbf{D}$ by replacing all the elements of its $i$-th row with zero, and $\mathbf{d}_i^T$ denotes the $i$-th row of $\mathbf{D}$. Thus, for $i = m$, Eq. (7.20) gives the vector of ALVs (see Eq. (7.19)), with the $m$-th element of $\boldsymbol{\omega}_m$ representing the "value of labour power". However, nothing guarantees that system (7.20) is consistent. Moreover, even if the system is consistent, it is possible to have more than one solution. In the case where the vector of "additive commodity $i$ values" is uniquely determined, then the solution of system (7.20) is given by

$$\boldsymbol{\omega}_i^T = \mathbf{d}_i^T \left[ \mathbf{V} - \mathbf{D}_{(i)} \right]^{-1} \qquad (7.21)$$

However, even in this case, nothing guarantees that the solution is economically relevant. Thus, in the case of joint production, is *a priori* unknown if the empirical investigation of the relationships between AVs and "additive commodity $i$ values" is economically meaningful.

## 7.3.2  Empirical Investigation

To the best of our knowledge, there is not any empirical study that has taken into account alternative value bases in the exploration of the relationships between AVs and LVs in joint production economies. In what follows, we investigate the relationships between AVs and "additive commodity $i$ values" in joint production economies using data from the SUTs of the Finnish (for the year 2004) and Japanese (for the year 2000) economies.[16]

The application of the previous analysis to the SUTs of the Finnish (for the year 2004) and Japanese (for the year 2000) economies gives the following results:

(i). The matrices $\mathbf{B}$ and $[\mathbf{V} - \mathbf{D}_{(i)}]$ are non-singular. Consequently, $\mathbf{p}^T$ and $\boldsymbol{\omega}_i^T$ can be uniquely estimated from Eqs. (7.18) and (7.21), respectively.

---

[16]The systems of the Finnish and Japanese economies are also investigated in Chap. 5 of the present book. For the available input–output data as well as the construction of the relevant variables, see the Appendix in that chapter.

(ii). The matrices $[\mathbf{B} - \mathbf{A}]^{-1}$ contain negative elements. Consequently, the systems under consideration are not all-productive and, therefore, they do not have the usual properties of single production systems.

(iii). The system of ALPVs of the Finnish economy has 21 positive and 36 complex conjugate solutions for $r$, and only economically irrelevant solutions for $\mathbf{p}^T$. On the other hand, the system of ALPVs of the Japanese economy has a unique, positive solution for $[r, \mathbf{p}^T]$, and $(1 + r)^{-1}$ is the dominant eigenvalue of the matrix $\mathbf{CB}^{-1}$. Thus, it is found that the actual uniform profit rate of the Japanese economy is almost 39%.

(iv). The vector of ALVs of the Finnish economy contains one negative element, which corresponds to commodity 37 ("Secondary raw materials"). On the other hand, the vector of ALVs of the Japanese economy is positive.

(v). In the case of the Finnish economy, 29 from the 57 estimated vectors of "additive commodity values (ACVs)" are economically irrelevant. More specifically, economically irrelevant are the vectors of ACVs that correspond to the following value bases (by CPA code): 01, 02, 05, 10, 13, 14, 15, 16, 20, 23 $\oplus$ 11, 24, 26, 27, 28, 29, 30, 31, 33, 37, 40, 41, 45, 52, 70, 72, 80, 85, 93, 95. The vectors of ACVs associated with commodities 01, 05, 13, 14, 15, 16, 20, 23, 24, 26, 27, 28, 29, 31, 33, 40, 41, 45, 52, 70, 72, 80, 85, 93 and 95 have one negative element that corresponds to commodity 37. The vectors of ACVs associated with commodities 02, 30, and 37 have one negative element that corresponds to commodities 10, 32, and 14, respectively. Finally, the vector of ACVs associated with commodity 10 has two negative elements that correspond to commodities 23 $\oplus$ 11 and 37. Since we have already estimated that the vector of ALVs is economically irrelevant, it follows that, in the case of the Finnish economy, the exploration of the empirical relationships between AVs and "additive commodity $i$ values" is without economic meaning.

(vi). In the case of the Japanese economy, all the 24 estimated vectors of ACVs are positive. Therefore, in this case, it is economically relevant to explore the empirical relationships between AVs and "commodity $i$ values".

Table 7.5 and Fig. 7.5 report the deviations of AVs from "additive commodity $i$ values" for the Japanese economy. Table 7.5 is constructed with the same logic as the Tables 7.1, 7.2, 7.3, 7.4, 7.5 in Sects. 7.2.2.1 and 7.2.2.2. In Fig. 7.5 we display the ALPV–ACV and MV–ACV deviations. The ALPV (MV)–ACV deviations are displayed in the vertical (horizontal) axis, while the AV–ALV deviations are taken as the origin of the axes. Thus, the points below (above) the horizontal axis indicate ALPV–ACV deviations that are less (greater) than the ALPV–ALV deviation, while the points on the left (right) of the vertical axis indicate MV–ACV deviations that are less (greater) than the MV–ALV deviation.

**Table 7.5** Value deviations: Japanese economy, year 2000

| | $dD^{-1}$ (%) | |
|---|---|---|
| Value base | ALPVs vs. "commodity $i$ values" | MVs vs. "commodity $i$ values" |
| Labour | 16.3 | 44.2 |
| "Agriculture, forestry, and fishing" | 23.8 | 49.4 |
| "Mining" | 27.8 | 56.3 |
| "Food products and beverages" | 20.8 | 46.5 |
| "Textiles" | 21.5 | 51.8 |
| "Pulp, paper, and paper products" | 25.3 | 54.0 |
| "Chemicals" | 20.0 | 54.1 |
| "Petroleum and coal products" | 22.4 | 53.9 |
| "Non-metallic mineral products" | 23.6 | **37.8** |
| "Basic metals" | 31.6 | 50.4 |
| "Fabricated metal products" | 23.5 | **39.3** |
| "Machinery" | 23.5 | 48.9 |
| "Electrical machinery, equipment and supplies" | 23.3 | 49.3 |
| "Transport equipment" | 19.0 | 46.2 |
| "Precision instruments" | 20.3 | 47.3 |
| "Other manufacturing products" | **15.0** | 49.2 |
| "Construction" | 24.5 | **21.0** |
| "Electricity, gas, and water supply" | **13.3** | 51.1 |
| "Wholesale and retail trade" | 18.5 | 45.2 |
| "Finance and insurance" | 18.3 | **36.3** |
| "Real estate" | 19.1 | **22.4** |
| "Transport and communications" | 17.3 | 48.0 |
| "Service activities" | 16.8 | **40.8** |
| "Government services" | 19.3 | **41.7** |
| "Private non-profit services to households" | 18.4 | 44.6 |
| Average value deviations | 20.9 | 45.2 |

From the Table 7.5 and the associated numerical results, we arrive at the following conclusions:

(i). The deviation of the vector of ALPVs (MVs) from the vector of ALVs is almost 16.3% (44.2%).

(ii). The average deviation of ALPVs (MVs) from ACVs is in the area of 20.9% (45.2%).

(iii). The deviation of ALPVs from the vectors of ACVs associated with the commodities "Other manufacturing products" and "Electricity, gas, and water supply" is less than the corresponding ALPV–ALV deviation.

(iv). The deviation of MVs from the vectors of ACVs associated with the commodities "Non-metallic mineral products", "Fabricated metal products", "Construction", "Finance and insurance", "Real estate", "Service activities",

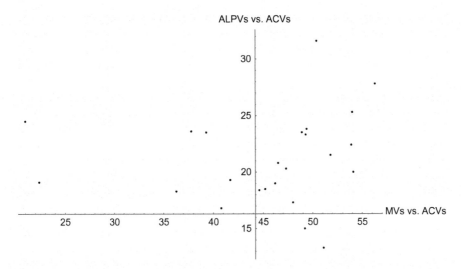

**Fig. 7.5** Value deviations (%): Japanese economy, year 2000

and "Government services" is less than the corresponding MV–ALV deviation.

(v). The smallest (largest) ALPV–"additive commodity $i$ value" deviation is 13.3% (31.6%) and corresponds to the vector of ACVs associated with the commodity "Electricity, gas, and water supply" ("Basic metals").

(vi). The smallest (largest) MV–"additive commodity $i$ value" deviation is 21.0% (56.3%) and corresponds to the vector of ACVs associated with the commodity "Construction" ("Mining").

The next issue that comes up is whether the systems under consideration are "$r_0$– all-engaging" (see Sects. 4.2.1 and 5.3.1). The estimation of the characteristic values and vectors associated with the pairs $\{\mathbf{B}, \mathbf{A}\}$ of the Finnish and Japanese economies gives the following result: the eigen-system of the Finnish economy has 20 positive (and simple) eigenvalues, while that of the Japanese economy has 7 positive (and simple) eigenvalues. However, there are no positive left and right eigenvectors and, therefore, the considered systems are not $r_0$– all-engaging.

## 7.4   Concluding Remarks

The extension of the empirical investigation of the relationships amongst "labour values", long-period values, and market values to the framework of alternative "value bases" pointed out that there are cases in which "commodity values" and "additive commodity values" are better approximations of actual values than "labour values" and "additive labour values", respectively. These findings do not or, more precisely, cannot provide support to an alternative value theory. On the contrary, by taking into account the detection of economically irrelevant long-period values, "additive commodity values" and/or "additive labour values" in the empirically relevant case of joint production, these findings indicate that the claim that actual economies can be coherently analysed in terms of "labour values" cannot be sustained.

Thus, given the analysis developed so far in this book, it should be concluded that the classical–Marxian hypothesis that the main determinant of commodity prices in the real world is the corresponding quantities of labour "embodied" constitutes one of the most controversial issues in economic thought. Although this hypothesis is not completely rejected in the context of extremely simplistic representations of actual economies, it is devoid of economic sense and, in actual fact, not empirically testable in the realistic cases of heterogeneous labour, open economies, and joint production. In particular, any attempt to empirically test this hypothesis is, *at best*, circular, since:

(i). Wage differentials are used to homogenize the direct labour inputs. Hence, the estimated "labour values" depend on market price ratios.

(ii). In open economies, both absolute and relative "labour values" either depend on market price ratios or are indeterminate.

(iii). In joint production economies, the "labour values" are either not necessarily positive or indeterminate. And the conversion of Supply and Use Tables into Symmetric Input–Output Tables rests on the tacit assumption that there is a single production system hidden in the Supply and Use Tables characterizing the real world.

## Appendix: Data Sources and Construction of Variables

The SIOTs and the corresponding levels of sectoral employment of the French and Swedish economies were obtained from the Eurostat website (http://ec.europa.eu/eurostat). The input–output tables describe 59 products, which are classified according to CPA ("Classification of Product by Activity"). The described products and their correspondence to CPA are the following:

1. (CPA: 01). Products of agriculture, hunting, and related services
2. (02). Products of forestry, logging, and related services
3. (05). Fish and other fishing products; services incidental of fishing
4. (10). Coal and lignite; peat
5. (11). Crude petroleum and natural gas; services incidental to oil and gas extraction excluding surveying
6. (12). Uranium and thorium ores
7. (13). Metal ores
8. (14). Other mining and quarrying products
9. (15). Food products and beverages
10. (16). Tobacco products
11. (17). Textiles

12. (18). Wearing apparel; furs
13. (19). Leather and leather products
14. (20). Wood and products of wood and cork (except furniture); articles of straw and plaiting materials
15. (21). Pulp, paper, and paper products
16. (22). Printed matter and recorded media
17. (23). Coke, refined petroleum products, and nuclear fuels
18. (24). Chemicals, chemical products, and man-made fibres
19. (25). Rubber and plastic products
20. (26). Other non-metallic mineral products
21. (27). Basic metals
22. (28). Fabricated metal products, except machinery and equipment
23. (29). Machinery and equipment n.e.c.
24. (30). Office machinery and computers
25. (31). Electrical machinery and apparatus n.e.c.
26. (32). Radio, television, and communication equipment and apparatus
27. (33). Medical, precision and optical instruments, watches and clocks
28. (34). Motor vehicles, trailers, and semi-trailers
29. (35). Other transport equipment
30. (36). Furniture; other manufactured goods n.e.c.
31. (37). Secondary raw materials
32. (40). Electrical energy, gas, steam, and hot water
33. (41). Collected and purified water, distribution services of water
34. (45). Construction work
35. (50). Trade, maintenance and repair services of motor vehicles and motorcycles; retail sale of automotive fuel
36. (51). Wholesale trade and commission trade services, except of motor vehicles and motorcycles
37. (52). Retail trade services, except of motor vehicles and motorcycles; repair services of personal and household goods
38. (55). Hotel and restaurant services
39. (60). Land transport; transport via pipeline services
40. (61). Water transport services
41. (62). Air transport services
42. (63). Supporting and auxiliary transport services; travel agency services
43. (64). Post and telecommunication services
44. (65). Financial intermediation services, except insurance and pension funding services
45. (66). Insurance and pension funding services, except compulsory social security services
46. (67). Services auxiliary to financial intermediation
47. (70). Real estate services
48. (71). Renting services of machinery and equipment without operator and of personal and household goods
49. (72). Computer and related services

50. (73). Research and development services
51. (74). Other business services
52. (75). Public administration and defence services; compulsory social security services
53. (80). Education services
54. (85). Health and social work services
55. (90). Sewage and refuse disposal services, sanitation and similar services
56. (91). Membership organization services n.e.c.
57. (92). Recreational, cultural, and sporting services
58. (93). Other services
59. (95). Private households with employed persons

In the SIOTs of the French economy, all the elements associated with product 37 ("Secondary raw materials") for both years; and product 12 ("Uranium and thorium ores") for the year 2005 equal zero and, therefore, we remove them from our analysis. Thus, in the case of the French economy, we derive SIOTs of dimensions $58 \times 58$ for the year 1995 and $57 \times 57$ for the year 2005. In the SIOTs of the Swedish economy, all the elements associated with product 12 equal zero and, therefore, we remove them from our analysis. Furthermore, Statistics Sweden has aggregated, due to confidentiality reasons, products 14 ("Other mining and quarrying products") and 16 ("Tobacco products") with products 13 ("Metal ores") and 15 ("Food products and beverages"), respectively, while products 51 ("Wholesale trade and commission trade services, except of motor vehicles and motorcycles") and 52 ("Retail trade services, except of motor vehicles and motorcycles; repair services of personal and household goods") are aggregated with product 50 ("Trade, maintenance, and repair services of motor vehicles and motorcycles; retail sale of automotive fuel"). Additionally, for the year 2005, products 32 ("Radio, television, and communication equipment and apparatus") and 74 ("Other business services") are aggregated with products 31 ("Electrical machinery and apparatus n.e.c.") and 73 ("Research and development services"), respectively. Finally, since the labour input that corresponds to the production of product 11 ("Crude petroleum and natural gas; services incidental to oil and gas extraction excluding surveying") equals zero for both of the years, we aggregate product 11 with product 13. Thus, in the case of the Swedish economy, we derive SIOTs of dimensions $53 \times 53$ for the year 1995 and $51 \times 51$ for the year 2005.

The MVs of all products are taken to be equal to 1; that is to say, the physical unit of measurement of each product is that unit which is worth of a monetary unit. Thus, the matrices of input–output coefficients, $\mathbf{A}$, are obtained by dividing element-by-element the inputs in each industry by its gross output (i.e. by its "Output at basic prices").

In accordance with most of the relevant empirical studies, we use wage differentials to homogenize the sectoral employment, i.e. the vector of inputs in direct homogeneous labour, $\mathbf{l}^T \equiv [l_j]$, is determined as follows: $l_j = \left(L_j/x_j\right)\left(w_j^M/w_{min}^M\right)$, where $L_j, x_j, w_j^M$ denote the total employment, gross output, and money wage rate, in terms of MVs, of the $j$ th sector, respectively, and $w_{min}^M$ the minimum sectoral money wage rate in terms of MVs (also see Chap. 5, Appendix). Furthermore, by assuming that workers do not save and that their consumption has the same composition as the vector of the final consumption expenditures of the household sector, $\mathbf{h}$, directly obtained from the input–output tables, the vector of the real wage rate, $\mathbf{b} \equiv [b_i]$, is determined as follows: $\mathbf{b} = \left(w_{min}^M/\mathbf{e}^T\mathbf{h}\right)\mathbf{h}$, where $\mathbf{e}^T \equiv [1, 1, \ldots, 1]$ denotes the row summation vector identified with the vector of MVs. Finally, it must be noted that the available input–output tables do not include inter-industry data on fixed capital stocks and on non-competitive imports. As a result, our investigation is restricted to a closed economy with circulating capital.

# References

Bidard, C., & Ehrbar, H. G. (2007). Relative prices in the classical theory: Facts and figures. *Bulletin of Political Economy, 1*(2), 161–211.

Bródy, A. (1970). *Proportions, prices and planning. A mathematical restatement of the labor theory of value*. Amsterdam: North Holland.

Dmitriev, V. K. (1898). The theory of value of David Ricardo: An attempt at a rigorous analysis. In V. K. Dmitriev ([1904] 1974). *Economic essays on value, competition and utility* (pp. 37–95). Edited with an introduction by D. M. Nuti, London: Cambridge University Press.

Gintis, H., & Bowles, S. (1981). Structure and practice in the labor theory of value. *Review of Radical Political Economics, 12*(4), 1–26.

Manresa, A., Sancho, F., & Vegara, J. M. (1998). Measuring commodities' commodity content. *Economic Systems Research, 10*(4), 357–365.

Mariolis, T. (2000). Positive (non-positive) surplus value with non-positive (positive) profits. *Political Economy. Review of Political Economy and Social Sciences, 7*, 81–126. (in Greek).

Mariolis, T. (2001). On V. K. Dmitriev's contribution to the so-called "transformation problem" and to the profit theory. *Political Economy. Review of Political Economy and Social Sciences, 9*, 45–60.

Mariolis, T. (2003a). Controllability, observability, regularity, and the so-called problem of transforming values into prices of production. *Asian–African Journal of Economics and Econometrics, 3*(2), 113–127.

Mariolis, T. (2003b). On the lack of correspondence between surplus value and profit. In A. Kalafatis, P. Livas, & T. Skountzos (Eds.), *Volume of essays in honor of Professor Apostolos Lazaris* (Vol. 1, pp. 199–218). Piraeus: University of Piraeus.

Mariolis, T. (2010). Norm bounds for a transformed price vector in Sraffian systems. *Applied Mathematical Sciences, 4*(9–12), 551–574.

Mariolis, T., & Rodousaki, E. (2011). Total requirements for gross output and intersectoral linkages: A note on Dmitriev's contribution to the theory of profits. *Contributions to Political Economy, 30*(1), 67–75.

Mariolis, T., & Soklis, G. (2007). On the empirical validity of the labour theory of value. In T. Mariolis (2010) (Ed.), *Essays on the logical history of political economy* (pp. 231–260). Athens: Matura (in Greek).

Mariolis, T., & Soklis, G. (2010). Additive labour values and prices: Evidence from the supply and use tables of the French, German and Greek Economies. *Economic Issues, 15*(2), 87–107.

Mariolis, T., & Tsoulfidis, L. (2016). *Modern classical economics and reality. A spectral analysis of the theory of value and distribution*. Tokyo: Springer.

Milana, C. (1985). Direct and indirect requirements for gross output in input–output analysis. *Metroeconomica, 37*(3), 283–292.

Parys, W. (1982). The deviation of prices from labor values. *The American Economic Review, 72* (5), 1208–1212.

Pasinetti, L. (1973). The notion of vertical integration in economic analysis. *Metroeconomica, 25* (1), 1–29.

Pasinetti, L. (1977). *Lectures on the theory of production*. New York: Columbia University Press.

Reati, A. (1986). La transformation des valeurs en prix non concurrentiels. *Economie Appliquée, 39* (1), 157–179.

Roemer, J. E. (1986). *Value, exploitation and class*. Chur: Harwood Academic Publishers.

Soklis, G. (2006). *Labour values and production prices: Exploration based on the joint production table of the Greek economy for the year 1999*. Master's Thesis, Athens: Department of Public Administration, Panteion University (in Greek).

Soklis, G. (2009). Alternative value bases and prices: Evidence from the input–output tables of the Swedish economy. *Journal of Applied Input–Output Analysis, 15*(1), 11–29.

Soklis, G. (2012). *Labour values, commodity values, prices and income distribution: Exploration based on empirical input–output tables*. Ph.D. Dissertation, Athens: Department of Public Administration, Panteion University (in Greek).

Soklis, G. (2014). Commodities' commodity content and prices: Empirical evidence from the input–output tables of the French economy. *Investigación Económica, 73*(288), 35–57.

Soklis, G. (2015). Labour versus alternative value bases in actual joint production systems. *Bulletin of Political Economy, 9*(1), 1–31.

Sraffa, P. (1960). *Production of commodities by means of commodities. Prelude to a critique of economic theory*. Cambridge: Cambridge University Press.

Szyrmer, J. M. (1986). Measuring connectedness of input–output models: 2. Total flow concept. *Environment and Planning A, 18*(1), 107–121.

Szyrmer, J. M. (1992). Input–output coefficients and multipliers from a total flow perspective. *Environment and Planning A, 24*(7), 921–937.

Szyrmer, J. M., & Walker, R. T. (1983). Interregional total flow: A concept and application to a U.S. input–output model. *Review of Regional Studies, 13*(1), 12–21.

# Chapter 8
# Capital Theory and Matrix Demand Multipliers in Sraffian Frameworks

**Abstract** This chapter provides a detailed exploration of matrix demand multipliers in Sraffian frameworks for both closed and open economies with linear processes of single and joint production. It reveals the characteristic features of these multipliers, and shows that they involve an autonomous demand–transfer payments curve, which turns out to be a useful tool for dealing with multiplier processes in heterogeneous capital worlds. Finally, it focuses on the dependence of long-run matrix demand multipliers on the exchange rate, income distribution and, therefore, changes in relative commodity prices. Thus, this chapter highlights the distinctive contribution of the Sraffian theory to both the political economy and economic policy of effective demand management.

**Keywords** Autonomous demand–transfer payments curve · Effective currency devaluation · Income distribution · Joint production · Matrix demand multipliers

## 8.1 Introduction

It need hardly be argued that the multiplier effects of autonomous demand are one of the most important areas of macroeconomics. For instance, Afanasyev (1983), a Soviet Marxist scholar, remarks:

> Keynes's multiplier theory is an important component of his market theory. [...] The theory of the multiplying process within the capitalist economy originated during the 1929–33 world economic crisis as a means of theoretically substantiating rising state expenditure for mollifying economic crises and unemployment which had assumed menacing proportions at the time. Having initially arisen in the form of the concept of employment multiplier, the theory was supplemented by Keynes with his theory of the multiplier of investment or income. [...] The multiplier theory has been a vital link in the chain of arguments aimed at justifying the need for state intervention in the capitalist economy. (pp. 174–176)

The multiplier concept, at least in its traditional form, was first introduced by Kahn (1931), and then further developed by Keynes (1936). It can also be traced in Kalecki's (1990, 1942) profit theory, although, as Sawyer (2008) argues, it does not

© Springer Nature Singapore Pte Ltd. 2021
T. Mariolis et al., *Spectral Theory of Value and Actual Economies*, Evolutionary
Economics and Social Complexity Science 24,
https://doi.org/10.1007/978-981-33-6260-4_8

occupy a central position in Kalecki's work (also see Łaski and Walther 2013). Furthermore, Screpanti and Zamagni (2005) note that

[s]igns of a rudimentary but deep insight into the multiplier process can be found in Marx. There is an interesting page in chapter 17 of the second volume of the *Theories of Surplus Value*, in which Marx tries to explain how a lack of effective demand in an industry with a high level of employment can be transmitted to the entire economy through a reduction in the production of that industry and the consequent reduction in employment and wages. [...] About thirty years after Marx, there were some shrewd insights, if not something more, in an unpublished work of 1896 by Julius Wulff and in one by Nicolaus A. L. J. Johannsen, who used the *"Multiplizirende Prinzip"*, as he called it, to account for the effects produced by an initial impulse of expenditure on the whole economy. However, the official date of birth of the multiplier is 1931. [...] In 1930 the multiplier principle was used by L. F. Giblin. Then in 1931 it was used by Jens Warming and by Ralph Hawtrey. Finally, the classic work of Richard Ferdinand Kahn, "The Relation of Home Investment to Unemployment", came out in *The Economic Journal* of 1931. Keynes understood immediately that it was an important missing piece in the puzzle he was trying to solve, and in 1936 he assigned it a central place in the *General Theory*. (p. 242)

Finally, approaching the issues from a different perspective, Buchanan et al. (1978) argue that

[i]n numerous newspaper articles, speeches and pamphlets in the 'twenties and early 'thirties, Keynes called for deficit-financed public works expenditures as a cure for unemployment. He brushed off as a "bogy" the possibility that this could, or would, lead to inflation [...] The *General Theory* (1936) attempted to provide a theoretical foundation for such views. But it did not make plain the precise implication of this analysis for economic policy. It contains the odd scornful aside on Gladstonian finance as "penny-wisdom" (p. 362), a cryptic call for "a somewhat comprehensive socialisation of investment" (p. 378), a neo-Mercantilist proposition that real wealth increases/decreases as the supply of gold increases/decreases (the effects of which can then be simulated by public works financed by fiat money creation) (pp. 129–30), and a general indication that aggregate output and employment could, and should, be determined by fiscal and interest-rate policies (p. 378). [...] None of this, however, constituted a very adequate or detailed specification of a Keynesian monetary–fiscal constitution. (pp. 51–52)

In any case, as is *now* known, the multiplier for real-world economies does not constitute a scalar, but a matrix quantity reflecting, in a complex way, the underlying inter-industry socio-technical linkages. More specifically, pouring "some water into the wine of traditional macroeconomics", Kurz (1985) introduced and explored the concept of the matrix multiplier of autonomous demand in Sraffian closed—without state—economy frameworks. Thus, he demonstrated that

there is no such thing as *"the"* multiplier. Rather the multiplier effects depend on the technical conditions of production, income distribution, consumption patterns and the physical composition of investment, as well as on savings ratios and the aggregate volume of investment. [...] [A] larger volume [in price terms] of investment could be associated with smaller levels of total income and employment. (pp. 134–135)

It could, furthermore, be shown that this matrix multiplier includes, as special versions or limiting cases, the usual Keynesian multipliers (Kurz 1985, pp. 126–127), the corresponding multipliers of the traditional input–output analysis, and their Marxian versions.[1]

This chapter (i) identifies the specific features of matrix demand multipliers in Sraffian frameworks and their spectral characteristics; (ii) shows that these multipliers involve an autonomous demand–transfer payments relationship, which exhibits formal similarities with the dual consumption–growth rate and wage–profit rate relationships in steady-state capital and growth theory;[2] and (iii) highlights the distinctive contribution of the Sraffian theory to the economics of effective demand. Section 8.2 constructs and explores matrix demand multipliers for the case of a closed economy of single production, circulating capital and homogeneous labour. Section 8.3 zeroes in on the relationships between autonomous demand and transfer payments. Section 8.4 extends the analysis to more realistic cases, including those of heterogeneous labour, open economy systems, and pure joint production. Section 8.5 deals with an open economy model, with heterogeneous capital and linear processes of both single and joint production, from a long-run perspective, and explores the relationships between the exchange rate, the relative commodity prices, and the volume of total employment. Finally, Sect. 8.6 concludes.

## 8.2 The Matrix Demand Multiplier in the Base Framework

Consider a closed, linear system involving only single products, basic commodities, circulating capital, and homogeneous labour. Furthermore, assume that:

(i). The system is viable, i.e. the Perron–Frobenius (P–F hereafter) eigenvalue of the irreducible $n \times n$ matrix of direct technical coefficients, $\mathbf{A}$, is less than 1.[3]

(ii). There are no capacity or labour limitations to the multiplier process.

(iii). The net product is distributed between profits and wages that are paid at the end of the common production period.

---

[1] Also see Eatwell and Milgate (2011, Chap. 10). For Kaleckian and post-Keynesian explorations of the Kahn–Keynes and Kaldor (1955) multipliers, see Gnos and Rochon (2008). For the multipliers of the traditional input–output analysis, see, e.g. Miller and Blair (2009, Chap. 6), ten Raa (2005, Chap. 3). Finally, for Marxian versions of the aforesaid multipliers, see, e.g. Hartwig (2004), Lange (1970), Trigg and Philp (2008).

[2] For the latter two relationships and the duality between them, also see Sects. 2.3.1 and 2.3.2 of this book.

[3] The transpose of an $n$x1 vector $\boldsymbol{\chi} \equiv [\chi_i]$ is denoted by $\boldsymbol{\chi}^{\mathrm{T}}$, and the diagonal matrix formed from the elements of $\boldsymbol{\chi}$ is denoted by $\hat{\boldsymbol{\chi}}$. Furthermore, $\lambda_{\mathbf{A}1}$ denotes the P–F eigenvalue of a semi-positive $n \times n$ matrix $\mathbf{A} \equiv [a_{ij}]$, and $(\boldsymbol{\chi}_{\mathbf{A}1}, \boldsymbol{\psi}_{\mathbf{A}1}^{\mathrm{T}})$ the corresponding eigenvectors, while $\lambda_{\mathbf{A}k}$, $k = 2, \ldots, n$ and $|\lambda_{\mathbf{A}2}| \geq |\lambda_{\mathbf{A}3}| \geq \ldots \geq |\lambda_{\mathbf{A}n}|$, denote the non-dominant eigenvalues, and $(\boldsymbol{\chi}_{\mathbf{A}k}, \boldsymbol{\psi}_{\mathbf{A}k}^{\mathrm{T}})$ the corresponding eigenvectors. Finally, $\mathbf{e}$ denotes the summation vector, i.e. $\mathbf{e} \equiv [1, 1, \ldots, 1]^{\mathrm{T}}$, and $\mathbf{e}_i$ the $i$th unit vector.

(iv). The price of a commodity obtained as an output at the end of the production period is the same as the price of that commodity used as an input at the beginning of that period ("stationary prices").

(v). The input–output coefficients and the sectoral profit rates are given and constant; hence, relative commodity prices are also given and constant ("fix-price economy").[4]

On the basis of these assumptions, the price side of the system is described by

$$\boldsymbol{\pi}^{T} = w\mathbf{l}^{T} + \boldsymbol{\pi}^{T}\mathbf{A}[\mathbf{I} + \hat{\mathbf{r}}] \tag{8.1}$$

where $\boldsymbol{\pi}^{T}$ $(> \mathbf{0}^{T})$ denotes the $1 \times n$ vector of commodity prices, $w$ $(> 0)$ the money wage rate, $\mathbf{l}^{T}$ $(> \mathbf{0}^{T})$ the $1 \times n$ vector of direct labour coefficients, $\mathbf{I}$ the $1 \times n$ identity matrix, and $\hat{\mathbf{r}}$ $(r_j > 0)$ the $n \times n$ diagonal matrix of the sectoral profit rates.

In accordance with Keynes's (1936) approach, we shall consider the vertically integrated representation of the economy (Pasinetti 1973), and express all value magnitudes in terms of wage-units. Since the economy is assumed to be viable, $[\mathbf{I} - \mathbf{A}]^{-1} > \mathbf{0}$ and, therefore, Eq. (8.1) can be rewritten as

$$\mathbf{p}^{T} = \mathbf{v}^{T} + \mathbf{p}^{T}\mathbf{H} \tag{8.2}$$

where $\mathbf{p}^{T} \equiv w^{-1}\boldsymbol{\pi}^{T}$ denotes the vector of prices in terms of the wage rate or the vector of labour-commanded prices, $\mathbf{v}^{T} \equiv \mathbf{l}^{T}[\mathbf{I} - \mathbf{A}]^{-1}$ $(> \mathbf{0}^{T})$ the vector of vertically integrated labour coefficients, and $\mathbf{H} \equiv \mathbf{A}\hat{\mathbf{r}}[\mathbf{I} - \mathbf{A}]^{-1} (> \mathbf{0})$ may be considered as the $\hat{\mathbf{r}}$-vertically integrated technical coefficients matrix. Since $\mathbf{p}^{T} > \mathbf{0}^{T}$, it follows that $\lambda_{\mathbf{H}1} < 1$.

The quantity side of the system is described by

$$\mathbf{I}\mathbf{x} = \mathbf{A}\mathbf{x} + \mathbf{y}$$

or

$$\mathbf{x} = [\mathbf{I} - \mathbf{A}]^{-1}\mathbf{y} \tag{8.3}$$

and

$$\mathbf{y} = \mathbf{c}_w + \mathbf{c}_p + \mathbf{d} \tag{8.4}$$

where $\mathbf{x}$ denotes the $n \times 1$ vector of activity levels, $\mathbf{I}\mathbf{x}$ $(= \mathbf{x})$ the gross output vector, $\mathbf{y}$ the net output vector, which is conceived of as the vector of effective final demand, $\mathbf{c}_w$ the vector of consumption demand out of wages, $\mathbf{c}_p$ the vector of consumption demand out of profits, and $\mathbf{d}$ $(\geq \mathbf{0})$ the autonomous demand vector (government expenditures and private investment).

---

[4]What follows draws on Mariolis (2008, 2018).

If the semi-positive commodity vectors $\mathbf{f}_w$ and $\mathbf{f}_p$ denote the given and constant consumption patterns associated with the two types of income, $s_w$ ($s_p$) denotes the savings ratio out of wages (out of profits), where $0 < s_q < 1$, $q = w, p$, denotes the direct tax rate on wages (on profits), where $0 < \tau_q < 1$, then the consumption demands amount to

$$\mathbf{c}_w = \left[(1 - s_w)(1 - \tau_w)\left(\mathbf{l}^\mathsf{T}\mathbf{x}\right)\left(\mathbf{p}^\mathsf{T}\mathbf{f}_w\right)^{-1}\right]\mathbf{f}_w$$

or, since $\mathbf{l}^\mathsf{T}\mathbf{x} = \mathbf{v}^\mathsf{T}\mathbf{y}$ (consider Eq. (8.3)),

$$\mathbf{c}_w = \left[(1 - s_w)(1 - \tau_w)\left(\mathbf{v}^\mathsf{T}\mathbf{y}\right)\left(\mathbf{p}^\mathsf{T}\mathbf{f}_w\right)^{-1}\right]\mathbf{f}_w \tag{8.5}$$

and

$$\mathbf{c}_p = \left[\left(1 - s_p\right)\left(1 - \tau_p\right)\left(\mathbf{p}^\mathsf{T}\mathbf{A}\widehat{\mathbf{r}}\mathbf{x}\right)\left(\mathbf{p}^\mathsf{T}\mathbf{f}_p\right)^{-1}\right]\mathbf{f}_p$$

or, since $\mathbf{A}\widehat{\mathbf{r}}\mathbf{x} = \mathbf{H}\mathbf{y}$,

$$\mathbf{c}_p = \left[\left(1 - s_p\right)\left(1 - \tau_p\right)\left(\mathbf{p}^\mathsf{T}\mathbf{H}\mathbf{y}\right)\left(\mathbf{p}^\mathsf{T}\mathbf{f}_p\right)^{-1}\right]\mathbf{f}_p \tag{8.6}$$

where the terms in brackets represent the levels of consumption demands out of wages and profits, respectively.[5]

Substituting Eqs. (8.5) and (8.6) into Eq. (8.4), and setting $\sigma_q \equiv 1 - (1 - s_q)(1 - \tau_q)$, yields

$$\mathbf{y} = \left[(1 - \sigma_w)\left(\mathbf{p}^\mathsf{T}\mathbf{f}_w\right)^{-1}\left(\mathbf{v}^\mathsf{T}\mathbf{y}\right)\right]\mathbf{f}_w + \left[(1 - \sigma_p)\left(\mathbf{p}^\mathsf{T}\mathbf{f}_p\right)^{-1}\left(\mathbf{p}^\mathsf{T}\mathbf{H}\mathbf{y}\right)\right]\mathbf{f}_p + \mathbf{d}$$

or, since $(\mathbf{v}^\mathsf{T}\mathbf{y})\mathbf{f}_w = (\mathbf{f}_w\mathbf{v}^\mathsf{T})\mathbf{y}$ and $(\mathbf{p}^\mathsf{T}\mathbf{H}\mathbf{y})\mathbf{f}_p = (\mathbf{f}_p\mathbf{p}^\mathsf{T}\mathbf{H})\mathbf{y}$,

$$\mathbf{y} = \mathbf{C}\mathbf{y} + \mathbf{d} \tag{8.7}$$

where

$$\mathbf{C} \equiv (1 - \sigma_w)\left(\mathbf{p}^\mathsf{T}\mathbf{f}_w\right)^{-1}\mathbf{f}_w\mathbf{v}^\mathsf{T} + (1 - \sigma_p)\left(\mathbf{p}^\mathsf{T}\mathbf{f}_p\right)^{-1}\mathbf{f}_p\mathbf{p}^\mathsf{T}\mathbf{H} \geq 0$$

or, setting $\mathbf{C}_w \equiv \left(\mathbf{p}^\mathsf{T}\mathbf{f}_w\right)^{-1}\mathbf{f}_w\mathbf{v}^\mathsf{T}$ and $\mathbf{C}_p \equiv \left(\mathbf{p}^\mathsf{T}\mathbf{f}_p\right)^{-1}\mathbf{f}_p\mathbf{p}^\mathsf{T}\mathbf{H}$,

---

[5]Extended modelling could take into consideration debt-financed worker's consumption and the effects of wealth on capitalist's consumption; for one-commodity formulations, see, e.g. Abraham-Frois (1991), Azad (2012).

$$\mathbf{C} = (1 - \sigma_w)\mathbf{C}_w + (1 - \sigma_p)\mathbf{C}_p \tag{8.8}$$

is the "matrix of total consumption demand". The rank of $\mathbf{C}_q$ is equal to 1 and, therefore, $rank[\mathbf{C}] \leq 2$ and $\mathbf{C}$ has at least $n - 2$ zero eigenvalues. Moreover, $\lambda_{C1}$ is a decreasing function of $\sigma_q$, while $\lambda_{C1} < 1$ (see Kurz 1985, pp. 135–136) or, in terms of lower and upper bounds (see Appendix 1 at the end of this chapter),

$$1 - \max\{\sigma_q\} \leq \lambda_{C1} \leq 1 - \min\{\sigma_q\} \tag{8.8a}$$

Hence, Eq. (8.7) has a unique, positive solution for $\mathbf{y}$:

$$\mathbf{y} = \mathbf{M}\mathbf{d} \tag{8.9}$$

where

$$\mathbf{M} \equiv [\mathbf{I} - \mathbf{C}]^{-1} = \sum_{h=0}^{+\infty} \mathbf{C}^h \geq \mathbf{0} \tag{8.9a}$$

is the static matrix multiplier linking autonomous demand to net output. From relations (8.8a) and Eq. (8.9a) it follows that

$$\lambda_{Mi} = (1 - \lambda_{Ci})^{-1}, \quad (\max\{\sigma_q\})^{-1} \leq \lambda_{M1} \leq (\min\{\sigma_q\})^{-1}$$

and it is remarkable that these bounds for $\lambda_{M1}$ correspond to the bounds for the long-run investment multiplier in a one-commodity world that have been determined by Kaldor (1955, pp. 95–97).

Substituting Eq. (8.8) into Eq. (8.9a), and using the Woodbury matrix identity,[6] yields

$$\mathbf{M} = \mathbf{M}_w + \left[1 - (1 - \sigma_p)(\mathbf{p}^T\mathbf{f}_p)^{-1}\mathbf{p}^T\mathbf{H}\mathbf{M}_w\mathbf{f}_p\right]^{-1}(1 - \sigma_p)\mathbf{M}_w\mathbf{C}_p\mathbf{M}_w$$

where

$$\mathbf{M}_w \equiv [\mathbf{I} - (1 - \sigma_w)\mathbf{C}_w]^{-1} = \mathbf{I} + \left[\mathbf{p}^T\mathbf{f}_w - (1 - \sigma_w)\mathbf{v}^T\mathbf{f}_w\right]^{-1}(1 - \sigma_w)\mathbf{f}_w\mathbf{v}^T$$

It then follows that the elements of $\mathbf{M}$ are non-increasing functions of the savings ratios and the tax rates, while the multiplier effects also depend, in a complicated way, on the:

(i) technical conditions of production;
(ii) sectoral profit rates;

---

[6]See Chap. 2, footnote 30.

(iii) consumption patterns; and

(iv) physical composition and aggregate volume of autonomous demand (also see Kurz 1985, pp. 128–133, which follows a different analytical approach).

We now turn to some characteristic special cases:

(i). If there is a uniform, across income types, consumption pattern, i.e. $\mathbf{f}_w = \mathbf{f}_p = \mathbf{f}$, then $\mathbf{C}$ reduces to a rank-one matrix. Equations (8.2), (8.9a) and the Woodbury matrix identity imply that

$$\mathbf{M} = \mathbf{I} + \left[ (\sigma_w \mathbf{v}^{\mathrm{T}} + \sigma_p \mathbf{p}^{\mathrm{T}} \mathbf{H}) \mathbf{f} \right]^{-1} \mathbf{f} \left[ \mathbf{p}^{\mathrm{T}} - (\sigma_w \mathbf{v}^{\mathrm{T}} + \sigma_p \mathbf{p}^{\mathrm{T}} \mathbf{H}) \right]$$

and, therefore,

$\lambda_{\mathrm{M1}} = [\sigma_w + (\sigma_p - \sigma_w)(\mathbf{p}^{\mathrm{T}} \mathbf{f})^{-1} \mathbf{p}^{\mathrm{T}} \mathbf{H} \mathbf{f}]^{-1} > 1$, $\lambda_{\mathrm{Mk}} = 1$, where $(\mathbf{p}^{\mathrm{T}} \mathbf{f})^{-1} \mathbf{p}^{\mathrm{T}} \mathbf{H} \mathbf{f}$ equals the share of profits in the vertically integrated sector producing consumption commodities.[7] The P–F eigenvalue corresponds to Kaldor's (1955) long-run investment multiplier and could be conceived of as *the* system's multiplier. Moreover, the Schur triangularization theorem implies that, in the present case, $\mathbf{M}$ can be transformed, via a semi-positive similarity matrix $\mathbf{\Gamma}$, into

$$\tilde{\mathbf{M}} \equiv \mathbf{\Gamma}^{-1} \mathbf{M} \mathbf{\Gamma} = \begin{bmatrix} \lambda_{\mathrm{M1}} & \tilde{\mathbf{m}}_{12}^{\mathrm{T}} \\ \mathbf{0}_{(n-1) \times 1} & \mathbf{I}_{(n-1) \times (n-1)} \end{bmatrix}$$

where the first column of $\mathbf{\Gamma}$ is $\boldsymbol{\chi}_{\mathrm{M1}}$ (the remaining columns are arbitrary), and $\tilde{\mathbf{m}}_{12}^{\mathrm{T}}$ is a $1 \times (n-1)$ positive vector.[8] That is, the original system is economically equivalent to systems in which *only* one (single) commodity is consumed.

(ii). If $\mathbf{f}_w = \mathbf{f}_p = \mathbf{f}$ and $\sigma_p = \sigma_w = \sigma$, then $\mathbf{M} = \mathbf{I} + (\sigma^{-1} - 1)(\mathbf{p}^{\mathrm{T}} \mathbf{f})^{-1} \mathbf{f} \mathbf{p}^{\mathrm{T}}$, $\lambda_{\mathrm{M1}} = \sigma^{-1}$, which, in a one-commodity world, merge into the textbook equation $\mathbf{M} = \sigma^{-1}$.

Furthermore, from Eqs. (8.3) and (8.9) it follows that

$$L = \mathbf{v}^{\mathrm{T}} \mathbf{M} \mathbf{d} \tag{8.10}$$

where $L \equiv \mathbf{l}^{\mathrm{T}} \mathbf{x}$ denotes the volume of total employment and, therefore, $\mathbf{v}^{\mathrm{T}} \mathbf{M}$ is the vector multiplier linking autonomous demand to total employment (*à la* Kahn 1931) and, at the same time, to aggregate wages; while, as is easily checked, $\mathbf{p}^{\mathrm{T}} \mathbf{H} \mathbf{M}$ is the vector multiplier linking autonomous demand to aggregate profits. Hence, as Kurz (1985) pointed out,

---

[7]In this case, and for $(\sigma_w, \sigma_p) \to (0, 1)$, $\mathbf{M}$ tends to a Marxian multiplier defined by Trigg and Philp (2008).

[8]If, for instance, $\mathbf{\Gamma} = [\boldsymbol{\chi}_{\mathrm{M1}}, \mathbf{e}_2, \ldots, \mathbf{e}_n]$, then $\tilde{\mathbf{m}}_{1212}^{\mathrm{T}} = (\lambda_{\mathrm{M1}} - 1)(\boldsymbol{\psi}_{\mathrm{M1}}^{\mathrm{T}} \boldsymbol{\chi}_{\mathrm{M1}})^{-1}[\psi_{2\mathrm{M1}}, \psi_{3\mathrm{M1}}, \ldots, \psi_{n\mathrm{M1}}]$. Also see Eq. (2.64).

an *increase* in the volume of [autonomous demand] in price terms, or an increase in primary employment [i.e. $\mathbf{v}^T\mathbf{d}$], could be associated with a *decrease* in the volume of total employment (or total net income). [...] [T]he view, occasionally expressed in economic policy discussions, according to which the employment effect of investment (or some other component of effective demand) is the greater, the greater is the *direct* labour intensity in the production of the goods demanded, cannot generally be sustained. It is in fact the vector $\mathbf{v}^T$ and not $\mathbf{l}^T$ that is of interest in this connection. Since relative prices, in general, deviate from [relative vertically integrated labour coefficients, $\mathbf{v}^T$], the employment effect of a given investment in price terms is the greater, the greater is the quantity of labour that is necessary, directly and indirectly, in the production of the investment goods demanded. (pp. 130–131; using our symbols)

We could also consider, for instance, the simplest two-industry system, i.e. reducible and without self-reproducing non-basics (see Sect. 2.3.3), where $\mathbf{f}_w = \mathbf{f}_p = \mathbf{f} = [0, 1]^T$ , and assume that $\hat{\mathbf{r}} = r\mathbf{I}$ (uniform profit rate), $r < a_{11}^{-1} - 1$, and $\mathbf{d} = \mathbf{d}^I \equiv [1, 0]^T$ or, alternatively, $\mathbf{d} = \mathbf{d}^{II} \equiv [0, 1]^T$. From Eq. (8.10) it finally follows that

$$L^1\left(L^{II}\right)^{-1} = \left[l_1(l_2 - \delta)^{-1}\right]\left[l_2 - \left(1 + s_p r\right)\delta\right]\left[l_2 - (1 + r)\delta\right]^{-1}$$

where $\delta \equiv a_{11}l_2 - a_{12}l_1$ , $\delta > 0$ iff the capital-commodity industry is more capital-intensive than the consumption-commodity industry, $l_2 - (1 + r)\delta > 0$, and $l_1(l_2 - \delta)^{-1}$ equals $v_1 v_2^{-1}$ . Hence, it is concluded that: (i) iff $v_1 > (<) v_2$ and $\delta < (>) 0$, then it would be possible that $L^1(L^{II})^{-1} = 1$; (ii) iff $\delta > 0$, then $L^1(L^{II})^{-1}$ is a strictly decreasing (increasing) function of $s_p$ (of $r$); and (iii) $L^1(L^{II})^{-1}$ is a strictly increasing (decreasing) function of both $a_{11}$ and $l_1$ (of both $a_{12}$ and $l_2$).

Without delving into a quantitative analysis, Afanasyev (1983) claims that

the volume of employment is closely dependent on a change in an increment in investment. The employment multiplier theory in a certain degree reflects this objective relationship, but only in its very general form, without account in many cases of the specific nature of the capitalist economy. [...] Yet since the multiplier concept is linked with the effect of inter-sector relations on the size of the market, it provides a far from full and a distorted reflection on the dependence of the capacity of the market on the degree of division of social labour. What it further leaves out of consideration is that the size of employment will depend not only on the volume of investment, but also to a considerable extent on the nature of this investment, on the organic structure of both accumulating and already functioning of capital. With an increase in the amount of functioning capital and a growth in its organic structure there may arise a situation where employment not only does not rise, it will actually fall. Keynes does not investigate this decisive dependence of the volume of employment on the organic structure of capital; he presents it in a very general way, in the form of a brief note: "[I]n the more generalised case it [the multiplier] is also a function of the physical conditions of production in the investment and consumption industries respectively." [Keynes 1936, p. 117, footnote 1]. (pp. 176–177)

It should finally be stressed that any change in relative commodity prices, induced by changes in income distribution, alters the multipliers and, therefore, the total multiplier effects become ambiguous. For instance, differentiation of Eq. (8.10) gives

$$dL = \mathbf{v}^{\mathrm{T}}(d\mathbf{M})\mathbf{d} + \mathbf{v}^{\mathrm{T}}\mathbf{M}(d\mathbf{d})$$

which implies that, in the general case, the direction of change in employment is a priori unknown, even if $d\mathbf{d} \geq \mathbf{0}$. As we will see later in this chapter, this ambiguity is a salient feature of the multiplier process in Sraffian frameworks.

## 8.3 Autonomous Demand–Transfer Payments Relationships

Let $\bar{\mathbf{d}}$ be the vector representing the given and constant physical composition of autonomous demand, and let E $(> 0)$ denote the level of autonomous demand. Thus, $\mathbf{d} = E\bar{\mathbf{d}}$ and Eqs. (8.7) and (8.10) are written as

$$\mathbf{y} = \mathbf{C}\mathbf{y} + E\bar{\mathbf{d}} \tag{8.11}$$

and

$$L = E\mathbf{v}^{\mathrm{T}}\mathbf{M}\bar{\mathbf{d}} \tag{8.12}$$

respectively. For any given and constant value of $L$, differentiation of Eq. (8.12) gives

$$0 = (dE)\mathbf{v}^{\mathrm{T}}\mathbf{M}\bar{\mathbf{d}} + E\mathbf{v}^{\mathrm{T}}(d\mathbf{M})\bar{\mathbf{d}}$$

or, invoking Eqs. (8.8) and (8.9a),

$$0 = \left\{ (dE)\mathbf{v}^{\mathrm{T}} + E\mathbf{v}^{\mathrm{T}}\mathbf{M}\left[ (1 - s_w)(d\tilde{\tau}_w)\mathbf{C}_w + \left(1 - s_p\right)\left(d\tilde{\tau}_p\right)\mathbf{C}_p \right] \right\}\mathbf{M}\bar{\mathbf{d}}$$

where $\tilde{\tau}_q \equiv -\tau_q$ can be conceived of as transfer payments rates. It then follows that Eq. (8.12) defines a "$E - \tilde{\tau}_w - \tilde{\tau}_p$ iso-employment frontier", in which each variable is inversely related to each of the others.

Now we (i) consider the net output and level of autonomous demand per unit of labour employed, i.e. $\mathbf{u} \equiv L^{-1}\mathbf{y}$, which implies that $\mathbf{v}^{\mathrm{T}}\mathbf{u} = 1$, and $\varepsilon \equiv L^{-1}E$, respectively; and (ii) assume that the "relative tax factor", $\rho \equiv (1 - \tau_w)^{-1}(1 - \tau_p)$, is given, i.e. $d\tau_p = \rho d\tau_w$.[9] Thus, Eq. (8.11) is written as

$$\mathbf{u} = (1 + \tilde{\tau})\mathbf{G}\mathbf{u} + \varepsilon\bar{\mathbf{d}} \tag{8.13}$$

---

[9]You and Dutt (1996, pp. 339–340) define this case as "a 'fair' tax hike or cut".

where $\mathbf{G} \equiv (1 - \tau)^{-1}\mathbf{C}$, $\widetilde{\tau} = -\tau$, $\tau = \tau_w$ or $\tau_p$ iff $\rho < 1$ or $\rho > 1$, respectively, and $\lambda_{\mathbf{G}1} < 1$ since $(1 - \tau)^{-1}(1 - \sigma_w)$ and $(1 - \tau)^{-1}(1 - \sigma_p)$ are both less than unity (consider relations (8.8a)).

If $\varepsilon = 0$, then Eq. (8.13) implies that $(1 + \widetilde{\tau})^{-1}$ is the P–F eigenvalue of $\mathbf{G}$, or $\widetilde{\tau} = \mathrm{T} \equiv \lambda_{\mathbf{G}1}^{-1} - 1$, and $\mathbf{u}$ is the corresponding right eigenvector. If $-1 < \widetilde{\tau} < \mathrm{T}$, then

$$\mathbf{u} = \varepsilon[\mathbf{I} - (1 + \widetilde{\tau})\mathbf{G}]^{-1}\overline{\mathbf{d}} = \varepsilon \sum_{h=0}^{+\infty} [(1 + \widetilde{\tau})\mathbf{G}]^h\overline{\mathbf{d}} \tag{8.14}$$

and, pre-multiplying by $\mathbf{v}^{\mathrm{T}}$ and solving for $\varepsilon$,

$$\varepsilon = \left(\mathbf{v}^{\mathrm{T}}[\mathbf{I} - (1 + \widetilde{\tau})\mathbf{G}]^{-1}\overline{\mathbf{d}}\right)^{-1}$$

$$= \det[\mathbf{I} - (1 + \widetilde{\tau})\mathbf{G}]\left(\mathbf{v}^{\mathrm{T}}\mathrm{adj}[\mathbf{I} - (1 + \widetilde{\tau})\mathbf{G}]\overline{\mathbf{d}}\right)^{-1} \tag{8.15}$$

where both the determinant and adjoint of $[\mathbf{I} - (1 + \widetilde{\tau})\mathbf{G}]$ are positive. From Eq. (8.15) it follows that $\varepsilon(-1) = \left(\mathbf{v}^{\mathrm{T}}\overline{\mathbf{d}}\right)^{-1}$, $\varepsilon(0) = \left(\mathbf{v}^{\mathrm{T}}[\mathbf{I} - \mathbf{G}]^{-1}\overline{\mathbf{d}}\right)^{-1}$, where $\varepsilon(-1) > \varepsilon(0)$, $d\varepsilon/d\widetilde{\tau} < 0$ and $\varepsilon$ tends to zero as $\widetilde{\tau}$ tends to T. Equation (8.15) defines a trade-off between $\varepsilon$ and $\widetilde{\tau}$, indicating that (i) the higher the level of autonomous demand is, the lower the transfer payments rates must be in order to maintain a given level of employment; and (ii) if $\varepsilon > \varepsilon(0)$, then transfer payments must be converted into taxes. This trade-off is formally similar to the trade-off between the consumption (wage) and growth (profit) rates in the Sraffian single production framework (see Appendix 2 at the end of this chapter).

A possible way to close the system is to impose the governmental budget constraint.[10] Assume that (i) the level of the government budget deficit per unit of labour employed, $\overline{b}$ ($> 0$), is exogenously fixed and (ii) autonomous demand consists only of government expenditures (namely, for the sake of brevity, there is no private investment). In this case, total private savings equal the government budget deficit and, therefore, we can write

$$s_w(1 - \tau_w)\mathbf{v}^{\mathrm{T}}\mathbf{u}(\widetilde{\tau}) + s_p(1 - \tau_p)\mathbf{p}^{\mathrm{T}}\mathbf{H}\mathbf{u}(\widetilde{\tau}) = \overline{b}$$

where $\mathbf{u}(\widetilde{\tau})$ is defined by substituting Eq. (8.15) into Eq. (8.14). By invoking Eq. (8.2) and $\mathbf{v}^{\mathrm{T}}\mathbf{u}(\widetilde{\tau}) = 1$, the definitions of $\rho$, $\widetilde{\tau}$, and assuming, for instance, that $\rho < 1$, we get that

$$(1 + \widetilde{\tau})\left[s_w + \rho s_p\left(\mathbf{p}^{\mathrm{T}}\mathbf{u}(\widetilde{\tau}) - 1\right)\right] = \overline{b} \tag{8.16}$$

or, if $\widetilde{\tau} > -1$,

---

[10]For traditional macroeconomic treatments, see Benavie (1973), Perkins (1980, pp. 34–35).

$$s_w + \rho s_p \left( \mathbf{p}^\mathrm{T} \mathbf{u}(\widetilde{\tau}) - 1 \right) = \overline{b}(1 + \widetilde{\tau})^{-1} \tag{8.16a}$$

where $\mathbf{p}^\mathrm{T} \mathbf{u}(\widetilde{\tau})$ is a ratio of polynomials of the first degree and, therefore, a strictly monotonic function of $\widetilde{\tau}$, while its denominator equals that of the expression giving the "$\varepsilon - \widetilde{\tau}$ curve". Moreover, for $-1 \leq \widetilde{\tau} \leq \mathrm{T}$, it necessarily holds that denominator is positive and $\mathbf{p}^\mathrm{T} \mathbf{u}(\widetilde{\tau}) > 1$. Hence, the left-hand side of Eq. (8.16a) is positive, strictly monotonic and bounded, while its right-hand side is a strictly decreasing function of $\widetilde{\tau}$. Finally, from Eqs. (8.13) and (8.16) we get that:

(i) $\widetilde{\tau} = -1$ for $\overline{b} = 0$;

(ii) $\widetilde{\tau} = 0$ for $\overline{b} = \overline{b}^* \equiv \left[ s_w + \rho s_p (\mathbf{p}^\mathrm{T} \mathbf{u}(0) - 1) \right]$; and

(iii) $\widetilde{\tau} = \mathrm{T}$ for $\overline{b} = \overline{b}^{**} \equiv \lambda_{\mathrm{G1}}^{-1} \left[ s_w + \rho s_p (\mathbf{p}^\mathrm{T} \mathbf{u}(\mathrm{T}) - 1) \right]$, where $\mathbf{u}(0) = \varepsilon(0)[\mathbf{I} - \mathbf{G}]^{-1}\overline{\mathbf{d}}$ and $\mathbf{u}(\mathrm{T}) = (\mathbf{v}^\mathrm{T} \boldsymbol{\chi}_{\mathrm{G1}})^{-1} \boldsymbol{\chi}_{\mathrm{G1}}$. Consequently, for $0 < \overline{b} \leq \overline{b}^{**}$, $\widetilde{\tau}$ $(-1 < \widetilde{\tau} \leq \mathrm{T})$ is determined by Eq. (8.16a) (for a numerical example, see Appendix 3 at the end of this chapter).

## 8.4 Some Extensions

The analysis can be extended to the cases of (i) indirect taxes and changes in income distribution; (ii) changes in the technical production conditions; (iii) heterogeneous labour and open economy systems; and (iv) pure joint production. It is reasonable to deal with these cases in turn.

### 8.4.1 Indirect Taxes and Changes in Income Distribution

In the case of indirect taxes levied on profits, the price system becomes $\boldsymbol{\pi}^\mathrm{T} = w\mathbf{l}^\mathrm{T} + \boldsymbol{\pi}^\mathrm{T} \mathbf{A}[\mathbf{I} + \widehat{\mathbf{r}}[\mathbf{I} + \widehat{\mathbf{z}}]]$ or $\mathbf{p}^\mathrm{T} = \mathbf{v}^\mathrm{T} + \mathbf{p}^\mathrm{T} \mathbf{H}_{\mathbf{z}}$, where $\widehat{\mathbf{z}} \equiv [z_i]$ ($> 0$) denotes the diagonal matrix of indirect tax rates, and $\mathbf{H}_{\mathbf{z}} \equiv \mathbf{H} + \mathbf{A}\widehat{\mathbf{r}}\widehat{\mathbf{z}}[\mathbf{I} - \mathbf{A}]^{-1}$. It then follows directly that an increase in any indirect tax or profit rate raises the elements $\mathbf{p}^\mathrm{T}$ and, therefore, reduces the wage shares $\theta_q \equiv (\mathbf{p}^\mathrm{T} \mathbf{f}_q)^{-1} \mathbf{v}^\mathrm{T} \mathbf{f}_q$ (for other types of indirect taxation, which lead to the same result, see Erreygers 1989; Metcalfe and Steedman 1971). Thus, if $\rho < 1$ and $(1 - s_p)\rho > (1 - s_w)$, then the maximum feasible value, T, of the transfer payments rate increases (consider Appendix 1 at the end of this chapter) and this, in its turn, implies that, at least for "high" values of $\widetilde{\tau}$, the $\varepsilon - \widetilde{\tau}$ curve (defined by Eq. (8.15)) shifts to the "right". That is to say, for these values of $\widetilde{\tau}$, the multiplier effects become weaker.

### 8.4.2   Changes in the Technical Production Conditions

Assume that two production techniques, $[\mathbf{A}, \mathbf{l}]$ and $[\mathbf{A}^*, \mathbf{l}^*]$, are cost-minimizing at the exogenously given values of the profit rates, $r_j$. Then $\mathbf{p}^{*T} = \mathbf{l}^{*T} + \mathbf{p}^{*T}\mathbf{A}^*[\mathbf{I} + \widehat{\mathbf{r}}]$ and $\mathbf{p}^* = \mathbf{p}$ (see, e.g. Kurz and Salvadori 1995, Chap. 5), which imply that

$$\Delta\mathbf{l}^T + \mathbf{p}^{*T}(\Delta\mathbf{A})[\mathbf{I} + \widehat{\mathbf{r}}] = \mathbf{0}^T, \Delta\mathbf{l}^T \equiv \mathbf{l}^{*T} - \mathbf{l}^T, \Delta\mathbf{A} \equiv \mathbf{A}^* - \mathbf{A} \qquad (8.17)$$

or, equivalently,

$$\Delta\mathbf{v}^T + \mathbf{p}^{*T}(\Delta\mathbf{H}) = \mathbf{0}^T, \Delta\mathbf{v}^T \equiv \mathbf{v}^{*T} - \mathbf{v}^T, \Delta\mathbf{H} \equiv \mathbf{H}^* - \mathbf{H} \qquad (8.18)$$

Now, consider a "capital-saving (capital-using)" form of technical change characterized by $\Delta\mathbf{A} \leq (\geq) \mathbf{0}$. From condition (8.17), the definition equation of $\mathbf{H}$ and condition (8.18) it necessarily follows, in turn, that $\Delta\mathbf{l}^T \geq (\leq) \mathbf{0}^T,$[11] $\Delta\mathbf{H} \leq (\geq) \mathbf{0}$, $\Delta\mathbf{v}^T > (<) \mathbf{0}^T$ and, therefore, the wage shares $\theta_q$ rise (fall). Thus, if $\rho < 1$ and $(1 - s_p)\rho > (1 - s_w)$, then both $\varepsilon(-1)$ and T decrease (increase) and this, in its turn, implies that, at least for both low and high values of $\widetilde{\tau}$, the $\varepsilon - \widetilde{\tau}$ curve shifts to the left (right). It seems, however, that, in the general case, the direction of the effects of mixed forms of technical change is *a priori* ambiguous.

### 8.4.3   Heterogeneous Labour and Open Economy Systems

In the case of $m$ ($\geq 2$) types of heterogeneous labour, the price system becomes $\boldsymbol{\pi}^T = \mathbf{w}^T\mathbf{L} + \boldsymbol{\pi}^T\mathbf{A}[\mathbf{I} + \widehat{\mathbf{r}}]$  or  $\boldsymbol{\pi}^T = \mathbf{w}^T\mathbf{V} + \boldsymbol{\pi}^T\mathbf{H}$, where $\mathbf{w}^T \equiv [w_\mu]$ ($w_\mu > 0$, $\mu = 1, 2, \ldots, m$) denotes the $1 \times m$ vector of money wage rates, $\mathbf{L}$ ($\geq 0$) the $m \times n$ matrix of direct labour coefficients, and $\mathbf{V} = \mathbf{L}[\mathbf{I} - \mathbf{A}]^{-1}$ the $m \times n$ matrix of vertically integrated labour coefficients. As is easily checked, the matrix of total consumption becomes (consider Eq. (8.8))

$$\mathbf{C} = \sum_{\mu=1}^{m} \left(1 - \sigma_{w\mu}\right)\left(\boldsymbol{\pi}^T\mathbf{f}_{w\mu}\right)^{-1} w_\mu\left(\mathbf{e}_\mu^T\mathbf{V}\right)\mathbf{f}_{w\mu} + \left(1 - \sigma_p\right)\left(\boldsymbol{\pi}^T\mathbf{f}_p\right)^{-1}\mathbf{f}_p\boldsymbol{\pi}^T\mathbf{H}$$

where $\mathbf{f}_{w\mu}$ denotes the consumption pattern associated with $w_\mu$. Therefore, the main difference involved here is that $rank[\mathbf{C}] \leq \min\{m + 1, n\}$, whereas relations (8.8a) continue to be valid with $q = w\mu, p$ (consider the vector $\mathbf{e}^T\widehat{\boldsymbol{\pi}}\mathbf{C}\widehat{\boldsymbol{\pi}}^{-1}$ as in Appendix 1

---

[11]It may be noted that $\Delta\mathbf{l}^T \geq (\leq) \mathbf{0}^T$ does not necessarily imply that $\Delta\mathbf{A} \leq (\geq) \mathbf{0}$.

at the end of this chapter).[12] Finally, in an $n$−country world economy, where country $j$ produces only commodity $j$, and labour is nationally homogeneous, the matrix of total consumption becomes

$$\mathbf{C} = \sum_{j=1}^{n} \left(1 - \sigma_{wj}\right)\left(\boldsymbol{\pi}^{\mathrm{T}}\mathbf{f}_{wj}\right)^{-1} w_j\left(\mathbf{e}_j^{\mathrm{T}}\mathbf{V}\right)\mathbf{f}_{wj} + \left(1 - \sigma_{pj}\right)\left(\boldsymbol{\pi}^{\mathrm{T}}\mathbf{f}_{pj}\right)^{-1}\mathbf{f}_{pj}\boldsymbol{\pi}^{\mathrm{T}}\mathbf{H}_j$$

where $\mathbf{V}$ is defined as above, but $\mathbf{L}$ now denotes the $n \times n$ diagonal matrix of direct labour coefficients, $\mathbf{H}_j \equiv \mathbf{A}\widehat{\mathbf{r}}_j[\mathbf{I} - \mathbf{A}]^{-1}$, $\widehat{\mathbf{r}}_j$ the diagonal matrix formed from the profit rate, $r_j$, in country $j$, and $\mathbf{f}_{qj}$ the consumption patterns in country $j$. This world economy model provides the basis for a more general treatment of the issues posed by the traditional open economy multiplier analysis.[13]

### 8.4.4 Pure Joint Production

In the case where the economy uses $n$ processes of pure joint production, the price system becomes

$$\boldsymbol{\pi}^{\mathrm{T}}\mathbf{B} = w\mathbf{l}^{\mathrm{T}} + \boldsymbol{\pi}^{\mathrm{T}}\mathbf{A}[\mathbf{I} + \widehat{\mathbf{r}}]$$

or, provided that $[\mathbf{B} - \mathbf{A}]$ is non-singular,

$$\mathbf{p}^{\mathrm{T}} = \mathbf{v}_{\mathbf{B}}^{\mathrm{T}} + \mathbf{p}^{\mathrm{T}}\mathbf{H}_{\mathbf{B}}$$

where $\mathbf{B}\ (\geq \mathbf{0})$ denotes the $n \times n$ output coefficients matrix, $\mathbf{v}_{\mathbf{B}}^{\mathrm{T}} \equiv \mathbf{l}^{\mathrm{T}}[\mathbf{B} - \mathbf{A}]^{-1}$ the vector of "additive labour values" (see Sects. 4.2.1 and 6.2.2.3), and $\mathbf{H}_{\mathbf{B}} \equiv \mathbf{A}\widehat{\mathbf{r}}[\mathbf{B} - \mathbf{A}]^{-1}$. The main difference involved here is that $\mathbf{v}_{\mathbf{B}}$ and/or $\mathbf{H}_{\mathbf{B}}$ and, therefore, the matrix of total consumption can contain negative elements (although $\mathbf{p}^{\mathrm{T}} > \mathbf{0}^{\mathrm{T}}$). In that case, there is not necessarily a trade-off between either consumption (wage) and growth (profit) rates or autonomous demand and transfer payments.[14]

---

[12]For aggregate post-Keynesian–Kaleckian models that include different types of labour and, thus, examine the effects of increasing employment and wage flexibility on growth and income distribution, see Dutt et al. (2015).

[13]For a compact survey of the traditional analysis, see Gandolfo (2002, Chap. 8). For a post-Keynesian–Sraffian one-country model, see Appendix 4 at the end of the present chapter. That model is convenient for empirical work (see Chap. 9 of this book).

[14]For the former relationships, see Sect. 4.2. For a numerical example of the latter relationship, see Appendix 5 at the end of this chapter, which builds on the example provided by Steedman (1977, Chaps. 11 to 13).

## 8.5    Effective Currency Devaluation and Multiplier Effects in the Long-Run

### 8.5.1    The Single Production Case

In a pioneering paper, Metcalfe and Steedman (1981) modelled the relationships between the exchange rate, the long-run relative prices, the volume of total employment, the national income, and the trade balance, in the context of single-product economies with *produced* means of production. The main attributes of their model may be summarized as follows:

> [W]e assume fixed proportions in consumption and fixed proportions in production. (p. 3) [...] All the [domestically produced] commodities are dual purpose commodities in that they may be consumed or utilized as means of production. [...] In addition, the economy may obtain dual purpose imported commodities from other countries; there are no *competitive* imports. We shall assume that the foreign currency prices of the imported commodities, whether they be consumed and/or used as material inputs, are independent of the volume of the economy's imports but that it must lower the foreign currency prices of exports in order to increase their volume. Thus the terms of trade are not given for this economy. (pp. 4–5) [...] We should emphasize that the multiplier relations which we derive are long-period multiplier relations in which stocks of inputs are fully adjusted to production requirements. (p. 12) [...] We consider an economy following a balanced, steady path of expansion at rate $g$. The time horizon for our analysis will be such that growth at this given rate remains consistent with our assumptions that the economy is small on the import side but large on the export side. The rate $g$ is treated as a constant. The aggregate value of investment at this growth rate then depends on the sectoral composition of domestic output and on the structure of relative prices. The value of investment in terms of numeraire is thus not a constant but is determined endogenously within our production framework. Our multipliers are therefore equilibrium "super-multipliers". (pp. 12–13)

Thus, they proved the following *ceteris paribus* statements:

S1. If the profit rate (the real wage) is held constant, *effective* currency devaluation, i.e. an increase in the money exchange rate relative to the money wage, must reduce the real wage (the profit rate):

> [A]n effective [currency] devaluation [...] necessarily reduces *at least* one of [real wage and profit rates]. The precise outcome will depend on the proximate forces which determine the distribution of income. In a "classical" world, with the real wage as a datum, the full incidence of an effective [currency] devaluation must fall on the rate of profits. [...] [This] conclusion [...] may have particularly important implications for the growth rate and long-run competitive strength of an economy, to the extent that these factors are influenced by the rate of return on invested capital. In a "post-Keynesian" world, where firms can maintain a given rate of profits, the full incidence of an effective devaluation must fall on the real wage rate. Of course, if firms can maintain the profits rate *and* workers are unwilling to concede any reduction in real wages then, in this impasse, an *effective* change in the exchange rate is logically impossible (for given [foreign import prices and technical conditions]). The only consequence of a money devaluation, in this situation, will be an equal proportionate increase in the money wage and in all money prices of domestically produced commodities. [...] The literature which explicitly links devaluation to variations in the real *wage* clearly allows for only one of several possibilities. (pp. 7–8)

S2. As with any kind of technical regress, an increase in any foreign import price shifts the "real wage rate, real exchange rate, profit rate frontier" in towards the origin. At least one of real wage, profit and real exchange rates must therefore fall.

S3. An effective devaluation improves the competitiveness of domestic output, since it cheapens all domestic products relative to all imported commodities.

S4. For *given* prices and distribution, extra exports produce extra employment in the aggregate.

S5. An effective devaluation changes the *relative* prices of domestically produced commodities and, therefore, alters the multiplier link between exports and gross output. Given that these changes are complicated, it follows that the effects on employment, national income, and trade balance of a devaluation-induced increase in exports (see S3) are ambiguous:

> For given prices and distribution, our analysis of the export–employment multiplier is an entirely traditional (but disaggregated) application of the theory of effective demand. Extra exports produce extra employment in the aggregate. However, it is equally clear that any change in prices or distribution will, in general, *change* the linkage between employment and the export vector. [. . .] [A]n effective devaluation operates by changing relative prices and the distribution of income, and these considerations immediately suggest that the conventional "fix-price", foreign trade multiplier cannot be readily integrated with the traditional elasticity analysis to deduce the effect[s] of an exchange rate change upon employment [, net outputs, aggregate wages and profits, and trade balance]. [. . .] In brief, there is no possibility of analysing the effect of devaluation in terms of "the" multiplier effects of the increased exports. "The" multiplier itself responds to the devaluation—and in an ambiguous way. [. . .] We can thus offer support both (neither) to those who suggest a positive, effective demand based, relation and (nor) to those who suggest an inverse, supply and demand based, relation between employment levels and real wage rates. (pp. 15–16)[15]

In what follows, we will show that in "square" systems of pure joint production, S1 to S4 cease to be of general validity and, therefore, there is a further source of ambiguity in the consequences of an effective devaluation (or of a change in any foreign import price).

## 8.5.2   The Joint Production Case

### 8.5.2.1   The Model

Our analysis is wholly based on the model formulated by Metcalfe and Steedman (1981). However, we assume that the open economy under consideration produces $n$ commodities and has $n$ (for simplicity's sake) linear processes of joint production. Hence, the following equations and inequalities need to be satisfied:

---

[15]For a relevant, but less general, approach, see Krugman and Taylor (1978).

$$\boldsymbol{\pi}^{T}\mathbf{B} \leq w\mathbf{l}^{T} + (1+r)\big(\boldsymbol{\pi}^{T}\mathbf{A} + e\boldsymbol{\pi}^{*T}\mathbf{A}^{*}\big) \qquad (8.19)$$

$$\boldsymbol{\pi}^{T}\mathbf{B}\mathbf{x} = w\mathbf{l}^{T}\mathbf{x} + (1+r)\big(\boldsymbol{\pi}^{T}\mathbf{A} + e\boldsymbol{\pi}^{*T}\mathbf{A}^{*}\big)\mathbf{x} \qquad (8.20)$$

$$\boldsymbol{\pi}^{T}\mathbf{f}_{1} + e\boldsymbol{\pi}^{*T}\mathbf{f}_{2} = 1 \qquad (8.21)$$

$$\mathbf{B}\mathbf{x} \geq cL\mathbf{f}_{1} + (1+g)\mathbf{A}\mathbf{x} + \mathbf{EX} \qquad (8.22)$$

$$\boldsymbol{\pi}^{T}\mathbf{B}\mathbf{x} = cL\boldsymbol{\pi}^{T}\mathbf{f}_{1} + (1+g)\boldsymbol{\pi}^{T}\mathbf{A}\mathbf{x} + \boldsymbol{\pi}^{T}\mathbf{EX} \qquad (8.23)$$

$$\boldsymbol{\pi}^{T} \geq \mathbf{0}^{T}, \mathbf{x} \geq \mathbf{0}, \mathbf{EX} \geq \mathbf{0}, [w, r, e, c] \geq \mathbf{0}^{T} \qquad (8.24)$$

where $\boldsymbol{\pi}^{T}$ now denotes the price vector of domestically produced commodities, $\mathbf{B}$ the output coefficient matrix, $w$ the uniform money wage rate, $r$ the uniform profit rate, $\mathbf{l}^{T}$, $\mathbf{A}$ the direct labour coefficients vector and input coefficients matrix for domestically produced commodities, respectively, $e$ the nominal exchange rate, $\boldsymbol{\pi}^{*T}$ the given vector of "gold" import prices, $\mathbf{A}^{*}$ the input coefficients matrix of the non-competing imports (for a pure consumption import the corresponding row of $\mathbf{A}^{*}$ is null), $\mathbf{x}$ the vector of activity levels, $\mathbf{f} \equiv \big[\mathbf{f}_{1}^{T}, \mathbf{f}_{2}^{T}\big]^{T}$ a given commodity vector representing the uniform, across income types, consumption pattern ($\mathbf{f}_{1}$ corresponds to domestically produced commodities, whereas $\mathbf{f}_{2}$ corresponds to imported commodities), $g$ ($\geq 0$) the given uniform growth rate, $c$ the level of consumption per unit of labour employed, $L$ ($\equiv \mathbf{l}^{T}\mathbf{x}$) the volume of total employment, and $\mathbf{EX}$ the vector of commodities exported.

In fact, we treat imported means of production as a primary input (also see Metcalfe and Steedman 1981, p. 11, footnote 15) and then we apply the relevant analysis of joint production systems (see Sect. 4.2 of this book). Thus, we could consider the economy as closed, and $\mathbf{EX}$ as a final, additional demand for consumer goods (also see Malinvaud 1959; Morishima 1960). Furthermore, it is assumed that the composition of $\mathbf{EX}$ may depend upon the relative prices of exports, while the volume of exports is a decreasing function of their foreign currency prices. However, it is not necessary to introduce the demand functions for exports explicitly. Relation (8.19) implies that no process is able to pay extra profits. Equation (8.20) implies, also because of relations (8.24), that when a process is not able to pay the ruling profit rate, it is not operated. Relation (8.22) implies that the total demand is satisfied. Equation (8.23), also because of relations (8.24), is the "rule of free goods", i.e. overproduced commodities fetch a zero price. Finally, Eq. (8.21) fixes the *numéraire*; hence, $w$ and $e$ also symbolize the level of the real wage rate and the real exchange rate (i.e. the number of bundles of the *numéraire* which exchange for a unit of gold), respectively.

### 8.5.2.2  Joint Versus Single Production

In order to be in a position to compare this system directly with single-product systems, we presuppose that: (i) the matrix $[\mathbf{B} - (1+g)\mathbf{A}]$ is invertible; and (ii) there exist economically relevant intervals of $r$ and $(w, e)$, in which $\boldsymbol{\pi}^T > \mathbf{0}^T$ and $\mathbf{x} > \mathbf{0}$. In these intervals, for $[w, e] > \mathbf{0}^T$ and iff the matrix $[\mathbf{B} - (1 + r)\mathbf{A}]$ is invertible, relations (8.19) and (8.22) hold with equality. Thus, we may write (also see Metcalfe and Steedman 1981, pp. 4–5 and 13–14)

$$\boldsymbol{\pi}^T = w\boldsymbol{\beta}_I^T(r) + e\boldsymbol{\beta}_{II}^T(r) \tag{8.25}$$

$$w\left[\boldsymbol{\beta}_I^T(r)\mathbf{f}_1\right] + e\left[\boldsymbol{\beta}_{II}^T(r)\mathbf{f}_1 + \boldsymbol{\pi}^{*T}\mathbf{f}_2\right] = 1 \tag{8.26}$$

$$\mathbf{Bx} = (1 - s)\left[wL + r(\boldsymbol{\pi}^T\mathbf{A} + e\boldsymbol{\pi}^{*T}\mathbf{A}^*)\mathbf{x}\right]\mathbf{f}_1 + (1 + g)\mathbf{Ax} + \mathbf{EX}$$

or

$$\mathbf{Bx} = \left[(1 - s)\boldsymbol{\beta}_{III}^T\mathbf{x}\right]\mathbf{f}_1 + (1 + g)\mathbf{Ax} + \mathbf{EX}$$

or, given that $(\boldsymbol{\beta}_{III}^T\mathbf{x})\mathbf{f}_1 = \mathbf{f}_1(\boldsymbol{\beta}_{III}^T\mathbf{x}) = \mathbf{f}_1\boldsymbol{\beta}_{III}^T\mathbf{x}$,

$$[\mathbf{I} - \mathbf{Z}]\boldsymbol{\Delta}^{-1}\mathbf{x} = \mathbf{EX} \tag{8.27}$$

where

$$\boldsymbol{\beta}_I^T(r) \equiv \mathbf{1}^T[\mathbf{B} - (1 + r)\mathbf{A}]^{-1}$$

$$\boldsymbol{\beta}_{II}^T(r) \equiv (1 + r)\boldsymbol{\pi}^{*T}\mathbf{A}^*[\mathbf{B} - (1 + r)\mathbf{A}]^{-1}$$

$$\mathbf{Z} \equiv \mathbf{Z}(s, r, w, e, g) \equiv (1 - s)\mathbf{f}_1\boldsymbol{\beta}_{III}^T\boldsymbol{\Delta} \tag{8.27a}$$

$$\boldsymbol{\beta}_{III}^T = \boldsymbol{\beta}_{III}^T(r, w, e) \equiv w\boldsymbol{\beta}_{IV}^T(r) + e\boldsymbol{\beta}_V^T(r)$$

$$\boldsymbol{\beta}_{IV}^T(r) = \mathbf{1}^T + r\boldsymbol{\beta}_I^T(r)\mathbf{A}$$

$$\boldsymbol{\beta}_V^T(r) \equiv r(\boldsymbol{\beta}_{II}^T(r)\mathbf{A} + \boldsymbol{\pi}^{*T}\mathbf{A}^*)$$

$$\boldsymbol{\Delta} \equiv \boldsymbol{\Delta}(g) \equiv [\mathbf{B} - (1 + g)\mathbf{A}]^{-1}$$

$s$ denotes the given fraction of income saved (for brevity's sake, we assume that $0 < s < 1$), and $\boldsymbol{\beta}_{III}$ is the vector of "values added" per unit activity level. The gold prices of domestically produced commodities, $e^{-1}\boldsymbol{\pi}^T$, are determined by Eq. (8.25). Equation (8.26) defines a "real wage rate, real exchange rate, profit rate frontier" for this open economy, and Eq. (8.27) defines a relation between $\mathbf{EX}$ and $\mathbf{x}$.

As is well known, *single* production models have the following key properties:

(i). Each element in $\boldsymbol{\beta}_I(r)$ and $\boldsymbol{\beta}_{II}(r)$ is positive and increases with $r$, tending to infinity as $r$ approaches its maximum feasible value, $r = R$.

(ii). For $r$ (and $g$) $< R$, the matrix $\boldsymbol{\Theta} \equiv [\mathbf{I} - \mathbf{Z}]$ in Eq. (8.27), where $\mathbf{B} = \mathbf{I}$, is invertible and its inverse is (semi-)positive (see Sect. 8.2). That is,

$$\mathbf{x} = \Delta\boldsymbol{\Theta}^{-1}\mathbf{E}\mathbf{X}$$

or

$$\mathbf{x} = \mathbf{M}^{\mathbf{x}}\mathbf{E}\mathbf{X}, \mathbf{M}^{\mathbf{x}} \equiv \Delta\boldsymbol{\Theta}^{-1} \qquad (8.28)$$

and

$$L = [\mathbf{m}^L]^{\mathrm{T}}\mathbf{E}\mathbf{X}, \quad [\mathbf{m}^L]^{\mathrm{T}} \equiv \mathbf{1}^{\mathrm{T}}\mathbf{M}^{\mathbf{x}} \qquad (8.29)$$

where $\mathbf{M}^{\mathbf{x}}$ is a (semi-)positive matrix of "super-multipliers" linking exports to gross output, and $\mathbf{m}^L$ is a vector of super-multipliers linking exports to total employment.[16]

By contrast, in the *joint* production case none of the said properties is given a priori:

(i). Setting aside the trivial case where $[\mathbf{B} - \mathbf{A}]^{-1} \geq \mathbf{0}$ (see Chaps. 5 and 7), each element in $\boldsymbol{\beta}_{\mathrm{I}}(r)$ and $\boldsymbol{\beta}_{\mathrm{II}}(r)$ is not necessarily a positive increasing function of $r$. This entails that statements S1 to S3 cease to be of general validity, and that the validity of S1–S2 may depend on the consumption pattern, $\mathbf{f}$.

(ii). Given that the determinant of $\boldsymbol{\Theta}$ equals $1 - (1 - s)\boldsymbol{\beta}_{\mathrm{III}}^{\mathrm{T}}\Delta\mathbf{f}_1$,[17] it follows that $\boldsymbol{\Theta}$ can be non-invertible. In that case:

(a) post-multiplying Eq. (8.27a) by $\mathbf{f}_1$ gives $\mathbf{Z}\mathbf{f}_1 = \mathbf{f}_1$, i.e. $\mathbf{f}_1$ is an eigenvector of $\mathbf{Z}$ associated with an eigenvalue that equals 1;

(b) pre-multiplying Eq. (8.27) by $\boldsymbol{\beta}_{\mathrm{III}}^{\mathrm{T}}\Delta$ gives[18]

$$\boldsymbol{\beta}_{\mathrm{III}}^{\mathrm{T}}\Delta\mathbf{E}\mathbf{X} = 0 \qquad (8.30)$$

i.e. the value added by the "sub-system" (Sraffa 1960, Appendix A) producing the vector

$$\begin{bmatrix} [\mathbf{B} - \mathbf{A}]\Delta\mathbf{E}\mathbf{X} \\ -\mathbf{A}^*\Delta\mathbf{E}\mathbf{X} \end{bmatrix}$$

equals zero;[19] and, consequently,

---

[16]Using the Woodbury matrix identity, Eq. (8.28) can be rewritten as

$$\mathbf{x} = \Delta\Big[\mathbf{I} + \big[1 - (1 - s)\boldsymbol{\beta}_{\mathrm{III}}^{\mathrm{T}}\Delta\mathbf{f}_1\big]^{-1}\big[(1 - s)\mathbf{f}_1\boldsymbol{\beta}_{\mathrm{III}}^{\mathrm{T}}\Delta\big]\Big]\mathbf{E}\mathbf{X}$$

(compare with Eqs. (11), (12) and (13) in Metcalfe and Steedman 1981, p. 14).

[17]See footnote 16 of this chapter.

[18]If $\boldsymbol{\Theta}$ is noninvertible (invertible) and Eq. (8.30) does not hold (holds), then Eq. (8.27) is inconsistent (then $\mathbf{x}$ has at least one negative element). Hence there is a contradiction.

[19]Let *TB* be the trade balance measured in *numéraire*. Then $TB = S - I$, where $S$ ($I$) denotes the aggregate net savings (net investment), and Eq. (8.30) imply that

(c) $\mathbf{x}$ is not uniquely determined. Hence, the vectors of super-multipliers linking exports to aggregate consumption, total employment, national income, and trade balance (see Metcalfe and Steedman 1981, pp. 14–18) are not uniquely defined. It goes without saying that the system can be analysed in terms of relative supply and demand curves for domestically produced commodities. Thus, the existence of non-unique solutions for $\mathbf{x}$ means that the said relative demand curve is not uniquely determined. Furthermore, it may be noted that Eq. (8.27) can be rewritten as

$$\mathbf{x} = \mathbf{N}\mathbf{x} + \boldsymbol{\kappa} \tag{8.27b}$$

where $\mathbf{N} \equiv \boldsymbol{\Delta}\mathbf{Z}\boldsymbol{\Delta}^{-1}$ and $\boldsymbol{\kappa} \equiv \boldsymbol{\Delta}\mathbf{E}\mathbf{X}$. The general solution of Eq. (8.27b) is

$$\mathbf{x} = \boldsymbol{\Xi}^{-}\boldsymbol{\kappa} + [\mathbf{I} - \boldsymbol{\Xi}^{-}\boldsymbol{\Xi}]\boldsymbol{\psi}$$

where $\boldsymbol{\Xi} \equiv \mathbf{I} - \mathbf{N}$, $\boldsymbol{\Xi}^{-}$ is a (1)-inverse of $\boldsymbol{\Xi}$, i.e. $\boldsymbol{\Xi}\boldsymbol{\Xi}^{-}\boldsymbol{\Xi} \equiv \boldsymbol{\Xi}$, and $\boldsymbol{\psi}$ is an arbitrary $n$–vector (see, e.g. Barnett 1990, pp. 260–273). Iff $\mathbf{Z}$ is semi-convergent, i.e. iff the limit

$$\lim_{h \to +\infty} \mathbf{Z}^{h} = \lim_{h \to +\infty} \boldsymbol{\Delta}^{-1}\mathbf{N}^{h}\boldsymbol{\Delta}$$

exists, then Eq. (8.27b) can be "expanded" as

$$\lim_{h \to +\infty} \left[ \left[ \mathbf{I} + \mathbf{N} + \mathbf{N}^{2} + \ldots + \mathbf{N}^{h-1} \right]\boldsymbol{\kappa} + \mathbf{N}^{h}\boldsymbol{\psi} \right] = \mathbf{x}^{*}$$

where

$$\mathbf{x}^{*} \equiv \boldsymbol{\Xi}^{D}\boldsymbol{\kappa} + \left[ \mathbf{I} - \boldsymbol{\Xi}^{D}\boldsymbol{\Xi} \right]\boldsymbol{\psi}$$

is a solution to Eq. (8.27b), and $\boldsymbol{\Xi}^{D}$ is the Drazin inverse of $\boldsymbol{\Xi}$ (see Meyer and Plemmons 1977). The determinant of $\mathbf{Z}$ always equals zero. Thus, when $n = 2$ and $\boldsymbol{\Theta}$ is non-invertible, $\mathbf{Z}$ is idempotent and, therefore, semi-convergent.

---

$$TB = scL\boldsymbol{\beta}_{\mathrm{III}}^{\mathrm{T}}\boldsymbol{\Delta}\mathbf{f}_{1} - g\left( \boldsymbol{\pi}^{\mathrm{T}}\mathbf{A} + e\boldsymbol{\pi}^{*\mathrm{T}}\mathbf{A}^{*} \right)\mathbf{x}$$

Thus, when $g = 0$, we obtain

$$TB = scL\boldsymbol{\beta}_{\mathrm{III}}^{\mathrm{T}}[\mathbf{B} - \mathbf{A}]^{-1}\mathbf{f}_{1} \quad (>0)$$

or, recalling that in this case the value of commodities exported, $\boldsymbol{\pi}^{\mathrm{T}}\mathbf{E}\mathbf{X}$, equals $e\boldsymbol{\pi}^{*\mathrm{T}}\mathbf{A}^{*}[\mathbf{B} - \mathbf{A}]^{-1}\mathbf{E}\mathbf{X}$, and the vector of commodities imported equals $\mathbf{A}^{*}\mathbf{x} + cLf_{2}$,

$$TB = -ecL\boldsymbol{\pi}^{*\mathrm{T}}\left[ \mathbf{A}^{*}[\mathbf{B} - \mathbf{A}]^{-1}\mathbf{f}_{1} + \mathbf{f}_{2} \right]$$

(iii). The vector of super-multipliers $\mathbf{m}^L$ (see Eq. (8.29)) can have negative elements. Hence S4 ceases to be of general validity.

(iv). Finally, consider a square system of joint production by means of unassisted labour paid at the beginning of the production period ($\mathbf{A} = \mathbf{0}, \mathbf{A}^* = \mathbf{0}, \boldsymbol{\pi}^T > \mathbf{0}^T$, $\mathbf{x} > \mathbf{0}$). Then,

$$\boldsymbol{\beta}_I^T(r) = (1 + r)\mathbf{l}^T\mathbf{B}^{-1}$$

$$\boldsymbol{\beta}_{II}(r) = \boldsymbol{\beta}_V(r) = \mathbf{0}$$

$$\boldsymbol{\beta}_{IV}^T(r) = (1 + r)\mathbf{l}^T$$

$$cL = (1 - s)(1 + r)wL$$

the quantity side of the economy is described by

$$\mathbf{Bx} = cL\mathbf{f}_1 + wL\mathbf{f}_1 g + \mathbf{EX}$$

and Eq. (8.27) takes the form

$$[\mathbf{I} - \mathbf{Z}']\mathbf{Bx} = \mathbf{EX}$$

where

$$\mathbf{Z}' \equiv [(1 - s)(1 + r) + g]w\mathbf{f}_1\mathbf{l}^T\mathbf{B}^{-1}$$

Hence, the determinant of $\boldsymbol{\Theta}' \equiv [\mathbf{I} - \mathbf{Z}']$ equals $(\boldsymbol{\pi}^T\mathbf{EX})(\boldsymbol{\pi}^T\mathbf{Bx})^{-1}$, $[\boldsymbol{\Theta}']^{-1} > \mathbf{0}$, and each element in $[\mathbf{m}^L]^T = \mathbf{l}^T\mathbf{B}^{-1}[\boldsymbol{\Theta}']^{-1}$ is positive. Thus, it can be stated that iff joint production *co-exists* with produced means of production, then S1 to S4 cease to be of general validity.

Since in the real-world joint production constitutes the rule, these findings seem to be of some importance. In any case, however, they tend to *reinforce* S5 or, equivalently, the central message of Metcalfe and Steedman (1981), that is:

> Any change in the effective exchange rate means a change in relative prices and in distribution, so that the macroeconomic effects of such a change cannot be discussed independently of the microeconomic determinants of relative prices and the relationship between prices, distribution and effective demand. (p. 18)

### 8.5.2.3   Numerical Examples

The following two numerical examples illustrate the results:[20]

---

[20]These examples have been built by modifying Examples 4.1 and 4.2 (Sect. 4.2.1).

## Example 8.1

Consider the following economy:

$$\mathbf{B} = \begin{bmatrix} 13.05 & 12.95 \\ 2.95 & 4.05 \end{bmatrix}, \quad \mathbf{A} = \begin{bmatrix} 12 & 12 \\ 2 & 3 \end{bmatrix}, \quad \mathbf{A}^* = [0.5, 1],$$

$$\mathbf{l}^T = [1, 1], \quad \mathbf{f}_1 = [1, 1]^T, \quad f_2 = 0$$

It is obtained that $[w, e] > \mathbf{0}^T$ and $w\boldsymbol{\beta}_I(r) + e\boldsymbol{\beta}_{II}(r) > \mathbf{0}$ (see Eq. (8.25)) iff $0 \le r < r^* \equiv 0.1$ and $v^* < v$, where $v \equiv we^{-1}$ and

$$v^* \equiv [\pi^*(1+r)(0.5r - 0.425)](r - 0.1)^{-1} \tag{8.31}$$

Assuming that (i) $0 \le r < r^*$ and $v^* < v$ hold; and (ii) the values of $s$, $g$ and the pattern of exports imply that *both* processes operate, it follows that the equation giving the $w - e - r$ frontier" (see Eq. (8.26)) is

$$w(0.2 - r) + e\pi^*(1+r)(0.15 - 5.5r) = 12r^2 - 2.45r + 0.2$$

or

$$w\Phi_2(r) + ef\Phi_1(r) = 1 \tag{8.32}$$

where the function $\Phi_1(r)$ is strictly decreasing for $0 \le r < r^*$, and positive (negative) for $0 \le r < r_1$ (for $r_1 < r < r^*$), the function $\Phi_2(r)$ is positive for $0 \le r < r^*$, and strictly increasing (decreasing) for $0 \le r < r_2$ (for $r_2 < r < r^*$), $r_1 \equiv 3/110 \cong 0.027$ and $r_2 \equiv 0.2 - (\sqrt{57}/60) \cong 0.074$.

Consider first that $r$ is treated as a datum. For $0 \le r < r_1$, $w$ and $e$ are inversely related, while an increase in $\pi^*$, given $e$ (given $w$), is associated with a reduction in $w$ (in $e$). At $r = r_1$, the $w = w(e)$ curve is horizontal and insensitive to $\pi^*$. Finally, for $r_1 < r < r^*$, $w$ and $e$ are directly related, while an increase in $\pi^*$, given $e$ (given $w$), is associated with an increase (a reduction) in $w$ (in $e$). Consequently, S1–S2 are valid for $0 \le r < r_1$.[21]

---

[21]If $\mathbf{f}_1 = [1, 0]^T$, then the equation giving the $w - e - r$ frontier is

$$w(0.1 - r) + e\pi^*(0.5r - 0.425) = 12r^2 - 2.45r + 0.2$$

or

$$w\Phi_4(r) + ef\Phi_3(r) = 1$$

where $\Phi_3(r)$ is negative and strictly decreasing for $0 \le r < r^*$, and $\Phi_4(r)$ is positive for $0 \le r < r^*$, and strictly increasing (decreasing) for

Now consider that $w$ is treated as a datum. Let a dot indicate the first derivative with respect to $r$. Thus, Eqs. (8.31) and (8.32) imply that

$$\left[v(\pi^*)^{-1}\dot{\Phi}_2(r) + \dot{\Phi}_1(r)\right]dr + \left[e^{-1}\Phi_1(r)\right]de = 0$$

and

$$\left[v^*(\pi^*)^{-1}\dot{\Phi}_2(r) + \dot{\Phi}_1(r)\right] \geq (<0) \quad \text{for } r \leq (>)r_3 \tag{8.32a}$$

$$\left[v(\pi^*)^{-1}\dot{\Phi}_2(r) + \dot{\Phi}_1(r)\right] \geq 0 \quad \text{or} \quad <0 \quad \text{for } r_3 < r < r_2 \tag{8.32b}$$

$$\left[v(\pi^*)^{-1}\dot{\Phi}_2(r) + \dot{\Phi}_1(r)\right] < 0 \quad \text{for } r_2 \leq r \tag{8.32c}$$

where $r_1 < r_3 (\cong 0.041) < r_2$. Hence, for $0 \leq r < r_1$, S1–S2 are valid. At $r = r_1$, $r$ is insensitive to $e$ and to $\pi^*$. For $r_1 < r \leq r_3$, $r$ and $e$ are directly related (see relation (8.32a)), while an increase in $\pi^*$, given $e$ (given $r$), is associated with an increase (a reduction) in $r$ (in $e$). For $r_3 < r < r_2$, the response of $r$ to a change in $e$ (or, given $e$, to a change in $\pi^*$) depends on the initial value of $v$ (see relation (8.32b)), while an increase in $\pi^*$, given $r$, is associated with a reduction in $e$. Finally, for $r_2 \leq r < r^*$, S1–S2 are valid (see relation (8.32c)).

Furthermore, for $0 \leq r < r^*$, $\boldsymbol{\beta}_1(r)$ is positive[22] and has a non-monotonic element. Hence, if $r$ (if $w$) is fixed, an effective devaluation improves (does not necessarily improve) competitiveness (for instance, consider the behaviour of the gold price of commodity 1 for $r_2 \leq r$).

Consequently, the validity of S1 to S3 depends on the values of the variables of the income distribution, and may depend on whether it is $r$ or $w$ that is given exogenously. Moreover, the validity of S1–S2 depends on $\mathbf{f}$.

Now assume that $\pi^* = 1$, $r = 10g = 0.099$ ($> r_2$), and $v = 1250/3$ ($> v^* \cong 412.7$). If $s > s_1 \cong 0.01996$ and $EX_1(EX_2)^{-1} = 1$, where $EX_i$ is the $i$th element of $\mathbf{EX}$, then both processes operate, $\mathbf{M}^{\mathbf{x}}$ ($\equiv \mathbf{B\Delta\Theta}^{-1}$) has two negative elements (for $s < s_2 \cong 0.08574$) or a negative element (for $s > s_2$), and $\mathbf{m}^L$ has a negative element (for $s < s_3 \cong 0.09057$) or it is positive (for $s > s_3$). Iff $EX_1(EX_2)^{-1} = 56299/2000$, then Eq. (8.30) holds. Thus, at $s = s_1$, $\boldsymbol{\Theta}$ is noninvertible, and $\mathbf{x}$ is not uniquely determined. Consequently, the validity of S4 depends on both the value of $s$ and the pattern of exports.

---

$$0 \leq r < 0.1 - 0.025\sqrt{10} \cong 0.021 \quad (\text{for } 0.1 - 0.025\sqrt{10} < r < r^*)$$

Consequently, for $0 \leq r < r^*$, $w$ and $e$ directly related, while an increase in $\pi^*$, given $e$ (given $w$), is associated with an increase (a reduction) in $w$ (in $e$).

[22]The opposite case appears in Example 8.2.

***Example 8.2***

Consider the following economy:

$$\mathbf{B} = \begin{bmatrix} 5 & 8 \\ 8 & 3 \end{bmatrix}, \quad \mathbf{A} = \begin{bmatrix} 1 & 3 \\ 3 & 0 \end{bmatrix}, \quad \mathbf{A}^* = [0, 5, 1], \quad \mathbf{l}^\mathrm{T} = [1, 1]$$

Let $\beta_{\mathrm{I}i}(r)$ be the $i$th element $\boldsymbol{\beta}_{\mathrm{I}}(r)$. For $0.5 \le r \le 17/30$ and $\eta^* < v^{-1}$, where

$$\eta^* \equiv (1 - 2r)[\pi^*(1 + r)(2.3r - 1.5)]^{-1}$$

we obtain $v\boldsymbol{\beta}_{\mathrm{I}}(r) + \boldsymbol{\beta}_{\mathrm{II}}(r) > \mathbf{0}$ and $\beta_{\mathrm{I}2}(r) \le 0$. For $17/30 < r < r_1 \equiv \left(9 - \sqrt{29}\right)/6$ and $\eta^* < v^{-1} < \eta^{**}$, where

$$\eta^{**} \equiv (2 - 3r)[\pi^*(1 + r)(3r - 1.7)]^{-1}$$

we obtain $v\boldsymbol{\beta}_{\mathrm{I}}(r) + \boldsymbol{\beta}_{\mathrm{II}}(r) > \mathbf{0}$ and $\beta_{\mathrm{I}2}(r) < 0$. For $r_1 < r < 15/23$ (At $r = 15/23$) and $\eta^{**} < v^{-1} < \eta^*$ (and for $\eta^{**} < v^{-1}$), we obtain $v\boldsymbol{\beta}_{\mathrm{I}}(r) + \boldsymbol{\beta}_{\mathrm{II}}(r) > \mathbf{0}$ and $\beta_{\mathrm{I}1}(r) < 0$. Finally, for $15/23 < r \le 2/3$ and $\eta^{**} < v^{-1}$, we obtain $v\boldsymbol{\beta}_{\mathrm{I}}(r) + \boldsymbol{\beta}_{\mathrm{II}}(r) > \mathbf{0}$ and $\beta_{\mathrm{I}1}(r) \le 0$. Consequently, at a given $r$ such that $0.5 \le r \le 2/3$ and[23] $r \ne r_1$ (and given that the system can be square with $[w, e] > \mathbf{0}^\mathrm{T}$ and $\boldsymbol{\pi}^\mathrm{T} > \mathbf{0}^\mathrm{T}$), S3 is not valid.

## 8.6   Concluding Remarks

This chapter revealed the characteristic features of matrix demand multipliers in Sraffian frameworks. It has also been detected that the matrix demand multiplier in a single production, circulating capital and homogeneous labour framework involves an autonomous demand–transfer payments curve, which exhibits formal similarities with the trade-off between consumption (wage) and growth (profit) rates. This curve constitutes a useful tool for dealing with multiplier processes in heterogeneous capital worlds, and has also been determined for cases of indirect taxes, heterogeneous labour, open economy systems, pure joint production, and changes in income distribution and technical production conditions. It has furthermore been emphasized that, in the joint production case and depending on the values of the relative tax factor and savings ratios, there is not necessarily a trade-off between the level of autonomous demand and the rate of transfer payments. Finally, it has been pointed out that the effects on employment, national income, and trade balance of a currency

---

[23] At $r = r_1$ the determinant of $[\mathbf{B} - (1 + r)\mathbf{A}]$ equals zero and, therefore, the system may be square iff $v^{-1}$ equals $\eta^*$ $(= \eta^{**})$. In that case, however, non-unique solutions arise. Finally, with regard to S1–S2, note that, for $0.5 \le r < 17/30$ and for $15/23 < r \le 2/3$, the element $\beta_{\mathrm{II}1}(r)$ (element $\beta_{\mathrm{II}2}(r)$) is positive (is positive) and decreases (increases) with $r$.

devaluation-induced increase in exports are ambiguous, while in the case of joint production of commodities by means of commodities, there is a further source of ambiguity:

(i). Effective currency devaluation has ambiguous long-run effects on both the income distribution and the competitiveness of domestic output.

(ii). The matrix of super-multipliers linking exports to gross output is not always uniquely defined.

(iii). The volume of exports and the volume of total employment may be inversely related, even if prices and income distribution do not change.

As it will be seen in the next chapter of this book, since the multiplier effects of autonomous demand are a central focus of the macroeconomic analysis of actual economies and since in the post-2008 world there are intense, policy-oriented debates on the "size of the fiscal multiplier", these Sraffian findings are also of interest for both structural and policy studies.

## Appendix 1: On the Eigenvalues of the Matrix of Total Consumption and a Dynamic Multiplier Process

Let $\mathbf{C}^*$ denote the matrix $\hat{\mathbf{p}}\mathbf{C}\hat{\mathbf{p}}^{-1}$, which is similar to $\mathbf{C}$. From Eq. (8.8) it follows that

$$\mathbf{e}^{\mathrm{T}}\mathbf{C}^* = (1 - \sigma_w)\mathbf{v}^{\mathrm{T}}\hat{\mathbf{p}}^{-1} + (1 - \sigma_p)\mathbf{p}^{\mathrm{T}}\mathbf{H}\hat{\mathbf{p}}^{-1}$$

Thus, applying the Frobenius bounds (see, e.g. Meyer 2001, p. 668) we get

$$\min\left\{ \left[(1 - \sigma_w)v_j + (1 - \sigma_p)\mathbf{p}^{\mathrm{T}}\mathbf{He}_j\right]p_j^{-1} \right\} \leq \lambda_{\mathrm{C}1}$$
$$\leq \max\left\{ \left[(1 - \sigma_w)v_j + (1 - \sigma_p)\mathbf{p}^{\mathrm{T}}\mathbf{He}_j\right]p_j^{-1} \right\}$$

or, since Eq. (8.2) implies that $(v_j + \mathbf{p}^{\mathrm{T}}\mathbf{He}_j)p_j^{-1} = 1$,

$$1 - \max\{\sigma_q\} \leq \lambda_{\mathrm{C}1} \leq 1 - \min\{\sigma_q\} \qquad (8.33)$$

As Kurz (1985, pp. 135–136) showed, the non-zero eigenvalues of $\mathbf{C}$ are the roots of the quadratic equation: $\lambda^2 - \beta\lambda + \gamma = 0$, where

$$\beta \equiv (1 - \sigma_w)\theta_w + (1 - \sigma_p)(1 - \theta_p) = \lambda_{\mathrm{C}1} + \lambda_{\mathrm{C}2} \qquad (8.34)$$
$$\gamma \equiv (1 - \sigma_w)(1 - \sigma_p)(\theta_w - \theta_p) = \lambda_{\mathrm{C}1}\lambda_{\mathrm{C}2} \qquad (8.35)$$

and $\theta_q \equiv (\mathbf{p}^T \mathbf{f}_q)^{-1} \mathbf{v}^T \mathbf{f}_q < 1$ equals the share of wages in the vertically integrated sector producing consumption out of wages or profits, respectively. As is easily checked, Eqs. (8.34) and (8.35) imply that:

(i) iff $\theta_w > (<) \theta_p$, then $\lambda_{C2} > (<) 0$;

(ii) if $\sigma_q = \sigma$, then $\lambda_{C1} = 1 - \sigma$ and $\lambda_{C2} = (1 - \sigma)(\theta_w - \theta_p)$;

(iii) if $\lambda_{C2} = 1 - \sigma_q$, then $\sigma_q = \sigma$ and $\lambda_{C1} = (1 - \sigma)(\theta_w - \theta_p)$, i.e. $\lambda_{C1} < \lambda_{C2}$, which is a contradiction; hence, $\lambda_{C2} \neq 1 - \sigma_q$;

(iv) iff $\theta_q = \theta$, then $\lambda_{C1} = 1 - \sigma_p + (\sigma_p - \sigma_w)\theta$ and $\lambda_{C2} = 0$;

(v) $(\lambda_{C1}, \lambda_{C2}) \to (1 - \min \{\sigma_q\}, 1 - \max \{\sigma_q\})$ as $(\theta_w, \theta_p) \to (1, 0)$; and

(vi) $(\lambda_{C1}, \lambda_{C2}) \to (\lambda^*, -\lambda^*)$, where $\lambda^* \equiv \sqrt{(1 - \sigma_w)(1 - \sigma_p)}$, as $(\theta_w, \theta_p) \to (0, 1)$.

Differentiating Eqs. (8.34) and (8.35) with respect to $\theta_q$, and solving for the first derivatives of the eigenvalues gives:

$$\partial \lambda_{C1} / \partial \theta_w = (1 - \sigma_w)(1 - \sigma_p - \lambda_{C1})(\lambda_{C2} - \lambda_{C1})^{-1}$$

$$\partial \lambda_{C1} / \partial \theta_p = -(1 - \sigma_p)(1 - \sigma_w - \lambda_{C1})(\lambda_{C2} - \lambda_{C1})^{-1}$$

$$\partial \lambda_{C2} / \partial \theta_w = -(1 - \sigma_w)(1 - \sigma_p - \lambda_{C2})(\lambda_{C2} - \lambda_{C1})^{-1}$$

$$\partial \lambda_{C2} / \partial \theta_p = (1 - \sigma_p)(1 - \sigma_w - \lambda_{C2})(\lambda_{C2} - \lambda_{C1})^{-1}$$

From these equations and relations (8.33) and $\lambda_{C2} \neq 1 - \sigma_q$ it follows that:

(i) if $\sigma_q > (<) \sigma_w$, then $\lambda_{C1}$ is an increasing (a decreasing) function of $\theta_w$ and $\theta_p$; and

(ii) $\partial \lambda_{C2} / \partial \theta_w |_{\theta_w = \theta_p} > 0$ and $\partial \lambda_{C2} / \partial \theta_p |_{\theta_p = \theta_w} < 0$ (since $\theta_w = \theta_p$ implies that $\lambda_{C2} = 0$) and, therefore, $\lambda_{C2}$ is an increasing (a decreasing) function of $\theta_w$ (of $\theta_p$).

Now consider the special case where $\mathbf{v}^T$ is the P–F eigenvector of $\mathbf{H}$ (or, equivalently, $\mathbf{l}^T$ is the P–F eigenvector of $[\mathbf{I} - \mathbf{A}]^{-1} \mathbf{A}\hat{\mathbf{r}}$, which is similar to matrix $\mathbf{H}$). Equation (8.2) implies that $\mathbf{p}^T = \mathbf{v}^T [\mathbf{I} - \mathbf{H}]^{-1}$. Hence, in this case,

$$\mathbf{p}^T \mathbf{H} = (1 - \lambda_{H1})^{-1} \lambda_{H1} \mathbf{v}^T, \qquad \theta_w = \theta_p = 1 - \lambda_{H1}$$

and, therefore, $\mathbf{C}$ is a rank-one matrix (see Eq. (8.8)), $\lambda_{Ck} = 0$, $\mathbf{v}^T$ is the P–F eigenvector of $\mathbf{C}$, the columns of $\mathbf{C}^*$ are all equal to each other, and

$$\lambda_{C1} = (1 - \sigma_w)(1 - \lambda_{H1}) + (1 - \sigma_p)\lambda_{H1}$$

Finally, it is added that, since $\lambda_{C1} < 1$, the dynamic multiplier process defined by

$$\mathbf{y}_t = \mathbf{C}\mathbf{y}_{t-1} + \Delta \mathbf{d}, \qquad t = 1, 2, \ldots$$

where $\Delta \mathbf{d}$ denotes the change in autonomous demand (see, e.g. Chipman 1950), is stable. The number $- \log \lambda_{C1}$ provides a measure for the "convergence rate" (see, e.g. Berman and Plemmons 1994, Chap. 7) of $\mathbf{y}_t$ to $\mathbf{M}(\Delta \mathbf{d})$, and the smallest damping ratio, $|\lambda_{C2}|^{-1}\lambda_{C1}$, can be considered as a lower measure of the intrinsic resilience of $\mathbf{y}_t$ to disturbance (see Sect. 3.2.2). The above eigenvalue derivatives imply that if, for instance, $\sigma_p > \sigma_w$ and $\theta_w > (<) \theta_p$, then the smallest damping ratio increases with increasing $\theta_p$ ($\theta_w$), whereas the convergence rate decreases.

## Appendix 2: The Formal Similarities Between the Trade-Offs

As is well known, in steady-growth equilibrium, the quantity and price sides of the economy can be described by

$$\chi = c\mathbf{f} + (1+g)\mathbf{A}\chi, \quad \mathbf{1}^{T}\chi = 1 \tag{8.36}$$

$$\pi^{T} = w\mathbf{1}^{T} + (1+r)\pi^{T}\mathbf{A}, \quad \pi^{T}\zeta = 1 \tag{8.37}$$

where $\chi$ denotes the vector of gross outputs per unit of labour employed, $\mathbf{f}$ the commodity vector that serves as the unit of consumption, $c$ the level of consumption per unit of labour employed, $g$ the uniform growth rate, $r$ the uniform profit rate, and $\zeta$ ($\geq \mathbf{0}$) the standard of value or *numéraire*. If $c = 0$ and $w = 0$, then Eqs. (8.36) and (8.37), respectively, imply that $(1 + g)^{-1}$ and $(1 + r)^{-1}$ are the P–F eigenvalue of $\mathbf{A}$, or $g = r = R \equiv \lambda_{A1}^{-1} - 1$, and $(\chi, \pi^{T})$ are the corresponding eigenvectors. If $-1 \leq (g, r) < R$, then

$$c = \left(\mathbf{1}^{T}[\mathbf{I} - (1+g)\mathbf{A}]^{-1}\mathbf{f}\right)^{-1} > 0, \quad dc/dg < 0$$

$$w = \left(\mathbf{1}^{T}[\mathbf{I} - (1+r)\mathbf{A}]^{-1}\zeta\right)^{-1} > 0, \quad dw/dr < 0$$

equations which define the trade-offs between the consumption and growth rates, on the one hand, and between the money wage and profit rates, on the other hand. It then follows that these two trade-offs are formally similar to each other, while in the case where the money wage rate is measured in terms of the unit of consumption, i.e. $\zeta = \mathbf{f}$, they become identical.

Taking now into account Eq. (8.15), it can be stated that the trade-off between the autonomous demand and transfer payments rates is formally similar to the trade-off between the consumption (wage) and growth (profit) rates. And, in the same vein, it is pertinent to note that, if $\mathbf{v}^{T}$ is the P–F eigenvector of $\mathbf{H}$ and, therefore, of $\mathbf{G}$ or, alternatively, if $\bar{\mathbf{d}}$ is the P–F eigenvector of $\mathbf{G}$, then Eq. (8.15) implies that

$$\varepsilon = \left[(1 + T)\mathbf{v}^{T}\bar{\mathbf{d}}\right]^{-1}(T - \tilde{\tau})$$

i.e. the $\varepsilon - \tilde{\tau}$ curve is linear, as in a one-commodity world. Leaving aside these rather restrictive cases, the curve becomes linear if $\mathbf{u}$ is normalized by setting $\psi_{G1}^{T}[\mathbf{I} - \mathbf{G}]^{-1}\mathbf{u} = 1$, with $\psi_{G1}^{T}\bar{\mathbf{d}} = 1$, where the left P–F eigenvector of $\mathbf{G}$ could be conceived of as a particular price vector associated with this matrix, i.e. $\boldsymbol{\psi}_{G1}^T = (1 + T)\boldsymbol{\psi}_{G1}^T \mathbf{G}$, and used for the evaluation of the system quantities. These normalization conditions, which correspond to those that have been proposed by Pasinetti (1992) (for the system (8.36)), imply that

$$\varepsilon = 1 - \widetilde{\tau} T^{-1}$$

which is formally equivalent to Sraffa's (1960, Chap. 4) linear wage–profit curve.

There is, however, a difference in the (possible) shapes of these trade-offs. The functional form of the consumption (wage)–growth (profit) rate curve is, in the general case, a ratio between a polynomial of the $n$th degree and one of the $(n - 1)$th degree and, therefore, may admit up to $3n - 6$ inflection points. Now we turn to the $\varepsilon - \widetilde{\tau}$ curve. If $\mathbf{X_G}$ and the diagonal matrix $\widehat{\boldsymbol{\lambda}}_\mathbf{G}$ are matrices formed from the right eigenvectors and the eigenvalues of $\mathbf{G}$, respectively, then $\mathbf{G} = \mathbf{X_G}\widehat{\boldsymbol{\lambda}}_\mathbf{G}\mathbf{X_G}^{-1}$ and, therefore, Eq. (8.15) can be written as

$$\varepsilon = \left( \boldsymbol{\omega}^T \left[ \mathbf{I} - (1 + \widetilde{\tau})\widehat{\boldsymbol{\lambda}}_\mathbf{G} \right]^{-1} \overline{\boldsymbol{\delta}} \right)^{-1} \tag{8.38}$$

where $\boldsymbol{\omega}^T \equiv \mathbf{v}^T\mathbf{X_G}$, $\overline{\boldsymbol{\delta}} \equiv \mathbf{X_G}^{-1}\overline{\mathbf{d}}$, $\omega_1 > 0$ and $\overline{\delta}_1 > 0$. Since $rank[\mathbf{G}] = rank\,[\mathbf{C}] \leq 2$, it follows that (i) $\lambda_{Gh} = 0$, where $h = 3, 4, \ldots, n$; and (ii) $\mathbf{G}\boldsymbol{\chi}_{Gh} = \mathbf{0}$, which implies that $\mathbf{v}^T\boldsymbol{\chi}_{Gh} = 0$ or $\omega_h = 0$ (and $\mathbf{p}^T\mathbf{H}\boldsymbol{\chi}_{Gh} = 0$). Hence, Eq. (8.38) reduces to

$$\varepsilon = [1 - (1 + \widetilde{\tau})\lambda_{G1}]$$
$$\times [1 - (1 + \widetilde{\tau})\lambda_{G2}]\{[1 - (1 + \widetilde{\tau})\lambda_{G2}]\omega_1\overline{\delta}_1 + [1 - (1 + \widetilde{\tau})\lambda_{G1}]\omega_2\overline{\delta}_2\}^{-1} \tag{8.39}$$

namely, the $\varepsilon - \widetilde{\tau}$ curve is formally similar to the consumption (wage)–growth (profit) rate curve of a *two*-sector economy and, therefore, has no inflection points (see Sect. 2.3.3).


## Appendix 3: Closing the System: A Numerical Example

Consider the following economy:

$$\mathbf{A} = \begin{bmatrix} 0.1 & 0.2 & 0.2 \\ 0.3 & 0.1 & 0.1 \\ 0.2 & 0.1 & 0.2 \end{bmatrix}, \quad \mathbf{l}^T = [1, 2, 1], \quad \hat{\mathbf{r}} = [0.05, 0.1, 0.15]\mathbf{I}, \quad \mathbf{f}_w = [1, 1.5, 2]^T,$$

$\mathbf{f}_p = [1, 0.5, 0.25]^T$, $s_w = 0.05$, $s_p = 0.70$, $\tau_w = 0.20$ and $\tau_p = 0.30$, i.e. $\rho = 7/8$. It is readily calculated that $\lambda_{G1} \cong 0.881$ or $T \cong 0.135$, and $T' \equiv \lambda_{G2}^{-1} - 1 \cong -293.183$.

Furthermore, assume that $\overline{\mathbf{d}}^{\mathrm{I}} = [1, 1, 1]^{\mathrm{T}}$ or, alternatively, $\overline{\mathbf{d}}^{\mathrm{II}} = [0, 0, 1]^{\mathrm{T}}$. It then follows that the $\varepsilon - \tilde{\tau}$ curves are (see Eq. (8.39))

$$\varepsilon^{\mathrm{I}} \cong -0.003(\mathbf{T} - \tilde{\tau})(\mathbf{T}' - \tilde{\tau})(8.017 + 0.017\tilde{\tau})^{-1},$$

$$\varepsilon^{\mathrm{I}}(-1) = 1/8 = 0.125, \quad \varepsilon^{\mathrm{I}}(0) \cong 0.015$$

or, alternatively,

$$\varepsilon^{\mathrm{II}} \cong -0.003(\mathbf{T} - \tilde{\tau})(\mathbf{T}' - \tilde{\tau})(2.327 + 0.033\tilde{\tau})^{-1},$$

$$\varepsilon^{\mathrm{II}}(-1) \cong 0.436, \quad \varepsilon^{\mathrm{II}}(0) \cong 0.051$$

where $d^2\varepsilon^{\mathrm{I}}/d\tilde{\tau}^2 < 0$ and $d^2\varepsilon^{\mathrm{II}}/d\tilde{\tau}^2 > 0$. From Eqs. (8.14) and (8.15) we get

$$\mathbf{p}^{\mathrm{T}}\mathbf{u}^{\mathrm{I}}(\tilde{\tau}) \cong (533.6 + 3.470\tilde{\tau})(480.3 + \tilde{\tau})^{-1},$$

$$d(\mathbf{p}^{\mathrm{T}}\mathbf{u}^{\mathrm{I}}(\tilde{\tau}))/d\tilde{\tau} > 0$$

or, alternatively,

$$\mathbf{p}^{\mathrm{T}}\mathbf{u}^{\mathrm{II}} \cong (77.8 - 1.706\tilde{\tau})(69.6 + \tilde{\tau})^{-1}, \quad d(\mathbf{p}^{\mathrm{T}}\mathbf{u}^{\mathrm{II}}(\tilde{\tau}))/d\tilde{\tau} < 0$$

where $\mathbf{p}^{\mathrm{T}}\mathbf{u}^{\mathrm{I}}(\mathbf{T}) = \mathbf{p}^{\mathrm{T}}\mathbf{u}^{\mathrm{II}}(\mathbf{T}) \cong 1.112$. Finally, the economically relevant $\tilde{\tau} - \overline{b}$ curves are determined by Eq. (8.16) and depicted in Fig. 8.1: $\overline{b}^{*\mathrm{I}} \cong 0.118$, $\overline{b}^{*\mathrm{II}} \cong 0.122$, $\overline{b}^{**} \cong 0.134$, $d^2\tilde{\tau}^{\mathrm{I}}/d\overline{b}^2 < 0$ and $d^2\tilde{\tau}^{\mathrm{II}}/d\overline{b}^2 > 0$.

## Appendix 4: A Post-Keynesian–Sraffian One-Country Model

Consider a one-country model where (i) there are no non-competitive imports; (ii) labour is homogeneous within each industry but heterogeneous across industries; (iii) $\mathbf{f}_w = \mathbf{f}_p = \mathbf{f} > \mathbf{0}$ and $\tau_q = 0$; (iv) the irreducible matrix of imported input–output coefficients, $\mathbf{A}^{\mathrm{m}}$, is given and constant;[24] and (v) the diagonal matrix, $\hat{\boldsymbol{\mu}}$, of imported commodities for final demand per unit of gross output of each commodity is given and constant. The price side of the economy is described by

---

[24]In the real world, the total input–output coefficients are technologically given, whereas both the imported and domestic input–output coefficients depend on the relationships between installed capacity, effective demand and trade impediments (see Levy 1982, pp. 51–53).

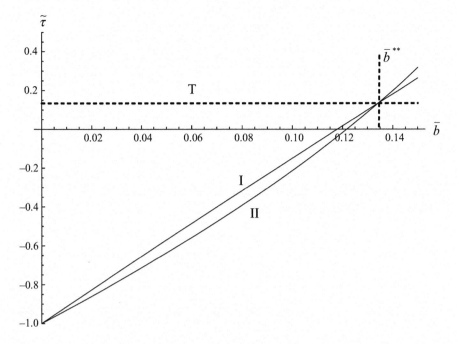

**Fig. 8.1** The government budget deficit–transfer payments curves

$$\boldsymbol{\pi}^T = \mathbf{w}^T\widehat{\mathbf{l}} + \boldsymbol{\pi}^T\mathbf{A}[\mathbf{I} + \widehat{\mathbf{r}}]$$

or

$$\boldsymbol{\pi}^T = \mathbf{w}^T\mathbf{V} + \boldsymbol{\pi}^T\mathbf{H}$$

where $\widehat{\mathbf{l}}$ denotes the $n \times n$ diagonal matrix of direct labour coefficients, and $\mathbf{V} \equiv \widehat{\mathbf{l}}[\mathbf{I} - \mathbf{A}]^{-1}$. The quantity side of the economy is described by

$$\mathbf{y} = \mathbf{c}_w + \mathbf{c}_p - \mathbf{IM} + \mathbf{d}$$

or

$$\mathbf{y} = \mathbf{c}_w + \mathbf{c}_p - [\mathbf{A}^m + \widehat{\boldsymbol{\mu}}]\mathbf{x} + \mathbf{d}$$

where $\mathbf{IM} = [\mathbf{A}^m + \widehat{\boldsymbol{\mu}}]\mathbf{x}$ denotes the import demand vector, and $\mathbf{d}$ the autonomous demand vector for domestically produced commodities (government consumption expenditures, investments, and exports). Hence, it follows that

$$\mathbf{y} = \left[\mathbf{C} - \widetilde{\mathbf{A}}^{m}\right]\mathbf{y} + \mathbf{d} \tag{8.39}$$

where $\widetilde{\mathbf{A}}^{m} \equiv [\mathbf{A}^{m} + \widehat{\boldsymbol{\mu}}][\mathbf{I} - \mathbf{A}]^{-1}$ is the matrix of total import demand, and

$$\mathbf{C} \equiv \mathbf{f}\widetilde{\boldsymbol{\pi}}^{\mathrm{T}}$$

where

$$\widetilde{\boldsymbol{\pi}}^{\mathrm{T}} \equiv \left(\boldsymbol{\pi}^{\mathrm{T}}\mathbf{f}\right)^{-1}\left[(1 - s_{w})\mathbf{w}^{\mathrm{T}}\mathbf{V} + (1 - s_{p})\boldsymbol{\pi}^{\mathrm{T}}\mathbf{H}\right]$$

is the matrix of total consumption demand, which has rank equal to 1.[25]
   Equation (8.39) can be written as

$$\left[\mathbf{I} - \mathbf{C} + \widetilde{\mathbf{A}}^{m}\right]\mathbf{y} = \mathbf{d}$$

or, since $\mathbf{y} = [\mathbf{I} - \mathbf{A}]\mathbf{x}$,

$$\mathbf{Kx} = \mathbf{d} \tag{8.40}$$

where

$$\mathbf{K} \equiv \left[\mathbf{I} - \mathbf{C} + \widetilde{\mathbf{A}}^{m}\right][\mathbf{I} - \mathbf{A}]$$

or, since $\widetilde{\mathbf{A}}^{m}[\mathbf{I} - \mathbf{A}] = \mathbf{A}^{m} + \widehat{\boldsymbol{\mu}}$ and $\mathbf{A} = \mathbf{A}^{d} + \mathbf{A}^{m}$, where $\mathbf{A}^{d}$ denotes the matrix of domestic input–output coefficients,

$$\mathbf{K} = \mathbf{I} - \mathbf{A}^{d} - \mathbf{C}[\mathbf{I} - \mathbf{A}] + \widehat{\boldsymbol{\mu}} \tag{8.41}$$

$$\mathbf{C}[\mathbf{I} - \mathbf{A}] = \left(\boldsymbol{\pi}^{\mathrm{T}}\mathbf{f}\right)^{-1}\mathbf{f}\left[(1 - s_{w})\mathbf{w}^{\mathrm{T}}\widehat{\mathbf{l}} + (1 - s_{p})\boldsymbol{\pi}^{\mathrm{T}}\mathbf{A}\widehat{\mathbf{r}}\right] (> \mathbf{0}) \tag{8.42}$$

and

$$\boldsymbol{\pi}^{\mathrm{T}}\mathbf{K} = \boldsymbol{\pi}^{\mathrm{T}}\left[\mathbf{I} - \mathbf{A}^{d}\right] - \left[(1 - s_{w})\mathbf{w}^{\mathrm{T}}\widehat{\mathbf{l}} + (1 - s_{p})\boldsymbol{\pi}^{\mathrm{T}}\mathbf{A}\widehat{\mathbf{r}}\right] + \boldsymbol{\pi}^{\mathrm{T}}\widehat{\boldsymbol{\mu}}$$

or, since $\mathbf{w}^{\mathrm{T}}\widehat{\mathbf{l}} + \boldsymbol{\pi}^{\mathrm{T}}\mathbf{A}\widehat{\mathbf{r}} = \boldsymbol{\pi}^{\mathrm{T}}\left[\mathbf{I} - (\mathbf{A}^{d} + \mathbf{A}^{m})\right]$,

---

[25]What follows draws on Mariolis (2020).

$$\pi^T K = s_w w^T \hat{1} + s_p \pi^T A \hat{r} + \pi^T (A^m + \hat{\mu}) \ (> 0^T) \qquad (8.43)$$

i.e. $\pi^T K$ equals the monetary value of the sum of savings and imports per unit of gross output of each commodity. Since (i) all the off-diagonal elements of $K$ are non-positive (see Eqs. (8.41) and (8.42)), i.e. $K$ is a "Z-matrix"; and (ii) there exist a positive vector such that its product with $K$ is positive (see Eq. (8.43)), it follows that $K$ is a non-singular "M-matrix" (see, e.g. Berman and Plemmons 1994, pp. 134–138), i.e. the real part of each eigenvalue of $K$ is positive, and $K^{-1} > 0$. Hence, Eq. (8.40) has a unique, positive solution for $x$:

$$x = M^x d \qquad (8.44)$$

where

$$M^x \equiv K^{-1} = [I - A]^{-1} \left[ I - C + \tilde{A}^m \right]^{-1}$$

is a positive matrix of multipliers linking autonomous demand to gross output, while its elements are decreasing functions of the savings ratios. The net output associated with $d$ is therefore given by

$$y = Md \qquad (8.45)$$

where $M \equiv [I - A]M^x$ or

$$M = \left[ I - C + \tilde{A}^m \right]^{-1} = \left[ I + [I - C]^{-1} \tilde{A}^m \right]^{-1} [I - C]^{-1}$$

Setting $M_I \equiv [I - C]^{-1}$ and using the Woodbury identity, we get

$$M_I = I + (1 - \lambda_{C1})^{-1} C$$

and

$$M = M_{II} M_I$$

where $M_{II} \equiv \left[ I + M_I \tilde{A}^m \right]^{-1}$ contains negative elements (since the matrix $I + M_I \tilde{A}^m$ is positive) and, therefore, $M$ may contain negative elements. Nevertheless, (i) $\pi^T M > 0^T$ (since $\pi^T [I - A] > 0^T$ and $M^x > 0$); and (ii) all the diagonal elements of $M$ are positive.[26] Moreover, since (i) $M^{-1}[I - A] = K$; and (ii) both $[I - A]$ and

---

[26]It holds that (i) $Cy = C[I - A]M^x d > 0$ (see Eqs. (8.42), (8.44) and (8.45)), $\pi^T[I - C]y > 0$ (which implies that the monetary value of savings is positive) and $\tilde{A}^m y = [A^m + \hat{\mu}]M^x d > 0$ for

**K** are M-matrices, it follows that $\mathbf{M}^{-1}$ is a "hidden M-matrix" or "mime (i.e. M-matrix and Inverse M-matrix Extension)" and, therefore, a "P-matrix" (see Tsatsomeros 2002, p. 126), i.e. all its principal minors are positive, and all its real eigenvalues are positive. Hence, **M** is a "P-matrix".

Now we turn to the following two *heuristic* cases:

(i). If $\mathbf{A}^{d} = \mathbf{0}$ and $\widehat{\boldsymbol{\mu}} = \mathbf{0}$, then $\mathbf{A}^{m} = \mathbf{A}$ and $\mathbf{K} = \mathbf{I} - \mathbf{C}[\mathbf{I} - \mathbf{A}]$ (see Eq. (8.41)). Using the Woodbury matrix identity yields

$$\mathbf{M}^{x} = \mathbf{K}^{-1} = \mathbf{I} + \left[1 - \left(\lambda_{C1} - \widetilde{\boldsymbol{\pi}}^{T}\mathbf{Af}\right)\right]^{-1}\mathbf{C}[\mathbf{I} - \mathbf{A}]$$

where $\left(\lambda_{C1} - \widetilde{\boldsymbol{\pi}}^{T}\mathbf{Af}\right)$ is the P–F eigenvalue of $\mathbf{C}[\mathbf{I} - \mathbf{A}]$. Hence, it follows that the P–F eigenvalue of $\mathbf{M}^{x}$ equals $\left[1 - \left(\lambda_{C1} - \widetilde{\boldsymbol{\pi}}^{T}\mathbf{Af}\right)\right]^{-1}$ ($> 1$), while all other eigenvalues equal 1. Although, in that case,

$$\mathbf{M} = [\mathbf{I} - \mathbf{A}]\mathbf{M}^{x} = [\mathbf{I} - \mathbf{A}] + \left[1 - \left(\lambda_{C1} - \widetilde{\boldsymbol{\pi}}^{T}\mathbf{Af}\right)\right]^{-1}[\mathbf{I} - \mathbf{A}]\mathbf{C}[\mathbf{I} - \mathbf{A}]$$

is a rank-one perturbation of $[\mathbf{I} - \mathbf{A}]$, there is no such simple relationship for the eigenvalues of $\mathbf{M}$.[27] For instance, consider the following "circulant" system:[28]

$$\mathbf{A}^{m} = \mathbf{A} = \text{circ}[0, a, 0, 0], 0 < a < 1, \mathbf{C} = 40^{-1}\begin{bmatrix} 4 & 3 & 2 & 1 \\ 8 & 6 & 4 & 2 \\ 12 & 9 & 6 & 3 \\ 16 & 12 & 8 & 4 \end{bmatrix}$$

where the eigenvalues of **A** are $\{\pm a, \pm ia\}$, $i \equiv \sqrt{-1}$, and $\lambda_{C1} = 2^{-1}$, while $\mathbf{C}[\mathbf{I} - \mathbf{A}] > \mathbf{0}$ for $a < 2^{-1}$. Figure 8.2 displays the moduli of the eigenvalues of the Leontief matrix, $[\mathbf{I} - \mathbf{A}]$ (depicted by dotted lines), and the moduli of the eigenvalues of **M** (depicted by solid lines) as functions of $a$ ($< 2^{-1}$). It is noted that (a) $\mathbf{M}^{-1}$ is a Z-matrix for $a \leq a_{1} \cong 0.075$; (b) **M** is positive for $a < 6^{-1}\left(\sqrt{31} - 5\right) \cong 0.095$; and (c) **M** has real eigenvalues for $a \leq a_{2} \cong 0.146$ and $a \geq a_{3} \cong 0.378$.

If, however, either **f** or $\widetilde{\boldsymbol{\pi}}^{T}$ happen to be P–F eigenvectors of $\mathbf{A}^{m}$ ($= \mathbf{A}$), then **M** reduces to

---

each $\mathbf{d} \geq \mathbf{0}$; and (ii) the $i$th diagonal element of **M** is the $i$th element of the net output vector, $\mathbf{y}_{i}$, associated with $\mathbf{d} = \mathbf{e}_{i}, i = 1, 2, \ldots, n$. Pre-multiplying $\mathbf{M}^{-1}\mathbf{y}_{i} = \mathbf{e}_{i}$ by the diagonal matrix $\widehat{\boldsymbol{\pi}}$, formed from the elements of $\boldsymbol{\pi}^{T}$, gives $\widehat{\boldsymbol{\pi}}[\mathbf{I} - \mathbf{C}]\mathbf{y}_{i} = -\widehat{\boldsymbol{\pi}}\widetilde{\mathbf{A}}^{m}\mathbf{y}_{i} + \pi_{i}\mathbf{e}_{i}$. If the $i$th element of $\mathbf{y}_{i}$ is non-positive, then all the elements of the vector $\widehat{\boldsymbol{\pi}}[\mathbf{I} - \mathbf{C}]\mathbf{y}_{i}$ are negative (since $\mathbf{Cy}_{i} > \mathbf{0}$ and $-\widehat{\boldsymbol{\pi}}\widetilde{\mathbf{A}}^{m}\mathbf{y}_{i} < \mathbf{0}$), and, therefore, $\mathbf{e}^{T}\widehat{\boldsymbol{\pi}}[\mathbf{I} - \mathbf{C}]\mathbf{y}_{i} = \boldsymbol{\pi}^{T}[\mathbf{I} - \mathbf{C}]\mathbf{y}_{i} < 0$. Hence there is a contradiction.

[27]Consider, e.g. Bierkens and Ran (2014) and the references therein.

[28]For the circulant economies, see Sect. 2.3.4.

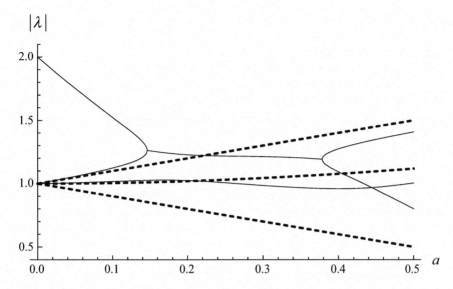

**Fig. 8.2** The moduli of the eigenvalues of the Leontief matrix (dotted lines), and of the matrix multiplier linking autonomous demand to net output (solid lines), as functions of the input–output coefficient

$$\mathbf{M} = [\mathbf{I} - \mathbf{A}] + [1 - \lambda_{\mathbf{C}1}(1 - \lambda_{\mathbf{A}1})]^{-1}(1 - \lambda_{\mathbf{A}1})\mathbf{C}[\mathbf{I} - \mathbf{A}]$$

or, respectively, to

$$\mathbf{M} = [\mathbf{I} - \mathbf{A}] + [1 - \lambda_{\mathbf{C}1}(1 - \lambda_{\mathbf{A}1})]^{-1}(1 - \lambda_{\mathbf{A}1})[\mathbf{I} - \mathbf{A}]\mathbf{C}$$

Hence, the eigenvalues of $\mathbf{M}$ are[29]

$$\left\{ \left[ (1 - \lambda_{\mathbf{A}1})^{-1} - \lambda_{\mathbf{C}1} \right]^{-1}, 1 - \lambda_{\mathbf{A}k} \right\}, \quad k = 2, 3, \ldots, n$$

(ii). When $\mathbf{A}^{\mathrm{m}} = \hat{\boldsymbol{\mu}} = \mathbf{0}$ and, therefore, $\mathbf{A}^{\mathrm{d}} = \mathbf{A}$ (the *corresponding* closed economy case), $\mathbf{K}$ reduces to $\mathbf{K_I} \equiv [\mathbf{I} - \mathbf{C}][\mathbf{I} - \mathbf{A}]$. Hence, the matrix multiplier linking autonomous demand to gross output reduces to

$$\mathbf{M_I^x} \equiv \mathbf{K_I^{-1}} = [\mathbf{I} - \mathbf{A}]^{-1}\mathbf{M_I}$$

where $\mathbf{M_I^x} > \mathbf{M^x}$ (since both $\mathbf{K_I}$ and $\mathbf{K}$ are M-matrices, and $\mathbf{K_I} < \mathbf{K}$; see, e.g. Horn and Johnson 1991, p. 117), and $\mathbf{p}^{\mathrm{T}}(\mathbf{M_I^x} - \mathbf{M^x})\mathbf{d}$ provides an aggregate measure of the import "leakages" that dampen the multiplier process in the domestic actual

---

[29]Consider the theorem mentioned in footnote 7 of Chap. 2.

economy. Finally, the matrix multiplier linking autonomous demand to net output reduces to $\mathbf{M_I}$ .

Finally, it should be added that:

(i). In the more realistic case of direct taxation, the terms $(1-s_q)$, $q = w, p$, should be replaced by $(1 - s_q)(1 - \tau_q)$. Furthermore, since all elements of $\mathbf{K}$ are strictly increasing functions of $s_q$, and $\mathbf{K}$ is an M-matrix, it follows that all elements of the gross output multiplier matrix, $\mathbf{M^x}$ ($\equiv \mathbf{K}^{-1}$), are strictly decreasing functions of $s_q$ (and $\tau_q$). Hence, since $\boldsymbol{\pi}^T\mathbf{M} > \mathbf{0}^T$, it follows that all individual industry multipliers, $\boldsymbol{\pi}^T\mathbf{Me}_i$, are strictly decreasing functions of $s_q$ (and $\tau_q$).

(ii). Taking into consideration traditional methods for the measurement of inter-industry linkages (see, e.g. Miller and Blair 2009, Chap. 12) and—especially—Dietzenbacher's (1997) re-interpretation of the Ghosh (1958) model, the net output multipliers $\boldsymbol{\pi}^T\mathbf{Me}_i$ can be considered as indices of socio-technical "total backward" linkages and leakages, respectively.[30] Hence, it seems that the formulation of the dual, price model (to the quantity model defined by Eq. (8.39)), where commodity prices change as a result of changes in autonomous components of values added per unit activity level, whereas commodity physical quantities are assumed to be constant, provides the basis for the derivation of socio-technical "forward" linkage and leakage indices. To the best of our knowledge, however, *such* a dual model is not yet available in the literature and, therefore, should be the subject of future research efforts.

## Appendix 5: A Numerical Example for the Joint Production Case

Consider the following economy:

$$\mathbf{B} = \begin{bmatrix} 6 & 3 \\ 1 & 12 \end{bmatrix}, \quad \mathbf{A} = \begin{bmatrix} 5 & 0 \\ 0 & 10 \end{bmatrix}, \quad \mathbf{l}^T = [1, 1], \quad \widehat{\mathbf{r}} = 0.2\mathbf{I}$$

It is obtained that

$$\mathbf{v_B^T} = [-1, 2], \quad \mathbf{p}^T = [1/3, 1], \quad \mathbf{H_B} = \begin{bmatrix} -2 & 3 \\ 2 & -2 \end{bmatrix}$$

and $\mathbf{x} = [\mathbf{B} - \mathbf{A}]^{-1}\mathbf{y} > \mathbf{0}$ iff $1 < y_1y_2^{-1} < 3/2$.

Furthermore, assume that

---

[30]It would also be possible to apply the logic of modern methods, such as the "hypothetical extraction method". For a comprehensive analysis of this method, see Miller and Lahr (2001).

$$s_w = 4/100, \quad \rho < 1, \quad \mathbf{f}_w = \mathbf{f}_p = \mathbf{f} = [1, 5/3]^T \text{ and } \bar{\mathbf{d}} = [1, 2/5]^T$$

As is easily checked,

(i) $rank[\mathbf{G}] = 1$ and $\lambda_{\mathbf{G}1} = (28/25) - (1/6)(1 - s_p)\rho$, while iff $s_p < 1 - (18/25)\rho^{-1}$, then $\mathbf{G} > \mathbf{0}$ and $\lambda_{\mathbf{G}1} < 1$.

(ii) iff $s_p = s_p^* \equiv 1 - (36/175)\rho^{-1}$, then $\mathbf{G}\bar{\mathbf{d}} = \lambda_{\mathbf{G}2}\bar{\mathbf{d}} = \mathbf{0}$ and, therefore, $\varepsilon = (\mathbf{v}^T\bar{\mathbf{d}})^{-1} = -5$ and $x_1 x_2^{-1} = -4/3$;

(iii) the level of autonomous demand as a function of $\tilde{\tau}$, $s_p$ and $\rho$ is given by

$$\varepsilon(\tilde{\tau}, s_p, \rho) = [54 + 504\tilde{\tau} - 75(1 + \tilde{\tau})(1 - s_p)\rho]\{5[18 - 95(1 + \tilde{\tau})(1 - s_p)\rho]\}^{-1}$$

with $\partial\varepsilon/\partial s_p > (<) 0$ and $\partial\varepsilon/\partial\rho < (>) 0$ for $\tilde{\tau} < (>) \tilde{\tau}^* \equiv -3/38 \cong -0.079$, while $\partial\varepsilon/\partial\tilde{\tau} < (>) 0$ iff $s_p < (>) s_p^*$; and

(iv) iff $\rho \leq 36/175$ ($\cong 0.206$), $0 < s_p < 1$ and $\Phi < \tilde{\tau} < \phi$ or iff $\rho > 36/175$, $s_p < (>)s_p^*$ and $\phi < (>) \tilde{\tau} < (>) \Phi$, then $x_1 x_2^{-1} > 0$, where

$$\Phi \equiv -[18 + 475(1 - s_p)\rho][1368 + 475(1 - s_p)\rho]^{-1},$$

$$\partial\Phi/\partial s_p > 0, \quad \partial\Phi/\partial\rho < 0$$

$$\phi \equiv [72 - 475(1 - s_p)\rho][228 + 475(1 - s_p)\rho]^{-1},$$

$$\partial\phi/\partial s_p > 0, \quad \partial\phi/\partial\rho < 0$$

$$\Phi(s_p^*, \rho) = \phi(s_p^*, \rho) = \tilde{\tau}^*$$

and

$$\varepsilon(\Phi) = 10/19 \cong 0.526, \quad \varepsilon(\phi) = 45/19 \cong 2.368$$

These bounds determine the *economically* relevant intervals of $\tilde{\tau}$ and $\varepsilon$, where the latter interval is independent of the value of $s_p$.

It then follows that iff $\rho > 36/175$, then the $\varepsilon - \tilde{\tau}$ curve may be increasing. For instance, the graphs in Figs. 8.3 and 8.4 correspond to the value $\rho = 16/19$ ($\cong 0.842$), which implies that $s_p^* = 529/700$ ($\cong 0.756$), and display the functions $\phi$, $\Phi$ ($\phi > 0$ for $s_p > 41/50 = 0.820$) and, respectively, the economically relevant segments of the $\varepsilon - \tilde{\tau}$ curves for different, representative values of $s_p$.

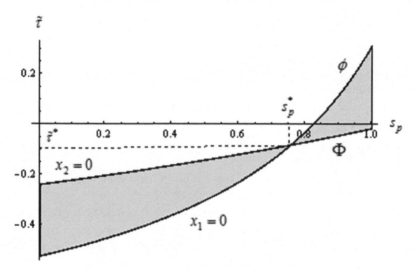

**Fig. 8.3** The economically relevant intervals of the transfer payments rate as functions of the savings ratio out of profits; the relative tax factor is equal to 16/19

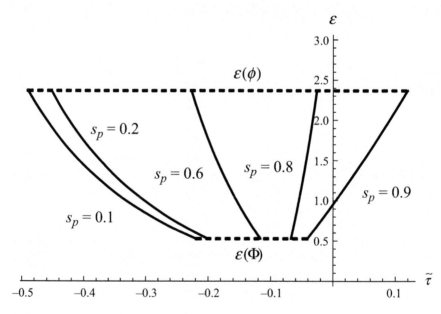

**Fig. 8.4** Economically relevant segments of the autonomous demand–transfer payments curves for different values of the savings ratio out of profits; the relative tax factor is equal to 16/19

# References

Abraham-Frois, G. (1991). Corporate behavior, valuation ratio and macroeconomic analysis. In E. J. Nell & W. Semmler (Eds.), *Nicholas Kaldor and mainstream economics. Confrontation or Convergence?* (pp. 190–204). London: Palgrave Macmillan.

Afanasyev, V. (1983). *Bourgeois economic thought 1930s–1970s*. Moscow: Progress Publishers.

Azad, R. (2012). A Steindlian model of concentration, debt and growth. *Metroeconomica, 63*(2), 295–334.

Barnett, S. (1990). *Matrices. Methods and applications*. Oxford: Oxford University Press.

Benavie, A. (1973). Policy impact multipliers and the budget constraint. *Metroeconomica, 25*(3), 272–287.

Berman, A., & Plemmons, R. J. (1994). *Nonnegative matrices in the mathematical sciences*. Philadelphia: Society for Industrial and Applied Mathematics.

Bierkens, J., & Ran, A. (2014). A singular M-matrix perturbed by a nonnegative rank one matrix has positive principal minors; is it D-stable? *Linear Algebra and Its Applications, 457*, 191–208.

Buchanan, J. M., Burton, J., & Wagner, R. E. (1978). *The consequences of Mr Keynes*. London: Institute of Economic Affairs.

Chipman, J. S. (1950). The multi-sector multiplier. *Econometrica, 18*(4), 355–374.

Dietzenbacher, E. (1997). In vindication of the Ghosh model: A reinterpretation as a price model. *Journal of Regional Science, 37*(4), 629–651.

Dutt, A. K., Charles, S., & Lang, D. (2015). Employment flexibility, dual labour markets, growth, and distribution. *Metroeconomica, 66*(4), 771–807.

Eatwell, J., & Milgate, M. (2011). *The fall and rise of Keynesian economics*. Oxford: Oxford University Press.

Erreygers, G. (1989). On indirect taxation and weakly basic commodities. *Journal of Economics, 50* (2), 139–156.

Gandolfo, G. (2002). *International finance and open-economy macroeconomics*. Berlin: Springer.

Ghosh, A. (1958). Input–output approach in an allocation system. *Economica, 25*(97), 58–64.

Gnos, C., & Rochon, L.-P. (Eds.). (2008). *The Keynesian multiplier*. London and New York: Routledge.

Hartwig, J. (2004). Keynes's multiplier in a two-sectoral framework. *Review of Political Economy, 16*(3), 309–334.

Horn, R. A., & Johnson, C. R. (1991). *Topics in matrix analysis*. Cambridge: Cambridge University Press.

Kahn, R. F. (1931). The relation of home investment to unemployment. *The Economic Journal, 41* (162), 173–198.

Kaldor, N. (1955). Alternative theories of distribution. *The Review of Economic Studies, 23*(2), 83–100.

Kalecki, M. (1990). *Essay on the business cycle theory*. In J. Osiatyński (Ed.), *Collected works of Michal Kalecki. Capitalism: Business cycles and full employment* (Vol. 1, pp. 65–106). Oxford: Clarendon Press.

Kalecki, M. (1942). A theory of profits. *The Economic Journal, 52*(206/207), 258–267.

Keynes, J. M. (1936). *The general theory of employment, interest and money*. London: Macmillan.

Krugman, P., & Taylor, L. (1978). Contractionary effects of devaluation. *Journal of International Economics, 8*(3), 445–456.

Kurz, H. D. (1985). Effective demand in a "classical" model of value and distribution: The multiplier in a Sraffian framework. *The Manchester School, 53*(2), 121–137. Reprinted in H. D. Kurz (1990). *Capital, distribution and effective demand. Studies in the "classical" approach to economic theory* (pp. 174–191). Cambridge: Polity Press.

Kurz, H. D., & Salvadori, N. (1995). *Theory of production. A long-period analysis*. Cambridge: Cambridge University Press.

Lange, O. (1970). *Introduction to economic cybernetics*. Oxford: Pergamon Press.

Łaski, K., & Walther, W. (2013). *Kalecki's profit equation after 80 years*. Wiiw Working Papers, No. 100, April 2013.

Levy, S. (1982). Foreign trade and its impact on employment: The Mexican case. *Journal of Development Economics, 10*(1), 47–65.

Malinvaud, E. (1959). Programmes d'expansion et taux d'intérêt. *Econometrica, 27*(2), 215–227.

Mariolis, T. (2008). Pure joint production, income distribution, employment and the exchange rate. *Metroeconomica, 59*(4), 656–665.

Mariolis, T. (2018). A Sraffian (no) trade-off between autonomous demand and transfer payments. *Metroeconomica, 69*(2), 473–487.

Mariolis, T. (2020). *Some spectral properties of the matrix demand multiplier in a single production model for actual economies*. Internal Report of the Study Group on Sraffian Economics, 31 Jan 2020. Athens: Department of Public Administration, Panteion University (in Greek).

Metcalfe, J. S., & Steedman, I. (1971). Some effects of taxation in a linear model of production. *The Manchester School, 39*(3), 171–185.

Metcalfe, J. S., & Steedman, I. (1981). Some long-run theory of employment, income distribution and the exchange rate. *The Manchester School, 49*(1), 1–20.

Meyer, C. D. (2001). *Matrix analysis and applied linear algebra*. New York: Society for Industrial and Applied Mathematics.

Meyer, C. D., Jr., & Plemmons, R. J. (1977). Convergent powers of a matrix with applications to iterative methods for singular linear systems. *Society for Industrial and Applied Mathematics Journal on Numerical Analysis, 14*(4), 699–705.

Miller, R. E., & Blair, P. D. (2009). *Input–output analysis: Foundations and extensions*. New York: Cambridge University Press.

Miller, R. E., & Lahr, M. L. (2001). A taxonomy of extractions. In M. L. Lahr & R. E. Miller (Eds.), *Regional science perspectives in economic analysis. A festschrift in memory of Benjamin H. Stevens* (pp. 407–441). Amsterdam: Elsevier Science.

Morishima, M. (1960). Economic expansion and the interest rate in generalized von Neumann models. *Econometrica, 28*(2), 352–363.

Pasinetti, L. L. (1973). The notion of vertical integration in economic analysis. *Metroeconomica, 25* (1), 1–29.

Pasinetti, L. L. (1992). "Standard prices" and a linear consumption/growth-rate relation. In L. L. Pasinetti (Ed.), *Italian economic papers* (Vol. 1, pp. 265–277). Oxford: Oxford University Press.

Perkins, J. O. N. (1980). Using the macroeconomic mix to stop stagflation. *Journal of Economic Studies, 7*(1), 28–50.

Sawyer, M. (2008). Kalecki and the multiplier. In C. Gnos & L.-P. Rochon (Eds.), *The Keynesian multiplier* (pp. 153–167). London and New York: Routledge.

Screpanti, E., & Zamagni, S. (2005). *An outline of the history of economic thought* (2nd ed.). Oxford: Oxford University Press.

Sraffa, P. (1960). *Production of commodities by means of commodities. Prelude to a Critique of economic theory*. Cambridge: Cambridge University Press.

Steedman, I. (1977). *Marx after Sraffa*. London: New Left Books.

ten Raa, T. (2005). *The economics of input–output analysis*. Cambridge: Cambridge University Press.

Trigg, A. B., & Philp, B. (2008). *Value magnitudes and the Kahn employment multiplier*. Paper presented to Developing Quantitative Marxism, Bristol, 3–5 April 2008. Retrieved Sept 15, 2019, from http://carecon.org.uk/QM/Conference%202008/Papers/Trigg.pdf.

Tsatsomeros, M. J. (2002). Generating and detecting matrices with positive principal minors. *Asian Information-Science-Life. An International Journal, 1*(2), 115–132.

You, J.-I., & Dutt, A. K. (1996). Government debt, income distribution and growth. *Cambridge Journal of Economics, 20*(3), 335–351.

# Chapter 9
# Effective Demand and Devaluation Policies: Evidence from Input–Output Tables for Eurozone Economies

**Abstract** Using input–output data and Sraffian frameworks, this chapter provides empirical estimations of demand multipliers and the medium- and long-run effects of wage and currency devaluations on international price competitiveness and income distribution for Eurozone economies. The findings (i) reveal certain differentiated socio-technical production conditions in the economies under consideration (i.e. Greece, Italy, Spain, and the Eurozone as a whole); (ii) seem to be in accordance with the observed deep Southern Eurozone recession; (iii) cast doubt on the "horizontal" policy measures implemented in the post-2010 Eurozone economy; and (iv) provide an alternative framework for formulating well-targeted effective demand management and structural policy programs.

**Keywords** Management of effective demand · Matrix multipliers · "PIIGS" versus Eurozone economies · Sraffian modelling · Wage versus currency devaluation

## 9.1 Introduction

During 2008 and 2009, the so-called PIIGS economies, i.e. Portugal, Ireland, Italy, Greece, and Spain, faced serious external and fiscal imbalances. At that time, it was argued by several researchers that although such imbalances were related (to one degree or another) to significant competitiveness divergences in the Eurozone system, exiting the single currency union would lead to vicious cycles of currency devaluations, cost-push inflation, lack of capital inflows, monetary financing of deficits, and recessions. Thus, the implementation of contractionary fiscal and wage devaluation policy measures emerged as a possible, although painful, way to tackle the "PIIGS crisis".

Indeed, as, for instance, De Grauwe and Ji (2016) remark,

since 2008–9 quite dramatic turnarounds of the relative unit labour costs have occurred (internal devaluations) in Ireland, Spain, and Greece, and to a lesser extent in Portugal and Italy. These internal devaluations have come at a great cost in terms of cost output and employment in the debtor countries mainly because the expenditure-reducing effects of these

© Springer Nature Singapore Pte Ltd. 2021
T. Mariolis et al., *Spectral Theory of Value and Actual Economies*, Evolutionary Economics and Social Complexity Science 24,
https://doi.org/10.1007/978-981-33-6260-4_9

internal devaluations were more intense than the expenditure switching (competitiveness) effects. (p. 61)

In addition, according to the International Labour Organization (2016, pp. 12–13), in 2015 the average real wage rates in Ireland, Italy, Greece and Spain were still below the levels of 2007 (in Greece, real wages have dropped by approximately 25% since that year). On the other hand, however, there were no processes of significant internal revaluations in the creditor Eurozone economies:

> Thus, one can conclude that at the insistence of the creditor nations, the burden of the adjustments to the imbalances in the Eurozone has been borne almost exclusively by the debtor countries in the periphery. This has created a deflationary bias that explains why the Eurozone has been pulled into a double-dip recession in 2012–13, and why real GDP has stagnated since 2008, in contrast with what has happened in the non-Euro EU countries and in the USA. (De Grauwe and Ji 2016, p. 62)

In October 2012, the International Monetary Fund (2012, pp. 41–43) stated that the projections for the measures applied and/or proposed (from 2010 onwards) to the Greek economy were based on the false premise that the fiscal multiplier was around 0.50, whereas the "actual" fiscal multiplier was in the range of 0.90 to 1.70. The annual report of the Bank of Greece for the year 2012 mentioned that

> [a]ccording to a recent IMF staff report, fiscal adjustment had a substantially larger impact on GDP than initially projected. In particular, during the early years of the crisis, the average fiscal multiplier was 2–3 times higher than the original estimates (0.5; see IMF Report, March 2012, *Greece: Request for Extended Arrangement Under the Extended Fund Facility-Staff report*, p. 15). See Blanchard, O. and D. Leigh (2013), "Growth Forecast Errors and Fiscal Multipliers", IMF Working Paper 13/1; and IMF, *World Economic Outlook*, Autumn 2012. However, the ECB [European Central Bank] and the European Commission voiced their disagreement to both the results of the IMF study and the methodology used to estimate fiscal multipliers. See European Commission (2012), *Autumn Economic Forecasts*, and ECB (2012), *Monthly Bulletin*, December. In this light, the IMF January 2013 report suggests that the average fiscal multiplier for Greece is estimated at around 1 (see *Greece: First and Second Reviews*, IMF Country Report No. 13/20, p. 13). (Bank of Greece 2013, pp. 127–128)

One year earlier, it was estimated, on the basis of almost trivial calculations, that the usual Keynesian multiplier of autonomous demand for the Greek economy was around 1.71 and, therefore, an attempt to eliminate the state budget primary deficit would result in cumulative Gross Domestic Product (GDP) losses of about 29% (Mariolis 2011a). And regarding the Eurozone (EZ) as a whole, it has been estimated that, between 2011 and 2013, the fiscal consolidation actions

> had a considerable negative impact on GDP, with the decline of GDP relative to the no-consolidation case increasing to 7.7% by the end of 2013. As a consequence of this GDP decline, the reduction of the primary balance achieved by fiscal consolidation is quite low, and peaks at only 0.2% of GDP. This is far less than the total consolidation effort of 3.9%. A more gradual and backloaded consolidation scenario, where the fiscal tightening would have set in during the recovery of the Euro Area economy, would have cost half the output lost (3.7%) and would have led to a much stronger primary balance improvement (2.1% of GDP) due to the lower multiplier effects that prevail in such a scenario. (Gechert et al. 2016, p. 1138)

Furthermore, empirical evidence suggests that, especially in Portugal, Greece and Spain, the possible rebalancing-price competitiveness effects of that "internal devaluation strategy" were also negatively affected by (i) the increases in profit margins and indirect taxes; and (ii) the nominal appreciation of the euro from the second quarter of 2012 to the second quarter of 2014. Thus, it has been argued that the observed

> improvement in external balances is mainly explained by the collapse of imports in these countries, and this is a consequence of low relative demand and not of the (weak) improvement in competitiveness. (Uxó et al. 2014, p. 1)[1]

At the same time, as Pianta (2014) stressed,

> [t]he crisis of 2008 has brought Europe to a stagnation. In the first quarter of 2014 real GDP in the 28 countries of the EU has grown by 0.3% only compared to the previous quarter. The continent has been divided between a slow-growing "centre" with financial and political power, and a "periphery" in depression, with no political influence, high public debt, high unemployment. [...] With 2008 values for industrial production [defined as real output in mining, manufacturing, public utilities; construction is excluded] equal to 100, in 2013 only Germany, Austria and the Netherlands had an index that had suffered limited slumps during the recession and had returned to pre-crisis levels. [...] Southern Europe has experienced a dramatic loss of industrial production; 2013 values are 88 for Portugal, 79 for Italy, 76 for Spain, 73 for Greece. As a result of the prolonged European crisis, a permanent loss of production capacity is taking place in most industries and most countries, with a major destruction of economic activities in the Southern "periphery". (pp. 281–282)

At the end of 2014, the Eurozone inflation rate turned negative, while the subsequent announcement of the European Central Bank's asset purchase program (on 22 January 2015), the so-called Quantitative Easing Program of 1 trillion euro, led to considerable depreciations of the euro against major international currencies. In fact,

> between early May 2014 and end-May 2015, the euro depreciated by 23% vis-à-vis the US dollar and by 12% in nominal effective terms (against a basket of currencies of 38 major trading partners of the euro area). (European Central Bank 2015, p. 11)

According to estimates by the European Commission (2015),

> [o]n average, a 5% depreciation of the euro's NEER[2] increases import prices by some 4% after one year, with most of the impact occurring in just one quarter. By contrast, it takes around three quarters until changes in import prices are passed on to consumer prices and the response is generally small, as final goods prices incorporate substantial shares of domestically produced inputs (retail, transport, marketing costs). Yet the extent of the response of consumer prices differs slightly across Member States, partly because of different consumption patterns (a high proportion of services in some countries, a high proportion of energy in others). On average, a 5% depreciation of the euro's NEER leads to an increase in euro area consumer prices of about 0.3% after one year. However, as commodities are largely priced in

---

[1]Also, see Bilbao-Ubillos and Fernández-Sainz (2019) and Myant et al. (2016).

[2]That is, the nominal effective exchange rate used by the European Commission: A weighted average of bilateral exchange rates (monthly averages) against 42 trading partners, using double export weights.

US dollars and the dollar has appreciated strongly, the impact of recent exchange rate changes on prices may be larger than suggested by these estimates. Export prices in the euro area appear to be less responsive to permanent changes in the NEER than import prices. A 5% depreciation of the euro's NEER lowers export prices in foreign currencies by about 2% after one year. The limited pass-through of exchange rate changes to (foreign currency) export prices may be partly explained by offsetting effects from higher imported interme-diate input costs and partly by mark-up adjustments. [...] [A] 5% depreciation of the euro's NEER [...] may increase real GDP in the euro area by around 0.3% in the first year and another 0.2% in the second year. [...] [T]he impact on Member States' real economies also depends on how strongly export demand responds to changes in relative prices. Empirical evidence suggests that price elasticities differ widely across countries and industries. For example, the price elasticity of Germany's exports is estimated to be smaller than that of other large Member States (notably Italy and Spain). Through this channel, the depreciation of the euro may support intra-euro area rebalancing. (pp. 51–52)

All these facts and figures suggest that (i) the magnitudes of the demand multi-pliers; (ii) both medium- and long-run effects of wage and/or exchange rate changes on prices, income distribution and growth; and (iii) the differentiated features of each economy should be carefully taken into consideration before the adoption of any policy measures.

However, one of the underlying issues is that, in the post-2008 world, there are both policy-oriented and theoretical debates on the "size of the demand multipliers" (and especially of "the fiscal multiplier"). For instance, several empirical estimates of the fiscal multipliers tend to fall in the 0.5 to 2.0 range, suggesting that fiscal multipliers increase more in a recession than they decrease in an expansion, and that fiscal spending multipliers tend to be (but are not necessarily) larger than fiscal revenue multipliers (see, e.g. Batini et al. 2014; Mineshima et al. 2014).[3] In fact, it has been estimated that, for economies in recession or, *a fortiori*, in a "liquidity trap", the fiscal spending multiplier might be in the range of 1.7 to 3.7 (see the summary overview provided by Krugman et al. 2018, pp. 522–524), whereas Ramey (2019) sustains that

[f]or multipliers on general government purchases, the evidence from developed countries suggests that they are positive but less than or equal to unity, meaning that government purchases raise GDP but do not stimulate additional private activity and may actually crowd it out. [...] The evidence for higher spending multipliers during recessions or times of high unemployment is fragile, and the most robust results suggest multipliers of one or below during these periods. The evidence for higher government spending multipliers during periods in which monetary policy is very accommodative, such as zero lower bound periods, is somewhat stronger. Recent time series estimates for the United States and Japan suggest that multipliers could be 1.5 or higher during those times. Estimated and calibrated New Keynesian models for the United States and Europe also imply higher multipliers under certain conditions. For tax rate change multipliers, the estimates implied by the leading

---

[3]For summaries of the issues involved and reviews of the existing empirical evidence, from (post-) Keynesian viewpoints, see Charles (2016), Charles et al. (2015, 2018), Leão (2013) and Palley (2009). For recent estimations of input–output multipliers, see, e.g. Antonopoulos et al. (2014), Athanassiou et al. (2014), and Kolokontes et al. (2018) (Greece); Garbellini et al. (2014) (EZ); Ksenofontov et al. (2018) (Russian Federation); Portella-Carbó (2016) (Spain, Italy, France, Germany, UK, US, Japan and P. R. China); Pusch (2012) (European Union).

methods do not agree. [. . .] Fiscal multipliers might be different in the wake of a financial crisis. However, the evidence for larger national multipliers on the 2009 Obama stimulus package is at best weak. Quantitative New Keynesian models do not find larger fiscal multipliers. Multipliers estimated on cross-state data appear larger at first, but shrink once they are adjusted to be nationally representative. The latest studies on multipliers during the fiscal consolidations in Europe suggest that they were not higher than usual, either. (pp. 90–91)

Finally, Castelnuovo and Lim (2019) conclude their recent survey of the literature as follows:

More work is needed before we have a consensus about the size of fiscal policy multipliers. [. . .] [T]he construction of long historical datasets appears to be a promising avenue to sharpen econometric estimates of the fiscal multipliers [. . .] the response of a broad set of variables should be studied to have a deeper understanding of the transmission mechanism (s) driving the output effects of fiscal spending. [. . .] [F]or open economies like, for example, Australia, the response of net exports and the exchange rate should also be scrutinised. (pp. 87–88)

This chapter provides empirical estimations and policy-oriented analysis of (i) the output, import and employment matrix demand multipliers for two representative "PIIGS economies", i.e. Greece and Spain, and for the EZ economy as a whole; and (ii) the medium- and long-run effects of wage and currency devaluations on international price competitiveness and income distribution by focusing *exclusively* on the input–output configurations of Greece and Italy, i.e. two "PIIGS economies" that are characterized, however, by different levels and structures of production[4] and, at the same time, have experienced significantly different rates of wage devaluation.

For this purpose, we use:

(i) Input–output data from the Supply and Use Tables (SUTs) and the Symmetric Input–Output Tables (SIOTs) for the "pre-adjustment" year of 2010.

(ii) Input–output models based on the Sraffian framework(s) developed in Chap. 8. Nevertheless, the particular structures of these models are imposed not only by the purpose (and underlying assumptions) of the present chapter, but also by the available SUTs and SIOTs, which provide no data on the different types of labour employed in each industry, fixed capital stock matrices, non-competitive imports, natural resources (such as land of different qualities), and consumption patterns associated with wages and profits.[5]

The remainder of the chapter is structured as follows. Section 9.2 deals with the output, import and employment matrix multipliers. Section 9.3 deals with the medium- and long-run effects of wage and currency devaluations on international price competitiveness and income distribution. Finally, Sect. 9.4 concludes.

---

[4]See, e.g. Ciccarone and Saltari (2015), Ferretti (2008), Mariolis (2017, 2018) and Tarancón et al. (2018).

[5]For the case of the Greek economy, the SUTs also provide no data on imported intermediate inputs.

## 9.2    Matrix Demand Multipliers in a Joint Production Framework: A Comparative Analysis of the Greek, Spanish and Eurozone Economies

### 9.2.1    The Analytic Framework

Consider an open, linear system involving only circulating capital and producing $n$ commodities by $n$ industries of pure joint production. Furthermore, assume that:

(i) There are no capacity or labour limitations to the multiplier process.

(ii) There are no non-competitive imports.

(iii) The net product is distributed to profits and wages that are paid at the end of the common production period.

(iv) The price of a commodity obtained as an output at the end of the production period is the same as the price of that commodity used as an input at the beginning of that period ("stationary prices").

(v) The input–output coefficients and the sectoral profit and money wage rates are given and constant; hence, the commodity prices are also given and constant ("fix-price economy").

(vi) The imports per unit of gross output of each commodity are given, constant and can be expressed by a diagonal matrix.

(vii) Labour is homogeneous within each industry but heterogeneous across industries.

(viii) There is a uniform, across income types, given and constant consumption pattern.

On the basis of these assumptions, the price side of the system is described by[6]

$$\mathbf{p}^T\mathbf{B} = \mathbf{w}^T\widehat{\mathbf{l}} + \mathbf{p}^T\mathbf{A}[\mathbf{I} + \widehat{\mathbf{r}}]  \qquad (9.1)$$

where $\mathbf{B}$ $(\geq \mathbf{0})$ denotes the $n \times n$ output coefficients matrix, $\mathbf{A}$ $(\geq \mathbf{0})$ the $n \times n$ input coefficients matrix, $\mathbf{I}$ the $n \times n$ identity matrix, $\widehat{\mathbf{l}}$ $(l_j > 0)$ the $n \times n$ diagonal matrix of direct labour coefficients, $\mathbf{p}^T$ $(> \mathbf{0}^T)$ the $1 \times n$ vector of commodity prices, $\mathbf{w}^T$ $(w_j > 0)$ the $1 \times n$ vector of money wage rates, and $\widehat{\mathbf{r}}$ $(r_j > 0)$ the $n \times n$ diagonal matrix of the sectoral profit rates.[7]

Provided that $[\mathbf{B} - \mathbf{A}]$ is non-singular, Eq. (9.1) can be rewritten as

---

[6]The diagonal matrix formed from the elements of an $n \times 1$ vector vector $\mathbf{x}$ is denoted by $\widehat{\mathbf{x}}$. Moreover, $\mathbf{e}$ denotes the summation vector, and $\mathbf{e}_i$ the $i$th unit vector.

[7]In fact, the positivity of *all* sectoral profit rates is a convenient but not necessary assumption. Moreover, as is well known, $\widehat{\mathbf{r}} > \mathbf{0}$ does not necessarily hold true for actual economies.

$$\mathbf{p}^T = \mathbf{w}^T \mathbf{V} + \mathbf{p}^T \mathbf{H} \tag{9.2}$$

where $\mathbf{H} \equiv \mathbf{A}\hat{\mathbf{r}}[\mathbf{B} - \mathbf{A}]^{-1}$ may be considered as the $\hat{\mathbf{r}}$–vertically integrated technical coefficients matrix, and $\mathbf{V} \equiv \hat{\mathbf{l}}[\mathbf{B} - \mathbf{A}]^{-1}$ denotes the matrix of direct and indirect labour requirements per unit of net output for each commodity.[8]

The quantity side of the system is described by

$$\mathbf{Bx} = \mathbf{Ax} + \mathbf{y}$$

or

$$\mathbf{x} = [\mathbf{B} - \mathbf{A}]^{-1}\mathbf{y} \tag{9.3}$$

and

$$\mathbf{y} = \mathbf{c}_w + \mathbf{c}_p - \mathbf{IM} + \mathbf{d}$$

or, setting $\mathbf{IM} = \hat{\boldsymbol{\mu}}\mathbf{Bx}$,

$$\mathbf{y} = \mathbf{c}_w + \mathbf{c}_p - \hat{\boldsymbol{\mu}}\mathbf{Bx} + \mathbf{d} \tag{9.4}$$

where $\mathbf{x}$ denotes the $n \times 1$ activity level vector, $\mathbf{y}$ the vector of effective final demand, $\mathbf{c}_w$ the vector of consumption demand out of wages, $\mathbf{c}_p$ the vector of consumption demand out of profits, $\mathbf{IM}$ the import demand vector, $\mathbf{d}$ ($\geq \mathbf{0}$) the autonomous demand vector for domestically produced commodities (government consumption expenditures, investments, and exports), and $\hat{\boldsymbol{\mu}}$ the diagonal matrix of imports per unit of gross output of each commodity.

If $\mathbf{f}$ ($\geq \mathbf{0}$) denotes the given, uniform and constant consumption pattern (associated with the two types of income), and $s_w$ ($s_p$) denotes the savings ratio out of wages (out of profits), where $0 \leq s_w < s_p \leq 1$, then Eqs. (9.2) and (9.3) imply that the consumption demands amount to

$$\mathbf{c}_w = \left[(1 - s_w)\left(\mathbf{w}^T \mathbf{V}\mathbf{y}\right)\left(\mathbf{p}^T \mathbf{f}\right)^{-1}\right]\mathbf{f} \tag{9.5}$$

$$\mathbf{c}_p = \left[(1 - s_p)\left(\mathbf{p}^T \mathbf{H}\mathbf{y}\right)\left(\mathbf{p}^T \mathbf{f}\right)^{-1}\right]\mathbf{f} \tag{9.6}$$

where the terms in brackets represent the levels of consumption demands out of wages and profits, respectively.

Substituting Eqs. (9.5) and (9.6) into Eq. (9.4) finally yields

---

[8]Both $\mathbf{H}$ and $\mathbf{V}$ are not necessarily semi-positive matrices (see Sect. 4.2.1).

$$\mathbf{y} = \left[\mathbf{C} - \widetilde{\mathbf{A}}\right]\mathbf{y} + \mathbf{d} \tag{9.7}$$

where

$$\mathbf{C} \equiv \left(\mathbf{p}^{\mathsf{T}}\mathbf{f}\right)^{-1}\mathbf{f}\left[(1 - s_w)\mathbf{w}^{\mathsf{T}}\mathbf{V} + (1 - s_p)\mathbf{p}^{\mathsf{T}}\mathbf{H}\right]$$

is the matrix of total consumption demand, and

$$\widetilde{\mathbf{A}} \equiv \widehat{\boldsymbol{\mu}}\mathbf{B}[\mathbf{B} - \mathbf{A}]^{-1}$$

is the matrix of total import demand.

Provided that $\left[\mathbf{I} - \mathbf{C} + \widetilde{\mathbf{A}}\right]$ is non-singular,[9] Eq. (9.7) can be uniquely solved for $\mathbf{y}$:

$$\mathbf{y} = \mathbf{M}\mathbf{d} \tag{9.8}$$

where $\mathbf{M} \equiv \left[\mathbf{I} - \mathbf{C} + \widetilde{\mathbf{A}}\right]^{-1}$ is the static multiplier linking autonomous demand to net output, i.e. a matrix multiplier in a Sraffian joint production and open economy framework. It is a multiplier of commodities (instead of industries) and the multiplier effects depend, in a rather complicated way, on the: (i) technical conditions of production; (ii) imports per unit of gross output; (iii) distributive variables ($w_j^{-1}\mathbf{w}$ and $\widehat{\mathbf{r}}$); (iv) savings ratios out of wages and profits; (v) consumption pattern; and (vi) physical composition of autonomous demand.[10] It goes without saying that, in general, any change in relative commodity prices, induced, directly or indirectly, by changes in income distribution, alters the elements of this matrix multiplier and, therefore, the total multiplier effects become ambiguous. This ambiguity is a salient feature of the multiplier process in Sraffian frameworks (see Sect. 8.5.2.2).

Finally, Eqs. (9.3) and (9.8) imply that the volumes of employment, $\mathbf{L} \equiv \widehat{\mathbf{l}}\mathbf{x}$, associated with $\mathbf{d}$ are given by

$$\mathbf{L} = \mathbf{V}\mathbf{M}\mathbf{d} \tag{9.9}$$

Thus, the employment effects of $\mathbf{d}$ can be decomposed (Kahn 1931) into "primary employment" effects, i.e.

$$\mathbf{L}_{\mathrm{I}} = \mathbf{V}\mathbf{d} \tag{9.9a}$$

and "secondary employment" effects, i.e.

---

[9]See Sect. 8.5.2.2 and Appendix 4 of Chap. 8.

[10]In the (more realistic) case of direct taxation, the term $(1 - s_q)$, $q = w, p$, should be replaced by $(1 - s_q)(1 - \tau_q)$, where $\tau_q$ denotes the tax rates (see Sect. 8.2).

$$\mathbf{L}_{II} \equiv \mathbf{L} - \mathbf{L}_I = \mathbf{V}[\mathbf{M} - \mathbf{I}]\mathbf{d} \tag{9.9b}$$

From Eqs. (9.8) and (9.9), it follows that the changes on (i) the monetary value of net output, $\Delta_y^i$ (net output multiplier); (ii) the monetary value of imports, $\Delta_{Im}^i$ (import multiplier); and (ii) total employment, $\Delta_L^i$ (total employment multiplier), induced by the increase of one unit in the autonomous demand for commodity $i$, are given by

$$\Delta_y^i \equiv \mathbf{p}^T \mathbf{M} \mathbf{e}_i \tag{9.10}$$

$$\Delta_{Im}^i \equiv \mathbf{p}^T \widetilde{\mathbf{A}} \mathbf{M} \mathbf{e}_i \tag{9.11}$$

and

$$\Delta_L^i \equiv \mathbf{e}^T \mathbf{V} \mathbf{M} \mathbf{e}_i \tag{9.12}$$

respectively.[11]

### 9.2.2 Main Empirical Results and Evaluation

The application of our analytic framework to the SUTs of the Greek (GR), Spanish (SP) and EZ economies for the year 2010 ($n = 63$) gives the following main results:[12]

(i) The matrices $[\mathbf{B} - \mathbf{A}]^{-1}$ exist and contain negative elements (nevertheless, their diagonal elements are all positive). Consequently, the actual economies under consideration do not have the usual properties of single-product systems.

---

[11]It should be clarified that we do not introduce the summation vector as an operator for the reduction of different types of labour to homogeneous labour (see Chaps. 4 to 6), but only to provide empirically convenient indices for the total employments effects. Nevertheless, these indices (like *any* other scalar indices) cannot replace the information gained from the actual matrices **VM**. As Kurz (1985) remarks, "With different qualities of labour it is not only total employment that is of interest, but also the quantities of employment of the different qualities of labour. Clearly, changes in the physical composition of a given volume of investment in price [...] terms in general entail not only changes in employment as a whole but also changes in the employment of the various kinds of labour. Moreover, with labour of different kinds available in fixed amounts in the short period, different physical specifications of investment demand will generally result in different degrees of employment and, perhaps, pose the problem of bottlenecks to the multiplier expansion." (p. 134).

[12]What follows draws on Mariolis et al. (2018a). For the available input–output data as well as the construction of the relevant variables, see Appendix 1 at the end of this chapter. Appendix 2 at the end of this chapter provides a dissection of the input–output structure of the Greek economy for the years 2005 and 2010. For updated estimates, which take into account the COVID-19 multiplier effects on the Greek economy, see Mariolis et al. (2020b, c).

(ii) Table 9.1 reports the estimations for the net output, $\Delta_y^i$, and import, $\Delta_{Im}^i$, multipliers (see Eqs. (9.10) and (9.11)) for the case where $s_w = 0$ and $s_p = 1$.[13] The last two columns give the percentage deviations of the EZ multipliers from those of the Greek and Spanish economies, and the last row gives the arithmetic mean of the multipliers for the total economy (TE), i.e. the changes on the monetary values of net output and imports, respectively, induced by a simultaneous increase of $1/n$ units in the autonomous demand for every commodity $i = 1, 2, \ldots, 63$. Finally, it is noted that the diagonal elements of the matrices $\mathbf{M}$ and $\widetilde{\mathbf{A}}\mathbf{M}$ are all positive.

(iii) Table 9.2 reports the estimations for the total employment multipliers, $\Delta_L^i$ (see Eq. (9.12)), the primary employment multipliers, $\Delta_{LI}^i \equiv \mathbf{e}^{\mathsf{T}}\mathbf{V}\mathbf{e}_i$, and the secondary employment multipliers, $\Delta_{LII}^i \equiv \mathbf{e}^{\mathsf{T}}\mathbf{V}[\mathbf{M} - \mathbf{I}]\mathbf{e}_i$, as percentages of the total employment multipliers, i.e. $\Delta_{LII}^i(\Delta_L^i)^{-1}$ (see Eqs. (9.9a) and (9.9b)). The last column gives the percentage deviations of the EZ total employment multipliers from those of the Greek and Spanish economies, and the last row gives the arithmetic means for the total economy. Finally, it is noted that the diagonal elements of the matrices $\mathbf{VM}$ are all positive. The graphs in Figs. 9.1, 9.2 and 9.3 give a visual representation of the values of the elements in matrices $\mathbf{M}$, $\widetilde{\mathbf{A}}\mathbf{M}$, and $\mathbf{VM}$, respectively: near zero values are shown in a shade of grey, while negative (positive) values tend to be bluish (reddish).

From these results it is deduced that:

(i) In terms of all multipliers, the EZ economy is more correlated with the Spanish economy rather than with the Greek one. More specifically, Table 9.3 gives the correlation matrix between the economies' net output, import and total employment multipliers. It follows that, for all economies under consideration, there is a significant negative linear correlation between the net output and import multipliers, and a significant positive linear correlation between the net output and total employment multipliers. However, in the case of the Greek economy, the former correlation is more intense, while the latter is less intense. These findings are in accordance with the figures reported in Table 9.2, which show that the *secondary* employment effects are significantly weaker in the Greek economy.[14]

---

[13]All the numerical results reported hereafter correspond to this case. Nevertheless, the graphs in Appendix 3 at the end of this chapter display the arithmetic means of the net output multipliers, $\overline{\Delta}_y^i$, as functions of the savings ratios for (a) $s_w = 0$ and $0 < s_p \leq 1$; and (b) $0 \leq s_w \leq 1$ and $s_p = 1$. We consider that this parametric analysis also captures the case of direct taxation (see footnote 10 of this chapter). Typical findings in many empirical studies suggest that there is a strong positive relationship between personal savings ratios and lifetime income (see, e.g. Dynan et al. 2004), $s_w < s_p$ and the difference between $s_w$ and $s_p$ is significant (say, in the range of 30% to 50%; see, e.g. Onaran and Galanis 2012, and the references therein). Thus, we presume that the results for the (polar) case $s_w = 0$ and $s_p = 1$ are sufficiently representative.

[14]Also consider the autonomous demand–transfer payments iso-employment curves for the Greek economy in Appendix 2 (Fig. 9.11) at the end of this chapter.

**Table 9.1** Net output and import multipliers, and their percentage deviations: Greek (GR), Spanish (SP) and Eurozone (EZ) economies, year 2010

| | GR | | SP | | EZ | | Percentage deviations $\Delta_y^i$ | | Percentage deviations $\Delta_{lm}^i$ | |
|---|---|---|---|---|---|---|---|---|---|---|
| $i$ | $\Delta_y^i$ | $\Delta_{lm}^i$ | $\Delta_y^i$ | $\Delta_{lm}^i$ | $\Delta_y^i$ | $\Delta_{lm}^i$ | EZ–GR | EZ–SP | EZ–GR | EZ–SP |
| 1 | 0.79 | 0.37 | 0.87 | 0.37 | 1.02 | 0.31 | 29.2% | 16.7% | −17.0% | −15.9% |
| 2 | 1.07 | 0.46 | 1.21 | 0.24 | 1.16 | 0.21 | 8.4% | −4.3% | −54.5% | −13.6% |
| 3 | 0.89 | 0.28 | 0.82 | 0.60 | 0.97 | 0.41 | 8.6% | 18.6% | 46.8% | −31.1% |
| 4 | 0.17 | 0.92 | 0.21 | 0.89 | 0.23 | 0.85 | 34.9% | 5.1% | −7.3% | −4.0% |
| 5 | 0.77 | 0.53 | 0.91 | 0.48 | 1.18 | 0.31 | 53.3% | 29.8% | −42.1% | −36.2% |
| 6 | 0.40 | 0.81 | 0.46 | 0.77 | 0.73 | 0.60 | 83.0% | 58.3% | −26.5% | −23.1% |
| 7 | 0.79 | 0.73 | 1.00 | 0.58 | 1.19 | 0.33 | 50.2% | 18.6% | −54.9% | −43.1% |
| 8 | 0.40 | 0.85 | 0.80 | 0.59 | 1.11 | 0.37 | 180.0% | 38.3% | −56.0% | −36.7% |
| 9 | 1.02 | 0.56 | 1.37 | 0.37 | 1.39 | 0.24 | 37.0% | 1.8% | −56.5% | −35.3% |
| 10 | 0.23 | 0.86 | 0.16 | 0.91 | 0.37 | 0.76 | 62.1% | 135.7% | −11.7% | −16.2% |
| 11 | 0.28 | 0.86 | 0.58 | 0.69 | 0.93 | 0.45 | 233.2% | 62.2% | −47.2% | −34.4% |
| 12 | 0.28 | 0.85 | 0.38 | 0.81 | 0.83 | 0.49 | 196.9% | 118.6% | −42.3% | −39.3% |
| 13 | 0.50 | 0.77 | 0.76 | 0.64 | 1.11 | 0.40 | 123.3% | 46.4% | −48.3% | −37.8% |
| 14 | 0.75 | 0.65 | 1.05 | 0.53 | 1.20 | 0.34 | 59.0% | 13.8% | −48.0% | −36.1% |
| 15 | 0.55 | 0.72 | 0.71 | 0.66 | 0.86 | 0.53 | 56.9% | 20.6% | −27.5% | −20.0% |
| 16 | 0.84 | 0.60 | 0.95 | 0.59 | 1.27 | 0.33 | 51.9% | 34.1% | −45.1% | −44.5% |
| 17 | 0.07 | 0.98 | 0.22 | 0.89 | 0.51 | 0.75 | 598.3% | 134.4% | −23.9% | −16.5% |
| 18 | 0.41 | 0.78 | 0.60 | 0.71 | 0.96 | 0.47 | 135.2% | 61.4% | −39.7% | −33.2% |
| 19 | 0.41 | 0.83 | 0.60 | 0.72 | 1.10 | 0.42 | 168.4% | 83.3% | −49.6% | −42.1% |
| 20 | 0.16 | 0.93 | 0.55 | 0.76 | 1.06 | 0.44 | 573.0% | 93.2% | −53.1% | −42.5% |
| 21 | 0.06 | 1.00 | 0.68 | 0.68 | 0.84 | 0.56 | 1217.9% | 24.1% | −43.7% | −17.3% |
| 22 | 0.44 | 0.78 | 0.75 | 0.66 | 0.95 | 0.48 | 114.1% | 26.2% | −38.4% | −26.2% |
| 23 | 0.99 | 0.13 | 1.29 | 0.38 | 1.39 | 0.28 | 40.4% | 7.9% | 115.0% | −27.0% |
| 24 | 0.77 | 0.49 | 0.88 | 0.40 | 0.94 | 0.37 | 21.2% | 7.0% | −25.9% | −8.6% |
| 25 | 1.33 | 0.37 | 1.24 | 0.35 | 1.33 | 0.17 | 0.2% | 7.8% | −54.8% | −52.3% |
| 26 | 1.02 | 0.43 | 1.02 | 0.50 | 1.29 | 0.24 | 26.7% | 27.4% | −45.2% | −52.6% |
| 27 | 1.04 | 0.40 | 1.30 | 0.36 | 1.40 | 0.22 | 34.2% | 7.3% | −45.7% | −39.8% |
| 28 | 1.24 | 0.24 | 1.32 | 0.37 | 1.50 | 0.20 | 21.2% | 13.7% | −18.2% | −46.1% |
| 29 | 1.16 | 0.39 | 1.47 | 0.33 | 1.41 | 0.19 | 20.9% | −4.1% | −50.8% | −41.9% |
| 30 | 1.31 | 0.29 | 1.51 | 0.27 | 1.49 | 0.16 | 13.7% | −0.8% | −45.7% | −41.6% |
| 31 | 1.12 | 0.35 | 1.18 | 0.42 | 1.37 | 0.24 | 22.3% | 16.6% | −31.7% | −43.3% |
| 32 | 0.91 | 0.36 | 1.09 | 0.40 | 1.11 | 0.28 | 21.5% | 1.5% | −21.5% | −30.1% |
| 33 | 0.84 | 0.50 | 1.06 | 0.54 | 1.01 | 0.47 | 20.8% | −4.8% | −7.0% | −13.5% |
| 34 | 0.50 | 0.74 | 1.32 | 0.36 | 1.29 | 0.27 | 159.0% | −2.2% | −63.8% | −24.9% |
| 35 | 1.26 | 0.48 | 1.71 | 0.39 | 1.67 | 0.26 | 32.9% | −2.5% | −46.8% | −35.0% |
| 36 | 1.05 | 0.33 | 1.25 | 0.30 | 1.33 | 0.18 | 27.5% | 6.3% | −44.4% | −39.1% |
| 37 | 1.00 | 0.54 | 1.19 | 0.46 | 1.36 | 0.21 | 35.5% | 13.8% | −61.6% | −55.7% |
| 38 | 1.09 | 0.47 | 1.25 | 0.34 | 1.28 | 0.21 | 17.5% | 2.0% | −55.1% | −37.4% |

(continued)

**Table 9.1**  (continued)

| | GR | | SP | | EZ | | Percentage deviations $\Delta_y^i$ | | Percentage deviations $\Delta_{lm}^i$ | |
|---|---|---|---|---|---|---|---|---|---|---|
| $i$ | $\Delta_y^i$ | $\Delta_{lm}^i$ | $\Delta_y^i$ | $\Delta_{lm}^i$ | $\Delta_y^i$ | $\Delta_{lm}^i$ | EZ–GR | EZ–SP | EZ–GR | EZ–SP |
| 39 | 1.16 | 0.24 | 1.05 | 0.29 | 1.18 | 0.20 | 1.8% | 11.8% | −16.5% | −30.8% |
| 40 | 1.10 | 0.42 | 1.38 | 0.41 | 1.50 | 0.23 | 36.5% | 8.7% | −44.6% | −42.6% |
| 41 | 1.25 | 0.36 | 1.44 | 0.31 | 1.36 | 0.19 | 8.8% | −5.3% | −47.3% | −38.9% |
| 42 | 0.97 | 0.43 | 1.30 | 0.24 | 1.39 | 0.21 | 43.2% | 7.1% | −51.9% | −13.1% |
| 43 | 1.33 | 0.29 | 1.30 | 0.26 | 1.42 | 0.18 | 6.4% | 9.7% | −37.3% | −32.2% |
| 44 | 1.34 | 0.18 | 1.09 | 0.07 | 0.50 | −0.03 | −62.6% | −54.2% | −115.6% | −138.0% |
| 45 | 1.25 | 0.29 | 1.43 | 0.33 | 1.34 | 0.21 | 7.3% | −6.7% | −28.3% | −36.3% |
| 46 | 1.11 | 0.31 | 1.37 | 0.38 | 1.40 | 0.21 | 25.5% | 1.6% | −29.8% | −43.7% |
| 47 | 1.31 | 0.43 | 1.41 | 0.30 | 1.39 | 0.32 | 6.6% | −1.2% | −25.5% | 7.9% |
| 48 | 1.20 | 0.36 | 1.37 | 0.39 | 1.25 | 0.27 | 4.5% | −8.7% | −23.8% | −30.8% |
| 49 | 1.16 | 0.33 | 1.43 | 0.30 | 1.13 | 0.24 | −3.0% | −21.1% | −25.4% | −19.0% |
| 50 | 1.00 | 0.32 | 0.89 | 0.43 | 0.91 | 0.30 | −8.4% | 2.1% | −5.4% | −29.2% |
| 51 | 1.70 | 0.39 | 1.91 | 0.39 | 1.89 | 0.20 | 11.5% | −1.0% | −49.0% | −49.2% |
| 52 | 1.15 | 0.38 | 1.26 | 0.38 | 1.32 | 0.23 | 14.7% | 4.9% | −39.7% | −40.2% |
| 53 | 1.43 | 0.37 | 1.53 | 0.46 | 1.50 | 0.23 | 5.0% | −1.9% | −37.2% | −49.6% |
| 54 | 1.50 | 0.35 | 1.68 | 0.34 | 1.67 | 0.19 | 11.1% | −0.7% | −46.9% | −45.9% |
| 55 | 1.66 | 0.35 | 1.77 | 0.36 | 1.87 | 0.18 | 12.6% | 5.7% | −48.1% | −48.7% |
| 56 | 1.18 | 0.29 | 1.52 | 0.41 | 1.55 | 0.17 | 31.3% | 1.8% | −42.1% | −58.3% |
| 57 | 1.25 | 0.53 | 1.56 | 0.39 | 1.81 | 0.19 | 45.4% | 15.8% | −63.9% | −50.3% |
| 58 | 1.06 | 0.20 | 1.32 | 0.28 | 1.37 | 0.18 | 29.0% | 4.2% | −12.3% | −37.3% |
| 59 | 1.37 | 0.37 | 1.57 | 0.36 | 1.48 | 0.17 | 8.1% | −6.1% | −55.6% | −54.0% |
| 60 | 1.37 | 0.43 | 1.54 | 0.44 | 1.75 | 0.20 | 27.2% | 13.9% | −53.2% | −54.6% |
| 61 | 0.96 | 0.15 | 1.34 | 0.45 | 1.41 | 0.22 | 46.5% | 5.0% | 43.3% | −52.1% |
| 62 | 1.33 | 0.21 | 1.18 | 0.29 | 1.25 | 0.13 | −5.9% | 6.5% | −40.2% | −55.5% |
| 63 | 1.93 | 0.45 | 2.02 | 0.41 | 2.11 | 0.20 | 9.6% | 4.6% | −56.9% | −52.3% |
| TE | 0.95 | 0.49 | 1.13 | 0.46 | 1.24 | 0.30 | 29.9% | 9.1% | −38.9% | −34.5% |

(ii) Unfavourable multiplier values are concentrated in industrial commodities, whereas favourable multiplier values are concentrated in service commodities. This view is further supported by the figures in Tables 9.4 and 9.5. Table 9.4 reports the arithmetic means of multipliers for the primary production, industrial and service commodities, and commodities that are primarily related to government activities (i.e. commodities 54 to 57; see Appendix 1 at the end of this chapter), while the figures in parentheses indicate the percentage deviations of the sectoral multiplier values from those of the total economy. It seems that these findings (in combination with those reported in Tables 9.1 and 9.2) are not in contrast with the observed recessions of the Greek and Spanish economies and, to the extent that they correspond to reality, reveal the inter-sectoral dimensions of these prolonged recessions. At the same time, they do not contradict those of some other studies (although using

**Table 9.2** Employment multipliers, decomposition and percentage deviations: GR, SP and EZ economies, year 2010

| | GR | | | SP | | | EZ | | | Percentage deviations $\Delta_L^i$ | |
|---|---|---|---|---|---|---|---|---|---|---|---|
| $i$ | $\Delta_L^i$ | $\Delta_{LII}^i$ | $\Delta_{LII}^i(\Delta_L^i)^{-1}$ (%) | $\Delta_L^i$ | $\Delta_{LII}^i$ | $\Delta_{LII}^i(\Delta_L^i)^{-1}$ (%) | $\Delta_L^i$ | $\Delta_{LII}^i$ | $\Delta_{LII}^i(\Delta_L^i)^{-1}$ (%) | EZ-GR | EZ-SP |
| 1 | 57.7 | 69.2 | −19.9% | 22.8 | 26.6 | −17.1% | 27.6 | 28.7 | −4.1% | −52.2% | 21.2% |
| 2 | 81.9 | 100.8 | −23.1% | 28.0 | 25.1 | 10.4% | 20.3 | 17.2 | 15.5% | −75.2% | −27.4% |
| 3 | 23.4 | 25.9 | −10.7% | 21.0 | 27.6 | −31.2% | 21.2 | 22.4 | −5.7% | −9.1% | 1.1% |
| 4 | 3.2 | 17.4 | −446.3% | 3.4 | 15.0 | −346.2% | 2.6 | 9.3 | −259% | −18.4% | −23.1% |
| 5 | 28.9 | 40.6 | −40.3% | 18.0 | 20.8 | −15.7% | 23.2 | 20.4 | 12.0% | −19.8% | 29.0% |
| 6 | 13.7 | 37.6 | −174.6% | 10.1 | 23.0 | −128.4% | 14.9 | 21.0 | −41.1% | 9.0% | 47.9% |
| 7 | 41.8 | 66.5 | −58.8% | 23.7 | 25.6 | −8.0% | 49.5 | 50.8 | −2.7% | 18.2% | 108.7% |
| 8 | 10.6 | 28.0 | −164.0% | 13.2 | 16.1 | −22.2% | 17.8 | 14.8 | 16.7% | 67.8% | 34.5% |
| 9 | 29.3 | 30.0 | −2.5% | 27.6 | 21.4 | 22.5% | 25.8 | 18.3 | 29.0% | −11.9% | −6.7% |
| 10 | 3.0 | 15.6 | −422.4% | 1.9 | 14.2 | −633.1% | 4.6 | 9.7 | −113% | 52.8% | 135.5% |
| 11 | 6.6 | 24.4 | −268.9% | 7.5 | 12.4 | −65.6% | 13.1 | 12.1 | 8.0% | 98.7% | 76.0% |
| 12 | 6.2 | 22.0 | −253.1% | 4.3 | 9.9 | −127.6% | 10.6 | 10.7 | −0.5% | 70.3% | 144.0% |
| 13 | 12.2 | 24.6 | −102.0% | 12.8 | 16.3 | −27.3% | 18.6 | 15.7 | 15.8% | 52.9% | 45.0% |
| 14 | 18.1 | 22.3 | −22.9% | 19.1 | 17.9 | 6.0% | 20.5 | 15.7 | 23.2% | 12.9% | 7.1% |
| 15 | 11.3 | 21.0 | −85.8% | 11.3 | 15.2 | −34.7% | 13.8 | 14.1 | −2.3% | 22.0% | 21.8% |
| 16 | 21.6 | 26.2 | −21.3% | 17.7 | 18.4 | −3.9% | 22.7 | 17.3 | 23.8% | 5.1% | 27.8% |
| 17 | 1.8 | 23.4 | −1228.0% | 2.9 | 12.6 | −328.0% | 8.2 | 14.8 | −80.6% | 365.6% | 178.7% |
| 18 | 8.6 | 20.7 | −141.4% | 8.9 | 14.2 | −59.8% | 15.5 | 14.9 | 4.0% | 81.6% | 75.2% |
| 19 | 12.1 | 30.3 | −150.9% | 8.6 | 13.4 | −56.2% | 18.2 | 15.5 | 14.8% | 50.7% | 111.3% |
| 20 | 4.0 | 25.6 | −545.2% | 9.7 | 17.2 | −77.5% | 17.2 | 15.0 | 12.3% | 332.4% | 77.0% |
| 21 | 2.6 | 70.1 | −2553.2% | 9.8 | 13.6 | −39.7% | 14.0 | 15.6 | −11.6% | 430.1% | 43.4% |
| 22 | 17.7 | 44.3 | −150.3% | 16.7 | 23.8 | −42.5% | 19.5 | 21.6 | −11.1% | 9.8% | 16.7% |

(continued)

**Table 9.2** (continued)

| | GR | | | SP | | | EZ | | | Percentage deviations $\Delta_L^i$ | |
|---|---|---|---|---|---|---|---|---|---|---|---|
| $i$ | $\Delta_L^i$ | $\Delta_{LI}^i$ | $\Delta_{LII}^i(\Delta_L^i)^{-1}$ (%) | $\Delta_L^i$ | $\Delta_{LI}^i$ | $\Delta_{LII}^i(\Delta_L^i)^{-1}$ (%) | $\Delta_L^i$ | $\Delta_{LI}^i$ | $\Delta_{LII}^i(\Delta_L^i)^{-1}$ (%) | EZ–GR | EZ–SP |
| 23 | 9.8 | 9.7 | 0.8% | 22.3 | 17.0 | 24.0% | 24.2 | 16.8 | 30.5% | 146.7% | 8.3% |
| 24 | 10.1 | 13.0 | −28.8% | 8.2 | 9.6 | −17.5% | 9.7 | 8.3 | 14.6% | −3.8% | 18.6% |
| 25 | 25.8 | 17.7 | 31.5% | 18.3 | 13.8 | 24.5% | 17.7 | 11.4 | 35.5% | −31.5% | −3.4% |
| 26 | 17.6 | 15.9 | 10.0% | 17.7 | 17.3 | 2.3% | 20.6 | 14.9 | 27.8% | 16.7% | 16.3% |
| 27 | 30.5 | 29.4 | 3.6% | 23.7 | 18.3 | 22.7% | 26.1 | 18.7 | 28.3% | −14.4% | 10.5% |
| 28 | 28.9 | 22.9 | 20.8% | 25.9 | 20.1 | 22.2% | 29.5 | 20.3 | 31.1% | 2.3% | 14.2% |
| 29 | 25.5 | 21.0 | 17.7% | 30.2 | 22.4 | 26.0% | 23.4 | 15.8 | 32.3% | −8.4% | −22.6% |
| 30 | 50.2 | 42.3 | 15.6% | 41.2 | 32.5 | 21.1% | 37.5 | 28.5 | 24.1% | −25.2% | −9.1% |
| 31 | 30.3 | 26.9 | 11.2% | 23.9 | 20.6 | 13.9% | 24.3 | 17.0 | 30.0% | −19.8% | 1.9% |
| 32 | 12.3 | 13.5 | −10.4% | 16.1 | 14.0 | 13.3% | 14.6 | 11.4 | 21.6% | 19.1% | −9.3% |
| 33 | 14.3 | 15.8 | −10.5% | 16.7 | 14.7 | 12.0% | 15.9 | 13.6 | 14.4% | 11.1% | −5.0% |
| 34 | 9.3 | 16.5 | −78.1% | 22.6 | 17.0 | 24.9% | 20.5 | 14.7 | 28.5% | 121.1% | −9.3% |
| 35 | 33.8 | 26.7 | 21.2% | 44.0 | 31.9 | 27.4% | 37.2 | 25.5 | 31.4% | 10.1% | −15.4% |
| 36 | 32.8 | 33.6 | −2.7% | 23.7 | 19.6 | 17.1% | 28.3 | 22.4 | 20.8% | −13.6% | 19.5% |
| 37 | 21.3 | 19.8 | 6.9% | 19.4 | 15.7 | 19.1% | 20.6 | 13.8 | 32.8% | −3.4% | 6.0% |
| 38 | 28.0 | 26.3 | 6.1% | 17.7 | 13.1 | 25.9% | 18.2 | 12.7 | 30.2% | −35.2% | 2.3% |
| 39 | 10.2 | 5.4 | 47.3% | 9.7 | 8.0 | 17.9% | 13.9 | 10.1 | 27.7% | 37.0% | 43.6% |
| 40 | 24.9 | 21.7 | 12.8% | 24.1 | 17.5 | 27.4% | 24.1 | 14.7 | 38.9% | −3.0% | 0.0% |
| 41 | 18.3 | 10.9 | 40.7% | 17.9 | 10.0 | 44.3% | 16.9 | 9.8 | 41.8% | −7.9% | −5.7% |
| 42 | 17.6 | 16.2 | 7.8% | 17.8 | 12.5 | 29.3% | 20.2 | 12.8 | 36.7% | 15.0% | 13.7% |
| 43 | 37.1 | 28.8 | 22.2% | 23.2 | 18.1 | 22.0% | 23.1 | 15.3 | 33.7% | −37.7% | −0.6% |
| 44 | 8.9 | 0.8 | 91.4% | 5.8 | 4.2 | 28.0% | −0.9 | 7.8 | 1016% | −109.6% | −114.7% |

| | | | | | | | | | | | |
|---|---|---|---|---|---|---|---|---|---|---|---|
| 45 | 25.3 | 19.0 | 24.7% | 30.4 | 23.5 | 22.6% | 22.3 | 16.1 | 28.0% | −11.7% | −26.5% |
| 46 | 41.1 | 39.1 | 4.9% | 27.7 | 21.4 | 22.7% | 25.1 | 17.9 | 28.8% | −38.8% | −9.4% |
| 47 | 30.0 | 22.5 | 25.0% | 23.1 | 16.0 | 30.9% | 26.3 | 19.3 | 26.6% | −12.4% | 13.5% |
| 48 | 21.4 | 15.9 | 26.0% | 27.4 | 21.2 | 22.6% | 22.8 | 18.1 | 20.7% | 6.3% | −17.0% |
| 49 | 28.7 | 24.7 | 13.9% | 34.8 | 27.3 | 21.8% | 22.1 | 19.9 | 10.1% | −23.0% | −36.6% |
| 50 | 23.9 | 23.9 | −0.1% | 12.3 | 13.0 | −5.6% | 9.0 | 8.3 | 7.8% | −62.2% | −26.6% |
| 51 | 53.5 | 36.8 | 31.2% | 67.2 | 51.5 | 23.4% | 48.9 | 33.3 | 31.9% | −8.5% | −27.2% |
| 52 | 28.5 | 24.8 | 13.2% | 24.7 | 20.4 | 17.4% | 24.0 | 17.9 | 25.5% | −16.0% | −3.0% |
| 53 | 42.2 | 32.2 | 23.7% | 47.8 | 41.8 | 12.5% | 37.8 | 29.5 | 22.1% | −10.4% | −20.8% |
| 54 | 33.6 | 21.7 | 35.6% | 33.7 | 22.0 | 34.7% | 29.2 | 17.1 | 41.4% | −13.2% | −13.6% |
| 55 | 43.4 | 27.6 | 36.4% | 35.1 | 21.8 | 37.8% | 36.2 | 20.7 | 42.8% | −16.4% | 3.3% |
| 56 | 24.2 | 20.2 | 16.4% | 27.2 | 17.9 | 34.1% | 28.3 | 18.4 | 35.1% | 17.1% | 4.0% |
| 57 | 48.3 | 43.0 | 10.9% | 37.4 | 27.5 | 26.3% | 46.6 | 32.1 | 31.0% | −3.5% | 24.8% |
| 58 | 17.5 | 15.2 | 13.1% | 24.0 | 18.6 | 22.6% | 24.8 | 18.1 | 27.3% | 42.0% | 3.3% |
| 59 | 47.7 | 38.8 | 18.7% | 33.0 | 23.1 | 29.8% | 29.2 | 20.6 | 29.6% | −38.9% | −11.4% |
| 60 | 46.4 | 38.0 | 18.1% | 39.0 | 29.8 | 23.6% | 38.3 | 24.8 | 35.2% | −17.6% | −1.9% |
| 61 | 20.5 | 21.2 | −3.3% | 39.9 | 33.8 | 15.2% | 28.5 | 21.0 | 26.1% | 38.9% | −28.7% |
| 62 | 64.7 | 56.8 | 12.3% | 38.6 | 37.2 | 3.6% | 30.1 | 25.6 | 14.9% | −53.5% | −22.0% |
| 63 | 89.8 | 67.7 | 24.7% | 89.1 | 71.5 | 19.8% | 102.9 | 83.2 | 19.2% | 14.5% | 15.5% |
| TE | 26.1 | 28.7 | −10.1% | 23.2 | 20.8 | 10.5% | 23.8 | 19.0 | 20.3% | −8.9% | 2.4% |

**Fig. 9.1** Representation of the net output multiplier matrices: GR, SP and EZ economies, year 2010

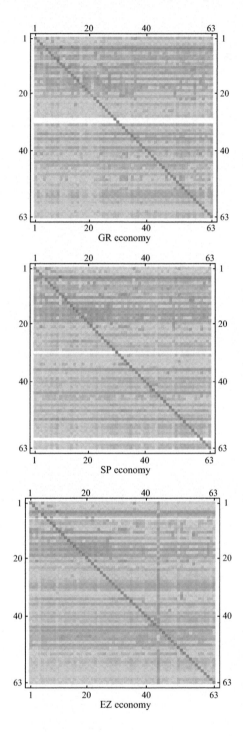

**Fig. 9.2** Representation of
the import multiplier
matrices: GR, SP and EZ
economies, year 2010

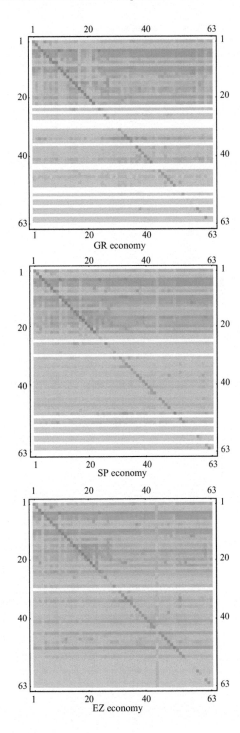

GR economy

SP economy

EZ economy

**Fig. 9.3** Representation of
the total employment
multiplier matrices: GR, SP
and EZ economies,
year 2010

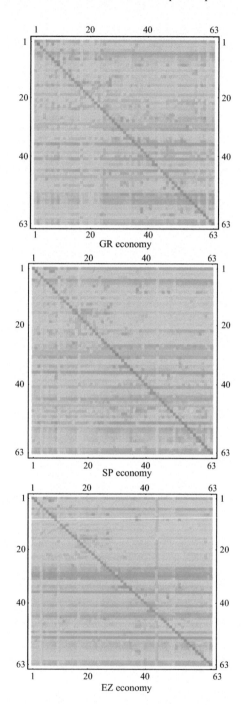

**Table 9.3** Correlation matrix between net output, import and total employment multipliers: GR, SP and EZ economies, year 2010

|  |  | $\Delta_{Im}^i$ | | | $\Delta_y^i$ | | | $\Delta_L^i$ | | |
|---|---|---|---|---|---|---|---|---|---|---|
|  |  | EZ | GR | SP | EZ | GR | SP | EZ | GR | SP |
| $\Delta_{Im}^i$ | EZ | 1.00 | | | | | | | | |
|  | GR | 0.80 | 1.00 | | | | | | | |
|  | SP | 0.91 | 0.84 | 1.00 | | | | | | |
| $\Delta_y^i$ | EZ | −0.72 | −0.53 | −0.58 | 1.00 | | | | | |
|  | GR | −0.83 | −0.82 | −0.80 | 0.78 | 1.00 | | | | |
|  | SP | −0.82 | −0.71 | −0.79 | 0.90 | 0.91 | 1.00 | | | |
| $\Delta_L^i$ | EZ | −0.41 | −0.27 | −0.28 | 0.78 | 0.61 | 0.67 | 1.00 | | |
|  | GR | −0.53 | −0.44 | −0.50 | 0.64 | 0.70 | 0.65 | 0.76 | 1.00 | |
|  | SP | −0.54 | −0.47 | −0.46 | 0.81 | 0.76 | 0.82 | 0.90 | 0.80 | 1.00 |

quite different frameworks; see, e.g. Blanchard and Leigh 2013; Gechert and Rannenberg 2015; International Monetary Fund 2012, pp. 41–43), while De Cos and Moral-Benito (2016), applying a smooth transition vector autoregression (STVAR) model, estimated Spain's fiscal multiplier at 1.40 for crisis (or turbulent) times and 0.60 for tranquil times. Furthermore, Charles (2016) and Charles et al. (2015, 2018) argue, both empirically (also especially regarding Southern Eurozone economies) and theoretically (within aggregate post-Keynesian–Kaleckian models), that, during important recessions, decreases in the savings ratio out of profits and/or the propensity to import are large enough to increase the fiscal multiplier value. Finally, Leão (2013) concludes that:

> real world multipliers [of government spending] are manifestly high enough to ensure that, below full employment, an increase in government spending reduces the debt-to-GDP ratio. (p. 463)[15]

Table 9.5 reports the percentage deviations and the "mean absolute deviation" (MAD) of the EZ sectoral multipliers from those of the Greek and Spanish economies. The figures suggest that the most remarkable deviations between the EZ and

---

[15]Ilzetzki et al. (2013), using a quarterly dataset of government expenditure in 44 countries (20 high-income and 24 developing) and the structural vector autoregression (SVAR) approach, found that (i) the output effect of an increase in government consumption is larger in industrial than in developing countries; (ii) the fiscal multiplier is relatively large in economies operating under predetermined exchange rates but is zero in economies operating under flexible exchange rates; and (iii) fiscal multipliers in open economies are smaller than in closed economies. Findings (i) and (ii) are not fully consistent with the findings in Mariolis et al. (2020a), which uses input–output data from the World Input–Output Database (WIOD) for the year 2014 (latest available data), and provides estimations of the net output, import and employment matrix demand multipliers in a post-Keynesian–Sraffian single production framework (see Appendix 4 of Chap. 8 of the present book) for the world's ten largest economies, i.e. United States of America, People's Republic of China, Japan, Germany, France, United Kingdom of Great Britain and Northern Ireland, Brazil, India, Italy, and Canada, which account for about 70% of the world's GDP.

**Table 9.4** Sectoral multipliers, and their percentage deviations from those of the total economy (TE): GR, SP and EZ economies, year 2010

| | GR | | | SP | | | EZ | | |
|---|---|---|---|---|---|---|---|---|---|
| | $\bar{\Delta}_y^i$ | $\bar{\Delta}_{lm}^i$ | $\bar{\Delta}_L^i$ | $\bar{\Delta}_y^i$ | $\bar{\Delta}_{lm}^i$ | $\bar{\Delta}_L^i$ | $\bar{\Delta}_y^i$ | $\bar{\Delta}_{lm}^i$ | $\bar{\Delta}_L^i$ |
| Primary production | 0.92 (−3.2%) | 0.37 (−24.5%) | 54.3 (108.0%) | 0.97 (−14.2%) | 0.40 (−13.0%) | 23.9 (3.0%) | 1.05 (−15.3%) | 0.31 (3.3%) | 23.1 (−2.9%) |
| Industry | 0.57 (−40.0%) | 0.70 (42.9%) | 14.5 (−44.4%) | 0.77 (−31.8%) | 0.62 (34.8%) | 13.2 (−43.1%) | 1.01 (−18.5%) | 0.43 (43.3%) | 17.9 (−24.8%) |
| Services | 1.19 (25.3%) | 0.36 (−26.5%) | 30.8 (18.0%) | 1.36 (20.4%) | 0.35 (−23.9%) | 29.3 (26.3%) | 1.37 (10.5%) | 0.22 (−26.7%) | 26.9 (13.0%) |
| Government activities | 1.40 (47.4%) | 0.38 (−22.4%) | 37.4 (43.3%) | 1.63 (44.2%) | 0.37 (−19.6%) | 33.4 (44.0%) | 1.73 (39.5%) | 0.18 (−40.0%) | 35.1 (47.5%) |
| TE | 0.95 | 0.49 | 26.1 | 1.13 | 0.46 | 23.2 | 1.24 | 0.30 | 23.8 |

**Table 9.5** Percentage deviations of the EZ sectoral multipliers from those of the GR and SP economies, year 2010

| | Percentage deviations $\overline{\Delta}_y^i$ | | Percentage deviations $\overline{\Delta}_{Im}^i$ | | Percentage deviations $\overline{\Delta}_L^i$ | |
|---|---|---|---|---|---|---|
| | EZ–GR | EZ–SP | EZ–GR | EZ–SP | EZ–GR | EZ–SP |
| Primary production | 14.1% | 8.2% | −16.2% | −22.5% | −57.5% | −3.3% |
| Industry | 77.2% | 31.2% | −38.6% | −30.6% | 23.4% | 35.6% |
| Services | 15.1% | 0.7% | −38.8% | −37.1% | −12.7% | −8.2% |
| Government activities | 23.5% | 6.1% | −52.6% | −51.4% | −6.1% | 5.1% |
| MAD | 35.5% | 13.4% | 31.2% | 30.1% | 31.2% | 15.7% |

Note: The MAD refers to the three main sectors of the economies

these two Southern Europe economies are, firstly, in the industry sector and, secondly, in the import dependencies of the government activity sector.[16] Nevertheless, the high value of the total employment multiplier (relative to the value of the net output multiplier) for the Greek primary sector is also noticeable, and rather indicates the low labour productivity (measured by $\overline{\Delta}_y^i \left(\overline{\Delta}_L^i\right)^{-1}$) of this sector.

(iii) Tables 9.1 and 9.2 also indicate that, in each economy, there are, on the one hand, commodities simultaneously characterized by net output, import and total employment multipliers that are better than those of the total economy (TE), and, on the other hand, commodities simultaneously characterized by net output, import and total employment multipliers that are worse than those of the total economy.[17] These findings could provide a basis for formulating well-targeted, scheduled and country-specific policy programs at the levels of individual commodities and industries. Nevertheless, to further analyze the demand management capabilities and specify the policy objectives at said levels, the *actual* composition of autonomous demand components (reported in the SUTs) as well as the governmental and external budget constraints should be taken into account,[18] while the—desirable—net output and employment multiplier effects should be weighted, in some way, by the—side—import multiplier effect. Regarding the latter issue, and given that both the Greek and Spanish economies faced serious external imbalances, and should strengthen their extraversion and export performance (consider, e.g. Collignon and Esposito 2017; Oelgemöller 2013), one possible way forward would be to focus exclusively on the tradable sectors (see Appendix 1 at the end of this chapter; Table 9.19) and combine the net output, import and total employment multipliers into the following composite index (of Cobb–Douglas type) for each tradable commodity:

---

[16]These findings are compatible with those on the "inter-sectoral linkages and leakages" in the Greek economy (see Appendix 2 at the end of this chapter).

[17]The highly import-dependent commodities (see Appendix 2 at the end of this chapter; Tables 9.28 and 9.30) tend to be characterized by low net output and employment multipliers and, at the same time, by high import multipliers.

[18]Consider Mariolis and Soklis (2018, pp. 127–131), and Sect. 8.3 of this book.

$$CI^i \equiv \left(\Delta_y^i\right)^\alpha \left(\Delta_L^i\right)^{1-\alpha} \left(\Delta_{Im}^i\right)^{-1}$$

or

$$CI^i = \left(\Delta O^i\right)^\alpha \left(\Delta E^i\right)^{1-\alpha}$$

where $\Delta O^i \equiv \Delta_y^i \left(\Delta_{Im}^i\right)^{-1}$, $\Delta E^i \equiv \Delta_L^i \left(\Delta_{Im}^i\right)^{-1}$ are the indices of net output and total employment multiplier effects relative to import multiplier effects, respectively, and $0 < \alpha < 1$. Hence, by assigning quite different weights to the indices $\Delta O^i$ and $\Delta E^i$, i.e. by setting $\alpha = 0.10$ and, alternatively, $\alpha = 0.90$, we define as "key commodities" (as "anti-key commodities") *for* effective demand management policies the commodities ranked in the top ten (in the bottom ten) positions according to both values of $CI^i$ (also consider, e.g. the reflections offered by Díaz et al. 2006, pp. 299–302). The results are reported in Table 9.6, where the numbers in parentheses indicate the rank order according to the two values of $CI^i$, while commodities which are common amongst the economies under consideration are denoted by bold characters. Thus, it is observed that, in all economies, the vast majority of key commodities belong to services, while the vast majority of anti-key commodities belong to industry and tend to be common across these three economies.[19]

### 9.2.3  Conclusions

Using input–output data from the Supply and Use Tables for the year 2010 and a joint production framework, we estimated the static net output, import and employment multipliers for the Greek, Spanish and Eurozone economies. It has been detected that:

(i) Although both Southern economies diverge to a considerable extent from the EZ economy, the latter is, however, more correlated with the Spanish economy rather than the Greek. This differentiated correlation probably results from, firstly, the heavy dependence, both direct and indirect, of the Greek industry sector on imports and, secondly, the high value of the total employment multiplier for the Greek primary sector.

(ii) The relatively high import dependencies of both the Greek and Spanish government activity sectors are noticeable. Nevertheless, in all the economies considered, the government activity sectors are characterized by favourable values for the net output and employment multipliers, casting doubt, therefore, on the fiscal consolidation measures implemented.

---

[19]Also compare Table 9.6 with Tables 9.30 and 9.31 (reported in Appendix 2 at the end of this chapter).

**Table 9.6** Key and anti-key tradable commodities for effective demand management policies: GR, SP and EZ economies, year 2010

| i | Key commodities | | | i | Anti-key commodities | | |
|---|---|---|---|---|---|---|---|
| | **GR** | **SP** | **EZ** | | **GR** | **SP** | **EZ** |
| 1 | – | (10, 10) | – | 4 | (34, 27) | (32, 25) | (39, 32) |
| 2 | (1, 10) | (2, 1) | (9, 9) | 6 | – | (28, 23) | (35, 29) |
| 3 | (7, 6) | – | – | 8 | (28, 24) | – | – |
| 29 | – | – | (4, 1) | 10 | (33, 26) | (34, 26) | (38, 31) |
| 34 | – | (8, 4) | – | 11 | (30, 25) | (30, 21) | (31, 26) |
| 35 | – | – | (2, 4) | 12 | (31, 25) | (31, 24) | (36, 27) |
| 40 | – | (9, 6) | (7, 7) | 13 | – | (25, 18) | – |
| 41 | – | (9, 2) | (10, 2) | 15 | – | (26, 19) | (33, 27) |
| 42 | – | – | (8, 5) | 17 | (36, 28) | (33, 25) | (37, 30) |
| 45 | (5, 2) | (4, 2) | (6, 7) | 18 | (29, 23) | (28, 21) | – |
| 46 | (4, 3) | (5, 4) | (5, 6) | 19 | – | (29, 21) | – |
| 47 | (10, 9) | – | – | 20 | (20, 27) | (28, 22) | – |
| 48 | – | (6, 5) | – | 21 | (35, 28) | (27, 20) | (34, 28) |
| 49 | (6, 4) | – | – | 24 | – | – | (32, 24) |
| 50 | (9, 7) | – | – | 34 | (27, 21) | – | – |
| 52 | (8, 8) | (7, 6) | – | Total number | 10 | 12 | 9 |
| 53 | – | (3, 5) | (1, 3) | | | | |
| 61 | (3, 1) | – | – | | | | |
| 62 | – | (1, 3) | – | | | | |
| Total number | 9 | 11 | 9 | | | | |

(iii) A sustainable (in fiscal terms) and growth-oriented policy could be directed towards, on the one hand, reallocation of government consumption and investment expenditures and, on the other hand, targeted increases in both domestic and foreign demand (i.e. for industries characterized by favourable multiplier values) by means of production and employment subsidies.

(iv) With regard to the tradable sectors, extremely unfavourable multiplier values tend to be concentrated in certain industrial commodities, whereas extremely favourable multiplier values are dispersed amongst various service and primary production commodities. This two-sided finding suggests that effective demand management policies are necessary, but not sufficient, for resetting the Eurozone system on viable paths of recovery. It rather calls, on the one hand, for a common intra-Eurozone industrial and trade policy reform, and, on the other hand, for per country and commodity-specific demand policies.

## 9.3  Wage versus Currency Devaluation in a Single Production Framework: A Comparative Analysis of the Greek and Italian Economies

### 9.3.1  The Analytic Framework

#### 9.3.1.1  Basic Assumptions and Price Equation

Consider an open, linear economy involving only single products, basic commodities, circulating capital and competitive imports.[20] Assume that:

(i) At least one commodity enters directly into its own production.

(ii) The economy is "viable"; namely, the Perron–Frobenius (P–F hereafter) eigenvalue of the "irreducible and primitive" matrix of total input–output coefficients is less than 1.[21]

(iii) Production imports are paid at the beginning of the common production period. Wages are paid at the end of the common production period, and there are no savings out of this income.

(iv) The input–output coefficients, output levels, nominal profit rates, sectoral net tax rates on gross output ("taxes less subsidies on products"), and foreign currency prices of the imported commodities are all given and constant.

(v) Labour is homogeneous within each industry but heterogeneous across industries.

---

[20]What follows draws on Mariolis et al. (2019b).

[21]The P–F eigenvalue of a semi-positive $n \times n$ matrix $\mathbf{A} \equiv [a_{ij}]$ is denoted by $\lambda_{\mathbf{A}1}$, while $\lambda_{\mathbf{A}k}, k = 2,$ ..., $n$ and $|\lambda_{\mathbf{A}2}| \geq |\lambda_{\mathbf{A}3}| \geq \ldots \geq |\lambda_{\mathbf{A}n}|$, denote the non-dominant eigenvalues.

Based on these assumptions we can write

$$\mathbf{p}^T = \left(\mathbf{p}^T \mathbf{A}_L^d + E\mathbf{p}^{*T}\mathbf{A}_L^m + \mathbf{p}^T\widehat{\mathbf{T}}\right)[\mathbf{I} + \widehat{\mathbf{r}}] + \mathbf{w}^T\widehat{\mathbf{l}} \qquad (9.13)$$

where $\mathbf{p}^T (> \mathbf{0}^T)$ denotes the $1 \times n$ stationary price vector of domestically produced commodities, $E (= 1)$ the single nominal exchange rate, and $\mathbf{p}^{*T}$ the $1 \times n$ vector of foreign currency prices of the imported commodities, $\mathbf{p}^T = E\mathbf{p}^{*T}$. Furthermore, $\mathbf{A}_L^d \equiv \left[a_{ijL}^d\right]$, $\mathbf{A}_L^m \equiv \left[a_{ijL}^m\right]$ denote the $n \times n$ domestic and imported direct input (or Leontief) coefficients matrices, respectively, $\widehat{\mathbf{T}} \equiv \left[\tau_j\right]$ the $n \times n$ matrix of net tax rates, $\widehat{\mathbf{r}}$ $(r_j > 0)$ the $n \times n$ matrix of the sectoral profit rates, $\mathbf{w}^T$ $(w_j > 0)$ the $1 \times n$ vector of money wage rates, and $\widehat{\mathbf{l}}$ $(l_j > 0)$ the $n \times n$ diagonal matrix of direct labour coefficients.

### 9.3.1.2   Wage Devaluation

Equation (9.13) can be rewritten as

$$\mathbf{p}^T = \mathbf{p}^T\mathbf{F} + E\mathbf{m}^T + \mathbf{w}^T\widehat{\mathbf{l}} \qquad (9.14)$$

where

$$\mathbf{F} \equiv \left[\mathbf{A}_L^d + \widehat{\mathbf{T}}\right][\mathbf{I} + \widehat{\mathbf{r}}]$$

and

$$\mathbf{m}^T \equiv \mathbf{p}^{*T}\mathbf{A}_L^m[\mathbf{I} + \widehat{\mathbf{r}}]$$

From Eq. (9.14) it directly follows that $\lambda_{\mathbf{F1}} < 1$, since $\mathbf{p}^T > \mathbf{0}^T$.

In order to estimate the price effect of wage devaluation we use the following dynamic version of system (9.14):

$$\mathbf{p}_{t+1}^T = \mathbf{p}_t^T\mathbf{F} + E\mathbf{m}^T + \mathbf{w}'^T\widehat{\mathbf{l}}, \quad t = 0, 1, 2, \ldots \qquad (9.15)$$

where $\mathbf{p}_0^T = \mathbf{p}^T$, $\mathbf{w}'^T \equiv (1 - w)\mathbf{w}^T$ and $w$ denotes the uniform devaluation rate, $0 < w < 1$. The solution of Eq. (9.15) is

$$\mathbf{p}_{t+1}^T = \mathbf{p}_0^T\mathbf{F}^{t+1} + \left(E\mathbf{m}^T + \mathbf{w}'^T\widehat{\mathbf{l}}\right)\left[\mathbf{F}^t + \mathbf{F}^{t-1} + \ldots + \mathbf{F} + \mathbf{I}\right] \qquad (9.16)$$

From Eqs. (9.13) and (9.15) it follows that the initial value of the actual average profit rate is given by

$$\bar{r}_0 \equiv \left(\mathbf{p}_0^T \mathbf{A}_L \hat{\mathbf{r}} \mathbf{x}\right) \left(\mathbf{p}_0^T \mathbf{A}_L \mathbf{x}\right)^{-1} \tag{9.17}$$

where

$$\mathbf{A}_L \equiv \mathbf{A}_L^d + \mathbf{A}_L^m + \hat{\mathbf{T}}$$

and $\mathbf{x}$ ($> \mathbf{0}$) denotes the $n \times 1$ vector of the actual gross outputs. The per period average inflation rate is defined as

$$\pi_t \equiv \left(\mathbf{p}_t^T \mathbf{x}\right) \left(\mathbf{p}_{t-1}^T \mathbf{x}\right)^{-1} - 1$$

and, therefore, the per period average real profit rate could be estimated by (see Sraffa 1932; Lager 2001)

$$\rho_t \equiv (\bar{r}_0 - \pi_t)(1 + \pi_t)^{-1} \tag{9.18}$$

Finally, the international price competitiveness of the economy could be estimated by the following "real exchange rate" index:

$$q_t \equiv E_t \left(\mathbf{p}_t^T \mathbf{EX}\right)^{-1} \tag{9.19}$$

where $\mathbf{EX}$ ($\geq \mathbf{0}$) denotes the $n \times 1$ vector of actual exports.

From Eqs. (9.15), (9.16), (9.18) and (9.19) it follows that:

(i) The price vector tends to

$$\mathbf{p}_\infty^T \equiv \left(E\mathbf{m}^T + \mathbf{w}'^T \hat{\mathbf{l}}\right)[\mathbf{I} - \mathbf{F}]^{-1}$$

since $\lambda_{\mathbf{F}1} < 1$; that is,

$$\mathbf{p}_\infty^T = \mathbf{p}_0^T - w\mathbf{w}^T \hat{\mathbf{l}}[\mathbf{I} - \mathbf{F}]^{-1}$$

and

$$\mathbf{p}_\infty^T > (1 - w)\mathbf{p}_0^T$$

The adjustment of the price vector towards its new equilibrium level depends on the magnitudes of $\lambda_{\mathbf{F}1}$ and $|\lambda_{\mathbf{F}k}|^{-1}\lambda_{\mathbf{F}1}$. More specifically, the number $-\log\lambda_{\mathbf{F}1}$ provides a measure for the convergence rate of $\mathbf{p}_{t+1}^T$ to $\mathbf{p}_\infty^T$, while the smallest damping ratio, $|\lambda_{\mathbf{F}2}|^{-1}\lambda_{\mathbf{F}1}$, can be considered as a lower measure of the intrinsic resilience of $\mathbf{p}_{t+1}^T$ to disturbance.

(ii) The price-movement is governed by $\mathbf{w}^T \hat{\mathbf{l}} \mathbf{F}'$, which could be conceived of as the series of "dated quantities" of direct labour needed for the production of the domestic commodities (see Sraffa 1960, pp. 34–35; Kurz and Salvadori 1995, p. 175), since

$$w^{-1}\left(\mathbf{p}_{t+1}^{\mathrm{T}} - \mathbf{p}_t^{\mathrm{T}}\right) = -\mathbf{w}^{\mathrm{T}}\widehat{\mathbf{l}}\mathbf{F}' \tag{9.20}$$

It then follows that the prices of "labour-intensive" commodities tend to, but not necessarily, decrease more than the prices of "capital-intensive" commodities (also see Sect. 2.3.3). In the extreme (and unrealistic) case where $\mathbf{F}$ has rank 1 and, therefore, $\lambda_{\mathbf{F}k} = 0$ for all $k$, i.e. the smallest damping ratio becomes infinite, Eq. (9.20) implies that, for $t \geq 1$, the difference vector $\mathbf{p}_{t+1}^{\mathrm{T}} - \mathbf{p}_t^{\mathrm{T}}$ becomes collinear to the left P–F eigenvector of $\mathbf{F}$.

(iii) The average real profit rate first increases and then decreases, tending to $\bar{r}_0$, since $\mathbf{p}_{t+1}^{\mathrm{T}} < \mathbf{p}_t^{\mathrm{T}}$ and $\pi_t$ tends to 0.

(iv) The international competitiveness increases and tends to $\left(\mathbf{p}_{\infty}^{\mathrm{T}}\mathbf{EX}\right)^{-1}$, since $E_t = E$.

### 9.3.1.3   Currency Devaluation Under Complete Wage Indexation

Let $\mathbf{B}_w$, $\mathbf{B}_w^*$ be the given and constant semi-positive $n \times n$ matrices of domestic and imported wage commodities per unit of labour employed, respectively. Then

$$\mathbf{w}^{\mathrm{T}} = \mathbf{p}^{\mathrm{T}}\mathbf{B}_w + E\mathbf{p}^{*\mathrm{T}}\mathbf{B}_w^*$$

and, therefore, Eq. (9.13) can be rewritten as

$$\mathbf{p}^{\mathrm{T}} = \mathbf{p}^{\mathrm{T}}\mathbf{G} + E\mathbf{h}^{\mathrm{T}} \tag{9.21}$$

where

$$\mathbf{G} \equiv \mathbf{F} + \mathbf{B}_w\widehat{\mathbf{l}}$$

and

$$\mathbf{h}^{\mathrm{T}} \equiv \mathbf{m}^{\mathrm{T}} + \mathbf{p}^{*\mathrm{T}}\mathbf{B}_w^*\widehat{\mathbf{l}}$$

From Eqs. (9.14) and (9.21) it directly follows that $\lambda_{\mathbf{F}1} < \lambda_{\mathbf{G}1} < 1$, since $\mathbf{F} \leq \mathbf{G}$ and $\mathbf{p}^{\mathrm{T}} > \mathbf{0}^{\mathrm{T}}$.

In order to estimate the price effect of currency devaluation we use the following dynamic version of system (9.21):

$$\mathbf{p}_{t+1}^{\mathrm{T}} = \mathbf{p}_t^{\mathrm{T}}\mathbf{G} + E'\mathbf{h}^{\mathrm{T}}, \quad t = 0, 1, 2, \ldots \tag{9.22}$$

where $\mathbf{p}_0^{\mathrm{T}} = \mathbf{p}^{\mathrm{T}}$, $E' \equiv (1 + \varepsilon)E$ and $\varepsilon \, (> 0)$ denotes the devaluation rate. The solution of Eq. (9.22) is

$$\mathbf{p}_{t+1}^{\mathrm{T}} = \mathbf{p}_0^{\mathrm{T}}\mathbf{G}^{t+1} + E'\mathbf{h}^{\mathrm{T}}\left[\mathbf{G}^t + \mathbf{G}^{t-1} + \ldots + \mathbf{G} + \mathbf{I}\right] \tag{9.23}$$

From Eqs. (9.18), (9.19), (9.22) and (9.23) it follows that:

(i) The price vector tends to

$$\mathbf{p}_\infty^{\mathrm{T}} \equiv E'\mathbf{h}^{\mathrm{T}}[\mathbf{I} - \mathbf{G}]^{-1}$$

since $\lambda_{\mathbf{G}1} < 1$; that is,

$$\mathbf{p}_\infty^{\mathrm{T}} = (1 + \varepsilon)\mathbf{p}_0^{\mathrm{T}}$$

Analogously to the case of the wage devaluation, the price adjustment process depends on the magnitudes of $\lambda_{\mathbf{G}1}$ and $\lambda_{\mathbf{G}1}|\lambda_{\mathbf{G}k}|^{-1}$.

(ii) The price-movement is governed by $\mathbf{h}^{\mathrm{T}}\mathbf{G}^t$, which could be conceived of as the series of dated quantities of imported inputs needed for the production of the domestic commodities, since

$$\varepsilon^{-1}\left(\mathbf{p}_{t+1}^{\mathrm{T}} - \mathbf{p}_t^{\mathrm{T}}\right) = \mathbf{h}^{\mathrm{T}}\mathbf{G}^t \tag{9.24}$$

It then follows that the prices of "imported input-intensive" commodities tend to, but not necessarily, increase more than the prices of "domestic input-intensive" commodities.

(iii) The average real profit rate first decreases and then increases, tending to $\bar{r}_0$, since $\mathbf{p}_t^{\mathrm{T}} < \mathbf{p}_{t+1}^{\mathrm{T}}$ and $\pi_t$ tends to 0.

(iv) The international competitiveness first increases and then decreases, returning to its initial value, since $\mathbf{p}_\infty^{\mathrm{T}} = (1 + \varepsilon)\mathbf{p}_0^{\mathrm{T}}$.

### 9.3.1.4    Long-Run Trade-Offs

Now we assume that the distributive variables ($w_j$ or/and $r_j$) exhibit stable structures in *relative* terms. Thus, Eq. (9.14) can be written as

$$\widetilde{\mathbf{p}}^{\mathrm{T}} = \widetilde{\mathbf{p}}^{\mathrm{T}}\mathbf{F} + \widetilde{E}\mathbf{m}^{\mathrm{T}} + \widetilde{w}\left(\overline{w}^{-1}\mathbf{w}^{\mathrm{T}}\right)\widehat{\mathbf{l}}$$

or, since $\lambda_{\mathbf{F}1} < 1$,

$$\widetilde{\mathbf{p}}^{\mathrm{T}}\widetilde{E}^{-1} = \left[\mathbf{m}^{\mathrm{T}} + \left(\widetilde{w}\widetilde{E}^{-1}\right)\left(\overline{w}^{-1}\mathbf{w}^{\mathrm{T}}\right)\widehat{\mathbf{l}}\right][\mathbf{I} - \mathbf{F}]^{-1} \tag{9.25}$$

where $\overline{w}$ denotes the economy's actual average wage rate, defined as

$$\overline{w} \equiv \left(\mathbf{w}^{\mathrm{T}}\widehat{\mathbf{l}}\mathbf{x}\right)\left(\mathbf{e}^{\mathrm{T}}\widehat{\mathbf{l}}\mathbf{x}\right)^{-1}$$

and $\widetilde{w}$ the "overall level" of wage rates. Furthermore, it is convenient (although not essential) to adopt the actual normalized export vector as the standard of value or *numéraire*, writing

$$\widetilde{\mathbf{p}}^{\mathrm{T}}\mathbf{z} = 1, \mathbf{z} \equiv \left(\mathbf{p}_0^{\mathrm{T}}\mathbf{EX}\right)^{-1}\mathbf{EX} \tag{9.26}$$

Thus, Eqs. (9.25) and (9.26) imply

$$\widetilde{w} = \left(1 - \widetilde{E}\mathbf{m}^{\mathrm{T}}[\mathbf{I} - \mathbf{F}]^{-1}\mathbf{z}\right)\left[\left(\overline{w}^{-1}\mathbf{w}^{\mathrm{T}}\right)\widehat{\mathbf{l}}[\mathbf{I} - \mathbf{F}]^{-1}\mathbf{z}\right]^{-1} \tag{9.27}$$

which defines the linear trade-off between "the" wage rate and the exchange rate, measured in terms of the normalized export vector $\mathbf{z}$. It is noted that (i) commodity prices are linear functions of $\widetilde{E}$; and (ii) the straight line defined by Eq. (9.27) passes through the point: ($\widetilde{E} = E = 1$, $\widetilde{w} = \overline{w}$), at which $\widetilde{\mathbf{p}}^{\mathrm{T}} = \mathbf{p}_0^{\mathrm{T}}$.

Equation (9.14) can also be written as

$$\widetilde{\mathbf{p}}^{\mathrm{T}} = \widetilde{\mathbf{p}}^{\mathrm{T}}\widetilde{\mathbf{F}}(\widetilde{r}) + \widetilde{E}\widetilde{\mathbf{m}}(\widetilde{r})^{\mathrm{T}} + \mathbf{w}^{\mathrm{T}}\widehat{\mathbf{l}}$$

or, if $\lambda_{\overline{\mathbf{F}}(\widetilde{r})\mathbf{l}} < 1$,

$$\widetilde{\mathbf{p}}^{\mathrm{T}}\widetilde{E}^{-1} = \left(\widetilde{\mathbf{m}}(\widetilde{r})^{\mathrm{T}} + \widetilde{E}^{-1}\mathbf{w}^{\mathrm{T}}\widehat{\mathbf{l}}\right)\left[\mathbf{I} - \widetilde{\mathbf{F}}(\widetilde{r})\right]^{-1} \tag{9.28}$$

where

$$\widetilde{\mathbf{F}}(\widetilde{r}) \equiv \left[\mathbf{A}_{\mathrm{L}}^{\mathrm{d}} + \widehat{\mathbf{T}}\right]\left[\mathbf{I} + \widetilde{r}(\overline{r}_0^{-1}\widehat{\mathbf{r}})\right]$$

$$\widetilde{\mathbf{m}}(\widetilde{r})^{\mathrm{T}} \equiv \mathbf{p}^{*\mathrm{T}}\mathbf{A}_{\mathrm{L}}^{\mathrm{m}}\left[\mathbf{I} + \widetilde{r}(\overline{r}_0^{-1}\widehat{\mathbf{r}})\right]$$

and $\widetilde{r}$ denotes the overall level of profit rates. Each element in $\left[\mathbf{I} - \widetilde{\mathbf{F}}(\widetilde{r})\right]^{-1}$ is positive and a strictly increasing convex function of $\widetilde{r}$, tending to plus infinity as $\lambda_{\widetilde{\mathbf{F}}(\widetilde{r})\mathbf{l}}$ approaches 1 from below (see, e.g. Kurz and Salvadori 1995, p. 116). Thus, Eqs. (9.26) and (9.28) imply

$$\tilde{E} = \left(1 - \mathbf{w}^T \hat{\mathbf{l}}\left[\mathbf{I} - \tilde{\mathbf{F}}(\tilde{r})\right]^{-1}\mathbf{z}\right)\left(\tilde{\mathbf{m}}(\tilde{r})^T\left[\mathbf{I} - \tilde{\mathbf{F}}(\tilde{r})\right]^{-1}\mathbf{z}\right)^{-1} \qquad (9.29)$$

which defines the trade-off between the exchange rate and "the" profit rate. It is noted that (i) commodity prices are *not* necessarily monotonic functions of $\tilde{r}$; and (ii) the curve defined by Eq. (9.29) passes through the point: $(\tilde{r} = \bar{r}_0, \tilde{E} = E = 1)$, at which $\tilde{\mathbf{p}}^T = \mathbf{p}_0^T$.

It will now be clear that, for $\tilde{E} = E = 1$, there is also a trade-off between the wage rate and the profit rate, defined by

$$\tilde{w} = \left(1 - \tilde{\mathbf{m}}(\tilde{r})^T\left[\mathbf{I} - \tilde{\mathbf{F}}(\tilde{r})\right]^{-1}\mathbf{z}\right)\left[(\bar{w}^{-1}\mathbf{w}^T)\hat{\mathbf{l}}\left[\mathbf{I} - \tilde{\mathbf{F}}(\tilde{r})\right]^{-1}\mathbf{z}\right]^{-1} \qquad (9.30)$$

The curve defined by Eq. (9.30) passes through the point: $(\tilde{r} = \bar{r}_0, \tilde{w} = \bar{w})$, at which $\tilde{\mathbf{p}}^T = \mathbf{p}_0^T$.

These three trade-offs yield the loci of all feasible *long-run* income (re)-distributions. Hence, taking also into account Eqs. (9.25) and (9.28), it follows that:[22]

(i) In terms of control system theory, the reciprocal of the functions defined by Eqs. (9.27), (9.29) and (9.30) constitute transfer functions of the dynamic systems defined by Eqs. (9.15) and (9.22).

(ii) If the wage rate (the profit rate) is held constant, an increase in the exchange rate *relative* to the wage rate, i.e. an "effective currency devaluation", must reduce the profit rate (the wage rate).

(iii) An effective currency devaluation improves the competitiveness of domestic output, since it cheapens all domestic products relative to all imported commodities.

(iv) Technical progress (i.e. a decrease in any of the elements of $\mathbf{A}_L^d$, $\mathbf{A}_L^m$, $\hat{\mathbf{l}}$), or a decrease in any foreign import price or net tax rate, necessarily implies that the trade-off curves move outwards from the origin. Hence, the areas under those curves can be conceived of as measures of the economy's overall performance (see Degasperi and Fredholm 2010).

The hitherto available empirical studies of the matrix multipliers of autonomous demand (see Sect. 9.2) do not take into account neither the underlying income distribution changes nor the possible underutilization of productive capacity (which may result in a non-inverse relationship between the distributive variables; see Chap. 11). Hence, the estimation of the *total* multiplier effects for actual economies is a pending issue.

In the late 1970's Kalman (1979) noted:

> If one is foolish enough to believe newspapers, "the depreciation of the dollar (against foreign currencies) has no effect on Americans unless they travel abroad." The professional

---

[22]See Chap. 2 and Sect. 8.5.

economic analysis is a good deal more sophisticated. According to the *basic Keynesian model*, the domestic price rise as a percentage of depreciation would correspond, at most, to the percentage of foreign trade in the national economy; thus, for the US, less than about 8 per cent of the lowered external value of the dollar would react back in the form of higher domestic prices. On the other hand, the so called *global monetary theory* implies that the effect would be, in the long run, 100 per cent. [...] Evidently both the Keynesian and global monetarist models represent attempts to grasp a piece of economic reality. As such, they are intuitively valuable. But they contribute little to modeling the economic system *as it really is*; their information value is too modest. The essential issues are of course of the *dynamic* type. The hedging phrases "short run" and "long run" simply reveal the inability of the simple models to cope with this aspect of the problem. Given that this is how things are, the effectiveness of economic theory for building models of predictive power is now and is likely to remain very limited. In the interests of modesty, it is well to bear in mind that the scenario is analogous with predicting the behavior, i.e., output, of a computer which has just been loaded with a big program about which little is known. The Keynesian will say: In the short run, the computer will put out many numbers. The global monetarist will say: In the long run the computer will stop but it will be warmer when it stops than when it has started. Such statements are trivial or irrelevant or misleading as far as the real system aspects are concerned. There is no substitute for finding out what the program actually is. It is well to bear in mind also (to rub in some conventional wisdom from the system field) that in the economics problem under discussion a simple and reliable answer may be expected only if it were true that the effect of exchange-rate change on domestic price level is *loosely* coupled to the rest of the economy. If a phenomenon is loosely coupled then we are in the classical-science situation area and there is no problem. (Very probably the problem has been solved already.) But, on the other hand, if the phenomenon is *not* loosely coupled, then we have a system-determined problem with all its attendant difficulties. Contemporary analytic economic theory shows little awareness of these elementary facts of life. (pp. 17–18)

## 9.3.2   Main Empirical Results and Evaluation

The application of our analytic framework to the SIOTs of the Greek and Italian economies, for the year 2010 ($n = 63$), gives the following main results:[23]

(i) Tables 9.7 and 9.8 report the estimations of the arithmetic mean values of the dated quantities of direct labour and imported inputs, i.e. $\mathbf{w}^T\widehat{\mathbf{I}}\mathbf{F}^t$ and $\mathbf{h}^T\mathbf{G}^t$ (see Eqs. (9.20) and (9.24), in the three main sectors of the economies, that is, primary production, industry, and services. Furthermore, Tables 9.9 and 9.10 report the sectoral compositions of imports and exports. It is noted that the Euclidean angle (measured in degrees) between the total import vectors of the two economies is almost 34.1°, while the relevant figure for the total export vectors is almost 75.6°: these figures further indicate the differences between the import–export structures of the two economies under consideration.

(ii) In a recent empirical study, Aydoğuş et al. (2018) introduce the following cost-push input–output price model (using our symbols):

---

[23]For the available input–output data as well as the construction of the relevant variables, see Appendix 4 at the end of this chapter.

**Table 9.7** Sectoral dated quantities of direct labour and imported inputs: Greece, year 2010

| Labour | Primary production | Industry | Services | Total economy | Imported inputs | Primary production | Industry | Services | Total economy |
|---|---|---|---|---|---|---|---|---|---|
| $\mathbf{w}^T\hat{\mathbf{I}}$ | 0.118 | 0.188 | 0.228 | 0.208 | $\mathbf{h}^T$ | 0.181 | 0.244 | 0.147 | 0.185 |
| $\mathbf{w}^T\hat{\mathbf{I}}\mathbf{F}$ | 0.110 | 0.095 | 0.105 | 0.101 | $\mathbf{h}^T\mathbf{G}$ | 0.169 | 0.145 | 0.135 | 0.140 |
| $\mathbf{w}^T\hat{\mathbf{I}}\mathbf{F}^2$ | 0.074 | 0.060 | 0.073 | 0.068 | $\mathbf{h}^T\mathbf{G}^2$ | 0.120 | 0.107 | 0.114 | 0.112 |
| $\mathbf{w}^T\hat{\mathbf{I}}\mathbf{F}^3$ | 0.049 | 0.042 | 0.051 | 0.047 | $\mathbf{h}^T\mathbf{G}^3$ | 0.091 | 0.085 | 0.096 | 0.092 |
| Sum | 0.351 | 0.385 | 0.457 | 0.425 | Sum | 0.561 | 0.581 | 0.492 | 0.528 |
| Total sum $\mathbf{w}^T\hat{\mathbf{I}}[\mathbf{I}-\mathbf{F}]^{-1}$ | 0.464 | 0.483 | 0.580 | 0.537 | Total sum $\mathbf{h}^T[\mathbf{I}-\mathbf{G}]^{-1}$ | 1.000 | 1.000 | 1.000 | 1.000 |

**Table 9.8** Sectoral dated quantities of direct labour and imported inputs: Italy, year 2010

| Labour | Primary production | Industry | Services | Total economy | Imported inputs | Primary production | Industry | Services | Total economy |
|---|---|---|---|---|---|---|---|---|---|
| $\mathbf{w}^T\widehat{\mathbf{l}}$ | 0.255 | 0.111 | 0.227 | 0.184 | $\mathbf{h}^T$ | 0.090 | 0.263 | 0.089 | 0.155 |
| $\mathbf{w}^T\widehat{\mathbf{l}}\mathbf{F}$ | 0.074 | 0.080 | 0.103 | 0.094 | $\mathbf{h}^T\mathbf{G}$ | 0.184 | 0.135 | 0.114 | 0.125 |
| $\mathbf{w}^T\widehat{\mathbf{l}}\mathbf{F}^2$ | 0.058 | 0.058 | 0.074 | 0.067 | $\mathbf{h}^T\mathbf{G}^2$ | 0.113 | 0.094 | 0.105 | 0.102 |
| $\mathbf{w}^T\widehat{\mathbf{l}}\mathbf{F}^3$ | 0.043 | 0.043 | 0.054 | 0.049 | $\mathbf{h}^T\mathbf{G}^3$ | 0.088 | 0.073 | 0.093 | 0.085 |
| Sum | 0.430 | 0.292 | 0.458 | 0.394 | Sum | 0.475 | 0.565 | 0.401 | 0.467 |
| Total sum $\mathbf{w}^T\widehat{\mathbf{l}}[\mathbf{I}-\mathbf{F}]^{-1}$ | 0.548 | 0.408 | 0.605 | 0.527 | Total sum $\mathbf{h}^T[\mathbf{I}-\mathbf{G}]^{-1}$ | 1.000 | 1.000 | 1.000 | 1.000 |

**Table 9.9** Sectoral compositions (%) of imports and exports: Greece, year 2010

|  | Imports | | | | |
|  | Intermediate consumption | Final consumption expenditure by households | Gross fixed capital formation | Total imports | Total exports |
|---|---|---|---|---|---|
| Primary production | 2.4 | 3.1 | 0.01 | 2.3 | 4.0 |
| Industry | 70.5 | 88.3 | 97.5 | 80.6 | 39.2 |
| Services | 27.1 | 8.6 | 2.4 | 17.1 | 56.8 |
| Total | 100 | 100 | 100 | 100 | 100 |

**Table 9.10** Sectoral compositions (%) of imports and exports: Italy, year 2010

|  | Imports | | | | |
|  | Intermediate consumption | Final consumption expenditure by households | Gross fixed capital formation | Total imports | Total exports |
|---|---|---|---|---|---|
| Primary production | 2.6 | 4.0 | 0.6 | 2.7 | 1.3 |
| Industry | 80.4 | 83.5 | 91.4 | 81.7 | 82.0 |
| Services | 17.0 | 12.5 | 8.0 | 15.6 | 16.7 |
| Total | 100 | 100 | 100 | 100 | 100 |

$$\mathbf{p}^T = \left( E\mathbf{p}^{*T}\mathbf{A}_L^m + \mathbf{w}^T\hat{\mathbf{l}} + \mathbf{s}^T \right)\left[ \mathbf{I} - \mathbf{A}_L^d \right]^{-1}$$

where $\mathbf{p}^T$ $(= E\mathbf{p}^{*T})$ is identified with $\mathbf{e}^T$, and $\mathbf{s}^T$ denotes the vector of "unit operational surplus (unit capital costs)", while the unit labour and capital costs, $\mathbf{w}^T\hat{\mathbf{l}} + \mathbf{s}^T$, are assumed to be constant. Thus, they estimate the *total* effect, both direct and indirect, of the nominal exchange rate change on the stationary commodity prices as: $\mathbf{e}^T\mathbf{A}_L^m\left[\mathbf{I} - \mathbf{A}_L^d\right]^{-1}$, i.e. as the sums of the column elements of $\mathbf{A}_L^m\left[\mathbf{I} - \mathbf{A}_L^d\right]^{-1}$.[24] The calculations are performed for 26 countries (including Italy, for the year 2010, but not Greece) and 27 sectors, using IO tables (from OECD Stan Database, Eurostat, and Izmir Regional Development Agency (IZKA) of Turkey):

> The estimates presented here should be considered to be upper limits; actual changes in the prices are likely to be lower. [. . .] The results range from 0.07 for US to 0.34 for Ireland [for

---

[24]Nevertheless, Aydoğuş et al. (2018) remark that "[i]t is possible to investigate a closed version of this model as well. The closed model endogenises labor costs and consumption. Any shock to the model would trigger an increase in labor costs, thus income. A rise in income causes an increase in consumption which, in turn, causes further expansion. Thus a closed model would be able to account for *induced* effects of a price change, as well. Such an expansion is performed, and the implied results are calculated. Unfortunately results that are obtained from a closed version of our model are too high to be realistic. This is probably due to the implicit assumption that any increase in prices is fully reflected in wages, which creates a balooning effect that leads to unrealistically high figures. So we do not report results from the closed version of our model." (p. 326).

Italy the result is 0.174]. The average is 0.18; on average, a unit change in the exchange rate causes a 0.18 unit change in the CPI [consumer price index]. (Aydoğuş et al. 2018, p. 327)

By applying that approach to *our* data, we obtained the following results for Greece: 0.138 (primary production), 0.234 (industry), 0.114 (services), 0.161 (total economy) and 0.139 (CPI), while for Italy the results were as follows: 0.112, 0.345, 0.115, 0.203 and 0.170, respectively.[25] It should be noted, however, that the sums of the column elements of $\mathbf{A}_L^m \left[ \mathbf{I} - \mathbf{A}_L^d \right]^{-1}$ coincide with both the vector of share of "foreign content (or foreign value added)" in final demand for domestically produced products and the vector of "total backward leakages".[26]

(iii) Figures 9.4 and 9.5 (the horizontal axes are plotted in logarithmic scale) display the moduli of the normalized eigenvalues, $|\lambda_{\bullet i}| \lambda_{\bullet 1}^{-1}$, of the system matrices, $\bullet \equiv \mathbf{F}, \mathbf{G}$. These figures also report the relevant convergence rates, smallest damping ratios and the arithmetic, *AM*, and geometric, *GM*, means of the non-zero non-dominant eigenvalues.

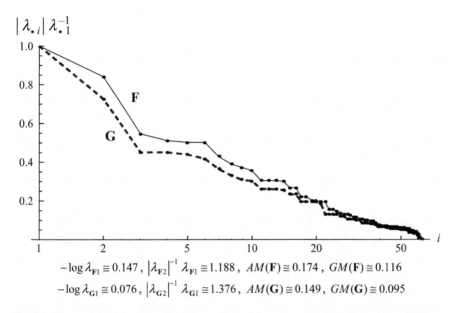

$$-\log \lambda_{\mathrm{F1}} \cong 0.147, \; \left| \lambda_{\mathrm{F2}} \right|^{-1} \lambda_{\mathrm{F1}} \cong 1.188, \; AM(\mathbf{F}) \cong 0.174, \; GM(\mathbf{F}) \cong 0.116$$

$$-\log \lambda_{\mathrm{G1}} \cong 0.076, \; \left| \lambda_{\mathrm{G2}} \right|^{-1} \lambda_{\mathrm{G1}} \cong 1.376, \; AM(\mathbf{G}) \cong 0.149, \; GM(\mathbf{G}) \cong 0.095$$

**Fig. 9.4** The moduli of the normalized eigenvalues of the system matrices: Greece, year 2010

---

[25]For an alternative, input–output modelling and estimation of the total effect, see De Grauwe and Holvoet (1978): the application to a group of "European Community-countries" (Belgium, France, Germany, Italy, Netherlands, and U.K.), for the year 1970, gave that, under no (under complete) wage indexation, a 1% devaluation increases the CPI by approximately 0.50% (0.67%) in all these countries (pp. 75–76). According to those authors, "the results of the model give no indication of the speed with which the price transmission operates. It could be that the time it takes for the price effects to be fully realised is three months, six months, a year or more." (p. 77).

[26]See Appendix 2 at the end of this chapter.

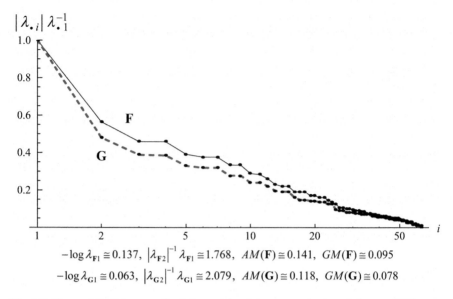

$$-\log \lambda_{F1} \cong 0.137, \ \left|\lambda_{F2}\right|^{-1} \lambda_{F1} \cong 1.768, \ AM(\mathbf{F}) \cong 0.141, \ GM(\mathbf{F}) \cong 0.095$$

$$-\log \lambda_{G1} \cong 0.063, \ \left|\lambda_{G2}\right|^{-1} \lambda_{G1} \cong 2.079, \ AM(\mathbf{G}) \cong 0.118, \ GM(\mathbf{G}) \cong 0.078$$

**Fig. 9.5** The moduli of the normalized eigenvalues of the system matrices: Italy, year 2010

(iv) Table 9.11 reports the estimations of the initial values of the actual average profit rates, $\bar{r}_0$ (see Eq. (9.17)), of the two economies, and their constituent components, i.e. the shares of profits and net taxes (on products) in the net product, the average wage rate, $\bar{w}$, the aggregate labour and capital productivities, and the aggregate capital intensity. These figures suggest that the considerable deviation between the values of $\bar{r}_0$ in the two economies is directly related to the deviation between the values of the aggregate capital productivities. It should also be noted that, with the exception of six product-industries, the elements of the vector of vertically integrated labour coefficients, defined as $\mathbf{e}^T \widehat{\mathbf{l}} \left[ \mathbf{I} - \left( \mathbf{A}_L^d + \mathbf{A}_L^m \right) \right]^{-1}$, are greater in the Greek than in the Italian economy; in fact, the "mean absolute deviation" between these vectors is almost 74.4%. By contrast, the P–F eigenvalues of the matrices $\mathbf{A}_L^d$, $\mathbf{A}_L^m$ and $\mathbf{A}_L^d + \mathbf{A}_L^m$ are greater in the Italian than in the Greek economy; in the case of the Italian economy, these eigenvalues are approximately equal to 0.455, 0.343 and 0.607, respectively, while in the case of the Greek

| **Table 9.11** The initial values of the actual average profit rates and their constituent components: Greece and Italy, year 2010 | | Greece | Italy |
|---|---|---|---|
| | $\bar{r}_0$ (%) | 84.7 | 54.3 |
| | Share of profits (%) | 64.7 | 63.4 |
| | Share of net taxes (%) | 4.5 | 2.8 |
| | $\bar{w}$ | 0.006 | 0.011 |
| | Labour productivity | 0.021 | 0.033 |
| | Capital productivity | 1.392 | 0.876 |
| | Capital intensity | 0.015 | 0.037 |

economy, they are approximately equal to 0.380, 0.196 and 0.500, respectively.[27] All these figures are in accordance with those on aggregate labour and capital productivities. Furthermore, Tables 9.12 and 9.13 report the estimations of the evolution of the average inflation rate, $\pi_t$, the consumer price index (CPI), and the "relative" average real profit rate, i.e. $\rho_t \bar{r}_0^{-1}$ (see Eq. (9.18)), $t = 1, \ldots, 4$, for the representative cases where $w = 20\%$ or $30\%$ and $\varepsilon = 30\%$ or $50\%$.[28]

**Table 9.12** The estimated evolution of the average inflation rate, CPI and average real profit rate (%): Greece, year 2010

| | Wage devaluation | | | | | | Currency devaluation | | | | | |
|---|---|---|---|---|---|---|---|---|---|---|---|---|
| | $w = 20\%$ | | | $w = 30\%$ | | | $\varepsilon = 30\%$ | | | $\varepsilon = 50\%$ | | |
| | $\pi_t$ | CPI | $\rho_t \bar{r}_0^{-1}$ | $\pi_t$ | CPI | $\rho_t \bar{r}_0^{-1}$ | $\pi_t$ | CPI | $\rho_t \bar{r}_0^{-1}$ | $\pi_t$ | CPI | $\rho_t \bar{r}_0^{-1}$ |
| $t = 1$ | −3.6 | −3.1 | 108.1 | −5.4 | −4.7 | 112.4 | 5.7 | 5.7 | 88.2 | 9.5 | 9.5 | 81.0 |
| $t = 2$ | −2.2 | −2.2 | 104.8 | −3.3 | −3.4 | 107.4 | 3.9 | 3.9 | 91.7 | 6.3 | 6.2 | 87.0 |
| $t = 3$ | −1.5 | −1.5 | 103.3 | −2.3 | −2.4 | 105.1 | 3.0 | 3.1 | 93.6 | 4.8 | 4.8 | 90.1 |
| $t = 4$ | −1.1 | −1.1 | 102.3 | −1.6 | −1.7 | 103.6 | 2.4 | 2.4 | 94.8 | 3.7 | 3.8 | 92.1 |

**Table 9.13** The estimated evolution of the average inflation rate, CPI and average real profit rate (%): Italy, year 2010

| | Wage devaluation | | | | | | Currency devaluation | | | | | |
|---|---|---|---|---|---|---|---|---|---|---|---|---|
| | $w = 20\%$ | | | $w = 30\%$ | | | $\varepsilon = 30\%$ | | | $\varepsilon = 50\%$ | | |
| | $\pi_t$ | CPI | $\rho_t \bar{r}_0^{-1}$ | $\pi_t$ | CPI | $\rho_t \bar{r}_0^{-1}$ | $\pi_t$ | CPI | $\rho_t \bar{r}_0^{-1}$ | $\pi_t$ | CPI | $\rho_t \bar{r}_0^{-1}$ |
| $t = 1$ | −3.2 | −2.8 | 109.3 | −4.7 | −4.2 | 114.1 | 4.4 | 3.8 | 87.9 | 7.4 | 6.4 | 80.4 |
| $t = 2$ | −2.0 | −2.1 | 105.9 | −3.1 | −3.2 | 109.1 | 3.5 | 3.4 | 90.4 | 5.7 | 5.6 | 84.7 |
| $t = 3$ | −1.5 | −1.6 | 104.4 | −2.3 | −2.5 | 106.8 | 2.8 | 2.8 | 92.2 | 4.5 | 4.5 | 87.8 |
| $t = 4$ | −1.1 | −1.2 | 103.2 | −1.7 | −1.9 | 105.0 | 2.3 | 2.4 | 93.5 | 3.6 | 3.7 | 90.0 |

---

[27]As is well known, the inverse of the vertically integrated labour coefficients can be considered as measures of the sectoral productivities of labour, while $\lambda_{\bullet 1}^{-1} - 1$, $\bullet = A_L^d, A_L^m, A_L^d + A_L^m$, can be considered as measures of the aggregate capital productivities. For a recent empirical study of the European Union economies, see Tarancón et al. (2018).

[28]Large one-off wage devaluations (in excess of, say, 30%) can result in strong socio-political tensions and, therefore, are not necessarily feasible. On the other hand, it has been estimated that, in the period 2010–2012, *only* a large currency devaluation, i.e. in excess of 57%–60%, could contribute to the recovery of the Greek economy (Katsinos and Mariolis 2012; Mariolis 2012, 2013). For a recent estimate of the so-called redenomination risk (i.e. the risk of defaults obtained by the redenomination of debts in a different currency) of Greek exit from the European Monetary Union, see Lapavitsas (2018). According to that estimate (which fits with the approaches by Nordvig and Firoozye 2012; Nordvig 2014; Durand and Villemot 2016), "The bulk of the redenomination risk is concentrated in the public sector, and there is no doubt at all that in the event of exit Greece would have to declare default and seek deep restructuring of its public debt. The net relevant positions of both the private (non-financial) sector and of the banking sector, however, are clearly positive and unlikely to change drastically in the near future. From the perspective of the private economy, therefore, the "balance sheet effect" of exit is likely to be positive, though the distribution of the effect across the non-financial and the banking sector is likely to be uneven, and hence some agents would be adversely affected. The distribution is not

(v) Tables 9.14 and 9.15 report the estimations of the evolution of the international competitiveness of the economies, expressed as $q_t q_0^{-1}$ (see Eq. (9.19)), $t = 1$, ..., 3, for the cases where the devaluation rates are in the range of 20% to 50%.

(vi) Tables 9.16 and 9.17 report the long-run effects of the two devaluations on the initial (actual) values of the distributive variables ($\widetilde{w} = \overline{w}$, $\widetilde{r} = \overline{r}_0$; see Table 9.11). More specifically, in Table 9.16, the values for the profit rate are estimated by Eq. (9.30), for $w = 20\%$ or $30\%$, while, in Table 9.17, the values of the wage and profit rates are estimated by Eqs. (9.27) and (9.29), respectively, for

**Table 9.14** The estimated evolution of the international competitiveness (%): Greece, year 2010

|  | Wage devaluation | | | |
|---|---|---|---|---|
|  | $w = 20\%$ | $w = 30\%$ | $w = 40\%$ | $w = 50\%$ |
| $t = 1$ | 102.3 | 103.5 | 104.7 | 105.9 |
| $t = 2$ | 104.1 | 106.2 | 108.5 | 110.8 |
| $t = 3$ | 105.3 | 108.2 | 111.3 | 114.5 |
| $t \rightarrow +\infty$ | 108.5 | 113.2 | 118.4 | 124.1 |
|  | Currency devaluation | | | |
|  | $\varepsilon = 20\%$ | $\varepsilon = 30\%$ | $\varepsilon = 40\%$ | $\varepsilon = 50\%$ |
| $t = 1$ | 112.6 | 118.3 | 123.7 | 128.8 |
| $t = 2$ | 109.7 | 113.9 | 117.8 | 121.4 |
| $t = 3$ | 107.9 | 111.2 | 114.3 | 117.1 |

**Table 9.15** The estimated evolution of the international competitiveness (%): Italy, year 2010

|  | Wage devaluation | | | |
|---|---|---|---|---|
|  | $w = 20\%$ | $w = 30\%$ | $w = 40\%$ | $w = 50\%$ |
| $t = 1$ | 102.3 | 103.5 | 104.8 | 106.1 |
| $t = 2$ | 104.1 | 106.3 | 108.6 | 111.0 |
| $t = 3$ | 105.4 | 108.4 | 111.5 | 114.8 |
| $t \rightarrow +\infty$ | 109.2 | 114.5 | 120.3 | 126.7 |
|  | Currency devaluation | | | |
|  | $\varepsilon = 20\%$ | $\varepsilon = 30\%$ | $\varepsilon = 40\%$ | $\varepsilon = 50\%$ |
| $t = 1$ | 114.2 | 120.7 | 127.0 | 133.0 |
| $t = 2$ | 111.4 | 116.5 | 121.3 | 125.8 |
| $t = 3$ | 109.5 | 113.7 | 117.5 | 121.0 |

---

possible to assess, given the data available at present. The more unpredictable and complex part of the redenomination risk concerns the Bank of Greece [BoG], and is a result of the support that the central bank has given to the Greek banking sector in the course of the crisis. The liabilities of the BoG, however, have a different legal and economic status compared to the debt of the public sector, leaving open the question of redenomination. In view especially of the accumulation of foreign securities by the BoG during the last several years, the position of the BoG is not as weak as it might appear at first sight." (pp. 242–243).

$\varepsilon = 30\%$ or $50\%$ (as in Tables 9.12 and 9.13). Finally, Table 9.18 reports the areas under the $\tilde{w} - \tilde{E}$, $\tilde{E} - \tilde{r}$ and $\tilde{w} - \tilde{r}$ curves.[29]

From these results, it is deduced that:

(i) In general lines, the shares of dated quantities of direct labour and, in particular, of imported inputs in the cost of outputs tend to be greater in the Greek than in the Italian economy. More specifically, in the case of the Greek economy, services is the most labour- and export-intensive sector and, at the same time, the less imported input-intensive one, whereas industry is the most imported input- and (total) import-intensive sector. Finally, the relatively high indirect dependencies of the primary production sector on both labour and imported inputs, as well as the relatively high direct dependence of industry on labour inputs, are also noticeable (see Tables 9.7 and 9.9). Thus, it can be concluded that the international competitiveness effects of wage devaluation tend to be more (less) favourable for the service

**Table 9.16** The estimated long-run effect of wage devaluation on the profit rate: Greece and Italy, year 2010

|         | Wage devaluation | |
|---------|-----------|-----------|
|         | $w = 20\%$ | $w = 30\%$ |
| Greece  | 91.6% | 95.0% |
|         | (−0.35) | (−0.32) |
| Italy   | 59.8% | 62.5% |
|         | (−0.43) | (−0.40) |

Note: The figures in parentheses give the arc elasticities of the profit rate with respect to the wage rate

**Table 9.17** The estimated long-run effects of currency devaluation on the wage and profit rates: Greece and Italy, year 2010

|         | Currency devaluation | | | |
|---------|-----------|-----------|-----------|-----------|
|         | $\varepsilon = 30\%$ | | $\varepsilon = 50\%$ | |
|         | Wage rate | Profit rate | Wage rate | Profit rate |
| Greece  | 0.003 | 68.4% | 0.001 | 57.7% |
|         | (−2.56) | (−0.82) | (−3.57) | (−0.95) |
| Italy   | 0.006 | 42.1% | 0.003 | 33.5% |
|         | (−2.25) | (−0.97) | (−2.86) | (−1.18) |

Note: The figures in parentheses give the arc partial elasticities of the distributive variables with respect to the exchange rate

**Table 9.18** The areas under the wage–exchange–profit rates curves: Greece and Italy, year 2010

|        | $\tilde{w} - \tilde{E}$ curve | | $\tilde{E} - \tilde{r}$ curve | | $\tilde{w} - \tilde{r}$ curve | |
|--------|-----------|----------|-----------|----------|-----------|----------|
|        | z(Greece) | z(Italy) | z(Greece) | z(Italy) | z(Greece) | z(Italy) |
| Greece | 0.0135 | 0.0128 | 1.7964 | 1.8830 | 0.0133 | 0.0113 |
| Italy  | 0.0223 | 0.0225 | 1.0826 | 1.0529 | 0.0130 | 0.0128 |

Note: The symbol z(•) indicates that the *numéraire* is the normalized export vector of the country: •

---

[29]The graphs in Appendix 5 at the end of this chapter depict these curves. Experiments show that the overall picture does not change significantly when the actual gross output vector (or, alternatively, the actual net output vector) is used as the *numéraire*.

(for the primary production) sector, while those of currency devaluation tends to be more (less) favourable for the service (for the industry) sector. In the case of the Italian economy, services is the most labour-intensive sector and, at the same time, the less imported input-intensive one, whereas industry is the most imported input-, import- and export- intensive sector and, at the same time, the less labour-intensive one. Finally, the high dependencies of the primary production sector on both direct labour and indirect imported inputs are also noticeable (see Tables 9.8 and 9.10). Thus, it can be concluded that the international competitiveness effects of wage devaluation tend to be more (less) favourable for the service (for the industry) sector, while those of currency devaluation tends to be more (less) favourable for the service (for the industry) sector.

(ii) Regarding the Greek economy and the case of currency devaluation, our abovementioned findings do not differ much from those reported by Katsinos and Mariolis (2012), which are based on the input–output table data for the year 2005 and on different model assumptions. This further support the view that the structural features of the Greek economy have been shaped well before the emergence of the so-called PIIGS crisis (see Appendix 2 at the end of this chapter). Our findings also seem to be compatible with those on the matrix multipliers of autonomous demand for the Greek economy (see Sect. 9.2), which suggest that:

(a) The industry sector is heavily dependent on imports and, therefore, diverges considerably from the industry sector in the Eurozone economy.
(b) The highly import-dependent industries tend to be characterized by low net output and employment multipliers and, at the same time, by high import multipliers.
(c) A well-targeted effective demand management policy could be mainly based on the service sector, and is necessary but not sufficient for resetting the economy on viable paths of recovery. Hence, industrial policy and structural transformation are also needed.

(iii) In both economies the convergence rate of the wage devaluation process is considerably greater than that of the currency devaluation process, while the damping ratios of the wage devaluation process tend to be less than those of the currency devaluation process (see Figs. 9.4 and 9.5).[30] These facts are reflected in the evolutions of the average inflation and real profit rates (see Tables 9.12 and 9.13) and of the international competitiveness of the two economies (see Tables 9.14 and 9.15). In particular, considering that, as already mentioned, large wage devaluations may not be feasible, the findings suggest, for instance, that a wage devaluation of 30% cannot increase competitiveness by more than 15% (that is, 13.2% in the case of the Greek economy, and 14.5% in the case of the Italian economy). On the other hand, two years after a currency devaluation of 50%, competitiveness could remain

---

[30]It is a key stylized fact in many empirical studies that, across countries and over time, the moduli of the first non-dominant normalized eigenvalues of the price system matrices fall markedly, whereas the rest constellate in much lower values, forming a "long tail" (see Chap. 3).

at least 21% higher than its initial level (that is, 21.4% in the case of the Greek economy, and 25.8% in the case of the Italian economy). Several decades ago, Friedman (1953) noted that

> [t]he argument for flexible exchange rates is, strange to say, very nearly identical with the argument for daylight saving time. Isn't it absurd to change the clock in summer when exactly the same result could be achieved by having each individual change his habits? All that is required is that everyone decide to come to his office an hour earlier, have lunch an hour earlier, etc. But obviously it is much simpler to change the clock that guides all than to have each individual separately change his pattern of reaction to the clock, even though all want to do so. The situation is exactly the same in the exchange market. It is far simpler to allow one price to change, namely, the price of foreign exchange, than to rely upon changes in the multitude of prices that together constitute the internal price structure. (p. 173)

In conclusion, our price pass-through estimations seem not to be in contradiction with the findings reported in some other studies on currency and wage devaluations (using either similar or different frameworks).[31] For instance, as Salvatore (2013) remarks, empirical evidence on large currency devaluations during the turbulent period 1997 (second quarter) to 1999 (third quarter) shows that

> except for Indonesia, the inflation rate in the [other] Asian countries considered [i.e. Thailand, Korea, and Malaysia] was less than one-third of the rate of depreciation of their currencies. In other words, about one-third of the price advantage that these nations received from currency depreciation was wiped out by the resulting [accumulated] inflation. In Indonesia, the rate was 72.5 percent (49.0/67.6). In Latin America, it was about 20 percent for Brazil and 46 percent for Chile. In Mexico, the rate of inflation was almost double the rate of depreciation of its currency. (p. 513)[32]

(iv) Both effective wage and currency devaluations imply significant effects on income distribution in the long-run, while the wage rate is more sensitive than the profit rate to currency devaluation (see Tables 9.16 and 9.17). Finally, the findings suggest a rather mixed picture of the economies' comparative long-run performance with respect to the two types of devaluation (see Table 9.18). This probably results from the fact that the Greek economy tends to be characterized by higher levels of sectoral capital productivities, whereas the Italian economy tends to be characterized by higher levels of sectoral labour productivities and shares of foreign content in final demand (or, equivalently, total backward leakages).

### 9.3.3  Conclusions

Using input–output data from the Symmetric Input–Output Tables for the year 2010 and relevant linear price models, we estimated the effects of wage and currency

---

[31]See, e.g. Angelini et al. (2015), Bahmani-Oskooee et al. (2008), Brancaccio and Garbellini (2015), Burstein et al. (2005), Donayre and Panovska (2016) and Uxó et al. (2014).

[32]Also, consider the relevant empirical evidence provided by Borensztein and De Gregorio (1999) and Frankel et al. (2012).

devaluations on sectoral price levels and overall levels of income distribution variables for the Greek and Italian economies. It has been detected that:

(i) The medium-run aggregate competitiveness effect of wage devaluation tends to be similar in the two economies considered, whereas those of currency devaluation are more favourable in the case of the Italian economy. This results from inter-country differences in sectoral (a) export compositions; and (b) dependencies on labour and imported inputs.

(ii) In terms of improving international competitiveness in the medium-run, wage devaluation appears as a slower and less efficient process than currency devaluation.

(iii) Although both devaluations may imply significant effects on income distribution, effective currency devaluation involves a range of alternative distributive regimes. In the long-run, the wage rate responds more strongly than the profit rate with respect to currency devaluation.

(iv) Given the inter-country differences in (a) labour and capital productivities; and (b) shares of foreign content in final demand, there is a rather mixed picture of the economies' comparative long-run performance with respect to the two types of devaluation.

## 9.4   Final Remarks

Using Sraffian frameworks, this chapter provided empirical estimations and policy-oriented analysis of (i) the net output, import and employment matrix multipliers; and (ii) the medium- and long-run effects of wage and currency devaluations on international price competitiveness and income distribution for three "PIIGS economies", i.e. Greece, Italy, and Spain. Our results cast doubt on the "horizontal" policy measures implemented in the post-2010 Eurozone economy and point to the limited effectiveness of both types of devaluation as key levers for the required economic adjustment and recovery. Hence, they rather call for a wider and more flexible strategy framework that includes, on the one hand, per country and sector-specific wage rate changes and demand management policies and, on the other hand, an intra-Eurozone industrial, trade and currency depreciation policy. In fact, the

> Commission calls on Member States to recognise the central importance of industry for boosting competitiveness and sustainable growth in Europe and for a systematic consideration of competitiveness concerns across all policy areas. [...] [T]he objective of revitalization of the EU economy calls for the endorsement of the reindustrialisation efforts in line with the Commission's aspiration of raising the contribution of industry to GDP to as much as 20% by 2020. (European Commission 2014)

Taking this into account, a well-targeted industrial policy programme should be formulated.

This Sraffian income distribution–effective demand–production modelling provides a useful alternative framework for estimating demand multiplier and devaluation effects and for exploring their very inter-industry nature. Nevertheless, future research work should use post-2014 input–output data for all the European Union economies, and incorporate (i) explicitly both the direct and the indirect taxation sides of the fiscal systems, as well as estimations of national autonomous demand–transfer payments iso-employment curves, which are analytical devices for comparing demand multiplier effects across time and countries; (ii) a sensitivity analysis of the multiplier effects to expected or predicted changes in income distribution, exchange rates, consumption pattern(s), propensities to import and production methods; (iii) a distinction between competitive and non-competitive imports, as well as fixed capital and the degrees of its utilization; and (iv) the international spillover effects of demand management policies by means of a multi-country model and relevant inter-country input–output data.

# Appendix 1: Data Sources and Construction of Variables for the Estimation of Demand Multipliers

The Supply and Use Tables (SUTs) and the corresponding levels of employment of the Greek, Spanish and Eurozone economies are provided via the Hellenic Statistical Authority, Spanish Statistical Office and Eurostat websites, respectively.[33] At the time of this research (September 2016), SUTs were available for the following years: 2005 through 2012 for the Greek economy; 2008 through 2010 for the Spanish economy; and 2008 through 2011 for the EZ economy.

The available SUTs describe 65 products and industries. However, the elements associated with the commodity "Services provided by extraterritorial organisations and bodies" are all equal to zero and, therefore, we remove them from our analysis. Moreover, since the labour input in the industry "Imputed rents of owner-occupied dwellings" equals zero, we aggregate it with the industry "Real estate activities excluding imputed rent". Thus, we derive SUTs that describe 63 products. The described products and their correspondence to CPA (Classification of Products by Activity) are reported in Table 9.19, where products 1 to 3 belong to "Primary production". Products 4 to 27 belong to "Industry": (i) product 4 corresponds to "Mining and quarrying"; (ii) products 5 to 23 correspond to "Processing products"; (iii) product 24 corresponds to "Energy"; (iv) products 25 and 26 correspond to "Water supply and waste disposal"; and (v) product 27 corresponds to "Construction". Finally, products 28 to 63 belong to "Services", while products 54 to 57 are primarily related to government activities. In the last column of Table 9.19, the

---

[33]http://www.statistics.gr/en/statistics/-/publication/SEL38/2010;  http://www.statistics.gr/en/statistics/-/publication/SEL21/2016;  http://www.ine.es/dyngs/INEbase/en/operacion.htm?c=Estadistica_C&cid=1254736165950&menu=resultados&secc=1254736195578&idp=1254735576581; http://ec.europa.eu/eurostat/web/esa-supply-use-input-tables/data/workbooks; and http://appsso.eurostat.ec.europa.eu/nui/show.do?dataset=nama_nace64_e&lang=en (retrieved Sept 6, 2016).

**Table 9.19** Product classification and tradable commodities: GR, SP and EZ economies, year 2010

| No | CPA | Nomenclature | Tradable Commodities | | |
|---|---|---|---|---|---|
| | | | GR | SP | EZ |
| 1 | A01 | Products of agriculture, hunting and related services | v | v | v |
| 2 | A02 | Products of forestry, logging and related services | v | v | v |
| 3 | A03 | Fish and other fishing products; aquaculture products; support services to fishing | v | v | v |
| 4 | B | Mining and quarrying | v | v | v |
| 5 | C10–C12 | Food products, beverages and tobacco products | v | v | v |
| 6 | C13–C15 | Textiles, wearing apparel and leather products | v | v | v |
| 7 | C16 | Wood and of products of wood and cork, except furniture; articles of straw and plaiting materials | v | v | v |
| 8 | C17 | Paper and paper products | v | v | v |
| 9 | C18 | Printing and recording services | – | – | – |
| 10 | C19 | Coke and refined petroleum products | v | v | v |
| 11 | C20 | Chemicals and chemical products | v | v | v |
| 12 | C21 | Basic pharmaceutical products and pharmaceutical preparations | v | v | v |
| 13 | C22 | Rubber and plastics products | v | v | v |
| 14 | C23 | Other non-metallic mineral products | v | v | v |
| 15 | C24 | Basic metals | v | v | v |
| 16 | C25 | Fabricated metal products, except machinery and equipment | v | v | v |
| 17 | C26 | Computer, electronic and optical products | v | v | v |
| 18 | C27 | Electrical equipment | v | v | v |
| 19 | C28 | Machinery and equipment n.e.c. | v | v | v |
| 20 | C29 | Motor vehicles, trailers and semi-trailers | v | v | v |
| 21 | C30 | Other transport equipment | v | v | v |
| 22 | C31–C32 | Furniture; other manufactured goods | v | v | v |
| 23 | C33 | Repair and installation services of machinery and equipment | – | – | – |
| 24 | D35 | Electricity, gas, steam and air-conditioning | – | – | v |
| 25 | E36 | Natural water; water treatment and supply services | – | – | – |
| 26 | E37–E39 | Sewerage; waste collection, treatment and disposal activities; materials recovery; remediation activities and other waste management services | v | v | v |
| 27 | F | Constructions and construction works | – | – | – |
| 28 | G45 | Wholesale and retail trade and repair services of motor vehicles and motorcycles | – | – | – |
| 29 | G46 | Wholesale trade services, except of motor vehicles and motorcycles | – | – | v |
| 30 | G47 | Retail trade services, except of motor vehicles and motorcycles | – | – | – |
| 31 | H49 | Land transport services and transport services via pipelines | – | v | – |
| 32 | H50 | Water transport services | v | v | v |
| 33 | H51 | Air transport services | v | v | v |

(continued)

**Table 9.19** (continued)

| | | | | | |
|---|---|---|---|---|---|
| 34 | H52 | Warehousing and support services for transportation | v | v | v |
| 35 | H53 | Postal and courier services | – | – | v |
| 36 | I | Accommodation and food services | – | – | – |
| 37 | J58 | Publishing services | v | v | – |
| 38 | J59–J60 | Motion picture, video and television programme production services, sound recording and music publishing; programming and broadcasting services | v | – | v |
| 39 | J61 | Telecommunications services | – | v | v |
| 40 | J62–J63 | Computer programming, consultancy and related services; information services | v | v | v |
| 41 | K64 | Financial services, except insurance and pension funding | v | v | v |
| 42 | K65 | Insurance, reinsurance and pension funding services, except compulsory social security | v | – | v |
| 43 | K66 | Services auxiliary to financial services and insurance services | – | – | – |
| 44 | L68A–L68B | Real estate activities | – | – | – |
| 45 | M69–M70 | Legal and accounting services; services of head offices; management consulting services | v | v | v |
| 46 | M71 | Architectural and engineering services; technical testing and analysis services | v | v | v |
| 47 | M72 | Scientific research and development services | v | – | v |
| 48 | M73 | Advertising and market research services | v | v | v |
| 49 | M74–M75 | Other professional, scientific and technical services; veterinary services | v | – | v |
| 50 | N77 | Rental and leasing services | v | v | v |
| 51 | N78 | Employment services | – | – | – |
| 52 | N79 | Travel agency, tour operator and other reservation services and related services | v | v | – |
| 53 | N80–N82 | Security and investigation services; services to buildings and landscape; office administrative, office support and other business support services | – | v | v |
| 54 | O84 | Public administration and defence services; compulsory social security services | – | – | – |
| 55 | P85 | Education services | – | – | – |
| 56 | Q86 | Human health services | – | – | – |
| 57 | Q87–Q88 | Social work services | – | – | – |
| 58 | R90–R92 | Creative, arts and entertainment services; library, archive, museum and other cultural services; gambling and betting services | – | – | – |
| 59 | R93 | Sporting services and amusement and recreation services | – | – | – |
| 60 | S94 | Services furnished by membership organisations | – | – | – |
| 61 | S95 | Repair services of computers and personal and household goods | v | – | – |
| 62 | S96 | Other personal services | – | v | – |
| 63 | T | Services of households as employers; undifferentiated goods and services produced by households for own use | – | – | – |
| | | Total number of tradable commodities | 38 | 37 | 40 |

symbol "v" indicates the "tradable commodities". They are conventionally defined as commodities for which the ratio of total trade (exports plus imports) to gross domestic production, i.e. the "openness ratio", is in the order of 10% or more (see De Gregorio et al. 1994; Piton 2017). It is noted, however, that, in the case of the Greek economy, products 36 ("Accommodation and food services") and 52 ("Travel agency, tour operator and other reservation services and related services"), which are related to tourism activities, display zero exports and imports because the relevant SUTs record only the total travel receipts and payments and not the respective payments for each commodity. These exports–receipts (imports–payments) constitute the 19.4% (the 3.1%) of the total exports (the total imports) of this economy. Thus, we decided to consider commodity 52 as tradable in the Greek economy.[34]

The construction of the variables is as follows:

(i) The price vector, $\mathbf{p}^T$, is identified with $\mathbf{e}^T$, i.e. the physical unit of measurement of each product is that unit which is worth of a monetary unit (in the present SUTs, the unit is set to 1 million euro).

(ii) The $63 \times 63$ Make and Use Matrices, which are directly obtained from the SUTs, are considered as the empirical counterpart of $\mathbf{B}$ and $\mathbf{A}$, respectively.

(iii) The $63 \times 1$ vector of consumption expenditures of the household sector, which is directly obtained from the Use Table, is considered as the empirical counterpart of $\mathbf{f}$.

(iv) The element "Compensation of employees" from the Use Table, which is an element of the "Value Added" of each industry, is considered as the empirical counterpart of total wages in industry $j$, $W_j$. Thus, the money wage rate for each industry is estimated as $w_j = W_j l_j^{-1}$, where $l_j$ denotes the total employment in the $j$th industry.

(v) The sectoral "profit factors" are estimated from

$$1 + r_j = \left( \sum_{i=1}^{n} b_{ij} - w_j l_j \right) \left( \sum_{i=1}^{n} a_{ij} \right)^{-1}$$

(vi) The $63 \times 1$ vector of imports, which is directly obtained from the Use Table, is considered as the empirical counterpart of $\mathbf{IM}$. Thus, we may estimate the matrix $\widehat{\boldsymbol{\mu}}$.

It should finally be stressed that, unlike the papers by Mariolis and Soklis (2015, 2018), we do not transform the Use Tables (which are measured in current "purchasers' prices") into current "basic prices" and, therefore, we take into account *ad valorem* taxes. Moreover, Mariolis and Soklis (2015, 2018) apply their framework to

---

[34]The openness ratios of product 36 are almost 6.0% (SP) and 4.3% (EZ), while those of product 52 are 18.5% (SP) and 3.3% (EZ).

an earlier SUT of the Greek economy for the year 2010, provided via the Eurostat website.[35] Thus, there are deviations between our and their empirical results for the Greek economy, which do not alter, however, the general picture of the structure of this economy.

## Appendix 2: The Input–Output Structure of the Greek Economy 2005–2010

During the period 2008–2010, the Greek economy faced serious external and fiscal imbalances. In 2010, the unemployment rate was at 12.7%, the government budget and current account deficits, amounted to 11.1% and 10.1% of GDP, respectively, while the trade balance deficit was 6.8% (according to Bank of Greece data). The public debt reached 146% of GDP, the "Net international investment position" was at minus 97.9% and, finally, the net national savings were minus 24 billion euro or 13% of the net national disposable income (according to Hellenic Statistical Authority data).[36]

The Greek governments attempted to correct those imbalances by the application of contractionary fiscal and internal devaluation policies, such as indiscriminate reductions in government expenditures, increases in taxes and cuts in unit labour costs ("internal devaluation strategy"). These policies resulted to a significant improvement of the state budget primary deficit but with a GDP contraction (for the period 2010–2013) of about 22.2% (in constant prices of 2010) and a rate of unemployment of about 27.5%. In the same period, the exports were reduced by 3.3% and the imports by 15.5% (in constant prices of 2010), while the export market share of world's total was reduced by 9.4% (according to Hellenic Statistical Authority and World Bank data).[37]

In this Appendix we analyze the input–output structure of the Greek economy. For this purpose, we—basically—use:[38]

---

[35]http://ec.europa.eu/eurostat/web/esa-supply-use-input-tables/data/workbooks. The same holds true for the estimations provided by Ntemiroglou (2016), which, in addition, are based on the levels of employees in each industry.

[36]After entering the European Monetary Union, the net annual national savings in Greece became systematically *negative*. During the period 2000–2010, the total net external borrowing of the country amounted to 148% of its total net investments. For a macroeconomic analysis of the falling tendency of savings in the Greek economy, see Katsimi and Moutos (2010) and Mariolis (2011b, 2017, Chap. 2).

[37]For more on these issues, see Lapavitsas and Mariolis (2017) and Lapavitsas et al. (2018). According to Jovanović et al. (2018), "The Greek agony has to a large extent been provoked by the lousy structure of the Eurozone, and also partly by the Greek mischief that such a structure permitted." (p. 337, footnote 22).

[38]What follows draws on Leriou (2018), Leriou and Mariolis (2018), Mariolis (2016, 2017, 2018) and Mariolis et al. (2019a).

(i) Data from the SIOTs of the Greek and Eurozone economies for the years 2005 and 2010;[39]

(ii) A system of basic and derivative indices associated with the constituent components of gross national expenditure and the external sector of the economy, respectively.

## *The System of Indices*

For each produced commodity $i(=1, 2, \ldots, n)$ it holds that

$$X_i = IC_i + C_i + I_i + EX_i - IM_i \tag{9.31}$$

where $X_i$ denotes the gross domestic production, $IC_i$ the intermediate consumption (domestic and imported), $C_i$ the total final consumption expenditure (by households and government), $I_i$ the gross capital formation (gross fixed capital formation and changes in inventories), $EX_i$ the exports, and $IM_i$ the imports of commodity $i$. The sum $IC_i + C_i + I_i$ denotes the gross national expenditure for commodity $i$, while $X_i - IC_i$ denotes the gross value added of commodity $i$.

Dividing Eq. (9.31) by $X_i$ we obtain

$$1 = \delta_{ICi} + \delta_{Ci} + \delta_{Ii} + \delta_{EXi} - \delta_{IMi} \tag{9.32}$$

where $\delta_{ICi} \equiv IC_i/X_i$, $\delta_{Ci} \equiv C_i/X_i$, $\delta_{Ii} \equiv I_i/X_i$, $\delta_{EXi} \equiv EX_i/X_i$, and $\delta_{IMi} \equiv IM_i/X_i$. When $\delta_{ICi} > 1$, the gross value added of commodity $i$ is negative.

Now, we can introduce the following derivative indices:

(i) Index of gross domestic savings: For each produced commodity we may write

$$S_i = I_i + EX_i - IM_i \tag{9.33}$$

where $S_i$ denotes the gross domestic savings in commodity $i$. Dividing Eq. (9.33) by $X_i$ we obtain

$$\delta_{Si} = \delta_{Ii} + \delta_{EXi} - \delta_{IMi} \tag{9.34}$$

or, invoking Eq. (9.32),

---

[39]The SIOTs of the Greek and Eurozone economies are provided via the Eurostat website, http://epp.eurostat.ec.europa.eu (retrieved Sept 6, 2016). The available SIOTs describe 65 products and industries. However, the elements associated with the products "Imputed rents of owner-occupied dwellings" and "Services provided by extraterritorial organisations and bodies" are all equal to zero and, therefore, we remove them from our analysis. Thus, we derive SIOTs that describe 63 product/industry groups. For the described products and their correspondence to CPA, see Table 9.19.

$$\delta_{Si} = 1 - (\delta_{ICi} + \delta_{Ci})$$

where $\delta_{Si} \equiv S_i/X_i$ denotes the index of gross domestic savings in commodity $i$.

(ii) Index of normalized trade balance:

$$\delta_{TBi} \equiv (EX_i - IM_i)/(EX_i + IM_i) = (\delta_{EXi} - \delta_{IMi})/(\delta_{EXi} + \delta_{IMi})$$

(iii) Index of "revealed comparative advantage" (see, e.g. Laursen 1998, 2015):

$$\delta_{RCAi} \equiv \alpha_i(\delta_{TBi} - \delta_{TB})$$

where

$$\alpha_i \equiv 2[(EX_i + IM_i)/(EX + IM)], \quad EX \equiv \sum_{i=1}^{n} EX_i, \quad IM \equiv \sum_{i=1}^{n} IM_i$$

is a coefficient of normalization, and

$$\delta_{TB} \equiv (EX - IM)/(EX + IM)$$

Positive (negative) values for $\delta_{RCAi}$ imply comparative advantage (disadvantage), while all values sum up to zero.

(iv) Index of intra-commodity trade (Grubel–Lloyd index):

$$\delta_{ICTi} \equiv 1 - [|EX_i - IM_i|/(EX_i + IM_i)] = 1 - [|\delta_{EXi} - \delta_{IMi}|/(\delta_{EXi} + \delta_{IMi})]$$

(v) Index of self-sufficiency:

$$\delta_{SSi} \equiv X_i/(X_i + IM_i - EX_i) = 1/(1 + \delta_{IMi} - \delta_{EXi}) \tag{9.35}$$

From Eqs. (9.31) and (9.35) it follows that

$$X_i = \delta_{SSi}(IC_i + C_i + I_i)$$

which implies that $\delta_{SSi}$ could be conceived of as a (partial) multiplier of gross national expenditure.

(vi) Index of total import dependency:

$$\delta_{IDEi} \equiv IM_i/(X_i + IM_i - EX_i) = \delta_{IMi}/(1 + \delta_{IMi} - \delta_{EXi}) \tag{9.36}$$

From Eqs. (9.31) and (9.36) it follows that

$$X_i = (1 - \delta_{\text{IDE}i})(IC_i + C_i + I_i) + EX_i$$

which implies that, for a given value of the exports, $1 - \delta_{\text{IDE}i}$ could be conceived of as a multiplier of gross national expenditure.

(vii) Index of import dependency of capital goods:

$$\delta_{\text{IDK}i} \equiv IM_i/(X_i + IM_i - EX_i - C_i) = \delta_{IM_i}/[1 + \delta_{IM_i} - (\delta_{EXi} + \delta_{Ci})] \qquad (9.37)$$

From Eqs. (9.31) and (9.37) it follows that

$$X_i = (1 - \delta_{\text{IDK}i})(IC_i + I_i) + C_i + EX_i$$

which implies that, for given values of both the total final consumption and the exports, $1 - \delta_{\text{IDK}i}$ could be conceived of as a multiplier of the sum of intermediate consumption and gross capital formation.

As is easily checked, when $\delta_{EXi} < 1$: (i) $\delta_{SSi}$ is positive and, when $\delta_{TBi} > (<) 0$, greater than (less than) 1; (ii) $\delta_{\text{IDE}i} < 1$; and (iii) $\delta_{\text{IDK}i} \geq \delta_{\text{IDE}i}$.

Finally, we should briefly consider some involved economic policy dilemmas or trade-offs. Thus, we call "effective" those economic policies (macroeconomic, trade or structural) that increase the index of self-sufficiency and, at the same time, decrease the two indices of import dependency, i.e. $\dot{\delta}_{SSi} > 0$ and $\dot{\delta}_{\text{IDE}i} < 0$, $\dot{\delta}_{\text{IDK}i} < 0$, where the superposed dot denotes differentiation with respect to time. Differentiation of Eq. (9.32) gives

$$0 = \dot{\delta}_{ICi} + \dot{\delta}_{Ci} + \dot{\delta}_{Ii} + \dot{\delta}_{EXi} - \dot{\delta}_{IMi}$$

or, setting $\delta_{Ki} \equiv \delta_{ICi} + \delta_{Ii}$,

$$\dot{\delta}_{Ci} + \dot{\delta}_{Ki} = -\left(\dot{\delta}_{EXi} - \dot{\delta}_{IMi}\right) \qquad (9.38)$$

Differentiation of Eqs. (9.35) and (9.36) gives

$$\dot{\delta}_{SSi} = \left(\dot{\delta}_{EXi} - \dot{\delta}_{IMi}\right)/(1 + \delta_{IMi} - \delta_{EXi})^2 \qquad (9.39)$$

and, respectively,

$$\dot{\delta}_{\text{IDE}i} = \left[\delta_{IMi}\dot{\delta}_{EXi} + (1 - \delta_{EXi})\dot{\delta}_{IMi}\right]/(1 + \delta_{IMi} - \delta_{EXi})^2 \qquad (9.40)$$

From Eqs. (9.38)–(9.40) it follows that an effective economic policy necessarily involves

$$\dot{\delta}_{Ci} + \dot{\delta}_{Ki} < 0$$

i.e. it reduces at least one of $\delta_{Ci}$ and $\delta_{Ki}$, and, when, for instance, $\delta_{EXi} < 1$,

$$\dot{\delta}_{IMi} < \dot{\delta}_{EXi} < [-(1 - \delta_{EXi})/\delta_{IMi}]\dot{\delta}_{IMi}$$

Furthermore, Eq. (9.37) can be written as $\delta_{IMi} = \delta_{IDKi}\delta_{Ki}$. Differentiating this latter equation and substituting into Eq. (9.38) yields

$$\dot{\delta}_{Ci} = -(1 - \delta_{IDKi})\dot{\delta}_{Ki} + \delta_{Ki}\dot{\delta}_{IDKi} - \dot{\delta}_{EXi} \qquad (9.41)$$

from which it follows that, *when* $\delta_{IDKi} \geq 1$, an effective economic policy $(\dot{\delta}_{IDKi} < 0)$ that does not decrease $\delta_{EXi}$ necessarily involves $\dot{\delta}_{Ci} < 0$ (even when $\dot{\delta}_{Ki} < 0$).

## Results

The application to the SIOTs of the Greek and Eurozone economies for the years 2005 and 2010 produced the following main results:[40]

(i) Using the indices (%) of revealed comparative advantage and normalized trade balance, the exported or/and imported commodities of the Greek economy can be categorized into three groups ("product mapping scheme"; Widodo 2008). Table 9.20 refers to the year 2005, and shows that there are twenty-seven commodities with comparative disadvantage ("Group C"): twenty of them (or 74%) are industrial commodities. By contrast, there are twenty-four commodities with comparative advantage ("Groups A and B"): two of them (or 8%) are industrial commodities (the symbol $\overline{\delta}$ indicates the arithmetic mean of an index). Table 9.21 refers to the year 2010, and shows that there are twenty-nine commodities with comparative disadvantage: nineteen of them (or 66%) are industrial commodities. By contrast, there are twenty-three commodities with comparative advantage: three of

**Table 9.20** Product mapping scheme for the Greek economy, year 2005

| Group A $\delta_{RCAi} > 0, \delta_{TBi} > 0$ | Group B $\delta_{RCAi} > 0, \delta_{TBi} < 0$ |
|---|---|
| $i = 3, 27, 28, 29, 30, 31, 32, 35, 39, 46, 48, 49, 53, 55, 56.$ Total Number $= 15$ $\overline{\delta}_{RCAi} = 3.2\%, \overline{\delta}_{TBi} = 44.3\%,$ $\overline{\delta}_{ICTi} = 55.7\%$ | $i = 1, 15, 33, 40, 42, 45, 47, 59, 61.$ Total Number $= 9$ $\overline{\delta}_{RCAi} = 0.2\%, \overline{\delta}_{TBi} = -12.9\%, \overline{\delta}_{ICTi} = 87.9\%$ |
| | Group C $\delta_{RCAi} < 0, \delta_{TBi} < 0$ |
| | $i = 2, 4, 5, 6, 7, 8, 9, 10, 11, 12, 13, 14, 16, 17, 18, 19, 20, 21, 22, 24, 26, 34, 37, 38, 41, 50, 58.$ Total Number $= 27$ $\overline{\delta}_{RCAi} = -1.9\%, \overline{\delta}_{TBi} = -64.1\%, \overline{\delta}_{ICTi} = 35.9\%$ |

---

[40]We obtain similar results using data form the SUTs (see Mariolis 2018).

**Table 9.21** Product mapping scheme for the Greek economy, year 2010

| Group A $\delta_{RCAi} > 0, \delta_{TBi} > 0$ | Group B $\delta_{RCAi} > 0, \delta_{TBi} < 0$ |
|---|---|
| $i = 3, 15, 27, 28, 29, 30, 31,$ 32, 33, 48, 55, 56. Total Number $= 12$ $\bar{\delta}_{RCAi} = 4.1\%, \bar{\delta}_{TBi} = 49.5\%,$ $\bar{\delta}_{ICTi} = 50.6\%$ | $i = 1, 10, 35, 39, 40, 45, 46, 47, 49, 53, 61.$ Total Number $= 11$ $\bar{\delta}_{RCAi} = 0.4\%, \bar{\delta}_{TBi} = -12.0\%, \bar{\delta}_{ICTi} = 88.0\%$ |
| | Group C $\delta_{RCAi} < 0, \delta_{TBi} < 0$ |
| | $i = 2, 4, 5, 6, 7, 8, 9, 11, 12, 13, 14, 16, 17, 18, 19, 20, 21,$ 22, 24, 26, 34, 37, 38, 41, 42, 50, 58, 59, 62. Total Number $= 29$ $|\bar{\delta}_{RCAi}| = -2.0\%, \bar{\delta}_{TBi} = -63.7\%, \bar{\delta}_{ICTi} = 36.3\%$ |

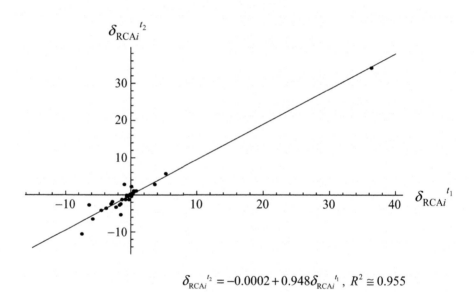

$$\delta_{RCAi}{}^{t_2} = -0.0002 + 0.948\delta_{RCAi}{}^{t_1}, \ R^2 \cong 0.955$$

**Fig. 9.6** Linear regression between the values of the revealed comparative advantage indices: Greek economy, years 2010 and 2005

them (or 13%) are industrial commodities. Finally, Fig. 9.6 shows the linear regression between the $\delta_{RCA}$ values of commodity $i$ at time $t_2 = 2010$ and those at time $t_1 = 2005$, i.e.

$$\delta_{RCAi}{}^{t_2} = \beta + \gamma\delta_{RCAi}{}^{t_1} + \varepsilon$$

where $\beta$ and $\gamma$ denote standard linear regression parameters, and $\varepsilon$ a residual term. Since both the values of $\gamma$ ($\cong 0.948$) and $\gamma/R$ ($\cong 0.970$) are not notably less than 1, it follows that there are *no* significant changes in the pattern and degree, respectively, of international specialization of the Greek economy (see Dalum et al. 1998).

(ii) Regarding the exported or/and imported commodities, there exist:

(a) Twenty (year 2005) or eighteen (year 2010) commodities with positive gross domestic savings. About 20% or 22% of them, respectively, belong to the industry sector.

(b) Thirty (year 2005) or thirty-three (year 2010) commodities with negative gross domestic savings. About 60% or 55% of them, respectively, belong to the industry sector.

For the positive-saving (the negative-saving) commodities, there is not (there is) a significant power function regression between the index of total import dependency, $\delta_{IDEi}$, and the index of gross domestic savings, $\delta_{Si}$. These findings seem to indicate that positive savings are more correlated with gross capital formation than with trade balance, while negative savings are more correlated with trade balance than with gross capital formation (consider Eqs. (9.34) and (9.36)).

(iii) There appears to be an underlying pattern in our empirical results: Bad index values are concentrated in industrial commodities, whereas good index values are concentrated in service commodities. Moreover, the findings for the year 2010 do not differ much from those for the year 2005, which probably suggests that the structural features of the economy have been shaped well *before* the emergence of the so-called Greek (or PIIGS) crisis (for earlier work in this vein, see Mariolis 1999, 2011c; Mariolis et al. 1997, 2012). These views are further supported by the figures in Tables 9.22, 9.23, 9.24, 9.25, 9.26 and 9.27, which report the arithmetic means, *AM*, of the basic and derivative indices for the primary production, industrial and service commodities in both the Greek and Eurozone economies ($\delta_{ICi}^m$ denotes the imported intermediate consumption index). Thus, it can be stated that the industry sector is the "weak link" in the Greek economy and, at the same time, diverges considerably from the industry sector in the Eurozone economy. On the other hand, the service sectors in these economies exhibit rather similar performance, whereas the primary production sector in the Eurozone economy is characterized by relatively unfavourable index values.

(iv) In the year 2010, there are fourteen industrial and two service commodities in the Greek economy that are simultaneously characterized by a "low" self-sufficiency

**Table 9.22** The arithmetic means of the basic indices for the primary production, industrial and service commodities: Greek economy, year 2005

|  | $\overline{\delta}_{ICi}$ | $\overline{\delta}_{ICi}^m$ | $\overline{\delta}_{ICi}^m/\overline{\delta}_{ICi}$ | $\overline{\delta}_{Ci}$ | $\overline{\delta}_{Ii}$ | $\overline{\delta}_{EXi}$ | $\overline{\delta}_{IMi}$ |
|---|---|---|---|---|---|---|---|
| Primary production | 37.2 | 7.4 | 19.9 | 70.8 | −4.1 | 12.4 | 16.2 |
| Industry | 108.3 | 62.3 | 57.5 | 91.6 | 77.2 | 27.2 | 204.3 |
| Services | 54.2 | 9.8 | 18.1 | 47.6 | 2.6 | 7.3 | 11.7 |
| Total economy (*AM*) | 74.0 | 29.7 | 40.1 | 65.4 | 30.7 | 15.1 | 85.3 |

**Table 9.23** The arithmetic means of the derivative indices for the primary production, industrial and service commodities: Greek economy, year 2005

|  | $\bar{\delta}_{Si}$ | $\bar{\delta}_{TBi}$ | $\bar{\delta}_{RCAi}$ | $\bar{\delta}_{ICTi}$ | $\bar{\delta}_{SSi}$ | $\bar{\delta}_{IDEi}$ | $\bar{\delta}_{IDKi}$ |
|---|---|---|---|---|---|---|---|
| Primary production | −8.0 | −13.5 | 0.3 | 55.4 | 98.5 | 14.9 | 102.2 |
| Industry | −99.9 | −58.6 | −1.9 | 37.0 | 63.1 | 48.3 | 348.5 [70.9][(iii)] |
| Services | −1.8 [4.7][(i)] | 5.7 | 1.6 | 61.8 | 162.0 [97.5][(ii)] | 6.5 | 9.8 |
| Total economy (AM) | −39.5 [−36.4][(i)] | −23.2 | 0 | 50.8 | 121.3 [84.2][(ii)] | 22.8 | 143.2 [36.9][(iii)] |

Notes: (i) excluding commodity 34 ($\delta_{Si} = -229.1\%$); (ii) excluding commodity 32 ($\delta_{SSi} = 2418.6\%$); and (iii) excluding commodity 6 ($\delta_{IDKi} = 6733.7\%$)

**Table 9.24** The arithmetic means of the basic indices for the primary production, industrial and service commodities: Greek economy, year 2010

|  | $\bar{\delta}_{ICi}$ | $\bar{\delta}^m_{ICi}$ | $\bar{\delta}^m_{ICi}/\bar{\delta}_{ICi}$ | $\bar{\delta}_{Ci}$ | $\bar{\delta}_{Ii}$ | $\bar{\delta}_{EXi}$ | $\bar{\delta}_{IMi}$ |
|---|---|---|---|---|---|---|---|
| Primary production | 39.9 | 7.2 | 18.0 | 57.2 | 1.4 | 15.4 | 14.0 |
| Industry | 116.6 | 72.3 | 62.0 | 74.5 | 126.2 | 29.3 | 246.7 |
| Services | 53.2 | 9.5 | 17.9 | 48.0 | 2.9 | 7.3 | 11.4 |
| Total economy (AM) | 76.7 | 33.3 | 43.4 | 58.6 | 49.8 | 16.1 | 101.2 |

**Table 9.25** The arithmetic means of the derivative indices for the primary production, industrial and service commodities: Greek economy, year 2010

|  | $\bar{\delta}_{Si}$ | $\bar{\delta}_{TBi}$ | $\bar{\delta}_{RCAi}$ | $\bar{\delta}_{ICTi}$ | $\bar{\delta}_{SSi}$ | $\bar{\delta}_{IDEi}$ | $\bar{\delta}_{IDKi}$ |
|---|---|---|---|---|---|---|---|
| Primary production | 2.8 | −4.3 | 0.5 | 57.5 | 104.0 | 13.7 | 35.7 |
| Industry | −91.2 | −55.0 | −1.8 | 41.2 | 64.4 | 47.3 | 369.7 [73.9][(iii)] |
| Services | −1.2 [4.3][(i)] | −6.0 | 1.4 | 57.4 | 157.7 [97.1][(ii)] | 7.2 | 11.6 |
| Total economy (AM) | −35.3 [−32.7][(i)] | −26.6 | 0 | 50.5 | 119.6 [84.8][(ii)] | 22.8 | 149.2 [34.2][(iii)] |

Notes: (i) excluding commodity 34 ($\delta_{Si} = -194.2\%$); (ii) excluding commodity 32 ($\delta_{SSi} = 2280.0\%$); and (iii) excluding commodity 6 ($\delta_{IDKi} = 7174.0\%$)

**Table 9.26** The arithmetic means of the basic indices for the primary production, industrial and service commodities: Eurozone economy, year 2010

|  | $\bar{\delta}_{ICi}$ | $\bar{\delta}^m_{ICi}$ | $\bar{\delta}^m_{ICi}/\bar{\delta}_{ICi}$ | $\bar{\delta}_{Ci}$ | $\bar{\delta}_{Ii}$ | $\bar{\delta}_{EXi}$ | $\bar{\delta}_{IMi}$ |
|---|---|---|---|---|---|---|---|
| Primary production | 67.8 | 9.9 | 14.6 | 40.1 | 5.6 | 5.9 | 19.4 |
| Industry | 83.3 | 29.1 | 34.9 | 22.3 | 11.9 | 25.0 | 42.5 |
| Services | 51.9 | 4.0 | 7.6 | 41.9 | 3.5 | 7.7 | 5.0 |
| Total economy (AM) | 64.6 | 13.8 | 21.4 | 34.3 | 6.8 | 14.2 | 20.0 |

**Table 9.27** The arithmetic means of the derivative indices for the primary production, industrial and service commodities: Eurozone economy, year 2010

|  | $\overline{\delta}_{Si}$ | $\overline{\delta}_{TBi}$ | $\overline{\delta}_{RCAi}$ | $\overline{\delta}_{ICTi}$ | $\overline{\delta}_{SSi}$ | $\overline{\delta}_{IDEi}$ | $\overline{\delta}_{IDKi}$ |
|---|---|---|---|---|---|---|---|
| Primary production | −7.8 | −50.1 | −0.5 | 49.9 | 88.6 | 16.6 | 31.7 |
| Industry | −5.6 [11.8]$^{(i)}$ | 10.0 | −0.4 | 74.7 | 98.7 | 25.9 | 37.2 |
| Services | 6.2 | 23.6 | 0.3 | 64.3 | 104.6 | 5.2 | 8.2 |
| Total economy (AM) | 1.0 [7.6]$^{(i)}$ | 14.9 | 0 | 67.6 | 101.6 | 13.7 | 20.4 |

Note: (i) excluding commodity 4 ($\delta_{Si} = -400.5\%$)

**Table 9.28** The highly import-dependent commodities in the Greek economy, year 2010

| $i$ | $\delta_{ICi}$ | $\delta_{ICi}^{m}$ | $\delta_{Si}$ | $\delta_{TBi}$ | $\delta_{RCAi}$ | $\delta_{ICTi}$ | $\delta_{SSi}$ | $\delta_{IDEi}$ | $\delta_{IDKi}$ |
|---|---|---|---|---|---|---|---|---|---|
| 4 | 717.8 | 630.5 | −617.8 | −96.1 | −10.48 | 3.9 | 14.1 | 87.7 | 87.7 |
| 5 | 23.1 | 6.8 | −18.1 | −44.3 | −2.43 | 55.7 | 84.3 | 25.5 | 128.7 |
| 6 | 40.8 | 17.0 | −153.2 | −56.0 | −2.78 | 44.0 | 46.6 | 74.4 | 7174.0 |
| 8 | 100.8 | 73.6 | −55.9 | −79.1 | −1.18 | 20.9 | 54.5 | 51.5 | 73.6 |
| 11 | 165.7 | 125.7 | −167.9 | −65.4 | −3.60 | 34.6 | 36.9 | 79.8 | 128.1 |
| 12 | 102.9 | 83.2 | −197.4 | −66.5 | −3.36 | 33.5 | 35.6 | 80.7 | 262.1 |
| 13 | 117.2 | 53.5 | −40.3 | −44.7 | −0.48 | 55.3 | 71.4 | 46.3 | 55.5 |
| 16 | 98.3 | 23.3 | −16.7 | −74.6 | −1.84 | 25.4 | 73.4 | 31.1 | 36.0 |
| 17 | 371.7 | 347.9 | −495.4 | −100 | −4.12 | 0.0 | 5.6 | 94.4 | 108.0 |
| 18 | 77.3 | 60.5 | −26.0 | −29.5 | −0.15 | 70.5 | 63.7 | 79.8 | 115.6 |
| 19 | 24.9 | 19.2 | 72.1 | −64.1 | −1.99 | 35.9 | 39.4 | 77.5 | 78.4 |
| 20 | 76.2 | 66.3 | −317.0 | −94.7 | −2.59 | 5.3 | 15.2 | 87.2 | 181.0 |
| 21 | 61.9 | 58.5 | −120.5 | −72.1 | −5.28 | 27.9 | 6.9 | 111.1 | 124.8 |
| 22 | 71.3 | 51.3 | −68.9 | −83.1 | −2.33 | 16.9 | 46.7 | 58.7 | 107.9 |
| 34 | 280.6 | 211.6 | −194.2 | −77.9 | −6.42 | 22.1 | 34.0 | 75.4 | 79.0 |
| 42 | 59.1 | 20.5 | −24.1 | −39.9 | −0.27 | 60.1 | 80.6 | 34.1 | 71.6 |
| AM | 149.4 | 115.6 | −152.6 | −68.0 | −3.1 | 32.0 | 44.3 | 68.5 | 550.8 |

index and "high" import dependency indices.[41] These "highly import-dependent commodities" are reported in Table 9.28: it is observed that they all belong to Group C of Table 9.21, and it should also be noted that, in value terms, their imports correspond to about 566% of their exports and 76% of the economy's total imports, while their exports correspond to 22% of the economy's total exports. At least nine of these commodities, i.e. those with $\delta_{IDKi} > 1$, could be the immediate objective of a "vertical" industrial policy programme, based on export subsidies, joint ventures between Greek and foreign firms, and technology transfers, in order to increase the

---

[41] Hereafter, the term "low" ("high") shall mean "lower (higher) than the arithmetic mean of the total economy", i.e. in the present case, lower than 84.8%, and higher than 22.8% and 34.2% (see the last row and the notes in Table 9.25).

**Table 9.29** The lowly import-dependent commodities in the Greek economy, year 2010

| $i$ | $\delta_{ICi}$ | $\delta^m_{ICi}$ | $\delta_{Si}$ | $\delta_{TBi}$ | $\delta_{RCAi}$ | $\delta_{ICTi}$ | $\delta_{SSi}$ | $\delta_{IDEi}$ | $\delta_{IDKi}$ |
|---|---|---|---|---|---|---|---|---|---|
| 1  | 58.1 | 8.5  | 0.2  | −7.1  | 0.94    | 92.9 | 98.0   | 14.7 | 24.8 |
| 3  | 27.6 | 2.8  | 22.9 | 57.4  | 0.68    | 42.6 | 126.7  | 9.9  | 26.7 |
| 27 | 13.6 | 0.2  | 81.7 | 38.3  | 0.97    | 61.7 | 101.4  | 1.1  | 1.2  |
| 28 | 32.6 | 0.00 | 13.4 | 100   | 1.05    | 0    | 107.1  | 0    | 0    |
| 29 | 40.4 | 0.00 | 19.1 | 100   | 5.63    | 0    | 110.5  | 0    | 0    |
| 30 | 40.6 | 0.00 | 19.0 | 100   | 2.91    | 0    | 110.4  | 0    | 0    |
| 31 | 27.2 | 1.1  | 0.8  | 15.5  | 0.27    | 84.5 | 100.8  | 2.2  | 8.1  |
| 32 | 2.3  | 0.3  | 95.6 | 99.1  | 34.06   | 0.9  | 2280.0 | 9.7  | 18.4 |
| 35 | 96.5 | 1.8  | −0.7 | −25.8 | 0.00025 | 74.2 | 99.3   | 1.8  | 1.9  |
| 39 | 46.2 | 2.1  | −0.7 | −9.5  | 0.20    | 90.5 | 99.3   | 4.2  | 9.2  |
| 40 | 62.1 | 12.5 | 36.8 | −6.4  | 0.25    | 93.6 | 97.7   | 19.2 | 19.4 |
| 45 | 22.2 | 0.00 | 4.3  | −14.5 | 0.15    | 85.5 | 98.5   | 5.9  | 6.3  |
| 46 | 89.5 | 5.4  | −0.6 | −11.5 | 0.07    | 88.5 | 99.4   | 2.9  | 3.3  |
| 48 | 99.3 | 3.9  | 0.6  | 7.8   | 0.16    | 92.2 | 100.7  | 3.9  | 3.9  |
| 49 | 86.8 | 7.5  | −1.8 | −11.3 | 0.08    | 88.7 | 98.3   | 8.6  | 10.1 |
| 53 | 93.4 | 1.4  | −0.3 | −10.1 | 0.05    | 89.9 | 99.7   | 1.5  | 1.6  |
| 55 | 1.9  | 0.1  | 0.1  | 27.0  | 0.04    | 73.0 | 100.1  | 0.1  | 5.9  |
| 56 | 2.2  | 0.01 | 0.1  | 27.0  | 0.06    | 73.0 | 100.1  | 0.2  | 7.7  |
| 61 | 39.6 | 2.2  | −0.7 | −6.4  | 0.04    | 93.6 | 99.3   | 5.5  | 13.9 |
| AM | 46.0 | 2.6  | 15.3 | 24.7  | 1.6     | 64.5 | 217.2  | 4.9  | 8.6  |

index of self-sufficiency and, at the same time, to decrease the two indices of import dependency.[42] By contrast, there are two primary production, one industrial and sixteen service commodities that are simultaneously characterized by a high self-sufficiency index and low import dependency indices. These "lowly import-dependent commodities" are reported in Table 9.29: it is observed that they all belong to Groups A and B of Table 9.21, and it should also be noted that, in value terms, their imports correspond to about 17% of their exports and 6% of the economy's total imports, while their exports correspond to 57% of the economy's total exports. Finally, in Tables 9.30 and 9.31 the symbol "v" indicates the "highly import-dependent commodities" and the "lowly import-dependent commodities", respectively, in two "non-PIIGS" (i.e. France (FR) and Germany (GER)) and three "PIIGS" (i.e. Greece (GR), Italy (IT) and Spain (SP)) economies, as well as for the EZ economy as a whole. It is thus observed that:

---

[42]For basic dilemmas that such a policy would inevitably face, see Eq. (9.41). Furthermore, according to Chow (2015), "Without foreign competition, the protected domestic producers have no incentive to improve their products or change their technology. [. . .] [T]hrough the subsidies, the government knows exactly the cost involved in helping to develop the industry concerned. By imposing import restrictions, the government does not know this cost and therefore may not care about the economic loss involved; only the consumers suffer." (p. 321).

**Table 9.30** The highly import-dependent commodities in Eurozone economies, year 2010

| i | GER | FR | GR | IT | SP | EZ |
|---|---|---|---|---|---|---|
| 1 | v | – | – | v | – | v |
| 2 | – | – | – | v | – | – |
| 3 | v | v | – | v | v | v |
| 4 | v | v | v | v | v | v |
| 5 | – | – | v | v | – | – |
| 6 | – | v | v | – | v | v |
| 8 | – | v | v | v | – | – |
| 10 | v | v | – | – | v | v |
| 11 | – | v | v | v | v | – |
| 12 | – | v | v | v | v | – |
| 13 | – | v | v | – | v | – |
| 15 | v | – | – | v | – | v |
| 16 | – | – | v | – | – | – |
| 17 | v | v | v | v | v | v |
| 18 | – | v | v | – | v | – |
| 19 | – | v | v | – | v | – |
| 20 | – | v | v | v | – | – |
| 21 | v | – | v | – | – | – |
| 22 | v | v | v | – | v | v |
| 32 | v | – | – | – | – | – |
| 33 | – | – | – | v | – | – |
| 34 | – | – | v | – | – | – |
| 42 | – | – | v | – | – | – |
| 50 | – | – | – | – | – | v |
| 61 | – | – | – | v | – | – |
| Total number | 9 | 13 | 16 | 13 | 11 | 9 |
| Industrial commodities | 67% | 92% | 88% | 62% | 91% | 67% |

(a) Commodities 4 ("Mining and quarrying") and 17 ("Computer, electronic and optical products") are common "highly import-dependent commodities" amongst these economies, while commodities 11 ("Chemicals and chemical products") and 12 ("Basic pharmaceutical products and pharmaceutical preparations") are common "highly import-dependent commodities" amongst these "PIIGS economies".

(b) Commodities 28 ("Wholesale and retail trade and repair services of motor vehicles and motorcycles") and 29 ("Wholesale trade services, except of motor vehicles") are common "lowly import-dependent commodities" amongst these economies, while there are also one industrial commodity (i.e. "Construction")

**Table 9.31** The lowly import-dependent commodities in Eurozone economies, year 2010

| $i$ | GER | FR | GR | IT | SP | EZ |
|---|---|---|---|---|---|---|
| 1 | – | – | v | – | – | – |
| 3 | – | – | v | – | – | – |
| 5 | – | – | – | – | v | – |
| 9 | v | – | – | v | v | v |
| 14 | v | – | – | v | v | v |
| 16 | v | – | – | v | – | v |
| 23 | v | – | – | v | v | v |
| 24 | – | – | – | – | v | – |
| 25 | – | – | – | v | v | – |
| 26 | – | v | – | – | – | – |
| 27 | – | – | v | v | v | – |
| 28 | v | v | v | v | v | v |
| 29 | v | v | v | v | v | v |
| 30 | – | v | v | v | v | v |
| 31 | – | v | v | v | v | v |
| 32 | – | v | v | v | v | v |
| 33 | – | – | – | – | v | – |
| 34 | – | – | – | v | v | – |
| 35 | – | – | v | v | v | – |
| 36 | – | – | – | – | v | – |
| 37 | v | – | – | v | – | – |
| 38 | – | – | – | v | v | v |
| 39 | – | – | v | v | v | – |
| 40 | v | – | v | – | v | v |
| 41 | v | – | – | v | v | v |
| 42 | v | – | – | – | v | – |
| 43 | – | – | – | v | v | – |
| 44 | – | – | – | v | v | – |
| 45 | – | – | v | v | v | – |

(continued)

**Table 9.31**  (continued)

| 46 | V | – | V | V | V | V |
|----|---|---|---|---|---|---|
| 47 | – | – | – | V | V | – |
| 48 | – | – | V | V | V | – |
| 49 | – | – | V | V | V | – |
| 50 | – | V | – | – | – | – |
| 51 | V | – | – | V | V | – |
| 52 | – | – | – | V | – | – |
| 53 | – | – | V | V | V | – |
| 54 | – | – | – | V | V | – |
| 55 | – | – | V | V | V | – |
| 56 | – | – | V | V | V | – |
| 57 | – | – | – | V | V | – |
| 58 | – | – | – | V | – | – |
| 59 | – | – | – | V | V | – |
| 60 | – | – | – | V | V | – |
| 61 | – | – | V | – | V | – |
| 62 | – | – | – | V | – | – |
| 63 | – | – | – | V | – | – |
| Total number | 12 | 7 | 19 | 36 | 37 | 13 |
| Industrial commodities | 33% | 14% | 5% | 17% | 19% | 31% |

and twelve service commodities which are common "lowly import-dependent commodities" amongst these "PIIGS economies".

(c) The EZ economy seems to be more correlated with the German economy rather than with the other economies.

(v) The values of the domestic intermediate consumption index, $\delta^d_{ICi} = \delta_{ICi} - \delta^m_{ICi}$, are equal to the row-sums of the domestic direct output coefficients (or Ghosh) matrix, $\mathbf{A}^d_G$, while the values of the imported intermediate consumption index, $\delta^m_{ICi}$, are equal to the row-sums of the imported direct output coefficients matrix, $\mathbf{A}^m_G$. Figures 9.7 and 9.8 refer to the Greek economy, for the year 2010, and show that there are significant linear regressions between:

(a) $\delta^d_{ICi}$ and the inter-industry "forward linkages", FLINK$_i$ , i.e. the row-sums of the matrix $\left[\mathbf{I} - \mathbf{A}^d_G\right]^{-1}$; and

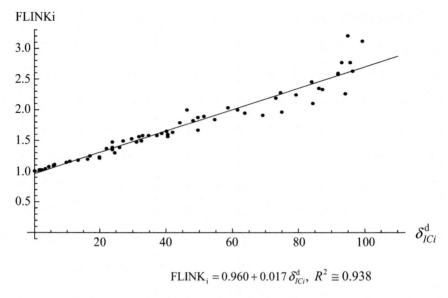

$$FLINK_i = 0.960 + 0.017\,\delta^{d}_{ICi}, \ R^2 \cong 0.938$$

**Fig. 9.7** Inter-industry forward linkages versus domestic intermediate consumption indices: Greek economy, year 2010

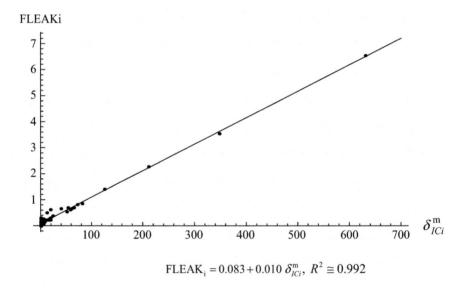

$$FLEAK_i = 0.083 + 0.010\,\delta^{m}_{ICi}, \ R^2 \cong 0.992$$

**Fig. 9.8** Inter-industry forward leakages versus imported intermediate consumption indices: Greek economy, year 2010

(b) $\delta_{ICi}^{m}$ and the inter-industry "forward leakages", FLEAK$_i$, i.e. the row-sums of the matrix $\left[\mathbf{I} - \mathbf{A}_G^d\right]^{-1}\mathbf{A}_G^m$, respectively.[43]

Finally, it is detected that there are fourteen commodities characterized by high forward leakages, while eleven of them are highly import-dependent commodities (see Table 9.28).

(vi) Figures 9.9 and 9.10 refer to the Greek economy, for the year 2010, and show:[44]

(a) The share of domestic content (or domestic value added) in final demand, measured by the elements of the vector

$$\mathbf{\omega}^{dT} \equiv \mathbf{\omega}^T\left[\mathbf{I} - \mathbf{A}_L^d\right]^{-1}$$

and the share of foreign content (or foreign value added) in final demand, measured by the elements of

$$\mathbf{\omega}^{mT} \equiv \mathbf{e}^T\mathbf{A}_L^m\left[\mathbf{I} - \mathbf{A}_L^d\right]^{-1}$$

where $\mathbf{\omega}^T$ denotes the $1 \times 63$ vector of (direct) gross value added per unit activity level, $\mathbf{A}_L^d$ the domestic direct input coefficients (or Leontief) matrix, $\mathbf{A}_L^m$ the imported direct input coefficients matrix, and $\mathbf{e}^T = \mathbf{\omega}^{dT} + \mathbf{\omega}^{mT}$ (see Hummels et al. 2001).[45] In Fig. 9.9, the horizontal line gives the arithmetic mean of the shares of domestic content in final demand. It is detected that there are twenty-six industries with low shares of domestic content (one primary production and eighteen industrial industries), while eleven of them correspond to highly import-dependent commodities (see Table 9.28).

(b) The domestic value added of industry $i$ "embodied" in the economy's exports, measured by

$$\mathbf{DV} \equiv [DV_i] \equiv \widehat{\mathbf{\omega}}\left[\mathbf{I} - \mathbf{A}_L^d\right]^{-1}\mathbf{EX}$$

where $\widehat{\mathbf{\omega}}$ denotes the matrix formed from the elements of $\mathbf{\omega}^T$, and $\mathbf{EX}$ the $63 \times 1$ vector of exports. In Fig. 9.10, the horizontal line gives the arithmetic mean of $DV_i$. It is detected that there are eighteen industries with high $DV_i$ (one primary production and seven industrial industries; see Table 9.32). Table 9.33 reports the sectoral domestic content shares of exports,

---

[43]For the measurement of the inter-industry linkages and leakages, see Reis and Rua (2009).

[44]For the numerical results, see Mariolis et al. (2017).

[45]The elements of $\mathbf{\omega}^{mT}$ also give the inter-industry "backward leakages".

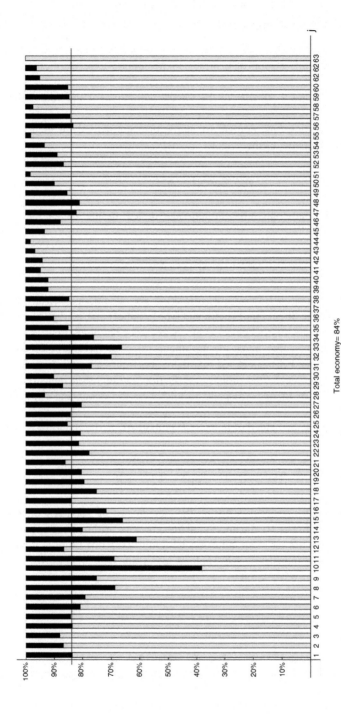

**Fig. 9.9** The shares (%) of domestic content (grey colour) and foreign content (black colour) in final demand: Greek economy, year 2010

Total economy= 84%

Primary production = 86%, Industry = 77%, Services = 89%

$$DVS = \left(\boldsymbol{\omega}^{T}\left[\mathbf{I} - \mathbf{A}_{L}^{d}\right]^{-1}\mathbf{EX}\right)/\left(\mathbf{e}^{T}\mathbf{EX}\right)$$

(vii) Finally, Fig. 9.11 refers to the Greek economy, for the year 2010, and displays two estimated autonomous demand–transfer payments iso-employment curves (see Sect. 8.3). More specifically, the solid line corresponds to the actual

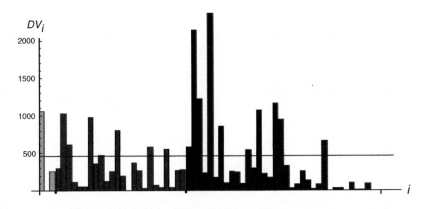

Total economy= 459.0

Primary production = 442.1 (or 4.6%), Industry = 329.0 (or 27.3%), Services = 547.0 (68.1%)

**Fig. 9.10** The domestic value added (in million euros) of industry $i$ "embodied" in the economy's exports: Greek economy, year 2010

**Table 9.32** The industries with high domestic value added (in million euros) "embodied" in the economy's exports: Greek economy, year 2010

| $i$ | $DV_i$ |
|---|---|
| 1 | 1057.2 |
| 5 | 1032.7 |
| 6 | 618.1 |
| 10 | 984.2 |
| 12 | 469.6 |
| 15 | 803.6 |
| 21 | 583.6 |
| 24 | 553.8 |
| 28 | 579.3 |
| 29 | 2141.1 |
| 30 | 1222.0 |
| 32 | 7405.2 |
| 34 | 862.3 |
| 39 | 546.7 |
| 41 | 1073.2 |
| 44 | 1164.6 |
| 45 | 946.0 |
| 53 | 665.8 |

**Table 9.33** The sectoral domestic content shares of exports (*DVS*): Greek economy, year 2010

|  | *DVS* | Export shares | Export-weighted *DVS* |
|---|---|---|---|
| Primary production | 84.9% | 4.0% | 3.4% |
| Industry | 66.6% | 39.2% | 26.1% |
| Services | 75.9%. | 56.8% | 43.1% |
|  |  |  | Total economy = 72.6% |

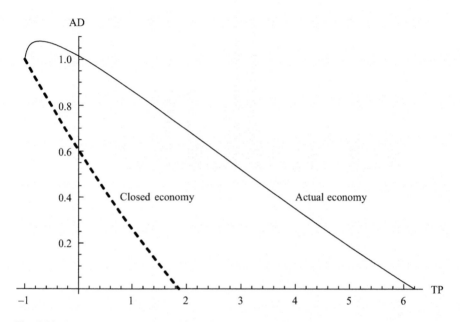

**Fig. 9.11** Autonomous demand–transfer payments curves: Greek economy, year 2010

economy, and is found to be *non*-monotonic, while the dashed line corresponds to the heuristic case where the economy is closed to international trade, and, as expected, is found to be monotonic ("AD" denotes the level of autonomous demand, and "TP" the transfer payments rate).[46] Since the area under an autonomous demand–transfer payments curve can be conceived of as a measure of the

---

[46]For the estimations see Mariolis et al. (2018b). It is noted that Eq. (9.4) is now written as:

$$\mathbf{y} = \mathbf{c}_w + \mathbf{c}_p - \left[\mathbf{A}_L^m + \widehat{\boldsymbol{\mu}}\right]\mathbf{x} + \mathbf{d}$$

where $\widehat{\boldsymbol{\mu}}$ now denotes the diagonal matrix of imported commodities for final demand per unit of gross output of each commodity (see Appendix 4 of Chap. 8). Moreover, it has been assumed that $s_w = 0$, $s_p = 1$ and, in accordance with data from the Tax Policy Department of the Greek Ministry of Finance, $\tau_w = 7.09\%$ and $\tau_p = 9.37\%$.

economy's overall multiplier performance, it follows that the import "leakages" dampen this performance by 213.7%.[47] Thus, it can be stated that the external sector plays a key role in the multiplier process in the Greek economy.

## Conclusions

This inter-sectoral analysis identified main structural features of the Greek economy. It has been detected that a well-targeted effective demand management policy is necessary but not sufficient for the recovery of this economy; that is to say, industrial policy and structural transformation are also needed. More specifically, demand policy could be mainly based on the service and the primary production sectors, which include the vast majority of the revealed comparative advantage and lowly import-dependent commodities. By contrast, the industry sector includes the vast majority of the revealed comparative disadvantage and highly import-dependent commodities; it is also characterized by negative gross domestic savings, low intra-commodity specialization, and low domestic content in exports. Industrial policy could primarily focus on nine industrial commodities that exhibit particularly high direct import dependency of capital goods.

## Appendix 3: The Arithmetic Means of the Net Output Multipliers as Functions of the Savings Ratios

The graphs in Fig. 9.12 display the arithmetic means of the net output multipliers as functions of the savings ratios. Thus, it is observed that (i) they are all strictly decreasing functions of the savings ratios (as in the case of single-product systems; see Sect. 8.2), and more sensitive to changes in the savings ratio out of profits; and (ii) the arithmetic mean of the net output multiplier for the EZ economy is no less than 1, regardless of the values of the savings ratios. Since actual economies may be in different phases of the business cycle, while there is literature evidence that, during important recessions, decreases in the savings ratio out of profits (and/or the propensities to import) are large enough to increase "the" fiscal multiplier value, and since changes in the savings ratios are, in our modelling, formally equivalent to changes in the direct tax rates, the present sensitivity analysis could be particularly useful for policy purposes (and

---

[47]For $s_w = 0$ and $s_p = 0.80$, this figure reduces to 139.7%.

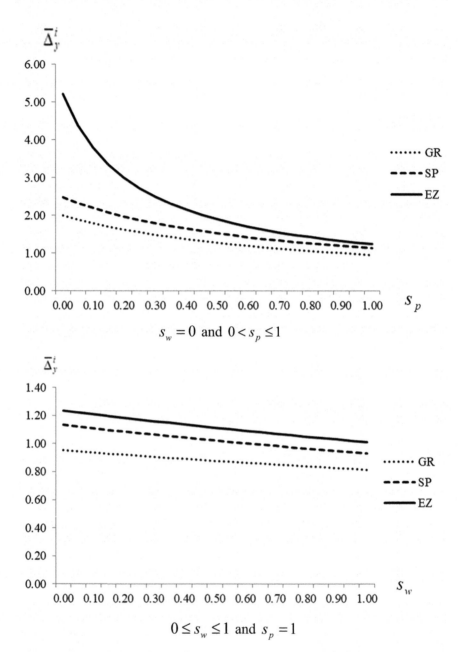

**Fig. 9.12** The arithmetic means of the net output multipliers as functions of the savings ratios: GR, SP and EZ economies, year 2010

should be extended to include changes in the determinants of the demand for imports).

# Appendix 4: Data Sources and Construction of Variables for the Estimation of the Effects of Wage and Currency Devaluations

The SIOTs and the corresponding sectoral levels of employment are provided via the Hellenic Statistical Authority, Italian National Institute of Statistics, and Eurostat websites.[48] The available SIOTs describe 65 products and industries. However, all the elements associated with the industry "Services provided by extraterritorial organisations and bodies" are all equal to zero and, therefore, we remove them from our analysis. Moreover, since the labour input in the industry "Imputed rents of owner-occupied dwellings" equals zero, we aggregate it with the industry "Real estate activities excluding imputed rent". Thus, we derive SIOTs that describe 63 industries.

The construction of the variables is as follows:

(i) The price vector, $\mathbf{p}^T$, is identified with $\mathbf{e}^T$, i.e. the physical unit of measurement of each product is that unit which is worth of a monetary unit (in the present SIOTs, the unit is set to 1 million euro).

(ii) The matrix of direct labour coefficients, $\widehat{\mathbf{l}}$, is obtained by dividing element-by-element the relevant inputs in each industry by its gross output (i.e. by its "Output at basic prices", which is directly obtained from the SIOT). The matrix of net tax rates, $\widehat{\mathbf{T}}$, is obtained in a similar way.

(iii) The element "Wage and salaries" from the SIOT, which is an element of the "Value added at basic prices" of each industry, is considered as the empirical counterpart of total wages in industry $j$, $W_j$. Thus, the money wage rate for each industry is estimated as $w_j = W_j(l_j x_j)^{-1}$, where $x_j$ denotes the gross output of the $j$th industry.

(iv) The sectoral "profit factors" are estimated from

$$1 + r_j = \left(1 - w_j l_j\right)\left(\sum_{i=1}^{n} a_{ijL}^d + a_{ijL}^m + \tau_j\right)^{-1}$$

(v) The vector of exports, which is directly obtained from the SIOT, is considered as the empirical counterpart of $\mathbf{EX}$.

---

[48]http://www.statistics.gr/en/statistics/-/publication/SEL38/2010; http://dati.istat.it/?lang=en& SubSessionId=7e7a1f62-9daa-4cc1-919b-6479cb641095; and http://ec.europa.eu/eurostat/web/ esa-supply-use-input-tables/data/workbooks (retrieved Sept 6, 2016).

(vi) The matrices of domestic, $\mathbf{B}_w$, and imported, $\mathbf{B}_w^*$, wage commodities per unit of labour employed are estimated from

$$\mathbf{B}_w = \left(\mathbf{p}^T\mathbf{c} + E\mathbf{p}^{*T}\mathbf{c}^*\right)^{-1}\mathbf{c}\mathbf{w}^T = \left[\mathbf{e}^T(\mathbf{c} + \mathbf{c}^*)\right]^{-1}\mathbf{c}\mathbf{w}^T$$

and

$$\mathbf{B}_w^* = \left(\mathbf{p}^T\mathbf{c} + E\mathbf{p}^{*T}\mathbf{c}^*\right)^{-1}\mathbf{c}^*\mathbf{w}^T = \left[\mathbf{e}^T(\mathbf{c} + \mathbf{c}^*)\right]^{-1}\mathbf{c}^*\mathbf{w}^T$$

where $\mathbf{c}$, $\mathbf{c}^*$ denote the vectors of final consumption expenditure by households for domestically produced and imported commodities, respectively, which are directly obtained from the SIOT. Finally, the "consumer price index" (CPI) is estimated as $[\mathbf{e}^T(\mathbf{c} + \mathbf{c}^*)]^{-1}(\mathbf{c} + \mathbf{c}^*)$.

## Appendix 5: The Long-Run Wage–Profit–Exchange Rates Trade-Offs for the Greek and Italian Economies

The graphs in Figs. 9.13, 9.14 and 9.15 depict the long-run trade-offs in terms of the normalized export vectors of the two economies under consideration. It is noted that, with the exception of one element, the other elements of the vector $\left(\overline{w}^{-1}\mathbf{w}^T\right)\widehat{\mathbf{l}}[\mathbf{I} - \mathbf{F}]^{-1}$ (see the denominator in Eq. (9.27)) are greater in the Greek than in the Italian economy; in fact, the mean absolute deviation between these vectors is almost 82.3%. On the other hand, the signs of the difference between the vectors $\mathbf{m}^T[\mathbf{I} - \mathbf{F}]^{-1}$ (see the numerator in Eq. (9.27)) are mixed, and the same holds true with respect to the components of the other two curves. Hence, it seems that nothing useful can be said, *a priori*, about the relative position of the curves. For instance, the graphs in Fig. 9.16 depict the difference, $\delta$, between the Greek and Italian economies' scalars $\left(\overline{w}^{-1}\mathbf{w}^T\right)\widehat{\mathbf{l}}\left[\mathbf{I} - \widetilde{\mathbf{F}}(\widetilde{r})\right]^{-1}\mathbf{z}$ (see the denominator in Eq. (9.30)) as a function of the profit rate (the curve depicted in the second graph is non-monotonic).

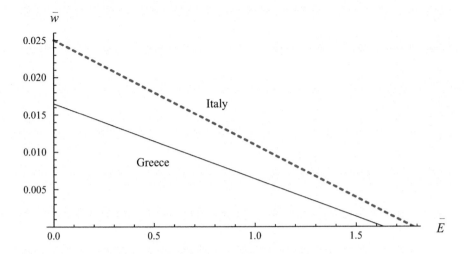

*Numéraire*: the normalized export vector of the Greek economy

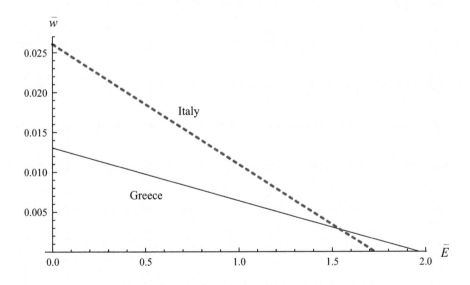

*Numéraire*: the normalized export vector of the Italian economy

**Fig. 9.13** The wage–exchange rates trade-off: Greek and Italian economies, year 2010

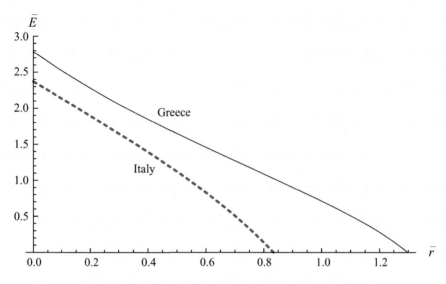

*Numéraire*: the normalized export vector of the Greek economy

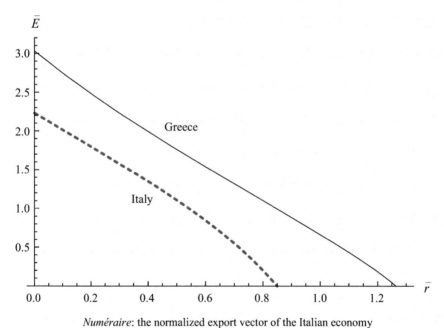

*Numéraire*: the normalized export vector of the Italian economy

**Fig. 9.14** The exchange–profit rates trade-off: Greek and Italian economies, year 2010

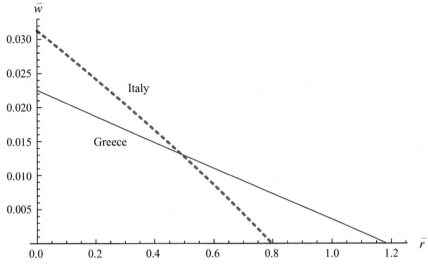

*Numéraire*: the normalized export vector of the Greek economy

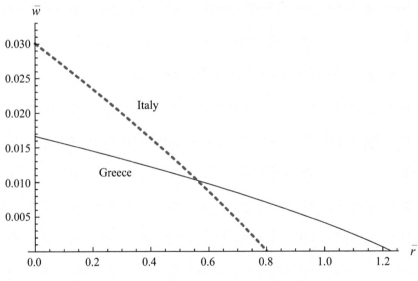

*Numéraire*: the normalized export vector of the Italian economy

**Fig. 9.15** The wage–profit rates trade-off: Greek and Italian economies, year 2010

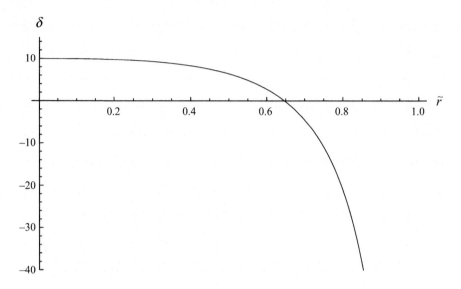

*Numéraire*: the normalized export vector of the Greek economy

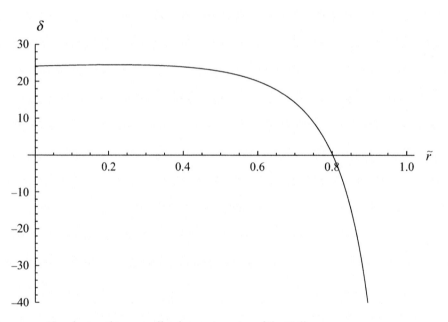

*Numéraire*: the normalized export vector of the Italian economy

**Fig. 9.16** The difference between the denominator components of the wage–profit rates trade-off as a function of the profit rate: Greek and Italian economies, year 2010

# References

Angelini, E., Dieppe, A., & Pierluigi, B. (2015). Modelling internal devaluation experiences in Europe: Rational or learning agents? *Journal of Macroeconomics, 43*, 81–92.

Antonopoulos, R., Adam, A., Kim, K., Masterson, T., & Papadimitriou, D. B. (2014, April). *Responding to the unemployment challenge: A job guarantee proposal for Greece.* Levy Economics Institute, Retrieved Nov 30, 2019, from http://www.levyinstitute.org/pubs/rpr_apr_14.pdf

Athanassiou, E., Tsekeris, T., & Tsouma, E. (2014). Input–output analysis and multiplier effects for the Greek economy. *Greek Economic Outlook, 24*, 63–72.

Aydoğuş, O., Değer, Ç., Çalışkan, E. T., & Günal, G. G. (2018). An input–output model of exchange-rate pass-through. *Economic Systems Research, 30*(3), 323–336.

Bahmani-Oskooee, M., Hegerty, S. W., & Kutan, A. M. (2008). Do nominal devaluations lead to real devaluations? Evidence from 89 countries. *International Review of Economics and Finance, 17*(4), 644–670.

Bank of Greece. (2013). *Annual report of the bank of Greece.* Athens: Bank of Greece, February 2013.

Batini, N., Eyraud, L., Forni, L., & Weber, A. (2014). *Fiscal multipliers: Size, determinants, and use in macroeconomic projections.* IMF Technical Notes and Manuals, International Monetary Fund, Fiscal Affairs Department, 14/04, September 2014.

Bilbao-Ubillos, J., & Fernández-Sainz, A. (2019). A critical approach to wage devaluation: The case of Spanish economic recovery. *The Social Science Journal, 56*(1), 88–93.

Blanchard, O. J., & Leigh, D. (2013). Growth forecast errors and fiscal multipliers. *The American Economic Review, 103*(3), 117–120.

Borensztein, E., & De Gregorio, J. (1999). *Devaluation and inflation after currency crises.* International Monetary Fund, Mimeo, February 1999.

Brancaccio, E., & Garbellini, N. (2015). Currency regime crises, real wages, functional income distribution and production. *European Journal of Economics and Economic Policies: Intervention, 12*(3), 255–276.

Burstein, A., Eichenbaum, M., & Rebelo, S. (2005). Large devaluations and the real exchange rate. *Journal of Political Economy, 113*(4), 742–784.

Castelnuovo, E., & Lim, G. (2019). What do we know about the macroeconomic effects of fiscal policy? A brief survey of the literature on fiscal multipliers. *The Australian Economic Review, 52*(1), 78–93.

Charles, S. (2016). An additional explanation for the variable Keynesian multiplier: The role of the propensity to import. *Journal of Post Keynesian Economics, 39*(2), 187–205.

Charles, S., Dallery, T., & Marie, J. (2015). Why the Keynesian multiplier increases during hard times: A theoretical explanation based on rentiers' saving behaviour. *Metroeconomica, 66*(3), 451–473.

Charles, S., Dallery, T., & Marie, J. (2018). Why are Keynesian multipliers larger in hard times? A Palley–Aftalion–Pasinetti explanation. *Review of Radical Political Economics, 50*(4), 736–756.

Chow, G. C. (2015). *China's economic transformation.* Chichester: Wiley Blackwell.

Ciccarone, G., & Saltari, E. (2015). Cyclical downturn or structural disease? The decline of the Italian economy in the last twenty years. *Journal of Modern Italian Studies, 20*(2), 228–244.

Collignon, S., & Esposito, P. (2017). *Measuring European competitiveness on the sectoral level.* Brussels: European Trade Union Institute (ETUI).

Dalum, B., Laursen, K., & Villumsen, G. (1998). Structural change in OECD export specialisation patterns: De-specialisation and "stickiness". *International Review of Applied Economics, 12*(3), 423–443.

De Cos, P. H., & Moral-Benito, E. (2016). Fiscal multipliers in turbulent times: The case of Spain. *Empirical Economics, 50*(4), 1589–1625.

De Grauwe, P., & Holvoet, C. (1978). On the effectiveness of a devaluation in the E.C.-countries. *Tijdschrift voor Economie en Management, 23*(1), 67–82.

De Grauwe, P., & Ji, Y. (2016). Crisis management and economic growth in the Eurozone. In F. Caselli, M. Centeno, & J. Tavares (Eds.), *After the crisis. Reform, recovery, and growth in Europe* (pp. 46–72). Oxford: Oxford University Press.

De Gregorio, J., Giovannini, A., & Wolf, H. C. (1994). International evidence on tradables and nontradables inflation. *European Economic Review, 38*(6), 1225–1244.

Degasperi, M., & Fredholm, T. (2010). Productivity accounting based on production prices. *Metroeconomica, 61*(2), 267–281.

Díaz, B., Moniche, L., & Morillas, A. (2006). A fuzzy clustering approach to the key sectors of the Spanish economy. *Economic Systems Research, 18*(3), 299–318.

Donayre, L., & Panovska, I. (2016). State-dependent exchange rate pass-through behavior. *Journal of International Money and Finance, 64*, 170–195.

Durand, C., & Villemot, S. (2016). Balance sheets after the EMU: An assessment of the redenomination risk. *Documents de Travail de l'OFCE*, (2016–31).

Dynan, K. E., Skinner, J., & Zeldes, S. P. (2004). Do the rich save more? *Journal of Political Economy, 112*(2), 397–444.

European Central Bank. (2015). *The international role of the euro*. Frankfurt am Main: European Central Bank, July.

European Commission. (2014). *For a European industrial renaissance*. Retrieved Nov 30, 2019, from http://eur-lex.europa.eu/legal-content/EN/NOT/?uri=CELEX:52014DC0014

European Commission. (2015). *European economic forecast. Winter 2015*. Brussels: European Commission. Directorate-General for Economic and Financial Affairs, February.

Ferretti, F. (2008). Patterns of technical change: A geometrical analysis using the wage–profit rate schedule. *International Review of Applied Economics, 22*(5), 565–583.

Frankel, J. A., Parsley, D., & Wei, S.-J. (2012). Slow pass-through around the world: A new import for developing countries? *Open Economies Review, 23*(2), 213–251.

Friedman, M. (1953). *Essays in positive economics*. Chicago and London: The University of Chicago Press.

Garbellini, N., Marelli, E., & Wirkierman, A. L. (2014). Domestic demand and global production in the Eurozone: A multiregional input–output assessment of the global crisis. *International Review of Applied Economics, 28*(3), 336–364.

Gechert, S., Hallett, A. H., & Rannenberg, A. (2016). Fiscal multipliers in downturns and the effects of Euro Area consolidation. *Applied Economics Letters, 23*(16), 1138–1140.

Gechert, S., & Rannenberg, A. (2015). The costs of Greece's fiscal consolidation. *Vierteljahrshefte zur Wirtschaftsforschung, 84*(3), 47–59.

Hummels, D., Ishii, J., & Yi, K.-M. (2001). The nature and growth of vertical specialization in world trade. *Journal of International Economics, 54*(1), 75–96.

Ilzetzki, E., Mendoza, G. E., & Végh, A. C. (2013). How big (small?) are fiscal multipliers? *Journal of Monetary Economics, 60*(2), 239–254.

International Labour Organization. (2016). *Global wage report 2016/2017. Wage inequality in the workplace*. Geneva: International Labour Office.

International Monetary Fund. (2012). *World economic outlook: Coping with high debt and sluggish growth*. Washington: International Monetary Fund, October.

Jovanović, M. N., Damnjanović, J., & Njegić, J. (2018). Among the central and eastern European countries of the European Union, who gained and who lost? *Economia Internazionale/International Economics, 71*(3), 317–370.

Kahn, R. (1931). The relation of home investment to unemployment. *The Economic Journal, 41*(162), 173–198.

Kalman, R. E. (1979). A system-theoretic critique of dynamic economic models. In B. Lazarević (Ed.), *Global and large scale system models* (pp. 3–24). Berlin: Springer.

Katsimi, M., & Moutos, T. (2010). EMU and the Greek crisis: The political-economy perspective. *European Journal of Political Economy, 26*(4), 568–576.

Katsinos, A., & Mariolis, T. (2012). Switch to devalued drachma and cost-push inflation: A simple input–output approach to the Greek case. *Modern Economy, 3*(2), 164–170.

Kolokontes, D. A., Kontogeorgos, A., Loizou, E., & Chatzitheodoridis, F. (2018). Key-sectors attractiveness of the Greek economy: An input–output approach. *Applied Econometrics and International Development, 18*(1), 35–54.

Krugman, P. R., Obstfeld, M., & Melitz, M. J. (2018). *International economics. Theory and policy.* Harlow, England: Pearson.

Ksenofontov, M. Y., Shirov, A. A., Polzikov, D. A., & Yantovskii, A. A. (2018). Assessing multiplier effects in the Russian economy: Input–output approach. *Studies on Russian Economic Development, 29*(2), 109–115.

Kurz, H. D. (1985). Effective demand in a "classical" model of value and distribution: The multiplier in a Sraffian framework. *The Manchester School, 53*(2), 121–137. Reprinted in H. D. Kurz (1990). *Capital, distribution and effective demand. Studies in the "classical" approach to economic theory* (pp. 174–191). Cambridge: Polity Press.

Kurz, H. D., & Salvadori, N. (1995). *Theory of production. A long-period analysis.* Cambridge: Cambridge University Press.

Lager, C. (2001). A note on non-stationary prices. *Metroeconomica, 52*(3), 297–300.

Lapavitsas, C. (2018). The redenomination risk of exiting the Eurozone: An estimation based on the Greek case. *European Law Journal, 24*(2–3), 226–243.

Lapavitsas, C., & Mariolis, T. (2017). *Eurozone failure, German policies, and a new path for Greece. Policy analysis and proposals.* Edited with the collaboration of C. Gavrielides. Berlin: Rosa Luxemburg Stiftung. Retrieved Nov 30, 2019, from https://www.rosalux.de/en/publication/id/14546/eurozone-failure-german-policies-and-a-new-path-for-greece/

Lapavitsas, C., Mariolis, T., & Gavrielides, C. (2018). *Economic policy for the recovery of Greece.* Preface by E. Screpanti. Athens: Livanis (in Greek).

Laursen, K. (1998). *Revealed comparative advantage and the alternatives as measures of international specialization.* Danish Research Unit for Industrial Dynamics, Working paper 98–30, December 1998.

Laursen, K. (2015). Revealed comparative advantage and the alternatives as measures of international specialization. *Eurasian Business Review, 5*(1), 99–115.

Leão, P. (2013). The effect of government spending on the debt-to-GDP ratio: Some Keynesian arithmetic. *Metroeconomica, 64*(3), 448–465.

Leriou, E. (2018). *Analysis of the external sector of the Greek and Eurozone economies 2005–2010: Comparative findings.* Post-Doctoral Dissertation, Athens: Department of Public Administration, Panteion University (in Greek).

Leriou, E., & Mariolis, T. (2018). *The input–output structures of Eurozone economies 2005–2010: Comparative findings for the French, German, Greek, Italian, Spanish and Eurozone economies.* Mimeo (in Greek).

Mariolis, T. (1999). The new international division of labor. In T. Mariolis & G. Stamatis (2000). *The EMU epoch: Globalization, EMU, drachma, stock exchange market* (pp. 25–40). Athens: Stachy (in Greek).

Mariolis, T. (2011a). *The economic policy in and out of the Eurozone.* Paper presented at the conference: "Stop of Payments: The Next Few Hours", Athens, 26 September 2011. Enlarged version in T. Mariolis (Ed.). (2018). *Essays on the work of Dimitris Batsis: "The heavy industry in Greece"* (pp. 445–465). Athens: Tziola Publications (in Greek).

Mariolis, T. (2011b). The wages–profits–growth relationships and the peculiar case of the Greek economy. In T. Mariolis (Ed.). (2018). *Essays on the work of Dimitris Batsis: "The heavy industry in Greece"* (pp. 67–78). Athens: Tziola Publications (in Greek).

Mariolis, T. (2011c). *Greece, European Union and economic crisis.* Athens: Matura (in Greek).

Mariolis, T. (2012). Unemployment, external sector, and developmental structural change of the Greek economy. In T. Mariolis (Ed.). (2018). *Essays on the work of Dimitris Batsis: "The heavy industry in Greece"* (pp. 501–527). Athens: Tziola Publications (in Greek).

Mariolis, T. (2013). Currency devaluation, external finance and economic growth: A note on the Greek case. *Social Cohesion and Development, 8*(1), 59–64.

Mariolis, T. (2016). *The foreign-trade leakages in the Greek economy.* Paper presented at the workshop: "What is the future for Europe?", European Research Network on Social and Economic Policy & Research on Money and Finance, SOAS, Thessaloniki, 26–27 April 2016, Aristotle University of Thessaloniki.

Mariolis, T. (2017). *A New Economic Policy Programme for Greece.* Athens: Korontzis (in Greek).

Mariolis, T. (2018). The foreign-trade leakages in the Greek economy: Evidence from the supply and use table for the year 2010. *East–West Journal of Economics and Business, 21*(1–2), 135–155.

Mariolis, T., Economidis, C., Stamatis, G., & Fousteris, N. (1997). *Quantitative evaluation of the effects of devaluation on the cost of production. Based on the input–output table of the Greek economy for the year 1988.* Athens: Kritiki (in Greek).

Mariolis, T., Leriou, E., & Soklis, G. (2019b). Dissecting the input–output structure of the Greek economy 2005–2010. *Economia Internazionale/International Economics, 72*(4), 453–474.

Mariolis, T., Moutos, T., & Soklis, G. (2017). *The dynamic industries of the Greek economy.* Mimeo (in Greek).

Mariolis, T., Ntemiroglou, N., & Soklis, G. (2018a). The static demand multipliers in a joint production framework: Comparative findings for the Greek, Spanish and Eurozone economies. *Journal of Economic Structures, 7*, 18. https://doi.org/10.1186/s40008-018-0116-0.

Mariolis, T., Ntemiroglou, N., & Soklis, G. (2018b). The Sraffian autonomous demand–transfer payments curve for the Greek economy. *Statistical Review, Journal of the Greek Statistical Association, 11–12*, Special issue in honor of Professor Ioannis Vavouras, 24–37 (in Greek).

Mariolis, T., Ntemiroglou, N., & Soklis, G. (2020a). *Estimating the static matrix demand multipliers for the world's ten largest economies in a post-Keynesian–Sraffian one-country model.* Internal Report of the Study Group on Sraffian Economics, 27 Jun 2020. Athens: Department of Public Administration, Panteion University.

Mariolis, T., Rodousakis, N., & Katsinos, A. (2019a). Wage versus currency devaluation, price pass-through and income distribution: A comparative input–output analysis of the Greek and Italian economies. *Journal of Economic Structures, 8*, 9. https://doi.org/10.1186/s40008-019-0140-8.

Mariolis, T., Rodousakis, N., & Soklis, G. (2020b). The COVID-19 multiplier effects of tourism on the Greek economy. *Tourism Economics* (forthcoming). https://doi.org/10.1177/1354816620946547.

Mariolis, T., Rodousakis, N., & Soklis, G. (2020c). Inter-sectoral analysis of the greek economy and the COVID-19 multiplier effects. *European Politics and Society*, Special issue "Eurozone and economic crisis in Greece at 2020: Current challenges and prospects". https://doi.org/10.1080/23745118.2021.1895555.

Mariolis, T., & Soklis, G. (2015, June). *The Sraffian multiplier for the Greek economy: Evidence from the supply and use table for the year 2010.* Centre of Planning and Economic Research, Discussion Paper No. 142, Athens. Retrieved Nov 30, 2019, from https://www.kepe.gr/index.php/en/research/recent-publications/discussion-papers/item/2736-dp_142

Mariolis, T., & Soklis, G. (2018). The static Sraffian multiplier for the Greek economy: Evidence from the supply and use table for the year 2010. *Review of Keynesian Economics, 6*(1), 114–147.

Mariolis, T., Soklis, G., & Groza, E. (2012). Estimation of the maximum attainable economic dependency ratio: Evidence from the symmetric input–output tables of four European economies. *Journal of Economic Analysis, 3*(1), 52–71.

Mineshima, A., Poplawski-Ribeiro, M., & Weber, A. (2014). Size of fiscal multipliers. In C. Cottarelli, P. Gerson, & A. Senhadji (Eds.), *Post-crisis fiscal policy* (pp. 315–372). Cambridge, MA: The MIT Press.

Myant, M., Theodoropoulou, S., & Piasna, A. (Eds.). (2016). *Unemployment, internal devaluation and labour market deregulation in Europe.* European Trade Union Institute (ETUI): Brussels.

Nordvig, J. (2014). *Cost and Benefits of Eurozone Breakup: The role of contract redenomination and balance sheet effects in policy analysis.* Mimeo.

Nordvig, J., & Firoozye, N. (2012, June). *Rethinking the European monetary union.* Wolfson Economics Prize 2012. Final submission. Retrieved Nov 30, 2019, from https://www.researchgate.net/publication/319873989

Ntemiroglou, N. (2016). The Sraffian multiplier and the key-commodities for the Greek economy: Evidence from the input–output tables for the period 2000–2010. *Bulletin of Political Economy, 10*(1), 1–24.

Oelgemöller, J. (2013). Revealed comparative advantages in Greece, Ireland, Portugal and Spain. *Intereconomics, 48*(4), 243–253.

Onaran, Ö., & Galanis, G. (2012). *Is aggregate demand wage-led or profit-led? National and global effects.* Conditions of Work and Employment Series No. 40. Geneva: International Labour Office.

Palley, T. I. (2009). Imports and the income–expenditure model: Implications for fiscal policy and recession fighting. *Journal of Post Keynesian Economics, 32*(2), 311–322.

Pianta, M. (2014). An industrial policy for Europe. *Seoul Journal of Economics, 27*(3), 277–305.

Piton, S. (2017). A European disease? Non-tradable inflation and real interest rate divergence. *CESifo Economic Studies, 63*(2), 210–234.

Portella-Carbó, F. (2016). Effects of international trade on domestic employment: An application of a global multiregional input–output supermultiplier model (1995–2011). *Economic Systems Research, 28*(1), 95–117.

Pusch, T. (2012). Fiscal spending multiplier calculations based on input–output tables – an application to EU member states. *European Journal of Economics and Economic Policies: Intervention, 9*(1), 129–144.

Ramey, V. A. (2019). Ten years after the financial crisis: What have we learned from the renaissance in fiscal research? *Journal of Economic Perspectives, 33*(2), 89–114.

Reis, H., & Rua, A. (2009). An input–output analysis: Linkages versus leakages. *International Economic Journal, 23*(4), 527–544.

Salvatore, D. (2013). *International economics* (11th ed.). New York: Wiley.

Sraffa, P. (1932). Dr. Hayek on money and capital. *Economic Journal, 42*(165), 42–53.

Sraffa, P. (1960). *Production of commodities by means of commodities. Prelude to a critique of economic theory.* Cambridge: Cambridge University Press.

Tarancón, M.-A., Gutiérrez-Pedrero, M.-J., Callejas, F. E., & Martínez-Rodríguez, I. (2018). Verifying the relation between labor productivity and productive efficiency by means of the properties of the input–output matrices. The European case. *International Journal of Production Economics, 195*, 54–65.

Uxó, J., Paúl, J., & Febrero, E. (2014). *Internal devaluation in the European periphery: The story of a failure.* Working Papers DT 2014/2, Albacete, University of Castilla – La Mancha.

Widodo, T. (2008). Dynamic changes in comparative advantage: Japan "flying geese" model and its implications for China. *Journal of Chinese Economic and Foreign Trade Studies, 1*(3), 200–213.

# Chapter 10
# Wrestling with Goodwin's Distributive Growth Cycle Modelling: Theory and Empirical Evidence

**Abstract** This chapter investigates Goodwin's distributive growth cycle model and some of its extensions, focusing on (i) its stability properties under the assumptions of a variable elasticity of substitution (VES) production function and endogenous labour productivity growth; and (ii) the implications of capital heterogeneity, providing also an empirical test using actual input–output data. It is shown that the incorporation of a VES production function and endogenous labour productivity growth into Goodwin's model can considerably modify its dynamic behaviour, while the incorporation of heterogeneous capital indicates that the system's economic relevance and dynamics depend on the eigenvalues of the matrix of input–output coefficients, underlining the importance of Sraffa's contribution.

**Keywords** Endogenous labour productivity growth · Goodwin's models · Heterogeneous capital · Principal coordinates · Variable elasticity of substitution production function

## 10.1 Introduction

In *A Growth Cycle* (1967, 1972), Goodwin developed a dynamic model that describes the inter-dependences amongst income distribution, capital accumulation, and (un)employment. More specifically, by taking into account the "Harrod–Domar" model as well as a "real Phillips curve", he established a model of endogenous economic fluctuations, where the share of wages and the employment rate constitute the model's state (phase) variables. Over time, this model has proved seminal in understanding economic cycles, having had a remarkable influence in the literature and still inspiring new works.

As is well known, Goodwin's growth cycle model lacks some important features of the actual economies, such as:

(i). The substitution between "capital and labour" (see, e.g. van der Ploeg 1985).

(ii). The endogeneity of technical progress; in particular, the model includes an assumption about technical progress (a "Harrod-neutral" technical progress), but

© Springer Nature Singapore Pte Ltd. 2021  
T. Mariolis et al., *Spectral Theory of Value and Actual Economies*, Evolutionary Economics and Social Complexity Science 24,  
https://doi.org/10.1007/978-981-33-6260-4_10

without explaining it. Furthermore, even in the case of the absence of this technical progress, its dynamics do not change significantly (see, e.g. Mariolis 2006, p. 122).

(iii). The heterogeneity of capital (in line with Sraffa 1960).[1]

This chapter, first, incorporates a production function with variable elasticity of substitution (VES; see, e.g. Revankar 1971) and endogenous labour productivity growth into Goodwin's model. Second, it focuses on two heterogeneous capital-extensions proposed by Goodwin (1976, 1984). According to Goodwin, (i) these extensions are always economically relevant and (ii) their dynamic behaviours are independent of the eigenvalues of the matrix of input–output coefficients. By contrast, we point out that their economic relevance and the dynamic behaviour of the overall system do depend on the said eigenvalues. And to concretize our argument, we test these extensions with actual input–output table data.

The remainder of the chapter is structured as follows: Section 10.2 presents the original model. Section 10.3 investigates the stability properties of this model when a VES production function and endogenous labour productivity growth are considered. Section 10.4 traces the implications of capital heterogeneity. Section 10.5 tests these implications, using the Symmetric Input–Output Tables (SIOTs) of the Greek economy for the years 2010 and 2015 and provides some generalized conclusions about the relevant dynamic behaviour of actual economies. Finally, Sect. 10.6 concludes.

## 10.2    Goodwin's Original Model

Consider a closed capitalist economy, with constant returns to scale, steady technical progress (disembodied), and steady growth of the labour force, producing only one commodity that can be used for consumption and investment purposes.[2] Homogeneous labour is the only primary input, and capital stock does not depreciate. There are only two classes, workers and capitalists, and two kinds of income, wages and profits. Wages are paid at the end of the production period and there are no savings out of this income, while all profits are saved and invested. Finally, fiscal and monetary considerations are ignored.

On the basis of these assumptions, we can write the following system of equations:

$$q = \min\{K\sigma^{-1}, L\alpha^{-1}\}, \quad \widehat{\alpha} = -\gamma \tag{10.1}$$

$$\widehat{N} = n \tag{10.2}$$

---

[1]Goodwin (1967) by himself stressed that the model is "starkly schematbed and hence quite unrealistic" (p. 54).

[2]This section draws on Mariolis (2006, Chap. 3, 2013), Rodousakis (2012a, Chap. 2, 2014, 2015).

$$\dot{K} = I = S = P \equiv (1 - M)q \tag{10.3}$$

$$\widehat{w} = \varepsilon E - \zeta, \ \zeta < \varepsilon \tag{10.4}$$

$$M \equiv wLq^{-1} \tag{10.5}$$

$$E \equiv LN^{-1} \tag{10.6}$$

where $\gamma$, $n$, $\varepsilon$, $\zeta$ are positive constants. A "dot" ("hat") above a variable denotes time derivative (logarithmic derivative with respect to time). Equation (10.1) is a Leontief production function (or a fixed proportions production function), where $q$ denotes the output (by definition equal to total income), $K$ the capital stock, $L$ the volume of employment, $\sigma$ the capital–output ratio (i.e. the reciprocal of capital productivity), and $\alpha^{-1}$ the labour productivity. Equation (10.2) states the assumption that the labour force, $N$, grows at a steady rate. Equation (10.3) captures the behavioural assumptions of workers and capitalists, where savings, $S$, are equal to investment, $I$, and profits, $P$, are completely reinvested. Equation (10.4) captures the assumption that the real wage rate, $w$, rises in the neighbourhood of full employment.[3] Finally, Eqs. (10.5) and (10.6) give the definitions of the share of wages in total income, $M$, and the employment rate, $E$, respectively.

The profit rate, $r$, is given by

$$r \equiv PK^{-1} = (1 - M)qK^{-1} \tag{10.7}$$

Hence, Eqs. (10.1), (10.3), and (10.7) define the capital accumulation (growth) rate, $g$, i.e.

$$g = r = \sigma^{-1}(1 - M) \tag{10.8}$$

Furthermore, from Eqs. (10.5) and (10.6) it follows that

$$\widehat{M} = \widehat{w} + \widehat{L} - \widehat{q} \tag{10.9}$$

$$\widehat{E} = \widehat{L} - \widehat{N} \tag{10.10}$$

From Eq. (10.1) it follows that

$$\widehat{q} = \widehat{L} - \widehat{\alpha}$$

hence, substituting Eqs. (10.1) and (10.4) into Eq. (10.9) yields

---

[3]In fact, it gives the wage bargaining equation, which is a linear real Phillips curve, i.e. real wage rate rises as employment rate increases. Goodwin introduced a nonlinear and strictly increasing function, $\widehat{w} = f(E)$, where $\widehat{w}$ tends to infinity (to a negative value) as $E$ tends to unity (to zero). However, he claimed that the substance of the results does not depend on the exact form of this function and, therefore, introduced Eq. (10.4).

$$\widehat{M} = \varepsilon E - (\zeta + \gamma) \tag{10.11}$$

In the same time, from Eq. (10.1) it follows that

$$\widehat{L} = g - \gamma$$

hence, Eqs. (10.2) and (10.10) imply that

$$\widehat{E} = g - \gamma - n$$

or, recalling Eq. (10.8),

$$\widehat{E} = \sigma^{-1}(1 - M) - (\gamma + n) \tag{10.12}$$

Consequently, the model can be reduced to the non-linear dynamical system of Eqs. (10.11) and (10.12), which can be written as

$$\dot{M} = (b_1 E - a_1)M \tag{10.13}$$

$$\dot{E} = (a_2 - b_2 M)E \tag{10.14}$$

where $a_1 \equiv \zeta + \gamma$, $b_1 \equiv \varepsilon$, $a_2 \equiv \sigma^{-1} - \gamma - n$, and $b_2 \equiv \sigma^{-1}$. The system of Eqs. (10.13) and (10.14) is easily recognized as a Lotka–Volterra (LV hereafter) predator–prey system (see, e.g. Hirsch and Smale 1974, Chap. 12).[4] In this case, the predator and prey variables are the share of wages and the employment rate, respectively.[5]

It has two equilibria with $\dot{E} = \dot{M} = 0$, namely

$$M^* = 0, \quad E^* = 0 \quad \text{and} \quad M^{**} = a_1 b_1^{-1}, E^{**} = a_2 b_2^{-1},$$

where the latter is economically relevant when[6]

---

[4]Another economic equivalent is Palomba's model (1939) of investment–consumption conflict; further see Gandolfo (2008). Moreover, the LV predator–prey system can be regarded as a special case of the Kolmogoroff's predator–prey system (1936). For the similarities between the two systems and a Kolmogoroff generalization of Goodwin's model, see Sportelli (1995).

[5]For two alternative interpretations, where (i) the employment rate is the predator, with the share of profits as its prey or (ii) the predator is "employed workers", while the prey is the "unemployed", i.e. capitalists are passive non-players, see Solow (1990).

[6]According to Gandolfo (1997), the validity of the condition $\sigma^{-1} > \gamma + n$ is confirmed by empirical evidence: "0.20 can be taken as a safe lower limit for [capital productivity], and 0.12 as a safe upper limit for the productivity-augmented $n$" (p. 461, footnote 14). It might be considered, however, that the validity of such conditions in growth cycle models should be postulated (see, e.g. Mariolis 2006, pp. 114–115, footnote 75).

$$\sigma^{-1} > \gamma + n \quad \text{and} \quad \zeta + \gamma < \varepsilon$$

The Jacobian matrix, $\mathbf{J} \equiv [J_{ij}]$, of the system of Eqs. (10.13) and (10.14) is

$$J_{11} \equiv \partial \dot{M} / \partial M = b_1 E - a_1$$

$$J_{12} \equiv \partial \dot{M} / \partial E = b_1 M$$

$$J_{21} \equiv \partial \dot{E} / \partial M = -b_2 E$$

$$J_{22} \equiv \partial \dot{E} / \partial E = a_2 - b_2 M$$

and is known as community matrix. At the trivial fixed point, $(M^*, E^*)$, the $\mathbf{J}^*$ is diagonal, with $J_{11}^* < 0$, $J_{22}^* > 0$; therefore, it is a saddle point (that is also for the original system of Eqs. (10.13) and (10.14). Next consider the non-trivial fixed point, $(M^{**}, E^{**})$. Then

$$\mathbf{J}^{**} = \begin{bmatrix} 0 & b_1 a_2 b_2^{-1} \\ -b_2 a_1 b_1^{-1} & 0 \end{bmatrix}$$

The eigenvalues of this matrix are both purely imaginary and conjugate to each other, $\lambda = \pm i \sqrt{a_1 a_2}$, $i \equiv \sqrt{-1}$. Hence, $(M^{**}, E^{**})$ is a centre for the linearized system, while is either a focus (stable or unstable) or a centre for the original system (see, e.g. Krüger 1985).[7] From Eqs. (10.13) and (10.14) it follows that

$$\dot{E}\dot{M}^{-1} \equiv dE/dM = (EM^{-1})(a_2 - b_2 M)(b_1 E - a_1)^{-1}$$

which is a separable differential equation, with general solution

$$-\ln \left( M^{a_2} E^{a_1} \right) + b_2 M + b_1 E = B$$

where $B$ is the constant of integration, which depends on the initial conditions. Therefore, we can draw the integral curves using the relation

$$\varphi_1(E)\varphi_2(M)^{-1} = C \tag{10.15}$$

---

[7]The linearization of the equations yields a solution similar to "simple harmonic motion" with $M$ trailing $E$ by 90° in the cycle (see, e.g. Tong 1983, p. 40).

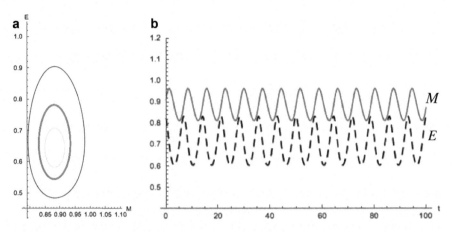

**Fig. 10.1** Closed orbits of Goodwin's model and the behaviour of the two state variables over time: (a) closed orbits for different initial conditions and (b) the dynamics of $M$ and $E$ over time

where $\varphi_1(E) \equiv E^{-a_1} e^{b_1 E}$, $\varphi_2(M) \equiv M^{a_2} e^{-b_2 M}$, and $C \equiv e^B$. Hence, from Eq. (10.19) it is obtained that $(M^{**}, E^{**})$ is a stable focus: the levels of $M$ and $E$ cycle and oscillate without damping around the fixed point.[8] The trajectory described depends upon the initial conditions and the parameters of the model. More specifically, it is obtained clockwise orbits with a unique centre in the $M - E$ phase plane (for the construction of the phase diagram, see Gabisch and Lorenz 1989, pp. 154–155; Gandolfo 1997, pp. 461–463).[9] However, it should be noted that it is possible $M$ (or $E$) to exceed unity, i.e. the state variables attaining unrealistic values.[10] Figure 10.1 summarizes the points made above, where $\varepsilon = 0.5$, $\zeta = 0.3$, $\gamma = 0.05$, $\sigma = 0.42$, and $n = 0.11$.

---

[8]These results can be extended also to the non-linear system, for the global dynamics of the system, see, e.g. Harvie et al. (2007) and Takeuchi (1996, Chap. 2).

[9]The period $T$ of Goodwin's cycles is determined by the model's parameters and it can be shown (Atkinson 1969; Harvie 2000) that around the centre

$$T = 2\pi \left[ (\zeta + \gamma)(\sigma^{-1} - (\gamma + n)) \right]^{-1/2}$$

Atkinson (1969) suggests a value of $T$ (in years) between 9.8 and 21.9, van der Ploeg (1983a) between 10 and 16, and Blatt (1983, p. 210) and Solow (1990, p. 40) between 8 and 10. Aguiar-Conraria (2001) and Dore (1993) compute a value of $T$ around 4. For the period of the non-linear system, see Evans and Findley (1999); Harvie et al. (2007); Shih and Chow (2004).

[10]Even though many authors have extended Goodwin's model by relaxing one or more of his assumptions, it is noteworthy that only a few appear to recognize the problem of the state variables attaining unrealistic values (see, e.g. Blatt 1983, p. 210; Desai et al. 2006; Harvie et al. 2007 and the references therein).

Goodwin (1967) summarized the whole mechanism as follows:

When profit is greatest, [...] employment is average, and the high growth rate pushes employment to its maximum [...], which squeezes the profit rate to its average value [...]. The deceleration in the growth employment (relative) to its average value again, where profit and growth are again at their nadir. This low growth rate leads to a fall in output and employment to well below full employment, thus restoring profitability to its average value because productivity is now rising faster than wage rates [...]. The improved profitability carries the seed of its own destruction by engendering a too vigorous expansion of output and employment, thus destroying the reserve army of labour and strengthening labour's bargaining power. This inherent conflict and complementarity of workers and capitalists is typical of symbiosis. (pp. 57–58)

Therefore, an increase in employment leads to an increase in the share of wages, which decreases the profit rate and thus capital accumulation. The outcome of lower capital accumulation is a decrease in the output and consequently in the employment, leading to a reduction in the share of wages and an increase in the profit rate. A higher profit rate leads to faster capital accumulation and, hence, an increase in output growth and employment. At this point the cycle restarts.

## 10.3   Goodwin's Original Model with a VES Production Function

### 10.3.1   The Model

Since Goodwin's system constitutes an economic equivalent of the LV predator–prey system, it is "structurally unstable", i.e. sensitive to perturbations in its functional structure.[11] In fact,

any influence on the rate of change of one or both of the two [state] variables which depends on the value of this variable is equivalent to the introduction of a dampening effect. The conservative dynamics of the original Lotka/Volterra equations will thus be destroyed and the emerging system turns into a dissipative dynamical system. [...] As soon as a dissipative structure prevails, a modified Goodwin model can exhibit converging or diverging oscillations as well as limit cycles depending on the assumed damping or forcing terms. (Lorenz 1989, p. 61)

Hence, even a slight perturbation of its structure can destroy the closed orbit character of its solution.[12] Van der Ploeg (1985) has shown, by using a constant

---

[11]This section draws on Rodousakis (2012a, 2014).

[12]In most of the literature on Goodwin's model structural instability is considered another major weakness of the model and several modifications of it are explicitly aimed at yielding a structurally stable limit cycle (Medio 1979; Sportelli 1995 and the references therein). However, there is no reason to believe that actual economies would necessarily be structurally stable, or that systems characterized by some degree of instability are uninteresting or residual. This suggests that the adoption of a structurally unstable model should be evaluated on a case-by-case basis, depending on

elasticity of substitution (CES) production function, that the substitution between "capital and labour" plays a crucial role in the dynamics of the model: it becomes asymptotically stable (i.e. it is equivalent to the assumption of a *positive friction* term).[13] Goodwin (1991) has shown that if we add endogenous productivity growth, then the system becomes unstable (i.e. it is equivalent to the assumption of a *negative friction* term). In what follows we investigate the role of a VES production function and of endogenous labour productivity growth within the Goodwin's original model.[14] Hence, we assume that:

(i). The efficiency of labour is influenced by the size of the capital stock (i.e. as Aguiar-Conraria 2008, p. 519, mentions "a Kaldorian technical progress function is considered")

$$L_e = Le^{\gamma t}K^{\beta} \tag{10.16}$$

where $\beta$ is a positive constant and $L_e$ denotes the "labour input in efficiency units" (van der Ploeg 1985, p. 222; Aguiar-Conraria 2008, pp. 519–520).[15]

(ii). A VES production function, i.e.[16]

$$q = K^{1-\delta\rho}[l + (\rho - 1)K]^{\delta\rho}, \ \ 0 \leq \delta\rho < 1 \tag{10.17}$$

that if $\rho = 1$, then Eq. (10.17) reduces to the Cobb–Douglas case, while if $\rho = 0$, then it reduces to the "*AK* model" production function.[17]

From the profit-maximizing conditions (Aguiar-Conraria 2008, p. 520; van der Ploeg 1985, p. 223), we obtain

---

the nature of the phenomenon investigated and the aims of the research (see, e.g. Vercelli 1982, 1991). In general, for the concept of structural stability, see Andronov and Pontryagin (1937).

[13]Consider Samuelson (1971, pp. 982–983) and, for example, Lorenz (1989, pp. 51–52).

[14]Aguiar-Conraria (2008) has considered both a CES production function and endogenous labour productivity growth and concluded that the stabilities properties of that system are *a priori* unknown (i.e. the equilibrium can be locally stable, unstable, or the system behaves locally like Goodwin's one). Also see Aguiar-Conraria (2001) and van der Ploeg (1983a, 1983b, 1987). Thus, contrary to Goodwin (1967), we relax the assumptions of "steady technical progress (disembodied)" and "constant capital–output ratio".

[15]It should be noted that if $\beta = 0$, then Eq. (10.16) is written as $L_e = Le^{\gamma t}$, i.e. it captures the assumption of steady technical progress.

[16]In contrast to CES production function, which restricts the elasticity of substitution to be constant along an isoquant, VES allows this substitution parameter to vary, i.e. a change in the intensity of capital affects the elasticity of substitution between capital and labour. In fact, empirical investigations have been concluded that the "the overall impression is that the VES functions are more realistic than the CES (C–D [Cobb–Douglas]) functions" (Sato and Hoffman 1968, p. 457); also see Kazi (1980), Lovell (1968), Lu and Fletcher (1968).

[17]Note that if $\rho \rightarrow \delta^{-1}$, then Eq. (10.17) reduces to the linear production function and, therefore, as $\rho$ increases from zero to $\delta^{-1}$, the elasticity of substitution increases steadily from zero to infinity (see Revankar 1971, p. 67). Also see Sato and Hoffman (1968) for a very similar production function.

$$\partial q / \partial L_e = w e^{-\gamma t} K^{-\beta} \tag{10.18}$$

Hence, from Eqs. (10.16) and (10.17) it follows that

$$\left\{ \delta \rho K^{1-\delta \rho} [L_e + (\rho - 1)K]^{\delta \rho - 1} L_e \right\} \left\{ A K^{1-\delta \rho} [L_e + (\rho - 1)K]^{\delta \rho} \right\}^{-1} = w L q^{-1}$$

or, recalling Eq. (10.5),

$$k = (\rho - 1)^{-1} \left[ (\delta \rho - M) M^{-1} \right] \tag{10.19}$$

where $k (\equiv K L_e^{-1})$ denotes the optimal factor demand ratio ("in efficiency units"). Hence, from Eqs. (10.17) and (10.19), the (optimal) capital–output ratio can be written as

$$\sigma = D^{-\delta \rho} \tag{10.20}$$

where $D \equiv [(\rho - 1)\delta \rho](\delta \rho - M)^{-1}$.[18] Furthermore, from the definition of labour productivity and Eqs. (10.16) and (10.17) it follows that

$$\alpha^{-1} = k \left[ k^{-1} + (\rho - 1) \right]^{\delta \rho} e^{\gamma t} K^{\beta}$$

or, recalling Eq. (10.20),

$$\alpha^{-1} = \delta \rho M^{-1} D^{\delta \rho - 1} e^{\gamma t} K^{\beta} \tag{10.21}$$

Logarithmic differentiation of Eq. (10.21) yields

$$\widehat{\alpha} = \left[ \delta \rho (1 - M - 1)(\delta \rho - M)^{-1} \right] \widehat{M} - \gamma - \beta \widehat{K} \tag{10.22}$$

Substituting Eq. (10.22) into Eq. (10.3) yields

$$\widehat{K} = (1 - M) D^{\delta \rho} \tag{10.23}$$

Since $\widehat{M} = \widehat{w} + \widehat{\alpha}$, from Eqs. (10.3), (10.22), and (10.23) it follows that

$$\dot{M} = (\delta \rho - 1)^{-1} \left[ \varepsilon E - (\gamma + \zeta) - \beta (1 - M) D^{\delta \rho} \right] (\delta \rho - M) \tag{10.24}$$

At the same time, from the definition of $E$ and

---

[18]For Eqs. (10.23) and (10.24) to be economically relevant, we must assume that $\delta \rho \neq M$ and $D > 0$.

$$\widehat{k} = (1 - \beta)\widehat{K} - \widehat{L} - \gamma$$

it follows that

$$\widehat{E} = (1 - \beta)\widehat{K} - \widehat{k} - \gamma - \widehat{N}$$

and, therefore, from

$$\widehat{k} = \left[\delta\rho(\delta\rho - M)^{-1}\right]\widehat{M}$$

and Eqs. (10.2), (10.19), and (10.23), it is obtained

$$\dot{E} = \left[(1 - \beta)(1 - M)D^{\delta\rho} + \delta\rho(\delta\rho - M)^{-1}\widehat{M} - (\gamma + n)\right]E \qquad (10.25)$$

Consequently, the model described above can be reduced to the non-linear dynamical system of Eqs. (10.24) and (10.25).

### 10.3.2   The Properties

We distinguish between the following two cases:

**Case 1:** Exogenous labour productivity growth, i.e. $\beta = 0$. If we consider $\rho = 1$, from the profit-maximizing conditions, i.e. Eq. (10.18), we obtain

$$w = \delta k^{1-\delta} e^{\gamma t} \qquad (10.26)$$

Hence, the model reduces to the non-linear system

$$\dot{k} = (1 - \delta)^{-1}[\varepsilon E - (\gamma + \zeta)]k \qquad (10.24a)$$

$$\dot{E} = \left[(1 - \delta)k^{-\delta} - \widehat{k} - (\gamma + n)\right]E \qquad (10.25a)$$

where the state variables are now $k$ and $E$.[19] The above system has a non-trivial fixed point, i.e.

$$k^* = (\gamma + n)^{-1/\delta}[(1 - \delta)]^{1/\delta}, E^* = (\gamma + \zeta)\varepsilon^{-1}$$

The Jacobian matrix of Eqs. (10.24a) and (10.25a) is

---

[19]The Cobb–Douglas production function implies constant share of wages and, therefore, the state variable $M$ is replaced by $k$ which is strongly associated with income distribution.

$$J_{11} \equiv \partial \dot{k}/\partial k = [\varepsilon E - (\gamma + \zeta)](1-\delta)^{-1}$$

$$J_{12} \equiv \partial \dot{k}/\partial E = \varepsilon k (1-\delta)^{-1}$$

$$J_{21} \equiv \partial \dot{E}/\partial k = -\delta E(1-\delta)k^{-\delta-1}$$

$$J_{22} \equiv \partial \dot{E}/\partial E = \varepsilon E(1-\delta)^{-1} + (1-\delta)k^{-\delta} - \widehat{k} - (\gamma + n)$$

Linearizing the system around $(k^*, E^*)$, we obtain

$$\dot{k} = (1-\delta)^{-1}\varepsilon k^* E'$$

$$\dot{E} = -\delta(1-\delta)E^*(k^*)^{-\delta-1}k' - (1-\delta)^{-1}\varepsilon E^* E'$$

where $k' \equiv k - k^*$ and $E' \equiv E - E^*$. Thus, the characteristic equation of the above system can be written as

$$\lambda^2 - \theta_1 \lambda + \theta_0 = 0$$

where

$$\theta_0 (\equiv \det[\mathbf{J}^*]) = \delta \varepsilon E^*(k^*)^{-\delta}$$

and

$$\theta_1 (\equiv \mathrm{tr}[\mathbf{J}^*]) = -(1-\delta)^{-1}\varepsilon E^*$$

Since $\theta_0$ is positive and $\theta_1$ is negative, the fixed point is locally asymptotically stable. The discriminant of the characteristic equation, $\Delta^* (\equiv \theta_1{}^2 - 4\theta_0)$, may be written as

$$\Delta^* = \left[\varepsilon E^* - 4\delta E^*(k^*)^{-\delta}(\delta-1)^2\right]/\mu_1 \tag{10.27}$$

where $\mu_1 \equiv (\delta - 1)^2(\varepsilon E^*)^{-1}$. It follows that for large (small) enough $\varepsilon$, Eq. (10.27) will be positive (negative) and, therefore, the fixed point is a stable node (focus).

Considering now that $\rho \in (0, 1) \cup (1, +\infty)$, the system of Eqs. (10.24) and (10.25) is written as follows:

$$\dot{M} = (\delta\rho - 1)^{-1}[\varepsilon E - (\gamma + \zeta)](\delta\rho - M) \tag{10.24b}$$

$$\dot{E} = \left[(1-M)D^{\delta\rho} + \delta\rho^{-1}(\delta\rho - M)\widehat{M} - (\gamma + n)\right]E \tag{10.25b}$$

The non-trivial fixed point of this system is equal to[20]

---

[20]To the non-trivial fixed point there may correspond more than one economically relevant value for $M$.

$$M^* = 1 - (\gamma + n)(D^*)^{-\delta\rho}, \quad E^* = (\gamma + \zeta)\varepsilon^{-1}$$

The Jacobian matrix of Eqs. (10.24b) and (10.25b) is

$$J_{11} \equiv \partial\dot{M}/\partial M = -(\delta\rho - 1)^{-1}[\varepsilon E - (\gamma + \zeta)]$$

$$J_{12} \equiv \partial\dot{M}/\partial E = \varepsilon(\delta\rho - M)(\delta\rho - 1)^{-1}$$

$$J_{21} \equiv \partial\dot{E}/\partial M$$

$$= \left\{ (1 - \delta\rho)M[(\delta\rho - M)]^{-1}D^{\delta\rho} - \delta\rho(\varepsilon E - \gamma - \zeta)[(\delta\rho - 1)M^2]^{-1} \right\}E$$

$$J_{22} \equiv \partial\dot{E}/\partial E = (1 - M)D^{\delta\rho} + \delta\rho[2\varepsilon E - (\gamma + \zeta)][(\delta\rho - 1)M]^{-1} - (\gamma + n)$$

Linearizing the system around $(M^*, E^*)$, we obtain

$$\dot{M} = \varepsilon(\delta\rho - M^*)(\delta\rho - 1)^{-1}E'$$

$$\dot{E} = \left\{ (D^*)^{\delta\rho}[(1 - \delta\rho)M^*](\delta\rho - M^*)^{-1}E^* \right\}E' + \left\{ (\varepsilon\delta\rho E^*)[(\delta\rho - 1)M^*]^{-1} \right\}E'$$

where $M' \equiv M - M^*$ and $D^* \equiv [(\rho - 1)\delta\rho](\delta\rho - M^*)^{-1}$ and, therefore,

$$\theta_0 = \varepsilon M^* E^* (D^*)^{\delta\rho}$$

and

$$\theta_1 = (\varepsilon\delta\rho E^*)[(\delta\rho - 1)M^*]^{-1}$$

Since $\theta_0$ is positive and $\theta_1$ is negative, the fixed point is locally asymptotically stable. Furthermore, the discriminant of the characteristic equation may be written as

$$\Delta^* = \left\{ \varepsilon E^* - 4M^*(D^*)^{\delta\rho}[(\delta\rho - 1)M^*]^2(\delta\rho)^{-2} \right\}\mu_2^{-1} \tag{10.28}$$

where $\mu_2 \equiv [(\delta\rho - 1)M^*]^2[\varepsilon E^*(\delta\rho)^2]^{-1}$. Hence, for large (small) enough $\varepsilon$, $\Delta^*$ will be positive (negative) and, therefore, the fixed point is a stable node (focus).

The following two numerical examples illustrate some of the points made above:

**Example 10.1**
Assume that $\varepsilon = 0.04$, $\zeta = 0.003$, $\gamma = 0.001$, $\rho = 1$, $\delta = 0.99$ and $n = 0.03$. It is obtained that (see Eqs. (10.24a) and (10.25a))

$$k^* \cong 0.318 \quad \text{and} \quad E^* \cong 0.1.$$

Therefore, we get $\theta_1 \cong -0.4$, $\theta_0 \cong 0.012$ and that the discriminant, $\Delta^* \cong 0.110$, is positive: the fixed point is a stable node.

**Example 10.2**
Assume that $\varepsilon = 0.04$, $\zeta = 0.003$, $\gamma = 0.001$, $\rho = 0.202$, $\delta = 0.99$ and $n = 0.03$. It is obtained that (see Eqs. (10.24b) and (10.25b))

$$M^* \cong 0.957 \quad \text{and} \quad E^* \cong 0.1.$$

Therefore, we get $\theta_1 \cong -0.001$, $\theta_0 \cong 0.0028$ and that the discriminant, $\Delta^* \cong -0.011$, is negative: the fixed point is a stable focus.

**Case 2:** Endogenous labour productivity growth, i.e. $\beta \neq 0$. If we consider $\rho = 1$, Eq. (10.26) is written as

$$w = \delta k^{1-\delta} e^{\gamma t} K^{\beta}$$

and, therefore,

$$\dot{k} = \left\{ [\varepsilon E - (\gamma + \zeta)](1 - \delta)^{-1} - \beta k^{-\delta} \right\} k \tag{10.24c}$$

$$\dot{E} = \left[ (1 - \beta)(1 - \delta)k^{-\delta} - \hat{k} - (\gamma + n) \right] E \tag{10.25c}$$

The non-trivial equilibrium point of this system is given by

$$k^* = (\gamma + n)[(1 - \beta)(1 - \delta)]^{-1/\delta}, M^* = \left[ (\gamma + \zeta) + \beta(1 - \delta)(k^*)^{-\delta} \right] \varepsilon^{-1}$$

The Jacobian matrix of Eqs. (10.24c) and (10.25c) is

$$J_{11} \equiv \partial \dot{k}/\partial k = [\varepsilon E - (\gamma + \zeta)](1 - \delta)^{-1} - (1 - \delta)\beta k^{-\delta}$$

$$J_{12} \equiv \partial \dot{k}/\partial E = \varepsilon k(1 - \delta)^{-1}$$

$$J_{21} \equiv \partial \dot{E}/\partial k = -k^{-\delta-1}\left[ (1 - \beta)(1 - \delta)k^{-\delta-1} - \beta \delta \right] E$$

$$J_{22} \equiv \partial \dot{E}/\partial E = (1 - \beta)(1 - \delta)\delta k^{-\delta} - \varepsilon E(1 - \delta)^{-1}$$

Hence, linearizing the system of Eqs. (10.24c) and (10.25c) around $(k^*, M^*)$, we obtain

$$\dot{k} = \beta \delta (k^*)^{-\delta} k' + \varepsilon k^* (1 - \delta)^{-1} E'$$

$$\dot{E} = \left[ -(1 - \beta)(1 - \delta)\delta(k^*)^{-\delta-1} - \beta A \delta(k^*)^{-\delta-1} \right] E^* k' - \varepsilon E^* (1 - \delta)^{-1} E'$$

and, therefore, we obtain

$$\theta_0 = \varepsilon E^* (1 - \beta)\delta(k^*)^{-\delta}$$

and

$$\theta_1 = \beta\delta(k^*)^{-\delta} - \varepsilon E^*(1-\delta)^{-1}$$

Since $\theta_0$ is positive and $\theta_1$ is negative, the fixed point is locally asymptotically stable.

Finally, if $\rho \in (0,1) \cup (1, +\infty)$, the model is described by the system of Eqs. (10.24) and (10.25). Its non-trivial fixed point is given by[21]

$$M^* = 1 - (\gamma + n)[(1 - \beta)]^{-1}(D^*)^{-\delta\rho}, E^* = \left[\beta(1 - M^*)(D^*)^{\delta\rho} + \gamma + \zeta\right]\varepsilon^{-1}$$

The Jacobian matrix of Eqs. (10.24) and (10.25) is

$$J_{11} = -(\delta\rho - 1)^{-1}\left[\varepsilon E - (\gamma + \zeta) - \beta(1 - M)D^{\delta\rho}\right] + \beta D^{\delta\rho}M$$

$$J_{12} = (\delta\rho - 1)^{-1}(\delta\rho - M)\varepsilon$$

$$J_{21} = D^{\delta\rho}ZE - \left[\varepsilon E - (\gamma + \zeta) - (1 - M)\beta D^{\delta\rho}\right]\delta\rho\left[(\delta\rho - 1)M^2\right]^{-1}E$$

$$J_{22} = (1 - \beta)(1 - M)D^{\delta\rho} + \delta\rho[(\delta\rho - M)]^{-1}\widehat{M} - (\gamma + n) + \delta\rho\varepsilon E[(\delta\rho - 1)M]^{-1}$$

where $Z \equiv [M - \beta M + \delta\rho(\beta - M + \beta M)](\delta\rho - M)^{-1}$. The linearized version of the system of Eqs. (10.24) and (10.25) around $(M^*, E^*)$ can be written as

$$\dot{M} = -\beta(D^*)^{\delta\rho}M^*M' + \varepsilon(\delta\rho - 1)^{-1}(\delta\rho - M^*)E'$$

$$\dot{E} = (D^*)^{\delta\rho}Z^*M' + \left\{(\varepsilon\delta\rho E^*)[(\delta\rho - 1)M]^{-1}E^*\right\}E'$$

Therefore, we obtain

$$\theta_0 = \varepsilon(1 - \beta)(D^*)^{\delta\rho}E^*M^*$$

and

$$\theta_1 = \beta(D^*)^{\delta\rho}M^* + (\varepsilon\delta\rho E^*)[(\delta\rho - 1)M^*]^{-1}$$

Since $\theta_0$ is positive, the local stability properties of the system of Eqs. (10.24) and (10.25) depend on the sign of $\theta_1$. Hence, we may distinguish the following cases:[22]

(i). When $\beta < -(\varepsilon\delta\rho E^*)[(\delta\rho - 1)(M^*)^2(D^*)^{\delta\rho}]^{-1}$, it follows that $\theta_1 < 0$: stable.

---

[21] See footnote 20 of this chapter.

[22] It should be noted that (i) for $\beta \neq 0$ (both for $\rho = 1$ and $\rho \in (0,1) \cup (1, +\infty)$), the sign of the discriminant of the characteristic equation is indeterminate; (ii) the dynamics of the system is somewhat analogous to that obtained for the CES production function (see Aguiar-Conraria 2008, pp. 521–522); and (iii) Aguiar-Conraria (2008, p. 522) notes that, in the case of CES, "only when the production function is extremely close to a Leontief technology does the system generate perpetual (and explosive) oscillations": however, the VES does not contain the Leontief production function as its special case.

(ii). When $\beta = -(\varepsilon\delta\rho E^*)[(\delta\rho - 1)(M^*)^2(D^*)^{\delta\rho}]^{-1}$, it follows that like in Goodwin's original model: centre. Hence, $(M^*, E^*)$ is either a focus (stable or unstable) or a centre for the original system (see, e.g. Andronov et al. 1987, pp. 278–280).

(iii). When $\beta > -(\varepsilon\delta\rho E^*)[(\delta\rho - 1)(M^*)^2(D^*)^{\delta\rho}]^{-1}$, it follows that $\theta_1 > 0$: unstable.

The following two numerical examples illustrate some of the points made above:

**Example 10.3**
Assume that $\varepsilon = 0.04, \zeta = 0.003, \gamma = 0.001, \beta = 0.5, \rho = 1, \delta = 0.99$ and $n = 0.03$. It is obtained that (see Eqs. (10.24c) and (10.25c))

$$k^* \cong 0.158 \quad \text{and} \quad E^* \cong 0.875.$$

Therefore, we get $\theta_1 \cong -0.430, \theta_0 \cong 0.108$ and that the discriminant, $\Delta^* \cong -0.248$, is negative: the fixed point is a stable focus.

**Example 10.4**
Assume that $\varepsilon = 0.04, \zeta = 0.003, \gamma = 0.001, \beta = 0.5, \rho = 0.202, \delta = 0.99$ and $n = 0.03$. It is obtained that (see Eqs. (10.24) and (10.25))

$$M^* \cong 0.916 \quad \text{and} \quad E^* \cong 0.875.$$

Therefore, we get $\theta_1 \cong 0.329, \theta_0 \cong 0.0118$ and that the discriminant, $\Delta^* \cong 0.061$, is positive: the fixed point is an unstable node.

Hence, it has been shown that the incorporation of a VES production function in Goodwin's model is equivalent to the introduction of a *dampening* effect; hence, the equilibrium becomes locally asymptotically stable. However, if we assume endogenous labour productivity growth, it is then concluded that (i) the local dynamic behaviour of the system depends on the "degree of endogeneity of labour productivity growth"; (ii) there are two opposite effects, the *destabilizing* effect of "endogenous labour productivity growth" and the *stabilizing* effect of the "elasticity of substitution"; and (iii) neither effect is, in general, dominant over the other. More specifically, the equilibrium in the case that the effect of the endogenous labour productivity growth is stronger than the effect of the elasticity of substitution is locally stable (*positive friction*), whereas that in the opposite case is unstable (*negative friction*). Finally, in the case of equality, the model exhibits perpetual oscillations (like in Goodwin's original model).

## 10.4 Goodwin's Disaggregated Models

Goodwin's model is in "aggregative form" and this has been recognized by Goodwin (1984) himself as the fundamental weakness of his model, i.e.

aggregated models, including my own, are less than totally satisfactory; they are useful in helping to conceptualize and as preliminary skirmishes prior to elaboration in disaggregative form. (p. 67)[23]

To overcome this weakness Goodwin developed two models, which were proposed in *Use of Normalised General Co-ordinates in Linear Value and Distribution Theory* (1976) (Goodwin's Disaggregated Model 1; GDM1 hereafter) and *Disaggregating Models of Fluctuating Growth* (1984) (GDM2 hereafter).[24] Those models: (i) capture the inter-relationships amongst the industries (sectors); (ii) do not describe the dynamics of the aggregate economy, but the dynamics of each industry (sector) of the economy; and (iii) generate dynamic behaviours which depend strongly on the matrix of input–output coefficients.[25]

### 10.4.1   GDM1: The One-Commodity Case

*Ceteris paribus*, the GDM1 may be described by the following relations:

$$y \equiv (1-a)x \tag{10.29}$$

$$x = \min\{Ka^{-1}, La^{-1}\}, \ \widehat{a} = -\gamma \tag{10.30}$$

$$\widehat{m} = \xi E - \psi, \ \psi < \xi \tag{10.3a}$$

$$g = r \equiv r_n - \widehat{p} \tag{10.31}$$

$$\widehat{p} = (a + \theta)(1 + r_n) - 1 \tag{10.32}$$

where $x(y)$ denotes the gross (net) output, $m$ the money wage rate, $r_n$ the nominal profit rate, $p$ the product price, and $\theta$ the unit labour cost. Equation (10.29) captures the assumption that capital lasts for one period of production. Equation (10.30) is a Leontief production function (also see Eq. (10.1)). Equation (10.3a) captures the assumption that the money wage rate rises in the neighbourhood of full employment. Equation (10.31) describes the relationship between the real and the nominal profit rate. Finally, the nominal profit rate is assumed to be fixed, whilst the cost in one period determines price in the next, i.e. $p(t+1) = (p(t)a + m(t)a(t))(1 + r_n)$, where $t$ denotes the time. Hence, from the last equation, "if we ignore the difference between differentials and differences" (Goodwin 1983, p. 147), we get Eq. (10.32).

Since $\theta \equiv map^{-1}$, the share of wages in net output, $M_y$, can be written as

---

[23]However, the model also neglects altogether any effective demand issues; see Chap. 11 of the present book.

[24]Also see Goodwin (1983, Chap. 7, 1986, 1989, pp. 125–140), Goodwin and Landesmann (1996, pp. 180–181), Goodwin and Punzo (1987, pp. 106–112).

[25]This section draws on Mariolis (2006, pp. 188–196), Rodousakis (2012a, Chap. 4, 2012b, 2016, 2019).

$$M_y \equiv mL(py)^{-1} = \theta(1-a)^{-1} \tag{10.33}$$

Substituting Eqs. (10.30), (10.3a), and (10.32) into

$$\widehat{M}_y = \widehat{\theta} = \widehat{m} + \widehat{a} - \widehat{p}$$

yields

$$\widehat{M}_y = \xi E - (\psi + \gamma) - (1 + r_n)\big[a + (1-a)M_y\big] + 1 \tag{10.34}$$

From Eqs. (10.29) and (10.30) it follows that

$$\widehat{y} = \widehat{L} + \gamma$$

hence, from Eqs. (10.2) and (10.31) and the definition of $E$, it is obtained

$$\widehat{E} = g - (\gamma + n) \tag{10.35}$$

In the same time, from Eqs. (10.3a) and (10.31) it follows that

$$g = (1 + r_n)[1 - (a + \theta)] \tag{10.36}$$

or, recalling Eq. (10.33),

$$g = (1 + r_n)(1-a)(1-M_y) \tag{10.37}$$

Hence, Eq. (10.35) is written as

$$\widehat{E} = (1 + r_n)(1-a)(1-M_y) - (\gamma + n) \tag{10.38}$$

Consequently, the model reduces to the non-linear system of Eqs. (10.34) and (10.38), which has one equilibria with $\dot{M}_y = \dot{E} = 0$, namely

$$M_y^* = 1 - (\gamma + n)[(1 + r_n)(1-a)]^{-1} \quad \text{and} \quad E^* = (r_n + \psi - n)\xi^{-1}$$

The Jacobian matrix of Eqs. (10.34) and (10.38) is

$$J_{11} \equiv \partial \dot{M}_y / \partial M_y = -(1 + r_n)\big[2(1-a)M_y + a\big] + \xi E - (\psi + \gamma) + 1$$

$$J_{12} \equiv \partial \dot{M}_y / \partial E = \xi M_y$$

$$J_{21} \equiv \partial \dot{E} / \partial M_y = -(1 + r_n)(1-a)E$$

$$J_{22} \equiv \partial \dot{E}/\partial E = (1 + r_n)(1 - a)(1 - M_y) - (\gamma + n)$$

where

$$\theta_0 = \xi(1 + r_n)(1 - a)E^* M_y^*$$

and

$$\theta_1 = -(1 + r_n)(1 - a)M_y^*$$

Since $\theta_0$ is positive and $\theta_1$ is negative, the fixed point is locally asymptotically stable. Hence, in the long-run $\widehat{p} = r_n - (\gamma + n)$, $g = \gamma + n$, and $\widehat{w} = \gamma$.

### 10.4.2   GDM2: The One-Commodity Case

*Ceteris paribus*, we assume that "operating profit equals investment and growth" (Goodwin 1984), i.e.

$$\widehat{x} = \Pi \equiv 1 - \alpha - wa \tag{10.39}$$

where $\Pi$ denotes the profits per unit activity level. Furthermore, we assume that all prices are constant and, hence, Eq. (10.3a) is replaced by Eq. (10.3).

Since $M_y = \theta(1 - a)^{-1}$,[26] from Eq. (10.39) it follows that

$$\widehat{x} = (1 - a)(1 - M_y) \tag{10.40}$$

Equations (10.29) and (10.30) imply that

$$\widehat{L} = \widehat{y} - \gamma \tag{10.41}$$

Substituting Eqs. (10.3a) and (10.41) into

$$\widehat{M}_y = \widehat{w} + \widehat{L} - \widehat{y}$$

yields

---

[26]Goodwin (1984, p. 69) hypothesized that $M_x \equiv \theta$ denotes the share of wages in gross output. However, it would make no relevant difference to what follows to take into account this consideration.

$$\widehat{M}_y = \varepsilon E - (\gamma + \zeta) \tag{10.42}$$

Furthermore, since $\widehat{x} = \widehat{y}$, from Eqs. (10.40) and (10.41) it follows that

$$\widehat{L} = (1 - a)(1 - M_y) - \gamma$$

or, recalling Eq. (10.2) and the definition of $E$,

$$\widehat{E} = (1 - a)(1 - M_y) - (\gamma + n) \tag{10.43}$$

Consequently, the model reduces to the non-linear system of Eqs. (10.42) and (10.43), which is dynamically equivalent to Goodwin's original system (1967).

## 10.4.3   Goodwins's Method of Principal Coordinates

Consider a closed, linear system, involving only single products, circulating capital and homogeneous labour. Furthermore, assume that (i) the input–output coefficients are fixed; (ii) the system is viable, i.e. the Perron–Frobenius (P–F hereafter) eigen-value of the $n \times n$ matrix of input–output coefficients, $\mathbf{A}$, is less than 1, and diagonalizable; (iii) wages are paid at the beginning of the common production period; and (iv) the profit (growth) rate, $r$ $(g)$, is uniform.

On the basis of these assumptions, we can write

$$\mathbf{p}^T = (1 + r)(m\mathbf{b}^T + \mathbf{p}^T\mathbf{A}), \quad m \equiv \mathbf{p}^T\mathbf{w} \tag{10.44}$$

$$\mathbf{x} = (1 + g)(\mathbf{c} + \mathbf{A}\mathbf{x}), \quad \mathbf{c} \equiv \mathbf{w}\mathbf{b}^T\mathbf{x} \tag{10.45}$$

where $\mathbf{p}$ denotes a vector of long-period values, i.e. production prices, $m$ the money wage rate, $\mathbf{b}$ the vector of direct labour coefficients, $\mathbf{w}$ the vector of the real wage rate, $\mathbf{x}$ the vector of gross outputs, and $\mathbf{c}$ the consumption vector.[27] Goodwin has proposed a "reformulation" of the two systems of equations represented above based on a simple "coordinate transformation".

Consider all the eigenvectors of $\mathbf{A}$ to be linearly independent. By the diagonal canonical form transformation, we then have

$$< \mathbf{\Lambda} >= \mathbf{H}^{-1}\mathbf{A}\mathbf{H} \tag{10.46}$$

---

[27]System (10.44) is essentially the same as Sraffa's (1960, Chap. 2) price system, except that, following Goodwin, we hypothesize that wages are paid ex ante.

where $<\Lambda>$ is a diagonal matrix having all the eigenvalues of $\mathbf{A}$ on the main diagonal, and $\mathbf{H} \equiv [h_{ij}]$ $\left(\mathbf{H}^{-1} \equiv \left[h'_{ij}\right]\right)$ is a matrix having $n$ linearly independent right-hand side (left-hand side) eigenvectors of $\mathbf{A}$ in its columns (rows), i.e. it denotes the "modal matrix" of $\mathbf{A}$.

The two equations system of Eqs. (10.51) and (10.52) may therefore simply be written as

$$\mathbf{P}^{\mathrm{T}} = (1+r)\left( m\mathbf{a}^{\mathrm{T}} + \mathbf{P}^{\mathrm{T}} < \Lambda > \right) \tag{10.47}$$

$$\mathbf{X} = (1+g)(\mathbf{k}+ < \Lambda > \mathbf{X}) \tag{10.48}$$

where $\mathbf{P}^{\mathrm{T}} \equiv \mathbf{p}^{\mathrm{T}}\mathbf{H}$, $\mathbf{a}^{\mathrm{T}} \equiv \mathbf{b}^{\mathrm{T}}\mathbf{H}$, $\mathbf{X} \equiv \mathbf{H}^{-1}\mathbf{x}$, and $\mathbf{k} \equiv \mathbf{H}^{-1}\mathbf{c}$. As observed by Goodwin, this transformation defines $n$ independent, one-commodity, simpler systems (known as eigen-sectors), i.e. the system of Eqs. (10.44) and (10.45) is transformed from its own "original coordinates" to another set of normalized "principal coordinates" (see Goodwin and Punzo 1987, Chap. 2, Sect. 5). There are of course the difficulties that:

(i).These systems are fictitious, i.e. "these eigen-sectors do not exist—they are mere accounting devices: no decisions are taken by such fictitious units" (Goodwin and Punzo 1987, p. 60).

(ii). In general, they have no economic interpretation, in the sense that the eigenvalues of $\mathbf{A}$ can be negative or complex (with only exception the P–F eigenvalue which is always real and positive, i.e. the Sraffa's 1960, Chap. 4, "Standard system").

Regarding this, Goodwin observed that we can always go back to the original coordinates where these difficulties disappear, i.e. according to Goodwin and Punzo (1987):

> [The] transformation suppresses, without ignoring, the great difficulties of inter-dependence. Certain problems can be solved with ease, and then, in transforming back to [original] Cartesian coordinates, full account is taken of the overwhelming unity of the economic system, the dependence of each sector on all the others. (p. 54)

What is really remarkable is that such a transformation solves the problem of synthesizing the structure of an economic system "not by aggregating into one commodity", but by rearranging sectors into "pseudo-producing sectors", i.e. into the eigen-sectors. In these terms, all inter-dependences disappear and each eigen-sector takes up the analytical characteristics of "Ricardo's Corn Economy", with all well-known analytical simplifications attached to such concepts. Thus, as Goodwin (1984) mentioned, the main advantage of the transformation under discussion is that

> [b]y separating variables, the complications of inter-dependence have been removed, without being ignored since when transforming back the solutions they are taken account of. (p. 68)[28]

---

[28]For this reason, the systems of Eqs. (10.44) and (10.45), and Eqs. (10.47) and (10.48) are strictly equivalent to each other. See Sect. 2.2 of this book.

**Fig. 10.2** The logic of Goodwin's method of principal coordinates

The method can be summarized as follows: through the "coordinate transformation" the original system is substituted by a fictitious eigen-system; hence, we are able to analyse it in terms of eigen-sector and, then, by transforming it back to the original coordinates we can evaluate our results in original terms. The logic behind the method is illustrated in Fig. 10.2.

Thus, due to this method the system of Eqs. (10.34) and (10.38) (or, respectively, of Eqs. (10.42) and (10.43)) can be written in disaggregative form.[29]

### 10.4.4   GDM1: The Heterogeneous Capital Case

As observed by Goodwin (1976), if we consider $n$ sectoral labour and product markets in principal coordinates, the GDM1 can be generalized into an $n$ eigen-sector model. Hence, from Eqs. (10.34) and (10.38), we can write the following $n$ 2D-systems of differential equations in state variables $l_j$ and $\beta_j$:

$$\widehat{l}_j = \xi_j \beta_j - (\gamma_j + \psi_j) - [\lambda_j + (1 - \lambda_j)l_j](1 + r_{nj}) + 1 \tag{10.49}$$

$$\widehat{\beta}_j = (1 + r_{nj})(1 - \lambda_j)(1 - l_j) - (\gamma_j + n_j) \tag{10.50}$$

where $l_j \left( \equiv \left[ \left( m_j p_j^{-1} \right) L_j \right] y_j^{-1} \right)$ and $\beta_j \left( \equiv L_j N_j^{-1} \right)$ denote the share of wages and the employment rate of the $j$th eigen-sector, respectively.

From the non-linear system of Eqs. (10.49) and (10.50), we cannot derive any result for the dynamics of the "original system", in the sense that its solutions cannot be expressed in terms of the original coordinates. The way out of this problem is to linearize the system around the equilibria. Hence, linearizing these systems around the non-zero fixed points $\left( l_j^*, \beta_j^* \right) = \left( \delta_j e_j^{-1}, c_j d_j^{-1} \right)$, where $\delta_j \equiv (1 + r_{nj})$ $(1 - \lambda_j) - (\gamma_j + n_j)$, $e_j \equiv (1 + r_{nj})(1 - \lambda_j)$, $c_j \equiv r_{nj} + \psi_j - n_j$, $d_j \equiv \xi_j$, $l_j' \equiv l_j - l_j^*$, and $\beta_j' \equiv \beta_j - \beta_j^*$, we obtain

$$\dot{l}_j = -\delta_j l_j' + (d_j \delta_j)e_j^{-1}\beta_j' \tag{10.51}$$

---

[29]For this Goodwin's contribution, see Aruka (1991), Boggio (1991) as well as Chap. 2 of this book.

$$\dot{\beta}_j = -(e_j c_j) d_j^{-1} l'_j \tag{10.52}$$

Equation (10.51) can be written as

$$\ddot{l}_j = -\delta_j \dot{l}_j + (d_j \delta_j) e_j^{-1} \dot{\beta}_j$$

or, recalling Eq. (10.52),

$$\ddot{l}_j = -\delta_j \dot{l}_j - \delta_j c_j l'_j \tag{10.53}$$

Hence, the system of Eqs. (10.52) and (10.53) can be written in matrix form as

$$\ddot{\mathbf{l}} = - <\mathbf{K}> \dot{\mathbf{l}} - <\mathbf{N}> \mathbf{l}' \tag{10.54}$$

$$\dot{\boldsymbol{\beta}} = - <\boldsymbol{\Omega}> \mathbf{l}' \tag{10.55}$$

where $\ddot{\mathbf{l}} \equiv [\ddot{l}_j]$, $\dot{\mathbf{l}} \equiv [\dot{l}_j]$, $\mathbf{l}' \equiv \mathbf{l} - \mathbf{l}^*$, $\mathbf{l} \equiv [l_j]$, $\mathbf{l}^* \equiv [l^*_j]$, and $\dot{\boldsymbol{\beta}} \equiv [\dot{\beta}_j]$, while <**K**>, <**N**>, and <**Ω**> denote the diagonal matrices formed from the elements $<\delta_j>$, $<\delta_j c_j>$, and $<e_j(c_j/d_j)>$, respectively.

Going back to the original coordinates, i.e. pre-multiplying Eqs. (10.54) and (10.55) by **H** and taking into account that the vector $\mathbf{u} \equiv [u_j] \equiv \mathbf{Hl}$ ($\mathbf{v} \equiv [v_j] \equiv \mathbf{H\beta}$) denotes the *sectoral* shares of wages (the *sectoral* employment ratess) of the original system, we obtain

$$\ddot{\mathbf{u}} = -\mathbf{K}\dot{\mathbf{u}} - \mathbf{N}\mathbf{u}' \tag{10.56}$$

$$\dot{\mathbf{v}} = -\boldsymbol{\Omega}\mathbf{u}' \tag{10.57}$$

where $\ddot{\mathbf{u}} \equiv [\ddot{u}_j]$, $\dot{\mathbf{u}} \equiv [\dot{u}_j]$, $\mathbf{u}' \equiv \mathbf{u} - \mathbf{u}^*$, $\mathbf{u}^* \equiv [u^*_j]$, $\dot{\mathbf{v}} \equiv [\dot{v}_j]$, $\mathbf{K} \equiv \mathbf{Q} <\mathbf{K}> \mathbf{Q}^{-1}$, $\mathbf{N} \equiv \mathbf{Q} <\mathbf{N}> \mathbf{Q}^{-1}$, and $\boldsymbol{\Omega} \equiv \mathbf{Q} <\boldsymbol{\Omega}> \mathbf{Q}^{-1}$.[30] Equation (10.56) is easily recognizable as a "free vibration of damped multiple degree of freedom system". It is not too difficult to show that if some eigenvalues of the matrix of input–output coefficients are complex, then Goodwin's assumptions of $r_{nj}$, $n_j$, $\gamma_j$, $\psi_j$ lead to a system (of coupled equations) which is economically irrelevant.[31] Conversely, if we assume them as uniform across eigen-sectors, then all the elements of **K**, **N** and **Ω** are real. Therefore, in this *special* case, to which is difficult to provide an economic rationale, the system of Eqs. (10.56) and (10.57) exhibits the following dynamic: "A given initial condition chooses one of the curves, and each sector spiral on to its stable equilibrium point" (Goodwin 1976, p. 599). It should be noted that the exact

---

[30]Of course, the same results would be obtained if we had solved the system of Eqs. (10.51) and (10.52) and then transformed our findings back to their original coordinates.

[31]For the proofs, see Appendix 1 at the end of this chapter.

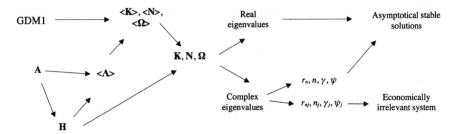

**Fig. 10.3** The dynamics of GDM1 in the heterogeneous capital case

dynamic patterns of the system (monotonic or fluctuating) depend on the eigenvalues of **A**. Figure 10.3 summarizes the points made above.

The following two numerical examples illustrate some of the points made above:

***Example 10.5***
Consider the system

$$
\mathbf{A} = \begin{bmatrix} 0.1 & 0.015 & 0.001 \\ 0.16 & 0.35 & 0.06 \\ 0.14 & 0.14 & 0.275 \end{bmatrix}
$$

with

$$
\mathbf{H} \cong \begin{bmatrix} 0.035 & -0.040 & -0.841 \\ 0.700 & -0.364 & 0.452 \\ 0.713 & 0.930 & 0.297 \end{bmatrix}
$$

$$
\mathbf{H}^{-1} \cong \begin{bmatrix} 0.670 & 0.976 & 0.411 \\ -0.145 & -0.773 & 0.766 \\ -1.154 & 0.077 & -0.019 \end{bmatrix}
$$

and

$$
\lambda_1 \cong 0.419, \quad \lambda_2 \cong 0.214, \quad \lambda_3 \cong 0.0916.
$$

Also, assume that $\gamma_j = \gamma$, $r_{nj} = r_n$, $\psi_j = \psi$, $\xi_j = \xi$, and $n_j = n$, where $j = 1, 2, 3$. Hence,
for $\gamma = 0.03$, $r_n = 0.1$, $\psi = 65.55$, $\xi = 85.49$, and $n = 0.004$, we get

$$
\mathbf{K} \cong \begin{bmatrix} 0.056 & 0.043 & -0.015 \\ 0.315 & -0.642 & 0.060 \\ 0.153 & -0.174 & 0.763 \end{bmatrix}
$$

and

$$\mathbf{N} \cong \begin{bmatrix} 0.003 & 0.002 & -0.001 \\ 0.016 & 0.033 & -0.003 \\ 0.008 & -0.009 & 0.039 \end{bmatrix}$$

Therefore, we get

$$u_1' = e^{-1.443t}\left[0.015e^{0.672t} - 0.064e^{0.902t} + 0.107e^{1.385t} - 0.011e^{1.387t}\right.$$
$$\left. +0.758e^{1.424t}\cos(0.039) + 17.373e^{1.424t}\sin(0.039)\right]$$
$$u_2' = e^{-1.443t}\left[0.101e^{0.672t} - 1.236e^{0.902t} + 2.065e^{1.385t} - 0.110e^{1.387t}\right.$$
$$\left. -0.421e^{1.424t}\cos(0.039) - 9.639e^{1.424t}\sin(0.039)\right]$$
$$u_3' = e^{-1.443t}\left[-0.254e^{0.672t} - 1.248e^{0.902t} + 2.086e^{1.385t} + 0.277e^{1.387t}\right.$$
$$\left. -0.261e^{1.424t}\cos(0.039) + 5.978e^{1.424t}\sin(0.039)\right]$$

If we set $C_1 = C_2 = C_3 = 0$, where $C_{1,\,2,\,3}$ are the constants of integration of $\dot{\mathbf{v}} = -\mathbf{\Omega}\mathbf{u}'$, then from the above solution, we obtain

$$v_1' = -0.015e^{-0.770t} + 0.098e^{-0.540t} - 1.535e^{-0.058t} + 0.231e^{-0.056t}$$
$$-475.024e^{-0.0185t}\cos(0.040) - 195.841e^{-0.0185t}\sin(0.040)$$
$$v_2' = -0.147e^{-0.770t} + 1.896e^{-0.540t} - 29.635e^{-0.058t} + 2.218e^{-0.056t}$$
$$+263.561e^{-0.0185t}\cos(0.040) - 108.659e^{-0.0185t}\sin(0.040)$$
$$v_3' = 0.371e^{-0.770t} + 1.952e^{-0.540t} - 29.921e^{-0.058t} - 5.568e^{-0.056t}$$
$$+163.449e^{-0.0185t}\cos(0.040) + 67.386e^{-0.0185t}\sin(0.040)$$

Figures 10.4 and 10.5 represent the path of $u_j'$ and $v_j'$, respectively.

***Example 10.6***
Consider the system

$$\mathbf{A} = \begin{bmatrix} 0.4 & 0.9 & 0.02 \\ 0.08 & 0.1 & 0.2 \\ 0.4 & 0.21 & 0.009 \end{bmatrix}$$

with

$$\mathbf{H} \cong \begin{bmatrix} -0.802 & 0.128 - 0.621i & 0.128 + 0.621i \\ -0.274 & 0.117 + 0.385i & 0.117 - 0.385i \\ -0.531 & -0.660 & -0.660 \end{bmatrix}$$

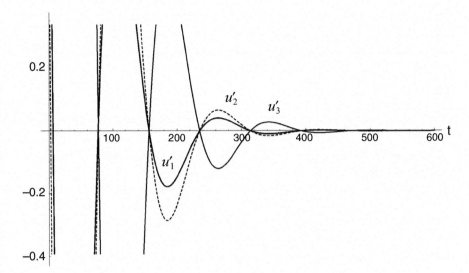

**Fig. 10.4** The path of $u'_{1,2,3}$ in the case of GDM1: real eigenvalues

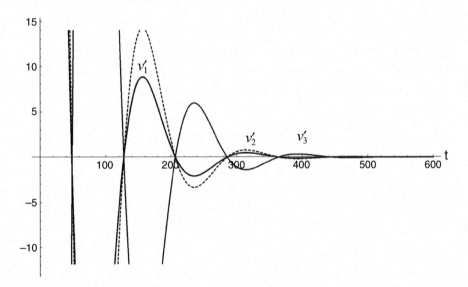

**Fig. 10.5** The path of $v'_{1,2,3}$ in the case of GDM1: real eigenvalues

$$\mathbf{H}^{-1} \cong \begin{bmatrix} -0.667 & -1.075 & -0.321 \\ 0.268 + 0.319i & 0.432 - 0.784i & -0.628 - 0.077i \\ 0.268 - 0.319i & 0.432 + 0.784i & -0.628 + 0.077i \end{bmatrix}$$

and

$$\lambda_1 \cong 0.721, \quad \lambda_2 \cong -0.106 + 0.253i, \quad \lambda_3 \cong -0.106 - 0.253i$$

Furthermore, assume that $\gamma = 0.005$, $r_n = 0.1$, $\psi = 0.03$, $\xi = 0.04$, and $n = 0.06$. Thus, it is obtained that

$$\mathbf{K} \cong \begin{bmatrix} 0.595 & -0.99 & -0.022 \\ -0.088 & 0.925 & -0.22 \\ -0.44 & -0.231 & 1.025 \end{bmatrix}$$

and

$$\mathbf{N} \cong \begin{bmatrix} 0.0416 & -0.069 & -0.001 \\ -0.006 & 0.065 & -0.015 \\ -0.030 & -0.016 & 0.071 \end{bmatrix}$$

Therefore,

$$u_1' = e^{-1.272t} \left[ -0.066 e^{1.198t} \cos(0.001t) + 0.926 e^{1.151t} \cos(0.048t) - 0.061 e^{0.195t} \cos(0.280t) \right.$$
$$\left. + 0.104 e^{1.198t} \sin(0.001) + 14.578 e^{1.151t} \sin(0.048t) + 0.144 e^{0.195t} \sin(0.280t) \right]$$

$$u_2' = e^{-1.272t} \left[ 0.005 e^{1.198t} \cos(0.001t) + 0.317 e^{1.151t} \cos(0.048t) + 0.077 e^{0.195t} \cos(0.280t) \right.$$
$$\left. - 0.078 e^{1.198t} \sin(0.001) + 4.987 e^{1.151t} \sin(0.048t) - 0.062 e^{0.195t} \sin(0.280t) \right]$$

$$u_3' = e^{-1.272t} \left[ 0.120 e^{1.198t} \cos(0.001t) + 0.614 e^{1.151t} \cos(0.048t) - 0.134 e^{0.195t} \cos(0.280t) \right.$$
$$\left. + 0.045 e^{1.198t} \sin(0.001) + 9.659 e^{1.151t} \sin(0.048t) - 0.092 e^{0.195t} \sin(0.280t) \right]$$

and then from the above solution, we get

$$v_1' = -1.147 e^{-0.074t} \cos(0.001t) + 25.794 e^{-0.120t} \cos(0.048t) - 0.111 e^{-1.077t} \cos(0.280t)$$
$$+ 3.423 e^{-0.074t} \sin(0.001) + 54.479 e^{-0.120t} \sin(0.048t) + 0.286 e^{-1.077t} \sin(0.280t)$$

$$v_2' = -0.401 e^{-0.074t} \cos(0.001t) + 8.825 e^{-0.120t} \cos(0.048t) + 0.149 e^{-1.077t} \cos(0.280t)$$
$$- 2.258 e^{-0.074t} \sin(0.001) + 18.638 e^{-0.120t} \sin(0.048t) - 0.1268 e^{-1.077t} \sin(0.280t)$$

$$v_3' = 3.735e^{-0.074t}\cos(0.001t) + 17.090e^{-0.120t}\cos(0.048t) - 0.268e^{-1.077t}\cos(0.280t)$$
$$+ 0.448e^{-0.074t}\sin(0.001) + 36.095e^{-0.120t}\sin(0.048t) - 0.174e^{-1.077t}\sin(0.280t)$$

Figures 10.6 and 10.7 represent the path of $u_j'$ and $v_j'$, respectively.

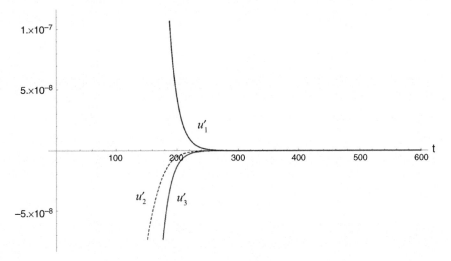

**Fig. 10.6** The path of $u_{1,2,3}'$ in the case of GDM1: complex eigenvalues

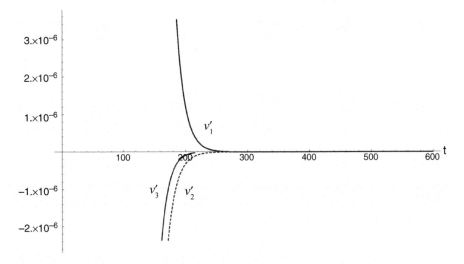

**Fig. 10.7** The path of $v_{1,2,3}'$ in the case of GDM1: complex eigenvalues

### 10.4.5   GDM2: The Heterogeneous Capital Case

If we consider $n$ sectoral labour and product markets in principal coordinates, the GDM2 can be generalized into an $n$ eigen-sector model and, hence, from Eqs. (10.42) and (10.43), we can write the following $n$ 2D-systems:

$$\widehat{l}_j = \varepsilon_j \beta_j - (\gamma_j + \zeta_j) \tag{10.58}$$

$$\widehat{\beta}_j = (1 - \lambda_j)(1 - l_j) - (\gamma_j + n_j) \tag{10.59}$$

As in the case of GDM1, the solutions of the non-linear system of Eqs. (10.58) and (10.59) cannot be expressed in terms of the original coordinates. Therefore, we linearize these systems around the non-zero fixed point $(l_j^*, \beta_j^*) = \left( \phi_j \chi_j^{-1}, s_j \iota_j^{-1} \right)$, where $\phi_j \equiv (1 - \lambda_j) - (\gamma_j + n_j)$, $\chi_j \equiv (1 - \lambda_j)$, $s_j \equiv \zeta_j + \gamma_j$, $\iota_j \equiv \varepsilon_j$ and we obtain

$$\dot{l}_j = (\iota_j \phi_j)\chi_j^{-1}\beta'_j \tag{10.60}$$

$$\dot{\beta}_j = -(\chi_j s_j)\iota_j^{-1}\beta'_j \tag{10.61}$$

Equation (10.60) can be written as

$$\ddot{l}_j = (\iota_j \phi_j)\chi_j^{-1}\dot{\beta}_j$$

or, recalling Eq. (10.61),

$$\ddot{l}_j = -\phi_j s_j l'_j \tag{10.62}$$

Hence, the system of Eqs. (10.61) and (10.62) can be written in matrix form as

$$\ddot{\mathbf{l}} = - <\mathbf{M}> \mathbf{l}' \tag{10.63}$$

$$\dot{\mathbf{\Phi}} = - <\mathbf{\Phi}> \mathbf{l}' \tag{10.64}$$

where $\boldsymbol{\beta}' \equiv \boldsymbol{\beta} - \boldsymbol{\beta}^*$, $\boldsymbol{\beta} \equiv [\beta_j]$, $\boldsymbol{\beta}^* \equiv \left[\beta_j^*\right]$, <M> and <$\boldsymbol{\Phi}$> are the diagonal matrices formed from the elements <$\phi_j s_j$> and $< (\chi_j s_j)\iota_j^{-1} >$, respectively.

Therefore, going back to the original coordinates, i.e. pre-multiplying Eqs. (10.63) and (10.64) by **H**, we obtain

$$\ddot{\mathbf{u}} = -\mathbf{M}\mathbf{u}' \tag{10.65}$$

$$\dot{\mathbf{v}} = -\mathbf{\Phi u}' \tag{10.66}$$

where $\mathbf{M} \equiv \mathbf{H} < \mathbf{M} > \mathbf{H}^{-1}$ and $\mathbf{\Phi} \equiv \mathbf{H} < \mathbf{\Phi} > \mathbf{H}^{-1}$.[32] The system (10.65) is easily recognized as a "free vibration of undamped $n$ degree of freedom system", where $\mathbf{I}$ and $\mathbf{M}$ are the "mass" and "stiffness" matrices, respectively (see, e.g. Shabana 1996, Chap. 6). Moreover, the examination of the system of Eqs. (10.65) and (10.66) or, alternatively, Eqs. (10.58) and (10.59) shows that its behaviour depends on the eigenvalues of the matrix $\mathbf{A}$. We distinguish between the following two cases:

**Case 1:** All eigenvalues are real. If all eigenvalues are real, then the result is a 2 $nD$-system, with $n$ LV oscillating pairs, i.e. all pairs $(u_j, v_j)$ will oscillate with different periods and phases. Moreover, taking into consideration that the "actual" system can be described as a "free vibration of undamped $n$ degree of freedom system", the motion of each actual sector ("general motions") will be bounded and can be expressed as a linear combination of those motions ("eigen-oscillations"), each of which has a definite frequency.[33] If the ratios of the frequencies are rational numbers, the motion of each sector will be periodic. Conversely, if one or more pairs of frequencies form an irrational ratio, the motions will be erratic, never repeating (see Goodwin and Punzo 1987, pp. 111–112). It should be noted that, in Goodwin's opinion, the system exhibits the above dynamics regardless of the eigenvalues of $\mathbf{A}$.

**Case 2:** Some eigenvalues are complex. In this case, Goodwin's assumptions about differential labour markets and growth rates of labour force and labour productivity imply that matrix $\mathbf{M}$ can be written as $\mathbf{B} + i\mathbf{F}$ and, therefore, the Eq. (10.65) takes the form

$$\ddot{\mathbf{u}} + \mathbf{B}\mathbf{u}' + i\mathbf{F}\mathbf{u}' = \mathbf{0} \tag{10.65a}$$

where $\mathbf{B}$ and $\mathbf{F}$ are the "stiffness" and "hysteric damping" matrices, respectively.[34] Thus, we conclude that the system is economically irrelevant.[35] Conversely, if we assume uniform $n_j$, $\gamma_j$, $\zeta_j$ across eigen-sectors, then all the elements of $\mathbf{M}$ are real. However, even in this *special* case the actual system cannot be studied by means of standard analytical methods (i.e. to the best of our knowledge, there is no mathematical method for solving system (10.65), since some of the eigenvalues of $\mathbf{M}$ are complex).[36] Thus, we apply simulation methods to investigate the dynamic behaviour of the system, a somewhat unsatisfactory procedure. Nevertheless the results are

---

[32]The same results would be obtained if we had solved the system of Eqs. (10.58) and (10.59) and then transformed our findings back to their original coordinates.

[33]It should be noted that it is possible to exceed unity; also see footnote 10 of this chapter.

[34]The system (10.65a) is known as a hysteretically damped $n$ degree of freedom system (see Maia and Silva 1997, pp. 62–64).

[35]See footnote 31 of this chapter.

[36]Taking into account that some of the eigenvalues of $\mathbf{A}$ are complex, it is then not too difficult to show that some of the eigenvalues of $\mathbf{M}$ are complex too.

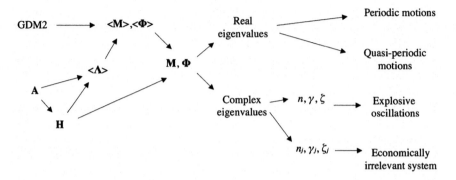

**Fig. 10.8** The dynamics of GDM2 in the heterogeneous capital case

interesting: numerical simulations show that all the $u'_j$ and $v'_j$ (may) oscillate with increasing amplitude.[37]

Figure 10.8 summarizes the points made above.

The following two numerical examples illustrate some of the points made above:

***Example 10.7***
Consider again the system

$$\mathbf{A} = \begin{bmatrix} 0.1 & 0.015 & 0.001 \\ 0.16 & 0.35 & 0.06 \\ 0.14 & 0.14 & 0.275 \end{bmatrix}$$

Also, assume that $\varepsilon_j = \varepsilon$, $\zeta_j = \zeta$, $\gamma_j = \gamma$, and $n_j = n$, where $j = 1, 2, 3$. Hence, for $\varepsilon = 0.04$, $\zeta = 0.03$, $\gamma = 0.005$, and $n = 0.06$, we get

$$\mathbf{M} \cong \begin{bmatrix} -0.029 & 0.0005 & 0.00004 \\ 0.006 & -0.020 & 0.002 \\ 0.005 & 0.005 & -0.023 \end{bmatrix}$$

and

$$\lambda_1^M \cong -0.030, \ \lambda_2^M \cong -0.025, \text{ and } \lambda_3^M \cong -0.018$$

where $\lambda_j^M$ denotes the $j$ eigenvalue of $\mathbf{M}$ and, therefore, we get

---

[37]We have experimented with a great number of different sets of parameters, and the results were similar. Finally, it should be remembered that the present analysis is restricted to the non-zero fixed point and its local properties and, therefore, it would be completely unwarranted to extend our results to the non-linear system (see e.g. Medio 1992, p. 51). This further indicates that although the linear system exhibits explosive oscillations, the system in its non-linear form may generate complex dynamic behaviours (including chaos).

$$u_1' = 0.007 \cos{(0.134t)} + 0.0006 \cos{(0.159t)} + 0.092 \cos{(0.172t)} +$$
$$0.054 \sin{(0.134t)} + 0.004 \sin{(0.159t)} + 0.536 \sin{(0.172t)}$$

$$u_2' = 0.144 \cos{(0.134t)} + 0.006 \cos{(0.159t)} - 0.050 \cos{(0.172t)} +$$
$$1.071 \sin{(0.134t)} + 0.035 \sin{(0.159t)} - 0.289 \sin{(0.172t)}$$

$$u_3' = 0.147 \cos{(0.134t)} - 0.014 \cos{(0.159t)} - 0.033 \cos{(0.172t)} +$$
$$1.092 \sin{(0.134t)} - 0.089 \sin{(0.159t)} - 0.190 \sin{(0.172t)}$$

If we set $C_1 = C_2 = C_3 = 0$, then we get (see Eq. (10.66))

$$v_1' = 0.203 \cos{(0.134t)} + 0.016 \cos{(0.159t)} + 2.482 \cos{(0.172t)} -$$
$$0.027 \sin{(0.134t)} - 0.003 \sin{(0.159t)} - 0.426 \sin{(0.172t)}$$

$$v_2' = 4.052 \cos{(0.134t)} + 0.152 \cos{(0.159t)} - 1.333 \cos{(0.172t)} -$$
$$0.544 \sin{(0.134t)} - 0.024 \sin{(0.159t)} + 0.229 \sin{(0.172t)}$$

$$v_3' = 4.131 \cos{(0.134t)} - 0.387 \cos{(0.159t)} - 0.876 \cos{(0.172t)} -$$
$$0.555 \sin{(0.134t)} + 0.0615 \sin{(0.159t)} + 0.150 \sin{(0.172t)}$$

Figures 10.9 and 10.10 represent the path of $u_j'$ and $v_j'$, respectively.

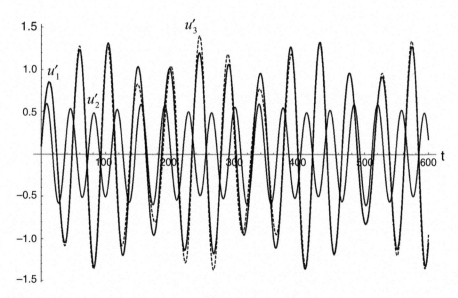

**Fig. 10.9** The path of $u_{1,2,3}'$ in the case of GDM2: real eigenvalues

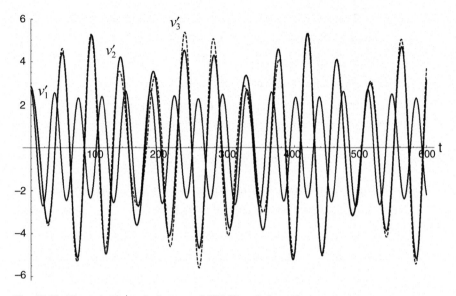

**Fig. 10.10** The path of $v'_{1,2,3}$ in the case of GDM2: real eigenvalues

*Example 10.8*

Consider the system

$$
\mathbf{A} = \begin{bmatrix} 0.4 & 0.9 & 0.02 \\ 0.08 & 0.1 & 0.2 \\ 0.4 & 0.21 & 0.009 \end{bmatrix}
$$

Furthermore, assume that $\varepsilon = 0.04$, $\zeta = 0.03$, $\gamma = 0.005$, and $n = 0.06$. Thus it is obtained that

$$
\mathbf{M} \cong \begin{bmatrix} -0.019 & 0.032 & 0.0007 \\ 0.003 & -0.029 & 0.007 \\ 0.014 & 0.007 & -0.032 \end{bmatrix}
$$

and

$$
\lambda_1^M \cong -0.036 - 0.009, \quad \lambda_2^M \cong -0.036 + 0.009, \quad \lambda_3^M \cong -0.007.
$$

Hence, we get

$$
u'_1 = e^{-0.023t}\left[0.165e^{0.023t}\cos{(0.087t)} + 0.046\cos{(0.192t)} - 0.112e^{0.046t}\cos{(0.192t)}\right.
$$
$$
\left. + 1.912e^{0.023t}\sin{(0.087t)} - 0.172\sin{(0.192t)} - 0.149e^{0.046t}\sin{(0.192t)}\right]
$$

$$u_2' = e^{-0.023t} \left[ 0.057e^{0.023t} \cos(0.087t) + 0.027 \cos(0.192t) + 0.017e^{0.046t} \cos(0.192t) \right.$$
$$\left. + 0.654e^{0.023t} \sin(0.087t) + 0.110 \sin(0.192t) + 0.117e^{0.046t} \sin(0.192t) \right]$$

$$u_3' = e^{-0.023t} \left[ 0.1106e^{0.023t} \cos(0.087t) - 0.185 \cos(0.192t) + 0.176e^{0.046t} \cos(0.192t) \right.$$
$$\left. + 1.267e^{0.023t} \sin(0.087t) - 0.011 \sin(0.192t) - 0.082e^{0.046t} \sin(0.192t) \right]$$

and

$$v_1' = -0.466 \sin(0.087t) + 11.233 \left[ 0.480 \cos(0.087t) - 0.080e^{-0.023t} \cos(0.192t) \right.$$
$$\left. - 0.073e^{0.023t} \cos(0.192t) - 0.013e^{-0.023t} \sin(0.192t) + 0.043e^{0.023t} \sin(0.192t) \right]$$

$$v_2' = -0.160 \sin(0.087t) + 11.233 \left[ 0.164 \cos(0.087t) + 0.049e^{-0.023t} \cos(0.192t) \right.$$
$$\left. + 0.054e^{0.023t} \cos(0.192t) - 0.017e^{-0.023t} \sin(0.192t) - 0.002e^{0.023t} \sin(0.192t) \right]$$

$$v_3' = -0.309 \sin(0.087t) + 11.233 \left[ 0.318 \cos(0.087t) + 0.004e^{-0.023t} \cos(0.192t) \right.$$
$$\left. - 0.029e^{0.023t} \cos(0.192t) + 0.085e^{-0.023t} \sin(0.192t) - 0.084e^{0.023t} \sin(0.192t) \right]$$

Figures 10.11 and 10.12 represent the path of $u_j'$ and $v_j'$, respectively.

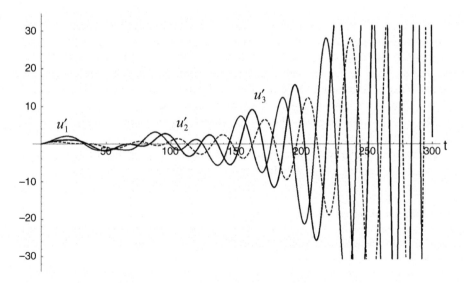

**Fig. 10.11** The path of $u_{1,2,3}'$ in the case of GDM2: complex eigenvalues

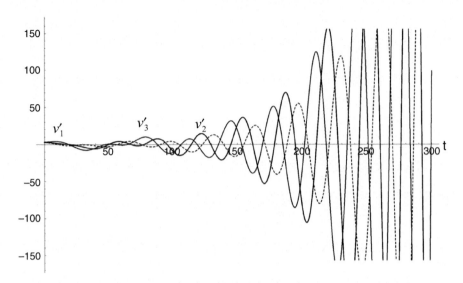

**Fig. 10.12** The path of $v'_{1,2,3}$ in the case of GDM2: complex eigenvalues

## 10.5   Empirical Testing

The application of the previous analysis to data from the SIOTs of the Greek economy, and for the latest available years,[38] i.e. 2010 and 2015,[39] gives the results summarized in Tables 10.1 and 10.2 and Figs. 10.13, 10.14, and 10.15.[40] The parameters $n$, $\gamma$, $\psi$, $\xi$, $\varepsilon$, $\zeta$, and $r_n$ have been estimated following Harvie (2000), Grasselli and Maheshwari (2017), Mariolis et al. (2006), and Tsoulfidis and Mariolis (2007). Table 10.1 shows the parameters of the two models.[41]

Table 10.2 shows the eigenvalues of the matrix **A** for the Greek economy and for the years 2010 and 2015.

For reasons of clarity of presentation and economy of space, the following set of figures is associated only with industry 1 ("agriculture, hunting, forestry, and

---

[38]We use input–output data from the OECD database (https://stats.oecd.org).

[39]For the estimation of $n$, $\gamma$, $\psi$, $\xi$, $\varepsilon$, $\zeta$ we deal with aggregate data from the AMECO database from 1960 to 2018 (https://knoema.com/ECAMED2020May/annual-macro-economic-database-may-2020).

[40]There have been significant attempts to empirically evaluate Goodwin's aggregated model and its extensions; see, e.g. Atkinson (1969), Desai (1984), Grasselli and Maheshwari (2017, 2018), Harvie (2000), Solow (1990), Araujo et al. (2019) and the references therein. However, the empirical evidence is mixed. There are some researchers who claim that there are short cycles around a long-period clockwise motion (see, e.g. Harvie 2000; Solow 1990). Some others (see, e.g. Farkas and Kotsis 1992) interpret Goodwin cycles as "long run secular waves" and adopt "an approach which attempts to argue for a large phase length and amplitude of this growth cycle" (Flaschel and Groh 1995, p. 295).

[41]This section draws on Rodousakis (2016, 2018, 2019).

**Table 10.1** The parameters of GDM1 and GDM2

| Parameters | |
|---|---|
| $n$ | 0.0085 |
| $\gamma$ | 0.0101 |
| $\xi$ | 0.9525 |
| $\psi$ | 0.7654 |
| $\varepsilon$ | 0.2204 |
| $\zeta$ | 0.1829 |
| $r_n$ | 0.5043 |

**Table 10.2** The eigenvalues of the matrix **A**: Greek economy, years 2010 and 2015

| 2010 | 2015 |
|---|---|
| 0.489216 | 0.502482 |
| 0.300401 | 0.272688 |
| 0.267292 | $0.220236 + 0.0186367\,i$ |
| 0.236773 | $0.220236 - 0.0186367\,i$ |
| $0.191262 + 0.046835\,i$ | 0.20282 |
| $0.191262 - 0.046835\,i$ | $0.163039 + 0.0938888\,i$ |
| 0.191704 | $0.163039 - 0.0938888\,i$ |
| 0.127775 | 0.178728 |
| $-0.0562392 + 0.106686\,i$ | 0.173328 |
| $-0.0562392 - 0.106686\,i$ | 0.140174 |
| $0.0835502 + 0.0736308\,i$ | $0.136446 + 0.0129018\,i$ |
| $0.0835502 - 0.0736308\,i$ | $0.136446 - 0.0129018\,i$ |
| $0.0722823 + 0.0156656\,i$ | 0.132024 |
| $0.0722823 - 0.0156656\,i$ | 0.0871959 |
| $0.00444074 + 0.0723437\,i$ | $0.0767178 + 0.01094\,i$ |
| $0.00444074 - 0.0723437\,i$ | $0.0767178 - 0.01094\,i$ |
| 0.0622318 | 0.0757863 |
| $0.0502977 + 0.0351575\,i$ | 0.0612991 |
| $0.0502977 - 0.0351575\,i$ | 0.0560732 |
| $-0.0473007$ | $-0.0302332 + 0.04631\,i$ |
| 0.0467386 | $-0.0302332 - 0.04631\,i$ |
| $0.0444321 + 0.00566242\,i$ | 0.0445254 |
| $0.0444321 - 0.00566242\,i$ | 0.0373671 |
| 0.0378407 | $0.0304509 + 0.0172821\,i$ |
| 0.0288366 | $0.0304509 - 0.0172821\,i$ |
| $-0.0232857$ | 0.030305 |
| 0.021882 | 0.0251007 |
| $-0.014648 + 0.0115345\,i$ | $-0.0243602$ |
| $-0.014648 - 0.0115345\,i$ | 0.0128062 |
| 0.013918 | $0.0044413 + 0.0087087\,i$ |
| 0.0125239 | $0.0044413 - 0.0087087\,i$ |
| $-0.004343 + 0.00340395\,i$ | $-0.00492798 + 0.00340323\,i$ |
| $-0.004343 - 0.00340395\,i$ | $-0.00492798 - 0.00340323\,i$ |
| 0.00431072 | $0.00241034 + 0.000287202\,i$ |
| 0.00137223 | $0.00241034 - 0.000287202\,i$ |
| 0 | 0 |

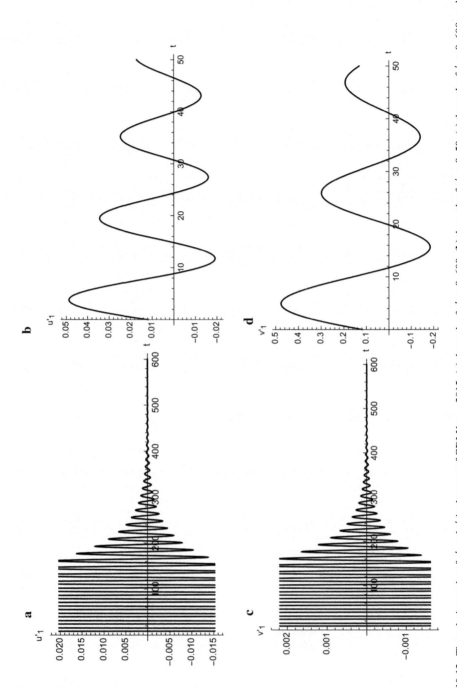

**Fig. 10.13** The solution paths of $u_1'$ and $v_1'$ in the case of GDM1; $t_0 = 2015$: (**a**) the path of $u_1'$, $t$: 0–600; (**b**) the path of $u_1'$, $t$: 0–50; (**c**) the path of $v_1'$, $t$: 0–600; and (**d**) the path of $v_1'$, $t$: 0–50

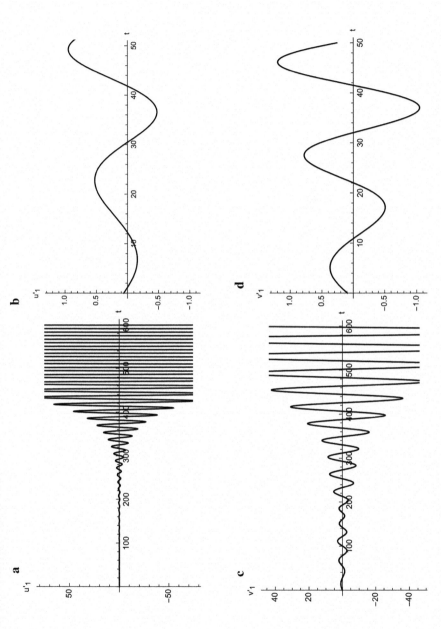

**Fig. 10.14** The solution paths of $u_1'$ and $v_1'$ in the case of GDM2; $t_0=2015$: (**a**) the path of $u_1'$, $t$: 0–600; (**b**) the path of $u_1'$, $t$: 0–50; (**c**) the path of $v_1'$, $t$: 0–600; and (**d**) the path of $v_1'$, $t$: 0–50

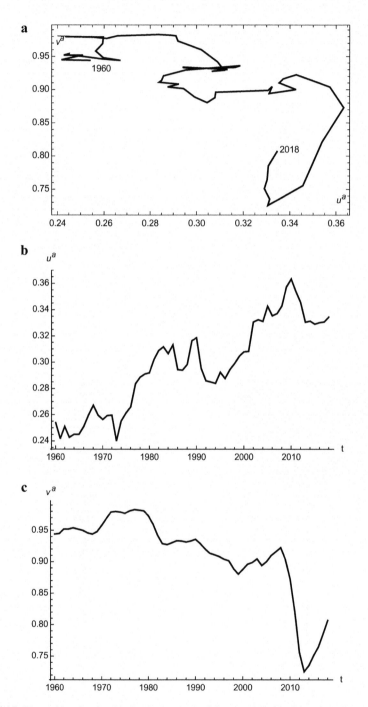

**Fig. 10.15** The trajectories for the Greek economy of the actual share of wages and the employment rate, 1960–2018: (**a**) the $u^a v^a$-trajectories; (**b**) the path of $u^a$; and (**c**) the path of $v^a$

fishing") and the year 2015. Figures 10.13 and 10.14 display the solution paths of $u'_1 (v'_1)$ which are associated with GDM1 and GDM2, respectively.

Finally, the *actual* trajectories of the share of wages of national income, $u^a$, and the employment rate, $v^a$, over the period 1960–2018 are shown in Fig. 10.15. The results suggest the existence of a three-quarter cycle over the period 1960–2018, initiating with low $u^a$/high $v^a$ and ending with low $u^a$/low $v^a$.[42]

On the basis of these estimates, we may remark that:

(i). Regarding the results obtained with GDM1, each industry exhibits damped oscillations, i.e. both $u'_j$ and $v'_j$ become smaller over time, tending to zero as $t$ tends to infinity (see, e.g. Fig. 10.13) and, therefore, it follows that the overall system is asymptotically stable. This evidence can be compared with the actual aggregative share of wages–employment rate trajectories for the Greek economy (see Fig. 10.15).[43] The evaluation of the results shows that from a qualitative as well as a quantitative point of view, GDM1 is found to be inadequate: it predicts damped oscillations and, therefore, cannot exhibit the cyclical behaviour of the actual system.

(ii). Regarding the results obtained with GDM2, each $u'_j$ and $v'_j$ oscillate with increasing amplitude (see, e.g. Fig. 10.14). At first they exhibit cyclical oscillations (see, e.g. Fig. 10.14b), then a critical value of $t$ is reached for which the oscillations become explosive (see, e.g. Fig. 10.14a). As in the case of GDM1, one can say that the dynamic behaviour (the motion) of the overall system is "equivalent" to the motions of the industries of the economy. Comparing now this motion with the motion of the actual system (see Fig. 10.15), from a qualitative point of view the model is found to be adequate to exhibit the cyclical movements of the share of wages and the employment rate. However, since there is a critical value of $t$ for which the oscillations become explosive, it follows that the model cannot describe long-run cycles. Finally, from a quantitative point of view, the model is found to be inadequate: both the share of wages and the employment rate exceed unity, while in the long-run they become "exotic".

From the findings, it becomes apparent that, for both models, the dynamics observed for the year 2010 are quite similar to those for the year 2015.[44] This is not unexpected, since the GDM1 tends to equilibrium, independently of its parameters, and the dynamic behaviour of GDM2 strongly depends on the eigenvalues of the matrix of input–output coefficients (see Sect. 10.2). Finally, it should be stressed that since there is a tendency towards uniformity in the eigenvalue distribution across

---

[42]Within the three-quarter cycle over the period 1960–2018, there appear, in addition, to be sub-cycles. However, some of the sub-cycles could well be small external shocks.

[43]The motion of the actual industries of the Greek economy cannot be estimated from the given data; therefore, it is reasonable to compare the result of our investigation with the aggregate data.

[44]We have also applied the models to data from the 19 industry-detail SIOTs of the Greek economy, and for the period 1988–1997 (see Appendix 2). The findings do not differ much from those reported for the years 2010 and 2015.

**Table 10.3** Aggregated input–output table: Greek economy, year 2015, millions of euros

| Outputs Inputs | Agriculture | Industry | Services | Total output |
|---|---|---|---|---|
| Agriculture | 1500.0556 | 13,956.0084 | 1058.8346 | 12,077.6628 |
| Industry | 2113.1061 | 19,095.9666 | 20,016.5154 | 72,002.7633 |
| Services | 1583.5580 | 12,106.9660 | 45,278.7159 | 196,054.8936 |
| Total output | 12,077.6628 | 72,002.7633 | 196,054.8936 | 280,135.3198 |

countries and over time (see Chap. 3), the dynamic patterns that emerge from the eigenvalues are expected to be quite similar across countries and over time.

However, in the cases of input–output systems with high level of aggregations, the possibility all the eigenvalues of **A** to be real numbers cannot be neglected. For better understanding, let us take a simple but representative SIOT for the Greek economy, and the year 2015, aggregated into three sectors (agriculture, industry, and services). This three-by-three input–output table is presented in Table 10.3.

The market prices, i.e. the market values, of all products are taken to be equal to 1; that is to say, the physical unit of measurement of each product is that unit which is worth of a monetary unit. Thus, **A** is obtained by dividing element-by-element the inputs of each industry by its gross output. So, we finally get[45]

$$A = \begin{bmatrix} 0.124200818 & 0.1938260 & 0.00540070 \\ 0.17495985 & 0.26521157 & 0.102096484 \\ 0.131114606 & 0.168145853 & 0.230949175 \end{bmatrix}$$

with

$$H \cong \begin{bmatrix} -0.374286 & -0.649476 & -0.661884 \\ -0.461857 & -0.079552 & 0.88338 \\ -0.845036 & 0.525583 & 0.098372 \end{bmatrix},$$

$$H^{-1} \cong \begin{bmatrix} -0.56393 & -0.837392 & -0.37025 \\ -0.339213 & -0.71207 & 0.89054 \\ -0.748206 & 0.760084 & -0.322735 \end{bmatrix}$$

and

$$\lambda_1 \cong 0.470086, \quad \lambda_2 \cong 0.147256, \quad \lambda_3 \cong 0.003010907.$$

---

[45]The subscripts 1, 2, and 3 correspond to the three sectors agriculture, industry, and services, respectively.

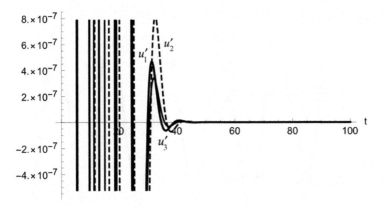

**Fig. 10.16** The path of $u'_{1,2,3}$ in the case of GDM1: $t_0 = 2015$

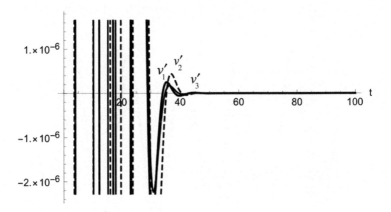

**Fig. 10.17** The path of $v'_{1,2,3}$ in the case of GDM1: $t_0 = 2015$

Therefore, the application of the GDM1 and GDM2 gives the results summarized in Figs. 10.16, 10.17, 10.18, and 10.19.[46] Hence, in the case of GDM1, we derive that each sector exhibits damped oscillations (see Figs. 10.16 and 10.17) and, therefore, it cannot exhibit the cyclical behaviour of the actual system. Conversely, in the case of GDM2, all $u'_j$ and $v'_j$ exhibit cyclical oscillations (see Figs. 10.18 and 10.19). Comparing now these oscillations with the motion of the actual economy (see Fig. 10.15), from a qualitative and, as well, a quantitative point of view, the model is found to be adequate to exhibit the cyclical movements of the share of wages and the employment rate.

---

[46]We have, as for the 36 industry-detail case, applied the models to the data for the year 2010, and the findings do not differ much from those reported here.

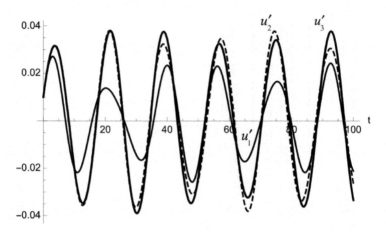

**Fig. 10.18** The path of $u'_{1,2,3}$ in the case of GDM2: $t_0 = 2015$

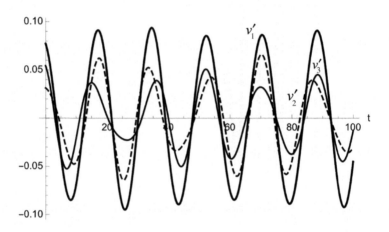

**Fig. 10.19** The path of $v'_{1,2,3}$ in the case of GDM2: $t_0 = 2015$

## 10.6   Concluding Remarks

This chapter investigated the stability properties of Goodwin's distributive growth cycle model under the considerations of a VES production function and endogenous labour productivity growth. It has been shown that the inclusion of a VES production function into Goodwin's model is equivalent to the introduction of a dampening effect and, hence, the system's equilibrium becomes locally asymptotically stable. If we assume endogenous labour productivity growth, then there are two opposite effects: the stabilizing effect of the elasticity of substitution and the destabilizing effect of endogenous labour productivity growth, where neither is, in general, dominant over the other. Furthermore, it examined two extensions of Goodwin's model that allow for capital heterogeneity, where the main difference between these extensions lies in the fact that one is characterized by a "nominal Phillips curve" and the other by a "real Phillips curve". Contrary to Goodwin's approach, it is found that both the economic relevance and the dynamic behaviour of the system depend on the eigenvalues of the matrix of input–output coefficients. In particular, if some eigenvalues are complex, then Goodwin's assumptions about differential (across industries) labour markets and growth rates of the labour force lead to an economically irrelevant system. However, even if we avoid these assumptions, numerical simulations showed that the model characterized by a "real Phillips curve" exhibits explosive oscillations. The latter is also verified through empirical tests using actual input–output table data. These insights on Goodwin's model in disaggregative forms result from the existence of complicated inter-relationships amongst industries in the empirically relevant case of production of commodities by means of commodities.


# Appendix 1: Proofs


Let us consider a $3 \times 3$ matrix $\mathbf{A}$ with one real eigenvalue (the P–F eigenvalue), $\lambda_1(<1)$, and a pair of complex conjugate eigenvalues $\lambda_2$ and $\lambda_3$. From Eq. (10.56) we get

$$\mathbf{K} \equiv \mathbf{Q} < \mathbf{K} > \mathbf{Q}^{-1}$$

where

$$< \mathbf{K} > = \begin{bmatrix} \alpha_1 & 0 & 0 \\ 0 & \alpha_2 & 0 \\ 0 & 0 & \alpha_3 \end{bmatrix}$$

From the above equation after rearrangement, we obtain

$$\mathbf{K}= \begin{bmatrix} \delta_1 h_{11} h'_{11}+\delta_2 h_{12} h'_{21}+\delta_3 h_{13} h'_{31} & \delta_1 h_{11} h'_{12}+\delta_2 h_{12} h'_{22}+\delta_3 h_{13} h'_{32} & \delta_1 h_{11} h'_{13}+\delta_2 h_{12} h'_{23}+\delta_3 h_{13} h'_{33} \\ \delta_1 h_{21} h'_{11}+\delta_2 h_{22} h'_{21}+\delta_3 h_{23} h'_{31} & \delta_1 h_{21} h'_{12}+\delta_2 h_{22} h'_{22}+\delta_3 h_{23} h'_{32} & \delta_1 h_{21} h'_{13}+\delta_2 h_{22} h'_{23}+\delta_3 h_{23} h'_{33} \\ \delta_1 h_{31} h'_{11}+\delta_2 h_{32} h'_{21}+\delta_3 h_{33} h'_{31} & \delta_1 h_{31} h'_{12}+\delta_2 h_{32} h'_{22}+\delta_3 h_{33} h'_{32} & \delta_1 h_{31} h'_{13}+\delta_2 h_{32} h'_{23}+\delta_3 h_{33} h'_{33} \end{bmatrix}$$

Since $\lambda_1$ is the P–F eigenvalue, the first column (row) of $\mathbf{H}$ (of $\mathbf{H}^{-1}$) is real and positive. The corresponding eigenvectors to $\lambda_2$ and $\lambda_3$ will ordinary involve negative and complex numbers. Therefore, the element $\kappa_{11}$ of $\mathbf{K}$ can be expressed as

$$\kappa_{11} = \delta_1 h_{11} h'_{11} + (\pm\tau \pm \varpi i)(\pm\eta \pm \omega i)(\pm\vartheta \pm \upsilon i)$$
$$+ (\pm\tau \mp \varpi i)(\pm\eta \mp \omega i)(\pm\vartheta \mp \upsilon i)$$

where $\eta$, $\omega$, $\vartheta$, $\upsilon \geq 0$ and $\tau, \varpi, \delta_1 h_{11} h'_{11} > 0$. The above relation is a sum of real numbers, and, therefore the element $\kappa_{11}$ is real. By contrast, if $n_2 \neq n_3$ or $\gamma_2 \neq \gamma_3$ or $r_{n2} \neq r_{n3}$, then $\delta_2 \neq \delta_3$ and $\kappa_{11}$ is complex (and the same holds true for any $\kappa_{ij}$ of a $n \times n$ matrix). Hence, if matrix $\mathbf{A}$ has complex eigenvalues and each eigen-sector has its particular $n_j$, $\gamma_j$, $r_{nj}$, then the elements of matrix $\mathbf{K}$ will be complex.

In the same way, it can be proved that the elements of the matrices $\mathbf{N}$ and $\mathbf{\Omega}$ ($\mathbf{M}$ and $\mathbf{\Phi}$) are real *iff* the parameters $\gamma_j$, $n_j$, $\zeta_j$, $r_{nj}$ ($\gamma_j$, $n_j$, $\psi_j$) are the same in all eigen-sectors.

## Appendix 2: The Solution Paths of $u'_1$ and $v'_1$ for the period 1988–1997

We have also applied the GDM1 and GDM2 to the data from the SIOTs of the Greek economy and for the period 1988–1997 (for a detailed analysis, see Rodousakis 2016). As in Sect. 10.5, the following set of figures is associated only with industry 1 and the year 1988. Figures 10.20 and 10.21 display the solution paths of $u'_1 (v'_1)$ which is associated with GDM1 and GDM2, respectively.

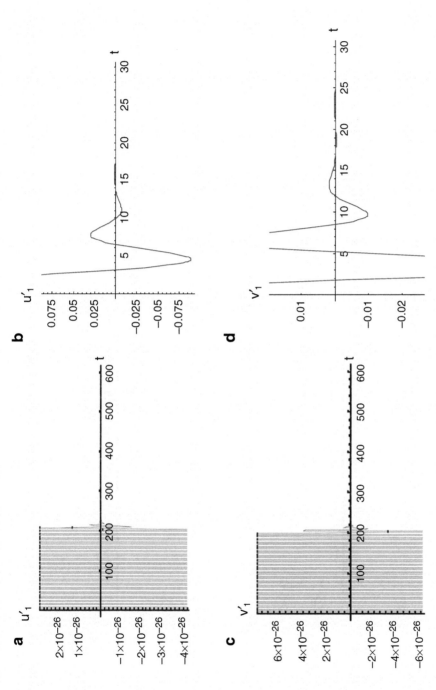

**Fig. 10.20** The solution paths of $u'_1$ and $v'_1$ in the case of GDM1; $t_0 = 2015$: (**a**) the path of $u'_1$, $t$: 0–600; (**b**) the path of $u'_1$, $t$: 0–600; (**c**) the path of $v'_1$, $t$: 0–600; and (**d**) the path of $v'_1$, $t$: 0–30

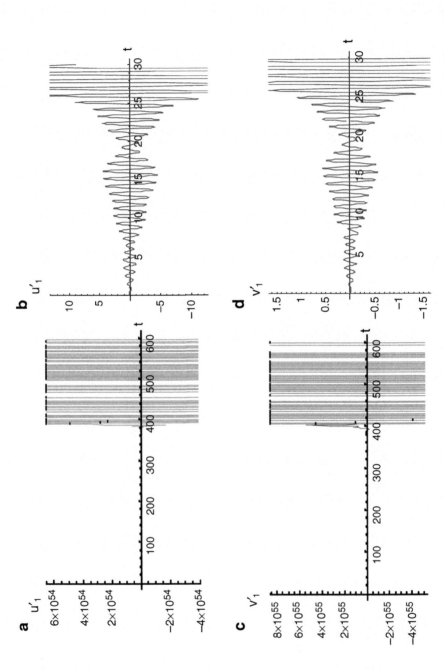

**Fig. 10.21** The solution paths of $u'_1$ and $v'_1$ in the case of GDM2; $t_0 = 2015$: (**a**) the path of $u'_1$, $t$: 0–600; (**b**) the path of $u'_1$, $t$: 0–30; (**c**) the path of $v'_1$, $t$: 0–600; and (**d**) the path of $v'_1$, $t$: 0–30

# References

Aguiar-Conraria, L. (2001). *The stability properties of Goodwin's growth cycle model*. NIPE WP 10/2001. Retrieved October 1, 2018, from http://www3.eeg.uminho.pt/economia/nipe/docs/2001/NIPE_WP_10_2001.PDF

Aguiar-Conraria, L. (2008). A note on the stability properties of Goodwin's predator–prey model. *Review of Radical Political Economics, 40*(4), 518–523.

Andronov, A. A., & Pontryagin, L. S. (1937). Coarse systems. *Doklady Akademmi Nauk, 14*(5), 247–251.

Andronov, A. A., Vitt, A. A., & Khaikin, S. E. (1987). *Theory of oscillators*. New York: Dover Publications.

Araujo, R. A., Dávila-Fernández, J. M., & Moreira, H. N. (2019). Some new insights on the empirics of Goodwin's growth–cycle model. *Structural Change and Economic Dynamics, 51*(3), 42–54.

Aruka, Y. (1991). Generalized Goodwin's theorems on general coordinates. *Structural Change and Economic Dynamics, 2*(1), 69–91. Reprinted In Y. Aruka (Ed.), (2011). *Complexities of production and interacting human behaviour* (pp. 39–66). Heidelberg: Physica–Verlag.

Atkinson, B. A. (1969). The timescale of economic models: How long is the long run? *The Review of Economic Studies, 36*(2), 137–152.

Blatt, J. M. (1983). *Dynamic economic systems: A post-Keynesian approach*. Sussex: Wheatsheaf.

Boggio, L. (1991). On Goodwin's method of principal coordinates. *Structural Change and Economic Dynamics, 2*(1), 93–98.

Desai, M. H. (1984). Econometric models of the share of wages in national income, U.K. 1855–1965. In R. M. Goodwin, M. Krüger, & A. Vercelli (Eds.), *Nonlinear models of fluctuating growth* (pp. 253–277). Heidelberg: Springer–Verlag.

Desai, M. H., Mosley, B. A., & Malcolm, P. (2006). A clarification of the Goodwin model of the growth cycle. *Journal of Economic Dynamics and Control, 30*(12), 2661–2670.

Dore, M. (1993). *The macrodynamics of business cycles: A comparative evaluation*. Oxford: Basil Blackwel.

Evans, C. M., & Findley, G. L. (1999). Analytic solutions to a family of Lotka–Volterra related differential equations. *Journal of Mathematical Chemistry, 25*(2), 181–189.

Farkas, M., & Kotsis, M. (1992). Modelling predator–prey and wage–employment dynamics. In G. Feichtinger (Ed.), *Dynamic economic models and optimal control* (pp. 513–526). Amsterdam: North Holland.

Flaschel, P., & Groh, G. (1995). The classical growth cycle: Reformulation, simulation and some facts. *Economic Notes, 24*(1), 293–326.

Gabisch, G., & Lorenz, H.-W. (1989). *Business cycle theory*. Heidelberg: Springer–Verlag.

Gandolfo, G. (1997). *Economic dynamics*. Heidelberg: Springer–Verlag.

Gandolfo, G. (2008). Giuseppe Palomba and the Lotka–Volterra equations. *Rendiconti Lincei, 19*(4), 347–357.

Goodwin, R. M. (1967). A growth cycle. In C. H. Feinstein (Ed.), *Socialism, capitalism and economic growth: Essays presented to Maurice Dobb* (pp. 54–58). Cambridge: Cambridge University Press.

Goodwin, R. M. (1972). A growth cycle. In E. K. Hunt & J. G. Schwartz (Eds.), *A critique of economic theory* (pp. 442–449). Harmondsworth: Penguin.

Goodwin, R. M. (1976). Use of normalized general coordinates in linear value and distribution theory. In K. R. Polenske & J. V. Skolka (Eds.), *Advances in input–output analysis, proceedings of the sixth international conference on input–output techniques* (pp. 581–602). Cambridge: Ballinger.

Goodwin, R. M. (1983). *Essays in linear economic structures*. London: Macmillan.

Goodwin, R. M. (1984). Disaggregated models of fluctuating growth. In R. M. Goodwin, M. Krüger & A. Vercelli (Eds.), *Nonlinear models of fluctuating growth* (pp. 67–72). Heidelberg: Springer–Verlag.

Goodwin, R. M. (1986). Swinging along the turnpike with von Neumann and Sraffa. *Cambridge Journal of Economics, 10*(3), 211–224.

Goodwin, R. M. (1989). Swinging along the autostrada: Cyclical fluctuations along the von Neumann ray. In M. Dore, S. Chakravarty, & R. M. Goodwin (Eds.), *John von Neumann and moderns economics* (pp. 125–140). Oxford: Clarendon Press.

Goodwin, R. M., & Landesmann, M. (1996). Structural change and macroeconomic stability in disaggregated models. In R. M. Goodwin & R. Scazzieri (Eds.), *Production and economic dynamics* (pp. 167–187). Cambridge: Cambridge University Press.

Goodwin, R. M., & Punzo, L. F. (1987). *The dynamics of a capitalist economy. A multi-sectoral approach*. Cambridge: Polity Press.

Goodwin, R. M. (1991). Economic evolution, chaotic dynamics and the Marx–Keynes–Schumpeter system. In G. M. Hodgson & E. Screpanti (Eds.), *Rethinking economics: Markets, technology and economic evolution* (pp. 138–152). Aldershot: Edward Elgar.

Grasselli, M., & Maheshwari, A. (2017). A comment on testing Goodwin: Growth cycles in ten OECD countries. *Cambridge Journal of Economics, 41*(6), 1761–1766.

Grasselli, M., & Maheshwari, A. (2018). Testing a Goodwin model with general capital accumulation rate. *Metroeconomica, 69*(3), 619–643.

Harvie, D. (2000). Testing Goodwin: Growth cycles in ten OECD countries. *Cambridge Journal of Economics, 24*(3), 349–376.

Harvie, D., Kelmanson, M. A., & Knapp, D. G. (2007). A dynamical model of business-cycle asymmetries: Extending Goodwin. *Economic Issues, 12*(1), 53–92.

Hirsch, M. W., & Smale, S. (1974). *Differential equations, dynamical systems and linear algebra*. New York: Academic Press.

Kazi, U. A. (1980). The variable elasticity of substitution production function: A case study from Indian manufacturing industries. *Oxford Economic Papers, 32*(1), 163–175.

Kolmogoroff, A. N. (1936). Sulla teoria di Volterra della lotta per l'esistenza. *Giornale dell'Istituto Italiano degli Attuari, 7*, 74–80 (in Italian; English translation in Kolmogoroff, A. N. (1978). On Volterra's theory of the struggle for existence). In F. M. Scudo & J. R. Ziegler (Eds.), *The Golden age of theoretical ecology, 1923–1940: A collection of works by V. Volterra, V. A. Kostitzin, A. J. Lotka, and A. N. Kolmogoroff* (pp. 287–292). Berlin: Springer–Verlag.

Krüger, M. (1985). A reconsideration of the stability properties of Goodwin's model of the growth cycle. *Economic Notes, 14*(1), 22–37.

Lorenz, H.-W. (1989). *Nonlinear dynamical economics and chaotic motion*. Heidelberg: Springer–Verlag.

Lovell, C. A. K. (1968). Capacity utilization and production function estimation in postwar American manufacturing. *Quarterly Journal of Economics, 82*(2), 219–239.

Lu, Y., & Fletcher, B. L. (1968). A generalization of the CES production function. *Review of Economics and Statistics, 50*(4), 449–452.

Maia, N. M., & Silva, J. M. (1997). *Theoretical and experimental modal analysis*. Hertfordshire: Research Studies Press Ltd.

Mariolis, T. (2006). *Introduction to the theory of endogenous economic fluctuations. Linear and nonlinear economic oscillators*. Athens: Typothyto (in Greek).

Mariolis, T. (2013). Goodwin's growth cycle model with the Bhaduri–Marglin accumulation function. *Evolutionary and Institutional Economics Review, 10*(1), 131–144.

Mariolis, T., Rodousakis, N., & Tsoulfidis, L. (2006). The rate of profit in the Greek economy, 1988–1997. An input–output analysis. *Archives of Economic History, 18*(2), 177–190.

Medio, A. (1979). *Teoria non lineare del ciclo economico*. Bologna: Il Mulino.

Medio, A. (1992). *Chaotic dynamics. Theory and applications to economics*. Cambridge: Cambridge University Press.

Palomba, G. (1939). *Introduzione allo studio della dinamica economica*. Napoli: Jovene.

Revankar, N. S. (1971). A Class of variable elasticity of substitution production functions. *Econometrica, 39*(1), 60–71.

Rodousakis, N. (2012a). *Endogenous fluctuations in one-sector and multi-sector models à la Goodwin*. Ph.D. Dissertation, Athens: Department of Public Administration, Panteion University (in Greek).

Rodousakis, N. (2012b). Goodwin's Lotka–Volterra model in disaggregative form: A correction note. *Metroeconomica, 63*(4), 599–613.

Rodousakis, N. (2014). The stability properties of Goodwin's growth cycle model with a variable elasticity of substitution production function. *Studies in Microeconomics, 2*(2), 213–223.

Rodousakis, N. (2015). Goodwin's growth cycle model with the Bhaduri–Marglin accumulation function: A note on the C.E.S. case. *Evolutionary and Institutional Economics Review, 12*(1), 105–114.

Rodousakis, N. (2016). Testing Goodwin's growth cycle disaggregated models: Evidence from the input–output table of the Greek economy for the year 1988. *Bulletin of Political Economy, 10* (2), 99–118.

Rodousakis, N. (2018). Applying Goodwin's disaggregated Lotka–Volterra model to actual data, *Statistical Review, Journal of the Greek Statistical Association, 11–12*, Special Issue in Honor of Professor Ioannis Vavouras, 92–99 (in Greek).

Rodousakis, N. (2019). *Multi-sector models à la Goodwin–Sraffa: Theoretical and empirical investigation*. Paper presented at the 1st Conference of the Study Group on Sraffian Economics: "From the Capital Theory Controversy in the 1960s to Greece's Virtual Bankruptcy in 2010", 11–12 April 2019, Panteion University, Athens, Greece (in Greek).

Samuelson, P. A. (1971). Generalized predator–prey oscillations in ecological and economic equilibrium. *Proceedings of the National Academy of Sciences USA, 68*(5), 980–983.

Sato, R., & Hoffman, F. (1968). Production functions with variable elasticity of substitution: Some analysis and testing. *Review of Economics and Statistics, 50*(4), 453–460.

Shabana, A. A. (1996). *Theory of vibration: An introduction*. Heidelberg: Springer–Verlag.

Shih, S.-D., & Chow, S.-S. (2004). A power series in small energy for the period of the Lotka–Volterra system. *Taiwanese Journal of Mathematics, 8*(4), 569–591.

Solow, R. (1990). Goodwin's growth cycle. In K. V. Velupillai (Ed.), *Nonlinear and multisectoral macrodynamics* (pp. 31–41). London: Macmillan.

Sportelli, M. (1995). A Kolmogoroff generalized predator–prey model of Goodwin's growth cycle. *Journal of Economics, 61*(1), 35–64.

Sraffa, P. (1960). *Production of commodities by means of commodities. Prelude to a critique of economic theory*. Cambridge: Cambridge University Press.

Takeuchi, Y. (1996). *Global dynamical properties of Lotka–Volterra systems*. Singapore City: World Scientific.

Tong, H. (1983). *Threshold models in non-linear time series analysis*. Heidelberg: Springer–Verlag.

Tsoulfidis, L., & Mariolis, T. (2007). Labour values, prices of production and the effects of income distribution: Evidence from the Greek economy. *Economic Systems Research, 19*(4), 425–437.

van der Ploeg, F. (1983a). Economic growth and conflict over the distribution of income. *Journal of Economic Dynamics and Control, 6*(3), 253–279.

van der Ploeg, F. (1983b). Predator–prey and neo-classical models of cyclical growth. *Journal of Economics, 43*(3), 235–256.

van der Ploeg, F. (1985). Classical growth cycles. *Metroeconomica, 37*(2), 221–230.

van der Ploeg, F. (1987). Growth cycles, induced technical change, and perpetual conflict over the distribution of income. *Journal of Macroeconomics, 9*(1), 1–12.

Vercelli, A. (1982). Is instability enough to discredit a model? *Economic Notes, 11*(3), 173–189.

Vercelli, A. (1991). *Methodological foundations of macroeconomics: Keynes and Lucas*. Cambridge: Cambridge University Press.

# Chapter 11
# Marxian Distributive–Effective Demand Dynamics and the "Law" of Rising Profit Rate

**Abstract** Marx's treatment of capitalist accumulation fluctuations constitutes a structured whole composed of distributive cycles, effective demand, and biased technological change sub-theories. This chapter dissects and re-investigates Marx's treatment on the basis of post-Keynesian and Sraffian frameworks. It (i) incorporates the Bhaduri–Marglin accumulation function into the Goodwin distributional conflict model, and deals with alternative, relevant versions of this extended model; (ii) zeroes in on Marx's so-called "law of the tendency of the profit rate to fall"; and (iii) points out that the "long-wave version" of the falling profit rate theory of crisis lacks logical consistency. Hence, it is concluded that Marx's sub-theory of biased technological change over-determines his sub-theories of distributive cycles and of effective demand, while the Sraffa–Kalecki–Goodwin modelling of endogenous circular causation provides the appropriate analytical framework for dealing with the capitalist accumulation process.

**Keywords** Bhaduri–Marglin accumulation function · Distributive–effective demand–technological change dynamics · Endogenous circular causation · Post-Keynesian and Sraffian frameworks · Profit mass and rate

## 11.1 Introduction

A critical reconstruction of Marx's overall theory of capitalist accumulation fluctuations can show that this theory constitutes a system of three discrete sub-theories:

1. Distributive cycles, i.e. cycles caused by income distribution–capital accumulation–unemployment inter-actions, in the absence of effective demand issues and technological change (Marx 1982, Chap. 25, Sect. 1).
2. Effective demand (see, e.g. Marx 1968, Chap. 17; Marx 1971, Chap. 19, Sects. 11–13, and 20, pp. 117–123; Marx 1982, pp. 208–209; Marx 1992; Marx 1991, pp. 614–615).

© Springer Nature Singapore Pte Ltd. 2021

T. Mariolis et al., *Spectral Theory of Value and Actual Economies*, Evolutionary Economics and Social Complexity Science 24,

https://doi.org/10.1007/978-981-33-6260-4_11

3. Biased technological change and consequent long-term fall in the profit rate (Marx 1968, Chaps. 12–24; Marx 1971, Chaps. 13–14).

Marx's sub-theory-1, distributive cycles, was clarified by Goodwin's (1967) modelling (see Chap. 10 of this book). It is interesting to remark that in the section entitled "The Progressive Production of a Relative Surplus Population or Industrial Reserve Army", Marx 1982, Chap. 25) approached the phenomenon of alternation between economic expansion and contraction through the concepts of endogenous circular causation and constant periodicity:

> The superficiality of political economy shows itself in the fact that it views the expansion and contraction of credit as the cause of the *periodic* alternations in the industrial cycle, whereas it is a mere *symptom* of them. Just as the heavenly bodies always repeat a certain movement, once they have been flung into it, so also does social production, once it has been flung into this movement of alternate expansion and contraction. *Effects become causes in their turn*, and the various vicissitudes of the whole process, which always reproduces its own conditions, take on the form of *periodicity*. When this periodicity has once become consolidated, even political economy sees that the production of a relative surplus population—i.e. a population surplus in relation to capital's average requirements for valorization—is a necessary condition for modern industry. (p. 786; emphasis added)

Setting aside the "reproduction schemes" (Volume Two of *Capital*), Marx's sub-theory-2, effective demand, was in an embryonic stage; it was developed by Kalecki (1971), who also attempted to synthesize sub-theories-1 and -2. Sub-theory-3, biased technological change, was clarified and further developed by Okishio (1961, 1972, 1977),[1] Steedman (1971, 1977, Chap. 9), Steedman (1980), Salvadori (1981), and Bidard (1986). Lenin (1893) provided a first combined investigation of Marx's expanded reproduction and technological change analyses (also see Voronin 1989 and the references therein), while Glombowski (1983) and Harris (1983) synthesized sub-theory-3 with basic aspects of sub-theory-1. Finally, Marx (and—possibly—Engels's editorial work) left only a few and very confusing pages for his—explicit—*overall* theory of economic fluctuations (see Marx 1991, Chap. 15).

Meanwhile, many scholars stressed that the Goodwin (1967) model of distributional conflict neglects altogether any effective demand issues, and this has been generally recognized as one of the fundamental weaknesses of the model. More recently, Marglin and Bhaduri (1988), Bhaduri and Marglin (1990), and Kurz (1990) showed, by means of generalized, static post-Keynesian models, that income redistribution (between profits and wages) has ambiguous effects on the equilibrium rates of capacity utilization, profits, and accumulation. Within those post-Keynesian models, (1) there is an independent Kaleckian accumulation (or investment) function;[2] (2) the commodities market is in equilibrium; and (3) the share of profits in

---

[1] Also see the exchange between Himmelweit (1974) and Okishio (1974).

[2] For a critical investigation, both theoretical and empirical, of Kaleckian accumulation functions, see Skott (2012).

total income (or, equivalently, the real wage rate) is treated as an exogenous variable. However, as it has also been remarked, the Bhaduri–Marglin context

remains the short run of Keynes and Kalecki. It may be objected at the outset that an exogenous short-run determination of the real wage is somewhat implausible. The approach is, nevertheless, worth pursuing particularly if it is understood as clearing the ground for more comprehensive dynamic analysis in which some aspect of the short-run outcome (say the rate of unemployment) feeds back into the wage rate (perhaps via a real Phillips curve). (Mainwaring 1991, p. 632)

The purpose of this chapter is to critically investigate the Marxian distributive–effective demand–technological change dynamics in the light of post-Keynesian and Sraffian theories. Section 11.2 incorporates the Bhaduri–Marglin accumulation function into the Goodwin (1967) model or, conversely, closes the Bhaduri–Marglin model by means of Goodwin's endogenous determination of income distribution,[3] and traces the implications of capital heterogeneity.[4] Section 11.3 extends the analysis of the one-commodity model to the cases of (1) constant elasticity of substitution (CES) production functions; and (2) disequilibrium between investment and savings. Section 11.4 focuses on Marx's sub-theory of biased technological change and consequent movements of the rate and mass of profits. Finally, Sect. 11.5 concludes.

## 11.2   The Goodwin Model with the Bhaduri–Marglin Accumulation Function

### 11.2.1   The One-Commodity Case

The model is presented in two successive stages: (a) the static "core" of the model and the relevant comparative static properties; and (b) the complete, dynamic, version (dynamization) of the model.[5]

---

[3]For this research line, see, e.g. Dutt (1992), Skott (1989), Sordi (2003), who do not use the Bhaduri–Marglin accumulation function, and Barbosa-Filho and Taylor (2006), Canry (2005), Flaschel et al. (2009), Kiefer and Rada (2015), Nikiforos and Foley (2012), Sasaki (2013), Tavani et al. (2011), von Arnim and Barrales (2015), who use, explicitly or otherwise, the said function.

[4]For the Goodwin models with heterogeneous capital and without excess capacity, see Sect. 10.4 of this book.

[5]This section draws on Mariolis (2006a, pp. 202–214), Mariolis (2006b, 2011, pp. 74–82), Mariolis (2013), Mariolis et al. (2019).

## 11.2.1.1   The Static Core

Consider a linear, closed, one-commodity and excess capital capacity economy, without capital depreciation and inflation. Competitive conditions are taken to be close to free competition,[6] while homogeneous labour is the only primary input and in perfectly elastic supply. Furthermore, assume that:

1. Workers are employed in proportion to the level of production, i.e. there is no supplementary or "overhead" labour. Hence, $L = \pi_L^{-1} Y$, where $L$ denotes the volume of employment, $\pi_L$ the technologically fixed labour productivity, and $Y$ the actual output.
2. Actual output is distributed between profits and wages. Wages are paid at the end of the production period, and there are no savings out of this income, while a given and constant fraction of profits is saved. That is, $S \equiv s_p P$, where $S$ denotes total savings, $s$, $0 < s_p \leq 1$, the savings ratio, and $P$, $0 \leq P \leq Y$, the profits.
3. The rate of capacity utilization, $u$, is defined as the ratio of actual output to potential output, $\widetilde{Y}$, where the latter is taken to be proportional to the capital stock in existence, $K$. That is, $u \equiv Y\widetilde{Y}^{-1}$ and $\widetilde{Y} = \pi_K K$, where $0 < u \leq 1$, and $\pi_K$ denotes the technologically fixed capital productivity.
4. The desired rate of capital accumulation, $g^I$, is a strictly increasing function of both the rate of capacity utilization and the share of profits in total income, $h \equiv PY^{-1}$.
5. Commodities market is in equilibrium and, moreover, the responsiveness of savings to changes in the rate of capacity utilization exceeds that of investment; therefore, the commodities market equilibrium is stable ("Keynesian stability condition"; see Bhaduri 2008).
6. Technological change,[7] fiscal and monetary considerations are ignored.

On the basis of these assumptions, we can write the following relations:[8]

---

[6]"This allows us to interpret the underutilization of productive capacity as caused essentially by an insufficient effective demand" (Kurz 1995, pp. 96–97). Furthermore, see Kurz (1993a, b, 1994).

[7]As Kurz (1990) stresses, "within the framework of the present model the choice of technique problem cannot generally be considered to be decided in terms of the technical conditions of production alone: the degree of capacity utilization matters too. The latter, however, reflects a multiplicity of influences, such as the state of income distribution and savings and investment behavior [...]. In particular, there is the possibility that, assessed in terms of the degree of utilization associated with the existing technique, a new technique proves superior, while in terms of its own characteristic steady-state degree of utilization it turns out to be inferior" (pp. 232–233).

[8]The first derivative of a function $\psi = \psi(\chi_1, \chi_2)$ with respect to the variable $\chi_j$ is denoted by

$$\psi_{\chi_j} \equiv \partial \psi / \partial \chi_j$$

$$r \equiv PK^{-1} = \left(PY^{-1}\right)\left(Y\tilde{Y}^{-1}\right)\left(\tilde{Y}K^{-1}\right) = hu\pi_K \tag{11.1}$$

$$w = \pi_L(1 - h) \tag{11.2}$$

$$g^S \equiv SK^{-1} = s_p PK^{-1} = s_p hu\pi_K \tag{11.3}$$

$$g^I = g^I(u, h), \quad g_u^I > 0, \quad g_h^I > 0 \tag{11.4}$$

$$g^S = g^I \tag{11.5}$$

$$g_u^S - g_u^I > 0 \text{ or } s_p \pi_K h > g_u^I \tag{11.6}$$

where $r$ denotes the profit rate, $w$ the real wage rate, and $g^S$ the savings–capital stock ratio. Equations (11.1) and (11.2) give the proximate determinants of the income distribution variables. Equation (11.3) gives the proximate determinants of the savings–capital stock ratio. Equation (11.4) introduces the accumulation function. Finally, Eq. (11.5) defines the commodities market equilibrium, and relation (11.6) gives the Keynesian stability condition for this market. The real wage rate or, equivalently, the share of profits is exogenously given, while the capacity utilization, capital accumulation (or growth), and profit rates are endogenously determined.

Using the "normalized profit rate", $r^N \equiv ru^{-1}$, Eqs. (11.1) and (11.2) define a linear wage–normalized profit rate curve, i.e.

$$r^N = \pi_K\left(1 - \pi_L^{-1}w\right)$$

the elasticity, $e_1$, of which equals the negative of the wage–profit ratio, i.e.

$$e_1 \equiv \left(dr^N/dw\right)w\left(r^N\right)^{-1} = -\pi_L^{-1}w\left(1 - \pi_L^{-1}w\right)^{-1} = -(1-h)h^{-1} \tag{11.7}$$

Equations (11.3), (11.4), and (11.5) define an implicit relation between the share of profits and the rate of capacity utilization, $u = u(h)$, or "IS-curve" (non-Hicksian), i.e.

$$s_p hu\pi_K = g^I(u, h)$$

the elasticity, $e_2$, of which is given by

$$e_2 = \left(g_h^I - s_p u(h)\pi_K\right)\left(s_p h\pi_K - g_u^I\right)^{-1} h(u(h))^{-1} \tag{11.8}$$

Since the term $s_p h\pi_K - g_u^I$ is positive (condition (11.6)), $e_2 > 0$ iff $g_h^I > s_p u(h)\pi_K$, i.e. the responsiveness of investment to changes in $h$ exceeds that of savings. Finally, differentiation of $r = hu(h)\pi_K$ (see Eq. (11.1)) with respect to $h$ gives

$$dr/dh = (1 + e_2)u(h)\pi_K \qquad (11.9)$$

from which it follows that an elastic, negatively sloped *IS*-curve necessarily implies that $dr/dh < 0$.

It then follows that the system is able to generate three alternative sets of steady-state equilibria (according to Kurz's 1990, pp. 222–226, terminology):

1. A "regime of overaccumulation", characterized by $\{du/dh < 0, dr/dh > 0\}$, prevails when

$$u(h)g_u^l < hg_h^l < s_p hu(h)\pi_K$$

2. A "regime of underconsumption", characterized by $\{du/dh < 0, dr/dh < 0\}$, prevails when

$$hg_h^l < u(h)g_u^l$$

In other words, an increase in the real wage rate implies higher profit and growth rates because the positive effect of demand is greater than the negative effect of higher costs ("paradox of costs"). It is easily checked that, for instance, a linear accumulation function,

$$g^l = a_0 + a_1 u + a_2 h$$

where $a_0 \ (\geq 0)$ represents the level of Keynesian "animal spirits", necessarily implies that $e_2 < 0$, and may imply a non-monotonic relationship between $r$ and $h$, since the two roots of the equation $r_h = 0$ have opposite signs, i.e.

$$h_{1,2} = \left[ a_1 a_2 \pm \sqrt{a_1 a_2 (a_1 a_2 + a_0 s_p \pi_K)} \right] (a_2 s_p \pi_K)^{-1}$$

where $h_1$ increases with $a_0$, $a_1$, and decreases with the remaining parameters. Hence, when $h_1 < 1$ and $h$ rises, the economy moves from the underconsumption regime to the overaccumulation regime.

3. A "Keynesian regime", characterized by $\{du/dh > 0, dr/dh > 0\}$, prevails when

$$s_p u(h)\pi_K < g_h^l$$

As Kurz (1990) remarks,

Keynes in the *General Theory* (1936) was of the opinion that a higher level of net investment a thus a higher rate of accumulation is of necessity tied to lower real wages, which will be brought about prices rising relative to money wages. However, in response to several critics Keynes later retracted this view [in his article "Relative movements of real wages and output", published in 1939]. Hence the label used above is meant to refer loosely to the Keynes of the *General Theory*. (p. 236, note 16)

Bhaduri and Marglin (1990) refer to both the overaccumulation and underconsumption regimes as "stagnationist (or wage-led) regimes without or, respectively, with cooperation between labour and capital". On the other hand, they refer to the Keynesian regime as "exhilarationist (or profit-led) regime", and point out that it involves cooperation between labour and capital iff

a given increase in the profit share stimulates the level of demand and capacity utilisation sufficiently to increase aggregate employment and the wage *bill*. (p. 384)

i.e. iff $(1 - h)u$ increases with increasing $h$ or, equivalently, $e_2 e_1 < -1$.

It should be added that, in the linear accumulation function–*open* economy case, $e_2$ is not necessarily negative. In that case, it holds

$$g^S = s_p h u \pi_K - tb$$

where $tb$ denotes the trade balance–capital stock ratio. Hence, the *IS*-curve is given by

$$u = (a_0 + tb + a_2 h)\left(s_p h \pi_K - a_1\right)^{-1}$$

and, therefore, $e_2 > (<) 0$ iff

$$s_p(a_0 + tb)\pi_K < (>) - a_1 a_2$$

or, in other words, there is a negative value for $tb$, i.e. the value

$$\widetilde{tb} \equiv -\left[a_1 a_2 \left(s_p \pi_K\right)^{-1} + a_0\right]$$

at which the economy moves to the Keynesian regime. The profit rate is given by

$$r = \left[(a_0 + tb)h + a_2 h^2\right]\pi_K \left(s_p h \pi_K - a_1\right)^{-1}$$

which implies that the economy is in the underconsumption regime when, and only when,

$$s_p a_2 h^2 \pi_K - 2 a_1 a_2 h - (a_0 + tb)a_1 < 0$$

Finally, when $tb = \widetilde{tb}$, it follows that

$$u = a_2(s_p \pi_K)^{-1} \quad \text{and} \quad r = h a_2 s_p^{-1}$$

namely, the profit rate increases linearly with the share of profits.[9]

### 11.2.1.2 Dynamization

Now, following Goodwin (1967), also assume that:

1. The labour force, $N$, grows at the steady rate $n$, i.e.[10]

$$\widehat{N} = n \qquad (11.10)$$

Steady-state growth at full employment (Harrod–Domar–Kaldor growth path) requires that the "natural" growth rate, $n$, must be less than the actual rate of capital accumulation corresponding to the maximum feasible value of the share of profits, $h = 1$, and to any actual value of the degree of capacity utilization, $u = \widetilde{u}$, i.e.

$$n < s_p \pi_K \widetilde{u} \qquad (11.10a)$$

(see Eq. 11.3).[11]

2. The real wage rate rises in the neighbourhood of full employment, i.e.

$$\widehat{w} = \varepsilon E - \zeta \qquad (11.11)$$

where $E \equiv L N^{-1}$ denotes the employment rate, and $\varepsilon, \zeta$ are positive constants.

Equations (11.2) and (11.7) imply that $\widehat{w} = e_1^{-1}\widehat{h}$ or, solving for $\widehat{h}$, and invoking Eq. (11.11),

---

[9]The terms "overaccumulation (or overproduction)" and "underconsumption" have a long history in the Marxist tradition but not, always, a sound or clear analytical meaning. See, e.g. Glombowski (1982), Glombowski and Krüger (1986), Krüger (1988), Lenin (1897), Lenin (1917, Sects. 4 and 8), Moszkowska (1935), Ségal (1936, Chaps. 9 and 10), Sherman (1971, 1979).

[10]A "dot" over a variable denotes the time derivative of that variable, while a "hat" denotes the logarithmic derivative with respect to time.

[11]This formulation is inherently different from that in Zamparelli (2015), who assumes no population growth (and $u = 1$). Meanwhile, it shares some common features with that by Tavani (2012) (despite assuming that $u = 1$) whose model: "evolves so as to achieve a Harrod-neutral path of technical progress, and a constant employment rate. [...] [E]quilibrium unemployment is not 'natural', in the sense that its role is not to prevent an accelerating inflation. Instead, in the spirit of Goodwin (1967), the role of equilibrium unemployment is to put the class-conflict between capital and labour to rest." (p. 124).

$$\dot{h} = e_1(\varepsilon E - \zeta)h \tag{11.12}$$

Since $L = \pi_L^{-1}\pi_K u K$ and $g^S = \widehat{K}$, it follows that $\widehat{L} = \widehat{u} + g^S$ or, recalling Eqs. (11.3) and (11.8),

$$\widehat{L} = e_2\widehat{h} + s_p hu(h)\pi_K \tag{11.13}$$

or, recalling Eq. (11.12),

$$\widehat{L} = e_2 e_1(\varepsilon E - \zeta) + s_p hu(h)\pi_K \tag{11.14}$$

Finally, substituting Eqs. (11.10) and (11.14) into

$$\widehat{E} = \widehat{L} - \widehat{N}$$

yields

$$\dot{E} = \left[e_2 e_1(\varepsilon E - \zeta) + s_p hu(h)\pi_K - n\right]E \tag{11.15}$$

Consequently, the model reduces to the non-linear system of Eqs. (11.12) and (11.15), which has two equilibria with $\dot{h} = \dot{E} = 0$, namely

$$h^* = 1, \quad E^* = 0 \tag{11.16}$$

and

$$h^{**} = n(s_p u(h^{**})\pi_K)^{-1}, \quad E^{**} = \zeta\varepsilon^{-1} \tag{11.16a}$$

where the latter is economically relevant ($0 < h^{**}, E^{**} < 1$) when

$$n < s_p u(h^{**})\pi_K \quad \text{and} \quad \zeta < \varepsilon \tag{11.16b}$$

To relations (11.16a) and (11.16b) there corresponds a unique value for $g^S$, i.e. $g^S = n$, and may correspond, when $e_2^{**} < 0$, more than one economically relevant value for $h$ and, therefore, for $u$ and $w$.[12]

The relevant Jacobian matrix, $\mathbf{J} \equiv [J_{ij}]$ is (take into account Eq. (11.9)[13]

---

[12]Consider, for instance, the case of a linear accumulation function (which, as we have already seen, necessarily implies that $e_2 < 0$).

[13]Since $\partial(\dot{E}E^{-1})/\partial(1 - h) < 0$ does not necessarily hold true (see Eq. (11.17c)), this system does not correspond to the Kolmogoroff "predator $(1 - h)$–prey $(E)$ system" (see, e.g. May 1972, p. 901). When $\partial(\dot{E}E^{-1})/\partial(1 - h) > 0$, the "two species are in symbiosis" (see Hirsch and Smale 1974, p. 273).

$$J_{11} \equiv \partial \dot{h}/\partial h = \varepsilon E - \zeta \tag{11.17a}$$

$$J_{12} \equiv \partial \dot{h}/\partial E = -\varepsilon(1 - h) \tag{11.17b}$$

$$J_{21} \equiv \partial \dot{E}/\partial h$$
$$= \left\{ \left[ (de_2/dh)e_1 + e_2 h^{-2} \right] (\varepsilon E - \zeta) + s_p (1 + e_2) u(h) \pi_K \right\} E \tag{11.17c}$$

$$J_{22} \equiv \partial \dot{E}/\partial E = e_2 e_1 (2\varepsilon E - \zeta) + s_p h u(h) \pi_K - n \tag{11.17d}$$

At the trivial fixed point, $(h^*, E^*)$: $e_1^* = 0$ and $\mathbf{J}^*$ is diagonal, with $J_{11}^* < 0$ and $J_{22}^* > 0$ (take into account relation (11.10a)); therefore, it is a saddle point, precisely like in the Goodwin model.

Next, consider the non-trivial fixed point(s), $(h^{**}, E^{**})$. Then $J_{11}^{**} = 0$, $J_{12}^{**} < 0$, and there are the following cases:

1. When $e_2^{**} > 0$, it follows that tr $[\mathbf{J}^{**}] < 0$ and det $[\mathbf{J}^{**}] > 0$: locally stable.
2. When $e_2^{**} = 0$, it follows that tr $[\mathbf{J}^{**}] = 0$ and det $[\mathbf{J}^{**}] > 0$ (like in the Goodwin model): centre. Hence, $(h^{**}, E^{**})$ is either a focus (stable or unstable) or a centre for the original system (depending on the precise form of $u(h)$; see, e.g. Andronov et al. 1987, pp. 278–280).
3. When $-1 < e_2^{**} < 0$, it follows that tr $[\mathbf{J}^{**}] > 0$ and det $[\mathbf{J}^{**}] > 0$: unstable.
4. When $e_2^{**} = -1$, it follows that tr $[\mathbf{J}^{**}] > 0$ and det $[\mathbf{J}^{**}] = 0$ $(J_{21}^{**} = 0)$: unstable.
5. When $e_2^{**} < -1$, it follows that tr $[\mathbf{J}^{**}] > 0$ and det $[\mathbf{J}^{**}] < 0$: saddle point.[14]

It is then concluded that the local dynamic behaviour of the system depends on the elasticity of the *IS*-curve, which, in its turn, depends on the form of the accumulation function. This elasticity determines the effect of a rising share of profits on the volume of employment, and may be conceived of as a "friction coefficient" (see Chap. 10) that alters the conservative dynamics of the Goodwin system: The equilibrium in the Keynesian regime $(e_2^{**} > 0$: positive friction) is locally stable, whereas that in the overaccumulation regime $(-1 < e_2^{**} < 0$: negative friction) is unstable. And in the border between these two regimes $(e_2^{**} = 0)$, the possible existence of cyclic paths cannot be excluded. Finally, the equilibrium in the underconsumption regime $(e_2^{**} < -1)$, where det $[\mathbf{J}^{**}]$ switches from positive to negative, is saddle-path stable.

The following three numerical examples illustrate some of the points made above:

***Example 11.1***
Consider a linear accumulation function,

$$g^I = a_0 + a_1 u + a_2 h$$

---

[14]The inclusion of the money market may not significantly alter the dynamic properties of the system (Mariolis and Michaelides 2020).

and assume that $a_0 = 0.01$, $a_1 = 0.03$, $a_2 = 0.05$, while $s_p \pi_K = 1$. It is obtained that (see Eqs. (11.8) and (11.9))

$$u = (0.01 + 0.05h)(h - 0.03)^{-1}$$

$$e_2 = -0.23h[(0.17 + h)h - 0.006]^{-1}$$

$\{u > 0, e_2 < 0\}$ for $h > 0.03$, $u = 1$ at $h \cong 0.042$, and $e_2 = -1$ at $h \cong 0.113$. Now assume that $\varepsilon = 0.004$, $\zeta = 0.003$ and $n = 0.03$. Hence, it is obtained that (see Eq. (11.16a))

$$h_{1,2}^{**} = 0.2 \pm \sqrt{5550}^{-1}, \quad E^{**} = 0.75$$

At $h_1^{**} \cong 0.348$ we get $e_2^{**} \cong -0.459$, tr $[\mathbf{J}^{**}] \cong 0.003$, det $[\mathbf{J}^{**}] \cong 0.001$ and that the discriminant,

$$\Delta^{**} \equiv (\text{tr } [\mathbf{J}^{**}])^2 - 4\det [\mathbf{J}^{**}]$$

is negative: the fixed point is an unstable focus. At $h_2^{**} \cong 0.052$ we get $e_2^{**} \cong -2.157$ : the fixed point is a saddle point.

### Example 11.2
Consider a "power" accumulation function,

$$g^I = a_0 u^{a_1} h^{a_2}$$

and assume that $a_0 = 1$, $a_1 = 0.8$, $a_2 = 1.3$, while $s_p \pi_K = 1$, $\varepsilon = 0.004$, $\zeta = 0.003$ and $n = 0.03$. It is obtained that $u = h^{e_2}$, $e_2 = (a_2 - 1)(1 - a_1)^{-1} = 1.5$, $h^{**} = n^{0.4} \cong 0.246$, $E^{**} = 0.75$, tr $[\mathbf{J}^{**}] \cong -0.014$, det $[\mathbf{J}^{**}] \cong 0.001$ and $\Delta^{**} < 0$: the fixed point is a stable focus. Finally, by letting $n$ vary parametrically, we get

$$\Delta^{**}(n) = 0.003(1 - n^{0.4})n^{-0.8}[0.00675(1 - n^{0.4}) - 10n^{1.4}]$$

from which it follows that $\Delta^{**}(n) \geq 0$, i.e. the fixed point is a stable node, for $n \leq 0.005$ (approximately).

### Example 11.3
Consider the accumulation function

$$g^I = u^{1/6}\phi_1(h)$$

where

$$\phi_1(h) \equiv a_0 + a_1 h - h^2 + h^3, \quad a_0 > 0$$

and

$$d\phi_1/dh > 0$$

for

$$a_1 > 3^{-1}$$

Assume that $a_0 = 0.005$, $a_1 = 0.35$, and $s_p \pi_K = 2$: it is obtained that

$$u = \left[0.5\left(0.005h^{-1} + 0.35 - h + h^2\right)\right]^{6/5}$$

i.e. the *IS*-curve is "U-shaped" (also see Marglin and Bhaduri 1988, pp. 22–23; Bhaduri and Marglin 1990, pp. 392–393),

$$e_2 = \left[1.2h\left(-0.005h^{-2} - 1 + 2h\right)\right]\left(0.005h^{-1} + 0.35 - h + h^2\right)^{-1}$$

$u = 1$ at $h \cong 0.00302$, $u \cong 0.12561$ at $h = 1$, $e_2 = 0$ at $h = \tilde{h} \cong 0.50963$, and $e_2 = -1$ at $h \cong 0.00291$ or $0.27045$ or, finally, $0.37370$ (also see Fig. 11.1). Now, assume that $\varepsilon = 0.004$, $\zeta = 0.003$ and $n = \tilde{n} \cong 0.0313517$. Hence, it is obtained that $h^{**} = \tilde{h}$, $E^{**} = 0.75$, $e_2^{**} = 0$ and

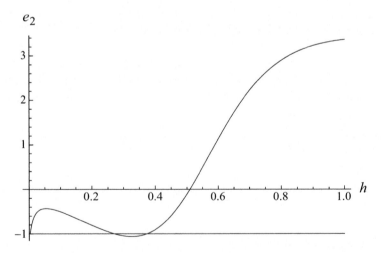

**Fig. 11.1** The elasticity of the *IS*-curve as a function of the share of profits: $h > 0.00302$

$$d(\text{Re}\lambda(a_0))/da_0 > 0 \quad \text{at} \quad a_0 = 0.005$$

where $\text{Re}\lambda(a_0)$ denotes the real part of the eigenvalues of $\mathbf{J}^{**}(a_0)$, since, as is easily checked,

$$\partial e_2/\partial a_0 < 0$$

We can therefore conclude that a "U-shaped" *IS*-curve may generate a Hopf bifurcation of periodic solutions.

### 11.2.1.3 Evidence from Econometric Estimations

To transform the theoretical model into an econometrically estimable one, we introduce a linear approximation of the *IS*-curve, i.e.

$$u(h) = \beta_0 + \beta_1 h$$

where $\beta_0$, $\beta_1$ are real-valued parameters. Thus, Eq. (11.15) reduces to

$$\dot{E}E^{-1} = \left[ e_2 e_1 \varepsilon E + \beta_0 s_p h \pi_K + \beta_1 s_p h^2 \pi_K - (e_2 e_1 \zeta + n) \right] \tag{11.18}$$

For given $E$, $\dot{E}E^{-1}$, $s_p h \pi_K$, and $s_p h^2 \pi_K$, based on the economy's aggregate data, the estimation of Eq. (11.18) is straightforward. This procedure provides us with direct estimates of $\beta_0$ and $\beta_1$. Also, it provides us with an estimate of $e_2 e_1 \varepsilon$. Given that (now)

$$e_1 = -(1 - \bar{h})\bar{h}^{-1}, \quad e_2 = \beta_1 \bar{h}(\beta_0 + \beta_1 \bar{h})^{-1}$$

we obtain an estimate of $\varepsilon$, where $\bar{\chi}$ denotes the average value of variable $\chi$. Similarly, given that $n$ is exogenous, and can be routinely estimated using the available data, from the estimate of the intercept in Eq. (11.18), we obtain the value of $\zeta$, since $e_1$ and $e_2$ are estimated as above. This econometric model leads to a single-equation estimate of a relationship between distribution and economic activity that should be interpreted as the joint outcome of the random shocks to distribution and utilization and the inherent dynamic behaviour of these variables (see, e.g. Kiefer and Rada 2015, pp. 1338–1339).

The estimation of the model for the case of the US economy and the time period 1960–2012, using structural breaks and a modern Bayesian sequential Monte Carlo method, gave the following results (Mariolis et al. 2019): The sub-period 1960–1973 is characterized by a Keynesian (or profit-led) regime, involving "cooperation between capital and labour" (since $e_2 e_1 < -1$), and the economy seems to be in a stable path. A similar picture arises for the sub-periods 1979–2006 and 2007–2012, that is, after the "second oil crisis" and the "subprime crisis", respectively.

Nevertheless, the sub-period 1974–1978 is characterized by an underconsumption regime, meaning that an increase in the real wage rate implies higher profit and growth rates, and the economy is saddle-path stable. These findings seem to be in accordance with the relevant literature, according to which the US economy consistently displays "counter-clockwise" cycles between employment rate and labour share of income, utilization rate, and labour share of income as well as utilization and employment rates (see Barrales and von Arnim 2017). And the results of the estimation of a similar model (although econometrically simpler) for the case of the German economy and the time period 1992–2007 suggested that, for both sub-periods 1992–2000 and 2000–2007, the economy is saddle-path stable (Konstantakis et al. 2014).

Although it is theoretically expected that open economies running "large" trade deficits *tend* to be profit-led (see Sect. 11.2.1.1 and, e.g. Ribeiro et al. 2017; von Arnim et al. 2014), the hitherto available empirical evidence provides, however, mixed results. Thus, Blecker (2016) and Santos and Araujo (2020) argue that the profit-led regime tends to dominate in the short term, whereas the wage-led regime tends to become dominant over the long term. Finally, taking into account the interdependence between national economies over the "second globalization era" (1990s–2010s), it could be added that increasing mobility of money capital implies a tendency towards the equalization of national profit rates and, therefore, specific relationships amongst national shares of wages, wage rates, and productivities.[15] In

---

[15]For brevity's sake, consider a two-economy (A and B) framework and abstract from capacity utilizations, taxes and exchange rate changes. Then $r^A = r^B = \tilde{r}$ and equations Eqs. (11.1) and (11.2) imply that

$$h^A \left(h^B\right)^{-1} = \pi_K^B \left(\pi_K^A\right)^{-1}$$

and

$$w^A \left(w^B\right)^{-1} = \pi_L^A \left(\pi_L^B\right)^{-1} \left[1 - \tilde{r}\left(\pi_K^A\right)^{-1}\right] \left[1 - \tilde{r}\left(\pi_K^B\right)^{-1}\right]^{-1}$$

or

$$w^A \left(w^B\right)^{-1} = \tilde{w} \equiv \pi_I \left(\pi_K^A - \tilde{r}\right)\left(\pi_K^A - \pi_{II}\tilde{r}\right)^{-1}$$

or, using the Taylor expansion about $\tilde{r} = 0$,

$$w^A \left(w^B\right)^{-1} = \tilde{w} \approx \pi_I \left[1 + (\pi_{II} - 1)\tilde{r}\left(\pi_K^A\right)^{-1}\right]$$

where $\pi_I \equiv \pi_L^A \left(\pi_L^B\right)^{-1}$, $\pi_{II} \equiv \pi_K^A \left(\pi_K^B\right)^{-1}$ and $\tilde{r} < \min\left\{\pi_K^A, \pi_K^B\right\}$ (for the relative profit rate, $\tilde{r}\pi_K^{-1}$, see Sect. 2.3.1 and Chap. 3 of this book). These relationships amongst national shares of wages, wage rates, and productivities could be conceived of as a fundamental economic law of equilibrium of the currency areas and especially of the Eurozone (Mariolis 2015). When $w^A \left(w^B\right)^{-1} > (<) \tilde{w}$, the price competitiveness of economy B (economy A) improves, and this implies that the national economies-members of currency areas are involved in a game of wage devaluations. According to fact, evidence from a panel of thirteen OECD countries over the period 1970–2012 suggests that, although demand is profit-led, there are long-term declines in both the shares of wages and the rates of capacity utilization, which appear to be correlated with the implementation of economic policies seeking to promote exports through income redistribution from wage incomes, with low propensities to save, to profit incomes, with high propensities to save (Kiefer and Rada 2015). At the same time, empirical evidence from the ten largest countries (in terms of their share of world GDP) suggests that, due to a "global saving glut", the world interest rate is currently low, relatively to the world growth rate, and this explains the new stylized fact that the current account and the trade balances are positively correlated during the "second globalization" (whereas they were negatively correlated during the "first globalization", 1870s–1910s; see Eugeni 2016, and compare with Lenin 1917). Although important, these mechanisms lie, however, outside the domain of our model.

## 11.2.2   The Heterogeneous Capital Case

Consider an identical economy that produces, however, many basic commodities by linear processes of single production, and assume that: (1) the production period is uniform across sectors; (2) the degree of capacity utilization is uniform both within and across sectors; (3) the desired rate of accumulation is a strictly increasing function of both the degree of capacity utilization and the aggregate share of profits; (4) workers and capitalists have identical and rigid consumption patterns; and (5) the consumption vector is adopted as the *numéraire*.[16]

In this case, the negatively sloped wage–normalized profit rate curve is not necessarily linear, while the elasticity of a non-linear $w - r^N$ curve no longer represents the ratio of income shares; moreover, the aggregate productivities of labour and capital are not given independently of, and prior to, prices, income distribution, and growth and, in fact, can change in a complicated way as distribution changes (see Chaps. 2 and 3). As Panico and Salvadori (1993) stress:

> The debate on capital theory has shown in a definite way that if single production holds and no primary input except labour is utilized, then the function $(\pi_K(r^N))^{-1}$ exists and has the following properties:

---

Rodrik (2011), "[d]ifferences in productivity account for between 80 to 90% of the variation in wages around the world" (p. 192), while for estimations of the levels and trends in the capital profitability across the world (1995–2007), see Chou et al. (2016).

[16]It need hardly be emphasized that assumptions (2) and (3) are rather crude; it seems, however, that more realistic assumptions lead to major complications. Assumptions (4) and (5) imply that the money wage rate equals the real wage rate.

$$r^N\big(\pi_K(r^N)\big)^{-1} < 1 \ \text{ if } \ 0 \le r^N < \lambda^{-1}$$

$$\lambda^{-1}\big(\pi_K(\lambda^{-1})\big)^{-1} = 1$$

[where $\lambda$ denotes the Perron–Frobenius eigenvalue of the capital coefficients matrix, and $\lambda^{-1}$ is the maximum feasible value of $r^N$, i.e. the value corresponding to $h = 1$ and to positive commodity prices]. Any other property attributed to this function requires the introduction of limiting assumptions. For instance, the usual neoclassical properties also require single production of one good only, which can be consumed or used as input for itself along with labour. (p. xx; using our symbols)[17]

Hence Eqs. (11.8) and (11.9) should be replaced by[18]

$$e_2 = \big[g_h^l - (1 + e_3)s_p u(h)\pi_K\big]\big(s_p h\pi_K - g_u^l\big)^{-1} h(u(h))^{-1}$$

and

$$dr/dh = (1 + e_3 + e_2)u(h)\pi_K$$

or

$$dr/dh = \big[hg_h^l - (1 + e_3)u(h)g_u^l\big]\pi_K\big(s_p h\pi_K - g_u^l\big)^{-1}$$

where $e_3$ denotes the elasticity of $\pi_K$ with respect to $h$, and consists of a "value effect" and a "composition effect". Nevertheless, $h$ continues to be a strictly increasing function of $r^N$ (see Franke 1999, pp. 46–49, where $u = 1$ holds by assumption) and, therefore, $h = \pi_K^{-1}r^N$ implies that $1 + e_3 > 0$. Thus, although $e_2 \ge 0$ implies that $dr/dh > 0$, the condition $s_p u(h)\pi_K < g_h^l$ does not necessarily imply that $e_2 > 0$, and $e_2 < -1$ does not necessarily imply that $dr/dh < 0$. Now:

1. The overaccumulation regime prevails when

$$(1 + e_3)u(h)g_u^l < hg_h^l < (1 + e_3)s_p hu(h)\pi_K$$

2. The underconsumption regime prevails when

$$hg_h^l < (1 + e_3)u(h)g_u^l$$

---

[17]For a comprehensive analysis of the said function, see Kurz and Salvadori (1995, pp. 475–480).

[18]For a detailed derivation, as well as for alternative savings assumptions (savings out of wages, by rentiers, and by workers), see Mariolis (2007).

3. The Keynesian regime prevails when

$$(1 + e_3)s_p u(h)\pi_K < g_h^l$$

Furthermore, Eq. (11.13) should be replaced by

$$\widehat{L} = (e_3 - e_4 + e_2)\widehat{h} + s_p hu(h)\pi_K \tag{11.19}$$

where $e_4$ denotes the elasticity of $\pi_L$ with respect to $h$, and the difference $e_4 - e_3$ equals the elasticity of capital intensity, $\pi_L \pi_K^{-1}$, with respect to $h$. Hence Eqs. (11.10), (11.11), and (11.19) imply that the model reduces to the following system:

$$\dot{h} = \eta_1(\varepsilon E - \zeta)h, \quad \eta_1 \equiv e_1(1 + e_3)^{-1} \leq 0$$

$$\dot{E} = [\eta_2\eta_1(\varepsilon E - \zeta) + s_p hu(h)\pi_K - n]E, \quad \eta_2 \equiv e_3 - e_4 + e_2$$

which includes the system of Eqs. (11.12) and (11.15) as a special case (i.e. $e_1 + (1 - h)h^{-1} = e_3 = e_4 = 0$).

Although, like in the one-commodity case (see Eq. (11.17)),

$$J_{11}^{**} = 0$$

$$J_{12}^{**} = \eta_1^{**}h^{**}\varepsilon < 0$$

and

$$J_{21}^{**} = s_p\left(1 + e_2^{**}\right)u(h^{**})\pi_K\zeta\varepsilon^{-1}$$

the sign of

$$J_{22}^{**} = \eta_2^{**}\eta_1^{**}\zeta$$

depends on the sign of the friction coefficient $\eta_2^{**}$, which, in its turn, depends not only on the sign of $e_2^{**}$ but also on that of the relevant elasticity of capital intensity. It is therefore concluded that there are no unambiguous relationships amongst the types of dynamic equilibrium, the regimes of accumulation, and the elasticity of the *IS*-curve.

## 11.3   Extensions of the One-Commodity Model

### 11.3.1   CES Production Functions

Assume a CES production function (see, e.g. Arrow et al. 1961),[19] i.e.

$$\widetilde{Y} = [(1 - \alpha)L^{-\omega} + \alpha K^{-\omega}]^{-1/\omega} \tag{11.20}$$

where $\alpha$, $0 < \alpha < 1$, denotes the share parameter; $-1 < \omega < 0$ or $\omega < 0$, and the elasticity of substitution between capital and labour equals $(1 + \omega)^{-1}$. It goes without saying that as $\omega \to 0$, Eq. (11.20) becomes the Cobb–Douglas production function, while as $\omega \to +\infty$, it becomes the Leontief production function.[20]
The profit-maximizing problem may be written as

$$\max \widetilde{Y} - rKu^{-1} - wLu^{-1}$$

and, therefore, from Eq. (11.20), it is obtained

$$wu^{-1} = (1 - \alpha)[(1 - \alpha)L^{-\omega} + \alpha K^{-\omega}]^{-(1+\omega)/\omega}L^{-1-\omega} \tag{11.21}$$

or, from Eq. (11.20) and the definition of $u$,

$$w[(1 - \alpha)L^{-\omega} + \alpha K^{-\omega}]^{-1/\omega}Y^{-1} = (1 - \alpha)[(1 - \alpha)L^{-\omega} + \alpha K^{-\omega}]^{-(1+\omega)/\omega}L^{-1-\omega}$$

and taking into account that $h = 1 - wLY^{-1}$ and the definition of $e_1$,

$$k = (\alpha e_1)^{1/\omega}(\alpha - 1)^{-1/\omega} \tag{11.22}$$

where $k \equiv KL^{-1}$ denotes the "optimal factor demand ratio".
Given the definition of $\pi_K$, from Eq. (11.20), it follows that

$$\pi_K = K^{-1}[(1 - \alpha)L^{-\omega} + \alpha K^{-\omega}]^{-1/\omega}$$

or

$$\pi_K = [(1 - \alpha)k^{\omega} + \alpha]^{-1/\omega}$$

or, taking into account Eq. (11.22),

---

[19]This section draws on Rodousakis (2012, 2015, 2019).
[20]Note that as $\omega \to -1$, Eq. (11.20) becomes the linear production function and, therefore, as $\omega$ increases from –1 to infinity, the elasticity of substitution decreases steadily from infinity to zero.

$$\pi_K = (-\alpha e_1 + \alpha)^{-1/\omega}$$

or, recalling the definition of $e_1$,

$$\pi_K = \left(h a^{-1}\right)^{1/\omega} \tag{11.23}$$

Finally, given the definitions of $k$ and $\pi_L$, and Eq. (11.20), it follows that

$$\pi_L = [(1 - \alpha) + \alpha k^{-\omega}]^{-1/\omega} u$$

or, taking into account Eq. (11.22) and the definition of $e_1$,

$$\pi_L = (h e_1)^{1/\omega} (\alpha - 1)^{-1/\omega} u \tag{11.24}$$

Equations (11.2), (11.11), and (11.24) imply that

$$\widehat{h} = e_1 \omega [(\varepsilon E - \zeta) - \widehat{u}](\omega + 1)^{-1} \tag{11.25}$$

Furthermore, the elasticity of the *IS*-curve is given by

$$e_2 = \left\{ [g_h^l - s_p u \pi_K - s_p h u (d\pi_K/dh)] \left(s_p h \pi_K - g_u^l\right)^{-1} \right\} h u^{-1} \tag{11.26}$$

Hence substituting Eqs. (11.23) and (11.26) into Eq. (11.25) yields

$$\dot{h} = [e_1 \omega h(\varepsilon E - \zeta)][(\omega + 1) + \omega e_1 e_2]^{-1} \tag{11.27}$$

Since

$$g^S \equiv \widehat{K} = s_p h u \pi_K \quad \text{and} \quad \widehat{k} = \widehat{K} - \widehat{L}$$

from Eqs. (11.22) and (11.23) it follows

$$\widehat{L} = s_p h^{(1+\omega)/\omega} u(h) \alpha^{-1/\omega} - (\omega e_1 h)^{-1} \widehat{h} \tag{11.28}$$

Substituting Eqs. (11.10), (11.26), and (11.27) into $\widehat{E} = \widehat{L} - \widehat{N}$ yields

$$\dot{E} = \left\{ s_p h^{(1+\omega)/\omega} u(h) \alpha^{-1/\omega} - (\varepsilon E - \zeta)[(\omega + 1)h + \omega h e_1 e_2]^{-1} - n \right\} E \tag{11.29}$$

Consequently, the present model reduces to the non-linear system of Eqs. (11.27) and (11.29), and we distinguish between the following two cases:

**Case 1:** $\omega \to 0$ (Cobb–Douglas production function). Equation (11.21) is written as

$$wu^{-1} = (1 - \alpha)k^{\alpha} \qquad (11.21a)$$

and, therefore, recalling the definitions of $u$, $h$, and $k$, we obtain

$$h = \alpha$$

Furthermore, from Eq. (11.21a), it follows that

$$\widehat{k} = \alpha^{-1}(\widehat{w} - \widehat{u})$$

and, therefore, recalling Eq. (11.11), and given that $e_5 \equiv \widehat{u}\widehat{k}^{-1}$, where $e_5$ denotes the elasticity of $u$ with respect to $k$, we obtain

$$\dot{k} = \left[(\varepsilon E - \zeta)(\alpha + e_5)^{-1}\right]k \qquad (11.30)$$

Since $\pi_K = k^{\alpha - 1}$, it follows that

$$g^S = s_p u(k)\alpha k^{\alpha - 1}.$$

Therefore, Eq. (11.28) should be replaced by

$$\widehat{L} = s_p u(k)\alpha k^{\alpha-1} - (\varepsilon E - \zeta)(\alpha + e_5)^{-1} \qquad (11.28a)$$

Finally, from Eqs. (11.10) and (11.28a) and the definition of $E$, it is obtained

$$\dot{E} = \left[s_p u(k)\alpha k^{\alpha-1} - (\varepsilon E - \zeta)(\alpha + e_5)^{-1} - n\right]E \qquad (11.31)$$

The system of Eqs. (11.30) and (11.31) has an equilibria with $\dot{k} = \dot{E} = 0$, namely

$$k^* = n^{1/(\alpha-1)}(s_p u(k)\alpha)^{-1/(\alpha-1)}, \quad E^* = \zeta\varepsilon^{-1}$$

to which there may correspond more than one economically relevant value for $k$.[21]
The Jacobian matrix of the system of Eqs. (11.30) and (11.31) is

$$J_{11} \equiv \partial\dot{k}/\partial k = (\varepsilon E - \zeta)\left[(\alpha + e_5)^{-1} - k(de_3/dk)(\alpha + e_5)^{-2}\right]$$

$$J_{12} \equiv \partial\dot{k}/\partial E = \varepsilon k(\alpha + e_5)^{-1}$$

---

[21]The equilibria is economically relevant when $n < s_p k^{1 - \alpha}u(k^*)$, $k \neq 0$, $\zeta < \varepsilon$ and $e_5^* \neq -\alpha$.

$$J_{21} \equiv \partial \dot{E}/\partial k = \left\{ s_p \alpha u(k) k^{\alpha-2}(e_5 + \alpha - 1) + [(\varepsilon E - \zeta)(de_5/dk)](\varepsilon + e_5)^{-2} \right\} E$$

$$J_{22} \equiv \partial \dot{E}/\partial E = s_p u(k) \alpha k^{\alpha-1} - (2\varepsilon E - \zeta)(\varepsilon + e_3)^{-1} - n$$

The determinant and trace of $\mathbf{J}^*$ can be written as

$$\det[\mathbf{J}^*] = -\varepsilon k^*(\alpha + e_5^*)^{-1}\left[ s_p \alpha u(k^*)(k^*)^{\alpha-2}(e_5^* + \alpha - 1)\right] E^*$$

$$\mathrm{tr}[\mathbf{J}^*] = -\omega(\alpha + e_5^*)^{-1} E^*$$

Hence, there are the following cases:

1. When $-\alpha < e_5^* < 1 - \alpha$, it follows that $\mathrm{tr}[\mathbf{J}^*] < 0$ and $\det[\mathbf{J}^*] > 0$: locally stable.
2. When $e_5^* < -\alpha$ or $e_5^* > 1 - \alpha$, it follows that $\det[\mathbf{J}^*] < 0$: saddle point.
3. When $e_5^* = 1 - \alpha$, it follows that $\mathrm{tr}[\mathbf{J}^*] < 0$ and $\det[\mathbf{J}^*] = 0$: locally stable.

**Case 2:** $-1 < \omega < 0$ or $\omega > 0$. The model reduces to the system of Eqs. (11.27) and (11.29), which has two equilibria with $\dot{h} = \dot{E} = 0$, namely $h^* = 1$, $E^* = 0$ and

$$h^{**} = n^{\omega/(1+\omega)}\left(\alpha^{1/\omega}u(h^{**})\right)^{-\omega/(1+\omega)}, \quad E^{**} = \zeta\varepsilon^{-1}$$

to which there may correspond more than one economically relevant value for $h$.[22] The Jacobian matrix of the system of Eqs. (11.27) and (11.29) is

$$J_{11} \equiv \partial\dot{h}/\partial h = \{(\omega - 2\omega h)[(\omega+1)h + \omega h e_1 e_2] +$$
$$\omega h^2 e_1[(\omega+1) + \omega e_2 + \omega h e_1(de_2/dh)]\}(\zeta - \varepsilon E)[(\omega+1)h + \omega h e_1 e_2]^{-2}$$

$$J_{12} \equiv \partial\dot{h}/\partial E = -\omega\varepsilon h(1-h)[(\omega+1)h + \omega h e_1 e_2]^{-1}$$

$$J_{21} \equiv \partial\dot{E}/\partial h = \{s_p u(h)h^{1/\omega}\alpha^{-1/\omega}(e_2 + 1 + \omega^{-1}) -$$
$$(\zeta - \varepsilon E)[(\omega+1) + \omega e_2 + \omega h e_1(de_2/dh)][(\omega+1)h + \omega h e_1 e_2]^{-2}\}E$$

$$J_{22} \equiv \partial\dot{E}/\partial E = s_p u(h)h^{1/\omega+1}\alpha^{-1/\omega} + (\zeta - 2\varepsilon E)[(\omega+1)h + \omega h e_1 e_2]^{-1} - n$$

At the trivial fixed point, $(h^*, E^*)$, we obtain

$$\det[\mathbf{J}^*] = -\omega\zeta(1+\omega)^{-1}\left[ s_p\alpha^{-1/\omega}u(1) + \zeta(1+\omega)^{-1} - n\right]$$

$$\mathrm{tr}[\mathbf{J}^*] = (1-\omega)\zeta(1+\omega)^{-1} + s_p\alpha^{-1/\omega}u(1) - n$$

---

[22]The latter is economically relevant when $n < s_p(h\alpha^{-1})^{1/\omega}g'(h^{**})$ and $\zeta < \varepsilon$.

Hence, if $\omega > 0$, then $\det[\mathbf{J}^*] < 0$ (take into account relation (11.10a)); therefore, it is a saddle point. On the other hand, if $-1 < \omega < 0$, then $\text{tr}[\mathbf{J}^*] > 0$ and $\det[\mathbf{J}^*] > 0$; therefore, it is an unstable point.

Next consider the non-trivial fixed point(s), $(h^{**}, E^{**})$. Then, we obtain

$$\det[\mathbf{J}^{**}] = \left\{ \left( s_p(h^{**})^{1/\omega} \alpha^{-1/\omega} u(h^{**}) \right) \left[ e_2^{**} + (1+\omega)\omega^{-1} \right] E^{**} \right\}$$
$$\left\{ -\varepsilon\omega(h^{**})^2 e_1^{**} \left[ (\omega+1)h^{**} + \omega h^{**} e_1^{**} e_2^{**} \right]^{-1} \right\}$$

$$\text{tr}[\mathbf{J}^{**}] = -\varepsilon E^{**} \left[ (\varepsilon\omega+1)h^{**} + \omega h^{**} e_1^{**} e_2^{**} \right]^{-1}$$

Hence, if $\omega > 0$, then there are the following two cases:

1. When

$$-(1+\omega)\omega^{-1} < e_2^{**} < -(1+\omega)\left(\omega e_1^{**}\right)^{-1}$$

it follows that $\text{tr}[\mathbf{J}^{**}] < 0$ and $\det[\mathbf{J}^{**}] > 0$: locally stable.

2. When either

$$e_2^{**} < -(1+\omega)\omega^{-1}$$

or

$$e_2^{**} > -(1+\omega)\left(\omega e_1^{**}\right)^{-1}$$

it follows that $\det[\mathbf{J}^{**}] < 0$: saddle point.

On the other hand, if $-1 < \omega < 0$, we have the same two cases as before, but with

$$-(1+\omega)\omega^{-1} < e_2^{**} < -(1+\omega)\left(\omega e_1^{**}\right)^{-1}$$

replaced by

$$-(1+\omega)\left(\omega e_1^{**}\right)^{-1} < e_2^{**} < -(1+\omega)\omega^{-1}$$

and

$$e_2^{**} < -(1+\omega)\omega^{-1} \text{ or } e_2^{**} > -(1+\omega)\left(\omega e_1^{**}\right)^{-1}$$

replaced by

$$e_2^{**} < -(1+\omega)(\omega e_1^{**})^{-1} \quad \text{or} \quad e_2^{**} > -(1+\omega)\omega^{-1}$$

It is then concluded that the local dynamic behaviour of the present Goodwin–Bhaduri–Marglin one-commodity system depends on the elasticity of substitution between capital and labour, and is more complicated than that of the van der Ploeg (1985) system.[23] Firms can substitute labour for capital, and this implies that, at the non-trivial fixed point(s), the system is locally either stable or saddle-path stable. In the former case, the economy "stagnates" in a state of unemployment and excess capital capacity.

## 11.3.2 Commodities Market Disequilibrium

Now assume that the adjustment of actual output to effective demand is described by

$$\dot{Y} = \mu(I - S) \tag{11.32}$$

where $I$ denotes total investment.

Since $K = Y(u\pi_K)^{-1}$, from Eqs. (11.3), (11.4) and (11.32) it follows that

$$\widehat{Y} = \mu\left[g'(u,h)(u\pi_K)^{-1} - s_p h\right] \tag{11.33}$$

or, since $\widehat{Y} = \widehat{L}$,

$$\widehat{L} = \mu\left[g'(u,h)(u\pi_K)^{-1} - s_p h\right] \tag{11.34}$$

Hence from Eqs. (11.10) and (11.34) and the definition of $E$, it is obtained

$$\dot{E} = \left\{\mu\left[g'(u,h)(u\pi_K)^{-1} - s_p h\right] - n\right\}E \tag{11.35}$$

Finally, since $\widehat{u} = \widehat{Y} - g^S$, Eqs. (11.3) and (11.33) imply that

$$\dot{u} = \left\{\mu\left[g'(u,h)(u\pi_K)^{-1} - s_p h\right] - s_p h u \pi_K^{-1}\right\}u \tag{11.36}$$

Consequently, the model reduces to the system of Eqs. (11.12), (11.35), and (11.36), which has three equilibria with $\dot{h} = \dot{E} = \dot{u} = 0$, namely

---

[23] Also see Sect. 10.3 of the present book.

$$h^* = 1, \quad E^* = 0, \quad u^*$$

$$h^{**} = \mu g^l(u,h)(\mu s_p u \pi_K + s_p), \quad E^{**} = \zeta \varepsilon^{-1}, \quad u^{**} = \mu g^l(u,h)\left[\pi_K(\mu s_p h + n)\right]^{-1}$$

and

$$h^{***} = \left[g^l(u,h)(u\pi_K)^{-1} - n\mu^{-1}\right]s_p^{-1}, \quad E^{**} = \zeta \varepsilon^{-1}, \quad u^{***}$$

where $u^*$ and $u^{***}$ are the positive value(s) of the degree of capacity utilization for which

$$s_p \pi_K^{-1}(u^*)^2 + \mu s_p u^* - \mu g^l(u^*, 1)\pi_K^{-1} = 0$$

and

$$s_p h^{***} \pi_K^{-1}(u^{***})^2 + \mu s_p h^{***} u^{***} - \mu g^l(u^{***}, h^{***})\pi_K^{-1} = 0$$

respectively. The Jacobian matrix of Eqs. (11.12), (11.35), and (11.36) is

$$J_{11} \equiv \partial \dot{h}/\partial h = \varepsilon E - \zeta$$

$$J_{12} \equiv \partial \dot{h}/\partial E = -\varepsilon(1 - h)$$

$$J_{13} \equiv \partial \dot{h}/\partial u = 0$$

$$J_{21} \equiv \partial \dot{E}/\partial h = \mu\left[g_h^l(\pi_K u)^{-1} - s_p\right]E$$

$$J_{22} \equiv \partial \dot{E}/\partial E = \mu\left[g^l(u,h)(\pi_K u)^{-1} - s_p h\right] - n$$

$$J_{23} \equiv \partial \dot{E}/\partial u = \mu g_u^l E(\pi_K u^2)^{-1}$$

$$J_{31} \equiv \partial \dot{u}/\partial h = \left[\mu g_h^l(\pi_K u)^{-1} - \mu s_p - s_p u \pi_K\right]u$$

$$J_{32} \equiv \partial \dot{u}/\partial E = 0$$

$$J_{33} \equiv \partial \dot{u}/\partial u = \mu g_u^l \pi_K^{-1} - \mu s_p h - 2 s_p h u \pi_K$$

At the trivial fixed point $(h^*, E^*, u^*)$, the characteristic equation of the linearized system is

$$\lambda^3 + z_1 \lambda^2 + z_2 \lambda + z_3 = 0$$

where

$$\mathbf{J}^* \equiv \begin{bmatrix} J_{11}^* & 0 & 0 \\ 0 & J_{22}^* & 0 \\ J_{31}^* & 0 & J_{33}^* \end{bmatrix}$$

$$z_1 \equiv -\mathrm{tr}[\mathbf{J}^*] = -\left(J_{11}^* + J_{22}^* + J_{33}^*\right)$$

$$z_2 \equiv J_{22}^* J_{33}^* + J_{11}^* J_{33}^* + J_{11}^* J_{22}^*$$

$$z_3 \equiv -\det[\mathbf{J}^*] = -J_{11}^* J_{22}^* J_{33}^*$$

and $z_2$ denotes the sum of the principal minors' determinants. The necessary and sufficient condition for the local stability is that all eigenvalues of $\mathbf{J}^*$ have negative real parts, which, from the Routh–Hurwitz conditions, is equivalent to

$$z_1 > 0, \quad z_2 > 0, \quad z_3 > 0 \text{ and } z_1 z_2 - z_3 > 0$$

If

$$n > \mu\left[g'(u,h)(\pi_K u)^{-1} - s_p h\right]$$

the said conditions are fulfilled and, therefore, the trivial fixed point is locally asymptotically stable. If

$$n < \mu\left[g'(u,h)(\pi_K u)^{-1} - s_p h\right]$$

then $z_3$ is negative and, therefore, the conditions are violated.

Next consider the non-trivial fixed point(s) $(h^{**}, E^{**}, u^{**})$. The relevant characteristic equation is

$$\lambda^3 + z_1' \lambda^2 + z_2' \lambda + z_3' = 0$$

where

$$\mathbf{J}^{**} \equiv \begin{bmatrix} 0 & J_{12}^{**} & 0 \\ J_{21}^{**} & 0 & J_{23}^{**} \\ J_{31}^{**} & 0 & J_{33}^{**} \end{bmatrix}$$

$$z_1' \equiv -\mathrm{tr}[\mathbf{J}^{**}] = -J_{33}^{**}$$

$$z_2' \equiv -J_{12}^{**} J_{21}^{**}$$

$$z_3' \equiv -\det[\mathbf{J}^{**}] = J_{12}^{**}\left(J_{21}^{**} J_{33}^{**} - J_{23}^{**} J_{31}^{**}\right)$$

and

$$z_1'z_2' - z_3' = J_{12}^{**}J_{23}^{**}J_{31}^{**}$$

It then follows that nothing can be said a priori about the dynamic behaviour of the linearized system(s) and, therefore, it is necessary to account for the specific form of the accumulation function. If the accumulation function is linear, then $J_{12}^{**}, J_{23}^{**}, J_{31}^{**}$ are all negative and, therefore, $z_1'z_2' - z_3' < 0$, namely, the fixed point(s) is locally unstable.[24] Consider, for instance, the following numerical example:

**Example 11.4**
Assume that

$$g^l = 0.1 + 0.02u + 0.5h$$

$\mu = 0.5$, $s_p = 1$, $\pi_K = 1.11$, $\varepsilon = 0.03$, $\zeta = 0.05$, and $n = 0.2$. It is obtained that there is a unique, economically relevant, non-trivial fixed point,

$$(h^{**}, E^{**}, u^{**}) = (0.503, 0.6, 0.357)$$

while the system follows a cyclical path and, therefore, this fixed point is an unstable focus (see the graphs in Fig. 11.2).

It can, however, be shown that alternative accumulation function forms may lead to significantly different solutions (including limit cycles) and, more specifically, that the dynamic properties of the system depend crucially on both the form and parameter values of this function (Mariolis and Rodousakis 2020).

## 11.4 Technological Change, Profit Rate, and Profit Mass

### 11.4.1 The "Law" of Rising Profit Rate

In the one-commodity case (Sect. 11.2.1) it holds[25]

$$r = hu\pi_K$$

or, equivalently,

$$r = e_S(1 + e_S)^{-1}u\pi_K = \left[1 - (1 + e_S)^{-1}\right]u\pi_K$$

where $h \leq 1$, $h = 1$ for $w = 0$, $u \leq 1$, and

---

[24]The same holds for the other, non-trivial fixed point(s).
[25]This and the next section draw on Mariolis (2014a, b, 2018).

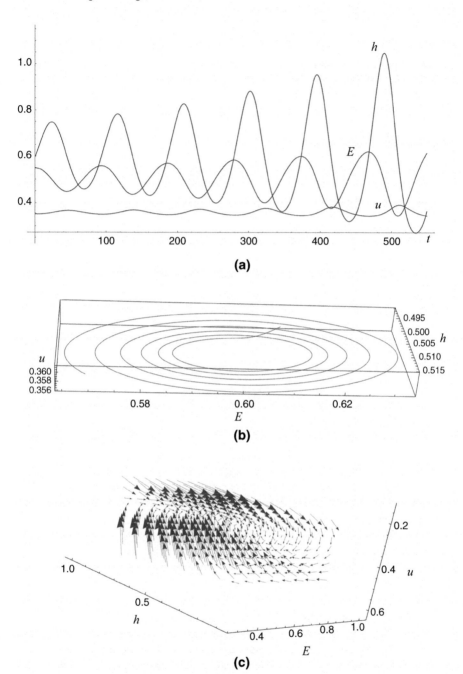

**Fig. 11.2** (**a**) The time dynamics of $h$, $E$, and $u$; (**b**) the system's path in the phase space; and (**c**) the *vector field* in the phase space: commodities market disequilibrium–linear accumulation function case

$$es = \pi_L w^{-1} - 1 = h(1 - h)^{-1}$$

denotes the "rate of surplus value", which tends to plus infinity as $w$ (as $h$) approaches zero (one) from below. It then follows that

$$r \leq \pi_K \tag{11.37}$$

Relation (11.37) implies that:

1. If capital productivity decreases with time, $t$, *and* tends to zero, then, irrespective of the magnitudes (and movements) of $h$ and $u$, the profit rate tends to zero (although not necessarily monotonically). Moreover, since

$$L = \kappa^{-1} uK, \quad \kappa = \pi_L \pi_K^{-1}, \quad \widehat{K} = s_p r, \quad s_p \leq 1$$

where $\kappa$ denotes the capital intensity (or Marx's "technical composition of capital"), it follows that

$$\widehat{L} \leq -\widehat{\kappa} + \widehat{u} + r$$

or

$$\widehat{L} \leq -(\widehat{\pi}_L - \widehat{\pi}_K) + \widehat{u} + \pi_K \tag{11.38}$$

Relation (11.38) implies that, if

$$\widehat{\pi}_K < 0, \quad \pi_K(t) \to 0, \quad \widehat{\pi}_L > 0 \tag{11.39}$$

then $\widehat{L}$ eventually becomes negative and, therefore, the employment rate, $E \equiv LN^{-1}$, eventually falls. Thus, it can be concluded that, if conditions (11.39) are fulfilled and the "rate of surplus value" eventually rises, without limit ($\widehat{\pi}_L > \widehat{w}$), then (a) capital intensity rises faster than labour productivity ($\widehat{\kappa} > \widehat{\pi}_L$); (b) the labour "value (organic) composition of capital",

$$VCC = [\pi_K(1 - h)]^{-1} = \pi_K^{-1}(1 + es)$$

eventually rises, without limit; (c) $r^N(t)(\pi_K(t))^{-1}$ tends to one and, therefore, the functions $r^N(t)$ and $\pi_K(t)$ are "asymptotically equivalent"; (d) the profit rate and, therefore, the ratio of profits to the sum of capital stock and profits, which equals $(1 + r^{-1})^{-1}$, tend to zero;[26] (e) the interest rate on loan capital tends to zero (since the

---

[26]When wages are paid at the beginning of the production period (as in Marx's definition of the profit rate; see, however, Marx 1982, pp. 277–278) and all capital is circulating, $(r^{-1} + 1)^{-1}$ equals the ratio of surplus product to gross output.

profit rate is an upper bound for this interest rate; see Marx 1991, Chap. 22) and, therefore, the price of land (as capitalized rent) rises (see Marx 1991, pp. 761 and 911–915); and (f) the economy is attracted to Goodwin's (1967) trivial fixed point. Nevertheless, if

$$\hat{\pi}_K < 0, \ \pi_K(t) \to \tilde{\pi}_K > 0$$

and the "rate of surplus value" rises without limit, then, although the "value composition of capital" rises without limit and $r^N(t)(e_S(t))^{-1}$ tends to zero,[27] the normalized profit rate may be strictly increasing.

2. If $\hat{\pi}_K \geq 0$, then a decrease in the normalized profit rate presupposes a decrease in the share of profits or, equivalently, in the "rate of surplus value".

The following two examples illustrate some of the points made above:

***Example 11.5***
Assume that

$$e_S(t) = e_S(0)e^{\beta t}, \ \beta > 0$$

and

$$\pi_K(t) = \pi_K(0)e^{-\gamma t}, \ 0 < \gamma < \beta$$

It then follows that $\hat{r}^N = 0$ at

$$t^* \equiv \beta^{-1} \ln\left[\delta(e_S(0))^{-1}\right]$$

where $\delta \equiv \beta\gamma^{-1} - 1 > 0, t^* > 0$ for $\delta > e_S(0)$, $t^*$ is a strictly decreasing function of $\gamma$ and $e_S(0)$, while $\partial t^*/\partial\beta = 0$ when

$$\ln\delta - \delta^{-1} - 1 = \ln e_S(0)$$

The monotonicity of $t^*$ with respect to $e_S(0)$ and to $\beta$ is explained by the fact that the partial elasticity of $r^N$ with respect to $e_S$ equals $(1 + e_S)^{-1}$; and this elasticity decreases with $e_S$.

Finally, when wages are paid at the beginning of the production period, the said elasticity equals

---

[27]As Engels noted, Marx insisted on investigating the difference $e_S - r^N$ (see Marx 1991, p. 162, footnote 10). When wages are paid at the beginning of the production period,

$$(e_S - r^N)e_S^{-1} = (1 + CVV^{-1})^{-1}$$

which implies that, if $CVV$ rises without limit, then this percentage difference tends to 1.

$$\left[1 + e_S(1 + \pi_K)^{-1}\right]^{-1}$$

while the partial elasticity of $r^N$ with respect to $\pi_K$ equals

$$\left[1 + \pi_K(1 + e_S)^{-1}\right]^{-1}$$

Hence, if $e_S$ increases without limit, while $\pi_K$ decreases and tends to zero, then the partial elasticity of $r^N$ with respect to $e_S$ (with respect to $\pi_K$) decreases (increases) and tends to zero (to one).

**Example 11.6**
Assume that

$$w(t) = w_1(t)w_2(t)$$

where

$$w_1(t) \equiv e^{0.01t}$$

$$w_2(t) \equiv 1 - 0.1\cos(0.2t)\sin(0.3t)t^{-0.1}$$

denote the "secular trend" and the "cyclic variation" components, respectively, of the real wage rate. Moreover, the evolution of labour and capital productivities is given by

$$\pi_L(t) = 1.1(w_1(t))^2$$

and

$$\pi_K(t) = (1 + t^{1.2})^{-1} + G(t), \quad G(t) \equiv 1.2e^{\pi(t)}, \quad \pi(t) \equiv -2e^{-0.0001t}$$

respectively, where $G(t)$ is a Gompertz curve (see, e.g. Winsor 1932). It is obtained that the share of profits tends to one, $VCC$ tends to increase without limit, $\widehat{\pi}_K > 0$ for $t > 118.19$, and $\pi_K(t)$ tends to 1.2. Finally, for $t < 8.87$, $r^N(t)$ fluctuates around a falling "trend"; it then fluctuates around a rising "trend", and, finally, is gradually "attracted" to the capital productivity trajectory (see the graphs in Fig. 11.3, where the dotted lines represent the "secular trends").

It is, thus, concluded that (1) the key role in Marx's "law" of the falling profit rate is played by the conditions

$$\widehat{\pi}_K < 0, \quad \pi_K(t) \to 0$$

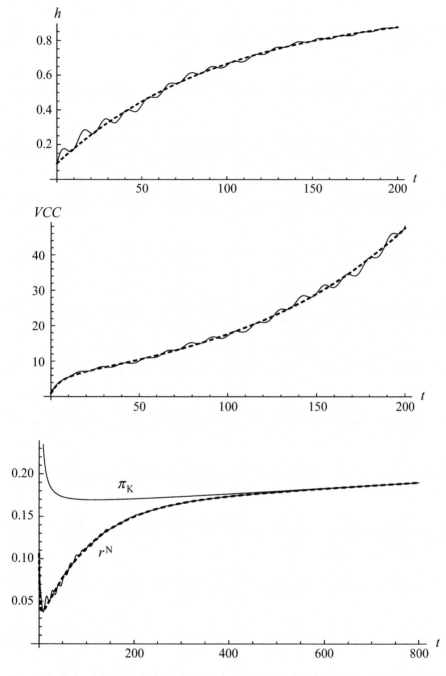

**Fig. 11.3** Share of profits tending to one, "value composition of capital" rising without limit, and non-falling normalized profit rate

and, therefore, (2) the only—possible—"counteracting factor" may be methods of production that entail, exceptionally,

$$\widehat{\pi}_L > 0, \ \widehat{\pi}_K \geq 0$$

Hence, the following, commonly repeated (in one form or another), statement cannot be sustained:

> [A] rise in the organic composition of capital leads to a lowering of the average rate of profit. There are a number of factors [such as, the rising rate of surplus value], however, which counteract the lowering of the rate of profit. [...] All these counteracting factors do not abolish but merely weaken the lowering of the rate of profit and convert it into a tendency. Thus, the raising of the organic composition of capital has as its inevitable consequence *the law of the tendency of the general (or average) rate of profit to fall.* (Academy of Sciences of the USSR 1957, p. 155)

Although Marx is not at all clear on this point, in his critical remarks on Antoine-Elisée Cherbuliez's book, *Richesse ou Pauvreté* (1841), we read:

> [Cherbuliez] obviously surmises that the mass of living labour employed declines relatively to past labour, although it increases absolutely, and that *therefore* the rate of profit must decline. But he never arrives at a clear understanding. (Marx 1971, p. 376)[28]

And in the French edition (1872–1875) of the first volume of *Capital*, Marx takes into account the biased technological change effects and, thus, revises his earlier view, on the constancy of the economic cycles' period,[29] as follows:

> Until now the duration of these [repeated self-perpetuating] cycles [whose successive phases embrace years, and always culminate in a general crisis, which is the end of one cycle and the starting-point of another] has been ten or eleven years, but there is no reason to consider this duration as constant. On the contrary, we ought to conclude, on the basis of *the laws of capitalist production as we have just expounded them,*[30] that the duration is variable, and that the length of the cycles will *gradually diminish.* (Marx 1982, p. 786, footnote; emphasis added)

It should now be added that, setting aside the issue of effective demand ($u(t) = 1$), differentiation of

$$Y = wL + rK$$

with respect to time gives

$$\widehat{Y} = (1 - h)\left(\widehat{w} + \widehat{L}\right) + h\left(\widehat{r} + \widehat{K}\right)$$

---

[28] Also see Marx (1993, pp. 746–749 and 762–764), Marx (1991, pp. 319, 333 and 369–370).

[29] See Sect. 11.1 of the present book.

[30] That is, $\widehat{w} < \widehat{\pi}_L < \widehat{\kappa}$.

or, rearranging terms and taking into account the definitions of capital intensity and productivities,

$$(1 - h)\widehat{w} + h\widehat{r} = \widehat{\pi}_L - h\widehat{\kappa}$$

or, finally,

$$(1 - h)\widehat{w} + h\widehat{r} = (1 - h)\widehat{\pi}_L + h\widehat{\pi}_K \tag{11.40}$$

*If* the technological conditions of production can be expressed by a neoclassical, constant returns to scale production function, i.e.

$$Y = AF(K, L) \tag{11.41}$$

where $A$ denotes the "total factor productivity", then differentiating Eq. (11.41) with respect to time, and taking into account the first-order conditions for cost-minimization, gives

$$\widehat{Y} = \widehat{A} + (1 - h)\widehat{L} + h\widehat{K}$$

or

$$(1 - h)\widehat{\pi}_L + h\widehat{\pi}_K = \widehat{A} \tag{11.42}$$

Hence, Eqs. (11.40) and (11.42) imply that

$$(1 - h)\widehat{w} + h\widehat{r} = (1 - h)\widehat{\pi}_L + h\widehat{\pi}_K = \widehat{A}$$

from which it follows that:

1. Iff $\widehat{A} > 0$, then simultaneous increases in $w$ and $r$, on the one hand, and in $\pi_L$ and $\pi_K$, on the other hand, are possible (also see Fig. 11.4).
2. When $\widehat{A} = 0$,

$$\widehat{\widehat{wr}}^{-1} = \widehat{\pi}_L \widehat{\pi}_K^{-1} = -e_S$$

which do not seem to contradict Marx's analyses. Nevertheless, the relative magnitudes of these changes depend on the underlying production function: for instance, in

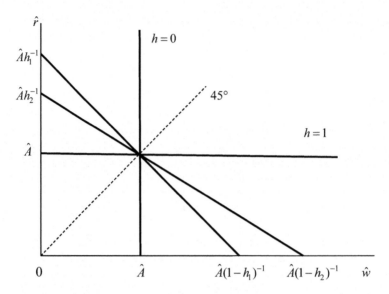

**Fig. 11.4** Possible combinations of simultaneous increases in the real wage and profit rates: $h_1 < h_2$ and "total factor productivity" growth case

the case of Cobb–Douglas production functions (and wages paid at the end of the production period), it holds that $\widehat{w} = \widehat{\pi}_L$ and, therefore, $\widehat{e}_S = 0$.

Finally, in the case of increasing returns to scale, $\widehat{A} = 0$ does not necessarily imply an inverse relationship between $\pi_L$ and $\pi_K$.[31]

The present argument about Marx's "law" of the falling profit rate also applies, in essence, to the corresponding heterogeneous capital case, since, as we have seen (Sect. 11.2.2), in this case it holds that

$$r^N < \pi_K\left(r^N\right) \quad \text{if} \quad 0 \leq r^N < \lambda^{-1}$$

and

$$\pi_K\left(\lambda^{-1}\right) = \lambda^{-1}$$

In actual fact, the essence of this argument applies to all those cases where there is a finite maximum value for the profit rate, and this underlines, in turn, the further importance of Sraffa's (1960) equation

---

[31]For a simple but interesting endogenous growth modelling of increasing returns to scale, see Anchishkin (1977, pp. 258–267). In Part Four ("The Production of Relative Surplus-Value") of *Capital*, Volume One, Marx (1982) analyzes laws of production implying "total factor productivity" growth and increasing returns to scale (also through the stimulation of workers' "animal spirits"; see pp. 443 and 447).

$$r^{\mathrm{N}} = R\left(1 - w^{\mathrm{S}}\right)$$

and relevant observation:

> The notion of a Maximum rate of profits corresponding to a zero wage has been suggested by Marx, directly through an incidental allusion to the possibility of a fall in the rate of profits "even if the workers could live on air"; but more generally owing to his emphatic rejection of the claim of Adam Smith and of others that the price of every commodity "either immediately or ultimately" resolves itself entirely (that is to say, without leaving any commodity residue) into wage, profit and rent—a claim which necessarily presupposed the existence of "ultimate" commodities produced by pure labour without means of production except land, and which therefore was incompatible with a fixed limit to the rise in the rate of profits. (p. 94)[32]

Empirical evidence provided by scholars with very different backgrounds suggests that, in the twentieth century, the prevailing "law" (i.e. trend) was that of non-decreasing capital productivity, $\widehat{\pi}_K \geq 0$. For instance, Osadchaya (1974), a Soviet Marxist scholar, emphasizes:

> [W]hen labour productivity tends to grow faster than the capital–labour ratio, [. . .] capital inputs per unit of output may decline or remain stable. The trend tendency for such a decline, signifying capital-saving technical progress, emerged in the 1920s. [. . .] Marx's analysis of the impact of technical progress on the value-composition of capital and, through it, on the value and physical structure of the product is taken as a basis by many Soviet economists in their research [. . .] Whatever the basis for these studies—whether the gross social product, including a repeated count of material input values, or the final social product—they all suggest the same conclusion: in the 1920s a new stage opened in the development of the productive forces of the industrialised countries, when the growing productivity of labour began to outstrip the capital–labour ratio, and when economies in labour, which always go hand in hand with technical progress, were supplemented with economies in capital inputs, both of fixed capital and raw and other materials. This tendency tends to be ever more pronounced with the advance of the scientific and technical revolution, with its vast potentialities for enhancing social productivity and reducing all types of inputs, both of living and of embodied labour. [. . .] Present-day development shows that the factors working against the reduction of the rate of profit on capital tend to exert an ever great effect. Statistical studies also show that in the past quarter-century tendencies working against any worsening of the proletariat's condition have become stronger. [. . .] As a result, the reduction of the working class share in the national income has slowed down in some countries at various periods. (pp. 175–178)[33]

And Samuelson and Nordhaus (2009) argue that

> [e]conomists studying the economic history of advanced nations have found that the following trends apply in most countries: (1) The capital stock has grown more rapidly than population and employment, resulting from capital deepening. (2) For most of the

---

[32]For Sraffa's equation in the case of additional primary inputs, see Metcalfe and Steedman (1972, pp. 156–157), while for the case of changes in the sectoral "total factor productivities", consider Sect. 4.3.1 of the present book (with $dr \neq 0$ and without necessarily assuming the existence of neoclassical production functions). Nevertheless, the joint production properties of real-world economies should also be taken into account (see Sects. 4.2, 6.2.2.3 and Chap. 5 of the present book).

[33]Is it not somewhat strange that Lenin (1915–1916, 1917) by-passes Marx's "law of the tendency of the profit rate to fall"?

period since 1900, there has been a strong upward trend in real average hourly earnings. (3) The share of labor compensation in national income has been remarkably stable over the last century. (4) There were major oscillations in real interest rates and the rate of profit, particularly during business cycles, but there has been no strong upward or downward trend over the post-1900 period. (5) Instead of steadily rising, which would be predicted by the law of diminishing returns with unchanging technology, the capital–output ratio has actually declined since the start of the twentieth century. (6) For most of the period since 1900, the ratios of national saving and of investment to GDP were stable. Since 1980, the national saving rate has declined sharply in the United States. (7) After effects of the business cycle are removed, national product has grown at an average rate of 3.3% per year. Output growth has been much higher than a weighted average of the growth of capital, labor, and resource inputs, suggesting that technological innovation must be playing a key role in economic growth. While the seven trends of economic history are not like the immutable laws of physics, they do portray fundamental facts about growth in the modern era. (pp. 512–514)

### 11.4.2    Falling Profit Rate with Rising Profit Mass

There are scholars arguing that Marx's "law of the falling profit rate" implies that the mass of profits eventually falls. For instance, Shaikh (1987, 1992) supports the thesis that (1) the mechanization and capitalization of production lead to rising "technical and organic compositions of capital"; (2) the "rate of surplus value" tends to rise over time (because real wages will not generally rise as fast as labour productivity); (3) even when the "rate of surplus value" rises without limit, the normalized profit rate eventually falls at a rate asymptotic to the fall of the capacity–capital ratio;[34] and (4) a secularly falling normalized profit rate necessarily produces a (single) "long wave" in the mass of profits, which first accelerates, then decelerates, stagnates, signalling the beginning of the crisis phase, and even falls. Thus, he argues that

> Marx's theory of a *secularly falling* rate of profit provides a natural foundation for a theory of long waves [...]. (Shaikh 1992, p. 175)

Consider a closed economy, without government intervention, and assume that $u(t) = 1$. Thus, we can write

$$P = rK \qquad (11.43)$$

$$g \equiv \widehat{K} = s_p r \qquad (11.44)$$

Differentiation of Eq. (11.43) with respect to time gives

$$\widehat{P} = \widehat{r} + \widehat{K}$$

or, recalling Eq. (11.44),

---

[34] As we have seen, however, this is necessarily true iff the capacity–capital ratio tends to zero.

$$\widehat{P} = \widehat{r} + s_p r \qquad (11.45)$$

where $\widehat{r}$ represents the "profit rate effect", and $s_p r$ represents the "capital accumulation effect" on $P$.

When, for instance, the profit rate falls at some given and constant rate (Shaikh 1992, p. 178), $a$, i.e.

$$r(t) = r(0)e^{-at}$$

where $0 < a < s_p r(0)$, Eq. (11.45) implies that

$$\widehat{P} = -a + s_p r(0)e^{-at} \qquad (11.46)$$

The general solution to the differential Eq. (11.46) is given by

$$P(t) = Ce^{\phi_2(t)}$$

where

$$\phi_2(t) \equiv -a^{-1}s_p r(0)e^{-at} - at$$

and $C$ denotes the constant of integration. It then follows that the profit mass is stagnant, i.e. $\widehat{P} = 0$, at

$$t^* \equiv a^{-1}\ln\left(s_p r(0)a^{-1}\right)$$

and tends to zero as $t$ tends to infinity (see, for instance, Fig. 11.5, where $r(0) = 1$, $a = 0.1$, $s_p = 0.5$, therefore, $t^* \cong 16.09$, and $C = 5$). Thus, Shaikh (1992) stresses:

> Marx calls the point of transition from normal accumulation to the crisis phase the "point of absolute overaccumulation of capital". It marks a *phase change* in all the major patterns of accumulation. The exact patterns in the long downturn phase depend on more concrete and conjunctural factors involving the credit system, on the role of the state *vis-à-vis* workers, businesses, and the banks, and on the strength of the class struggle. (pp. 179–180)

It should be added that, *ceteris paribus*, a strictly increasing $s_p$ (see Marx 1982, Chap. 24; Marx 1991, Chap. 15, Sect. 4) cannot invalidate the argument, since there is an upper limit ($=1$) for this parameter: when, for instance, it follows the logarithmically transformed Gompertz curve

$$s_p(t) = 1 - 0.5(0.1)^t$$

$\widehat{P}$ is maximized at $t \cong 1.08$, while it equals zero at $t_s^* \cong 23.03$ ($> t^*$; see Fig. 11.6). Now assume, however, that there is a *positive* limit for the falling profit rate, e.g.

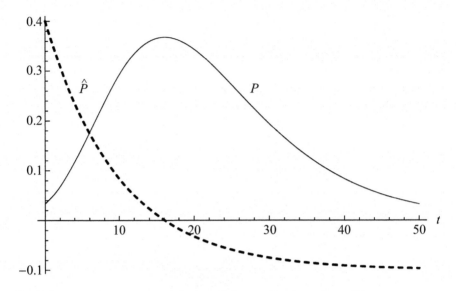

**Fig. 11.5** The profit mass and its relative rate of change, when the profit rate falls at a constant rate and the savings ratio remains constant

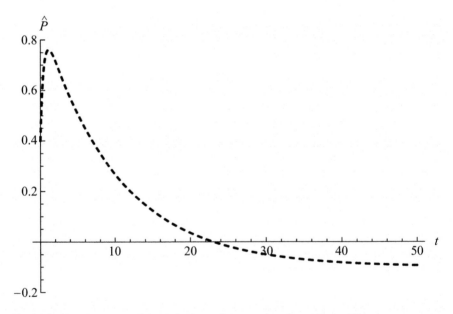

**Fig. 11.6** The relative rate of change in the profit mass, when the profit rate falls at a constant rate and the savings ratio increases

$$r(t) = r_{\min} + b^t \qquad (11.47)$$

where $0 < b < 1$, and that $s_p$ remains constant. The general solution to Eq. (11.45) is given by

$$P(t) = C(r_{\min} + b^t)e^{\phi_3(t)}$$

where

$$\phi_3(t) \equiv s_p\left[r_{\min}t + (\ln b)^{-1}b^t\right]$$

It then follows that $\widehat{P}$ may always be positive and, irrespective of the precise form of $r(t)$, tends to the value of $s_p r_{\min}$ (since $\widehat{r}$ tends to zero; see Eq. (11.45)) following a path that is not necessarily monotonic. For instance, see Fig. 11.7, where $r_{\min} = 0.02$, $b$ equals 0.80, 0.94 or 0.97, $s_p = 1$, and $C = 1$. For $b = 0.80$, $\widehat{P} = 0$ at $t_1^* \cong 7.66$ (maximum point for $P$) and $t_2^* \cong 27.40$ (minimum point for $P$), while for $b = 0.94$, $\widehat{P}$ is always positive and takes its minimum value at $t \cong 67.68$.

It is noted that, when wages are paid at the end of the production period, Eq. (11.47) can be derived from a Marglin (1984, p. 193)–Jones and Manuelli (1990) production function of the form:

$$Y = A_1 K + A_2 K^\alpha L^{1-\alpha}$$

where $A_1 > 0$, $A_2 > 0$, and $0 < \alpha < 1$; this production function is an additive combination of the $AK$ and Cobb–Douglas functions, and, therefore, violates one of the well-known Inada conditions, i.e. the first partial derivative of $Y$ with respect to $K$ tends to $A_1$ as $K$ tends to positive infinity. It is easy to see that the first-order conditions for cost-minimization imply that

$$r = A_1 + \gamma w^{-\beta}, \quad \beta \equiv \alpha^{-1}(1 - \alpha) \quad \gamma \equiv A_2^{\alpha^{-1}}\alpha(1 - \alpha)^\beta$$

Thus, by setting $A_1 = r_{\min}$ and $w = (\gamma b^{-t})^{\beta^{-1}}$, we get $r(t) = r_{\min} + b^t$.

It should also be stressed that the existence of a positive limit for the falling profit rate is an unnecessary condition for $\widehat{P} > 0$. When, for instance,

$$r(t) = b(c + dt)^{-1}$$

where $s_p b > d > 0$ and $c > 0$, the general solution to Eq. (11.45) is given by

$$P(t) = C(c + dt)^\nu$$

where $\nu \equiv s_p b d^{-1} - 1$. It then follows that $P$ is strictly increasing, while $\widehat{P}$ tends monotonically to zero.

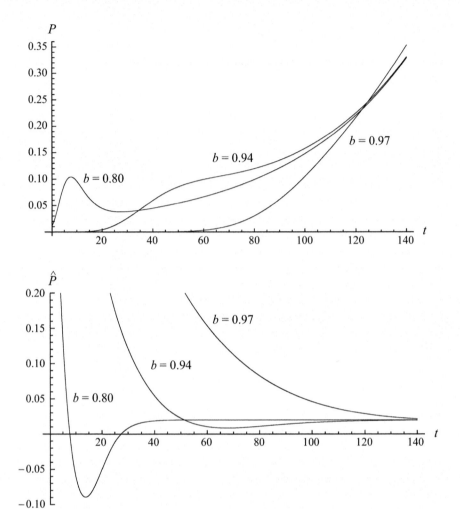

**Fig. 11.7** The profit mass and its relative rate of change, when the falling profit rate has a positive limit and the savings ratio remains constant

In fact, when $s_p$ remains constant, $\widehat{P} = 0$ for all $t$ iff

$$r(t) = \left(c + s_p t\right)^{-1}$$

where $c > 0$. So, for instance, for

$$r(t) = b\left(c + s_p t\right)^{-1}$$

where $b > (<) 1$, it holds that $\widehat{P} > (<) 0$, or for

$$r(t) = \left(c + s_p t\right)^{-\xi}$$

where $\xi > 0$, it holds that $\widehat{P} = 0$ (and $P > 0$) at

$$t^* \equiv s_p^{-1}\left(\xi^q - c\right)$$

which is not necessarily positive or even a maximum point for $P$, where $q \equiv (1 - \xi)^{-1}$, and $\xi^q$ strictly increases with $\xi$, and tends to 1.

At the same time, however, our overall analysis (in particular, consider Eq. (11.38)) implies that the following statement cannot be sustained either:

> The fall in the rate of profit does not mean a reduction in the *amount* of profit, i.e., in the total volume of surplus-value produced by the working class. On the contrary, *the amount of profit grows* both in connection with the rise in the rate of surplus-value and as a result of the growth in the number of workers exploited by capital. (Academy of Sciences of the USSR 1957, p. 155)

Finally, consider the more empirically relevant case of an open economy.[35] If the savings ratio out of profits applies to domestically generated profits plus net foreign income, then

$$s_p(P + iD) = gK + CA$$

or

$$g = s_p r - \left[tb + \left(1 - s_p\right)i\delta\right] \tag{11.48}$$

where $i$ denotes the rate of return on net external wealth, $D$ the stock of external assets,

$$CA \equiv TB + iD$$

the current account balance, $TB$ the trade balance, $tb \equiv TBK^{-1}$ and $\delta \equiv DK^{-1} (> -1$, i.e. the aggregate net wealth, $K + D$, is positive). It then follows that Eq. (11.45) should be replaced by

$$\widehat{P} = \widehat{r} + s_p r - \left[tb + \left(1 - s_p\right)i\delta\right]$$

---

[35]The case of government intervention is equally relevant and formally equivalent.

which implies that $\widehat{P}$ may always be positive even when the profit rate falls at a constant rate (provided only that the term in brackets is negative).[36] In that case, Marx's terminology and Shaikh's (1992) analysis imply that the "foreign (trade and income) effect" acts as a "counteracting influence" to the tendency of the profit *mass* to fall.

## 11.5   Synopsis and Final Remarks

The extension of Goodwin's distributive cycle model to include effective demand issues forms the basis for re-examining Marx's treatment of capitalist accumulation fluctuations. It has been shown that the incorporation of the Bhaduri–Marglin accumulation function into Goodwin's model amounts to the introduction of a sign-variable friction coefficient into the equations of motion and, hence, can considerably modify the system's behaviour. More specifically, the local dynamic properties of that extended system depend crucially on the elasticity of the $IS$-curve, which, in its turn, depends on the form of the accumulation function. Thus, the equilibrium in the profit-led (wage-led) growth regime is locally stable (unstable), whereas in the border between these two regimes, the possible existence of cyclic paths cannot be excluded. By contrast, in the heterogeneous capital case, where the economy-wide capital intensity changes with changes in income distribution, the system's friction coefficient depends on both the form of the accumulation function and the elasticity of capital intensity with respect to the share of profits and, therefore, the equilibrium in the wage-led (profit-led) regime may be locally stable (unstable). Nevertheless, this case should be re-examined by taking into account the uncontrollable/unobservable aspects of real-world economies (see Chap. 3). Finally, even in the one-commodity case, different assumptions regarding the substitution possibilities between "capital and labour" or the investment–savings gap can lead to significant differences in the economy's dynamic behaviour.

Marx's sub-theory of biased technological change, long-term fall in the profit rate, and rise in the "rate of surplus value" is based, in fact, on the decrease (to zero)

---

[36]Differentiation of $\delta \equiv DK^{-1}$ with respect to time gives

$$\dot{\delta} = \dot{D}K^{-1} - g\delta$$

Consequently, if the basic balance is zero, i.e. $\dot{D} = CA$, then

$$\dot{\delta} = tb + (i - g)\delta$$

or, recalling Eq. (11.48),

$$\dot{\delta} = tb + (i - s_p r + tb)\delta + (1 - s_p)i\delta^2$$

which is the equation of motion for $\delta$.

in capital productivity or, to be precise, on the decrease (to zero) in Sraffa's maximum profit rate, not on the increase in the "organic composition of capital". The internal consistency of this sub-theory partially depends on the explicit specification of both the technological and institutional-contractual conditions of production (such as the timing of wage payments) or, in other words, of aspects of the inter-connections between "productive forces and production relations". If, however, capital productivity tends to zero, while the "rate of surplus value" rises without limit, then the profit rate tends to zero (although not necessarily monotonically) and the economy is attracted to Goodwin's trivial fixed point. In this sense, it can be stated that Marx's sub-theory of biased technological change over-determines his sub-theories of distributive cycles and of effective demand. Empirical evidence suggests, however, that, in the twentieth century or, more precisely, since the 1920s, the prevailing "law" was that of non-decreasing capital productivity, which implies that a decrease in the normalized profit rate presupposes a decrease in the share of profits or, in other words, that Marx's "law" failed to hold.

It has also been shown that, when the normalized profit rate falls continuously (*by assumption*), nothing ensures the existence of a stagnation point for the profit mass, since the negative "profit rate effect" can be weaker than the positive "capital accumulation effect". In other words, the time path of the normalized profit rate, the proximate determinants of which are the evolution of the real wage rate and of the technical production conditions, also matters. Hence, the profit mass may be strictly increasing even when the normalized profit rate is strictly decreasing and, therefore, the "long-wave version" of the falling profit rate theory of crisis lacks logical consistency. In fact, the necessary coexistence of a strictly decreasing profit rate and one (or more) stagnation point for the profit mass is not a corollary of Marx's "law" of the falling profit rate, but a characteristic feature of Ricardo's system (see Pasinetti 1960, pp. 88–89), and, as Plekhanov 1947, pp. 62–63) emphatically remarks, similar views (on falling profit mass and rate) can be traced to Saint-Simonist writings.

Since capitalist accumulation is a process where "effects become causes in their turn", the Sraffa–Kalecki–Goodwin modelling of endogenous circular causation provides the appropriate analytical framework for dealing with that process.

# References

Academy of Sciences of the USSR. (1957). *Political economy. Textbook issued by the Institute of Economics of the Academy of Sciences of the USSR*. London: Lawrence & Wishart.

Anchishkin, A. (1977). *The theory of growth of a socialist economy*. Moscow: Progress Publishers.

Andronov, A. A., Vitt, A. A., & Khaikin, S. E. (1987). *Theory of oscillators*. New York: Dover.

Arrow, K. J., Chenery, H. B., Minhas, B. S., & Solow, R. M. (1961). Capital–labor substitution and economic efficiency. *The Review of Economics and Statistics, 43*(3), 225–250.

Barbosa-Filho, N. H., & Taylor, L. (2006). Distributive and demand cycles in the U.S. economy – a structuralist Goodwin model. *Metroeconomica, 57*(3), 389–411.

Barrales, J., & von Arnim, R. (2017). Longer-run distributive cycles: Wavelet decompositions for the US, 1948–2011. *Review of Keynesian Economics, 5*(2), 196–217.

Bhaduri, A. (2008). On the dynamics of profit-led and wage-led growth. *Cambridge Journal of Economics, 32*(1), 147–160.

Bhaduri, A., & Marglin, S. (1990). Unemployment and the real wage rate: The economic basis for contesting political ideologies. *Cambridge Journal of Economics, 14*(4), 375–393.

Bidard, C. (1986). Baisse tendancielle du taux de profit et marchandise-étalon in Piero Sraffa. *Economie Appliquee, 39*(1), 139–154.

Blecker, R. A. (2016). Wage-led versus profit-led demand regimes: The long and the short of it. *Review of Keynesian Economics, 4*(4), 373–390.

Canry, N. (2005). Wage-led regime, profit-led regime and cycles: A model. *Économie Appliquée, 58*(1), 143–163.

Chou, N.-T., Izyumov, A., & Vahaly, J. (2016). Rates of return on capital across the world: Are they converging? *Cambridge Journal of Economics, 40*(4), 1149–1166.

Dutt, A.-K. (1992). Conflict inflation, distribution, cyclical accumulation and crises. *European Journal of Political Economy, 8*(4), 579–597.

Eugeni, S. (2016). Global imbalances in the XIX, XX and the XXI centuries. *Economics Letters, 145*, 69–72.

Flaschel, P., Groh, G., Kauermann, G., & Teuber, T. (2009). The classical growth cycle after fifteen years of new observations. In P. Flaschel & M. Landesmann (Eds.), *Mathematical economics and the dynamics of capitalism* (pp. 69–77). London: Routledge.

Franke, R. (1999). Technical change and a falling wage share if profits are maintained. *Metroeconomica, 50*(1), 35–53.

Glombowski, J. (1982). A comment on Sherman's Marxist cycle model. *Review of Radical Political Economics, 14*(1), 42–49.

Glombowski, J. (1983). A Marxian model of long run capitalist development. *Journal of Economics, 43*(4), 363–382.

Glombowski, J., & Krüger, M. (1986). Some extensions of a classical growth cycle model. In W. Semmler (Ed.), *Competition, instability, and nonlinear cycles* (pp. 212–251). Berlin: Springer.

Goodwin, R. M. (1967). A growth cycle. In C. H. Feinstein (Ed.), *Socialism, capitalism and economic growth: Essays presented to Maurice Dobb* (pp. 54–58). Cambridge: Cambridge University Press.

Harris, D. J. (1983). Accumulation of capital and the rate of profit in Marxian theory. *Cambridge Journal of Economics, 7*(3–4), 311–330.

Himmelweit, S. (1974). A formal proof of Marx's two theorems: Comment. *Kobe University Economic Review, 20*, 93–95.

Hirsch, M. W., & Smale, S. (1974). *Differential equations, dynamical systems and linear algebra.* New York: Academic Press.

Jones, L. E., & Manuelli, R. (1990). A convex model of equilibrium growth: Theory and policy implications. *Journal of Political Economy, 98*(5), 1008–1038.

Kalecki, M. (1971). *Selected essays on the dynamics of the capitalist economy, 1933–1970.* Cambridge: Cambridge University Press.

Kiefer, D., & Rada, C. (2015). Profit maximising goes global: The race to the bottom. *Cambridge Journal of Economics, 39*(5), 1333–1350.

Konstantakis, K. N., Michaelides, P. G., & Mariolis, T. (2014). An endogenous Goodwin–Keynes business cycle model: Evidence for Germany (1991–2007). *Applied Economics Letters, 21*(7), 481–486.

Krüger, M. (1988). A general model of capital accumulation. In P. Flaschel & M. Krüger (Eds.), *Recent approaches to economic dynamics* (pp. 47–63). Frankfurt am Main: Peter Lang.

Kurz, H. D. (1990). Technical change, growth and distribution: A steady-state approach to "unsteady" growth. In H. D. Kurz (Ed.), *Capital, distribution and effective demand. Studies in the "classical" approach to economic theory* (pp. 211–239). Cambridge: Polity Press.

Kurz, H. D. (1993a). Accumulation et demande effective: Quelques notes. *Cahiers d'économie politique/Papers in Political Economy, 22*(1), 59–82.

Kurz, H. D. (1993b). Modèles classiques et projet keynésien: Réponse à Ch. Tutin. *Cahiers d'économie politique/Papers in Political Economy, 22*(1), 93–103.

Kurz, H. D. (1994). Growth and distribution. *Review of Political Economy, 6*(4), 393–420.

Kurz, H. D. (1995). The Keynesian project: Tom Asimakopoulos and the "other point of view". In G. C. Harcourt, A. Roncaglia, & R. Rowley (Eds.), *Income and employment in theory and practice: Essays in memory of Athanasios Asimakopoulos* (pp. 83–110). New York: St. Martin's Press.

Kurz, H. D., & Salvadori, N. (1995). *Theory of production. A long-period analysis.* Cambridge: Cambridge University Press.

Lenin, V. I. (1893). On the so-called market question. In V. I. Lenin (Ed.), *Collected works* (Vol. 1, pp. 79–125). Moscow: Progress Publishers.

Lenin, V. I. (1897). A characterisation of economic romanticism (Sismondi and our native Sismondists). In V. I. Lenin (Ed.), *Collected works* (Vol. 2, pp. 129–266). Moscow: Progress Publishers.

Lenin, V. I. (1915–1916). Notebooks on imperialism. In V. I. Lenin (Ed.), *Collected works* (Vol. 39). Moscow: Progress Publishers.

Lenin, V. I. (1917). Imperialism, the highest stage of capitalism. A popular outline. In V. I. Lenin (Ed.), *Collected works* (Vol. 22, pp. 185–304). Moscow: Progress Publishers.

Mainwaring, L. (1991). Review of the paper "Bhaduri, A., Marglin, S. (1990): Unemployment and the real wage rate: the economic basis for contesting political ideologies, *Cambridge Journal of Economics*". *European Journal of Political Economy, 7*(4), 632–634.

Marglin, S. A. (1984). *Growth, distribution, and prices.* Cambridge: Harvard University Press.

Marglin, S. A., & Bhaduri, A. (1988). *Profit squeeze and Keynesian theory.* World Institute for Development Economics Research of the United Nations University, Working Paper 39, April 1988.

Mariolis, T. (2006a). *Introduction to the theory of endogenous economic fluctuations. Linear and nonlinear economic oscillators.* Athens: Typothyto (in Greek).

Mariolis, T. (2006b). Distribution and growth in a multi-sector open economy with excess capacity. *Economia Internazionale/International Economics, 59*(1), 51–61.

Mariolis, T. (2007). Distribution and growth in an economy with heterogeneous capital and excess capacity. *Asian–African Journal of Economics and Econometrics, 7*(1–2), 365–375.

Mariolis, T. (2011). Interpretations of economic crises: A non-neoclassical and systemic analytical framework. In T. Mariolis (Ed.), *Greece, European Union and economic crisis* (pp. 59–93). Athens: Matura (in Greek).

Mariolis, T. (2013). Goodwin's growth cycle model with the Bhaduri–Marglin accumulation function. *Evolutionary and Institutional Economics Review, 10*(1), 131–144.

Mariolis, T. (2014a). Falling rate of profit and mass of profits: A note. *Review of Political Economy, 26*(4), 549–556.

Mariolis, T. (2014b). *Karl Marx's theory of economic crises.* Paper presented at the Sixteenth Conference of Greek Historians of Economic Thought, 6–7 June 2014, Department of Public Administration, Panteion University, Athens. MPRA Paper No 56831 (in Greek). Retrieved Mar 30, 2020, from https://mpra.ub.uni-muenchen.de/56831/.

Mariolis, T. (2015). The fundamental economic law of the Eurozone. In T. Mariolis (Ed.), *Essays on the work of Dimitris Batsis: "The heavy industry in Greece"* (pp. 633–642). Athens: Tziola Publications (in Greek).

Mariolis, T. (2018). *Marx's determination of the derivative function and the limit of the profit rate function.* Paper presented at the conference "200 Years since the Birth of Karl Marx: Economy, Society, State", 12–13 December 2018, Department of Public Administration, Panteion University, Athens (in Greek). Retrieved Mar 30, 2020, from https://www.researchgate.net/publication/330009383.

Mariolis, T., Konstantakis, K. N., Michaelides, P. G., & Tsionas, E. G. (2019). A non-linear Keynesian Goodwin-type endogenous model of the cycle: Bayesian evidence for the USA. *Studies in Nonlinear Dynamics and Econometrics, 23*(1), 137.

Mariolis, T., & Michaelides, P. G. (2020). *An endogenous money post-Keynesian cycle model.* Mimeo.

Mariolis, T., & Rodousakis, N. (2020). *A post-Keynesian commodities market disequilibrium model under alternative accumulation function forms.* Mimeo.

Marx, K. (1968). *Theories of surplus-value. Volume IV of Capital. Part II.* Moscow: Progress Publishers.

Marx, K. (1971). *Theories of surplus-value. Volume IV of Capital. Part III.* Moscow: Progress Publishers.

Marx, K. (1982). *Capital. A critique of political economy. Volume one.* Harmondsworth: Penguin Books.

Marx, K. (1991). *Capital. A critique of political economy. Volume three.* Harmondsworth: Penguin Books.

Marx, K. (1992). *Capital. A critique of political economy. Volume two.* Harmondsworth: Penguin Books.

Marx, K. (1993). *Grundrisse. Foundations of the critique of political economy (rough draft).* Harmondsworth: Penguin Books.

May, R. M. (1972). Limit cycles in predator–prey communities. *Science, 177*(4052), 900–902.

Metcalfe, J. S., & Steedman, I. (1972). Reswitching and primary input use. *The Economic Journal, 82*(325), 140–157.

Moszkowska, N. (1935). *Zur Kritik moderner Krisentheorien.* Prag: Michael Kacha.

Nikiforos, M., & Foley, D. K. (2012). Distribution and capacity utilization: Conceptual issues and empirical evidence. *Metroeconomica, 63*(1), 200–229.

Okishio, N. (1961). Technical change and the rate of profit. *Kobe University Economic Review, 7,* 85–99.

Okishio, N. (1972). A formal proof of Marx's two theorems. *Kobe University Economic Review, 18,* 1–6.

Okishio, N. (1974). A formal proof of Marx's two theorems: Reply. *Kobe University Economic Review, 20,* 95.

Okishio, N. (1977). Notes on technical progress and capitalist society. *Cambridge Journal of Economics, 1*(1), 93–100.

Osadchaya, I. (1974). *From Keynes to neoclassical synthesis. A critical analysis.* Moscow: Progress Publishers.

Panico, C., & Salvadori, N. (1993). Introduction. In C. Panico & N. Salvadori (Eds.), *Post Keynesian theory of growth and distribution* (pp. xiii–xxxi). Aldershot: Edward Elgar.

Pasinetti, L. L. (1960). A mathematical formulation of the Ricardian system. *The Review of Economic Studies, 27*(2), 78–98.

Plekhanov, G. V. (1947). *The development of the monist view of history.* London: Lawrence & Wishart.

Ribeiro, R. S. M., McCombie, J. S. L., & Lima, G. T. (2017). Some unpleasant currency-devaluation arithmetic in a post Keynesian macromodel. *Journal of Post Keynesian Economics, 40*(2), 145–167.

Rodousakis, N. (2012). *Endogenous fluctuations in one-sector and multi-sector models à la Goodwin.* Ph.D. Dissertation, Athens: Department of Public Administration, Panteion University (in Greek).

Rodousakis, N. (2015). Goodwin's growth cycle model with the Bhaduri–Marglin accumulation function: A note on the CES case. *Evolutionary and Institutional Economics Review, 12*(1), 105–114.

Rodousakis, N. (2019). *Generalizations of the Goodwin predator–prey model via the Bhaduri–Marglin investment function.* Paper presented at the 1st Conference of the Study Group on

Sraffian Economics: "From the Capital Theory Controversy in the 1960s to Greece's Virtual Bankruptcy in 2010", 11–12 April 2019, Panteion University, Athens, Greece (in Greek).

Rodrik, D. (2011). *The globalization paradox. Why global markets, states, and democracy can't coexist.* Oxford: Oxford University Press.

Salvadori, N. (1981). Falling rate of profit with a constant real wage. An example. *Cambridge Journal of Economics, 5*(1), 59–66.

Samuelson, P. A., & Nordhaus, W. D. (2009). *Economics* (19th ed.). New York: McGraw-Hill.

Santos, J. F. C., & Araujo, R. A. (2020). Using non-linear estimation strategies to test an extended version of the Goodwin model on the US economy. *Review of Keynesian Economics, 8*(2), 268–286.

Sasaki, H. (2013). Cyclical growth in a Goodwin–Kalecki–Marx model. *Journal of Economics, 108* (2), 145–171.

Ségal, L. (1936). *Principes d'économie politique.* Paris: Éditions Sociales Internationales.

Shaikh, A. (1987). The current economic crisis: Causes and implications. In Union for Radical Political Economics (Ed.), *The imperiled economy: Macroeconomics from a Left perspective* (pp. 115–126). New York: Union for Radical Political Economics.

Shaikh, A. (1992). The falling rate of profit as the cause of long waves: Theory and empirical evidence. In A. Kleinknecht, E. Mandel, & I. Wallerstein (Eds.), *New findings in long-wave research* (pp. 174–195). New York: St. Martin's Press.

Sherman, H. J. (1971). Marxist models of cyclical growth. *History of Political Economy, 3*(1), 28–55.

Sherman, H. J. (1979). A Marxist theory of the business cycle. *Review of Radical Political Economics, 11*(1), 1–23.

Skott, P. (1989). Effective demand, class struggle and cyclical growth. *International Economic Review, 30*(1), 231–247.

Skott, P. (2012). Shortcomings of the Kaleckian investment function. *Metroeconomica, 63*(1), 109–138.

Sordi, S. (2003). The interaction between growth and cycle in macrodynamic models of the economy. In N. Salvadori (Ed.), *The theory of economic growth. A "classical" perspective* (pp. 285–305). Cheltenham: Edward Elgar.

Sraffa, P. (1960). *Production of commodities by means of commodities. Prelude to a critique of economic theory.* Cambridge: Cambridge University Press.

Steedman, I. (1971). Marx on the falling rate of profit. *Australian Economic Papers, 10*(16), 61–66.

Steedman, I. (1977). *Marx after Sraffa.* London: New Left Books.

Steedman, I. (1980). A note on the "choice of technique" under capitalism. *Cambridge Journal of Economics, 4*(1), 61–64.

Tavani, D. (2012). Wage bargaining and induced technical change in a linear economy: Model and application to the US (1963–2003). *Structural Change and Economic Dynamics, 23*(2), 117–126.

Tavani, D., Flaschel, P., & Taylor, L. (2011). Estimated non-linearities and multiple equilibria in a model of distributive–demand cycles. *International Review of Applied Economics, 25*(5), 519–538.

van der Ploeg, F. (1985). Classical growth cycles. *Metroeconomica, 37*(2), 221–230.

von Arnim, R., & Barrales, J. (2015). Demand-driven Goodwin cycles with Kaldorian and Kaleckian features. *Review of Keynesian Economics, 3*(3), 351–373.

von Arnim, R., Tavani, D., & Carvalho, L. (2014). Redistribution in a neo-Kaleckian two-country model. *Metroeconomica, 65*(3), 430–459.

Voronin, A. Y. (1989). Analysis of the dynamics of expanded reproduction of intensive type using a two-commodity model. *Journal of Soviet mathematics, 45*(4), 1295–1302.

Winsor, C. P. (1932). The Gompertz curve as a growth curve. *Proceedings of the National Academy of Sciences of the United States of America, 18*(1), 1–8.

Zamparelli, L. (2015). Induced innovation, endogenous technical change and income distribution in a labor constrained model of classical growth. *Metroeconomica, 66*(2), 243–262.

# Index

© Springer Nature Singapore Pte Ltd. 2021
T. Mariolis et al., *Spectral Theory of Value and Actual Economies*, Evolutionary Economics and Social Complexity Science 24,
https://doi.org/10.1007/978-981-33-6260-4